The Virgin Birth of Christ

THE VIRGIN BIRTH OF CHRIST

by

J. GRESHAM MACHEN, D.D., Litt.D.

Professor of New Testament in
Westminster Theological Seminary, Philadelphia

BAKER BOOK HOUSE
Grand Rapids, Michigan

THE VIRGIN BIRTH OF CHRIST

ISBN: 0-8010-5885-6

Reprinted by
BAKER BOOK HOUSE COMPANY
with special permission

First printing, November 1965
Second printing, August 1967
Third printing, September 1971

PHOTOLITHOPRINTED BY CUSHING - MALLOY, INC.
ANN ARBOR, MICHIGAN, UNITED STATES OF AMERICA
1967

TO

MY MOTHER

PREFACE TO THE FIRST EDITION

THIS book may be regarded as containing in substance, though not in form, the Thomas Smyth Lectures which the author had the honor of delivering at Columbia Theological Seminary in the spring of 1927. The subject is here treated with much greater fullness than was possible in the lectures as they were delivered, and use is made of certain special studies which have been published from time to time in *The Princeton Theological Review*—particularly "The Virgin Birth in the Second Century," "The Hymns of the First Chapter of Luke," and "The Origin of the First Two Chapters of Luke," which appeared in 1912, and "The Integrity of the Lucan Narrative of the Annunciation," which appeared in 1927. The author is greatly indebted to John E. Meeter, Th.M., to whose careful scrutiny of the proof and correction of references and quotations the book owes much of whatever accuracy it may have attained. Profit has been received from Mr. Meeter's suggestions at many points.

1930. J. G. M.

PREFACE TO THE SECOND EDITION

IN THIS second edition, typographical errors have been corrected; additional references to recent discussion have been inserted here and there; and a number of other slight changes have been made. Page 121 has been partly re-written. The author is grateful to his brother, Arthur W. Machen, Jr., and to others who have made helpful suggestions.

It is impossible to comment here in any detail upon the way in which the book has been received; but in general it may be said that even those reviewers who disagree sharply with the author's position have for the most part been generous in according to the book at least some value as a compendium of information. The author is encouraged by such recognition, since he believes that truth is furthered by full and open debate.

If the book presents any distinctive feature, it is to be found, perhaps, in the argument for the integrity of the Lucan narrative which is contained in Chapter VI. That argument cannot, indeed, advance any particular claim to originality: even the stress which it lays upon the parallelism between the accounts of the annunciations to Zacharias and to Mary has been anticipated, as is indicated on pp. 152, 158, by other writers; and to the references there made should be added V. H. Stanton, *The Gospels as Historical Documents*, ii, 1909, p. 226. But the somewhat comprehensive presentation of the argument may, we hope, produce a certain cumulative effect.

At any rate, whatever distinctiveness there may be or may not be in this presentation of the argument, we do not think that the argument has been successfully answered. A careful literary criticism does, we think, in an extraordinarily decisive way, show that the belief in the virgin birth is an integral part of the Palestinian narrative underlying Lk. i.5-ii.52; and this fact has an important bearing upon the ultimate historical question as to the origin of the belief.

Our argument at this point has, indeed, been subjected to an able and extended criticism by Ferd. Kattenbusch, in an article entitled "Die Geburtsgeschichte Jesu als Haggada der Urchristologie (Zu J. Gr. Machen, The virgin birth of Christ)", in *Theologische Studien und Kritiken*, cii, 1930, pp. 454-474. The distinguished church historian, after certain bibliographical suggestions which we have found very useful in the preparation of the present edition, and after an exceedingly sympathetic and generous treatment of the book as a whole (despite disagreement with its main thesis), has here given renewed expression to essentially the same view as that which he adumbrated in 1900 in his comprehensive monograph on the Apostles' Creed. Two stages, he still maintains, are to be distinguished in the formation of the Lucan birth narrative. In the former stage, there was still no thought of a birth without human father, but the Spirit of God was regarded merely as connected with the very being of Jesus the Messiah in a peculiarly intimate way that could not be predicated of the Spirit's connection with any prophet. In the later stage, which appears with clearness only in the words, "seeing I know not a man," in Lk. i.34b, there was at least a suggestion of the virgin birth.

In reply to this article, the reader may still be referred to pp. 156-160, 317-319, below. Some parts of these pages would no doubt have to be re-written if the later rather than the earlier presentation of Dr. Kattenbusch's hypothesis were in view. For example, what is said on p. 318 regarding the doctrine of the preëxistence of Jesus does not apply to the recent article; and it should be observed also that Dr. Kattenbusch now suggests that in the formation of the idea of the virgin birth pagan stories of supernatural births, in addition to Is. vii.14, may have had a part, though only in providing a stimulus by way of contrast and not in providing anything like genuine models for the

Christian story. But, in the first place, the earlier form of the hypothesis is still interesting, both in itself and because of its effects upon subsequent criticism; and, in the second place, the main outlines of our objections to Dr. Kattenbusch's view remain as they were before. Particularly unconvincing, we are compelled to think, is what he says (on pp. 464f.) regarding the relation between the account of the birth of John the Baptist and that of the birth of Jesus in Lk. i.5-ii.52. He thinks it significant that the relation is not represented, more clearly than it is, as a relation between a lesser wonder and a greater one. But, as a matter of fact, it is difficult to see how anything could be clearer than Lk. i.36. According to Dr. Kattenbusch's theory, the angel ought to have been represented as saying to Mary: "And, behold, thy kinswoman Elisabeth, she also hath conceived a son who will be filled with the Spirit from his mother's womb; understand, therefore, that thy Son will be connected with the Spirit in an even more intimate way." As a matter of fact, what the angel did say, according to the narrative, is: "And, behold, thy kinswoman Elisabeth, she also hath conceived a son in her old age." Evidently the meaning is that the wonder in the case of Mary, though far greater, is analogous to the wonder in the case of Elisabeth in that it has to do with the physical fact of the conception of the child in the womb.

It is encouraging to observe that R. Bultmann (*Die Geschichte der synoptischen Tradition*, 2te Aufl., 1931, p. 322) expresses agreement with our insistence upon the intimate connection between Lk. i.34f. (including, of course, Lk. i.34b) and Lk. i.36f.; but his own hypothesis—that Lk. i.34-37 was composed by the author of the Gospel in imitation of Lk. i.18-20—is faced by serious special objections (which are set forth on pp. 138, 148, below) in addition to the objections that apply equally to all forms of the interpolation hypothesis.

The book has been criticized by a number of writers (for example, in *The Times Literary Supplement*, London, for April 10, 1930) on the ground that it weakens its case by attempting to prove too much—by attempting to establish a thoroughgoing trustworthiness for the birth narratives in Matthew and Luke, instead of admitting the presence of a "midrashic" element as does G. H. Box.

In reply to this criticism, the author desires to say how very highly he values the work of Canon Box (whose important book on the virgin birth has recently been supplemented, in a very interesting way, by two articles entitled "The Virgin Birth, A Survey of Some Recent Literature," in *Laudate*, ix, 1931, pp. 77-88, 147-155); and he also desires to say how sharply he distinguishes the view of this scholar, who accepts as historical the central miracle in the birth narratives and rejects details, from the views of those who accept only details and reject the central miracle. The author has taken occasion, moreover, to say (in *British Weekly*, for August 21, 1930), in reply to a very sympathetic review by H. R. Mackintosh (in the same journal, for July 17, 1930), that he does not adopt the apologetic principle of "all or nothing," and that he rejoices in the large measure of agreement regarding the birth narratives that unites him with scholars like Canon Box and the late Bishop Gore, who reject many things in the Bible that he regards as true. Nevertheless, the author still believes that a thoroughgoing apologetic is the strongest apologetic in the end; and, in particular, he thinks that when the objections to the supernatural have once been overcome, there are removed with them, in a much more far-reaching way than is sometimes supposed, the objections to the birth narratives as a whole.

Finally, the author desires to say how greatly encouraged he has been by the manner in which the book has been received by Roman Catholic scholars —for example, by the learned Abbot of Downside, Dom Chapman (in *The Dublin Review*, xcv, 1931, pp. 150-153), to whom students of the New Testament and of patristics have long been deeply indebted. The author is not, indeed, inclined to accept the dictum of John Herman Randall and John Herman Randall, Jr., when, from the point of view of those opposed to all traditional Christianity, they say (*Religion and the Modern World*, 1929, p. 136): "Evangelical orthodoxy thrives on ignorance and is undermined by education; Catholic orthodoxy is based on conviction, and has an imposing educational system of its own." He makes bold to think that the scholarly tradition of the Protestant Church is not altogether dead even in our day, and he looks for a glorious revival of it when the narrowness of our metallic age gives place to a new Renaissance. But if he disagrees with what these writers say about Protestantism, he agrees to the full with their high estimate of the Roman Catholic Church; and he rejoices greatly in the important contributions made by Roman Catholic scholars to the subject dealt with in the present book.

J. G. M.

March, 1932.

CONTENTS

The Virgin Birth of Christ

INTRODUCTION

ACCORDING to a universal belief of the historic Christian Church, Jesus of Nazareth was born without human father, being conceived by the Holy Ghost and born of the virgin Mary. It is the purpose of the following discussion to investigate the origin of this belief. Whatever may be thought of the virgin birth itself, the belief of the Church in the virgin birth is a fact of history which no one denies. How is that fact to be explained?

Two explanations are possible.

In the first place, it may be held that the Church came to believe in the virgin birth for the simple reason that the virgin birth was a fact; the reason why the creed came to say that Jesus was conceived by the Holy Ghost and born of the virgin Mary is that He was actually so conceived and so born.

In the second place, it may be held that the virgin birth was not a fact, but that the Church came to accept it as a fact through some sort of error. This second explanation, obviously, is capable of many subdivisions. If the idea of the virgin birth is not founded on fact, how did that idea originate? Whatever the final answer to this question may be, the question itself must certainly be raised by everyone who denies the historicity of the virgin birth. If the virgin birth of Christ was not a fact, the idea of the virgin birth certainly was; and as a fact it requires some explanation.

The former of the two hypotheses—the hypothesis that the belief in the virgin birth was founded upon fact—will be considered in Chapters I-XI; the latter, in Chapters XII-XIV.

The consideration of the former hypothesis consists essentially in an examination of the positive testimony to the virgin birth and of the objections that have been raised against it; the consideration of the latter hypothesis consists in an examination of the alternative theories that have been proposed to explain the origin of the idea of the virgin birth on the supposition that it was not founded upon fact.

Chapter I

THE VIRGIN BIRTH IN THE SECOND CENTURY[1]

THE examination of the testimony to the virgin birth will deal principally, of course, with the New Testament. But a consideration of the patristic evidence is not altogether without value. Can we be certain that the belief of the Church in the virgin birth came exclusively from the New Testament? May there not in the early period have been a tradition as to the birth of Jesus that was independent of Matthew and Luke? The question cannot be answered offhand. Certainly it is quite conceivable that belief in the virgin birth existed prior to the time when it was put into writing in our First and Third Gospels, and conceivably that oral tradition may still have made itself felt to some extent even after our Gospels appeared. So long as such a possibility exists, whether it may or may not be discovered finally to be in accordance with the facts, we shall not be treating our subject fairly unless we prefix to our consideration of the New Testament evidence some consideration of the other testimony of the early Church. Indeed, that testimony would be important even if it should prove to be altogether based upon the New Testament; for in that case it might at least serve to establish the early date and wide acceptance of the New Testament narratives and the absence of any alternative story of the birth of Jesus that could raise effective opposition to those narratives. From various points of view, therefore, it is important to investigate the attitude toward the virgin birth of Christ which was assumed by the Christian Church in the period immediately subsequent to the time when the Gospels were written.

In such an investigation, the natural starting-point may be found in the great Christian writers of the close of the second century. At that time, when extant Christian literature (outside of the New Testament) first becomes abundant, the virgin birth may easily be shown to have had as firm a place in the belief of the Church as it had at any subsequent time. The doctrine was indeed denied by isolated sects—and such denials, with their roots in the preceding decades, will be considered at some length in the discussion that follows—but

[1] Much of the material of this chapter will be found in an article by the present writer, entitled "The Virgin Birth in the Second Century," in *Princeton Theological Review*, x, 1912, pp. 529–580. Some of the detailed evidence given in that article is here omitted, and there is added some treatment of the recent literature.

those sects that denied the virgin birth were at any rate altogether excluded from the main body of the Church. Irenæus (who lived in his youth in Asia Minor and listened there to the teaching of the aged Polycarp), Clement of Alexandria in Egypt, and Tertullian in North Africa, all not merely attest their own belief in the virgin birth, but treat it as one of the essential facts about Christ which had a firm place in even the briefest summaries of the Christian faith.

There can be no doubt, then, that at the close of the second century the virgin birth of Christ was regarded as an absolutely essential part of Christian belief by the Christian Church in all parts of the known world. So much is admitted by everyone.

But far more than this must be admitted so soon as there is any closer examination of the facts.

In the first place, even if there were no earlier testimonies, the very fact that at the close of the second century there was such a remarkable consensus among all parts of the Church would show that the doctrine was no new thing, but must have originated long before. But as a matter of fact there are earlier testimonies of a very important kind.

Among these earlier testimonies should, no doubt, be reckoned the so-called "Apostles' Creed."[2] The form of that creed which we use today was produced in Gaul in the fifth or sixth century, but this Gallican form is based upon an old Roman baptismal confession, from which it differs for the most part only in minor details. The virgin birth appears as clearly in the older form of the creed as in the Gallican form.[3] The Roman confession, which was written originally in Greek, must be dated at least as early as A.D. 200, because it is the ancestor not only of our Gallican creed, but also of the many creeds used in various parts of the Western Church.[4] The use of the creed by Tertullian (North Africa) and Irenæus (Asia Minor and Gaul) pushes the date well back toward the middle of the second century. At that time, therefore, the virgin birth was part of the creed of the Roman Church; belief in it was solemnly confessed by every convert before baptism.

[2] The following discussion of the Apostles' Creed is for the most part not based upon independent investigation. All that is attempted is to point out the bearing which the commonly accepted conclusions in this field have upon the question of the virgin birth.

[3] The older form seems to have had simply "born of the Holy Ghost and the virgin Mary" (γεννηθέντα ἐκ πνεύματος ἁγίου καὶ Μαρίας τῆς παρθένου) instead of "conceived by the Holy Ghost, born of the virgin Mary." Whether the oldest form of all was simply "born of [or "through"] Mary the virgin" (γεννηθέντα ἐκ (διὰ) Μαρίας τῆς παρθένου) is an interesting question, but of minor importance for the present discussion. McGiffert (*The Apostles' Creed*, 1902) favors this short form. But compare Kattenbusch, *Das apostolische Symbolum*, ii, 1900, pp. 619 f.

[4] See Harnack, article "Apostolisches Symbolum," in Herzog-Hauck, *Realencyklopädie für protestantische Theologie und Kirche*, i, 1896, pp. 745 ff.

The importance of this fact should not be underestimated. In the first place, it is obvious that no new and strange doctrines could be incorporated in such a creed. Belief in the virgin birth was probably universal in the Roman Church and was probably required of every candidate for baptism long before it was given stereotyped expression in a definite baptismal confession. In the second place, the central position of the Roman Church makes it probable that what was regarded as essential Christian belief at Rome was also the belief of the Church at large. Finally, the character of the creed itself doubles the weight of the considerations just adduced. The old Roman creed is no elaborate compilation, but is very brief; the only facts about Jesus to which it gives a place are the virgin birth, the death, the resurrection, the ascension, the session at the right hand of God, and the future judgment. Evidently such an enumeration was intended as the very minimum of Christian belief. The virgin birth might well have been accepted by a large portion of the Church without finding a place in such a creed. Its presence there shows that it was regarded as one of the essentials, like the death and the resurrection.

The third quarter of the second century is not the earliest but almost the latest date which has been suggested by modern scholars for the origin of the old Roman creed. The question of an earlier dating depends to a considerable extent upon the question whether the creed does or does not exhibit a polemic character. McGiffert detects an anti-Marcionitic purpose in the creed, and places the date between A.D. 150 and 175; but a non-polemic interpretation is favored by Harnack [5] and Kattenbusch.[6] The creed, says Harnack, "originated in the missionary and catechetical function of the Church, and was at first purely a baptismal creed." [7] Surely this latter view is more likely to be correct. A polemic anti-Gnostic purpose would hardly have failed to appear much more clearly if it had actually been present. There is no reason, therefore, to place the creed later than the emergence of the great Gnostic systems; so far as the internal evidence goes, it might be put at a very much earlier time.

Striking parallels with the creed can be detected in writers whose activity lies wholly or partly in the former half of the second century, especially in Justin Martyr and in Ignatius. If such parallels are to be interpreted as indicating dependence upon the creed itself, then the creed must have been produced as early as A.D. 100. Moreover, the simplicity of form, and especially the brevity,

[5] Harnack, *Das apostolische Glaubensbekenntnis*, 26te Aufl., 1892, p. 18.

[6] In *Theologische Literaturzeitung*, xxxviii, 1913, column 598.

[7] "Es ist aus der missionirenden und katechetischen Function der Kirche hervorgegangen und war ursprünglich lediglich Taufsymbol" (*loc. cit.*).

of the creed speak strongly for a high antiquity. Could a compiler of A.D. 150 have resisted the temptation of guarding the faith definitely against heresy? [8]

This question of date is not so important as might at first sight be supposed. For even if the creed itself was not produced until a later time, the parallels in the early writers show that creed-like statements were prevalent in their day and that these creed-like statements included the virgin birth. It is merely a question, therefore, whether in those early formulations we have actual literary dependence upon the completed Apostles' Creed, or whether they represent rather the process by which the Apostles' Creed finally was compiled. In either case, the virgin birth appears in a central place in the faith of the Church.

Certainly if the Apostles' Creed was produced as late as A.D. 150, it is by no means the earliest second-century witness to the virgin birth.[9]

Justin Martyr, writing at about the middle of the century, regards the virgin birth as of fundamental importance, and defends it at length against Jewish and pagan objections. If he knew the Apostles' Creed, his insistence upon the virgin birth requires no comment. But even if he did not know the creed in its trinitarian form, he bears testimony to the existence of a Christological summary in which the virgin birth had a place.[10] The virgin birth comes naturally into his mind when he thinks of the fundamental facts of the life of Christ; and in one passage it appears rather clearly as part of a regular formula of exorcism.[11] As indicating the common belief of the Church a formula of exorcism is perhaps only less valuable than a baptismal confession. The details which it contains are mentioned not because of any particular relevancy under the circumstances, but merely as essential elements of the Christian conception of Christ. They are necessary to define His "name."

[8] Such internal evidence weighs very strongly with Kattenbusch, the author of the most elaborate modern monograph on the creed, who places the date at ±100 (*Das apostolische Symbolum*, ii, 1900, p. 328). Zahn (*Das apostolische Symbolum*, 2te Aufl., 1893, p. 47) supposes that the baptismal confession attained essentially the form which it has in the old Roman symbol at some time between 70 and 120.

[9] For second-century testimonies to the virgin birth, see especially Gore, *Dissertations on Subjects Connected with the Incarnation*, 1895, pp. 41 ff.; also Swete, *The Apostles' Creed*, 1894; and compare Hoben, "The Virgin Birth," in *American Journal of Theology*, vi, 1902, pp. 481 ff.

[10] See passages cited by Harnack in Gebhardt-Harnack-Zahn, *Patrum Apostolicorum Opera*, editio altera, I, ii, 1878, pp. 128–132.

[11] *Dial.*, 85 (Goodspeed, *Die ältesten Apologeten*, 1914, p. 197): "For every demon that is exorcised by the name of this very One, son of God and firstborn of all creation, and born through a virgin and become a man subject to suffering, and crucified under Pontius Pilate by your people, and dead, and risen from the dead, and ascended into heaven, is conquered and subdued." Compare Otto's note on this passage (in *Corpus apologetarum Christianorum*, editio tertia, ii, 1877, pp. 305 f.).

Aristides, whose "Apology"[12] may perhaps be dated at about A.D. 140,[13] regarded the virgin birth as one of the fundamental facts of Christianity.[14] Rendel Harris[15] supposes that the virgin birth formed part of the *symbolum fidei* as Aristides knew it. At any rate, it is given a place by Aristides in a very brief Christological summary. It appears clearly as one of the essential facts.

Ignatius, bishop of Syrian Antioch, who was martyred not later than A.D. 117, mentions the virgin birth clearly in several passages.[16] It is perfectly evident from these passages that Ignatius regarded the virginity of Mary as one of the essential facts about Christ. It is one of the "mysteries to be shouted aloud," one of the mysteries which were prepared by God in silence but now proclaimed to the ages by the wondrous star in the heavens. In one passage[17] the virgin birth forms part of a summary of the chief facts about Christ which is of the same general character as the summary which we detected in Justin Martyr. Harnack is therefore justified in saying that "Ignatius has freely reproduced a 'kerygma' of Christ which seems, in essentials, to be of a fairly

[12] The *Apology*, except for a fragment, was unknown until 1889, when a Syriac translation was discovered by J. Rendel Harris. Soon after, J. Armitage Robinson discovered that a Greek text had been preserved within the romance of *Barlaam and Josaphat*. For the reconstruction of the *Apology* and comprehensive discussions of Aristides, see especially Harris and Robinson, "The Apology of Aristides," second edition, in *Texts and Studies*, I, i, second edition, 1893; Seeberg, "Die Apologie des Aristides," in Zahn, *Forschungen zur Geschichte des neutestamentlichen Kanons*, v. Teil, 1893, pp. 159 ff; Geffcken, *Zwei griechische Apologeten*, 1907, pp. 1–96.

[13] So Seeberg. The date cannot be fixed with certainty, but the work bears marks of antiquity.

[14] See Harris and Robinson, *op. cit.*, 1893, pp. 29, 32, 36, 110, and p. 3 of the appended Syriac text; Seeberg, *op. cit.*, pp. 331 ff. The virgin birth is found in all three recensions—Armenian, Syriac and Greek. Without doubt it had a place in the original text.

[15] In Harris and Robinson, *op. cit.*, 1893, pp. 23 ff.

[16] Ignatius, *Eph.*, xviii.2–xix.1: "For our God, Jesus the Christ, was conceived in the womb by Mary, according to a dispensation, of the seed of David but also of the Holy Ghost; and He was born and was baptized that by His passion He might cleanse water. And hidden from the prince of this world were the virginity of Mary and her child-bearing and likewise also the death of the Lord—three mysteries to be cried aloud—the which were wrought in the silence of God." (Ὁ γὰρ Θεὸς ἡμῶν Ἰησοῦς ὁ Χριστὸς ἐκυοφορήθη ὑπὸ Μαρίας κατ' οἰκονομίαν, ἐκ σπέρματος μὲν Δαυεὶδ πνεύματος δὲ ἁγίου· ὃς ἐγεννήθη καὶ ἐβαπτίσθη ἵνα τῷ πάθει τὸ ὕδωρ καθαρίσῃ. Καὶ ἔλαθεν τὸν ἄρχοντα τοῦ αἰῶνος τούτου ἡ παρθενία Μαρίας καὶ ὁ τοκετὸς αὐτῆς, ὁμοίως καὶ ὁ θάνατος τοῦ Κυρίου· τρία μυστήρια κραυγῆς, ἅτινα ἐν ἡσυχίᾳ Θεοῦ ἐπράχθη). *Smyrn.*, i.1, 2: ". . . fully persuaded as touching our Lord that He is truly of the race of David according to the flesh, but Son of God by the Divine will and power, truly born of a virgin and baptized by John that *all righteousness might be fulfilled* by Him, truly nailed up in the flesh for our sakes under Pontius Pilate and Herod the tetrarch . . . ." (πεπληροφορημένους εἰς τὸν Κύριον ἡμῶν ἀληθῶς ὄντα ἐκ γένους Δαυεὶδ κατὰ σάρκα, υἱὸν Θεοῦ κατὰ θέλημα καὶ δύναμιν, γεγεννημένον ἀληθῶς ἐκ παρθένου, βεβαπτισμένον ὑπὸ Ἰωάννου ἵνα πληρωθῇ πᾶσα δικαιοσύνη ὑπ' αὐτοῦ, ἀληθῶς ἐπὶ Ποντίου Πιλάτου καὶ Ἡρώδου τετράρχου καθηλωμένον ὑπὲρ ἡμῶν ἐν σαρκί . . . . . .) In *Eph.*, vii.2 also (καὶ ἐκ Μαρίας καὶ ἐκ Θεοῦ), and in *Eph.*, xx (τῷ υἱῷ ἀνθρώπου καὶ υἱῷ Θεοῦ), Ignatius probably has the virgin birth definitely in mind. Text and translation in this note are derived from Lightfoot, *The Apostolic Fathers, Revised Texts with Short Introductions and English Translations*, 1907.

[17] *Smyrn.*, i.1, 2.

definite historical character and which contained, *inter alia,* the Virgin Birth, Pontius Pilate, and the ἀπέθανεν."[18]

The full importance of the testimony which Ignatius bears to the virgin birth can be appreciated only when the general purpose of his epistles is borne in mind.[19] Ignatius is arguing against docetists; to refute them it was not necessary to prove the virgin birth of Christ, but only to prove His real birth. "Born of a woman" would have been sufficient; indeed it might seem to be a more emphatic contradiction of docetism than "born of a virgin." Yet in *Smyrn.*, i.1 it is the latter phrase which Ignatius uses. The phrase seems to slip naturally from his pen.[20] He does not appear to be under the slightest necessity of defending it; apparently the opponents themselves accepted the virgin birth as over against an ordinary birth, but regarded it, as they did every other event in the earthly life of Christ, as a mere semblance. Ignatius clearly gives the impression that in his day the virgin birth was far beyond the reach of controversy, both in Antioch and in Asia Minor. Other errors had to be combated, but not an error which would make Jesus the son of Joseph by ordinary generation.

The testimony of Ignatius, therefore, is unequivocal. At about A.D. 110 belief in the virgin birth was no new thing; it was not a thing that had to be established by argument, but had its roots deep in the life of the Church. The value of this testimony, moreover, is enormously enhanced by the position and character of the person by whom it is borne. Ignatius was no neophyte, but bishop of the church at Syrian Antioch, the mother church of Gentile Christianity. The memory of such a person would of course stretch back for many years; and when we find him attesting the virgin birth not as a novelty but altogether as a matter of course, as one of the accepted facts about Christ, it becomes evident that the belief in the virgin birth must have been prevalent long before the close of the first century.

The other "Apostolic Fathers" do not mention the virgin birth, but their silence is entirely without evidential value.[21] The only extensive book among this little group of writings is the Shepherd of Hermas, and that curious work

[18] Harnack, article, "Apostolisches Symbolum," in Herzog-Hauck, *Realencyklopädie für protestantische Theologie und Kirche*, i, 1896, p. 751 (see the English translation, "*The Apostles' Creed*," 1901, pp. 59 f.). Similarly Bousset, *Kyrios Christos*, 2te Aufl., 1921, p. 269.

[19] For the argument which follows, see Swete, *op. cit.*, 1894, pp. 45 f.

[20] At other times, it is true, he does speak simply of the birth without mentioning the peculiar manner of it. See *Magn.*, xi, *Trall.*, ix.1.

[21] To call it "a uniform and notable silence" (Hoben, "The Virgin Birth," in *American Journal of Theology*, vi, 1902, p. 481) is misleading. The passages where Hoben supposes the virgin birth would have been mentioned if it had been accepted do not really lead to this conclusion.

scarcely mentions Christ at all. The other writings of the group are brief, and present no passages where it can be said that the virgin birth would have had to be mentioned if the writers accepted it. It is quite preposterous to expect the doctrine to be mentioned inevitably in every brief epistle and every moral treatise. How often is it mentioned today in the sermons and in the devotional writings even of those who insist most strongly upon it? The early Christian writers were not conscious that posterity would be dependent upon a few brief writings of theirs for its entire knowledge of the second-century Church. They were not concerned, therefore, to give a complete summary of their views about Jesus, but addressed themselves to special needs. Ignatius mentioned the virgin birth because the reality of Jesus' earthly life had been assailed. Against the docetic errorists, it was necessary to insist upon the birth of Jesus; and insistence upon the birth of Jesus meant insistence upon a virgin birth. Ignatius and his opponents were apparently not aware that any other kind of birth was being attributed to Jesus in the Church. The virgin birth of Christ, he says, is one of the great mysteries, and he insists upon the greatness of the mystery in order that his readers may see how important it is to hold, against the Docetists, that the mystery is a real thing and no mere semblance. The more marvellous the birth of Christ, the more important it becomes to vindicate its reality. Justin Martyr, on the other hand, mentioned the virgin birth because, in the first place, his plan was more comprehensive than that of the Apostolic Fathers. He was attempting a defence of Christianity as a whole, and therefore could not ignore such an essential element in Christian belief as the virgin birth of the Lord. In the second place, the virgin birth required special defence, because it was the object of special attack. But the attack came from outside the Church. The virgin birth was attacked by outsiders just because it was known as one of the characteristic Christian beliefs. The silence which early Christian writers preserve about the virgin birth when they are writing against schismatics and heretics, and Justin's elaborate defence of it against professed unbelievers, are alike indications of the firm position which it held in the faith of the Church.[22]

The preceding investigation has shown that a firm and well-formulated belief in the virgin birth extended back at least to the early years of the second century, and that the belief appears so much as a matter of course at that time that it could not possibly have been of recent origin.

The question arises, however, whether the testimony to the virgin birth was unanimous, even from the beginning of the second century on. May it not be

[22] Swete (*The Apostles' Creed*, 1894, pp. 46 f.) has rightly called attention to the testimony borne to the virgin birth even by heretics. Compare Bauer, *Das Leben Jesu im Zeitalter der neutestamentlichen Apokryphen*, 1909, pp. 37 ff. Those heretics who denied the virgin birth will be discussed below.

balanced by counter testimony to an ordinary human birth? Obviously the investigator must institute a careful search for positive denials of the virgin birth in the early period of the Christian Church.

Such denials are not hard to find; and they may be divided into two classes: (1) denials by opponents of Christianity, and (2) denials by professing Christians.

The denials that belong to the former of these two classes[23]—denials, that is, by opponents of Christianity—are not in themselves significant. No one could very well believe that Jesus came into the world by a stupendous miracle, and at the same time reject His lofty claims; opposition to Christianity as a whole necessarily involved opposition to the virgin birth. Denials by opponents of Christianity would, therefore, become significant only if the opponents should give evidence of possessing, positively, some alternative story of the birth of Jesus which might be regarded as historical as over against the New Testament story.

As a matter of fact, this condition is not satisfied by any of the denials of which we have knowledge. We should certainly not expect it to be satisfied by pagan denials[24] of Christianity; for it is hardly likely that at the time when Christianity had begun to claim the serious attention of the Græco-Roman world, the opponents would be able or willing to institute historical investigations in Palestine with regard to the birth of Jesus. Such a method of attack would be contrary to all that is known of the religious controversies of antiquity.

The case is a little different, however, with regard to the denials which proceeded from the Jews. From the very beginning, the Jews were in close contact with Jesus and with His followers, and the relation was for the most part one of active opposition. If the real facts of the birth of Jesus were concealed by the Christians, it is conceivable that the Jewish opponents could have handed down the true story. The Jewish view of the birth of Jesus must, therefore, be examined with some care.

The chief extant sources of information regarding early Jewish polemic against Christianity (in addition, of course, to the New Testament) are three in number: (1) Justin Martyr's Dialogue with Trypho, (2) Origen's treatise against Celsus, (3) the Talmud. In the earliest of these sources, Justin's Dialogue with Trypho, which was written about the middle of the second century, the Jew, Trypho, is not represented as adducing any concrete facts in opposition to the Christian story. The inconsistency of the virgin birth with the common

[23] See Bauer, *op. cit.*, pp. 458 ff.

[24] For the pagan denials, see Bauer, *op. cit.*, pp. 458 ff.

Jewish Messianic hopes is emphasized,[25] exception is taken to the Septuagint rendering at Isa. vii.14,[26] a discrediting similarity of the virgin birth to heathen myths such as the myth of the birth of Perseus from Danaë[27] is noticed, positive evidence against a virgin birth of the Messiah is adduced from the Old Testament.[28] But there is no alternative Jewish story of the actual circumstances of the birth of the man Jesus.[29]

Origen's treatise against Celsus[30] supplies what is lacking in Justin. The Jew whose anti-Christian polemic Celsus is repeating does not content himself with ordinary objections to the virgin birth or mere ridicule of it,[31] but seeks also to substitute for it an account of the true course of events, which Jesus Himself is said to have concealed by the miraculous story. Jesus, according to this Jewish polemic, was really the fruit of an adulterous union of Mary with a certain soldier whose name was Pantheras, and on account of her adultery His mother had been cast out of her home by her husband, the carpenter. Similar stories appear in the Talmud (but with wide divergences so far as names and circumstances are concerned), and reach their climax in the mediæval *Tōl'dōth Jēshū*. The same slander is also possibly alluded to by Tertullian.[32]

The Jewish polemic used by Celsus can hardly be put much later than the middle of the second century, and although the parts of the Talmud where the stories about Jesus occur are late, they are based upon earlier tradition. Furthermore, traces of this kind of Jewish polemic against the virgin birth have been discovered by some scholars in the Protevangelium of James,[33] and even in

25 *Dial.*, 49 (ed. Goodspeed, p. 147).

26 The objection is to the rendering παρθένος ("virgin") instead of νεᾶνις ("young woman"). See *Dial.*, 67 (ed. Goodspeed, p. 174). Compare *Dial.*, 43 (ed. Goodspeed, pp. 140 f.).

27 *Dial.*, 67 (ed. Goodspeed, p. 174).

28 *Dial.*, 68 (ed. Goodspeed, p. 177).

29 It has been suggested that there is an allusion to such an alternative story (which would resemble the one that will presently be examined) in *Dial.*, 23. There Justin calls Jesus, according to the manuscript reading, τὸν κατὰ τὴν βουλὴν τοῦ θεοῦ δίχα ἁμαρτίας τῆς ἀπὸ γένους τοῦ Ἀβραὰμ παρθένου γεννηθέντα υἱὸν θεοῦ Ἰησοῦν Χριστόν. If δίχα ἁμαρτίας is to be read, there may perhaps be an allusion to a story of a birth of Jesus out of wedlock; in saying that Jesus was born "apart from sin," Justin may perhaps be opposing that Jewish slander. But such an interpretation is very uncertain. Compare Otto's note. Goodspeed reads διὰ Μαρίας instead of δίχα ἁμαρτίας.

30 This work was itself written in the third century, but the work of Celsus against which it is directed dates from the latter part of the second century. That work of Celsus, though it was written by a pagan philosopher, seems to make use of the current Jewish polemic against Christianity, in which we are now interested.

31 *Contr. Cels.*, i. 39 (ed. Koetschau, i, 1899, p, 90).

32 *De spect.*, 30, "fabri aut quaestuariae filius," cited by Bauer (*op. cit.*, p. 458).

33 A. Meyer, in Hennecke, *Handbuch zu den neutestamentlichen Apokryphen*, 1904, pp. 99 f. There seems to be no necessity for supposing, as Meyer does, that the Protevangelium is directed also against a Jewish Christian (as distinguished from Jewish) belief in the birth of Jesus from Joseph and Mary.

the canonical Gospel of Matthew.[34] But however early the story of the adultery of Mary may be, it is now agreed by all serious historians that far from representing any independent tradition, it is based merely (by way of polemic) upon the Christian story of the virgin birth.[35] Hence the early Jewish slander is simply one testimony more, and that not an unimportant one, to the general belief of early Christianity in the virgin birth, and to the absence of any positive historical tradition that could contradict it. When the Jews set out to attack Christianity, it was necessary for them to attack the virgin birth, because that was an essential part of Christian belief; but what they put in opposition to it was not independent historical tradition, but either the obvious conjecture that Jesus was physically the son of His reputed father, Joseph, or else the utterly unbelievable slanderous story which has just been set forth.

Accordingly, the early denials of the virgin birth by opponents of Christianity have no weight whatever against the historicity of the event. The opponents presuppose the Christian doctrine, and have no historical tradition of their own to substitute for it. The mere fact of their opposition is of no importance whatever, for it is only what was to be expected. Unless they were to become Christians, they could hardly accept the virgin birth of Jesus Christ.

At first sight, however, it may not seem quite so easy to account for the other class of denials of the virgin birth—denials, namely, on the part of professing Christians. What except true historical tradition could lead any Christian to deny the miraculous conception of the Lord, provided he had once become acquainted with it? It becomes evident at once that Christian denials of the virgin birth demand very careful attention.[36]

When the virgin birth was denied, two possibilities were left open. If Jesus

[34] For example, by Zahn and by A. Meyer (*op. cit.*, p. 49). For an exposition and criticism of the view of Zahn, see below, pp. 230 f.

[35] The story of the illegitimate birth of Jesus was at least not excluded by Bahrdt (*Briefe über die Bibel im Volkston*, 1782, i, pp. 130 ff.) and was expanded into an elaborate narrative by Venturini, with detailed rationalizing not only of the canonical narratives, but also of the Protevangelium of James (Venturini, *Natürliche Geschichte des grossen Propheten von Nazareth*, 2te Aufl., 1806). According to Venturini, the true father of Jesus was connected with the Essenes; and afterwards Jesus Himself became an Essene. Venturini's romance was the source of the anonymous work, *Historische Enthüllungen über die wirklichen Ereignisse der Geburt und Jugend Jesu* (of which the second edition appeared at Braunschweig in 1849), which purported to be taken from an ancient manuscript! In more recent years, the biologist Haeckel has given credence to the Pandera story (*Welträthsel*, Neue Aufl., 1899, pp. 377–380; English translation, *The Riddle of the Universe*, 1901, pp. 328–330), but of course has not been followed by any serious historical student. Compare the refutations of Haeckel by Loofs, in *Christliche Welt*, xiii, 1899, columns 1069 f., and Hilgenfeld, in *Zeitschrift für wissenschaftliche Theologie*, xliii, 1900, pp. 271–277.

[36] The invaluable work of Bauer (*Das Leben Jesu im Zeitalter der neutestamentlichen Apokryphen*, 1909), which has already been cited a number of times, has been used very freely for the discussion that follows. Bauer (whose view about the fact of the virgin birth is, it is true, the opposite of our own) has collected the materials for investigation of this part of the subject with unparalleled fullness.

was not born of a virgin, He may have been begotten by Joseph, or else He may never have been born at all. Those who held the latter view [37] are of little importance for the present investigation, for their denial of the virgin birth evidently proceeded not from historical tradition, but from philosophical theory. To them, any birth, even a birth from a virgin, seemed to bring Christ into too intimate relation to the world.[38] If the story of the virgin birth is mythical, then Marcion's denial is not a refutation of the myth, but (if anything) a further development of it.[39]

Carpocrates and Cerinthus, who are included in Irenæus' account of early heretics, regarded Jesus as the son of Joseph and Mary. They differ from Marcion, therefore, in that what they substitute for the virgin birth is of itself easily believable. Hence their denial of the virgin birth, though it may turn out to be the product of philosophical speculation, may also turn out to be derived from historical tradition. The question cannot be quite so easily decided as in the case of Marcion.

Carpocrates [40] was a Gnostic thinker of the former half of the second century. The world he held to have been created by angels far inferior to the supreme Father. Jesus, he supposed, differed from other men only in greater strength of soul, which enabled Him to remember what He had seen in the presence of the supreme God. God sent a power upon Him, in order that He might escape from the creators of the world. Every soul that will imitate Jesus may accomplish as much as He. In order to escape further incarnations, men should strive to have experience of all kinds of actions. All morality consists in faith and love; everything else is good or bad only in human opinion, not in reality.

It will be seen at once how very slight is the connection of such a system with Christianity. It is not surprising that followers of Carpocrates at Rome placed representations of Jesus by the side of those of Pythagoras, Plato and Aristotle, very much after the manner followed at a later time by the Emperor Alexander Severus.[41]

Obviously the author of such a system would not require any historical evidence to induce him to deny the virgin birth, even if it were a universally

[37] For example, Marcion. See Bauer, *op. cit.*, pp. 34 ff.

[38] See the vigorous passage in Tertullian, *de carne Christi*, i (ed. Oehler, ii, 1854, pp. 425, 426).

[39] If, as was formerly supposed by some scholars, Marcion's Gospel, which contained no account of the birth of Jesus, represented the original form of the Gospel of Luke, of which our Third Gospel is an expansion, then Marcion could not be dismissed so readily. But that hypothesis has now generally been abandoned. It is now admitted that Marcion's Gospel is an abridgment of our Gospel of Luke.

[40] See, for example, G. Krüger, article "Karpokrates," in Herzog-Hauck, *op. cit.*, x, 1901, pp. 97–99.

[41] Irenæus, *haer.*, I. xxv (ed. Stieren).

accepted doctrine among the Christians of his day. For it was essential to his system that Jesus should start on an equality with other men, except for a greater freedom of soul. Only so could imitation of Him on the part of other men insure a success equal to His. If Jesus was born of a virgin, then a fundamental difference of nature, as well as of character, between Him and other men would have to be assumed; and His followers could have no assurance that it was not that different nature, unattainable to others, which procured Him His victory over the powers of the world. Of course, it may be held by some modern men that Carpocrates was quite correct in regarding Christianity as consisting simply in imitation of Jesus. But even then the whole character of his system, which is suffused with ideas of pagan philosophy, is hopelessly opposed to the view that such a correct interpretation of Christianity was anything more than a lucky guess. He is a bold historian who would trace the line of true primitive Christian tradition through Carpocrates rather than through Ignatius or Justin. As a matter of fact, Carpocrates cannot be regarded as a "Christian" except in a very loose sense of the word. His followers were only following out the teachings of their master when they claimed to be equal to Jesus or even stronger than He.[42] Carpocrates' denial of the virgin birth is perhaps not so very much more significant than that of Celsus.

Cerinthus is discussed by Irenæus[43] immediately after the discussion of Carpocrates. That his life must have fallen at a very early time is indicated by the familiar tradition of his encounter with the Apostle John in the bath-house at Ephesus. Like Carpocrates, he was a Gnostic, and like Carpocrates he regarded Jesus as the son of Joseph and Mary. But he supposed that after the baptism the Christ descended upon the man Jesus and enabled Him to proclaim the unknown Father and to work miracles, only to leave Him again before the crucifixion. It has been widely held by modern scholars that the view which dated the Messiahship and divine sonship of Jesus from the coming of the Spirit at the baptism represented an intermediate stage between the historical, purely humanitarian view of Jesus and the fully developed doctrine of the virgin birth, which extended the divine sonship back to the very beginning of Jesus' earthly life. If such was the development, Cerinthus may seem to be a witness to that intermediate view which had not yet relinquished the purely human birth of Jesus.[44]

Another explanation, however, will account at least equally well for the

[42] Irenæus, *haer.*, I. xxv. 2.

[43] *Haer.*, I. xxvi. 1.

[44] Compare Usener, *Das Weihnachtsfest*, 2te Aufl., 1911, pp. 122–131. Usener places the Christology of Cerinthus between that of Carpocrates and the later doctrine of the Church as it appears in the doctrine of the virgin birth.

absence of the virgin birth in the teaching of Cerinthus. It has just been observed that Cerinthus supposed the Christ to have departed from Jesus before the passion. Will it be supposed that such a view is more primitive than the view which held the Christ to have suffered on the cross in order that He might be raised up in glory? Is it not more likely that the teaching of Cerinthus on this point was due simply to a fear of bringing the Christ into too close relationship with the world? But if that is so, then the same dogmatic interest will account for Cerinthus' rejection of the virgin birth, supposing the doctrine to have been generally accepted in the Church of his day. Upon docetic principles, it was impossible for the Christ to be born at all, even from a virgin. Therefore He must have been united with the man Jesus only subsequently. But if the man Jesus thus had no relation with the Christ until His baptism, then there was no reason why He should be supposed to have been born of a virgin. Indeed, there was a positive reason to the contrary. For birth from a virgin was felt to involve divine sonship. Hence, if Cerinthus had accepted the virgin birth he would have been obliged to accept such a real incarnation of the Son of God as his exemption of the Christ from the passion shows him to have been anxious most of all to avoid. The virgin birth, therefore, was thoroughly abhorrent to the principles of Cerinthus, and his denial of it may well have been due to philosophical prepossession rather than to historical tradition.[45]

It may be objected that Cerinthus accepted the bodily resurrection of the man Jesus, even though he represented the Christ as having already departed from Jesus before the passion. Why should he have had any greater philosophical objection to the virgin birth of the man Jesus than he had to His resurrection? But to this objection there is a satisfactory reply. It is not true that the virgin birth was no more obviously inconsistent than was the resurrection with the dualistic principles of Cerinthus; for the virgin birth, at least to a man of Greek training, if not to a Jew, would seem to involve divine sonship far more clearly than would the resurrection. Mt. i.18-25 and Lk. i.35 might well have seemed to Cerinthus—falsely, indeed, but in view of Cerinthus' training quite naturally—to represent the supreme God as no more separate from the world than Zeus or the other divinities of Greek mythology; and if that representation were correct, then the whole dualistic system of Cerinthus would fall to the ground. We do not mean that in reading such a passage as Lk. i.35 Cerinthus would necessarily think of the divine begettings that are spoken of in Greek mythology—certainly such analogies are, as a matter of fact, exceed-

[45] Irenæus (*loc. cit.*) says that Cerinthus denied the virgin birth because it seemed to him to be impossible ("impossibile enim hoc ei visum est"). Does this mean that the objections of Cerinthus were philosophical rather than historical?

ingly remote. But at any rate the passage does speak of the human child Jesus distinctly as Son of God; and to any such designation of a human child the entire system of this early Gnostic is irreconcilably opposed.[46]

The denials of the virgin birth that have thus far been discussed [47] are alike in that they each proceeded from a single individual. This circumstance has facilitated the psychological exhibition of the motives for such denials. The system of Marcion, for example, is a fairly definite thing, and it can easily be shown that the virgin birth was inconsistent with it. The case is different, however, with the class of denials of the virgin birth which must next be examined; for the authors of these denials can be grouped under no more specific heading than "Jewish Christians" or at the best "Ebionites."

The Jewish Christian denial of the virgin birth appears for the first time, in our extant literature, in Justin Martyr's Dialogue with Trypho. The Jew Trypho, in that Dialogue, is represented as objecting to the preëxistence and virgin birth of Christ. These things, according to Trypho, being unlikely and incapable of proof, the whole Christian contention about Christ falls to the ground. In reply, Justin insists upon a certain division of the questions at issue. "Even if you deny the preëxistence and the virgin birth," he says in effect, "you may still accept the Messiahship; indeed, there are certain men of your own race who hold exactly that intermediate view:"

"For indeed, my friends, there are some," I said, "of your own race who confess that He is Christ but maintain that He was born a man from men; with whom I do not agree, nor would the majority of those who have come to the same way of thinking as I, since we have been commanded by Christ Himself to obey not human

[46] It is no decisive objection to this argument that the Ophites of Irenæus (*haer.*, I. xxx), though they held that the Christ descended upon Jesus at the baptism and departed from Him before the crucifixion, accepted the virgin birth (see Usener, *op. cit.*, pp. 137–139). On the contrary, that fact merely shows that the compulsion exerted upon Gnostic sects by the Christian tradition of the virgin birth was in some cases strong enough to overcome even the strongest philosophical prepossessions. Usener himself says (*op. cit.*, p. 138): "We observe how the virgin birth, after it had been received into the written Gospel, demanded recognition and forced even the most recalcitrant docetic systems to deal with it, and how the attempts at reconciliation were at first forced and awkward and then became more skillful." The only question is whether the contradictions did not arise on account of Gnostic innovations rather than (as Usener thinks) on account of innovations in our Gospel narratives.

[47] It is perfectly possible that other Gnostics besides the disciples of Carpocrates and Cerinthus denied the virgin birth (see Bauer, *op. cit.*, pp. 31 f.). With regard to the Gnostic Justin, the matter is perhaps not quite so clear as is sometimes assumed. It is not quite certain that this Justin regarded Jesus as begotten by Joseph, though he speaks of Him (Hippol., *Philos.* V. xxvi. 29, ed. Wendland, iii, 1916, p. 131) as son of Joseph and Mary. At any rate, any other Gnostics who may have denied the virgin birth are fully as unlikely as Carpocrates and Cerinthus to have been influenced in their denial by historical tradition.

teachings, but the things that were proclaimed through the blessed prophets and taught through Him."[48]

At the decisive point in this passage the manuscripts have until recently always been held to read "certain men of *our* race" instead of "certain men of *your* race"; and on that basis extensive use has been made of the passage in the attack on the early witnesses to the virgin birth. Justin Martyr, it has been insisted, recognizes men who deny the virgin birth as "men of our race"—that is, as Christians—hence he could not have regarded the virgin birth as one of the essential elements in Christian belief; the doctrine had, therefore, not yet become firmly established as part of the irreducible minimum of what a Christian must believe.

Other scholars, quite correctly, were unable to satisfy themselves with what in Justin would be an entirely unparalleled designation of the Christians as "men of our race"; and hence preferred, by a simple emendation of the text, to substitute *"your* race" for *"our* race."[49] "Your race" is in the Dialogue a common designation of the Jews, occurs in this immediate context, and is imperatively demanded by the thought. Never was an emendation more clearly required.

But then, after some scholars had based the most far-reaching arguments upon the reading "our race," and other scholars had argued learnedly in favor of a conjectural emendation "your race," Harnack conceived the idea of examining the basic manuscript for himself. And the result was that "your race" was found to have been the manuscript reading all along![50]

Accordingly, Justin does *not* say in this passage that those who denied the virgin birth are Christians. There is no contradiction, therefore, of what we have already shown to be the settled conviction of the same writer—namely,

[48] Justin Martyr, *dial.*, 48 (ed. Goodspeed, pp. 146 f.). For the translation some assistance has been received from Reith, in *Ante-Nicene Christian Library*, ii, 1867, pp. 148 f. The latter half of the sentence quoted is very obscure. For a different translation of it, see A. Lukyn Williams, *Justin Martyr, The Dialogue with Trypho*, 1930, p. 96.

[49] Reading ὑμετέρου instead of ἡμετέρου.

[50] The primary manuscript of the Dialogue is a dated manuscript of the year 1364, which is in the Bibliothèque nationale at Paris, the only other extant manuscript being regarded as clearly secondary and without much value. Harnack's discovery of the real reading of the Paris manuscript was reported in his *Dogmengeschichte*, 4te Aufl., i, 1909, p. 320. The present writer has examined the manuscript, and can report that the reading ὑμετέρου is perfectly plain. There could never have been any doubt but that the first letter of the word is υ and not η. The whole trouble was apparently caused by a mistake of the first publisher, Stephanus, which was copied by subsequent editors. Seldom has such a mistake been fraught with more disastrous consequences. Even after Harnack called attention to the error, we find such a scholar as James Moffatt (for example) drawing from the erroneous reading the conclusion that Justin recognizes as Christians those who reject the virgin birth (Moffatt, *Introduction to the Literature of the New Testament*, 3rd edition, 1918, printing of 1925, p. 10, footnote 2). Goodspeed has the correct reading in his edition of the Dialogue.

that the virgin birth was one of the fundamental things which every Christian apologist is called upon to defend. What he does say is merely that the Jew is illogical in rejecting the Messiahship of Jesus simply because he feels obliged to reject the preëxistence and the virgin birth. If the Jew could be induced to see that he was wrong at least about the Messiahship, then he might finally be convinced of his error about the virgin birth as well. Compared with full Christianity, and in itself, that mere recognition of the Messiahship of Jesus no doubt seemed to Justin entirely inadequate; but regarded simply and solely as a stepping-stone to higher things, it might serve Justin's immediate purpose.

The information to be derived from the passage, therefore, is simply that at the time of Justin Martyr there were certain men of Jewish descent who, although they accepted Jesus as the Messiah, regarded Him as merely human and born in the ordinary human way.[51] Certainly Justin does not say that all Jewish Christians denied the virgin birth;[52] indeed, the indefinite form of expression seems to suggest the exact opposite.[53] In the passage[54] just preceding the one here under discussion, Justin has been discussing the schismatic Jewish Christians at some length, and has divided them into two classes according to their position with regard to the necessity of Gentile Christian observance of the Mosaic law. Here, however, he refers to these believers in the Messiahship who denied the virgin birth as though they were entirely independent of the Jewish Christians whom he has just been discussing. If he had meant that all of the schismatic Jewish Christians, of both parties, rejected the virgin birth, surely he would have used some other expression than "certain men of your race" to designate them; he would naturally have spoken of them as "*these* men of your race, whom we have just been discussing," or the like. The reader certainly receives the impression that the "certain men" of Chapter 48 are comparatively few in number, and that they were left entirely out of account in the general division of schismatic Jewish Christianity which was set up in Chapter 47. Apparently Justin has to inform the Jew, as a thing not known before, or at least not prominently known, that there were men among his own race who denied the virgin birth and yet accepted the Messiahship of Jesus. The Jew had apparently jumped to the conclusion that in attacking the virgin birth he was attacking not merely part but all of the Christian conception of Christ; it seems never to have occurred to him that a man might conceivably reject the virgin birth and yet accept His Messiahship.

[51] *ἄνθρωπον . . . . . ἐξ ἀνθρώπων γενόμενον.*

[52] Bauer (*op. cit.*, p. 33) is entirely unwarranted in saying that the only Jewish Christians whom Justin knew were Jewish Christians who were not convinced of the virgin birth.

[53] Compare Zahn, *Geschichte des neutestamentlichen Kanons*, ii, 1890, p. 671, Anm. 2.

[54] *Dial.*, 47 (ed. Goodspeed, pp. 145 f.).

This passage, therefore, far from indicating that Justin knew no Jewish Christians except those who denied the virgin birth, proves rather that at the time of Justin the Jewish Christian opponents of the virgin birth—if we may use the term "Christian" for a moment in a loose sense—were so insignificant as to be ignored even by their own countrymen. Even among schismatic Jewish Christians they were apparently quite insignificant. And it must always be remembered that *schismatic* Jewish Christians, even including both of the two great classes mentioned in Chapter 47 of the Dialogue with Trypho, did not by any means include all the Jewish Christians. Many men of Jewish race no doubt united themselves simply with the main body of the Church and so lost their separate identity altogether. But the point that we are now making is that even among those who did not thus lose their separate identity, even among those who were unorthodox or schismatic, it is by no means clear, to say the least, that any considerable number, at the time of Justin, denied the virgin birth.

The next attestation of a Jewish Christian denial of the virgin birth appears in Irenæus' great work against heresies, which was written in the latter part of the second century. Here for the first time the term "Ebionites" occurs.[55] The relevant paragraph is as follows:[56]

> Those who are called Ebionites agree that the world was made by God; but their opinions with respect to the Lord are similar to those of Cerinthus and Carpocrates. They use the Gospel according to Matthew only, and repudiate the Apostle Paul, maintaining that he was an apostate from the law. As to the prophetical writings, they endeavour to expound them in a somewhat singular manner: they practise circumcision, persevere in the observance of those customs which are enjoined by the law, and are so Judaic in their style of life, that they even adore Jerusalem as if it were the house of God.

It is very difficult to determine from this tantalizingly brief passage what sort of sect the Ebionites were. Was their starting-point simply orthodox Pharisaic Judaism, or were they adherents of Gnostic views? In favor of the former alternative is to be placed their rejection of the Gnostic separation between a creator of the world on the one hand and a supreme God on the other, and

[55] Origen (*de princip.*, iv. 22) derives the name from a Hebrew word meaning "poor," and interprets it of the spiritual poverty of the sect. Perhaps it was originally a term used among the Jews to designate Christians in general, or else it may have been applied in a good sense by the Ebionites to themselves. Tertullian and others supposed that Ebion was the name of the founder of the sect, but this hypothesis, despite the vigorous defense of it by Hilgenfeld (compare also Dalman, *Die Worte Jesu*, 1898, p. 42, Anm. 2; English translation, *The Words of Jesus*, 1902, pp. 52 f., footnote 3), has generally been abandoned.

[56] Irenæus, *haer.*, I.xxvi. 2. The translation is that of Roberts and Rambaut in the *Ante Nicene Christian Library*, 1868.

also their strict adherence to the Mosaic law. But the matter is not so clear as is sometimes assumed. It is distinctly said that they held opinions with respect to the Lord "similar to those of Cerinthus and Carpocrates."[57] If this assertion is to be taken strictly, it might seem to involve the Ebionites in a Gnostic way of thinking; for Cerinthus, at least, held to the typically Gnostic separation between the man Jesus and the Christ who descended upon Him at the baptism. Carpocrates, it must be admitted, held a somewhat different view of the Lord; so that it might look as though Irenæus' ascription to the Ebionites of similarity to the views of Cerinthus and Carpocrates might refer only to the negative aspect of their views, especially to their rejection of the virgin birth. But even Carpocrates held that "a power descended upon him [the man Jesus] from the Father, that by means of it He might escape from the creators of the world."[58] This descent of a "power" upon Jesus may well have been essentially similar to Cerinthus' descent of the "Christ" upon Him; so that, after all, if the Ebionites were, as Irenæus says, similar to Cerinthus and Carpocrates in their view of the Lord, they may have been representatives not of a conservative Pharisaic Judaism, but of a Gnosticizing tendency.[59]

Another possible indication of Gnostic views in these Ebionites is found in the assertion that they endeavor to expound the prophetical writings "in a somewhat singular manner."[60] The curious expositions of Scripture here referred to may perhaps have involved Gnostic speculations. Schliemann[61] suggested a different interpretation. He held that what the passage really means is that the Ebionites sought to determine what things are prophetic. But this interpretation also may involve these Ebionites in affinity for Gnostic views; since it would enable us to discover a marked parallel between them and the Gnostic Ebionites of Epiphanius, who exercised criticism on the Old Testament.[62] The question must be left unsettled. It is not clear whether the sect that Irenæus here mentions was or was not of a Gnostic character.

57 On the removal of the "not," which occurs in the Latin text before "similar," see Harvey's edition of Irenæus, i, 1857, pp. 212 f.

58 Irenæus, *haer.*, I.xxv. 1 (translation of Roberts and Rambaut).

59 It is perhaps significant that Filastrius, in reproducing the lost *Syntagma* of Hippolytus (who is so largely dependent on Irenæus) brings the Ebionites into connection especially with Cerinthus rather than with Cerinthus and Carpocrates taken together. See Filastrius, c.ix (ed. Marx, 1898, p. 20, in the Vienna *Corpus*, vol. xxxviii): "Hebion discipulus eius Cerinthi, in multis ei similiter errans saluatorem nostrum hominem de Joseph natum carnaliter aestimabat, nihilque diuinitatis in eo fuisse docebat," etc.

60 "Quae autem sunt prophetica, curiosius exponere nituntur."

61 *Die Clementinen*, 1844, pp. 494–497. Compare Schmidtke, "Neue Fragmente und Untersuchungen zu den judenchristlichen Evangelien," in *Texte und Untersuchungen*, 37. Band, Heft 1. 1911, pp. 226 f.

62 See below, pp. 23–26.

Dependent upon Irenæus is Hippolytus, whose description of the Ebionites is as follows: [63]

> But the Ebionæi admit that the cosmos came into being by the God who is; and concerning Christ they invent the same things as Cerinthus and Carpocrates. They live according to Jewish customs, thinking that they will be justified by the Law and saying that Jesus was justified in practising the Law. Wherefore He was named by God Christ and Jesus, since none of them [64] has fulfilled the Law. For if any other had practised the commandments which are in the Law, he would be the Christ. And they say it is possible for them if they do likewise to become Christs; and that He was a man like unto all [men].

Here the well-known dependence of Hippolytus upon Irenæus appears in the first sentence. But in the rest of the passage the purely humanitarian way in which the Ebionites thought about Jesus is more clearly and fully expressed. Other men, Hippolytus says, could, according to the Ebionites, have been Christs, as Jesus was Christ, if like Him they should keep the law. There seems to be no hint here of Gnostic beliefs; though the notion that Jesus began on the same level with other men, so that they could emulate Him, is similar to views that Irenæus and Hippolytus attribute to Carpocrates. At any rate, the absence of any mention of distinctly Gnostic views in this passage is no clear proof that these Ebionites of Hippolytus were simple conservative or Pharisaic Jews. Other evidence may conceivably lead us to suspect that they were tinged with syncretistic if not Gnostic opinions. Certainly a view that made Jesus "Christ" only in a sense that might be possible for other men if only they should perfectly keep the law is far removed from any belief that could by any possibility be attributed to the primitive Palestinian Church.

When Tertullian [65] says that "Ebion" declared an "angel" to have been in Christ, as also in Zechariah, it is possible to think of some sort of Gnosticizing view of a union of the man Jesus with a heavenly being; but the passage is obscure.

In the writings of Origen, who lived in the former half of the third century, the Ebionites appear divided clearly into two classes, of which one accepted and the other denied the virgin birth. The matter appears with special clearness in a passage where Origen, with his characteristic allegorical method of exegesis, makes the Gospel incident of the healing of the blind man (or the two blind

[63] Hippolytus, *ref. omn. haer.*, vii. 34 (ed. Wendland, iii, 1916, p. 221). The translation is that of Legge, *Philosophumena* (in *Translations of Christian Literature*), 1921, ii, p. 93.

[64] Wendland conjectures, "none of the others," instead of "none of them."

[65] *De carne Christi*, 14 (ed. Oehler, ii, 1854, pp. 450 f.). Compare the translation by Holmes in the *Ante-Nicene Christian Library*.

men) at Jericho refer to the ecclesiastical conditions of his own time.[66] The blind beggar, Origen says, represents schismatic Jewish Christianity in its spiritual poverty. Jewish Christians show their poverty by the low view which they hold of the person of Christ; like the beggar, they address Jesus as "son of David" instead of by some higher title. They either suppose Him to have been born of Joseph and Mary, or else, admitting His birth from Mary and the divine Spirit, they deny His divinity.[67] The Gentile Christians rebuke the Jewish Christians for their low view of the person of Christ, as the crowd rebuked the beggar for his cry of "Son of David." The beggar, however, cried out all the more, and Jesus honored his real though inadequate faith by commanding him to be brought near. Then the beggar bethought himself of a higher title than "Son of David" and said "Rabbouni," "my Master." Not till then did the Saviour grant the restoration of sight. That lower view of the person of Christ is, therefore, according to Origen, insufficient for salvation; but it may serve as a stepping-stone to a more adequate faith.[68]

In this passage, apparently the only Jewish Christianity which Origen has in view is one which could be regarded by the crowds of Gentile Christians who were following after Jesus as an "Israelitish remnant sitting by the way." Yet even among men who held such a low, humanitarian view of the person of Christ there were not wanting some who accepted the virgin birth.

In the fifth book of Origen's treatise against Celsus,[69] Origen answers the charge of Celsus that the Christians do not differ from the Jews as follows:

> Suppose there are some who receive Jesus and on this ground boast that they are Christians, and yet wish to live according to the Jews' law like the mass of the Jews (and these are the twofold sect of Ebionites, who either acknowledge with us that Jesus was born of a virgin, or deny this, and maintain that He was begotten like other human beings) [70]—what does this fact establish against those of the Church, whom Celsus has designated "those of the multitude"? [71]

The name "Ebionites," which is here applied to these heretical Jewish Christians, was alluded to in the passage just cited from the Commentary on Matthew. The incidental use of the phrase, "the twofold Ebionites," [72] seems to show that the division between those Ebionites who denied the virgin birth

[66] Origen, *in evangelium Matt.*, xvi.10 ff. (ed. Lommatzsch, iv, 1834, pp. 32 ff.).

[67] ὁτὲ μὲν ἐκ Μαρίας καὶ τοῦ Ἰωσὴφ οἰωμένων αὐτὸν εἶναι, ὁτὲ δὲ ἐκ Μαρίας μὲν μόνης καὶ τοῦ θείου πνεύματος, οὐ μὴν καὶ μετὰ τῆς περὶ αὐτοῦ θεολογίας.

[68] Compare above, pp. 16 f., with respect to Justin Martyr.

[69] *Contr. Cels.*, v. 61 (ed. Lommatzsch, xix, 1846, pp. 283 f.).

[70] The translation of this parenthesis is that of Crombie, in the *Ante-Nicene Christian Library*.

[71] ἀπὸ τοῦ πλήθους. The translation of this phrase has been taken from Crombie, *loc. cit.*

[72] οἱ διττοὶ Ἐβιωναῖοι Compare *contr. Cels.*, v. 65 (ed. Lommatzsch, xix, 1846, p. 295), Ἐβιωναῖοι ἀμφότεροι.

and those who accepted it was no mere unimportant or fluctuating one.[73] The same division appears in Eusebius.[74] In Epiphanius and Jerome, who lived in the latter part of the fourth century and in the beginning of the fifth, the terminology (at least) differs; for by these writers those who accepted the virgin birth are called "Nazarenes,"[75] while the term Ebionites is reserved for those who denied it.[76]

Epiphanius' terminology has been followed by some scholars (for example by Zahn), the term "Nazarenes" being used for the more orthodox and milder class of Ebionites, "Ebionites" for the less orthodox. Whatever terminology be adopted, it is at least fairly plain that from the time of Origen to the time of Epiphanius there were two parties among the schismatic Jewish Christians, one of which denied the virgin birth, while the other accepted it.[77] In the period before Origen, Irenæus and, following him, Hippolytus mention only Ebionites who reject the virgin birth; but their failure to mention the other division of the schismatic Jewish Christians does not prove that it did not exist at the time when they wrote. For, in the first place, the less pronouncedly heretical character of those Jewish Christians who accepted the virgin birth might well cause them to be omitted from a catalogue of heresies;[78] and, in

[73] Harnack is, therefore, to say the least, venturing on doubtful ground when he says (*Dogmengeschichte*, 4te Aufl., i, 1909, p. 323): "[There was]—syncretistic (Gnostic) Jewish Christians being left out of account—only one group of Jewish Christians (with various shadings), which named itself from the beginning both 'Nazarenes' and 'Ebionites.'" Compare Harnack, *Chronologie der altchristlichen Litteratur*, i, 1897, pp. 633 f., Anm. 1; Zahn, *Geschichte des neutestamentlichen Kanons*, ii, 1890, p. 664, Anm. 2; McGiffert, "The Church History of Eusebius," in *Nicene and Post-Nicene Fathers*, on *hist. eccl.*, III. xxvii, note 1.

[74] *Hist. eccl.*, III. xxvii (ed. Schwartz, ii, 1903, pp. 254, 256).

[75] Epiphanius (*haer.*, xxix. 1, ed. Holl, i, 1915, pp. 321 f.) says that this term was originally applied to all Christians.

[76] Apparently Jerome does not say in so many words that the Ebionites denied the virgin birth. But he seems to contrast their view with the acceptance of the doctrine on the part of the Nazarenes. In one place, Epiphanius says that he does not know whether the Nazarenes regarded Jesus as a mere man or as begotten of the Holy Ghost and born of Mary (Epiphanius, *haer.*, xxix. 7, ed. Holl, i, 1915, pp. 329 f.). But evidently that doubt is merely due to the vagueness of Epiphanius' knowledge about this sect. The character of the sect is plainly indicated, so far as the belief in the virgin birth is concerned, by Jerome; and Epiphanius himself tells certain things about them which really imply their belief in the virgin birth.

[77] It should be noted that Origen regards both classes of Ebionites as standing outside the limits of the Church: he blames Celsus for confusing these errorists with "the men of the Church" (τοῖς ἀπὸ τῆς ἐκκλησίας). Compare *in Lucam homiliæ*, xvii (ed. Lommatzsch, v, 1835, pp. 148 f.), where, after remarking that all things which history narrates concerning the Saviour, including the virgin birth, are contradicted, Origen says that those who contradict are not those who believe in Christ.

[78] Thus Eusebius (*hist. eccl.*, VI. xvii) characterizes the Ebionites in general as those who deny the virgin birth, although in *hist. eccl.*, III. xxvii, he has mentioned Ebionites who accept it. Origen also, in the passage just cited from the *hom. in Luc.*, speaks of the Ebionites as those who deny the virgin birth, although he, too, as we have just shown, knew of Ebionites who accepted it. The passage is perhaps worthy of being quoted. "All things which the story about the Saviour narrates," says Origen, "are spoken against. The virgin is a mother—this is a sign

the second place, Irenæus and Hippolytus, since they lived in the West, can hardly be expected to give minute information about a Jewish Christianity that existed wholly or chiefly in the East.

Which of these two classes of Jewish Christians seems more likely to have preserved the correct tradition about the birth of Jesus? Unfortunately, the earliest detailed information, at least about the less heretical group, dates only from the latter half of the fourth century. It will be necessary to start from that point and work backwards.

In the latter half of the fourth century, the Ebionites, the less orthodox class of schismatic Jewish Christians, are described in some detail by Epiphanius.[79] His account is far from clear, and must be used with caution. Despite his faults, however, he has evidently preserved valuable information about the Ebionites which without him would have been lost.

According to Epiphanius, Ebion started from the sect of the Nazarenes, and began his special teaching after the destruction of Jerusalem, east of the Jordan, where the Nazarenes also had their seat. The Ebionites followed the Jewish law, and in washings even went beyond the Jews. In general the Ebionitic sect is divided into factions; a certain "Elxai"[80] introduced confusion. The Ebionites regard the sexual relation as impure,[81] and therefore do not partake of animal food.[82] Jesus they hold to have been begotten of a human father;[83] the Christ came down upon Him in the form of a dove. The Christ was not

---

that is spoken against. The Marcionites contradict this sign, and say that he was not born of a woman at all. The Ebionites [or "Ebionites," since Latin has no article] contradict the sign, saying that he was born of a man and a woman in like manner as we also are born." This passage is instructive as showing the way in which facts important in one connection may be left out of sight in another. There was no designation other than "Ebionites" for those schismatic Jewish Christians who believed that Jesus was born of Joseph and Mary; and here, in the broad contrast with the Marcionites who believed that Jesus was not born at all, the less characteristic body of Ebionites who accepted the virgin birth naturally do not come into Origen's mind. Compare McGiffert, in *Nicene and Post-Nicene Fathers*, on Eusebius, *hist. eccl.*, III. xxvii, note 5.

[79] *Haer.*, xxx (ed. Holl, i, 1915, pp. 333–382).

[80] The Elkesaites have generally been regarded as Gnostic Jewish Christians. But according to Brandt (*Elchasai*, 1912) the sect was at first not Christian at all, but simply Jewish. Elxai himself, Brandt believes, was a real individual, who in the days of Trajan produced, at least in substance, the book which was attributed to him. If the older view be held—that the Elkesaites were Christians—it is not quite impossible that the virgin birth was taught in the Elxai book (Hippol., *Philos.*, IX. xiv.1; X. xxix.1, 2, ed. Wendland, iii, 1916, pp. 252, 284).

[81] Epiphanius, *haer.*, xxx.15 (ed. Holl, i, p. 353). Yet Epiphanius also says that the Ebionites permit a plurality of marriages (haer., xxx. 18, ed. Holl, i, p. 357). The latter practice, he apparently thinks (*haer.*, xxx. 2, ed. Holl, i, pp. 334 f.), was a later development.

[82] *ἐμψύχων*.

[83] *ἐκ σπέρματος ἀνδρός*. Bauer (*op. cit.*, p. 31) is apparently mistaken when he says that Epiphanius represents the Ebionites as divided on the question of the birth of Jesus.

begotten by God the Father, but was created like one of the archangels, though He was greater than they; Christ came to abolish sacrifices. The Ebionites repudiate the work of Paul, and reject some of the Old Testament prophets.

The Ebionites use exclusively a single Gospel, which Epiphanius describes as a mutilated Matthew. They themselves call it the Hebrew Gospel or the Gospel according to the Hebrews. One of the fragments which Epiphanius has preserved refers to the apostles in the first person; the apostles are therefore perhaps represented as the authors of the book. Hence the Gospel might well be called the Gospel of the Twelve Apostles; and so it has often been identified with the work which is mentioned under that title by Origen.[84] The same fragment explains how the Gospel came to be called a Gospel of Matthew: Matthew is singled out by Jesus for direct address,[85] and so could be regarded as the representative of the other apostles in the composition of the book.[86]

The fragments which have been preserved by Epiphanius are amply sufficient to indicate the character of the Gospel. It is a Greek compilation based on our canonical Gospels of Matthew and Luke. That it is dependent on our Greek Gospels and was itself originally written in Greek is proved—among other indications—by the rather amusing substitution of the word "cake" for the word "locust" in the description of the food of John the Baptist; John the Baptist is said to have eaten, not locusts and wild honey, but "wild honey, whose taste was that of manna, as a cake with oil." The change is due to the vegetarian principles of the author.[87] But if some vegetable food was to be selected for John the Baptist, why were just cakes chosen? The reason is simply that the Greek word for "cake" happens to be very similar to the Greek word for "locust." [88] The same vegetarian principles of the author led him to change Lk. xxii.15, "With desire have I desired to eat this passover with you," into, "Have I with desire desired to eat this passover in the form of meat with you?" [89] The Ebionite opposition to sacrifices appears in the Gospel in the

[84] See Zahn, *Geschichte des neutestamentlichen Kanons*, ii, 1890, pp. 728 ff. Schmidtke ("Neue Fragmente und Untersuchungen zu den judenchristlichen Evangelien," in *Texte und Untersuchungen*, xxxvii. 1, 1911, pp. 170 ff.) protests vigorously against the identification; but it seems to be generally maintained by those who have written on the subject even after Schmidtke's book appeared.

[85] *καὶ σὲ τὸν Ματθαῖον.*

[86] See Zahn, *loc. cit.*

[87] See Zahn, *op. cit.*, ii, 1890, p. 733.

[88] *ἐγχρίς*, "cake"; *ἀκρίς*, "locust."

[89] *Μὴ ἐπιθυμίᾳ ἐπεθύμησα κρέας τοῦτο τὸ πάσχα φαγεῖν μεθ' ὑμῶν.* The apposition of *κρέας* and *τοῦτο τὸ πάσχα* is difficult to translate into English.

saying attributed to Jesus: "I came to put an end to sacrifices; and unless ye cease sacrificing, wrath shall not cease from you."[90]

This Gospel of the Ebionites contained no account of the birth and infancy of Jesus; but incidentally it displays dependence upon the first chapter of Luke, and perhaps also upon the second chapter of Matthew.[91] In the account of the baptism of Jesus, the three forms of the voice from heaven which were current in the early Church are simply placed side by side.[92]

From the confused and contradictory assertions by Epiphanius, at least so much would seem to be clear—that the Ebionites as he describes them were not simply Pharisaic Jews who accepted Jesus as the Messiah, but were strongly affected by peculiar (perhaps Gnostic or syncretistic) ideas. Their rejection of parts of the Old Testament, their views about sacrifice, and their interpretation of the event at the baptism would seem to place the matter beyond doubt.[93]

Hence the question arises whether the sect which is described by Epiphanius is or is not entirely distinct from all of the Ebionites mentioned by Jerome and by the earlier writers, Irenæus, Hippolytus, Origen, and Eusebius. The Ebionites of Jerome are not charged with any peculiarly Gnostic doctrines: so far as we could judge from what Jerome actually says about them, they might be held to differ from the Nazarenes merely by a stricter Judaism and by a lower view of the person of Christ. A similar absence of any definite mention of Gnostic doctrines appears in the descriptions of both of Eusebius' two classes of Ebionites. And both of Origen's two classes seem to be blamed for a grovelling, inadequate opinion rather than for unlawful speculations. In Irenæus, as we have already seen, the matter is not quite so clear; there may possibly be an

[90] Schmidtke (*op. cit.*, 1911, pp. 193 ff.) supposes that this citation was constructed by Epiphanius out of materials provided by the Clementine *Journeys of Peter* and that therefore it does not properly belong among the fragments of the Gospel of the Ebionites.

[91] It is said of John the Baptist, "who was said to be of the race of Aaron the priest, and a child of Zacharias and Elisabeth." Perhaps the historical error at the beginning of the Gospel: "It came to pass in the days of Herod the king of Judæa, John came baptizing," arose from a thoughtless repetition of the words "in the days of Herod the king" in Mt. ii.1. Since the author omitted the first two chapters of Matthew, the "in those days" with which Matthew introduces his account of John the Baptist became meaningless, and hence, apparently, the author turned back to Mt. ii.1 for an explanation of the word "those," in the phrase "those days," without stopping to think that Mt. ii.1 really referred to a very much earlier time. See Nicholson, *The Gospel According to the Hebrews*, 1879, p. 15.

[92] "And a voice came out of heaven saying, 'Thou art my beloved Son, in thee I am well pleased' [approximately Westcott and Hort's text in Mark and Luke], and again, 'I this day have begotten thee' [Western text in Luke]. And immediately there shone around the place a great light. Which having seen (it says) John says to him, 'Who art thou, Lord?'; and again a voice from heaven to him: 'This is my beloved Son, in whom I am well pleased' [approximately Westcott and Hort's text in Matthew]."

[93] Schmidtke (*op. cit.*, 1911, pp. 175–242) attributes the apparently Gnostic character of the Ebionites of Epiphanius simply to the undue use which Epiphanius made of the Clementine *Journeys of Peter* as a source of information about the sect.

allusion to Gnostic doctrines in what he says about the Ebionites. And even in the case of Origen, Eusebius, and Jerome, failure to mention Gnostic doctrines does not prove that those doctrines were not there.

At any rate, the evidence for the common view—that there was in addition to the Gnostic Ebionites of Epiphanius an entirely different sect of conservative, purely Pharisaic Ebionites existing at least from the second century on—is very far from amounting to positive proof. The other view, which would attribute to the Ebionites of Irenæus, and perhaps even to the deniers of the virgin birth who are mentioned by Justin Martyr, the germs of the peculiar doctrines described by Epiphanius, is also possible. It should be remembered that the extant descriptions of the Ebionites from the period before Epiphanius are very scanty, and that some of them come from men who had little opportunity for observation. To an outsider, the insistence of the Ebionites upon forms and ceremonies in general might be more noticeable than the exact difference of their ceremonies from those of the ordinary Jews; and their humanitarian views about Jesus might be more noticeable than their peculiar speculations about the Christ. Thus it is not quite impossible that all the Ebionites who denied the virgin birth were adherents of the Gnostic sect which is described, in its later manifestations, by Epiphanius. The Elxai book was probably produced at an early time; so that Gnostic Ebionism, even if based from the beginning upon that book,[94] may have originated before the time of Justin Martyr.[95]

The Nazarenes, of the time of Epiphanius and Jerome, must next be considered. Epiphanius' account of them is evidently not based upon personal observation; but Jerome, during his residence in the East, may well have come into close contact with them,[96] and therefore the scattered remarks about them in his writings deserve careful attention.

[94] If, on the other hand, Ebionism, though at first independent of Elxai, accepted the Elxai book later on, that fact would seem to indicate some original affinity for that book, so that even pre-Elkesaite Ebionism would perhaps not be altogether unlike the Ebionites of Epiphanius. The whole question is, however, very obscure.

[95] Compare the combination of an insistence upon Jewish observances with docetism in the errorists of the Ignatian Epistles. See *Magn.*, viii, with Lightfoot's note (in *The Apostolic Fathers*, second edition, II, ii, 1889, pp. 124 f.). The elimination from the pages of history of all non-Gnostic Jewish Christianity that denied the virgin birth is apparently favored by Zahn (*Das apostolische Symbolum*, 2te Aufl., 1893, p. 56). In opposition, see Harnack, *Chronologie*, i, 1897, p. 633, Anm. 1. For the view of Schmidtke, see below pp. 35–37. Whether Symmachus, who translated the Old Testament into Greek (perhaps about A.D. 200) was an Ebionite, is apparently not altogether certain. Schmidtke (*op. cit.*, p. 236, Anm. 2) regards him simply as a Jew. Harnack (*Dogmengeschichte*, 4te Aufl., i, 1909, pp. 322, Anm. 2, 327, Anm. 1) assigns him to the Gnostic branch of the Ebionites.

[96] Schmidtke (*op. cit.*, pp. 246 ff.), it is true, denies with very considerable show of reason that Jerome had ever really come into contact with the Nazarenes at all.

According to Jerome, the Nazarenes, who are scattered throughout all the synagogues of the East,[97] continue the observance of the Jewish law;[98] they try to be both Jews and Christians, and therefore fail of being either; they seek to put new wine into old bottles.[99] Yet they are to be estimated higher than the Ebionites, who merely pretend to be Christians.[100] While the Ebionites repudiate Paul as being a transgressor of the law,[101] the Nazarenes regard the preaching of Paul as a manifestation of the light that lightened the Gentiles.[102] And they recognize the divine sonship and virgin birth of Jesus.[103]

The Nazarenes used only one Gospel, which was written in Aramaic.[104] A copy was preserved in the library at Cæsarea, and Jerome was also permitted to copy the Gospel by the Nazarenes at Berœa in Syria. Indeed, he even says that he made both a Greek and a Latin translation of it. Despite the knowledge of its contents which he claims to possess and the frequent mention of it in his writings, his various designations of the Gospel have given a great deal of trouble. At times, he calls it the Gospel according to the Hebrews or the Gospel which is called that according to the Hebrews; at other times he speaks of it as though it were the Aramaic original of the Gospel of Matthew. Once he designates it as the Gospel which is called by many[105] the authentic Gospel of Matthew. The fullest single description of it is the following:

> In the Gospel according to the Hebrews which is written in the Chaldæan and Syrian language but in Hebrew letters, which the Nazarenes use until today, according to the apostles or, as very many think, according to Matthew, which also is kept in the Cæsarean library. . . .[106]

[97] Jerome, *ep.*, cxii.13 (ed. Hilberg, I. ii, 1912, p. 381). In criticism of this assertion, see Schmidtke, *op. cit.*, pp. 249 ff.

[98] On Isa. viii. 11 ff. (ed. Vall. et Maff., iv, 1845, col. 119).

[99] *Ep.*, cxii.13 (ed. Hilberg, I. ii, p. 382); on Ez. v.16 (ed. Vall. et Maff., v, 1845, col. 139).

[100] *Ep.*, cxii.13 (ed. Hilberg, I, ii, pp. 381 f.).

[101] On Mt. xii.2 (ed. Vall. et Maff., vii, 1845, col. 76).

[102] On Isa. ix.1 (ed. Vall. et Maff., iv, col. 125).

[103] *Ep.*, cxii (ed. Hilberg, I. ii, p. 381).

[104] "Chaldaico quidem Syroque sermone, sed Hebraicis litteris" (*adv. Pelagianos*, iii. 2, ed. Vall. et Maff., ii, 1845, col. 570). For the materials for studying the Gospel according to the Hebrews, see especially Zahn, *Geschichte des neutestamentlichen Kanons*, ii, 1890, pp. 642–723. The materials have also been collected by Schmidtke and by others.

[105] "Plerisque" (on Mt. xii.13, ed. Vall. et Maff., vii, col. 78).

[106] "In Evangelio iuxta Hebraeos, quod Chaldaico quidem Syroque sermone, sed Hebraicis litteris scriptum est, quo utuntur usque hodie Nazareni, secundum Apostolos, sive ut plerique autumant, iuxta Matthaeum, quod et in Caesariensi habetur bibliotheca . . ." (*adv. Pelagianos*, iii. 2, ed. Vall. et Maff., ii, col. 570).

The following is a possible explanation of this vacillation in Jerome's manner of speaking of the Gospel.[107] Jerome, we may suppose, had found an Aramaic Gospel, in use among the Nazarenes, which in part was parallel to our Greek Matthew. According to an early and widespread tradition, Matthew had written his Gospel originally in Aramaic ("Hebrew"). It was therefore natural at first sight for Jerome to suppose that the Nazarene Gospel was nothing less than the Aramaic Gospel of Matthew. Yet as a matter of fact—so our supposition runs—there were wide differences between that Nazarene Gospel and our Matthew; so that if that Gospel were the original Matthew, then our Gospel must be anything but a faithful translation. Jerome did not venture to draw this conclusion. Yet he could not bear to relinquish the appearance of being the only man in the Church who had in his hands the genuine Aramaic Matthew. And indeed in many cases the Greek Matthew could really be interpreted in a very plausible way by regarding the corresponding passages in the Nazarene Gospel as the original. Accordingly, where our Matthew and the Nazarene Gospel are parallel, Jerome treats the Nazarene Gospel as the original Aramaic Matthew; but where the two Gospels differ decisively, he calls the Nazarene Gospel by some other name, such as "Gospel according to the Hebrews."

We are far from regarding this hypothesis as being certainly correct. But at least it will explain the phenomena fairly well.

The Gospel according to the Hebrews is cited by Clement of Alexandria, Origen, and Eusebius, all of whom had first-hand acquaintance with its contents. It was also used by Hegesippus and perhaps even by Ignatius. Origen evidently distinguished it from that "Gospel of the Twelve Apostles" which we have already discussed. The latter Origen reckons among the apocryphal Gospels—it is one of the "attempts"[108] to which Luke alludes in his prologue, while the Gospel according to the Hebrews is apparently treated by Origen with respect,[109] though not as equal in authority to the four canonical Gospels. Formerly it was supposed that a connection of some kind existed between the two Jewish Christian Gospels—for instance, that the Ebionite Gospel was a later recension of the Nazarene Gospel, or that the two were different recensions of a common ancestor—but the investigations of Zahn, Handmann[110] and Harnack have caused the two to be regarded as entirely separate works.

[107] See Harnack, *Chronologie der altchristlichen Litteratur*, i, 1897, pp. 634 f.; and compare Zahn, *op. cit.*, ii, pp. 684 f.; Ropes, "Sprüche Jesu," in *Texte und Untersuchungen*, xiv. 2, 1896, pp. 84 f.

[108] As a matter of fact, this derogatory interpretation of the word ἐπεχείρησαν in Lk. i.1 is probably not correct.

[109] Compare, however, Schmidtke, *op. cit.*, pp. 154 ff.

[110] "Das Hebräer-Evangelium," in *Texte und Untersuchungen*, v. 3, 1888.

The external evidence makes it natural to suppose that the Gospel according to the Hebrews was written not later than the early part of the second century; and Harnack favors even a first-century date.[111] With regard to the relation of the work to the canonical Gospels, widely different views have been held. F. C. Baur supposed that the Gospel according to the Hebrews was the starting-point for the whole development of the Gospel history; others have held it to be based on our canonical Gospels; others have held intermediate views of various kinds. Zahn supposes that it was developed from the original Aramaic Matthew, but that, except from the purely linguistic point of view, it reproduces the original far less faithfully than our Greek Matthew. Harnack would regard it as independent of the Greek Matthew—partly more original, partly less original. Handmann identifies it with the *Logia* (designating by that term one of the two supposed common sources of our Matthew and Luke).

The problems of the book cannot here be solved. But at least so much seems to be clear—despite some things that look like fantastic elaborations of the Gospel history,[112] the Gospel according to the Hebrews contains tradition at least of great antiquity and is perhaps the most interesting of the non-canonical Gospels of which any considerable fragments have been preserved. It cannot, therefore, be a matter of complete indifference whether this Gospel did or did not contain an account of the virgin birth; and this question must now be briefly considered.[113]

In the first place, the designation of the Gospel as the Gospel of Matthew by Jerome and Epiphanius is better explained if it contained something corresponding to Mt. i-ii. The omission of two chapters at the beginning would have a far greater effect in producing the impression of a different work than very much greater divergences in the middle.[114] If the Gospel began with the baptism, like Mark, why should the report of it which came to Epiphanius have connected it so specifically with Matthew, and represented it, furthermore, as a "very complete" Matthew? It is true that Epiphanius himself did not understand wherein the completeness consisted—he is doubtful whether the Gospel contained the genealogy and does not know whether the readers of it accepted the virgin birth—but this very lack of understanding shows that

111 Harnack (*op. cit.*, i, pp. 635 ff.) is probably right in his contention (against Zahn) that a Greek translation of the Gospel existed long before Jerome, though Jerome did not see it.

112 A primitive character has probably never been successfully vindicated for the remarkable fragment (the fourth in Zahn's list), preserved both by Origen and by Jerome: "Just now my mother, the Holy Spirit, took me [Jesus] by one of my hairs and bore me away into the great mountain Tabor."

113 For a fuller discussion, see "The Virgin Birth in the Second Century," in *Princeton Theological Review*, x, 1912, pp. 562–570.

114 Compare V. H. Stanton, *The Gospels as Historical Documents*, i, 1903, p. 257.

Epiphanius did not invent the designation "very complete"; it must have been part of the indefinite report which was his only source of information about the book. As for Jerome, in order to explain his half conviction that the Gospel was nothing less than the Aramaic Matthew, the presence of a beginning corresponding to Mt. i-ii is even more imperatively required.

This requirement would perhaps be partially satisfied if the Gospel, though omitting all mention of the virgin birth—having, that is, nothing corresponding to Mt. i.18-25—contained the genealogy of Mt. i.1-16.[115] This hypothesis, however, is certainly incorrect. For if the Gospel contained the genealogy without alluding to the virgin birth, then the genealogy must have ended with some such sentence as "Joseph begat Jesus." But if the Gospel contained such a sentence as that without correction or explanation, it certainly could not have been treated with favor by Origen, Eusebius, and Jerome, every one of whom had independent and first-hand acquaintance with its contents.[116] Even if Hilgenfeld is correct in supposing that those Jewish Christian readers of the Gospel who accepted the virgin birth could explain the words, "Joseph begat Jesus," in harmony with the virgin birth,[117] certainly Origen and Eusebius (who had accepted the fourfold Gospel canon and were in no way prejudiced in favor of the Gospel according to the Hebrews) and the many Catholic Christians to whose opinion they seem to bear testimony could not and would not have done so. At the time of Eusebius no Catholic Christian would have placed a Gospel which closed the genealogy with "Joseph begat Jesus" in any

[115] This view has been held by Hilgenfeld ("Das Evangelium der Hebräer," in *Zeitschrift für wissenschaftliche Theologie*, vi, 1863, p. 353; *Evangelium sec. Hebraeos*, etc., 1884, pp. 15 ff.), and by Handmann (*op. cit.*, 1888, pp. 123, 138). Aside from the considerations mentioned in the text, the presence of the genealogy in the Gospel according to the Hebrews is thought to be favored by the assertion of Epiphanius (*haer.*, xxx, 14, ed. Holl, i, p. 351) that Cerinthus and Carpocrates used the genealogy of Matthew to prove that Jesus was the son of Joseph and Mary. But there is no real reason whatever for supposing that Cerinthus and Carpocrates used the Gospel according to the Hebrews. See Bauer, *op. cit.*, pp. 33 f.; Zahn, *op. cit.*, ii, pp. 730 f., Anm. 1; and especially Schmidtke, *op. cit.*, pp. 209 ff.

[116] See Zahn, *op. cit.*, ii, p. 686.

[117] Hilgenfeld, *Evangelium sec. Hebraeos*, etc., 1884, p. 19: "qui partum virginis concedebant Matth. hebr. I, 16 ad arbitrium interpretati videntur esse." The possibility of such an interpretation must certainly be conceded. For a Jew it was perfectly possible to understand the word "begat" in a putative rather than a physical sense. Indeed, we shall point out at a later stage of our discussion that even "if the Genealogy had ended with the uncompromising statement 'and Joseph begat Jesus' it would not prove that the Evangelist believed that Joseph was the natural father of Jesus" (Burkitt, *Evangelion da-Mepharreshe*, ii, 1904, p. 261). See below, pp. 185 f. But it is another question whether Jewish Christians who accepted the virgin birth, and who knew of Gospels that contained an account of it, would have been satisfied permanently with a Gospel which said nothing about the birth of Jesus except "Joseph begat Jesus." The use of the Gospel according to the Hebrews by the Nazarenes, who accepted the virgin birth, does, therefore, remain a strong argument in favor of supposing that it contained an account of the virgin birth—or at least a strong argument against supposing that, though not containing an account of the virgin birth, it contained a genealogy.

other category than that of the decidedly spurious books. It is quite certain, therefore, that if the Gospel according to the Hebrews contained no mention of the virgin birth, it also contained no genealogy. But if it contained no genealogy, it must have had a very different appearance at the very beginning from the Gospel of Matthew, and could hardly have been brought into such close connection with that Gospel by Epiphanius and Jerome.[118]

In the second place, the character of the readers of the Gospel is favorable to the supposition that it contained an account of the virgin birth. Jerome found it in use among the Nazarenes, who accepted the virgin birth.[119] Apparently Epiphanius did *not* find it in use among the Ebionites, who denied the virgin birth; they used the very different Gospel of which Epiphanius has preserved fragments. Eusebius[120] assigns it to the less unorthodox of his two classes of Ebionites—the class that accepted the virgin birth. In fact, there is no clear evidence that this Gospel ever was used by men who held Jesus to have been the son, by ordinary generation, of Joseph and Mary.

The only possible argument against this assertion is to be found in the testimony of Irenæus. In the passage which we have already quoted,[121] Irenæus says that the Ebionites who did not accept the virgin birth used only the Gospel according to Matthew. But what was this "Gospel according to Matthew"? A process of elimination might seem to point to an identification of it with the Gospel according to the Hebrews. The only two specifically Jewish Christian Gospels that we know—at least the only two that are known to have been called by the name of Matthew—are the Gospel according to the Hebrews and the Gospel of the Ebionites that is described by Epiphanius. Therefore, it might be argued, since the Gospel used by the Ebionites of Irenæus cannot possibly have been the Gospel of the Ebionites of Epiphanius, it must have been the Gospel according to the Hebrews.

But this reasoning is by no means conclusive. In the first place, the other horn of the dilemma is perhaps not so terrifying as is sometimes supposed. Is it so certain that the Gospel in question was not the one used by the Ebionites of Epiphanius? The prejudice against this view is due to the assumption that the Ebionites of Irenæus were at bottom simply conservative, Pharisaic Jews, and therefore were quite distinct from the curious sect described by Epiphanius. But this assumption is by no means certainly correct. If the considerations

[118] Compare Zahn, *op. cit.*, ii, p. 686.

[119] In one passage (on Mt. xii.13, ed. Vall. et Maff., vii, col. 78), indeed, he speaks of it as the Gospel which the Nazarenes *and Ebionites* use; but here he is probably inaccurate. Compare Schmidtke, *op. cit.*, p. 267. Jerome seems never to have come into close relations with the Ebionites.

[120] In accordance with the most probable interpretation of *hist. eccl.*, III.xxvii (ed. Schwartz ii, 1903. pp. 254, 256). See, however, for a criticism of this passage, Schmidtke, *op. cit.*, pp. 143 ff.

[121] Irenæus, *haer.*, I.xxvi. 2. See above, p. 18.

adduced above[122] have any weight whatever, then the purely Pharisaic and non-Gnostic or non-syncretistic character of the Ebionites of Irenæus is not so certain as is usually assumed. And if their teaching contained the germs of the Gnostic doctrines professed by the Ebionites of Epiphanius, then they may already have possessed that same Ebionite Gospel.

This identification of the "Matthew" used by the Ebionites of Irenæus with the Ebionite Gospel from which Epiphanius gives extracts has been gaining ground in recent years. It is adopted by Schmidtke,[123] Waitz,[124] Moffatt,[125] and Findlay.[126] If it is correct,[127] then the Ebionites of Irenæus, who denied the virgin birth, did *not* use the Gospel according to the Hebrews, so that they can no longer be used as a witness to the absence of a narrative of the virgin birth from that Gospel.

But, in the second place, even if the identification of the Gospel of Irenæus' Ebionites with the Gospel of Epiphanius' Ebionites be abandoned, the identification of the former Gospel with the Gospel according to the Hebrews does not necessarily follow. For these Ebionites of Irenæus may have used some Gospel which has been lost (the connection of which with Matthew is obscure); or they may have adapted the canonical Matthew in some such manner as Marcion adapted Luke. The assertion of Irenæus remains puzzling. But manifestly he is guilty, in any case, of error or incompleteness of one kind or another, since the Ebionites could not possibly, with their rejection of the virgin birth, have received the Gospel of Matthew as we know it (and as Irenæus knew it); and inferences drawn from such an erroneous assertion cannot be allowed to nullify clearer evidence.[128]

In the third place, there is some positive evidence to the effect that the Gospel according to the Hebrews, as it was known to Jerome, did contain a narrative corresponding to the second chapter of Matthew: for in several places[129] Jerome seems actually to cite such a narrative; he appeals to the

[122] Pp. 18 f.

[123] *Op. cit.*, 1911, p. 225.

[124] "Das Evangelium der zwölf Apostel," in *Zeitschrift für die neutestamentliche Wissenschaft*, xiv, 1913, pp. 121 f.

[125] Art. "Gospels (Uncanonical)," in Hastings, *Dictionary of the Apostolic Church*, i, 1916, p. 490. Moffatt uses the word "apparently" in referring to the identification.

[126] *Byways in Early Christian Literature*, 1923, p. 47. Findlay says that the identification is "probably" to be made.

[127] Compare, on the other side, Harnack, *Chronologie*, i, 1897, pp. 628, 630 f.

[128] What Gospel was used by the Jewish Christian opponents of the virgin birth mentioned by Justin Martyr and by Origen? It would be over-bold to answer that it was the Gospel according to the Hebrews, simply because no other definite answer can be given. In view of the scantiness of the sources, no definite answer can reasonably be expected. There is really no decisive objection against supposing that it was the Gospel of the Ebionites of Epiphanius.

[129] On Mt. ii.6 (ed. Vall. et Maff., vii, col. 26); *de vir. inl.*, iii (ed. Richardson, in *Texte und Untersuchungen*, xiv. 3, 1896, pp. 8 f.).

"Hebrew"[130] in the elucidation of Mt. ii.6, 15, 23 in a way that seems to show that what he means is his Aramaic "Matthew," or, in other words, the Gospel according to the Hebrews.[131] But if the Gospel according to the Hebrews contained the substance of Mt. ii, it was not altogether without an infancy section. And if it contained an infancy section, that section probably mentioned the virgin birth, since the users of the Gospel were not those who denied the virgin birth, but those who accepted it. A Gospel that contained no account of the birth of Jesus at all might conceivably have been used by believers in the virgin birth, but hardly a Gospel that contained an account of the birth and yet made no reference to the central miracle. The most natural inference to be drawn from Jerome's citations is that the Gospel according to the Hebrews had in it material corresponding to the whole of Mt. i-ii.

Two objections may be urged against our conclusion that the Gospel according to the Hebrews contained an account of the virgin birth.

In the first place, a stichometric list[132] of canonical, disputed, and apocryphal books attached to the "Chronography" of Nicephorus[133] makes the Gospel according to the Hebrews, with 2,200 stichoi, considerably shorter than the canonical Matthew, with 2,500 stichoi.[134] But the extant fragments of the Gospel according to the Hebrews appear to be longer rather than shorter than the corresponding passages of Matthew. Therefore—so the argument runs—the difference in length may best be accounted for by the absence from the Gospel according to the Hebrews of a narrative of the birth. But this argument, ingenious though it is, is by no means convincing; certainly it should not be allowed to discredit the far more definite evidence which we have adduced on the other side. The figure 2,200 may be incorrect,[135] or the greater length of Matthew may be accounted for by omissions in the Gospel according to the Hebrews other than the omission of the birth narrative.[136]

In the second place, the extant fragments of the Gospel are sometimes thought to be contradictory to the virgin birth, which, therefore, it is said,

130 "Ipsum hebraicum."

131 For a discussion of this question, see "The Virgin Birth in the Second Century," in *Princeton Theological Review*, x, 1912, pp. 565–568.

132 That is, a list giving the number of "stichoi" (the στίχος being a conventional measure of length) that various books contained.

133 Of the ninth century. For introduction and text, see Zahn, *op. cit.*, ii, 1890, pp. 295–301.

134 Mark is given 2,000 stichoi; John, 2,300; Luke, 2,600.

135 So Zahn, *op. cit.*, ii, p. 717, who appeals to other ancient errors in the figures of the St chometry.

136 Long stretches in the central part of Matthew are unrepresented in the extant fragments of the Gospel according to the Hebrews. See Zahn, *loc. cit.* It has been observed above (p. 29) that a great difference in the middle would affect the Matthæan appearance of the Gospel less unfavorably than a much smaller difference at the beginning.

could not well have been narrated in the same book. But this argument has little weight. In the account of the baptism, it is true, the Gospel according to the Hebrews says (in words attributed to the Spirit):

> My son, in all the prophets I was awaiting thee, that thou shouldst come and that I should rest in thee. Thou art my rest, thou art my firstborn Son who reignest to eternity.

But these words certainly do not mean that the divine sonship of Jesus did not exist prior to the baptism. The fragment in which Jesus speaks of the Spirit as "my Mother"[137] deserves somewhat closer attention; for in Mt. i.18-25 the activity of the Spirit may seem to take the place not of the mother, but of the father. But the designation of the Spirit as Mother contradicts not the canonical narratives themselves, but a crassly materialistic misinterpretation of them. The predominantly feminine gender of the Semitic word for "Spirit," which has probably given rise to the "my Mother"[138] of the fragment, was in the original Aramaic written or oral sources simply an additional safeguard (if, indeed, one was needed) of the lofty spiritual meaning of the birth story. As Jerome well says, "in the Godhead there is no sex."[139]

The preceding argument, though it does not make the presence of an account of the virgin birth in the Gospel according to the Hebrews altogether certain, at least makes it highly probable. The importance of this conclusion depends, to a considerable extent, upon the antiquity and value that are to be attributed to the book. If the book was written in the first century, as Harnack supposes, then its testimony becomes exceedingly valuable. But even if the dating of Zahn (for example)—after A.D. 135—is to be adopted, still the Gospel provides a valuable supplement of other evidence. The special importance of the testimony of the Gospel according to the Hebrews is that it is a testimony by Jewish Christians—indeed, even by schismatic Jewish Christians who did not accept without question the tradition of the Catholic Church. If not only Gentile Christians, but even Jewish Christians of this schismatic type, accepted the virgin birth before the close of the first century, then the legendary or mythical explanation of the origin of the doctrine becomes very difficult.

The foregoing discussion of the Jewish Christian Gospels has followed for

[137] See above, p. 29, footnote 112.

[138] ἡ μήτηρ μου.

[139] "In divinitate enim nullus est sexus," Jerome, on Isa. xl.11 (ed. Vall. et Maff., iv, col. 405). Compare *ep.*, xviii. 17 (ed. Hilberg I, i, 1910, p. 98): ". . . quando de superioribus disputatur, et masculinum aliquid, seu femininum ponitur, non tam sexum significari, quam idioma sonare linguae." Origen (*in Ioh.*, ii. 12, ed. Preuschen, iv, 1903, p. 67) compares the figurative use of the term "mother" in Jesus' words about him who does the will of God. All three passages are cited by Nicholson, *The Gospel according to the Hebrews*, 1879, pp. 80 f. (Nicholson's reference seems to be wrong in the case of the last passage).

the most part the trend of modern opinion prior to 1911, as influenced by Zahn, Handmann and Harnack. Despite important differences in detail, a considerable measure of unanimity had been attained. But in 1911 the whole question was reopened by the elaborate work of Schmidtke.[140] Schmidtke's investigations, which were exceedingly thorough and were based partly upon new materials, led him to an entirely new conception of the Jewish Christian Gospels and of their readers. It is an important question, therefore, whether Schmidtke is right, or whether the older view may still be held. That question cannot be answered here. All that can now be attempted is (1) a brief exposition of Schmidtke's view, (2) some estimate of its bearing upon the question of the virgin birth, and (3) some account of the way in which Schmidtke has influenced recent opinion.

At an early date, Schmidtke thinks, the Jewish Christians at Berœa in Syria, who had before simply formed part of the mixed church of that city, drifted apart, owing to the force of circumstances, from the Gentile Christians, and formed a separate community. These Jewish Christians of Berœa came to be designated as "Nazarenes." The assertion of Jerome that the Nazarenes were spread abroad through the synagogues of the East is entirely valueless; there never were Nazarenes outside of Berœa. The Nazarenes had formed part of the Catholic Church, and even after their separation differed from the Gentile Christians in little more than in their own devotion to Jewish customs. For example, they recognized the work of Paul with enthusiasm, and accepted the doctrine of the virgin birth. At some time after the writing of Ignatius' Epistle to the Smyrnæans, but before A.D. 150, the Nazarenes of Berœa translated the Greek Gospel of Matthew into their own language, the Aramaic. It was not a perfectly literal translation, being somewhat like a targum. But it did not differ from Matthew sufficiently to be regarded as a separate book. There is every reason to suppose, for example, that it contained Mt. i-ii.[141] This Aramaic Matthew of Berœa, though it was really a translation of the canonical Greek Matthew, came to be regarded as the original from which the Greek Matthew had been translated, and thus gave rise to the tradition of the "Hebrew" original of Matthew, which is attested by Papias in the middle of the second century and played a large rôle in Irenæus and subsequent writers. The Nazarene Gospel was used by Hegesippus (about A.D. 180), but was unknown except by hearsay to other writers prior to Eusebius. Eusebius had not

[140] "Neue Fragmente und Untersuchungen zu den judenchristlichen Evangelien," in *Texte und Untersuchungen*, xxxvii, 1, 1911.

[141] Schmidtke adduces evidence to show that the Nazarene Gospel could be quoted at Mt. i.6, 20 f. (*op. cit.*, pp. 24, 287). This evidence is to be added to the evidence for the presence of Mt. ii in the Nazarene Gospel, which has been discussed above.

seen the Gospel when he wrote his "Church History," but secured a copy before the appearance of his "Theophany." He regards the book as the original of Matthew. His copy was added to the library at Cæsarea, where it remained at the time of Jerome. But the author who brought the Gospel into prominence was Apollinaris of Laodicea. To him we owe the fragments which have been preserved by Jerome, and also those which have been preserved in the margin of certain Gospel manuscripts which are descendants of an edition of the Gospels that may be called the "Zion edition." This Nazarene Gospel was never regarded by anyone who was really familiar with its contents as a work distinct from the Gospel of Matthew, but was regarded as the original from which the canonical Gospel had been translated. It has nothing whatever to do with the Gospel according to the Hebrews.

Such is Schmidtke's view of the Nazarenes and of their Gospel. The Ebionites, Schmidtke thinks—to proceed to an exposition of his view about them—were a sect quite distinct from the Nazarenes. They were characterized by a denial of the virgin birth, though the name "Ebionites" was wrongly applied by Origen and Eusebius also to a sect that accepted the virgin birth. When Epiphanius wrote the first draught of his section on the Ebionites, he had no first-hand knowledge of them whatever. His description of the sect is vitiated by a confusion of the Ebionites with the Elkesaites, and by a wholesale employment of the material of the Clementine writings as the source of information about the Ebionites. All that he says about the Gnostic character of the Ebionites is based simply upon these groundless combinations. There never were any Gnostic Ebionites. But what Epiphanius says about the vegetarian principle of the Ebionites is correct. After writing the first draught of his chapter, Epiphanius received first-hand information about contemporary Ebionites on the island of Cyprus, and became acquainted with their Gospel. This later and correct information was simply added to the original draught of Epiphanius' work, and the result is the confused account which we have before us. The Ebionite Gospel from which Epiphanius gives extracts is to be identified, not with the Gospel of the Twelve Apostles,[142] but with the Ebionite Gospel which is mentioned by Irenæus as a Gospel of Matthew and is also mentioned and cited by Origen and others under the title "Gospel according to the Hebrews." The earliest trace of its use is in Hegesippus. To this Gospel according to the Hebrews are to be assigned the fragments in Epiphanius which have usually been assigned to the Gospel of the Twelve Apostles,[143] and also

[142] Compare above, p. 24.

[143] Schmidtke removes, however, from the list of these fragments the one which refers to the abrogation of sacrifices. See above, p. 25, footnote 90.

such fragments as the fragment in Origen which mentions the Holy Spirit as the mother of Jesus. This Greek Gospel according to the Hebrews has nothing whatever to do with the Aramaic Gospel of the Nazarenes; the two were kept quite separate by the early writers. Eusebius says of Hegesippus that he cited from the Gospel according to the Hebrews *and* from the Syriac (Gospel).[144] Here the two are placed clearly side by side. The common identification of the Gospel according to the Hebrews with the Aramaic Matthew of the Nazarenes is due altogether to the combined stupidity and deceitfulness of Jerome. Despite what he says about his Greek and Latin translation of the Gospel according to the Hebrews and about his opportunity of transcribing the Nazarene Gospel, he was not really familiar with either one. He saw the Aramaic Gospel in the library at Cæsarea, but on account of his ignorance of Aramaic was not able to use it to any great extent. His knowledge of the Gospel according to the Hebrews was derived from Origen; his knowledge of the Aramaic Matthew from Apollinaris of Laodicea. Since he was ignorant of both Gospels, it was possible for him to confuse them. He interpreted "according to the Hebrews" in the title of the Gospel according to the Hebrews erroneously in a linguistic sense, and so was led to identify this Gospel with the Aramaic Gospel of the Nazarenes. His designations of the Aramaic Gospel according to the Hebrews vary according to his sources of information and according to the exigencies of the occasion. In the Commentary on Matthew, for example, he could not well designate a Gospel which he referred to only occasionally as the original of Matthew; for if the Gospel was the original of Matthew, it was absurd for him not to refer to it oftener. As a matter of fact, he could not refer to it oftener, for the simple reason that his knowledge of it was limited to the citations that had been made by Apollinaris.

Even such a brief summary as the foregoing may suffice to exhibit the revolutionary character of Schmidtke's treatment of the Jewish Christian Gospels. The theory cannot here be examined critically. But such examination can be omitted with the better conscience because the importance of Schmidtke's investigation for the question of the historicity of the virgin birth is not so great as might be supposed. If Schmidtke's theory should prove to be correct, the second-century testimony to the virgin birth would not be weakened.

It is true that if Schmidtke is right the Nazarenes, who accepted the virgin birth, can no longer be regarded as a widespread sect, but become a local community at Berœa in Syria. It is true that the more orthodox "Ebionites,"

[144] *Hist. eccl.*, IV. xxii. 8: ἔκ τε τοῦ καθ' Ἑβραίους εὐαγγελίου καὶ τοῦ Συριακοῦ καὶ ἰδίως ἐκ τῆς Ἑβραΐδος διαλέκτου τινὰ τίθησιν. Compare, however, Nestle, *Einführung in das griechische Neue Testament*, 2te Aufl., 1899, pp. 77 f.

whom Origen and Eusebius represent as accepting the virgin birth, disappear from the pages of history.[145] It is true that the Nazarene Gospel, which contained an account of the virgin birth, can no longer be regarded as embodying independent tradition, but becomes a mere free translation of Matthew with some employment of the other canonical Gospels. It is true that the Ebionites of Epiphanius, who denied the virgin birth, are cleared of the charge of unhistorical Gnostic speculations. It is true that the Gospel according to the Hebrews mentioned by Hegesippus and other early writers can no longer be regarded as containing an account of the virgin birth. These features of Schmidtke's theory may appear to weaken the testimony to the virgin birth and enhance the value of the Jewish Christian denials of it.

But other features of the theory tend just as clearly in the opposite direction. In the first place, though the Nazarenes, on Schmidtke's theory, shrink to the proportions of a local community, their primitive appearance remains. And they accepted the virgin birth. It was the mere chance of their separation from their Gentile fellow-Christians that made them peculiar. Other Jewish Christians of similarly primitive character may be held simply to have been merged permanently in the Catholic Church. In the second place, the Nazarene Gospel, though it ceases, on Schmidtke's theory, to be a depository of independent tradition, becomes a valuable witness to the early acceptance of the Gospel of Matthew on the part of Jewish Christians. And the Gospel of Matthew contained an account of the virgin birth. In the third place, though the Ebionites, on Schmidtke's theory, cease to be Gnostic, they cannot on that account lay claim to any special primitiveness. The language, for example, was Greek, not Aramaic. Finally, though by Schmidtke's theory the Gospel according to the Hebrews is shown to have contained no account of the virgin birth, it is also shown to be utterly valueless. The only Gospel of these Jewish Christians who denied the virgin birth, the only Jewish Christian Gospel that did not contain the virgin birth, was a worthless Greek compilation based upon our Gospels of Matthew and Luke, a compilation which displays incidental dependence even upon those infancy sections that it omitted. The use of this Gospel by Hegesippus and the mention of it by Irenæus form simply further testimony to the early use of the canonical Gospels. And the employment of this Gospel, and of this Gospel only, by the Ebionites proves how entirely destitute they were of genuine historical tradition, except such as was embodied in the

[145] Schmidtke (*op. cit.*, p. 241) suggests that Origen's mention of a more orthodox class of "Ebionites," that accepted the virgin birth, is due simply to a false application of the name "Ebionites" to the Gnostic Jewish Christians, who, according to Schmidtke, accepted the virgin birth. It is the same confusion which Schmidtke sees in the connection which Epiphanius sets up between Elxai and the Ebionites. The suggestion is exceedingly bold.

canonical Gospels. Whatever the cause of their denial of the virgin birth, such denial was not based upon primitive tradition coming down from the time of Jesus. No sect whose sole Gospel was the one from which Epiphanius quotes in his chapter on the Ebionites has the slightest claim to be regarded as standing in any direct and peculiar relation to the primitive Jewish Church.

Schmidtke's theory has been variously estimated by subsequent writers. But on the whole it may be said that certain rather solid results are emerging from the discussion.[146] We have come to see at least that the fixed elements in the whole problem are the "Nazarene Gospel" quoted by Jerome and the "Ebionite Gospel" quoted by Epiphanius. The character of each of these is fairly clear: the Nazarene Gospel was an Aramaic (or Hebrew) Gospel that was somewhat similar to our Matthew; the Ebionite Gospel was a compilation made by an author of vegetarian principles, and probably of syncretistic (if not Gnostic) views, on the basis of our Greek Gospels, Matthew and Luke.

The difficulty comes when we seek to determine the relationship of these two gospels to the "Gospel according to the Hebrews" quoted by Clement and Origen. The older view identified this Gospel according to the Hebrews with the Nazarene Gospel. This identification was rejected by Schmidtke, and he has been followed in this particular by Waitz and Moffatt, and (with reservations) by Findlay, in the works already cited.[147] What then is to be done with the Gospel according to the Hebrews after it has thus been deprived of its identification with the Nazarene Gospel? Schmidtke identified it with the Ebionite Gospel, but that identification is generally rejected (and rightly so) by contemporary writers. Thus the Gospel according to the Hebrews is left hanging in the air, and we have at least three Jewish Christian Gospels instead of two.

What, then, is the bearing of this state of opinion upon the question of the virgin birth? Certainly it is by no means unfavorable to the historicity of the virgin-birth tradition.

[146] See Waitz, "Das Evangelium der zwölf Apostel," in *Zeitschrift für die neutestamentliche Wissenschaft*, xiii, 1912, pp. 338–348; xiv, 1913, pp. 38–64, 117–132; art. "Apokryphen des NT.s," in Herzog-Hauck, *Realencyklopädie*, xxiii, 1913, pp. 80–85; Moffatt, art. "Gospels (Uncanonical)," in Hastings, *Dictionary of the Apostolic Church*, i, 1916, pp. 489–495; Lagrange, "L'Évangile selon les Hébreux," in *Revue Biblique*, xxxi, 1922, pp. 161–181, 321–349; Findlay, *Byways in Early Christian Literature*, 1923, pp. 33–78; Dunkerley, "The Gospel According to the Hebrews," in *Expository Times*, xxxix, 1928, pp. 437–442, 490–495. To the last-named writer we are much indebted for his citation of the recent literature on the subject.

[147] The identification of the Gospel according to the Hebrews with the Nazarene Gospel has been maintained, against Schmidtke, by Lagrange (*op. cit.*), and by Dunkerley (*op. cit.*). Findlay (*op. cit.*, pp. 56 f.) suggests that the Gospel according to the Hebrews, though not the same as the Nazarene Gospel, may have had a good deal in common with it, so that the two may be regarded as different editions of the same book.

In the first place, it is now generally admitted that the Nazarene Gospel did contain an account of the virgin birth. The value of its testimony will of course depend largely upon what we think of that Gospel as a whole; but certainly the Gospel makes a far greater impression of primitiveness than is made by the only one of these Gospels that certainly omitted the virgin birth.

In the second place, the Ebionite Gospel, which omitted the virgin birth, though its compiler and users may be acquitted of actual Gnosticism, and though the date of it is often pushed farther back than was formerly done, retains its character as a distinctly secondary compilation based upon our Greek Gospels of Matthew and Luke. The identification of this Gospel with the "Gospel according to Matthew," which Irenæus says was in use among the Ebionites whom he mentions, greatly diminishes the evidence for a conservative, Pharisaical, and purely Jewish rejection of the virgin birth among professing Christians of Jewish race. The Ebionites of Irenæus, formerly thought to be the custodians of primitive Palestinian tradition, turn out to be affected by more or less syncretistic ideas; and their "Gospel according to Matthew," formerly thought to be of high importance, turns out to be a worthless compilation, dominated by a marked vegetarian tendency and based upon our Greek Gospels of Matthew and Luke. The earlier the date of this Gospel is placed,[148] the greater is the evidence for the early use of those two of our canonical gospels that contain an account of the virgin birth, and the smaller is the likelihood of there having been any really independent tradition that made Jesus the son, by ordinary generation, of Joseph and Mary.

In the third place, the "Gospel according to the Hebrews," properly so called, the Gospel mentioned under that title by Clement and Origen, being now deprived of its identification either with the Nazarene Gospel of Jerome or with the Ebionite Gospel of Epiphanius, is at least as likely as not to have contained an account of the virgin birth. If it is the same as the Gospel which is mentioned under the same title by Eusebius in the Church History,[149] then it probably did contain an account of the virgin birth; for it is assigned by Eusebius in that passage to those Ebionites who accepted the virgin birth tradition.[150] But even if it is regarded as different from that Gospel mentioned by Eusebius,[151] still there is at least no valid evidence that it did *not* contain an account of the virgin birth; and the respect with which it is treated by Clement

148 Waitz (*op. cit.*, pp. 127–130) is inclined to place it at the end of the first century.

149 Eusebius, *hist. eccl.*, III.xxvii. 4.

150 So Findlay, *op. cit.*, p. 58.

151 So Waitz, *op. cit.*, pp. 122 f. Against this view see Findlay, *op. cit.*, pp. 50–52. Waitz thinks that the Gospel which Eusebius mentions in the passage cited was the Ebionite Gospel. Surely, in view of the character of the sect of which Eusebius is speaking, that view is unlikely.

and Origen points toward its agreement, in the matter of the birth of Jesus, with the doctrine of the main body of the Church.

Neither by the older reconstruction, therefore, nor by the newer views which have gained vogue since the appearance of Schmidtke's book, has there really been found any Gospel of primitive appearance, in use among schismatic Jewish Christians, that ignored or denied the virgin birth of Christ.

It is now time to sum up the results of the preceding discussion concerning Jewish Christian denials of the virgin birth.

The virgin birth was denied, we have discovered, by the Gnostic or syncretistic Ebionites described by Epiphanius; but the character of this sect is such as to raise a very unfavorable presumption with regard to its traditions. These syncretistic Ebionites are as far removed as possible from all that primitive Jewish Christianity could possibly be conceived to have been. It is therefore exceedingly unlikely that they were united with Jesus or with His first disciples by a tradition which has elsewhere been lost. At any rate, the only Gospel which they are known to have used was a worthless compilation, which exhibits the most unscrupulous dogmatic alterations of the canonical material.[152]

The virgin birth has often been thought to have been denied also by certain Pharisaic Ebionites, who, aside from their humanitarian views about Jesus, differed from the Catholic Church merely by a strict insistence upon the Jewish law. If such Pharisaic Ebionites did exist, their denial of the virgin birth is not difficult to explain. They probably belonged to the stricter party of the Jewish Christians, which insisted upon the observance of the law by Gentiles as well as by Jews. They were more Jews than Christians; and to the orthodox Jew the virgin birth was an abomination.[153] It seemed out of harmony with his pride in the marriage relation and the begetting of children. It might seem to him to make void God's promise of a prince of David's line. It contradicted the one-sided transcendentalism of his idea of God, and seemed to make Jehovah no better than Zeus.

But as a matter of fact it is doubtful whether such Pharisaic Ebionites really existed at all. Certainly the trend of recent investigation has tended to diminish the evidence for their existence. It is by no means impossible that all the denials of the virgin birth among schismatic Jewish Christians came from men of the type that is represented by the Ebionite Gospel quoted by Epiphanius.

At any rate, the Jewish Christian denials of the virgin birth, of whatever kind they were, are more than neutralized by Jewish Christian affirmation of it.

[152] Compare Zahn, *Das apostolische Symbolum*, 1893, p. 56.

[153] Compare B. Weiss, *Leben Jesu*, 4te Aufl., i, 1902, pp. 210–214 (English transation, *The Life of Christ*, 1883, i, pp. 229, 232, footnote 2).

In the first place, the affirmation can be traced at least as far back as the denial. The denial appears for the first time in Justin Martyr, and it appears there in such a way as to suggest that it was by no means formidable. In the eyes of the non-Christian Jews, at any rate, it did not, apparently, loom very large; until corrected by Justin, the Jews seem to have been unaware that the Messiahship of Jesus could be accepted apart from the virgin birth. At the beginning of the second century, Ignatius, when arguing, apparently, against schismatic Jewish Christians, felt no need of correcting their view of the birth of Jesus. Let it not be said that this is due to indifference on the part of Ignatius, or to any lack of firmness in the way in which the virgin birth had been established at that time in the Church. Ignatius hardly yields to any later writer in the place he assigns to the virginity of Mary; it is to him one of the three great mysteries, the long-deferred revelation of which marks a new epoch in the history of the world. It is true, the argument from silence should be used with great caution. But the silence of Ignatius about Jewish Christian denial of the virgin birth is at least as significant as Justin's silence [154] about Jewish Christian acceptance of it. Furthermore, the Gospel according to the Hebrews is perhaps a direct witness to Jewish Christian belief in the virgin birth, from a time prior to that of Justin.[155]

In the second place, the character of those Jewish Christians who accepted the virgin birth raises a presumption in favor of their affirmation. Ritschl pointed out the close similarity between the views of the Nazarenes of Jerome and the view of the original apostles. Like the original apostles,[156] the Nazarenes for their own part continued the observance of the Jewish law; but, again like the original apostles, they recognized the freedom of the Gentile Christians and approved the work of Paul. The stricter Ebionites, on the contrary, who sought to force the observance of the law upon the Gentile converts [157] and regarded Paul as an apostate, were the spiritual successors not of the apostles, who had stood nearest to Jesus, but of the Judaizing "false brethren privily

[154] It has already been shown that this is hardly more than apparent silence.

[155] It is not improbable that very early (and probably Jewish Christian) testimonies to the virgin birth are to be found (1) in the *Ascension of Isaiah,* (2) in the *Testaments of the Twelve Patriarchs,* and (3) in the recently discovered *Odes of Solomon.* The passage in the *Ascension of Isaiah* which narrates the virgin birth is placed by Charles (*The Ascension of Isaiah,* 1900, pp. xxii. ff., xliv. f., 77) at the close of the first century. Compare, however, Harnack, *Chronologie,* i, 1897, pp. 574 ff.

[156] That is, in the early days of the apostolic Church. In the later days the original apostles may be held to have adopted the same practice as the Gentile Christians.

[157] For the distinction between the milder and the stricter party of the Jewish Christians, see Justin Martyr, *dial.,* 47, a passage which was referred to above, p. 17.

brought in."[158] In general, the Nazarenes, living in seclusion in the East and using their own ancient Gospel, produce an impression of conservatism and antiquity in marked contrast to the Ebionites of Epiphanius, with their doctrinal innovations and their worthless Gospel.

One fact deserves to be borne constantly in mind in the whole discussion—the fact, namely, that Jewish Christianity was not confined to the schismatic Jewish Christians included in lists of heresies. It has been shown above that even of the heretical Jewish Christians mentioned by Origen and others some accepted the virgin birth. But this whole discussion has left out of account the great numbers of Jewish Christians who in all probability simply became merged in the Catholic Church.[159] And everything points to the hypothesis that these, and not the schismatics of whatever opinion, were in possession of the most primitive historical tradition with regard to the life of Jesus.

The results of the foregoing investigation of the second-century testimony to the virgin birth may be summed up in two propositions:

1. A firm and well-formulated belief in the virgin birth extends back to the early years of the second century.

2. The denials of the virgin birth which appear in that century were based upon philosophical or dogmatic prepossession, much more probably than upon genuine historical tradition.

[158] Ritschl, *Entstehung der altkatholischen Kirche*, 2te Aufl., 1857, pp. 152 ff. No doubt the evidence will not warrant the definite division of schismatic Jewish Christianity into two parties, the milder party accepting the virgin birth and the stricter party denying it (against this see Nitzsch, *Grundriss der christlichen Dogmengeschichte*, 1870, pp. 42 ff.). But at any rate there is no evidence that any who held the milder view about the law, from the time of Justin to that of Jerome, denied the virgin birth, though a rather ambiguous passage in Eusebius (*hist. eccl.*, III. xxvii. 3–6) seems to mean that those who accepted the virgin birth were of the stricter way of thinking.

[159] Compare Schmidtke, *op. cit.*, pp. 247 ff., especially pp. 247 f., Anm. 4.

Chapter II

THE BIRTH NARRATIVE AN ORIGINAL PART OF THE THIRD GOSPEL

IT HAS been shown in the preceding chapter that the doctrine of the virgin birth, so far as the extant sources permit us to judge, was as firmly established at the beginning of the second century as it was at the close. Such is the most natural conclusion to be drawn in particular from the testimony of Ignatius, and there is nothing in the other extant information to invalidate it.

Obviously a doctrine which appears as so much a matter of course in the Ignatian Epistles could not have been an innovation, but must have had its roots in the previous period. Ignatius was no neophyte, but the bishop of a great church, the mother church of Gentile Christianity. At Antioch he was in a position by no means remote from the ultimate sources of information about the life of Jesus. Obviously, what he presents, without argument, as an essential part of Christian belief must already have been commonly believed in the Church for many years.

Even, therefore, if there were not a word about the subject in the New Testament, the second-century testimony would show that the belief in the virgin birth must have arisen, to say the least, well before the first century was over. As a matter of fact, however, the New Testament does contain an account of the virgin birth, and that account must now be examined.

The New Testament account of the birth of Jesus is contained in two of the New Testament books, the Gospel according to Matthew and the Gospel according to Luke. Since the narrative in Luke is more extended than that in Matthew and begins at an earlier point in the course of events, it may conveniently be considered first.

Of course our estimate of the Lucan account of the birth of Jesus will depend to a considerable extent upon what we think of the Third Gospel as a whole. Obviously that larger question cannot be considered here; consideration of it would require a separate treatise. It can merely be remarked in passing that there is just now an increasing tendency among scholars of widely diverse opinions to accept the traditional view that the Third Gospel and the Book of

Acts were actually written by Luke the physician, a companion of the Apostle Paul.

If this view is correct, very important consequences at once become evident. If the author of Luke-Acts was, as he is held to be by those who defend the traditional view of the authorship, identical with that companion of Paul who includes himself with Paul by the use of the first person plural in the so-called "we sections" of the Book of Acts, then at every point where the "we" occurs the author must have been present. The movements and relationships of the author can thus be traced. It can be shown by this method, for example, that the author came into contact, on the second missionary journey, not only with Paul, but also with Silas, who came originally from the Jerusalem Church. And, what is even more important, the significant "we" in the narrative extends into the very presence of James, the brother of the Lord, and of the Jerusalem Church itself.[1] The author was thus in Palestine at the beginning of the two years which Paul spent in prison at Cæsarea; and since at the end of that period he appears again in Palestine (where he took ship with Paul for Rome), it is natural to suppose that he spent all or part of the interval in that country. At that time, then, he could have had abundant opportunity to obtain information about the earthly life of Jesus from those who were best qualified to speak. If Luke was really the author of Luke-Acts, then there is a strong presumption in favor of the trustworthiness of the double work, not only where it deals with the missionary journeys of Paul, but also with regard to the life of Jesus and the early history of the Palestinian Church; and in particular it must be treated with respect where it deals with the events concerning the birth and infancy of the Lord.

It is not surprising, therefore, to find that the great majority of those who deny the historicity of the infancy narrative in the Third Gospel deny also the Lucan authorship of the book. The primary reason why they must do so is perfectly plain; it is simply that the Third Gospel and the Book of Acts, not only in the infancy narrative, but elsewhere as well, present a thoroughly supernaturalistic account of the life of Jesus and of the beginnings of the Christian Church. If a man rejects the supernatural, it is very difficult for him to suppose that an author who stood so close to the events as did Luke the physician, a companion of Paul, could have given so clearly supernatural and hence mistaken an account of what occurred. But just because of this consideration, it is the more significant that scholars like A. von Harnack of Berlin,[2] and the

[1] Acts xxi.18.

[2] See the well-known series of monographs beginning with *Lukas der Arzt*, 1906 (English translation, *Luke the Physician*, 1907).

distinguished historian, Eduard Meyer,[3] who themselves altogether reject the historicity of the miracles narrated in Luke-Acts, should have felt compelled to accept the traditional view of the authorship. Only very strong evidence in the sphere of literary criticism could so overcome the strong presumption against Lucan authorship which must exist in the minds of such opponents of the supernatural content of the books. And as a matter of fact that evidence is found upon independent examination to be very strong indeed. The more one examines the literary phenomena in connection with Luke-Acts, the more one is impressed by the evidence for the traditional view that the double work was written by Luke the physician, a companion of Paul.

It is, therefore, very significant that the account of the birth and infancy of Jesus in Lk. i-ii is a part of the Third Gospel. But this account of the birth and infancy constitutes not only a part of the Third Gospel, but a very peculiar part, a part which well deserves separate consideration.

The prologue of the Gospel, embracing the first four verses, is one of the most carefully constructed sentences in the whole New Testament. It is a typical "complex" sentence, in which the sense is held in abeyance until the end; and in the last clause, "in order that thou mayest know, concerning the things wherein thou has been instructed, *the certainty,*" the emphatic word of the whole sentence, "the certainty," is reserved to the last in an effective way which cannot be reproduced in any smooth English translation. It would be difficult to imagine a more skilfully formed, and more typically Greek, sentence than this.

Yet this typically Greek sentence is followed by what is probably the most markedly Semitic section in the whole New Testament, the section containing the account of the birth and infancy in Lk. i.5-ii.52. There could scarcely be a greater contrast in style. In passing from the complex Greek sentence of the prologue to the simple narrative style of the following section, which is like the style of the Old Testament historical books, one seems to be suddenly transplanted into a different world.

This contrast between the language of the birth narrative and the author's own style as it is found in the prologue might be expected, in a day of acuteness in the field of literary criticism, to lead to the hypothesis that Lk. i.5-ii.52 is a later addition, not found in the original form of the book. And indeed this hypothesis has not been altogether without its advocates. But the significant thing is that the advocates of it were perhaps more prominent one hundred and twenty-five years ago than they are today.

[3] *Ursprung und Anfänge des Christentums*, iii, 1923, pp. 23–36.

During the closing years of the eighteenth century the question was rather seriously raised whether the first two chapters, not merely of Matthew, but also of Luke, were later additions to the books. This hypothesis with regard to the Gospel of Luke (if we may confine our attention for the moment to that Gospel) has been favored in more recent times by Hilgenfeld,[4] Usener,[5] P. Corssen,[6] and F. C. Conybeare;[7] but it has failed signally to establish itself, and at present can claim comparatively little support.

The truth is that, despite the obvious differences of language and style that exist between Lk. i.5-ii.52 and other parts of Luke-Acts, a closer examination reveals also similarities of a very impressive kind. As early in the history of modern criticism as 1816, the language of this infancy section of the Gospel was carefully examined verse by verse by Gersdorf, with the result that a great number of "Lucan" words or usages—that is, words or usages found only or chiefly in the Lucan writings as compared with the other New Testament books—were discovered in it. Apparently without reference to Gersdorf, a similar process has been carried out in recent years by Zimmermann and Harnack, with entirely convincing results. An examination by the present writer, which was undertaken in order to test what proved to be an exaggeration by Harnack of the Lucan character of the section, yet resulted, so far as the present point is concerned, in a complete confirmation. It is perfectly clear that the hand of the author of the whole book has been at work in Lk. i.5-ii.52.[8]

Against this conclusion Hilgenfeld urged the hypothesis that the similarities between our section and the rest of the book were due to a redactor.[9] But surely the explanation is quite inadequate. The facts may be explained only if the author of the whole book, supposing he did use sources in Lk. i.5-ii.52, used them with freedom, preserving their peculiar quality and yet imparting to them something of his own style. Gradually the criticism of the Lucan writings is enabling us to construct something like a clear account of the literary methods of the author. And it is a very pleasing account indeed. We have here an author who had an admirable feeling for the beauty of the Old Testament narratives and of the Semitic narratives that came to him from Palestine, but

[4] "Das Vorwort des dritten Evangeliums (Luc. I, 1–4)," in *Zeitschrift für wissenschaftliche Theologie*, xliv, 1901, pp. 1–10; "Die Geburts- und Kindheitsgeschichte Jesu Luc. I, 5–II, 52," *ibid.*, pp. 177–235; "Zu Lucas III, 2," *ibid.*, pp. 466–468.

[5] *Das Weihnachtsfest*, 2te Aufl., 1911, pp. 52, 83–95; art. "Nativity," in *Encyclopædia Biblica*, iii, 1902, cols. 3347 f.

[6] In *Göttingische gelehrte Anzeigen*, clxi, 1899, pp. 325 f.

[7] "Ein Zeugnis Ephräms über das Fehlen von c. 1 und 2 im Texte des Lucas," in *Zeitschrift für die neutestamentliche Wissenschaft*, iii, 1902, pp. 192–197.

[8] For further information about the studies referred to in this paragraph, see below, pp. 102 ff.

[9] Hilgenfeld, "Die Geburts- und Kindheitsgeschichte Jesu Luc. I, 5–II, 52," in *Zeitschrift für wissenchaftliche Theologie*, xliv, 1901, p. 185.

who at the same time knew how to impart to his book a certain unity amid the diversity, which prevents it from being a mere compilation and makes it a genuine literary whole.

Thus the linguistic facts are strongly against the view that Lk. i.5-ii.52 constitutes an addition to the original Gospel. And a little examination will show that other arguments that have been adduced in favor of that view all break down.

In the first place, there is not the slightest external evidence in favor of the hypothesis. It is true that in the second century Marcion, the ultra-Pauline heretical teacher, used a form of the Gospel of Luke that did not contain the first two chapters. That fact was still used by Usener in 1889 to support his removal of Lk. i.5-ii.52 from the original form of the Gospel. Usener supposed that Marcion's Luke was derived from an earlier form of the Gospel from which our canonical Luke also comes, and that at this point the Marcionic form was more original.[10] But it would probably be difficult to find advocates of such a view today; it is now generally admitted that Marcion's form of the Gospel was due to a revision of our canonical form, a revision undertaken to support Marcion's peculiar views.[11] Thus it was impossible for Marcion to include in his Gospel any account of a birth of Jesus, to say nothing of a virgin birth, for the simple reason that he did not believe Jesus to have been born at all, but thought that He appeared full-grown upon the earth. As a witness to any form of the Third Gospel that did not include the first two chapters, Marcion is therefore altogether without significance.

Equally without significance for our purpose is a certain note to which F. C. Conybeare called attention, attached to a manuscript, dating from the year 1195, of the Armenian translation of Ephraem's Commentary on the Diatessaron. The manuscript in question is very late, and both text and interpretation of the note are very uncertain. It is not surprising that Conybeare's estimate of this piece of evidence has not received support from other scholars.[12]

[10] Usener, *Das Weihnachtsfest*, 1889, pp. 51 f., 80–91. These passages appear also in the second edition, which was published in 1911 under the care of Hans Lietzmann (pp. 51 f., 83–95).

[11] See, for example, Harnack, "Marcion," in *Texte und Untersuchungen*, 3. Reihe 15. Band, 2te Aufl., 1924, pp. 65 f.: "Therefore it is also an error to hold that when he [Marcion] omitted the infancy narrative he was influenced by the earlier tradition (supposed not to contain that narrative). It must be remembered that he also omitted the narrative of the baptism, which belongs to the oldest part of the Gospel material and in all probability was already present in the source 'Q'."

[12] Conybeare, "Ein Zeugnis Ephrāms über das Fehlen von c. 1 und 2 im Texte des Lucas," in *Zeitschrift für die neutestamentliche Wissenschaft*, iii, 1902, pp. 192–197. See "The New Testament Account of the Birth of Jesus," first article, in *Princeton Theological Review*, iii, 1905, pp. 643 f.

Thus there is complete unanimity among all the witnesses to the text in favor of including Lk. i.5-ii.52 in the original Third Gospel. The section was included in the earliest Gospel harmony, Tatian's Diatessaron, which was made in the second century; its presence in the Gospel is definitely attested by the Muratori Canon; and it is found in all the Greek manuscripts of the Gospel and in all the versions. Such unanimity among widely divergent lines of attestation makes it very adventurous, to say the least, to exclude the section from the original form of the Gospel according to Luke.

But if the attempts to find external evidence for excluding Lk. i.5-ii.52 from the Third Gospel have resulted in failure, equally unconvincing are the arguments which have been adduced from the Lucan writings themselves.

Thus when it is argued from Acts i.1—"The former treatise have I made, O Theophilus, concerning all things which Jesus began both to do and to teach, until the day when he was taken up"—that the Gospel (which is here called "the former treatise") could not have contained an account of anything that happened prior to the time when Jesus began to teach and to act, in other words, prior to the beginning of the public ministry,[18] surely that is a very pedantic way of understanding what is in reality just a reference to the main contents of the Gospel. Taken broadly, as over against the author's second book, the Book of Acts, the Gospel may surely be designated, even if it included the first two chapters, as an account of the things that Jesus began to do and to teach prior to the ascension. In a modern biography, it is considered perfectly proper for the author sometimes to go back even a number of generations in order that the reader may understand the better the life that is to be narrated in detail. So it was perfectly natural for a book concerned with what Jesus did and taught during His public ministry to include, at least by way of introduction, an account of events connected with His entrance into the world. And even though there were any objection to such a designation of the Gospel if the designation stood alone, the objection disappears when one observes the contrast that is implied with the contents of the author's second book. As over against the Book of Acts, with its account of the words and deeds of the apostles, it is not unnatural for the Gospel, even including the narrative of the birth and infancy, to be designated as an account of the words and deeds of Jesus. It should be observed, moreover, that in Acts i.1 no starting-point for the narrative of the former treatise is definitely mentioned. The author is thinking not of the starting-point of the Gospel, but of the end of it, where with the ascension of Jesus the transition was made to the subse-

[18] Hilgenfeld, *op. cit.*, p. 178.

quent progress of the gospel under the instrumentality of the apostles, which provides the subject-matter of the second book.

It is perhaps worthy of remark that even if the first two chapters of the Gospel were not present, the book would still begin, strictly speaking, with something other than the words and deeds of Jesus; for the first twenty verses of the third chapter are concerned with John the Baptist, whose preaching is reported at much greater length than in the other Synoptic Gospels. Just how much introductory material may be allowed in an account of what Jesus did and taught? Even if Lk. i.5-ii.52 be removed, there is a certain amount of such material. Who can say that the addition of that section would require a different designation of the book as a whole? Thus the argument from the prologue of Acts may be said to prove too much.

Equally unconvincing is Hilgenfeld's use of the prologue of the Gospel. When he argues that Christianity began with the baptism of Jesus, so that what happened before that could not be included among the things "fulfilled *among us*" (that is, in Christendom),[14] that is again a quite unwarranted pressing of the author's words. For refutation of it, one does not need to enter at length upon the vexed question of the interpretation of the prologue. Surely an account of the birth and infancy of Jesus could not be excluded from the things that have been fulfilled *among us* (that is, among Christians) even if Hilgenfeld is right in supposing that in the author's view Christianity began definitely with the baptism. Far more natural is it to say that the author desires to treat the whole complex of Christian facts, to which the birth of the Saviour and of His forerunner belonged. And it may even perhaps be argued that when this author speaks about his having followed all things *from the beginning* he is alluding to an earlier point of departure for his narrative than that which appeared in the works of some, at least, of his predecessors.

But is Hilgenfeld correct in designating the baptism of Jesus as being for this author the beginning of "Christianity"? That brings us to a consideration of the use to which some of the advocates of the theory which Hilgenfeld is defending have put the Lucan account of the baptism in Lk. iii.21-23 and the references to it in Acts i.22; x.37 f.; xiii.23 f. These passages, it is said, establish the baptism of Jesus by John, with the bestowal of the Spirit that accompanied it, as the true decisive "beginning" in the life of Jesus and thus as the beginning of the Christian facts with which the author of Luke and Acts was undertaking to deal.

[14] Hilgenfeld, "Das Vorwort des dritten Evangeliums (Luc. I, 1–4)", in *Zeitschrift für wissenschaftliche Theologie*, xliv, 1901, pp. 1–3; "Die Geburts- und Kindheitsgeschichte Jesu Luc. I, 5–II, 52," *ibid.*, pp. 177–179.

The argument is thought to be more powerful if, as has been done by a number of scholars, the reading of the "Western" text is adopted at Lk. iii. 22. In that verse, the great mass of witnesses to the text, including the Codex Vaticanus and the Codex Sinaiticus, have the reading with which we are familiar: "Thou art my beloved son, in thee I am well pleased." But the Codex Bezæ, supported by certain manuscripts of the Old Latin Version and by certain patristic citations, including apparently a reference in Justin Martyr at the middle of the second century, reads: "Thou art my son, this day have I begotten thee," thus making the divine utterance a quotation of the words in Ps. ii. 7. This reading, it is said, if it is original (and a number of scholars think that it is), places the beginning of the divine sonship of Jesus at the baptism, and so indicates that the same Gospel could not have placed it at the birth, as is plainly done in Lk. i.35.

In regard to this argument, it may be said in the first place that the Western text is in all probability incorrect at Lk. iii.22, as it is in so many other cases; and in the second place that even if it were correct it would not be nearly so significant as has sometimes been supposed. The passage in the Second Psalm, of which the Western text in Lk. iii.22 is a quotation, evidently designates, not the birth, but the induction into office, of the Messianic king. Accordingly it is applied by this same writer (in his report of a speech of Paul) to the resurrection.[15] If it were applied by the same writer both to the resurrection of Jesus and to the baptism, there would not really be the slightest incongruity; for in one sense the baptism and in another sense the resurrection constituted the induction of Jesus into his kingly function as "Son of God." Still less difficulty could be found in comparison with Lk. i.35, where the divine sonship of Jesus is brought apparently into connection with the virgin birth. The mere fact that after the virgin birth had been narrated the same writer should go on to apply a passage from the Psalms, in full accord with its obvious Old Testament sense, to the induction into office of the Messianic king at the beginning of the public ministry, surely need not be regarded as surprising at all.

Thus even if the Western reading were correct at Lk. iii.22 (as in all probability it is not), there would be nothing in this verse out of harmony with the birth narrative, and so nothing to show that that narrative could not have been included by the same author in the same book.

But even though the Western reading in this verse would not be sufficient, when taken alone, to show that the birth narratives were originally absent, may it not do so when taken in connection with certain other considerations?

[15] Acts xiii.33. Compare Rom. i.4.

Or even if the Western reading is not correct, is there not still enough evidence to show that for the author of Luke-Acts the baptism of Jesus, and not the birth, was the great "beginning," the beginning *par excellence,* to which he must be referring in the prologues of both his books? These questions deserve some consideration.

But here again the evidence will not at all bear the weight that is put upon it. It is indeed perfectly clear that to the author of Luke-Acts, on the basis of the information that came to him, the baptism of Jesus was an important event that did mark the beginning of something. But of what did it mark the beginning?

In the first place, it marked the beginning of that period in the life of Jesus to which the apostles could testify as eye-witnesses. That fact explains the reference in Acts i.22; for there it is represented as an important qualification for the man who was to take the place of Judas among the Twelve that he should have been with the disciples during all the time when Jesus went out and in among them beginning with the baptism of John. No other *terminus a quo* could have been designated, for the simple reason that none of the apostles, not even Peter himself, was with Jesus at an earlier time. The baptism clearly marks the beginning of the direct testimony of the apostles.

That fact really explains also the mention of the baptism in Acts x.37-39; for in that passage again Peter says: "And *we are witnesses* of all things which Jesus did in the country of the Jews and in Jerusalem." It was at the baptism that Peter began to be an eye-witness of the life of Christ upon earth. A similar consideration, if we may anticipate what will have to be said in another connection, serves to explain admirably the omission of the birth and infancy in the Gospel of Mark. That Gospel, according to a thoroughly credible tradition, embodies the teaching of Peter; and it seems to contain the things which would make a first impression rather than instruction of a more detailed and intimate kind. It is very natural that such a book should deal almost exclusively with things that Peter had himself seen and heard.

In Acts xiii.24, although there also the same consideration may be urged, the case is a little different; for in this passage, in the speech of Paul at Pisidian Antioch, the baptism of Jesus by John is not mentioned, and John appears rather as the last of the pre-Christian witnesses to Christ. But in the other two passages the prime consideration is that the baptism of Jesus by John marks the beginning of the period in the life of Christ to which the apostles could testify as eye-witnesses.

We are, indeed, far from wishing to assert that in the mind of the author of Luke-Acts, the baptism of Jesus was important only because it happened to be the point at which the apostles began to be eye-witnesses. On the contrary, this author, like the author of the other Gospels, represents the baptism as marking an important new beginning, not only for the disciples, but also for Jesus Himself.

The fact is no doubt indicated by the striking use of the absolute participle "beginning" at Lk. iii.23. That verse, literally translated, reads as follows: "And Jesus Himself was, when He began [in Greek, "beginning"], about thirty years old, being the son, as was supposed, of Joseph who was the son of Eli. . . ."[16] The words, "when He began," naturally give rise to question. The reader may be tempted to ask, "When He began *what?*"

Extreme answers have sometimes been given to this question. Thus it has been suggested, especially when the Western reading, "Thou art my son, this day have I begotten thee," is adopted in the preceding verse, that the "beginning" which is referred to in our verse is the beginning of the divine sonship of Jesus. Jesus has just been designated as having been begotten "this day" by God; hence His divine sonship, it is said, begins at that point. On this interpretation, the words, "as was supposed," in the phrase, "being the son, as was supposed, of Joseph," instead of being taken, in accordance with what is certainly the prevailing opinion, as a reference to the virgin birth of Jesus, have somewhere actually been taken as contrasting the physical sonship of Jesus as a child of Joseph and Mary—His sonship according to the outward appearance—with His real, or spiritual sonship, which began through the divine begetting at the time of the baptism. That divine begetting, on this interpretation, did not take place until Jesus, as a son of Joseph and Mary, had grown to full manhood. His apparent, or physical, or external, sonship had lasted for thirty years before His true, divine sonship began.

This interpretation of the words, "as was supposed," it may be remarked in passing, is rather unnatural. If the beginning of the divine, as distinguished from the human, sonship of Jesus is not regarded as having taken place before the baptism, then Jesus up to that time was not only apparently but really the son of Joseph. Therefore, to justify the interpretation of which we have been speaking, the sentence ought perhaps rather to have read: "And Jesus was, when He began, about thirty years of age, being, as was supposed, *still* (or *only*) the son of Joseph," or "being *according to the flesh* the son of Joseph." The words as they stand will hardly bear the meaning that is attributed to them. It would not be natural to set the divine begetting in a relation of contrast with the current opinion about the paternity of Joseph, as is done by the words, "as was supposed," except on the assumption that Joseph was not in a

[16] καὶ αὐτὸς ἦν Ἰησοῦς ἀρχόμενος ὡσεὶ ἐτῶν τριάκοντα, ὢν υἱός, ὡς ἐνομίζετο, Ἰωσὴφ τοῦ Ἡλεί. . . .

physical sense—that is, not in the sense that prevailed generally among the people—the father of Jesus.

It is not surprising, therefore, that the great majority (to say the least) of those who hold that the passage Lk. iii.22, 23 is incompatible with the birth of Jesus as it is narrated in the first two chapters, and that those chapters are therefore a later addition to the Gospel, admit that the words, "as was supposed," in verse 23 do constitute a reference to the virgin birth as it appears in Lk. i.34, 35, and hence admit that these words were interpolated by the same person who added the first two chapters to the Gospel. On that view, the words, "as was supposed," can no longer do duty as indicating that the baptism, and not the birth, of Jesus was the beginning of His divine sonship.

But even with this ordinary interpretation of these words, as they stand, as referring to the virgin birth (the interpretation which is no doubt held by nearly all scholars of all shades of opinion), and even with the ordinary, as distinguished from the Western, text in Lk. iii.22, does it not still remain true that the word "beginning" ("when He began") in verse 23 designates the event at the baptism as the decisive beginning, the beginning *par excellence,* which the author has in mind in the entire plan of his work, so that there could not originally have been prefixed to the account of this event an extended narrative of prior events such as that which we now have in the first two chapters?

In answer to this question it must freely be admitted, as indeed has already been done, that the baptism by John, or the event that immediately followed, is regarded by the author of Luke-Acts as an event of very great importance indeed. It is not at all surprising, therefore, that the time, or at least the general setting, of this event—or rather of the public appearance of John which was preliminary to it—should be fixed by the elaborate reference to contemporary political conditions in Lk. iii.1.

But surely the importance of the baptism of Jesus, in the mind of the Evangelist, does not carry with it any lack of importance for the birth and infancy. And as for the elaborate reference to contemporary conditions, it may be said, (1) that possibly the author did not possess equally detailed information regarding conditions at the time of the birth, (2) that such a chronological or political note would have been out of accord with the style chosen (for whatever reason) for the birth narrative, when a simple phrase, "in the days of Herod the King," alone suited the spirit of that narrative, (3) that in a reference to a time when Herod the Great ruled over all Palestine there was no need for the separate designation of the districts into which the country was later divided, so that for that earlier time an elaborate note like that in Lk. iii.1, 2 would have been impossible, (4) that the phrase, "in the days of

Herod the King," in Lk. i.5, coupled with the reference to the census and to Quirinius in Lk. ii.1 f., does show a desire on the part of the author to synchronize the birth of Jesus with surrounding political conditions which is somewhat similar, after all, to the treatment of the appearance of the Baptist in Lk. iii.1 f.

What, then, was the importance of the event at the baptism of Jesus, which caused that event to be designated by the somewhat surprising absolute use of the participle "beginning" (that is, in English, "when He began") in Lk. iii.23? The answer is simply that that event marked the beginning of the public ministry of Jesus. Up to that time He had been hidden; now He came forward publicly in His Messianic work. The account of the temptation, which immediately follows the account of the baptism, supports this understanding of that previous event. Jesus had just been designated by the voice from heaven as Son of God—that is (whatever deeper meaning there may be in the term), at least as Messiah. Thus the Western text, with its quotation of Ps. ii.7, secondary though it no doubt is, yet involves perhaps an essentially correct interpretation of the divine word; Jesus was, when the Spirit descended upon Him, designated as the Messianic king. The kingship had indeed been His before; but now He was to enter into the active exercise of it. But what kind of king should He be; how should He use His kingly power? That question it was which was asked by the Tempter, with his repeated "If thou be the son of God," and which Jesus answered in such a decisive way.

But, it is said, if the event at the baptism be taken in this fashion, not as making Jesus something that He had not been, but merely as designating His entrance into a work for which He had been qualified even before, what shall be thought of the descent upon Him of the Holy Spirit (Lk. iii.22)? Even if the words, "Thou art my son," could be understood not as the conferring of some new dignity or power that He had not possessed before, but merely as the announcement or confirmation of what was already His, how can the coming of the Holy Spirit upon Him be understood in this merely declarative way? Does not *that* event, at least, indicate that He now came to be something that He had not already been? And if so, how could it be supposed that not only had He possessed the Holy Spirit from His mother's womb, as was the case with John the Baptist,[17] but had owed to the Holy Spirit, in a supernatural conception, the very constitution of His being?[18] Finally, if that question is unanswerable, how could the same author have included two such incompatible representations in his book? And so must not the birth narratives, in which

[17] Lk. i.15.
[18] Lk. i.35.

the other representation is found, be a later addition not due to the original author of the book?

Such questions have sometimes been asked. And yet the objection that underlies them is not really by any means so serious as it may at first sight seem. It depends upon the assumption that the coming of the Holy Spirit in connection with the life of Jesus upon earth could take place, according to our Evangelist, only at one time and in one way. But surely that assumption is exceedingly uncertain, to say the least. The actions of the Spirit of God—we will not say, in reality, for that is not the question here—but according to the mind of the author of the Third Gospel, were very much more mysterious and very much more varied than they are thought to be by many modern scholars in their study-chambers. Who can say that because the Holy Spirit came upon the virgin mother of Jesus when He was conceived in the womb, therefore the same Spirit could not, according to the Evangelist, come upon Jesus again, and in other fashion, to fit Him for His public work as Messiah? Can the ineffable interactions between Jesus Christ and the Spirit of God be thus reduced to a set scheme? We think not; and in so thinking we are not merely voicing the conviction of Christendom throughout all the ages, but also are in full accord, no matter what the particular investigator's own convictions may be, with what a true historical exegesis must recognize as being in the mind of Luke. In order to understand a book like the Third Gospel, and like the other New Testament books, it is necessary to do something more than impose upon those books our own predilections; the true interpreter must rather seek to enter, as cannot be done by rule of thumb, into the very spirit of the writer. And when that is done, no contradiction will be found, but rather the deepest harmony, between the work of the Holy Spirit at the very beginning of Jesus' earthly life and the coming of the same Spirit upon Him when finally He went forth to begin His public ministry.

There is not the slightest reason, therefore, why we should not hold that the event at the baptism was important for Jesus, according to the author of the Third Gospel, not because it made Him something that He was not before, but because it designated His entrance upon His public work. What had been hidden before was now to become manifest to all the people. There had been a period of obscurity, but that period was preparatory to what was now at last to come.

That this interpretation is in accordance with the intention of the writer is not only probable in itself, but also is confirmed by one particular link between the birth narrative and what follows—a link which has generally escaped notice. In Lk. i.80 it is said that John the Baptist was in the deserts until the day of his "showing" to Israel.[19] Does that verse not lead the reader to look for the great "day" that is there held in prospect, the day when John should emerge from his obscurity and appear publicly as the forerunner of the Messianic salvation? Whenever that day should come, surely it would be heralded by the writer who included Lk. i.80 in his book, with all the solemnity that he could command. And just exactly that is done in Lk. iii.1 f. The period of obscurity and waiting in which the reader was left in the former passage at last is over; the forerunner emerges from the deserts and the day of Messianic salvation has dawned. What wonder that the concomitant political conditions are marked with all the precision that the writer can command; what wonder that rulers and high priests are marshalled to do honor to the great event that signalized their reign?

Thus is explained the fact that the elaborate synchronism of rulers in Lk. iii.1 f. marks not the baptism of Jesus, but the appearance or "showing forth" of His forerunner, John. In the clearest possible way the author has taken up the thread that for the moment was broken off. The forerunner was in obscurity in the deserts; He for whose coming he was to prepare was in humble subjection to earthly parents—and then the great day came, the day of the formal appearance of the herald in his great function of preparing for the Messianic king.

Far, therefore, from being an argument against regarding the first two chapters as part of the original form of the Gospel, the elaborate political note in Lk. iii.1 f. is an argument to the contrary. And even the way in which the Baptist is introduced in these two verses provides an incidental indication of the fact that the birth narrative has gone before. In contrast with what is found in the other Gospels, John is here designated, at his first appearance in connection with Jesus' public ministry, not as "the Baptist" or the like but as "Zacharias' son." It is truly surprising that Hilgenfeld actually finds in this phrase an argument *against* the original inclusion of the first two chapters in the Gospel.[20] Zacharias, the father of John, he says, is here mentioned as though for the first time, and therefore this Gospel could not have contained the account of him that now stands in Lk. i. Could there be any more complete reversal of the natural inference? Is it not perfectly clear that the reason why Luke, as distinguished from the other Evangelists, designates the Baptist as Zacharias' son, is that, unlike the other Evangelists, he has already given an account of

[19] The word for "showing," it may be remarked, is no ordinary word, but has a rather formal, solemn sound.

[20] Hilgenfeld, "Zu Lucas III, 2," in *Zeitschrift für wissenschaftliche Theologie*, xliv, 1901, pp. 466–468.

Zacharias at the beginning of his Gospel? Lk. iii.2 rather plainly refers back to Lk. i.5-25, 57-80.

A number of indications in detail, therefore, have been shown to unite the main body of the Third Gospel with the first two chapters. Careful search might reveal many others. And of course the words, "as was supposed," in Lk. iii.23, which have already been discussed in a slightly different connection, provide, as they stand, an additional link with the birth narrative. If that narrative is to be regarded as absent from the Gospel as it originally appeared, then these words must be an interpolation due to the man who expanded the Gospel into its present form. But obviously the necessity of removing such supposed interpolations in the body of the Gospel, before it can be separated from the first two chapters, overloads the hypothesis, and raises anew the question why it is that the original, shorter and uninterpolated, form of the book has so completely failed to leave any trace among the extant witnesses to the text.

Usener,[21] apparently, has an answer to this latter question. The Gospel, he thinks, was at first subject to repeated additions; it was not a work completed at one time and given to the world in definitive form, but was, rather, an agglomeration that was only gradually formed and was added to from time to time as the real or supposed needs of the Church might require. Thus, at first, according to Usener,[22] it did not even contain an account of the baptism of Jesus by John: the account of the baptism was then added; and last of all there was added the account of the birth. Why then is there such unanimity in the transmission of the text; why have those successive earlier forms left no trace? The answer, apparently, that Usener gave, at least the only answer that he could give, to this question is that the extant text, in all its lines of transmission, goes back to a canonized form of the Gospel that was fixed at some time in the second century to put an end to the misuse of the Gospels by what was regarded as heresy. This act of canonization it must have been, therefore, according to Usener's hypothesis, that stopped the process of agglomeration of Gospel material that had been going on before, and caused only the Gospels as we now have them to be handed down to us today.

To this entire hypothesis, however, there are the most serious objections. Where and when did this definitive canonization take place? If there was going on so free a process of addition to the Gospels as Usener supposes, if the contents of the Gospels were so completely in a state of flux, where, in the second century, was there a central ecclesiastical authority strong enough to

[21] *Das Weihnachtsfest*, 2te Aufl., 1911, especially pp. 95–101, 130–139.
[22] *Op. cit.*, 1911, pp. 51 f, 93.

put a stop to such a process all at once—strong enough to say to everyone who was freely adding to the agglomerations of material now called Gospels: "Thus far shalt thou go and no farther; this business of adding to the Gospels must stop; here and here only is the form of the Gospels which henceforth you must use"? And even if there was an authority strong enough to do that, would it have been efficient enough to destroy all the previous forms of the Gospels, widely used though they were in various parts of the Church, so completely that no trace of these forms should remain today in any of the many divergent lines of transmission of the text? It must be remembered that our text of the Gospels can be traced, through patristic citations and by the convergence of widely separated families of documents, to a time long prior to the production of the great uncial manuscripts. Could the supposed act of canonization have been so early and so complete as to dominate not one but all of the divergent lines of transmission?

If the thing had been attempted in the fourth or fifth century, conceivably it might have been possible. In the early fifth century, for example, the use of the Diatessaron was rooted out of the Syriac-speaking Church by ecclesiastical authority, and the use of the four separate Gospels was substituted for it. But, in the first place, that concerned only the Syriac-speaking Church, not the Church throughout the world; in the second place, it was not, as a matter of fact, completely successful, since, despite all ecclesiastical efforts, the Diatessaron, in translation at least, and through a commentary upon it, does remain to us today; and in the third place it was done in the fifth century, when ecclesiastical authority was far stronger than it was in the second century, which is the period with which Usener's hypothesis deals. Surely it would be difficult to find in that early period an ecclesiastical authority, not local but in the very fullest sense ecumenical, which could all at once put a stop to the transmission of the shorter forms of the Gospels which were being used in various churches and could suddenly impart to the Gospels a fixity of content which originally the Gospels did not at all possess. If the content of the Gospels was at first in such a complete state of flux, the process could never in the second century have been stopped so completely, and the earlier and shorter gospels so completely destroyed, as Usener's hypothesis really requires. No, there is only one way to explain the essential unanimity of our witnesses to the text, so far as the content of the Gospels is concerned. That way is to suppose that the Gospels were not mere agglomerations of material, as Usener apparently thinks they were, but in some sort literary units. No ecclesiastical authority in the second century could have produced the unanimity of transmission; only the authors themselves could have done it.

It might indeed be admitted, without the slightest danger to this conclusion, that a process of gradual agglomeration of originally separate material does, to some extent at least, underlie our Gospels. It might be admitted further that our Gospels, including the Gospel of Luke, do make use of earlier written sources, and that some, at least, if not all, of these sources were shorter than the Gospels as we now have them. These admissions would not at all involve us in the difficulties into which Usener's hypothesis falls; they would not at all cause us to be puzzled at the disappearance of some or all of the written sources that our Gospels used. The point is that the unanimity in the transmission of the contents of our Gospels, and the disappearance of some, at least, of the sources that they used, can be explained only if—contrary to Usener's view—the men to whom we owe our Gospels were not mere compilers, but in some sort (despite their use of previous materials), *authors,* who imparted a certain unity to their completed works and gave them to the Church with the authority of the authors' names. The facts of the transmission, we think, are explained only if our Gospels are not merely arbitrary fixations of impersonal and gradually forming agglomerations of materials, but genuine *books,* given to the world at definite points of time and possessed of the fixity of content which literary productions ordinarily have.

But if this conclusion alone, and not the hypothesis of Usener, does justice both to the state of ecclesiastical authority in the second century and to the unanimity in the transmission of the text, even more signally is it in accord with the characteristics of the Gospels themselves.

Are our Synoptic Gospels, as a matter of fact, merely loose conglomerations of material which could naturally be added to (or subtracted from) as need might require? The question must be answered with an emphatic negative, and most clearly of all as concerns the Gospel according to Luke. Whatever may be said of the other two, it is quite evident that the Third Gospel, at least, possesses, amid all the variety of its parts, a genuine literary unity. The whole recent history of literary criticism since Usener's book first appeared in 1889 has tended mightily against Usener's hypothesis. Through the researches of Harnack and others, and through a more sympathetic attention to the literary form of the New Testament books, which has been only one manifestation of a more sympathetic attitude in general toward the productions of the Hellenistic period in the history of the Greek language, it has been becoming increasingly evident that the writer of Luke-Acts was far more than a compiler, that he was, in fact, a genuine *author* who had his own plan for his work and who knew how, despite all his use of previously existing materials, to carry out that plan in detail.[23] There has not been for the most part, indeed, any return to the Tübingen over-emphasis upon the plan or "tendency" of the author; recent scholars have been less and less prone to find in the author of Luke-Acts a man who carried out his purpose for his book with ruthless disregard of the information that came to him. But that fact does not at all affect the point that we are now making. It does remain true that the whole tendency of recent criticism has been in favor of the literary unity of the Lucan writings.

This conviction as to the literary unity of Luke-Acts extends in the fullest measure, as we have observed, to the first two chapters. The more carefully those chapters are examined, the clearer become the indications in them of the hand of the author of the whole book. Those indications can never be explained by Hilgenfeld's elaborate hypothesis of a Pauline redactor who revised the birth narrative and also undertook a work of interpolation in the rest of the Gospel. This hypothesis seems rather obsolete today, not only because it displays a Tübingen assurance of discrimination between what is Pauline and what is not, which has come to be out of date—especially in view of the fact that many of Hilgenfeld's "Pauline" redactorial touches in Lk. i.5-ii.52 are paralleled in the Old Testament prophets—but also because the stylistic congruity between the birth narrative and the rest of Luke-Acts is too deep and too subtle to have been produced by a redactor. It could only have been due to a genuine author. If literary criticism has established anything at all, it has established the fact that the narrative of the birth and infancy is an integral part of the Third Gospel.[24]

[23] See especially Eduard Meyer, *Ursprung und Anfänge des Christentums*, i, 1921, pp. 1–3.

[24] Kattenbusch ("Die Geburtsgeschichte Jesu als Haggada der Urchristologie [Zu J. Gr. Machen, The virgin birth of Christ]", in *Theologische Studien und Kritiken*, cii, 1930, p. 456) criticizes the argument in this chapter on the ground that it does not take account of the hypothesis of B. H. Streeter (*The Four Gospels*, fourth impression, 1930, pp. 201–222) regarding a "Proto-Luke" which did not contain Lk. i. 5-ii. 52; and J. S. Bezzant (in his review in *The Journal of Theological Studies*, xxxiii, 1931, p. 74) mentions Vincent Taylor in the same connection, as another prominent advocate of the Proto-Luke hypothesis (*Behind the Third Gospel*, 1926). But in excluding Lk. i. 5-ii. 52 from Proto-Luke, Streeter and Vincent Taylor are holding merely that this section did not stand in one of the sources—a very important source, it is true—of the Third Gospel, rather than that it did not from the beginning stand in the Third Gospel itself. These scholars do, indeed, hold that the author of Proto-Luke was Luke himself, who was also the author of Luke-Acts; and they do, indeed, think that the elaborate way in which the appearance of John the Baptist is introduced in Lk. iii.1 f. is due to the fact that Proto-Luke began at this point (Streeter, *op. cit.*, p. 209; Vincent Taylor, *op. cit.*, pp. 193 f.). Nevertheless, a sharp distinction is to be drawn between their hypothesis and those of Hilgenfeld and Usener. Streeter (*op. cit.*, p. 216) regards the Third Gospel, as we now have it, not as a formless agglomeration of material, nor as a mere slightly enlarged second edition of an earlier work, but as a real book, whose parts are welded together by an author of considerable skill. And that book contained the birth narrative. Vincent Taylor (*The First Draft of St. Luke's Gospel*, [1927], p. 8) speaks of Proto-Luke as "no more than the first draft of a great work."

Chapter III

CHARACTERISTICS OF THE LUCAN NARRATIVE

IT HAS just been shown that the Lucan birth narrative was certainly an original part of the Third Gospel. That very important fact being established, we may now proceed to examine the narrative more in detail. Such examination will show that although this section plainly bears the marks of the Evangelist's hand, and is congruous in style and spirit with the rest of the book, yet also it possesses very marked characteristics of its own.

Those characteristics may be summed up in the fact to which attention has already been called, the fact that Lk. i.5-ii.52 is a strikingly Jewish and indeed Palestinian narrative.

That fact may be observed even in a translation into English or into any other modern language. Even in a translation, it becomes evident that we have here a style very similar to the style of the Old Testament historical books, and very dissimilar to the ordinary style of the Gentile author, as it is found, for example, in the prologue to the book. But in the original Greek the thing becomes even far more abundantly clear.

What strikes the reader most forcibly at the very beginning is the thoroughgoing "parataxis" that prevails throughout this narrative. Instead of long complex sentences, like that in the prologue with its wealth of subordinate clauses, we have here for the most part a series of short independent sentences, connected with one another by the conjunction "and." "There was a priest, by name Zacharias, and his wife from among the daughters of Aaron, and her name was Elisabeth"—so runs (if in order to exhibit the structure we may omit the simple qualifying phrases) the beginning of the narrative; and the beginning is typical of the whole.

Equally striking in the narrative is that thoroughgoing use of parallelism which is so marked a characteristic of Hebrew style. This feature appears with special prominence, as might be expected, in the poetical portions of the section—for example, the hymns of Mary and Zacharias; but it is evident also even in the prose narrative. Such parallelism is basic in Hebrew poetry, and its presence in our narrative contributes largely to the production of that Semitic flavor which connects the section so closely with the spirit of the Old Testament.

But the Semitic character of the narrative appears not only in the sentence-structure and in the style. It is equally evident in the vocabulary and in the details of the phraseology. One does not need to read very far in this narrative to discover the influence of Hebrew or Aramaic. Whatever subtractions may be made from any list of individual Hebraisms or Aramaisms,[1] the frequency of usages which, whether or not they occur also here and there in Greek literature or in papyri, are strikingly similar to Semitic usages, remains no doubt convincing enough. More convincing still, however, is the impression to be derived from reading the narrative through. That impression cannot adequately be expressed in any detailed analysis. The outstanding fact is that in this narrative we find ourselves in the indefinable but not the less unmistakable atmosphere of Palestine.

It is, moreover, not merely in language and style that the Semitic character of the narrative is revealed. Even more impressive are the indications to be found in the thought, as distinguished from the language, of the section. In the entire narrative there is no hint of any ideas derived from Gentile Christianity; indeed, there is no hint of any knowledge of anything that happened or that became known during or after the public ministry of Jesus. It may really be said, if the words are understood aright, that the narrative, with the hymns inserted in it, is not Christian, but pre-Christian throughout. What we really have here, in thought and spirit, as well as in language, is a bit of the Old Testament embedded in the midst of the New Testament.

Proof of this assertion may be found on the surface of the narrative from beginning to end. Thus the parents of John the Baptist are described in thoroughly Old Testament terms; the course of Abia is mentioned as though familiarity with priestly conditions were the most natural thing in the world; and the piety of Zacharias and Elisabeth is characterized in a way quite typical of the Old Testament and of Jewish feeling. The two, it is said, "walked in all the commandments and ordinances of the Lord blameless." There is certainly here no hint of any sharp Pauline distinction between righteousness under the law and the righteousness that comes through faith.

Faith, it is true, is highly exalted in this narrative; but such exaltation of faith does not transcend the teaching of the Old Testament. The Old Testament in its deepest import presents not a religion of merit, but a religion of grace; it really offers salvation as a gift of God. "Enter not into judgment with thy servant; for in thy sight shall no man living be justified"—these are words that really lie at the heart of the religion of Israel. And in the Old Testament,

[1] In the first edition, we cited the phrase "advanced in their days" (Lk. i.7) as a Hebraism. But compare the review by E. K. Simpson in *Bible League Quarterly*, for Jan.–March, 1931, p. 2.

as well as in the New Testament, confidence in the gracious promises of God is treated as the very basis of any true religious life.

Thus in the exaltation of faith in our narrative no Pauline or Gentile Christian influence need be detected. And the clear Pauline presentation of the contrast between the law and grace is conspicuous by its absence. The entire attitude of this narrative toward the law is just that which was found under the old dispensation; the religion of grace is there, but it is still implicit rather than explicit, or at any rate it is not yet in any sharp contrast to a righteousness to be obtained through the law.

In the verse which comes immediately after the characterization of Zacharias and Elisabeth, there is to be found, in conjunction especially with verse 25, one of the many little touches that indicate Jewish feeling. Elisabeth, it is said, was barren, and both she and Zacharias were "advanced in their days."[2] This barrenness was regarded as bringing upon Elisabeth "shame" or reproach.[3] Here we have the characteristic Jewish attitude toward child-bearing. It is to be doubted very much whether such an attitude could be paralleled in the Gentile world of that day, where exposure of infants was quite a common practice, and where at least the passionate Jewish desire for children and the feeling of shame when they were absent would have seemed to be rather a strange and foreign thing. Certainly our narrative has caught in a very delicate way at this point the finer shades of Jewish feeling.

In the words of the angel to Zacharias in Lk. i.13-20 there appears what is one of the most striking features of the narrative as a whole, namely, the complete absence of any specifically Christian, as distinguished from pre-Christian, features in the presentation of the Messianic hope. The angel says of the promised child that he will go before God to prepare His people; but there is no mention of a Messiah. Later on in the section the Messiah of course appears; but the promises concerning Him are couched in terms that display no knowledge of later events such as the resurrection, the beginning of the Gentile mission, or the destruction of Jerusalem. The Messianic hope appears essentially in Old Testament form.

We do not mean to say that the stupendous words of the angel in Lk. i.30-37 add nothing to the Old Testament presentation of the coming Messiah. On the contrary, they do render definite and plain the manner of the Messiah's entrance into the world, which had been prophesied indeed in Is. vii.14, but in mysterious terms that the Jews did not understand. They do, moreover, make explicit the superhuman nature of the Messiah, in a way that transcends in

[2] Lk. i.7.
[3] Lk. i.25.

definiteness even the majestic descriptions of the ninth chapter of Isaiah. Such an increase in plainness and definiteness is only to be expected if the appearance of the coming one was no longer in the dim and distant future, but was immediately at hand. Yet even so there is a complete absence of any detailed descriptions such as would have been natural only after the event. Even here the limits of true prophecy are preserved.

Even here, moreover, the kingdom of the promised Messiah is described in distinctly Old Testament terms. "The Lord God," it is said, "will give to Him the throne of David His father, and He will rule over the house of Jacob forever." There is a true, high sense in which that prophecy has been, and is being, gloriously fulfilled. But is it not unnatural that a Gentile Christian writer, after the destruction of Jerusalem or even after the beginning of the war that led to the destruction, would ever have spoken of the kingdom of Christ as a kingdom over the "house of Jacob"?

The same characteristic runs through the whole section. Thus in the song of Mary, called the Magnificat,[4] there is a complete absence of any definite allusions to events in the life of the coming Deliverer: indeed, the Deliverer is not mentioned at all; and the deliverance which God has brought or is to bring is described as help rendered to "Israel His servant" and as a fulfilment of His promise "to Abraham and to his seed."

Similar is the representation in the song of Zacharias, the so-called Benedictus.[5] There, it is true, the immediate occasion of the song becomes a little more definite than is the case in the Magnificat; the child of Zacharias is directly addressed by the words, "and thou, child, shalt be called a prophet of the Most High." But the specific events in the life of the child are not mentioned, and his mission as a prophet is described only in the most general terms. Indeed, there is in this hymn no clear allusion to the Messiah at all; the child is to go before Jehovah to prepare His people for Him, but in what particular way Jehovah is to appear is not said. And throughout the whole hymn the connection of the coming salvation with Israel is set forth in terms which would be very unnatural in a composition written with knowledge of the later events. Could a Gentile Christian writer, especially if he wrote after A.D. 70, ever have described the Messianic salvation as consisting in such a rescue of the Jewish people from the hands of its enemies that the people might have liberty to worship God without fear? It is true that the salvation which Israel, according to this hymn, is to receive is by no means purely political; by the agency of the forerunner who has just been born, the people is to be prepared morally for

[4] Lk. i 46–55.
[5] Lk. i.68–79.

the coming of Jehovah; the liberty which it is to receive is to be used for a worship of God in holiness and righteousness, and the salvation is to involve "the remission of sins." But this ethical element in the Messianic salvation does not at all transcend what is found in the Old Testament; it is presented in the most insistent fashion by the Old Testament prophets. There is, therefore, no indication whatever in the Benedictus which could stamp the hymn as a prophecy after the event; but on the contrary, there is every indication that the hymn was written before the calamity to the Jewish state which occurred in A.D. 70.

Similar is the impression which is made in the second chapter. Could anything be more unnatural to a Gentile Christian, writing after A.D. 70, or after the rejection of the Gospel by the mass of the Jewish people, than the description of Simeon as one who was awaiting the "consolation of Israel," or of the circle of pious folk to whom Anna spoke as those who were awaiting "the redemption of Jerusalem"? Such expressions are very natural in a Palestinian writer, living at a very early time; but they are as dissimilar as possible to what would be expected in the free composition of a later Gentile Christian. Everywhere in this chapter the Messianic hope is set forth in Old Testament terms.

It is true, indeed, that Lk. i-ii does contain expressions of a genuine universalism: the coming salvation is to be in the presence of all the peoples; it is to involve "light for a revelation to the Gentiles."[6] But such universalism does not at all transcend what is found in the Old Testament prophets. There could be nothing more uncritical than to regard every reference to a Gentile mission as an indication of a date subsequent to the founding of the Gentile Church at Antioch or to the Apostolic Council of Acts xv. It should never be forgotten that Judaism in the first Christian century, and in the immediately preceding period, was an active missionary religion; even the Pharisees, Jesus said, compassed sea and land to make one proselyte, and the Jewish synagogues throughout the world were attended by large numbers of Gentiles as well as by Jews. There was nothing revolutionary in the belief that the light of the true religion was to shine out from Israel to all the nations of the earth. What was really revolutionary in the Pauline mission, from the Jewish point of view, was found not in the fact that Gentiles were received, but in the terms on which they were received. All the discussion which the Gentile mission provoked was due to the fact that the Gentiles were received without being required to keep the law, and without being required to renounce their own nationality and become Jews.

[6] Lk. ii.31, 32.

Of that revolutionary form of universalism there is no trace in Lk. i-ii; in these chapters there is no hint that the prerogatives of Israel are to be broken down. On the contrary, just in the place where universalism appears most plainly, these prerogatives of Israel are preserved with special clearness; the light that shines upon the Gentiles is to be a glory to "thy people Israel"; the Jews are in a special sense God's people, and it is from them that light is to shine forth; Jerusalem is still conceived of as being the centre of the whole world.[7]

Such universalism is found, of course, in fullest measure in the great prophecies of the Old Testament. In our chapters, moreover, universalism may almost be said to be incidental; it is here the people of Israel that is everywhere primarily in view. Even in the words of the angels to the shepherds, this special reference to Israel is preserved; the "great joy" which is announced by the angels is to be not "to all people" (as the Authorized Version translates) but to "all the people,"[8] and the immediate reference is to "*the* people" in the Israelitish sense, or the covenant people of God. It would probably be a mistake, indeed, to take the words, "peace among men of good pleasure,"[9] in the angels' song, in a specifically particularistic way; it would probably be a mistake to identify the men of God's good pleasure with the people of Israel as such. But if particularism is here not explicit, neither is universalism; it is not said in any clear fashion that the men of God's good pleasure are to be found in the Gentile world as well as in Israel. Indeed, even if the reference is to men generally, to the whole human race, still the race as the recipient of God's favor might be conceived of as represented by the people whom God had chosen. God has given peace to men by the birth of the babe at Bethlehem; but it is not said which men are the recipients of that peace or of the "good pleasure" of God which is its ground.[10]

It is true, of course, that the salvation which is celebrated in our section is suited to all men and not merely to Jews. The good news that is connected here with the babe of Bethlehem is no doubt of such a character that ultimately it must be for the benefit of the whole human race. But this profound universalism, which inheres in the very essence of the gospel, hardly becomes any more explicit here than it does in certain passages of the Old Testament. The atmosphere of Lk. i-ii is the atmosphere of the old covenant. The gleams of

[7] Lk. ii.31 f.

[8] *παντὶ τῷ λαῷ*, Lk. ii.10.

[9] *εἰρήνη ἐν ἀνθρώποις εὐδοκίας*, Lk. ii.14.

[10] Compare, for example, Ps. viii.4: "What is man, that thou art mindful of him? and the son of man, that thou visitest him?" See also Völter, *Die evangelischen Erzählungen von der Geburt und Kindheit Jesu*, 1911, pp. 56 f.

a more glorious day, which are seen even in Old Testament prophecy, have become brighter; there is an expectancy in the air like the expectancy with which the earth awaits the coming of a new day; but still the sun has not yet risen fully above the horizon; prophecy has not yet ripened into complete fulfilment.

Thus the kind of universalism that appears in this narrative does not at all point to a date after the beginning of the Gentile mission in the Christian Church; there is no departure in this matter from the restraints proper to true prophecy.

But if so much be granted—if the universalism of the section be admitted not to constitute a *vaticinium ex eventu*—one specific point still requires consideration. It concerns the words in Lk. ii.34, 35, where the aged Simeon is represented as saying: "Behold, this child is set for the falling and rising of many in Israel; and for a sign that is spoken against—and through thine own soul shall pass a sword—in order that thoughts may be revealed out of many hearts." These words, it is said, are written in view of the conflicts in the life of Jesus and particularly in view of the Cross; they constitute, therefore, a *vaticinium ex eventu.*

With regard to this objection, it may be remarked, in the first place, that even if the objection were well founded it would not at all overthrow our argument for the Palestinian origin of this narrative: even if the words attributed to Simeon were not actually spoken by him, but were composed after the crucifixion of Jesus, that might conceivably have been done in Palestine in the early days of the Jerusalem Church as well as at some subsequent time; there would be no reason why the composition of the supposed *vaticinium ex eventu* should be attributed to a Gentile Christian, as distinguished from a Jewish Christian, author.

But, in the second place, we do not think that in point of fact the passage looks at all like a *vaticinium ex eventu*. It is true that the words, "And through thine own soul shall pass a sword," recall to our minds the scene of the *stabat mater dolorosa iuxta crucem lachrymosa;* inevitably we think of Mary as she stood at the foot of the cross. But because that scene is admirably characterized in its inner meaning by Simeon's words, it does not follow at all that it was definitely in mind when the words were first spoken or written. The whole prophecy is couched in very general terms: it declares that the child whom Simeon holds in his arms will make necessary a great decision, that the hidden thoughts of men's hearts will be revealed by their attitude toward Him, that there will be opposition, and that grief will pierce the mother's soul. The central thought in these words was not altogether unknown in pre-Christian times: for the prophets had spoken of the necessity of a great decision and of the suffering of God's righteous Servant; and John the Baptist, before the beginning of the public ministry of Jesus, spoke of a time of sifting, the separation of the wheat from the chaff, that was soon to come.

We do not, indeed, at all mean to deny the profound originality of Simeon's words. Without doubt, the thought of a suffering Messiah, though it is truly found in the Old Testament, had dropped out of sight in later Judaism. And although the expectation of a time of sifting might have come to a pious Israelite even without any supernatural revelation, yet the connection of such a time of sifting with a particular child whom Simeon held in his arms introduces an element that is quite fresh and new. No doubt, if these words were spoken before Jesus grew to manhood and entered upon His public ministry, they cannot be explained as due to merely natural insight, but constitute a true prophecy; and the attitude of the critic toward them will be determined by his attitude toward the possibility of supernatural revelation in general. But our point is that the words do not exceed the restraint which we find elsewhere observed in what we think to be genuine prophecy; such restraint is exceedingly difficult to explain as being exercised by a later writer who was freely composing speeches and prophecies to put into the mouths of his characters. The poetic, mysterious form in which Simeon's prophecy is couched —the wonderful characterization of the inner significance of the later conflict, coupled with a complete absence of the details that a Christian writer would know—creates an impression of great primitiveness.[11] The ultimate decision as to whether we have here genuine prophecy inspired by the Spirit of God depends upon considerations that lie beyond the sphere of merely literary, as distinguished from historical, criticism; but at least we can say that if ever a passage bore the internal marks of genuine prophecy and did *not* bear the marks of a *vaticinium ex eventu,* it is this prophecy attributed by the Third Gospel to the aged saint who had been "waiting for the consolation of Israel."

At any rate, however that may be, the passage certainly does not afford the slightest argument against the primitive Jewish and Palestinian character which we have found in the narrative as a whole.

This Palestinian character of the narrative, it may finally be observed, appears not only at the centre, but also at the circumference; it is found not only in the way in which the Messianic salvation is conceived, but also in the treatment of the details of life in Palestine. Evidently the narrator was inti-

[11] Compare Sweet, *The Birth and Infancy of Jesus Christ,* 1906, p. 76.

mately acquainted with the Temple ritual, with the arrangements for the service of the priests, and in general with the conditions of Jewish life.

That does not mean that all the details are definitely confirmed by independent sources of information. Thus it seems not to be known except from our narrative that an actual ceremony of presentation in the Temple was carried out for a first-born son in addition to the payment of the redemption-money, which payment could be made at the place of residence of the parents as well as at Jerusalem. But that such a ceremony of presentation should be carried out when circumstances permitted, and especially in view of the special hopes centring in the child Jesus, is altogether natural; there is not the slightest reason why we should not allow Lk. ii.22 to supplement at this point our other sources of information. Thus also it has been remarked that Lk. i.59 and ii.21 constitute the best extant attestation to the fact that the naming of a child was connected with the rite of circumcision.[12] But although such connection is not so well attested elsewhere, it is certainly the most natural and probable thing that could be imagined.

It must be remembered that our sources of information about Jewish life in Palestine in the first century are by no means so abundant as is often supposed. When we were at Sunday school in our youth, many of us had the impression that that mysterious company of persons known as "scholars" possessed vast stores of information about such matters—vast stores of information inaccessible to ordinary mortals. Such an impression was by no means altogether correct. We do not, indeed, desire at all to depreciate the researches of Wettstein, of Edersheim, of Schürer, and (more recently) of Strack-Billerbeck, as shedding light upon the environment of the life of Jesus; but, after all, the Rabbinical sources of information are late, and cannot be used without great caution for the earlier period; Josephus enters into little detail in describing the sacerdotal system; and in very many particulars, therefore, the New Testament is our best source of information about the Judaism of the first century. Certainly the points at which the allusions to Palestinian life in Lk. i-ii are confirmed either by the Old Testament or by later independent sources are so numerous as to raise a very favorable presumption with regard to the points at which such confirmation has not been found.

At one point, indeed, the accuracy of this section with regard to Jewish life has sometimes been impugned—namely, in the words, "their cleansing," in Lk. ii.22. The offering prescribed by the law for the conclusion of the period of ritual uncleanness or seclusion after childbirth is indeed quite correctly said

[12] Strack-Billerbeck, *Kommentar zum Neuen Testament aus Talmud und Midrasch*, ii, 1924, p. 107.

in this passage to consist of a pair of turtle-doves or two young pigeons;[13] and a distinctly favorable impression has always been produced by the fact that the alternative offering prescribed for less well-to-do persons is here represented, entirely without explanation, as having been made in the case of the mother of Jesus. But, it is objected, the ritual uncleanness after childbirth belonged, according to the law, to the mother alone; how, then, can the plural be correct in the phrase, "their cleansing"?

It may be remarked in passing that the transmission of the text is at this point not altogether uniform. A few witnesses read "*her* cleansing"; while the uncial Codex Bezæ, certain manuscripts of the Old Latin translation, and the Sinaitic Syriac manuscript of the Old Syriac translation, read "*his* cleansing." In the former reading, of course, all difficulty disappears; the cleansing according to that reading is attributed to the mother, exactly as would be expected according to the law. If the reading, "*his* cleansing" (or "*its* cleansing," since the masculine and the neuter are the same in Greek), be correct, no doubt the pronoun refers to the child, who is the only member of the holy family that is spoken of in the preceding verse. In that case the cleansing would be connected with the child because the child is the chief personage of the narrative; in connection with the circumcision and the giving of the name in the preceding verse, He alone is mentioned; Joseph and Mary are merely alluded to by the passive voice of the verb. So the cleansing, though the occasion of it was the ritual uncleanness, not of the child, but of the mother, might be spoken of as "his cleansing" because it was one of the successive events recorded about His life.

There is, however, no reason to depart from what is by far the best attested reading—namely, the reading, "their cleansing." That reading is commended by transcriptional probability, on the well-known principle that the more difficult reading is to be preferred to the easier; since both the other two readings may be accounted for as due to natural changes made by scribes. The reading, "her cleansing," may have been due simply to the influence of Leviticus, where in the basic passage, Lev. xii.6, the phrase runs, "When the days of *her* purifying are fulfilled." A scribe, in other words, may have felt the difficulty with which we are now dealing, and may also have yielded to the natural tendency to complete the verbal similarity to the closely parallel Old Testament passage by the simple change of "their" to "her." It is perhaps a little more difficult to explain the reading, "*his* cleansing": but possibly a scribe may have taken offence at the inclusion of Mary in the act of cleansing which is involved in the reading, "their cleansing." Such inclusion might have seemed

[13] Lk. ii.24. Compare Lev. xii.8.

to be contrary to the notion of the perpetual virginity of Mary, especially to the notion that the birth of Jesus took place *clauso utero,* which became prevalent in the Church. Thus the introduction of the singular masculine pronoun may possibly be explained as a dogmatic correction.

If "her cleansing" were in the original text, a similar consideration might, indeed, perhaps be used to explain the introduction of the reading, "their cleansing"; a scribe may have been shocked by the direct attribution of cleansing specifically and solely to Mary, and so may have introduced the plural pronoun in order to cause the phrase to be taken in some more general sense. But the reading, "her cleansing," is very weakly attested; and on the whole there seems to be no reason to depart from the reading, "their cleansing," which has an overwhelming preponderance of attestation in its favor.

But if that reading is to be regarded as correct, to what persons does the plural pronoun refer? It might conceivably refer to Mary and the child, and so it was taken, apparently, by Origen.[14] Something may perhaps be said in favor of such an interpretation. Joseph, it may be observed, is somewhat in the background throughout this whole narrative, and he is not mentioned in the preceding verse. It is true that Mary also is not mentioned in that verse; but she is alluded to by the mention of the naming of the child—"before He was conceived in the womb"—which refers, of course, to the scene described in Lk. i.26-38. Certainly Mary and the babe are the chief figures in this narrative; and it might be regarded as not altogether impossible that they should be linked together, to the exclusion of Joseph, in the use of the pronoun "their."

Nevertheless, this interpretation, despite all that can be said in favor of it, must be pronounced unnatural in the extreme. The only reference which any unsophisticated reader could give to the pronoun "their" surely would be provided by the subject of the verb in the same sentence. In the sentence, "When the days of *their* cleansing were fulfilled, according to the law of Moses, *they* brought him up to Jerusalem," surely the "their" refers to the same persons as the "they."

It must be admitted, therefore, that "their cleansing" means the cleansing of Joseph and Mary. But if so, how is the difficulty to be overcome? Does not the phrase attest the erroneous notion on the part of the narrator that the ritual cleansing after childbirth belonged to the father as well as to the mother? And could so erroneous a notion ever have been held by a Palestinian narrator?

[14] *Hom. in Luc.*, xiv, ed. Lommatzsch, v, 1835, pp. 133 f. Hilgenfeld ("Die Geburts- und Kindheitsgeschichte Jesu Luc. I,5–II,52," in *Zeitschrift für wissenschaftliche Theologie*, xliv, 1901, p. 227) favors this interpretation if the reading αὐτῶν is adopted.

Is not, therefore, the whole argument for the Palestinian provenience of the narrative very much weakened by the occurrence of this phrase?

In reply, it may be said that a very great weight is here being hung upon one phrase. The narrative elsewhere affords evidence of intimate acquaintance with the Jewish law and with Palestinian conditions. Is it not, therefore, only fair to approach the question with a certain favorable presumption; must not the passage be interpreted, if it is at all possible to do so, in a way that avoids ascription of a serious blunder to a narrator who elsewhere deals with these matters in so accurate a way? These questions, we think, should be answered in the affirmative. To do so does not involve any substitution of "apologetics" for scientific history; for it is not scientific, but highly unscientific, to accord to a witness who has already been shown to be generally reliable no more credence than would be accorded to a witness who is either demonstrably unreliable or else unknown.

If, therefore, the phrase, "their cleansing," may with any reasonableness be interpreted in a way that accords with the general accuracy with which the narrative deals with Palestinian conditions, surely such an interpretation must be adopted. And as a matter of fact such an interpretation does offer itself. The point of it is that the pronoun "their" does not refer to the impurity, but to the "purification." The impurity no doubt belonged to Mary alone: but the act of purification belonged also to Joseph; indeed, it was he who presumably bore the expense of the offering.

In other words, it is not clear that the genitive "their" in the phrase "their purification" is an objective, rather than a subjective, genitive: it is not clear that the phrase designates an "act by which they were cleansed"; for it may also designate an "act of cleansing which they carried out." And in the latter case there is no disharmony between this phrase and the terms of the Old Testament law.

On this interpretation—if we may anticipate a later phase of our discussion—there is no disharmony between this verse and the supernatural conception of Jesus, which is attested in Lk. i.34, 35. Whether physically the father of Jesus or not, Joseph could, in the sense just indicated, have a part in the offering by which the ceremonial impurity of the mother was removed. Indeed, for that matter, there would probably be no contradiction with Lk. i.34, 35 even if our interpretation of "their cleansing" were wrong, even if the phrase meant that the narrator did (erroneously) attribute the ceremonial impurity to Joseph as father as well as to Mary as mother. If the Mosaic law in the view of the narrator regarded the father as well as the mother as ceremonially unclean after the birth of a child, then since Joseph was publicly regarded as the father of this child it was natural that he should fulfil the legal requirements of purification, even though he was not actually the father. As Jesus later took part, according to all three Synoptic Gospels, in a baptism that was regarded as a baptism for the remission of sins, although in the view of all the Evangelists he certainly was guilty of no sin and so needed no remission, so here Joseph could be represented as fulfilling the legal duties of a father despite the mystery of the supernatural conception. That would in the mind of the narrator be merely another way in which (to use the phrase reported by Matthew) "all righteousness" was fulfilled. It is very rash indeed, therefore, to argue, on either interpretation of Lk. ii.22, that this verse contradicts the account of the supernatural conception that is given in Lk. i.34, 35.

But such considerations really belong to a later phase of our subject. What we are here interested in observing is that Lk. ii.22 need not at all be held to display such ignorance of the Mosaic law as would have been impossible in a Palestinian writer. No valid argument can be derived from this verse against the genuinely Palestinian character of the narrative, which is everywhere else so clear.

Chapter IV

THE HYMNS OF THE FIRST CHAPTER OF LUKE[1]

THE genuinely Palestinian character which has just been vindicated for Lk. i.5-ii.52 may conceivably be explained in a number of different ways; various hypotheses have been proposed to explain the production of such a narrative and the incorporation of it in our Third Gospel. But before these hypotheses are considered, it will be necessary to examine one particular part of the narrative with special care. The part to which we refer consists of the hymns that are embedded in the section: the Magnificat[2] and the Benedictus.[3] These hymns, because of their special characteristics, deserve something like separate consideration.

The impression of most readers has been that the hymns exhibit the Jewish or Palestinian characteristics which we have found in the whole section with even greater clearness than that which elsewhere appears. The diction is very largely that of the Old Testament; the style is characterized by that parallelism which is the basis of Hebrew poetry; the thought is marked by a striking absence of specifically Christian, as distinguished from pre-Christian, ideas. Certainly the *prima facie* evidence is strongly in favor of placing the origin of these hymns on Palestinian ground and at a very early time.

This obvious conclusion has, however, met a vigorous and able opponent in A. von Harnack of Berlin. In a detailed study which appeared in 1900,[4] supplemented by later works, he has attempted to show that the Magnificat and the Benedictus, far from being Palestinian hymns, are free compositions of the Gentile Christian author of the Gospel. The Old Testament coloring of the hymns, he maintains, was produced not by any familiarity of the author with Hebrew poetry in the original, but by a conscious imitation of the Septuagint translation. After subtraction of the Septuagint words and phrases, he says,

[1] This chapter is dependent upon the article by the present writer, "The Hymns of the First Chapter of Luke," in *Princeton Theological Review*, x, 1912, pp. 1–38; but much of the detailed proof has here been omitted, and account has been taken of recent investigations.

[2] Lk. i.46–55.

[3] Lk. i.68–79.

[4] Harnack, "Das Magnificat der Elisabet (Luc. 1, 46–55) nebst einigen Bemerkungen zu Luc. 1 und 2," in *Sitzungsberichte der königlich preussischen Akademie der Wissenschaften zu Berlin*, 1900, pp. 537–556.

what remains is so characteristically Lucan as to show that the hymns are due to Luke's own hand.

This argument of Harnack has not attained any general acceptance. It was opposed, for example, especially by Zimmermann,[5] Hilgenfeld,[6] Spitta,[7] and later by Gunkel.[8] In 1912 the present writer attempted some examination of it in detail, with decidedly negative result.[9]

The first question concerns the validity of Harnack's method. It has just been observed that Harnack tries to establish the Lucan authorship of the hymns by first subtracting from them the Septuagint words and phrases and then exhibiting the specifically Lucan character of what remains. But the trouble is that the subtraction of Septuagint words and phrases was not inclusive enough; many of the phrases which remain after Harnack's process of subtraction are found in the Septuagint, though in other passages than those which Harnack supposed the author of the hymns to have used.[10]

An attempt was indeed made by Harnack to overcome this objection. The occurrence of a word in the Septuagint, he said in effect, does not necessarily prevent it from being regarded as a mark of Luke's hand, if, within the New Testament, it occurs solely or chiefly in the Lucan writings; for the choice of the same word from the rich store of Septuagint usage, as well as coincidence of usage in other particulars, might show unity of authorship.[11] This answer was

5 "Evangelium des Lukas Kap. 1 und 2," in *Theologische Studien und Kritiken*, lxxvi, 1903, pp. 247–290, especially pp. 248–250, 257–259, 271.

6 "Die Geburts- und Kindheitsgeschichte Jesu Luc. I, 5–II, 52," in *Zeitschrift für wissenschaftliche Theologie*, xliv, 1901, pp. 177–235, especially pp. 205–215, 217–221.

7 "Das Magnifikat, ein Psalm der Maria und nicht der Elisabeth," in *Theologische Abhandlungen für Holtzmann*, 1902, pp. 61–94, especially pp. 78–83. Compare the later article, "Die chronologischen Notizen und die Hymnen in Lc. 1 u. 2," in *Zeitschrift für die neutestamentliche Wissenschaft*, vii, 1906, pp. 281–317.

8 "Die Lieder in der Kindheitsgeschichte Jesu bei Lukas," in *Festgabe . . . A. von Harnack zum siebzigsten Geburtstag dargebracht*, 1921, pp. 43–60, especially pp. 45, 52.

9 *Op. cit.*, 1912.

10 This objection was raised by Spitta ("Das Magnifikat, ein Psalm der Maria und nicht der Elisabeth," in *Theologische Abhandlungen für Holtzmann*, 1902, pp. 78–83) and was supported by him through a detailed examination of the Magnificat, which was extended to the Benedictus by the present writer.

11 Harnack, review of "The Hymns of the First Chapter of Luke," and "The Origin of the First Two Chapters of Luke" (*Princeton Theological Review*, x, 1912, pp. 1–38, 212–277), in *Theologische Literaturzeitung*, xxxviii, 1913, col. 7: "That this Lucan element comes to a very considerable extent from the Septuagint I have never denied, and it also does not affect my argument if the proofs for the part played by the Septuagint are extended still further; for the point is that the peculiarity and the constancy of the choice cause even the Septuagint elements to be specifically Lucan" ("Dass dieses lukanische Element zu einem sehr beträchtlichen Teile aus der LXX herrührt, habe ich nie bestritten, und es trifft meine Ausführungen auch nicht, wenn die Beweise für den Anteil dieser Quelle noch erweitert werden; denn die Eigenart und Konstanz der Auswahl macht eben auch die LXX-Elemente zu spezifisch lukanischen.").

anticipated to some extent on behalf of Harnack by Ladeuze,[12] and undoubtedly it has some weight. But it does not go the whole way toward removing the objection; and particularly does it fail to do so with regard to the hymns. If Harnack's original program could really be carried out, possibly his argument might be strong; if he could show (1) that part of the language of the Magnificat and Benedictus comes from the Septuagint, (2) that what is clearly *not* found in the Septuagint is distinctively Lucan, then possibly he might succeed in establishing Lucan authorship of the hymns. Even that, it is true, would be doubtful; for it would still be possible to hold to the hypothesis of Lucan revision or Lucan translation of originally Jewish Christian hymns. But as a matter of fact, Harnack's program cannot be carried out at all. When all the words and phrases commonly found in the Septuagint are subtracted from the hymns, very little remains; and it cannot be shown that that little was certainly due to the hand of Luke.

Only one really striking coincidence between the language of the hymns and that of the writer of Luke-Acts remains after the winnowing process just indicated has been carefully carried out.[13] That coincidence is found in the phrase, "through the mouth of his holy prophets from of old," in Lk. i.70, which appears in almost the same form in Acts iii.21.[14] The coincidence is more striking in the Greek original than it is in an English translation. Nevertheless, the argument based upon it can be shown not to be strong enough to bear anything like the full weight of Harnack's conclusion.

In the first place, it may possibly be questioned whether the text of the phrase translated "his holy prophets from of old" is correct in the passage in Acts.[15] In that passage, the so-called Western text, as represented by the Codex Bezæ, supported by certain other evidence, including citations in Irenæus, Tertullian and Origen, omits the words, "from of old"; and in the other witnesses

[12] "De l'origine du Magnificat et de son attribution dans le troisième Évangile à Marie ou à Élisabeth," in *Revue d'Histoire Ecclésiastique*, iv, 1903, p. 638, note. Compare "The Hymns of the First Chapter of Luke," in *Princeton Theological Review*, x, 1912, pp. 7 f., footnote 19.

[13] The only other coincidence which deserves special mention is found in the use of the phrase ἄφεσις ἁμαρτιῶν in Lk. i.77. That phrase occurs twice in the rest of the Gospel of Luke, five times in Acts, once in Matthew, once in Mark (Mk. i.4 = Lk. iii.3), and once in Paul. It does not occur at all in the Septuagint. But in view of Mk. i.4 (Lk. iii.3) the hypothesis suggests itself that the Greek expression is derived from a phrase current in the circles from which John the Baptist came. Compare ἀφήσει ἁμαρτίας in Ps. Sol. ix.14, which is cited by Ryle and James, ΨΑΛΜΟΙ ΣΟΛΟΜΩΝΤΟΣ *Psalms of the Pharisees commonly called Psalms of Solomon*, 1891, p. xcii.

[14] Lk. i.70, διὰ στόματος τῶν ἁγίων ἀπ' αἰῶνος προφητῶν αὐτοῦ; Acts iii.21, διὰ στόματος τῶν ἁγίων ἀπ' αἰῶνος αὐτοῦ προφητῶν.

[15] Zahn ("Die Urausgabe der Apostelgeschichte des Lucas," in *Forschungen zur Geschichte des neutestamentlichen Kanons*, ix, 1916) brackets the words in his reconstruction of the Western text, which he regards as the earlier of two editions of the book both of which he thinks were made by Luke.

there is some variation as to the place at which the words are inserted. If the witnesses for the omission are correct, then the distinctiveness of the language altogether disappears, and the similarity to Lk. i.70 ceases to be at all striking. And certainly something may be said in favor of following the Western text at this point. In the first place, there is the general presumption in favor of the "shorter reading." If the short text without "from of old" is correct, it is possible to account for the competing readings; they would represent various ways of inserting the gloss. The authority of the Western text is certainly greater where it omits something that the "Neutral text" contains than where it is longer than the Neutral text. In the second place, the desire of scribes to insert the gloss might be explained as due to the presence of the words in Lk. i.70; the insertion of the gloss would thus come under the head of "harmonistic corruptions." [16]

These arguments, it must be admitted, are by no means conclusive. In the first place, the phrase might have been omitted because of the unusual and somewhat difficult character of the expression which is found in the original text when the words are retained; in the second place, the documents which include the words do not insert them in exactly the place where they are found at Lk. i.70; and in the third place, despite the arguments for the omission drawn from transcriptional probability, the text of the Codex Bezæ and its associates, we hold, is generally so corrupt that it would be dangerous to follow it here.

In view of these considerations, we should probably print the words, "from of old," in the text of Acts iii.21 if we were making an edition of the Book of Acts; but at the same time a serious doubt does remain as to whether these words are genuine.

But if they are genuine, does the coincidence of expression with Lk. i.70 show that the Benedictus, in which the latter verse occurs, was composed by the author of Luke-Acts? We think that that is not the case.

In the first place, the phrase is not precisely the same in the two passages, since the pronoun "his" stands after the word "prophets" in Lk. i.70 and before the word "prophets" in Acts iii.21. It would, however, be a mistake to lay much stress upon this consideration. Certainly the similarity between the two phrases is very striking.

In the second place, it should be observed that the passage in Acts is part of the report of a speech attributed to Peter. Was that speech composed by the author of the book, or does it represent a report of what Peter actually said?

[16] Such arguments have led Souter (*Novum Testamentum Graece*, [1910]) to regard the words "from of old" with suspicion at Acts iii.21.

This question involves the general question of the speeches in the Book of Acts, and it will not be possible here to discuss it in detail. But certainly the speeches of Peter in the early part of the book do seem to possess a distinctive quality that prevents us from regarding them as free compositions of Luke. If, then, Acts iii.21 was not composed by Luke, similarity between that passage and Lk. i.70 does not show Lucan authorship of this latter passage. The similarity would, indeed, still require explanation. But various explanations would suggest themselves. One explanation would be that in his speech reported in the third chapter of Acts Peter himself was dependent upon the Benedictus—supposing that that was a hymn current in the primitive Jerusalem Church. But Peter's speech was probably spoken in Aramaic, and the verbal similarity of Acts iii.21 to Lk. i.70 could hardly have been produced in its present form except in the Greek language. Possibly, therefore, Peter himself, or whoever else first translated the report or summary of his speech into Greek, was influenced by the Greek form of the Benedictus, whether that hymn was originally composed in Greek or had been translated into Greek from Hebrew or Aramaic. This hypothesis is by no means beyond the bounds of possibility. If the Benedictus was actually composed by the father of John the Baptist, or if it was attributed to him at an early time, it may well have circulated among the disciples of John, and may have passed from them to the disciples of Jesus. There is nothing inherently improbable in supposing that the language of such a hymn might have become so well known in the primitive Church as to color the translation of a phrase in Peter's speech.

In the third place, if the form in which Peter's speech appears in the third chapter of Acts was not received by Luke from some previous record, but was composed by him, why may not he himself have been dependent upon the Benedictus—supposing that that hymn had come to him either separately or already embedded in the Jewish Christian narrative of the birth and infancy of John the Baptist and of Jesus? [17] Such dependence upon a Jewish Christian source would be altogether like what we know of this author's method. Evidently Luke had a keen appreciation of the style used in Palestinian sources; he has shown such appreciation clearly by the fact he has not used the typical

[17] Dependence of the author of Luke-Acts upon the songs of Lk. i–ii is accepted in the case of the Gloria in excelsis (Lk. ii.14) by Holtzmann (on Lk. xix.38 in *Hand-Commentar zum Neuen Testament*, 3te Aufl., i, 1901, p. 401). Compare also B. Weiss, on Lk. xix.38 in the ninth edition, 1901, of the Meyer Commentary; J. Weiss, *Die Schriften des Neuen Testaments*, 3te Aufl. (edited by Bousset and Heitmüller), i, 1917, p. 486. Wellhausen, (*Das Evangelium Lucae*, 1904, p. 109), on the other hand, instead of regarding Luke xix.38 as being derived from Lk. ii.14, reverses the relationship; while Spitta ("Die chronologischen Notizen und die Hymnen in Lc. 1 u. 2," in *Zeitschrift für die neutestamentliche Wissenschaft*, vii, 1906, p. 305) supposes that both are citations from a Jewish hymn.

Greek style of the prologue of his Gospel to narrate events that took place in Palestine, but has, both in the Gospel and in the early part of Acts, preserved the quality of narrative that was suited to the subject-matter. If such an author had become familiar with a Jewish Christian hymn attributed to the father of John the Baptist, what could be more natural than that the language of that familiar hymn should come readily to his pen, even, perhaps, without any conscious dependence, when he was introducing a similar thought in his report of a speech of Peter? It must be remembered that the coincidence of language in Lk. i.70 and Acts iii.21 appears in the expression of a thought that recurred again and again both among the Jews and in the early Church—namely, the thought that in the person and work of Jesus Old Testament prophecies were fulfilled. Might it not be natural that the phrase, "through the mouth of his holy prophets from of old," should, through its original use in the Greek translation of a Jewish Christian hymn, have become in some sort stereotyped in the primitive Church?

In the fourth place, the problem would be solved in a particularly satisfactory manner if Luke himself could be regarded as the translator of an Aramaic report of Peter's speech. In that case his use of a phrase which had already been used in a hymn incorporated in his earlier book would be admirably explained. It is by no means impossible that the author of Luke-Acts, despite the fact that he was a Gentile, should have been acquainted with the Aramaic language. If he was identical with the author of the "we-sections" of the Book of Acts, his presence in Palestine at the beginning and end of Paul's two-year imprisonment in that country can be definitely established. And whether or not he was a native of Syrian Antioch, as some modern scholars suppose, there is no decisive objection against the view—though also there may be no decisive argument in favor of it—that he lived in a partly Semitic environment in his early life. What is clear, at any rate, is that he had a warm sympathy with Jewish feeling and a delicate appreciation of Semitic style. It is certainly not beyond the bounds of possibility, therefore, that he should have been able to translate a Semitic document.

But if so, why may he not have been the translator, not merely of the speech of Peter in the third chapter of Acts, but also of the Benedictus itself, or even of the whole narrative contained in Lk. i.5-ii.52? That supposition, again, is not altogether impossible. And if it be correct, then the similarity between Acts iii.21 and Lk. i.70 is admirably explained, without supposing that either passage is a free composition of the author of the whole double work.

We are, indeed, far from giving assent to this hypothesis, or to any particular one of the hypotheses that have just been mentioned. Still other hypotheses might be suggested. But enough has been said to show that there are various possible ways of explaining the verbal coincidence between the two verses in question other than the way favored by Harnack. The Lucan characteristics which he finds in the Magnificat and Benedictus really reduce themselves, when properly sifted, to this one phrase; and this one phrase will by no means bear the whole weight of Harnack's theory regarding the composition of the hymns.

Harnack does not rely, indeed, merely upon the examination of details. The whole structure of the Magnificat, he thinks, is such that only a Gentile like Luke could have produced it;[18] the skilful management of the repeated pronouns,[19] and in general the elaborate character of the poetic composition, are thought to indicate the hand of the artist Luke. With regard to the Benedictus, Harnack is particularly confident. "The first three strophes of the Benedictus (verses 68-75; in all, there are five strophes with four lines each) are only superficially," he says, "put into the form of the Hebrew psalm; a closer examination reveals *a single, complicated, genuinely Greek period* which is altogether to the credit of the author of the prologue (Lk. i.1) and of numerous other excellent Greek sentences. The period is merely forced into the Hebraizing covering: the hands are Esau's hands, but the voice is the voice of Jacob."[20]

How many of the niceties of structure discovered by Harnack were intended by the authors of the hymns may well be doubted. At any rate, in order to prove Lucan authorship, Harnack should have exhibited by example (1) the likeness of these hymns to undisputed works of Luke and (2) their unlikeness to non-Lucan hymns.

The former requirement is incapable of fulfilment. Luke has unfortunately left to posterity no certain examples of his poetry, if he ever wrote any poetry at all. The most that could possibly be done would be to show that these hymns are Greek rather than Semitic in poetical form, or rather that they are such as only a man who used Greek as his native language would have produced, without a Semitic original, merely by moulding Hebrew materials into an imitation of a Hebrew poem. Examples of such a moulding of Hebrew materials by a Gentile are rather difficult to find; at any rate they have not been adduced by Harnack. What evidence is there, therefore, for placing the Magnificat and Benedictus in such a category?

[18] Harnack, "Das Magnificat der Elisabet (Luc. 1, 46–55) nebst einigen Bemerkungen zu Luc. 1 und 2," in *Sitzungsberichte der königlich preussischen Akademie der Wissenschaften zu Berlin*, 1900, pp. 544 f., 552–556; *Lukas der Arzt*, 1906, pp. 150–152 (English translation, *Luke the Physician*, 1907, pp. 214–218).

[19] That is, of μου and αὐτός in the Magnificat, and of αὐτός and ἡμεῖς in the Benedictus.

[20] Harnack, *Lukas der Arzt*, 1906, p. 152. Compare the English translation, *Luke the Physician*, 1907, p. 217.

The second requirement also is left unfulfilled by Harnack. If he is unable to exhibit the likeness of these hymns to undisputed Lucan works, or even to works composed by the method which he thinks Luke employed, he is also unable to exhibit their unlikeness to non-Lucan, and particularly Old Testament, hymns. Such an exhibition could only have been carried out by means of examples; and until it is carried out, Harnack's proof remains, to say the least, incomplete. If some Old Testament Psalms (in the Septuagint) were to be examined by the same kind of minute scrutiny which Harnack has applied to the hymns of Lk. i, perhaps similar peculiarities of composition might be discovered.

Harnack lays particular stress upon the former part of the Benedictus, Lk. i.68-75, which, he points out, constitutes one long sentence. But if he means to compare this sentence with the sentence that forms the Lucan prologue, Lk. i.1-4, the comparison is particularly disastrous for his conclusion. The two sentences are each of them long; but there the similarity ceases. In every other respect, it would be difficult to imagine a greater contrast. Lk. i.1-4 is not a compound, but a complex, sentence; it could not grammatically be broken off until almost the very end, since the sense is held in suspense; and the cadence of the sentence is obviously incomplete until it is rounded off by the last emphatic word, "the certainty."[21] Lk. i.68-75, on the other hand, consists of a large number of coördinate phrases and clauses put together in the loosest possible way; the passage could be broken off at the end of almost any one of the nine lines of which it is composed, and still make complete sense. The sentence is not planned as though the end were in view from the beginning, but is lengthened out by adding one epexegetical phrase or clause after another, loosely and almost as an after-thought. Is that a characteristic Greek form of sentence? Does it not rather look like the simplicity of Semitic poetry, forced into the restraints of Greek grammar?

A striking parallel to this sentence in the Benedictus is found in a passage in the so-called "Psalms of Solomon."[22] The Psalms of Solomon are extant in Greek, but the Greek is admittedly a translation from a Semitic original. Here we have, therefore, an example of admittedly Semitic poetry appearing in a Greek form. Comparison of these Psalms with the hymns of the first chapter of Luke ought, if Harnack's hypothesis be correct, to show a contrast; but as a matter of fact it shows a rather striking similarity. The passage to which we refer may be translated into English as follows:

[21] ἵνα ἐπιγνῷς περὶ ὧν κατηχήθης λόγων τὴν ἀσφάλειαν (Lk. i.4).

[22] At the end of the eighteenth Psalm of the collection. The text will be found in Ryle and James, *op. cit.*, p. 150.

Blessed are those who are born in those days
To see the good things of the Lord, which he will do for the coming generation,
Under the staff of the instruction of Christ the Lord in the fear of his God,
In the wisdom of the Spirit and of righteousness and strength,
To direct a man in the works of righteousness by the fear of God,
To establish them all in the fear of the Lord.

This sentence is, indeed, shorter than the sentence in the Benedictus; but the sentence-structure, if so very loose a conjunction of clauses and phrases may be called "structure" at all, is strikingly similar.

The Psalms of Solomon, from which this passage has been taken, afford material for other interesting comparisons with the hymns of the first chapter of Luke. Parallels have been cited by Ryle and James;[23] and although the similarities in detail may not often be very close, a certain affinity in spirit and in ideas cannot be denied. Here we have, therefore, another indication of the Palestinian and Semitic origin of the Lucan hymns, since the Psalms of Solomon reflect the events of the Palestinian invasion of Pompey, and were written in Palestine and in the Hebrew language at about the middle of the first century before Christ. The date of the Greek translation is placed by Ryle and James between 40 B.C. and A.D. 40.[24] There can be no thought of literary dependence one way or the other between these Psalms and the hymns of the first chapter of Luke; and the interesting hypothesis of Chase,[25] to the effect that the parallels are to be explained by a common dependence upon the "Greek Jewish prayers of the Hellenistic Synagogues" is unnecessary.[26] But the similarity of thought and feeling between the hymns of Lk. i-ii, on the one hand, and the Palestinian Psalms of Solomon and certain Palestinian Jewish prayers on the other, furnishes subsidiary evidence for a primitive Jewish Christian origin of the Magnificat and the Benedictus.

The primary, as distinguished from subsidiary, evidence is furnished simply

[23] *Op. cit.*, pp. lx, lxii, and especially xci f., where the parallels are cited in detail. Compare also Hillmann, "Die Kindheitsgeschichte Jesu nach Lukas," in *Jahrbücher für protestantische Theologie*, xvii, 1891, pp. 201 f.

[24] See Ryle and James, *op. cit.*, Introduction, especially pp. xxxvii–xliv. Frankenberg (*Die Datierung der Psalmen Salomos*, 1896) agreed with this view in holding to a Hebrew original for the Psalms, and even attempted a retranslation into Hebrew; but placed the date in an earlier period, that of the Syrian conflicts. He has, however, apparently won little support for this dating; and the accepted view is that the Psalms of Solomon were written in Hebrew in the first century before Christ. See Schürer, *Geschichte des Jüdischen Volkes*, 4te Aufl., iii, 1909, pp. 205–212; Gray, "Psalms of Solomon," in Charles, *Apocrypha and Pseudepigrapha of the Old Testament*, ii, 1913, pp. 625–630.

[25] "The Lord's Prayer in the Early Church," in *Texts and Studies*, edited by J. Armitage Robinson, i, 1891, No. 3, pp. 128 (note 1), 147–151.

[26] See "The Hymns of the First Chapter of Luke," in *Princeton Theological Review*, x, 1912, pp. 21 f.

by an examination of the two hymns themselves. It has already been observed that the Magnificat is made up almost altogether of Old Testament phrases. These phrases are derived from no one passage, but from the most various parts of the Old Testament Scriptures. The Magnificat is no mere imitation, for example, of the song of Hannah in I Sam. ii.1-10, though it does contain reminiscences of that song. Yet the various elements are welded together into a song of perfect unity and great beauty, which preserves the parallelism of Hebrew poetry in its noblest form. Harnack supposes that this result was accomplished by the conscious art of a Gentile. But it is no wonder that the vast majority of scholars as well as of simple readers are opposed to him. A single passage from the Old Testament might have been imitated; but that so very many passages should have been united without disclosing the joints, without making the slightest impression of artificiality, must always remain very improbable. The author of such a hymn must have lived in the atmosphere of the Old Testament, and must have been familiar from earliest childhood with its language. Only so could elements derived from so many sources have been incorporated without artificiality in a single poem. The synthesis must have been made in life, long before it was made in literary form.[27]

This employment of Old Testament phrases has indeed sometimes been regarded as a mark of artificiality. David Friedrich Strauss, for example, thought that if this hymn was inspired directly by the Holy Spirit it was somewhat surprising that the result should not be something more original, instead of being a mere collection of Old Testament reminiscences.[28] But surely this taunt displays an inadequate estimate of the Magnificat itself. If the Old Testament Scriptures themselves were given by inspiration of the Spirit of God, the use of them in a song of praise need not necessarily be unworthy of the same Spirit. And to regard such a use of Biblical language as a mark of artificiality is to do despite to the inmost heart of God's people in all ages. Our Lord Himself used the Scriptures in very similar fashion; the sacred words of prophets and Psalms came unbidden to His lips in moments of crisis and trial. T. D. Bernard[29] has aptly compared the modern use of Biblical phrases in prayer.[30] That is not artificial imitation, but the natural use of the language

[27] Compare Gunkel, "Die Lieder in der Kindheitsgeschichte Jesu bei Lukas," in *Festgabe . . . A. von Harnack zum siebzigsten Geburtstag dargebracht*, 1921, p. 52: " . . . Would the literary art of a Hellenist really have been able, by the use of collected citations from the Bible, to produce such genuineness of style? Is it not much more probable that a Jew, acquainted with the traditions of Hebrew poetry, here speaks to us—probably also in a Semitic language?"

[28] Strauss, *Leben Jesu*, 1835, p. 194; Hillmann, *op. cit.*, xvii, 1891, pp. 198 f.

[29] *The Songs of the Holy Nativity*, 1895, pp. 56 f.

[30] Compare C. C. Torrey, "Translations Made from the Original Aramaic Gospels," in *Studies in the History of Religions Presented to Crawford Howell Toy*, 1912, p. 293, footnote 9: "The fact that the language 'consists largely of reminiscences' is not a blemish. The devotional poetry of

dearest to the Christian heart. When a true saint of God uses the words of Holy Scripture to express his deepest feelings whether in prayer or praise, only a very cold and unsympathetic observer can suppose such language of the heart to have been put together, artificially, by the use of a concordance. It does require some sympathy, no matter how much learning the critic may possess, to enter into the soul of the devout Christian or the devout Jew. But when such sympathy is present, the hymns of the first chapter of Luke will seem to be not products of a study chamber, but spontaneous outpourings of devout and thankful hearts. Who can say that such outpourings are unworthy of having been inspired by the Spirit of God?

We have been speaking primarily of the Magnificat. But the other hymn, the Benedictus, presents essentially the same character. It may be, indeed, somewhat different in form—probably different enough to disprove Harnack's, and also Gunkel's,[31] contention that the two hymns must have been composed by the same person. The parallelism is not quite so simple; there are more subordinate clauses and appositions and epexegetical phrases;[32] the basic Old Testament passages are perhaps not capable of being quite so easily designated. But the Hebrew parallelism and the genuine Old Testament spirit are really just as clear as in the case of the Magnificat.[33]

The form of the hymns, then, is genuinely Semitic.[34] The Greek translation, like some of the better parts of the Septuagint, has preserved the spirit of the original, though without doing unnecessary violence to the idiom of the Greek language. But an even stronger argument for a primitive Palestinian origin is to be derived from the content of the hymns, as distinguished from the form. The argument has already been set forth incidentally, in connection with the argument for a Palestinian origin of the infancy narrative as a whole, and so need not be treated here at any length. There is nothing in the hymns which can by any possibility be stretched into an allusion to specifically Christian doctrine, or even to the details of the later history of Jesus. In the Magnificat

---

any religion of long standing must use familiar phrases; it could not otherwise have its intended effect."

[31] *Op. cit.*, 1921, p. 53.

[32] Compare Ladeuze, *op. cit.*, 1903, pp. 642 f.

[33] On the argument of Dalman (*Die Worte Jesu*, 1898, p. 183; English translation, *The Words of Jesus*, 1902, pp. 223 f.) against a Semitic original of ἐπεσκέψατο . . . . . ἀνατολὴ ἐξ ὕψους (Lk. i.78) see "The Hymns of the First Chapter of Luke," in *Princeton Theological Review*, x, 1912, pp. 23 f., footnote 90. Dalman's argument is by no means conclusive.

[34] Ladeuze, *op. cit.*, 1903, while opposing Harnack's contention for Lucan authorship of the hymns, supposes that Luke retouched the Magnificat here and there. That is perhaps possible, but cannot be proved.

there is no clear allusion even to the person of the Messiah at all.[35] In the Benedictus the allusion is merely to salvation in the house of David. The Messianic king has apparently come at last, or is about to come; but nothing more is known about Him than that which was contained in Old Testament prophecy. The child John is thought of as a forerunner, not particularly of the Messiah, but of Jehovah. The coming salvation is conceived of as applying not to the world, but, primarily at least, to Israel; Israel is to be delivered from the insolent oppressors.[36] That the salvation is to be not merely political, but also moral and religious, does not transcend the bounds of Old Testament prophecy.[37] If the words in Lk. i.79, "to appear to those who are sitting in darkness and the shadow of death," contain a hint of universalism, it is the universalism of Isaiah.

Against this overwhelming *prima facie* evidence, Harnack can urge only his linguistic argument. And that has been examined in detail and found insufficient. Harnack is indeed much more confident about the hymns than about the rest of Luke i-ii. In the case of the Magnificat and the Benedictus, he would exclude altogether the possibility, which he leaves open as regards the rest of the narrative, that Luke was merely the translator of an Aramaic source; and insists that the hymns were actually composed by him. But this decision should certainly be reversed. A linguistic examination of the hymns, when compared with an examination of the rest of Lk. i-ii, will show clearly that Harnack's evidence for Lucan authorship is far less convincing in the case of the Magnificat and Benedictus than in the rest of the section.[38] That the hymns were found by Luke in a Greek form is perhaps most probable; that they were translated by him from Hebrew or Aramaic is perfectly possible, but is by no means proved by the literary phenomena; that they were composed by him is practically out of the question.

[35] Völter (*Die evangelischen Erzählungen von der Geburt und Kindheit Jesu*, 1911, p. 23) calls attention to the fact that the closing words of the song of Hannah, *καὶ ὑψώσει κέρας χριστοῦ αὐτοῦ* (I Sam. ii.10) find no place in the Magnificat. If the Magnificat were composed to suit its present context on the basis of the song of Hannah, why should the author omit just those words in his Old Testament model which would seem to apply most directly to the Christian Messiah?

[36] Compare Loisy, *Les Évangiles synoptiques*, i, 1907, p. 312: "Cet idéal n'a rien de paulinien, et même un judéo-chrétien n'aurait pu s'exprimer de la sorte après la destruction de Jérusalem."

[37] Compare Hilgenfeld, "Die Geburts- und Kindheitsgeschichte Jesu Luc. I, 5–II, 52," in *Zeitschrift für wissenschaftliche Theologie*, xliv, 1901, p. 219: "Although this salvation is found not only in political liberation, but also in piety and righteousness, yet nothing carries us beyond the feelings of a Jew like the author of Ps. Sol. xvii, except that here the birth of the Messiah in the house of David is already apparently presupposed."

[38] Compare Feine, *Eine vorkanonische Überlieferung des Lukas*, 1891, p. 20; Stanton, *The Gospels as Historical Documents*, ii, 1909, pp. 223 ff. (where Harnack's argument about the hymns is singled out for particularly emphatic criticism).

The hypothesis of Harnack with regard to the composition of these hymns has been rather generally rejected by recent scholars. Indeed, so strong has been the impression produced by the genuinely Semitic quality of the form of the hymns, coupled with the absence of distinctly Christian ideas in the content of them, that a number of recent investigators have held that the hymns are not even Jewish Christian, but actually Jewish—that they were not originally intended to be placed in the mouths of Mary and Zacharias, but were simply Jewish songs composed to suit some entirely different occasions and then adapted to their present uses by the author of the infancy narrative.

This hypothesis, which has been advocated, at least for the Magnificat, in varying forms, by Hillmann,[39] Hilgenfeld,[40] Spitta,[41] Gunkel,[42] and others, would seem to be favored by the rather loose way in which the hymns are inserted in their present context and by the absence in them of any specific reference to the situation in which Mary and Zacharias stood. The Magnificat, in particular, contains no reference to the approaching birth of a son, and, at least superficially considered, might have been spoken under many different circumstances; there is nothing that points necessarily to the situation presupposed in the narrative. Indeed, the word translated "low estate" in verse 48—"for he hath regarded the low estate of his handmaiden"—has sometimes been regarded as introducing a discordant note. Wherein consisted the "low estate" of Mary? [43] The phrase, "from henceforth," or "from now on," of the same verse has also caused difficulty. Why should the blessing which all generations are to ascribe to Mary be dated just from her visit to Elisabeth, rather

[39] "Die Kindheitsgeschichte Jesu nach Lucas," in *Jahrbücher für protestantische Theologie*, xvii, 1891, pp. 197–213.

[40] "Die Geburts- und Kindheitsgeschichte Jesu Luc. I, 5–II, 52," in *Zeitschrift für wissenschaftliche Theologie*, xliv, 1901, pp. 208–215, 217–221.

[41] "Das Magnifikat, ein Psalm der Maria und nicht der Elisabeth," in *Theologische Abhandlungen für Holtzmann*, 1902, pp. 83–90. For the modification of Spitta's view or supplement to it, in his later article, "Die chronologischen Notizen und die Hymnen in Lc. 1 u. 2," in *Zeitschrift für die neutestamentliche Wissenschaft*, vii, 1906, pp. 281–317, see below p. 93; footnote 56.

[42] "Die Lieder in der Kindheitsgeschichte Jesu bei Lukas," in *Festgabe. . . . . A. von Harnack zum siebzigsten Geburtstag dargebracht*, 1921, pp. 43–60.

[43] This difficulty would become serious only if Völter (*op. cit.*, 1911, pp. 24 f.) were right in insisting that the word ταπείνωσις means not "low estate" or "humility," but "humiliation" —that is, that it denotes the descent from a higher estate into a lower. How, it might be asked, had Mary suffered such a fall? But the suffix -σις cannot always be interpreted so strictly (compare Wilkinson, *A Johannine Document in the First Chapter of St. Luke's Gospel*, 1902, p. 36); and if the word here means simply "low estate," then the expression is quite comprehensible on the lips of Mary. Wilkinson (*op. cit.*, p. 37) suggests that "the quotation ὅτι ἐπέβλεψεν ἐπὶ τὴν ταπείνωσιν τῆς δούλης αὐτοῦ quite naturally suits the feeling with which a native of Nazareth in Galilee would receive the news that she was destined to be the mother of Messiah (cf. St. John 1, 45)." But it is perhaps unnecessary to be so specific. The word ταπείνωσις may be simply an expression of natural humility on the lips of Mary; certainly the mother of Jesus according to this narrative did not belong among the "mighty" or the "rich" (verses 52, 53), to whom God might, if He judged according to the outward appearance, have had respect.

than from the conception of the child, or from the birth, or from some other important event? Again, it has sometimes been thought not to suit the character attributed to Mary in these chapters that she should utter a hymn of praise at all. Elsewhere in Lk. i-ii she is represented as silent and passive. The manner in which the hymn is introduced has also aroused objection. Elsewhere in the narrative, it is said, when similar poetical effusions are introduced, the presence of the Spirit is noted; here there is nothing but the simple words, "And Mary said." What follows the hymn has also been thought to be unnatural if Mary is regarded as the speaker: "And Mary abode with her about three months. . . ." If Mary has just been speaking, it is argued, her name would be omitted and Elisabeth's would be mentioned, instead of the reverse; that is, the sentence would read, "she abode with Elisabeth," instead of "Mary abode with her."

These difficulties have led a considerable number of recent scholars (including Harnack) to suppose that in the original text of the Gospel of Luke the Magnificat was attributed not to Mary but to Elisabeth.[44] This hypothesis is not quite devoid of manuscript support.[45] And apparently it overcomes some of the difficulties. The "low estate" of verse 48 now becomes thoroughly intelligible;[46] it is simply the humiliation (very acute to a Jewish woman) of childlessness, like the "humiliation" of Hannah, which in the Septuagint of I Sam. i.11 is expressed by the very same word in a clause very similar to the clause in the Magnificat.[47] The phrase "from henceforth" now dates the blessing pronounced upon Elisabeth from the first movement of her child in the womb. The reserve of Mary now remains unbroken. The presence of the Spirit in the speaker now does not need to be mentioned in verse 46, because it has just been mentioned in verse 41. Finally, the "Mary remained with her" (instead of "she remained with Elisabeth") of verse 56 now becomes natural, for Elisabeth has now just been the speaker and does not need to be mentioned again by name.

Spitta,[48] while admitting the validity of some of these arguments which have been urged against the common view that the narrator intended Mary to be regarded as the author of the hymn, is, on the other hand, unable to satisfy

[44] See, for example, Harnack, "Das Magnificat der Elisabet (Luc. 1, 46–55) nebst einigen Bemerkungen zu Luc. 1 und 2," in *Sitzungsberichte der königlich preussischen Akademie der Wissenschaften zu Berlin*, 1900, pp. 538–543.

[45] "Elisabeth" is read instead of "Mary" in certain manuscripts of the Old Latin version and in one citation in Irenæus. See Souter's note.

[46] The word could, moreover, now be interpreted in the strict sense of "humiliation."

[47] "If thou wilt indeed look upon the humiliation [or "low estate"] of thine handmaid," *ἐὰν ἐπιβλέπων ἐπιβλέψῃς (ἐπὶ) τὴν ταπείνωσιν τῆς δούλης σου* (I Sam. i.11).

[48] See the earlier of Spitta's two articles mentioned above, p. 76, footnote 7, and compare also the later one.

himself with the Elisabeth hypothesis. The external evidence for the omission of the subject of the verb "said" in verse 46, or for reading "Elisabeth" as the subject, is, he thinks, insufficient. It remains more probable, he argues, that the word "Mary" was first omitted by accident and then "Elisabeth" wrongly supplied in certain documents than that an original "Elisabeth" was changed to "Mary" in order that the hymn might be attributed to a more illustrious authoress.[49] Furthermore, if the Magnificat, as the song of the barren Elisabeth, were an imitation of the song of the barren Hannah, the indication of the barrenness of the singer, which appears so plainly in the song of Hannah,[50] would surely not have been omitted from the song of Elisabeth. The term "barren," being the very link which bound the two songs together, would not have been weakened into the general term "humiliation." Any other idea in Hannah's song, Spitta insists, would have been omitted more readily than that. Furthermore, the Elisabeth hypothesis, Spitta continues, explains no better than the Mary hypothesis the looseness with which the song is fitted into the narrative: if Elisabeth were regarded as the speaker, the hymn should have been inserted after Lk. i.25. At any rate, almost any place would have been more desirable for the insertion than that which was actually chosen. In verses 42-45, Elisabeth has greeted Mary as the mother of her Lord; Mary and her Son are here the all-important figures. Surely Elisabeth would not proceed at once, in such a situation, to such an extravagant praise of her own son. Moreover, Spitta says, the words "with her" of verse 56 follow admirably upon verse 45; whereas according to Old Testament usage, if the psalm had intervened, the name "Elisabeth" would have had to be mentioned even if Elisabeth had been represented as the speaker of the hymn. The phenomena, Spitta thinks, can be explained only by the hypothesis that the hymn was foreign to the original story. Originally, Spitta thinks, the hymn was intended by its unknown Jewish author merely to express an Israelitish woman's rejoicing over a happy turn in the history of the nation, for which her sons had fought; it is inserted here by the hand of the Evangelist redactor.

An important objection to this hypothesis is that the motive of the redactor is far from clear. How did the Evangelist ever come to insert the hymn? According to Spitta himself, the plan of the narrative in Lk. i-ii requires Mary to

[49] The view of Harnack is that in the original text of the Gospel there stood merely the words *καὶ εἶπεν*, the addition of Μαριάμ and of 'Ελισάβετ representing merely two ways of supplying the missing subject of the verb. Of these two glosses, the one by which 'Ελισάβετ was supplied was, Harnack thinks, in accordance with the intention of the author: for the author of course intended the unexpressed subject of *εἶπεν* to be simply the speaker of the preceding words; no change of speaker was meant.

[50] I Sam. ii.5: "so that the barren hath born seven; and she that hath many children is waxed feeble," *ὅτι στεῖρα ἔτεκεν ἑπτά, καὶ ἡ πολλὴ ἐν τέκνοις ἠσθένησεν.*

keep silent. If that plan is so clear to modern scholars, even after it has been spoiled by the insertion of the Magnificat, it should have been still clearer to the Evangelist before he made his insertion. He has respected it in other parts of the narrative; why has he upset it here? His action might indeed have been conceivable if he accomplished anything by it. If the Magnificat contained Lucan, or even merely Christian, ideas which the Evangelist was anxious to impress upon his readers, then the insertion of the hymn might be explicable. But Spitta himself has insisted that this is not the case. Or if the Evangelist had chanced upon a Jewish hymn that suited the situation of Mary in some remarkable way, conceivably he might have seized the opportunity of embellishing his narrative by inserting it. But that, too, is far from the fact. The situation implied in the Magnificat can be defined, on the basis of the hymn itself, only in general terms. How, then, came the hymn to be attributed to Mary?

By way of answer to this question, Spitta suggests that the Evangelist attributed the hymn to Mary and inserted it just at this point because of the phrase, "his handmaid," in Lk. i.48, which corresponds with Mary's words, "Behold the handmaid of the Lord," in verse 38, and because of the expression, "shall call me blessed," in verse 48, which corresponds with the words referring to Mary, "Blessed is she that believed," in verse 45.

It is interesting to observe at this point that the very verse (verse 48) which Spitta thus regards as being that in the original hymn which commended the use of the hymn to the Evangelist is excluded from the original hymn by Gunkel.[51] Gunkel regards the verse as an addition of the redactor, who thus suited the Jewish psalm to its present (Christian) use; he thinks (1) that it constitutes an intrusion of an individual or personal element into a psalm which otherwise, like most of the Old Testament Psalms, might have been spoken by every pious Israelite, and (2) that it breaks up the form of this psalm by introducing a future tense ("all generations *shall call* me blessed") into the midst of the aorists which elsewhere are used, and which alone are proper to an "eschatological hymn" in which future blessings are celebrated as though they were already past.

These arguments for the exclusion of verse 48 are surely insufficient. Even if Gunkel is right in supposing that most of the Old Testament Psalms lack references to peculiar individual experiences and might be sung by any pious Israelite, yet just the Old Testament Psalms will show that there are many exceptions, to say the least, to this rule. And the argument from the form of the hymn depends upon the view that the aorists are aorists proper to an

[51] *Op. cit.*, 1921, pp. 57 f. See also Klostermann, in *Handbuch zum Neuen Testament*, 2te Aufl., 5, 1929, pp. 19 f.; Bultmann, *Die Geschichte der synoptischen Tradition*, 2te Aufl., 1931, pp. 322 f.

eschatological hymn in which the future events are viewed as having already happened. That view is by no means certain. At any rate, the treatment of the hymn as a purely eschatological psalm seems to beg the question. The hymn may also very naturally be taken as a song of thanksgiving, possibly including future deeds of divine mercy, but spoken primarily in view of the event alluded to in verse 48.

But if Gunkel's excision of verse 48 from the original Jewish psalm were justified, the insertion of that psalm in the infancy narrative would become even more incomprehensible than it is when the verse is retained. For in the former case that poem would be merely an eschatological psalm, which might have been spoken at any time in the history of Israel. What could possibly have led the author of the infancy narrative to attribute such a psalm to the mother of Jesus?

Even if, however, verse 48, as is done by Hillmann, Hilgenfeld, and Spitta, be retained as part of the original Jewish composition, the insertion of the hymn in the infancy narrative still remains very strange. Even verse 48 fixes the situation presupposed by the hymn only in the most general way; it establishes a woman as the speaker, but it does not at all establish the nature of the benefit which is to proceed from her to all generations. Judith, for example, as the rescuer of Israel, might conceivably have uttered such a hymn.[52] No doubt the words of verse 48 do suit the situation of Mary at this point in the narrative, and no doubt also the blessing which all generations are to ascribe to Mary is in relation to the blessing which Elisabeth has already in verse 45 pronounced upon her; perhaps also the words, "his handmaid," in verse 48 may really be felt by the readers as corresponding to the words of Mary, "Behold the handmaid of the Lord," in verse 38. But although such correspondences may be easy to detect after the hymn has already been inserted, they would hardly have occurred to anyone in the reading of a Jewish song. The Evangelist, on Spitta's hypothesis, would almost have to be imagined as searching through a collection of Jewish songs in order to discover the one least unsuited to his purpose. What was the necessity of such a painful search? The narrative would have done very well without the Magnificat. Hillmann[53] considers it more probable that it was not the final redactor of the Gospel who inserted the Magnificat, but that the final redactor found it already inserted in the Jewish Christian narrative that he used in the first two chapters. That does not change the case

[52] Hilgenfeld (*op. cit.*, 1901, pp. 214 f.) supposes that not so much Hannah is thought of as Judith, probably in the general meaning of Judæa. "Nur möchte weniger die ihren Sohn dem Tempel weihende Hanna zu Grunde liegen als die Heldin Judith, wohl in der allgemeinen Bedeutung von Judäa."

[53] *Op. cit.*, 1891, p. 206.

essentially. In some respects, it would have been harder for a Jewish Christian writer to insert a purely Jewish, non-Christian hymn into his narrative than for a Gentile Christian to do so. A Jewish Christian writer might indeed be more likely to be familiar with such a hymn; it might conceivably have been familiar to him from childhood. But on the other hand he would be less likely to think that such a familiar Jewish hymn could be palmed off successfully as a hymn of Mary the mother of Jesus—unless, indeed, his idea was that Mary herself could be represented as making use of an already existing hymn to express her feelings in an hour of exultation, just as in the Church today we use familiar hymns to express our feeling at peculiar junctures of our lives. This last supposition would hardly be in accordance with the intention of the narrator. It would certainly not fit the case of the Benedictus, where in introducing the hymn the narrator says that Zacharias "was filled with the Holy Ghost and prophesied saying . . ."; for that form of introduction would hardly be used if the hymn were to be regarded merely as an already existing Jewish hymn that Zacharias used; and the strong presumption is that the supposition also does not fit the case of the Magnificat.

We are therefore brought back to the primary difficulty that faces the hypothesis which we have been discussing. How did this supposedly Jewish hymn ever come to be attributed to Mary, or, for that matter, to Elisabeth? In general, it is unlikely that a Jewish hymn would be inserted in such a narrative, and at such a place, by a Christian writer. Spitta points to similar cases in the Old Testament—for example, to the song of Hannah, which, he believes, was originally separate from its present context. But even granting for the sake of the argument the critical conclusions adopted by Spitta for the Old Testament passages, the present case is somewhat different. There, Hebrew writers would be adopting Hebrew hymns; here, a Christian writer would be adopting a Jewish hymn, and adopting it altogether without compulsion, for insertion in the most sacred part of his narrative. Would not the Christian consciousness of the newness of the Christian faith have precluded such disregard of the break between the old dispensation and the new?[54] If the Evangelist (or the author of the narrative lying back of Lk. i-ii) had revised the supposed Jewish song so as to make a Christian hymn of it, then his employment of it would perhaps be in accordance with the habit of certain ancient writers, though not, we think, with the habit of the author of Luke and Acts. But that he should insert a simple Jewish song without redaction or only with

[54] What Hillmann (*op. cit.*, 1891, pp. 204–206) says about other such purely Jewish elements in the New Testament is problematical. And even if they are really Jewish, they are, as they appear in the New Testament, made serviceable to Christian ideas. In the case of the Magnificat that would not be the case.

such redaction as would not at all change the essential character of the hymn [55] seems altogether beyond the bounds of probability. If the Evangelist were unscrupulous enough to put a simple Jewish hymn into the mouth of Mary, he would have been unscrupulous enough to make the hymn express his own ideas or refer to the later events in the life of Jesus.

The insertion by the Evangelist of this Jewish hymn would be explicable only if, when the Evangelist wrote, it was already regarded as a hymn of Mary. But that merely pushes the problem a step further back. How came the hymn to be attributed to Mary in the first place? If it were a Jewish song, it would very probably have been known as such by the primitive Jewish Christian community. How came that community, then, to put it into the mouth of the mother of the Lord, at a time, too, when she had probably not long been dead? [56]

The hypothesis, then, that the Magnificat was originally just a Jewish song, a foreign element inserted into the infancy narrative, must be rejected. Is it then simply a part of that narrative? Was it composed by the author of the narrative—that is, by the author of Luke's source in Lk. i-ii, since it has already been shown that composition by Luke himself is extremely unlikely? This hypothesis cannot altogether be excluded from consideration. The author of the source might conceivably have exercised the freedom of an ancient historian by attributing to his characters not words which they actually spoke, but words which, in view of the situation, they might fittingly have spoken.

[55] The view of Gunkel that verse 48 is due to a redactor has already been considered. Hilgenfeld accepted this verse as part of the original Jewish psalm, but supposed that the words, "to Abraham, and to his seed for ever," at the end of the hymn, in verse 55, constitute a Christian addition. Gunkel, on the other hand, lays great stress on just these latter words as being in accordance with the customary ending of a Jewish psalm. These questions are not important for our present argument. Our point is that neither of these additions, if additions they be, would at all make natural the inclusion of the Jewish hymns in the infancy narrative. If the redactor made interpolations in the hymns only to the extent that either Hilgenfeld's or Gunkel's view demands, his restraint is perhaps even more extraordinary than it would be if he made no interpolations at all. If he felt free to revise the hymns at all, why did he not make such revisions as would adapt them fully to his purpose?

[56] In a renewed discussion of the hymns of Lk. i–ii ("Die chronologischen Notizen und die Hymnen in Lc. 1 u. 2," in *Zeitschrift für die neutestamentliche Wissenschaft*, vii, 1906, pp. 303–317), Spitta suggests (pp. 316 f.) that the hymns came into the hands of the Evangelist under the titles, "Of Mary," "Of Zacharias," "Of Simeon," perhaps as parts of a collection dating from the early Christian period. Possibly, Spitta says, these names designated the persons that appear in Lk. i–ii. In that case, the hymns had been placed under the names of these persons by primitive Christianity without any real intention to represent them as the authors. But it is also possible, Spitta says further, that the hymns belonged originally to different persons, who really bore these same names. In that case those persons had nothing to do with the characters of the Christian narrative, but the chance similarity of name led the Evangelist to insert the hymns in their present positions. The former of these two suggestions by Spitta is liable to the objections urged above in the text; the latter is valuable chiefly as indicating some appreciation, on the part of the author, of the difficulties that beset all less adventurous suggestions.

An exceedingly strong objection to such a view arises from the absence, in the hymn, of specifically Christian ideas and of references to later events. A Christian writer, after the resurrection, in composing a hymn for the mother of the Lord, could hardly have failed to insert in it some more definite prophecy of the life or death or resurrection of her Son—unless indeed he were writing before the death of Mary, when such an anachronism would have provoked contradiction. But in this latter case he would scarcely have ventured to compose the hymn at all.

The force of this argument might perhaps be partially avoided if we could suppose that the Magnificat and Benedictus, in company with other parts of Lk. i, belonged originally to non-Christian tradition about John the Baptist, preserved in the circle of John's disciples. The hypothesis that there is such non-Christian Johannine tradition in the first chapter of Luke was favored by Völter,[57] with an elaborate documentary theory, and has received the weighty support of Harnack,[58] who, however, posits simply independent oral traditions about John and about Jesus, not independent documents. Of course, if the Magnificat and Benedictus were composed by non-Christian disciples of John the Baptist, then the absence from them of specifically Christian ideas no longer requires explanation. But the documentary theory of Völter is quite inadequately supported; and the more cautious theory of Harnack (more cautious because, since traditions are less easily studied than documents, assertions can be made about them with greater impunity) is also incapable of proof. Of course, the theory that both hymns were originally Johannine and non-Christian presupposes the view that the Magnificat belonged originally to Elisabeth rather than to Mary. But that view is beset with difficulties. It might conceivably be held in a form which would suppose the Magnificat to have been transferred by the Christian historian from Elisabeth to Mary.[59] But in view of the absence of specifically Christian ideas in the hymn, all motive for such transference was lacking. The most that might by any possibility be admitted is that if a choice had to be made between the view that the Magnificat was composed by a disciple of John and the view that it was simply a Jewish psalm, the former alternative might be preferable. But at best it would be merely the lesser of two improbabilities. At any rate, Harnack, as distinguished from Völter, cannot possibly use his theory of John-the-Baptist tradition to explain the absence of

[57] *Op. cit.*, 1911.

[58] *Neue Untersuchungen zur Apostelgeschichte*, 1911, pp. 108–110 (English translation, *The Date of the Acts and of the Synoptic Gospels*, 1911, pp. 153–156).

[59] Compare Spitta, "Die chronologischen Notizen und die Hymnen in Lc. 1 u. 2," in *Zeitschrift für die neutestamentliche Wissenschaft*, vii, 1906, pp. 311 f.

specifically Christian ideas in the hymns; because Harnack is quite certain that the hymns were composed by the Gentile Christian Luke.

One hypothesis alone overcomes all objections—the hypothesis that the Magnificat in its Greek form is actually derived from a Semitic song of Mary herself. That hypothesis explains, on the one hand, the absence from the hymn of specifically Christian ideas and of reference to later events in the life of Jesus; and it explains, on the other hand, the inclusion of such a hymn in a Christian narrative. It does justice, therefore, to the element of truth in Harnack's position as over against Gunkel's, and also to the element of truth in Gunkel's position over against Harnack's; but it avoids the errors which adhere to each of their positions. The more one studies alternative theories, the more one is led back to the simple view that the Magnificat was actually a song of Mary the mother of Jesus.

To many modern readers, no doubt, that will seem to be a highly adventurous conclusion. But it will seem so only because Joseph and Mary and Zacharias and Elisabeth as they appear in the infancy narrative are thought to be legendary figures. If, on the other hand, the narrative is based upon fact, why may not the mother of Jesus have been endowed with the gift of simple poetry, so that, under the immediate impression of her wonderful experience, she may have moulded her store of Scripture imagery, made part of her life from childhood, into this beautiful hymn of praise? Why must the mother of Jesus of Nazareth have been a nonentity? Just on naturalistic principles, the question may well be asked, to say nothing of the view which would make her the chosen vessel for the incarnation of the Son of God. Why may she not have possessed gifts that fitted her in some measure for her inestimable privilege? [60]

The hypothesis becomes more acceptable when one examines again the manner in which the hymn is introduced. Modern criticism is perhaps correct in observing that the Magnificat is inserted rather loosely in the narrative. Perhaps, indeed, the first impression of the reader is that the hymn is intended to be regarded as an immediate answer of Mary to the greeting of Elisabeth. But that is by no means certain. There is no perfectly clear indication of it either in the introductory words, "And Mary said," or in the hymn itself.[61] It

[60] Compare the significant admission of Harnack (*Neue Untersuchungen zur Apostelgeschichte*, 1911, p. 109, footnote; compare the English translation, *The Date of the Acts and of the Synoptic Gospels*, 1911, p. 155, footnote 1): "The stories [that is, the narrative of Jesus' birth and infancy that lies back of Lk. i–ii] are essentially unitary in character. The circle from which they came had high reverence for Mary and placed her in a significant manner by the side of her Son. That did not come of itself, but must go back to the impression of Mary . . . ." Compare also Resch, "Das Kindheitsevangelium," 1897, in *Texte und Untersuchungen*, x.5, p. 102.

[61] Spitta ("Das Magnifikat, ein Psalm der Maria und nicht der Elisabeth," in *Theologische Abhandlungen für Holtzmann*, 1902, pp. 89 f.) can even, without downright absurdity, venture the suggestion that perhaps the Evangelist thought of the Magnificat as arising not from the

looks as though the hymn may perhaps have circulated separately, as a hymn of Mary, produced during the visit to Elisabeth, but without any indication of the exact day and hour when it was first spoken. It would then, if this view be right, have been inserted in the narrative of the infancy at the proper place, as an answer to the greeting of Elisabeth, but without any indication whatever that it was spoken extemporaneously. It could be an answer to Elisabeth's greeting without being an immediate answer.

The words, "from henceforth," or (more literally) "from now on," in verse 48 constitute no insuperable objection to this view. These words may indeed refer to verse 45, "Blessed is she that believed"; they may represent Mary as seeing in this blessing just pronounced upon her by Elisabeth the first of a long series of similar pronouncements.[62] But this reference is by no means absolutely certain. The word "now" does not necessarily indicate the present moment, but may refer merely to a present period of time.[63] And even if the reference of the phrase to verse 45 is correct, still the hypothesis just suggested as to the composition of the hymn does not become impossible; the blessing by Elisabeth could still be in view as the occasion of the hymn even if the hymn was not actually composed in detail until afterwards.

We are far from asserting that this view is certainly correct. It is, indeed, perhaps preferable to the view of Resch, that the hymn had gradually taken form in Mary's mind between the annunciation and the visit of Elisabeth, so that without being in the strict sense extemporaneous it could be spoken immediately as an answer to Elisabeth's greeting. Still other views are possible. If, for example, it should be insisted that the hymn was an utterance directly inspired by the Holy Spirit and so not subject to the requirements of preparation that would otherwise be expected, we have no objection of principle to such a view; and it might be rendered more acceptable to the modern mind by the consideration that improvising of poetry may have been practised at that time and in that part of the world to a degree which is unknown in our modern Western civilization, so that the Spirit of God would not, according to the view in question, be using a method of utterance that was entirely out of connection with the natural habits of mind of the person through whom He would be speaking.

But our point is that the view which we outlined first is also not impossible, and it could be held in the fullest loyalty to the intention of the narrator. Hence the ridicule that has sometimes been vented upon the Lucan narrative,

---

situation in the house of Elisabeth, but from the situation to which the immediately preceding words point—namely, from the "fulfilment" (τελείωσις) of the promises made to Mary.

[62] So Ladeuze, *op. cit.*, 1903, p. 630.

[63] See Resch, *op. cit.*, 1897, p. 105.

for attributing to a simple Jewish maiden an improvised speech of such perfect artistic form, is misplaced. The sense of the narrative is not certainly violated if the Magnificat be regarded as the product of Mary's meditation during the three months which she spent in the hill country of Judæa.

Much of what has been said about the Magnificat could be repeated for the Benedictus. In the Benedictus, it is true, there is somewhat clearer indication of the occasion on which the hymn is intended to have been spoken, since the words, "And thou, child," etc., in verses 76-79, do point to a child, already born, as forerunner of the Messianic age. It is not surprising, therefore, that those who regard this hymn as an originally non-Christian Jewish poem suppose that these last four verses constitute a Christian addition. But even when these verses are regarded (as they certainly ought to be regarded) as an original part of the hymn, there is in the hymn the same absence, as in the case of the Magnificat, of specifically Christian ideas, and therefore there is the same difficulty of supposing that the hymn was composed by the author of the narrative. Moreover, the Benedictus is even more loosely inserted in the narrative than is the Magnificat. If the narrator had desired to put a hymn into the mouth of Zacharias, he would naturally have done so at Lk. i.64, when Zacharias regained his speech and "spake, blessing God." Instead, the hymn is inserted in a general description [64] of the growth of the child.[65] Surely a possible explanation is that the hymn was circulated separately, and was delivered to the author of the narrative as a hymn of Zacharias, but without definite indication of the time when it was produced.[66] Like the Magnificat it may well have been the product of partly conscious, though inspired, art.[67]

The absence, then, of specifically Christian ideas in the Magnificat and Benedictus, the absence of reference to facts in the life of Jesus, points to a time when the Messianic hope was still couched in the terms of Old Testament

[64] Lk. i.65–66, 80.

[65] The suggestion of Wilkinson (*op. cit.*, 1902, pp. 17, 32) that the compiler of the narrative regarded the Benedictus as an answer to the question, "What then shall this child be?" (verse 66), is not plausible.

[66] Compare James Cooper, article "Benedictus," in Hastings, *Dictionary of Christ and the Gospels*, i, 1908, p. 190: "Zacharias may have had it [the psalm] ready for the long anticipated moment; may have recited it then, and written it afterwards." That is perhaps possible, but there are some objections to it. And there is no clear indication in the narrative that the psalm was uttered at the time of the circumcision of John.

[67] Compare B. Weiss, *Leben Jesu*, 4te Aufl. i, 1902, p. 222: "This song of praise also exhibits the form of the Jewish Messianic hope in a primitiveness and purity which it did not retain in the later Christian period, and which could have been imitated only by a kind of artificial composition that was entirely foreign to that age. The song, moreover, is by no means put by the narrator into the mouth of Zacharias as an embellishment of the scene formed by the circumcision (i.64), but is inserted after the close of that scene as a memory from that time, which was still handed down in the hill country of Judæa." Compare the English translation, *The Life of Christ*, i, 1883, p. 242.

prophecy. On the other hand, the hymns are not simply Jewish hymns, composed in some unknown situation; for if they were, they could not have found a place in Lk. i-ii. They must, therefore, really have been produced by the persons to whom they are attributed in the narrative, and produced at a time when Old Testament prophecy had not yet been explained by its fulfilment. The fulfilment is at the door; it is no longer a thing of the dim and distant future: but the fashion of it is still unknown. The promised king has arrived at last, but the manner of His reign must still be learned only from the mysterious indications of prophecy. The Messiah is there, but He is still unknown. The hymns belong, in other words, exactly where the Evangelist has placed them.

If the hymns really were composed by Mary and by Zacharias, then they were no doubt composed either in Hebrew or in Aramaic. The former hypothesis would explain best of all the Old Testament spirit and coloring of this poetry. And that the priest Zacharias, at least, should have composed such a hymn in the sacred language, rather than in the language of every-day life, is by no means impossible; indeed, in view of the judgment of experts with regard to the language of Palestine at the time of Christ, it might almost be pronounced the more probable alternative. That a woman (Mary) should have composed a hymn in Hebrew is less natural,[68] though perhaps not altogether impossible. If the hymns were composed in Aramaic—and in the case of the Magnificat that is more probable—then the task of the Greek translator was harder. He would not be able to use Septuagint renderings which had already been formulated for the very expressions which lay before him, but might be forced to consider first (of course quite naturally, and almost unconsciously) the Old Testament Hebrew expressions which were equivalent to the Aramaic expressions of the hymns. In view of the similarity between Hebrew and Aramaic, the task would not be over-difficult, especially if the translator was at home in the Hebrew, Aramaic, and Greek Scriptures. Or else the Septuagint phrases might have occurred to the translator directly without reference to the Hebrew passages, as natural translations of the Aramaic. The suffusion of the original Aramaic hymns with the thought and language of the Old Testament would not be unnatural; for the Scriptures in an Aramaic form had become familiar to all through the oral translations in the synagogues.

The preceding discussion of the Magnificat and the Benedictus has at least served to refute the view of Harnack that the hymns were composed by the

[68] See Zahn, *Einleitung in das Neue Testament*, 3te Aufl., i, 1906, p. 4: "Also auch in den gesetzeseifrigen Familien verstanden die Frauen kein Hebräisch." Compare the English translation, *Introduction to the New Testament*, 1909, i, p. 7.

Gentile Christian Luke. Even if they were not actually spoken by the persons whose names they bear, and at the period of time dealt with in the infancy narrative, still their Palestinian origin might be, and has often been, maintained; they may be at least Jewish Christian even if they are not pre-Christian.

Thus Ladeuze[69] agrees with Spitta in supposing that the hymns were circulated separately, before they found a place in their present context. But he rightly rejects the view that they were simply Jewish psalms. They were found in use, he thinks, by Luke in the Christian communities of Palestine. "May they not be," he says, "both of them, simply that which, detached from the context, they seem to be, true psalms—Christian psalms spoken, under the action of the Spirit, in the meetings of the first communities in Palestine, and found by Luke at the same time as his Jewish Christian document concerning the infancy of Christ?"[70] Indeed, Ladeuze continues, Mary herself may have been the one who first sang the Magnificat among the believers. The concrete circumstances were already in the past; so she simply considered as a whole the work of which she had been the instrument.

This view, it may be remarked, does not explain so well as the view which we have advocated the absence from the hymn of definite references to the later events, such as the events in the public ministry of Jesus or such as the crucifixion and resurrection. But at least it preserves to the full the Palestinian character of the hymn.

J. Weiss, in the first and second editions of his commentary on the Gospels,[71] suggested that possibly the Magnificat may be regarded as a Jewish Christian psalm in which the Christian community gives thanks for the blessing which God has given it, verse 48 being an addition made in order to suit the song to its present context. The aorists in verses 51-54 refer, according to this hypothesis, to experiences of the Jewish Christian Church. The mighty act which, according to verse 51, God has performed is, Weiss suggests, the sending of Christ; the "lowly" of verse 52 are the members of the Christian community, who, strangely enough, were chosen from among the humbler classes of the people; the mighty ones who have been cast down from their thrones are, perhaps, Pilate and Herod, as also the persecutor Herod Agrippa, who died a sudden death in A.D. 44.

This interpretation of the psalm is, we think, hardly correct; the aorists of

[69] *Op. cit.*, 1903, pp. 638 ff.

[70] *Op. cit.*, 1903, p. 643.

[71] *Die Schriften des Neuen Testaments*, 2te Aufl., i, 1917, pp. 418 f. The hypothesis is stripped of many of its distinctive features in the third edition, which was revised, after Weiss's death, by Bousset.

the Magnificat may, for example, be understood, with Gunkel,[72] as referring to future events. Or, rather, *some* of the aorists may be understood in that way, since we see no reason why they must all be understood alike. The speaker of the hymn may already have experienced a mighty dispensation of God's grace; and then, in reflection upon that, and upon other acts of divine mercy in the past history of Israel, may in prophetic vision have included with these events of past and present other events that were still to come; the future glories may thus be regarded simply as the unfolding of what God had already done and as so necessarily involved in it that distinctions of time lost their importance.

It is perfectly true, as J. Weiss suggested, that even if the aorists of the Magnificat refer to the future, there must have been some special occasion for praising these future acts of God just at the particular time when the poet was writing. This occasion, however, was present to Mary, at the time described in Lk. i, as well as to a writer of the Jewish Christian Church. After the marvellous experience which Mary had undergone at the annunciation, the coming of the Messiah was to the eye of faith already accomplished, and also (in principle) all the acts of God's grace which are celebrated in verses 51-54.

The view of Wilkinson [73] with regard to the Magnificat is somewhat similar to that of J. Weiss, which has just been discussed; like Weiss he regards the hymn as "a hymn of the early Christian Church at Jerusalem." Only, unlike Weiss, he is not obliged to regard verse 48 as an interpolation into the original poem; for he supposes—in what, it must be confessed, is a very unnatural way—that the term "handmaiden" in that verse was originally applied (in a collective sense) to the Christian community.

No doubt there are objections to these views of Wilkinson and Weiss. But at least these scholars have performed a service by insisting (as over against the view of Harnack) upon the genuinely Palestinian character of the hymn. In that respect they join forces with the advocates of a merely Jewish, as distinguished from Jewish Christian, origin for the Magnificat and Benedictus. It is true that Weiss does believe that the original Magnificat has suffered interpolation (at verse 48) when it was incorporated in the narrative as we now have it; and he holds that in the Benedictus (the former part of which otherwise he regards as the work of a Jewish Christian poet) verses 76 f. (though not all of verses 76-79) constitute a later addition.[74] This latter opinion, as we have seen, is shared (with respect, however, to all of verses 76-79) quite generally by those scholars who regard the Benedictus as a merely Jewish

[72] "Die Lieder in der Kindheitsgeschichte Jesu bei Lukas," in *Festgabe. . . . A. von Harnack zum siebzigsten Geburtstag dargebracht*, 1921, pp. 53–57. Compare above, pp. 90 f.

[73] *A Johannine Document in the First Chapter of St. Luke's Gospel*, 1902, pp. 14 f., footnote 2.

[74] J. Weiss, *op. cit.*, 3te Aufl., i, revised by Bousset, pp. 406 f.

hymn. But a significant admission is made in this connection by one of the most distinguished of these scholars—namely by Gunkel.[75] The Christian writer who added verse 48 in the Magnificat and verses 76-79 in the Benedictus, he says, "knew the Old Testament well and perhaps wrote in a Semitic language," so that "his additions are not perfectly easy to distinguish." As a matter of fact, we think that the supposed "additions" are not to be distinguished at all, but are to be regarded as original parts of the hymns.[76] But at least it is interesting that so distinguished a student of Semitic language and literature as Gunkel supposes that even the Christian interpolator must have been thoroughly familiar with the Old Testament and probably wrote in a Semitic language. We have here a strong testimony, among many others, to the Palestinian origin of the hymns.

The whole trend of recent investigation, therefore, has been strongly opposed to the view of Harnack that the Magnificat and Benedictus are artificial compositions of a Gentile Christian. The Palestinian origin of the hymns is recognized both by those who regard the hymns as purely Jewish, and by those who regard them as hymns of the Jewish Christian Church, this second view constituting a salutary protest against the error in the first. The element of truth in both these two views can be conserved, we think, and the element of error avoided, only if we suppose that the hymns actually originated in the situations where they are now placed in the infancy narrative. But at any rate the Palestinian character of the hymns stands firm.

That conclusion tends to confirm our opinion with regard to the Palestinian character of the whole narrative in Lk. i-ii. It is conceivable, of course, that a Gentile Christian writer, freely composing a narrative of the birth and infancy of Jesus, should have embellished his work with two genuinely Palestinian psalms; but that is less likely than that a Jewish Christian writer should have done so. At least, it would have to be supposed that the Gentile Christian writer was familiar enough with Palestine to pick up what suitable poetic material that country afforded. We can say, at any rate—to speak cautiously—that the Magnificat and Benedictus, far from tending to weaken our conviction as to the Palestinian origin of the whole narrative, as would certainly be the case if Harnack's view of these hymns were right, really tend strongly to confirm that conviction. The character of these hymns is just what we should expect in a genuinely Palestinian narrative of the birth and infancy of Jesus.

[75] *Op. cit.*, 1921, p. 60.

[76] With regard to the Benedictus, Lagrange ("Le récit de l'enfance de Jésus dans S. Luc," in *Revue Biblique Trimestrielle*, iv, 1895, p. 168), appeals to the τοῦ δοῦναι, of verses 74, 77, as indicating the same author in both parts. In general it may be said that there is no adequate reason whatever for regarding verses 76–79 as an addition.

Chapter V

THE ORIGIN AND TRANSMISSION OF THE LUCAN NARRATIVE

IT HAS been shown in Chapter III that the whole narrative in Lk. i-ii is Semitic and Palestinian in character, and displays a striking lack of acquaintance with events in the later history of the apostolic Church. These characteristics, it has been shown further (in Chapter IV), appear with special clearness in the two hymns, the Magnificat and the Benedictus.

But how is this Palestinian character of the Lucan infancy narrative to be explained? Various hypotheses suggest themselves.

The most obvious hypothesis, of course, is that in this section the author of Luke-Acts made use of a Palestinian source, written originally in Hebrew or Aramaic, which either had already been translated into Greek or else was translated by Luke himself.

This hypothesis has been opposed in recent years especially by Harnack.[1] By a detailed examination of the language of the infancy narrative he has sought to show that after subtraction has been made of the words and phrases taken from the Septuagint what remains is so characteristically Lucan that Luke must have been the author, and not merely the editor, of the narrative. He does not, indeed, exclude the possibility that Luke may have used an Aramaic source in these chapters, but he insists that if Luke did so he must have translated the source himself; he could not have found it already existing in Greek; the Greek form of the infancy narrative must be due to Luke alone. And although Harnack admits this possibility that Luke translated an Aramaic source, he is evidently inclined to favor the other view, that in the composition of this narrative oral tradition only was used, so that Luke was in the fullest sense the author, and not merely the editor or the translator, of the written narrative.

How then does Harnack explain the Semitic coloring of the language in this section? He does so very largely by insisting upon conscious imitation, on the part of Luke, of the style of the Septuagint. In the prologue, he supposes, Luke is writing according to his own natural style; in the following narrative he is imitating the style of the Septuagint.

[1] It was also opposed by Dalman (*Die Worte Jesu*, 1898, pp. 31 f.; English translation, *The Words of Jesus*, 1902, pp. 38–40), and by Loisy (*Les Évangiles synoptiques*, i, 1907, pp. 170, 277).

At first sight the hypothesis may seem to be very unlikely, since it seems to attribute to the author of Luke-Acts a refinement of art which is hardly natural in an ancient writer. But possibly first impressions in this matter may have to be modified. As a matter of fact, imitations of the Septuagint, or, to say the least, detailed influence of the Septuagint, in the Lucan writings cannot altogether be denied. For example, despite his Greek literary affinities, Luke uses the Hebraistic phrase, "it came to pass,"[2] far more than it is used by any other New Testament writer. Evidently he had a keen appreciation for what may be called the "Bible style" of the Septuagint, and felt that that style was peculiarly fitted to be the vehicle of his own sacred narrative. Harnack's contention would simply lead us to say, in effect, that in treating in a poetical manner the events connected with the Saviour's birth, Luke carried the imitation of the Septuagint style somewhat farther than he did when he was narrating in a more matter-of-fact way the events of the public ministry, and very much farther than he did when he came to events that took place in a Gentile environment, like the events of the missionary journeys of Paul. In the case of the public ministry, we might say that Luke was hindered by his sources from carrying out his stylistic plans with perfect freedom; and in the case of the missionary journeys of Paul the subject-matter did not lend itself at all to imitation of the Septuagint. But in the infancy narrative there would be no such hindrances, and the style of the Septuagint could freely be employed if the author pleased.

Thus the hypothesis of Harnack cannot be regarded as inherently impossible. In support of it he has in a very careful way[3] gone through representative sections of Lk. i.5-ii.52, pointing out Lucan peculiarities—that is, words or usages which occur only in Luke-Acts among the New Testament writings or else occur more frequently there than in the rest of the New Testament and especially in Matthew and Mark. The work of Harnack has received a valuable supplement from Zimmermann,[4] who examined in detail those portions of the narrative which were left unexamined in Harnack's earlier discussion. In

[2] ἐγένετο δέ or καὶ ἐγένετο.

[3] Harnack, "Das Magnificat der Elisabet (Luc. 1, 46–55) nebst einigen Bemerkungen zu Luc. 1 und 2," in *Sitzungsberichte der königlich preussischen Akademie der Wissenschaften zu Berlin*, 1900, pp. 537–556; *Lukas der Arzt*, 1906, pp. 69–75, 138–152 (English translation, *Luke the Physician*, 1907, pp. 96–105, 199–218); compare also *Neue Untersuchungen zur Apostelgeschichte*, 1911, pp. 108–110 (English translation, *The Date of the Acts and of the Synoptic Gospels*, 1911, pp. 153–156).

[4] "Evangelium des Lukas Kap. 1 und 2," in *Theologische Studien und Kritiken*, lxxvi, 1903, pp. 247–290. Compare also Plummer, in his commentary (in the *International Critical Commentary*) and Stanton, *The Gospels as Historical Documents*, ii, 1909, pp. 291–295; Hawkins, *Horae Synopticae*, second edition, 1909, pp. 15–24, 27–29, 35–51. Compare also various observations in Vogel, *Zur Charakteristik des Lukas*, 2te Aufl., 1899; and in Friedrich, *Das Lukasevangelium und die Apostelgeschichte, Werke desselben Verfassers*, 1890.

Harnack's more recent work he has carried the examination through part of the sections that Zimmermann had already covered.[5]

These recent investigators were anticipated one hundred years ago by Gersdorf,[6] who defended the first two chapters of Matthew and Luke, as original parts of the First and Third Gospels, by an elaborate linguistic argument. The chapters in question were explored very much after the method that has been adopted by Harnack and Zimmermann. Lk. i-ii, for example, was traversed from beginning to end in order to exhibit those linguistic features which connect it with the rest of Luke-Acts as the work of the same writer. In thoroughness, Gersdorf was not one whit inferior to the more recent investigators. It is remarkable how very seldom Harnack or Zimmermann has detected a Lucan characteristic which Gersdorf had not already observed; and in a number of cases Gersdorf observed what his successors have overlooked. Gersdorf labored with insufficient textual materials and was too much inclined to emend the text in order to secure absolute uniformity of style; but such faults do not affect the permanent usefulness of his work. The neglect with which he has been treated, in recent years, even by scholars who have been over exactly the same ground,[7] is undeserved.

Harnack and Zimmermann agree in excluding a Greek written source for Lk. i.5-ii.52. The style of the passage, they maintain, is found, after due allowance is made for peculiarity of the subject-matter and for imitation of the Septuagint, to be so totally Lucan that Luke must have been something more than the mere editor; he must have been the first to treat the material in a Greek narrative. If he had used a Greek source, they maintain, the style of the source would necessarily appear in the use of a non-Lucan vocabulary and phraseology.

So far, Harnack and Zimmermann agree. But they differ in what they substitute for the rejected hypothesis of a Greek source. Zimmermann supposes that Luke used an Aramaic source which he translated himself; Harnack,

[5] The result is as follows:—i.5–15 has been examined both by Harnack and by Zimmermann; i.16–38, by Zimmermann; i.39–56, by Harnack, supplemented by Zimmermann; i.57–67, by Zimmermann; i.68–79 by Harnack, supplemented by Zimmermann; i.80–ii.14, by Zimmermann; ii.15–20, by Harnack, supplemented by Zimmermann; ii.21–40, by Zimmermann; ii. 41–52, by Harnack, supplemented by Zimmermann. It will be observed that the essay of Zimmermann was written after Harnack's earlier work, but before the later work. In his later work, Harnack displayed no acquaintance with Zimmermann's investigations. In i.5–15, therefore, Harnack and Zimmermann have investigated the same material independently. In view of their independence, the agreement of the investigators in many of the proofs urged with regard to this passage becomes significant.

[6] *Beiträge zur Sprach-charakteristik der Schriftsteller des Neuen Testaments*, 1816.

[7] Feine (*Eine vorkanonische Überlieferung des Lukas*, 1891, p. 19) constitutes an exception in that he does recognize the value of Gersdorf's work.

while admitting the possibility of an Aramaic source, apparently thinks it more probable that Luke depended merely upon oral tradition.

Harnack began his investigation with the Magnificat and the Benedictus, in the case of which, as we have already observed, he excluded the possibility, which he admits for the rest of the narrative, that Luke translated an Aramaic source. The language of the hymns, he maintained, is, after subtraction of the Septuagint element, so totally Lucan as to show unmistakably that the hymns are free compositions of the author of the whole double work. This contention has been refuted in the last chapter. Far from showing that the hymns were free compositions of Luke, Harnack has not even succeeded in showing that the hand of Luke has been at work on them at all; so far as the linguistic phenomena go, it is possible, though not obligatory, to hold that the hymns came to Luke in a Greek form and that he incorporated them in his work without change.

But if the arguments of Harnack are unconvincing with regard to the hymns, they are far from being without force for the rest of the narrative. In 1911 the present writer engaged in a rather detailed examination of the whole infancy narrative, in order to determine how many of the Lucan characteristics detected by Gersdorf, Harnack, Zimmermann and others, might more properly be regarded simply as characteristics of the Septuagint.[8] The result showed, indeed, that Harnack had not proved his point; many of the words and phrases which Harnack had listed as Lucan may equally well be placed in a different category. The phenomena are not such as definitely to exclude the use of a Greek written source in Lk. i-ii. Nevertheless, after all such deductions have been made, enough remains to show plainly that the hand of the author of the whole book has been at work in this section. That much, at least, has been demonstrated by Harnack. We do not, indeed, think that the Lucan characteristics, after the necessary deductions have been made, are sufficient to show that Luke was the first to put the narrative in a Greek form and sufficient to exclude the hypothesis that he used a Greek written source; but they are amply sufficient to show at least that if he did use a Greek written source he used it with freedom and made it conform in important particulars to the style of the rest of his great double work.

For one thing, the objection which Harnack raised to our method of examining his argument,[9] applies with very much more force to the whole narrative than it does to the hymns. Harnack had said, in effect, that when

[8] "The Hymns of the First Chapter of Luke" and "The Origin of the First Two Chapters of Luke," in *Princeton Theological Review*, x, 1912, pp. 1–38, 212–277.

[9] See Harnack's review of the two articles by the present writer (cited above), in *Theologische Literaturzeitung*, xxxviii, 1913, cols. 7 f.

the Septuagint element is removed, what remains is so characteristically Lucan that Luke must have been in the full sense the author, and not merely the editor, of the narrative. Our investigation showed, by a detailed use of the Hatch-Redpath concordance to the Septuagint, that the Septuagint element in the language of the narrative is very much greater than Harnack supposed, so that many of Harnack's Lucan characteristics are really just characteristics of the Septuagint, likely to be used by anyone who was influenced by the Septuagint style. In reply Harnack insisted, in effect, that even if the characteristics to which he points are also found in the Septuagint, that does not necessarily destroy their evidential value, since a choice of just the same usages from the rich store of Septuagint phraseology might indicate unity of authorship as well as it would be indicated by coincidence in other respects.

This reply, which had been anticipated by Ladeuze and to some extent by the present writer,[10] is by no means without weight. And yet we think it does not quite go the whole way. When it is observed that similarity in language between the Lucan writings in general, on the one hand, and the Septuagint, on the other, is far greater than that between the Septuagint and the other New Testament writers, then some, at least, of the coincidences in language between Lk. i-ii and the rest of Luke become less significant. Where else in the New Testament can a section be found which approximates so closely as does Lk. i-ii to the narrative of the Old Testament? Part of the exceptionally close affinity of Lk. iii-Acts xxviii to Lk. i-ii may be due simply to an exceptionally close affinity to the Septuagint in general. Other New Testament writers may be found to diverge more than Luke does from Lk. i-ii simply because they diverge more from the Septuagint. Thus Harnack's reply, although unquestionably it deserves to be borne carefully in mind, does not altogether destroy the damage to his extreme conclusion which comes from the discovery in the Septuagint of a large number of those words and phrases which he designated as specifically Lucan. The Lucan residuum being smaller, after subtraction of the Septuagint element, than he supposed, perhaps he ought to be content with the hypothesis of Lucan employment of a previously existing source, instead of insisting that Luke must have been the first to put the narrative in a Greek written form.

A second caution, moreover, needs to be borne in mind before Harnack's conclusion can be accepted in its entirety. May not some of the parallels between Lk. i-ii and the rest of Luke-Acts be explained as due probably to dependence of Luke upon various sources of a common type? With what part of Luke-Acts is Lk. i-ii to be compared in order to exhibit its completely Lucan char-

[10] See above, pp. 76 f.

acter? Obviously the comparison would best be made, if possible, with parts where Luke's own style appears in its purity. But this requirement is not certainly satisfied, for example, in the former part of Acts, especially in the speeches which are there attributed to Jewish Christians. Very probably Luke is there using sources, and sources of a Jewish Christian kind very much like the source that has been posited for Lk. i-ii. Therefore the affinity of Lk. i-ii with these early chapters in Acts does not necessarily prove full Lucan authorship. It may conceivably prove nothing more than authorship by a Jewish Christian, whose linguistic and religious environment was the same as that of the author or authors who produced the sources of Luke's account, in Acts, of the primitive Jerusalem Church.

Finally, even if Lk. i-ii is found to coincide in a certain usage with elements in Luke-Acts which may be admitted to be actually due to Luke himself, that still does not necessarily prove dependence of Lk. i-ii upon the Lucan usage in question. For the dependence may be the other way around. This possibility has indeed usually been neglected in the discussion of the subject. But such neglect is quite unjustifiable.

That Luke's style has been colored by at least one phrase in the Benedictus (regarded as a previously existing hymn) has already been shown to be possible,[11] and there is no good reason why the dependence may not have extended also to other parts of the infancy narrative.

One case of such possible dependence deserves special consideration. It is possible dependence upon the angelic doxology in Lk. ii.14. With that verse, which reads according to the correct text, "Glory to God in the highest, and on earth peace among men of [His] good pleasure,"[12] Gersdorf compared the latter part of Lk. xix.38, where the words of the multitude at the triumphal entry read, "In heaven peace, and glory in the highest."[13] These words are not in the other Gospels, but take the place in Luke of the "Hosanna in the highest"[14] of Matthew and Mark. But what is the relation between this Lucan addition and the angelic song in Lk. ii.14? The two have two things in common; the "glory in the highest" and the conjunction of this with "peace in. . . ." With regard to the former point, Ryle and James can cite an interesting parallel in the Psalms of Solomon: "glorious, dwelling in the highest."[15] This sug-

[11] See above, pp. 79 f.

[12] δόξα ἐν ὑψίστοις θεῷ καὶ ἐπὶ γῆς εἰρήνη ἐν ἀνθρώποις εὐδοκίας.

[13] ἐν οὐρανῷ εἰρήνη καὶ δόξα ἐν ὑψίστοις.

[14] ὡσαννὰ ἐν τοῖς ὑψίστοις.

[15] Psalms of Solomon, xviii.11 (xix.1). See Ryle and James, ΨΑΛΜΟΙ ΣΟΛΟΜΩΝΤΟΣ *Psalms of the Pharisees, commonly called Psalms of Solomon*, 1891, p. xcii. Compare Bruce in *Expositor's Greek Testament*, i, 1897, on Lk. ii.14; Resch, "Das Kindheitsevangelium," 1897, in *Texte und Untersuchungen*, x. 5, p. 47.

gests the possibility that the "glory in the highest" of Lk. ii.14 and of Lk. xix.38 may be quite independent. The idea was a natural one, and also the expression of it. The writer who first put the angelic song into Greek (supposing it to have existed first in Aramaic or Hebrew) may have written independently of the one who performed a similar service for whatever Semitic original there may have been for the words attributed to the multitude in Lk. xix.38. In the latter passage the "in the highest," at any rate, was already given, in the tradition lying back of the "Hosanna in the highest" of Matthew and Mark. The conjunction of "peace" with "glory in the highest" might also be explained as due to mere coincidence, especially since the order is reversed and since "peace" goes with "in heaven" in the first place and with "on earth" and "among men of [His] good pleasure" in the other.

However, in view of the rather striking parallel between the two passages, other solutions of the problem call for careful consideration. Wellhausen [16] is quite confident that Lk. ii.14 is dependent upon Lk. xix.38. This hypothesis, however, is apparently connected with the untenable [17] view that Lk. i-ii is an addition to the completed Gospel. The reverse hypothesis, that Lk. xix.38 is dependent upon Lk. ii.14, is favored by Holtzmann,[18] B. Weiss,[19] J. Weiss,[20] and Bruce.[21] In Lk. xix.38, Holtzmann supposes, the wording of the triumphant cry was exchanged for a reminiscence of the Gloria (Lk. ii.14), which had already become a hymn of the Christian congregation. There is nothing inherently impossible in this hypothesis, though if a correct view be held with regard to the date of the Gospel, the Gloria must have become a hymn of the Church long before Holtzmann would suppose to have been the case. If there is dependence, may it not be—rather than the reverse—dependence of the author of the Gospel, either upon the Gloria existing in separate form or else upon the Gloria already inserted in a source underlying Lk. i-ii?

Such dependence would not be irreconcilable with the trustworthiness of Luke as a historian. The cry of the multitude at the triumphal entry of Jesus into Jerusalem was not recorded, perhaps, with verbal exactness. Indeed, it was perhaps not stereotyped when it was first uttered. There were many persons who accompanied Jesus as He descended from the Mount of Olives; some, no doubt, said one thing, others another.[22] It is not surprising, therefore, that

[16] *Das Evangelium Lucae*, 1904, p. 109: "That Lk. xix.39 is the model for ii.14 cannot be doubted, although Weiss reverses the relationship."

[17] See above, Chapter II.

[18] *Hand-Commentar*, 3te Aufl., 1901, on Lk. xix.38.

[19] In Meyer's *Kommentar*, 9te Aufl., 1901, *in loc.*

[20] *Die Schriften des Neuen Testaments*, 3te Aufl., revised by Bousset, 1917, *in loc.*

[21] In *Expositor's Greek Testament*, 1897, *in loc.*

[22] Compare James Cooper, article "Hosanna," in Hastings, *Dictionary of Christ and the Gospels*, i, 1908, p. 750.

the tradition of what was said is not exactly uniform. The characteristic cry of the multitude—what was heard again and again during the descent into the city—might have impressed itself upon a hearer with greater or less fullness. The translation into Greek, moreover, necessarily brought divergence from the exact words that were spoken by any one person among the multitude. One Aramaic word, "Hosanna," has been preserved by three of the Evangelists. Luke, for the benefit of his Greek readers, may have substituted Greek words for it. His words, "in heaven peace, and glory in the highest," reproduce perhaps the general meaning of the "Hosanna in the highest" which has been preserved by Matthew and Mark. That latter phrase is not altogether clear to modern readers, as a glance at the commentaries will show; and possibly it may not have been clear to the first readers whom Luke had in view. In order to bring out the meaning of the original cry—that is, its real significance in the feeling of the original speakers—possibly literal translation was insufficient. There are cases where a certain amplification is the truest translation.

We are far, indeed, from affirming that this is the true way of explaining the divergence of Luke at this point from the other two Synoptic Gospels. To those who have not accepted without modification the current view of Luke's dependence solely upon Mark, it will seem more probable that Lk. xix. 38b is no mere amplification of "Hosanna in the highest," but rather a reproduction of independent tradition.

But the decision with regard to that question does not affect essentially the problem involved in the parallel with Lk. ii.14. For the tradition was not in the first place fixed in a Greek form; if it came to Luke in Greek, it came in a translation, which might be modified with more freedom than would have been permissible in the case of the wording in the original language. In any case, therefore, Luke may have made use of the words of the angelic doxology in determining the form, though not the content, of the triumphal cry as it was to appear in his Gospel. He may have done so consciously or unconsciously, more probably the latter. The song of the angels, as recorded in the infancy narrative, was, it may be held, familiar to him; the wording of it would then come naturally from his pen when he was putting the similar praise of the multitude into a form which would be both intelligible and impressive to himself and to his Greek readers.

Such a solution of the problem would be a compromise between two hypotheses; the hypothesis that Lk. ii.14 and Lk. xix.38 are completely independent of each other, and the hypothesis that the latter is dependent upon the former. The present form of Lk. xix.38, so the compromise hypothesis would hold, is partly due to a real coincidence in the praises originally rendered to God in the two cases, and partly to Luke's familiarity with the wording of the angelic hymn.

At any rate, the reverse hypothesis, that Luke received Lk. xix.38 in its present form, and then conformed the wording of the angelic hymn to it, is less probable. In view of what has just been said, Luke must be pronounced less likely to have conformed to something else the wording of the angelic hymn than the wording of the cry of the multitude; for in the former case the various special considerations that we have just adduced would not apply. At any rate, the view that Luke conformed Lk. ii.14 to the wording of Lk. xix.38 is very unlikely unless he was himself the first translator of the angelic song or of the whole narrative in which it is contained. In that case he may conceivably have allowed himself such freedom.

Against the view that he actually composed the angelic hymn himself various objections present themselves. For instance, the very bold Hebraism, "men of good pleasure,"[23] would be difficult to explain.

Enough, then, has been said to show that the similarity between Lk. ii.14 and Lk. xix.38 does not prove that Luke was the actual composer of the former. The most that could be held is that he was the first to put the angels' song into Greek. That would perhaps help to explain his familiarity with its wording and his natural employment of it in Lk. xix.38 without artificial imitation. But such an hypothesis is not necessary.

This instance may serve to show, not, indeed, that dependence of the rest of Luke-Acts upon a source underlying Lk. i-ii is certain, but that it is at least possible; so that for this reason, as for other reasons, even striking similarities of style between the infancy narrative and the rest of the work do not by any means indubitably prove that the author of the whole work composed that narrative without the use of sources. Some of those similarities may be due to dependence of the author in the rest of his work upon the language of the source that he used at the beginning.

It is true, the example which we have just discussed at some length is taken from a hymn—the angelic doxology—which may conceivably have existed in separate form; so that dependence upon that hymn would not necessarily prove dependence upon the infancy narrative as a whole. But who can say that this latter possibility must necessarily be ruled out of court? There is no real reason why the dependence of Luke should not be extended even to the narrative portions of Lk. i-ii, if he was really using a written source in that section of his Gospel. He was attracted, not unnaturally, by the simple grandeur and poetic dignity of the "Bible style," and followed, therefore, the Old Testament model,

[23] ἀνθρώποις εὐδοκίας.

as we have seen, in his own sacred narrative. But why should such linguistic influence have been exerted by the Old Testament alone? If Lk. i-ii is what at first sight it would seem to be, a poetic narrative produced on the very native soil of the Old Testament, at a time when the Old Testament type of language was still a living thing, and if this narrative fell into the hands of Luke, what would be more natural than that it, as well as the Old Testament, should impress itself permanently upon his mind and heart? Surely it is hardly inferior in beauty to the best of what the Old Testament can offer; and it is concerned with the events most stimulating to the Christian imagination. It may well have taken a place side by side with the Old Testament in moulding the literary gifts of the Greek historian for a sacred use.[24]

However, after all deductions have been made, the Lucan residuum in the style of Lk. i-ii remains amply sufficient to prove that the author of Luke-Acts certainly had a part in the production of the present form of the infancy narrative. Nothing that we have just been saying should be allowed to obscure that very important fact. Some of the "Lucan characteristics" discovered by Harnack were shown by our investigation of the Septuagint usage *not* to be also characteristic of the Septuagint. Many of them are to be found, moreover, not only in the former part of Acts, but also in the latter, and presumably more purely Lucan, part. Finally, some of them can be shown *not* to have been taken by Luke from Lk. i-ii, because they belong not to Semitizing Greek or even to popular Greek, but rather to the literary form of the Koiné. Hence Luke was certainly at least the editor of Lk. i-ii. That fact was established by Gersdorf one hundred years ago. It has been confirmed and not disproved by recent investigations—confirmed not only by Harnack, but also, we think, by our criticism of Harnack.

Thus the first (and perhaps the most important) result of the detailed examination to which in 1911 we tried to subject the argument which Harnack and Zimmermann had developed for detecting Lucan style in Lk. i-ii was a clear confirmation of that argument. In the birth narrative, we found, the hand of Luke has certainly been at work. Some of the supposed indications of Lucan style were eliminated; but the severity of the test exhibited only all the more clearly the cogency of the proof that remained.

[24] Compare Stanton, *The Gospels as Historical Documents*, ii, 1909, p. 291: "Luke may have been led to use the expressions in question [ἐγένετο, etc.] partly from his own familiarity with the LXX, partly from his having become accustomed to them in copying this document at the beginning." Compare also Feine, *Eine vorkanonische Überlieferung des Lukas*, 1891, p. 20: "The source which we are tracing is used only in this one Gospel; we have therefore no standard for judging it outside of the Third Gospel. Moreover, if this source bore a Hebraistic stamp, Luke himself also introduced Hebraizing turns of expression in his two writings, and also knew how to assimilate the linguistic material of his sources and use it further in an independent way."

On the other hand, however, the investigation resulted in a deepened impression of the affinity of Lk. i-ii for the Septuagint. Many of the supposed Lucan characteristics were shown to be merely characteristics of the Septuagint. Of course Harnack himself admitted the presence of a large Septuagint element in the language and style of Lk. i-ii. But our investigation showed that element to be much larger than Harnack supposed.

This remarkable affinity of Lk. i-ii with the language of the Old Testament points clearly to a Jewish Christian origin of the narrative. We are not forgetting that from the very beginning the Old Testament Scriptures were accepted as authoritative by the Gentile Christian Church as well as by the Jewish Christian Church. But an examination of patristic literature will show that despite the fact that the Old Testament was universally accepted as authoritative, and despite the fact that it is quoted at great length by the patristic writers, yet the style of the Gentile Christian writers remained their own and was by no means so suffused with Septuagint usages as is the case in Lk. i-ii. The close similarity of the language of Lk. i-ii to the language of the Old Testament does, therefore, still require some special explanation.

Moreover, our detailed examination only served to exhibit anew the Palestinian character of the narrative. That Palestinian character does not appear merely in those words and phrases that are also found in the Septuagint, but runs through the whole section. It appears, moreover, as we have seen,[25] not merely in the language but also in the thought. Recent researches have not in the slightest served to modify the first impression made upon an unprejudiced reader that we have in this section a genuinely Jewish and Palestinian narrative.

Even Harnack does not altogether deny the correctness of that impression; for although he holds that the narrative was composed by the Gentile Christian, Luke, he admits at the same time that in composing it Luke made use of Palestinian tradition. It must be remembered that according to Harnack the author of Luke-Acts was actually Luke the physician, a man who was demonstrably in Palestine at the beginning and end of the two years that Paul spent in prison at Cæsarea, and who, because of personal associations, would have had abundant opportunity to acquaint himself both then and at other times with what Palestinian disciples were saying. Harnack holds that the stories about John the Baptist which appear in the Lucan infancy narrative must have originated in a circle of John's disciples; and that the stories about Jesus must have come to Luke with the claim of having been derived from Mary, and therefore must certainly have come from Palestine.[26]

[25] See above, pp. 63-74.

[26] Harnack, *Neue Untersuchungen zur Apostelgeschichte*, 1911, pp. 108–110 (English translation, *The Date of the Acts and of the Synoptic Gospels*, 1911, pp. 153–156). See below, pp. 166–168.

What, then, is our conclusion regarding the hypothesis that Lk. i-ii was composed by the author of Luke-Acts himself without the use of written sources? That hypothesis, as we have already seen, must emphatically be rejected so far as the hymns are concerned. But with regard to the bulk of the narrative, the answer is not so simple. One form in which the hypothesis might be held must indeed certainly be excluded. Luke certainly did not compose the narrative simply by artificial imitation of the Septuagint and artificial adaptation of the details to Palestinian conditions of which he had no first-hand knowledge. Such a refinement of art is almost inconceivable in an ancient writer. If, therefore, the author of Luke-Acts actually composed the birth narrative himself, he must have been himself in close touch with Palestinian conditions. This supposition is by no means unnatural. Harnack [27] can even suggest that before he united himself with the Christian community the author of Luke-Acts had belonged to the disciples of John the Baptist and had already pursued investigations which he afterwards used for his Gospel. However that may be, he certainly—supposing him to be the person who speaks of himself in the first person in the we-sections of the Book of Acts—came to Palestine at the time of Paul's last visit to Jerusalem. At that time, or on previous occasions of which nothing definite is known, he may have acquainted himself intimately with Palestinian conditions. And certainly he may have come into possession of definite Palestinian tradition with regard to the birth of John and Jesus. If so—if he had himself been in Palestine, if he had come into possession of Palestinian oral tradition—and if, moreover, he put that tradition into written form without any long delay, then conceivably he might have composed the birth narrative without the aid of written sources. In this form, the hypothesis is perfectly possible. It was by no means rejected categorically when we examined the narrative in detail. All that was maintained is that the hypothesis has not been proved; all that we maintained (at this point) against Harnack is that the non-Semitic Lucan element in Lk. i-ii is insufficient to exclude the possibility, at least, of written sources.

The important thing to observe is that if Luke was the first to put the Lucan birth narrative into written form, even then the genuinely primitive Palestinian character of Lk. i-ii cannot be denied. If Harnack is right, if the linguistic phenomena show that Luke was the original author of Lk. i-ii, that proves not that Lk. i-ii is late, but that the whole of Luke-Acts is early. If it can be proved that this section was composed by the author of Luke-Acts, then we have simply one more weighty argument in favor of the Lucan authorship and early date of the entire work. The hypothesis that Luke composed

[27] *Op. cit.*, 1911, pp. 108 f. (English translation, pp. 153 f.).

Lk. i-ii on the basis of primitive Palestinian oral tradition, aided by first-hand acquaintance with Palestinian conditions, is very attractive. It explains admirably many of the facts. It may well be correct. But it has not been proved.

A second hypothesis to be considered is that for Lk. i-ii Luke himself translated an Aramaic written source.[28] This hypothesis would explain on the one hand the thoroughly Palestinian character of the content of Lk. i-ii and on the other hand the undeniable Lucan elements in the style. That Luke should have known sufficient Aramaic to translate an Aramaic document can hardly be pronounced impossible. Thus Harnack, who himself is inclined to reject the hypothesis of an Aramaic source for Lk. i-ii, supposes that Luke may have translated an Aramaic document in the early part of Acts, and adds that knowledge of Aramaic sufficient to translate a simple Aramaic text may well be attributed to a native of Antioch (as Harnack thinks Luke to have been) and a companion of Paul.[29] This hypothesis is possible. But like the first hypothesis it cannot be proved.[30]

The third hypothesis is that Luke employed a Greek written source. Our examination of the linguistic phenomena showed that this hypothesis, like the two others, is possible. After deducting from the language of Lk. i-ii what is characteristic of the Septuagint and what is natural in a Jewish Christian document, the Lucan element that remains is insufficient to prove anything more than Lucan revision of a previously existing document, though on the other hand it is sufficient to render actual Lucan composition—with the qualifications that we have noted above—also possible. The hypothesis of a Greek written source, like the other two hypotheses, is possible, but not certain.

If Luke was using in Lk. i-ii a Greek written source, then the source may have been composed originally in Greek, or the Greek form in which Luke used it may have been produced by previous translation from Hebrew or Aramaic.

[28] This view is held by Zimmermann, *op. cit.*, pp. 267–273.

[29] Harnack, *Lukas der Arzt*, 1906, p. 84, footnote 3 (English translation, *Luke the Physician*, 1907, p. 119, footnote 2). Compare Vogel, *op. cit.*, p. 14. For an opposite view of the Semitic attainments of Luke, see Dalman, *Die Worte Jesu*, 1898, p. 32 (English translation, *The Words of Jesus*, 1902, p. 40 f.). Compare Zahn, *Einleitung in das Neue Testament*, 3te Aufl., ii, 1907, pp. 408, 421, 430 (English translation, *Introduction to the New Testament*, iii, 1909, pp. 107 f., 129, 141.

[30] The hypothesis that Luke himself translated a Semitic document in Lk. i–ii is upheld by C. C. Torrey ("The Translations Made from the Original Aramaic Gospels," in *Studies in the History of Religions Presented to Crawford Howell Toy*, 1912, pp. 285–295). But Torrey thinks that the Semitic document was Hebrew, not Aramaic. This suggestion is worthy of consideration. That the author of Luke-Acts should have known Hebrew is perhaps less likely than that he should have known Aramaic; but in view of our ignorance concerning his birth and education, it cannot, perhaps, be pronounced impossible.

According to Resch,[31] Gunkel,[32] and C. C. Torrey,[33] the source was originally composed in Hebrew. That view would no doubt explain admirably the linguistic phenomena; for in the opinion of an expert like Dalman [34] a number of the Semitisms in Lk. i-ii—for example, the familiar narrative use of the phrase, "it came to pass"—are Hebraisms, not Aramaisms. But is it likely that such a narrative should have been composed in Hebrew in the first century after Christ? At that time Hebrew seems to have long ceased to be the ordinary language of Palestine.[35] Yet it also seems to have remained in use as the language of certain kinds of literature.[36] Perhaps we may say that if Lk. i-ii was originally written in Hebrew, then it was probably intended from the first to be in some sort a sacred narrative, for which the sacred language would be the fittest vehicle. In view of the lofty, poetical tone of the narrative, comparable to the best parts of the Old Testament, such a supposition is by no means impossible. The necessary knowledge of Hebrew would not have been lacking; for, despite linguistic changes among the people, the Old Testament continued to be read and studied in its original language. It is true, however, that the earliest Christian community, despite the presence of many priests,[37] was probably composed chiefly of persons who, in the sense that was true of the apostles,[38] were "unlearned and ignorant men." And in such a community the employment of the ordinary language of the country for such a work as the source of Lk. i-ii may perhaps be regarded as more natural than the employment of Hebrew.

The Hebraisms (as distinguished from Aramaisms) of Lk. i-ii have not always been regarded as overbalancing these *a priori* considerations. Indeed, they have sometimes been regarded as furnishing an argument not for, but positively against, any Semitic original for the narrative. For, it is said, Hebraisms are not Aramaisms; they might establish a Hebrew original, but certainly not an Aramaic original. But if a Hebrew original, it is argued, is impossible in view of the linguistic conditions prevailing in Palestine in the first century after

[31] "Das Kindheitsevangelium," in *Texte und Untersuchungen*, x. 5, 1897.

[32] *Zum religionsgeschichtlichen Verständnis des Neuen Testaments*, 1903, p. 67. According to Gunkel it is "very probable" that the narrative goes back to a Hebrew original.

[33] *Loc. cit.* It will be remembered (see above, note 30) that Torrey thinks that the Hebrew source was translated not by some previous translator, but by Luke himself.

[34] Compare C. C. Torrey, *op. cit.*, pp. 292 ff.

[35] Dalman, *op. cit.*, pp. 1–10 (English translation, pp. 1–12); Zahn, *op. cit.*, i, pp. 1–24 (English translation, i, pp. 1–33); Schürer, *Geschichte des jüdischen Volkes*, 4te Aufl., ii, 1907, pp. 23–21 (English translation, *A History of the Jewish People*, II. i, 1885, pp. 8–10).

[36] Dalman, *op. cit.*, pp. 10–13 (English translation, pp. 12–16).

[37] Acts vi.7.

[38] Acts iv.13. That sense is by no means exactly the one that we attach to the corresponding English words.

Christ, then the Hebraisms still require explanation. According to Dalman, they can be explained only as due to the Septuagint; in other words, they are not really Hebraisms, but "Septuagint Græcisms" or "Greek Biblicisms."[39] Of course the Hebraisms might conceivably be explained as due to an influence exerted upon the Aramaic of the source by the Hebrew Old Testament. The apparent Hebraisms would then be Aramaic Biblicisms. Thus, although the familiar Hebraistic phrase, "it came to pass," has no equivalent in the living Aramaic, yet in the (Aramaic) Targums the Hebrew usage is imitated.[40] It might have been imitated also in the Aramaic source of Lk. i-ii. But this Dalman regards as improbable, because (he evidently thinks) the imitation of a Targum is hardly to be attributed to Christian writers.[41] In general, says Dalman,[42] "the Jewish Aramaic, as it lived among the people, displayed even less tendency to adopt Hebrew expressions than did the Greek of the Synoptic Gospels." Hence Dalman can even enunciate the principle for the literary criticism of the New Testament: "the more Hebraisms, so much the more activity of Hellenistic redactors."[43] The Hebraisms in Lk. i-ii are thus made to afford merely another support for the view of Dalman that the narrative was originally composed in Greek.

Such questions certainly cannot be settled without first-hand knowledge of the dialects of Palestine. But even if one accepts most of what Dalman says with regard to these dialects, the possibility of an Aramaic source[44] does not seem to be altogether excluded. In the first place, it might be maintained (against Dalman) that the Aramaic source imitated the Hebrew of the Old Testament. That supposition, which certainly does not seem altogether unlikely, would explain some or all of the non-Aramaic Hebraisms of Lk. i-ii. Or else, in the second place, these non-Aramaic Hebraisms might be explained by imitation of the Septuagint on the part of the Greek translator.[45]

At any rate, if Lk. i-ii was composed originally in Greek, it was composed by some one thoroughly familiar with Palestinian conditions and in all prob-

[39] Dalman, *op. cit.*, p. 33 (English translation, pp. 41 f.).

[40] Dalman, *op. cit.*, pp. 25 f. (English translation, pp. 32 f.).

[41] Dalman, *op. cit.*, p. 16 (English translation, p. 20).

[42] *Op. cit.*, p. 34 (English translation, p. 42).

[43] Dalman, *loc. cit.*

[44] That the source was originally composed in Aramaic was designated by Klostermann, in the first edition of his commentary (*Handbuch zum Neuen Testament*, II. i, 1919, p. 364), as being the majority opinion. He cited in favor of it Plummer, Bousset, Gressmann.

[45] What has just been said about the possibility that Luke's source was originally written in Aramaic has obvious importance also for the hypothesis (discussed above) that Luke himself translated an Aramaic document.

ability in the very early days of the Jerusalem Church.[46] So much has been established by what has been said above about the Palestinian character both of the form and of the content of the narrative. That such a primitive Jewish Christian narrative should have been written in Greek is by no means impossible. The earliest Christian community at Jerusalem, which is described in the first chapters of Acts, was composed, to a very considerable extent, of Greek-speaking Jews.[47]

Some scholars have attempted to establish a Semitic original for Lk. i-ii by pointing out mistakes in translation in the extant Greek narrative. Gunkel[48] regards "Christ the Lord"[49] in Lk. ii.11 as the clearest indication of a Hebrew original. It looks, he thinks, like a mistranslation of "the Lord's anointed,"[50] which is certainly mistranslated thus in the Septuagint of Lam. iv.20. "Christ the Lord"—so no doubt Gunkel reasons, is an unprecedented phrase on Semitic ground; whereas a Christian translator, to whom the title "Lord" seemed natural as applied to Christ, would very naturally take the Hebrew phrase in this way. But the phrase, "Christ the Lord," in Greek occurs also in the Psalms of Solomon, xvii.36. It is true, some scholars have regarded it there also as a mistranslation. Nevertheless, every additional occurrence of the phrase makes the theory of mistranslation less likely.[51] Dalman,[52] who has been followed by Loisy,[53] supposes that "the Lord" was added by the Evangelist to explain "Christ," which is used here for the first time in the Gospel. The matter is problematical at best. "Christ the Lord" may well be a correct translation of the source. That the tense of the verb in the clause, "seeing I know not a man,"[54] in Lk. i.34 is due to a mistranslation has also not been proved. That passage will be discussed in the next chapter.

Our general conclusion is that many questions with regard to Lk. i-ii must be left undecided. It is uncertain whether the narrative was composed by Luke himself merely on the basis of Aramaic oral tradition (though we think that less likely), or whether he himself translated a Semitic document, or whether

[46] If, indeed, Luke himself was the composer of the narrative—a possibility which we have not entirely excluded—the date would have o be put a little later, unless Luke should be supposed to have composed the narrative during some early stay in Palestine and then incorporated it at a later time in his Gospel. But if Luke was not the composer, there is not the slightest reason to put the date of composition later than the very early days of the Jerusalem Church.

[47] Acts vi.1.

[48] *Zum religionsgeschichtlichen Verständnis des Neuen Testaments*, 1903, p. 67.

[49] Χριστὸς κύριος.

[50] As the phrase appears in the Hebrew Old Testament.

[51] See the defence of the correctness of the translation in Ps. Sol., xvii.36 by Ryle and James, *in loc.*

[52] *Op. cit.*, p. 249 (English translation, pp. 303 f.).

[53] *Les Évangiles synoptiques*, i, 1907, pp. 350 f., footnote 3.

[54] ἐπεὶ ἄνδρα οὐ γινώσκω.

he used a Greek written source. It is also uncertain whether the source, if it came into Luke's hands in a Greek form, was composed originally in Greek, or in Hebrew, or in Aramaic. But in the midst of so much uncertainty, two facts stand out clear. In the first place, the birth narrative formed an original part of the Third Gospel; and in the second place, it is genuinely primitive and Palestinian. These two facts are quite independent of the disputed questions. And they are the really important facts.

Chapter VI

THE INTEGRITY OF THE LUCAN NARRATIVE[1]

IT HAS been shown in the last three chapters that the Lucan narrative of the birth and infancy of Jesus in Lk. i.5-ii.52 is strikingly Jewish and Palestinian both in form and in content. That narrative attests the virgin birth of Christ. But if so, a serious difficulty emerges for those who deny the historicity of the virgin birth. It will be observed in Chapter XIV of our discussion that when the fact of the virgin birth is rejected, the idea of the virgin birth is usually thought to have been derived from pagan sources. The question then becomes acute how such a pagan idea could have found a place just in the most strikingly Jewish and Palestinian narrative in the whole New Testament.

This question has been answered by many modern scholars by a theory of interpolation. It is perfectly true, they say, that Lk. i.5-ii.52 is of Palestinian origin; and it is perfectly true that an attestation of the virgin birth now stands in that narrative; but, they say, that attestation of the virgin birth formed no original part of the narrative, but came into it by interpolation.

It would be difficult to exaggerate the importance of this question; indeed, we may fairly say that if the interpolation theory is incorrect the most prominent modern reconstruction proposed in opposition to the historicity of the virgin birth falls to the ground. The view as to the origin of the idea of the virgin birth which has been most widely held by those modern historians who deny the fact of the virgin birth stands or falls with the interpolation theory.

The interpolation theory[2] has been held in various forms. A classification of these various forms is possible from two points of view.

The first point of view concerns the sense in which the supposed interpolation is to be called an interpolation. A threefold division is here possible. In the first place, the interpolation may be regarded as an interpolation into the completed Gospel, a gloss introduced into the Third Gospel at some point

[1] This chapter reproduces with some additions, the article, "The Integrity of the Lucan Narrative of the Annunciation," in *Princeton Theological Review*, xxv, 1927, pp. 529–586.

[2] Compare "The New Testament Account of the Birth of Jesus," second article, in *Princeton Theological Review*, iv, 1906, pp. 50–61.

in the manuscript transmission. In the second place, the interpolation may be regarded as an interpolation made by the author of the Gospel himself into a Jewish Christian source which elsewhere he is following closely. In this case the words attesting the virgin birth would be an original part of the Gospel, but would not belong to the underlying Jewish Christian narrative. In the third place, the interpolation may be regarded as an interpolation made by the author himself, not into a source, but into the completed Gospel—that is, the author first finished the Gospel without including the virgin birth, and then inserted the virgin birth as an afterthought. This third possibility has been suggested—for the first time so far as we know—by Vincent Taylor, the author of the latest important monograph on the subject.[3]

The second point of view from which a classification is possible concerns the extent of the supposed interpolation. Whether the interpolation is to be regarded as an interpolation into the completed Gospel by a scribe, or into the source by the author of the Gospel, or into the completed Gospel by the author of the Gospel, how much is to be regarded as interpolated?

With regard to this latter question, there have been various opinions. The earliest and probably still the commonest view is that the interpolation embraces verses 34 and 35 of the first chapter. That view received its first systematic grounding from Hillmann in 1891.[4] It has since then been advocated by Usener, Harnack, Zimmermann, Schmiedel, Pfleiderer, Conybeare, Loisy, and others. A second view was suggested by Kattenbusch[5] and defended by Weinel.[6] It is to the effect that only the words, "seeing I know not a man,"[7] in Lk. i.34, are to be eliminated. A third view includes verses 36 and 37 with verses 34 and 35 in the supposed interpolation.[8]

With regard to the former classification—that is, the classification according to the sense in which the supposed interpolation is to be taken as an interpolation—it may be noticed at the start that the first view, which regards the interpolation as an interpolation made by a scribe into the completed Gospel, is opposed by the weight of manuscript attestation. There is really no external evidence worthy the name for the view that Lk. i.34, 35, or any part of it, is an interpolation. Manuscript b of the Old Latin Version, it is true, does substi-

[3] Vincent Taylor, *The Historical Evidence for the Virgin Birth*, 1920.

[4] Hillmann, "Die Kindheitsgeschichte Jesu nach Lucas," in *Jahrbücher für protestantische Theologie*, xvii, 1891, pp. 213–231.

[5] *Das Apostolische Symbol*, ii, 1900, pp. 621 f., 666–668 (Anm. 300).

[6] "Die Auslegung des Apostolischen Bekenntnisses von F. Kattenbusch und die neutestamentliche Forschung," in *Zeitschrift für die neutestamentliche Wissenschaft*, ii, 1901, pp. 37–39.

[7] ἐπεὶ ἄνδρα οὐ γινώσκω.

[8] So Bultmann, *op. cit.*, 1931, pp. 321 f. Clemen (*Religionsgeschichtliche Erklärung des Neuen Testaments*, 2te Aufl., 1924, p. 116) includes in the supposed interpolation even verse 38.

tute for verse 34 the words of verse 38: "And Mary said, Behold the handmaid of the Lord; be it unto me according to thy word," and then omits these words in verse 38; while manuscript e, also of the Old Latin Version, though it retains verse 34, agrees with b in the omission at verse 38.[9] But the omission of verse 34 by b is entirely isolated among the manuscripts of the New Testament; and never was a reading more clearly secondary.[10] As for the omission of the clause, "seeing I know not a man," in a quotation of the passage by John of Damascus in the eighth century, it is exceedingly doubtful whether the omission really represents anything that stood in manuscripts used by this writer; and in any case the testimony is too late to be of importance.[11]

Thus the unanimity of manuscript evidence for the inclusion of Lk. i.34, 35 is practically unbroken. And, in view of the many widely divergent lines of transmission in which the text of the Gospel has come down to us, it is difficult to see how such unanimity could have arisen if the verses were interpolated in the course of the transmission.

This argument, of course, applies only to that form of the interpolation hypothesis which regards the supposed insertion as having been made into the completed Gospel. It does not apply to the view that the author of the Gospel himself made the insertion into the narrative derived from his source or into the Gospel which he had already written but had not published. But possibly these forms of the hypothesis may be found to be faced by special difficulties of their own.

At any rate, what we shall now do is to examine these three forms of the interpolation hypothesis so far as possible together—noting, of course, as we go along, the cases where any particular argument applies only to one or to two of the three forms rather than to all.

[9] The reading of b was inaccurately cited in the first issue of the present book and that of e was not noticed. The author is grateful to J. S. Bezzant (in *The Modern Churchman*, xxi, 1931, p. 95, and in *Journal of Theological Studies*, xxxiii, 1931, p. 73) for pointing out the error.

[10] If it was not a mere careless blunder due to the fact that verses 34 and 38 begin with the same words (so A. C. Headlam, in *The Guardian* for March 25, 1903, p. 432), it was a pious emendation due to the desire of a scribe to save Mary from the appearance of unbelief which might be produced by her question in verse 34 (so, apparently, Zahn, *in loc.*). In substituting for the difficult words in verse 34 the eminently edifying words of submission in verse 38, the author of this reading has pursued the same tendency as that which is pursued by this same manuscript b and other Old Latin manuscripts (including e) in avoiding the word "father," as designating Joseph's relation to Jesus, at Lk. ii.33. It is strange to find Streeter (*The Four Gospels*, fourth impression, 1930, pp. 267 f., 525) so much inclined to attach importance to a reading which, if not an accidental blunder, is clearly an emendation made in the interests of the high dignity of the Virgin Mary. On the reading of b, see Headlam, *loc. cit.*, and in *The Guardian*, for April 8, 1903, pp. 501 f.; also Allen, in *The Interpreter*, i, 1905, pp. 116–118.

[11] A. C. Headlam (in *The Guardian*, for March 25, 1903, p. 432) thinks that the omission was "either accidental or due to a natural feeling of reticence."

The first consideration which we may notice as having been adduced in favor of the interpolation theory is of a general character. The rest of the narrative, it is said, outside of Lk. i.34, 35, is perfectly compatible with a birth of Jesus simply as the son of Joseph and Mary, indeed it is even contradictory to the notion of a virgin birth; if, therefore, we accomplish the simple deletion of these two verses, all inconsistency is removed and the story becomes perfectly smooth and easy.

With regard to this argument, it should be noticed, in the first place, that the simple deletion of Lk. i.34, 35 will not remove the virgin birth from the Third Gospel in general, or from the infancy narrative in particular; for the virgin birth is clearly implied in several other places.

The first of these places is found at Lk. i.26 f., where it is said: "And in the sixth month the angel Gabriel was sent from God unto a city of Galilee whose name was Nazareth, to a virgin betrothed to a man whose name was Joseph, of the house of David, and the name of the virgin was Mary.". Here Mary is twice called a virgin, and in what follows nothing whatever is said about her marriage to Joseph. This phenomenon is perfectly natural if the virgin birth was in the mind of the narrator, but it is very unnatural if the reverse is the case. Advocates of the interpolation theory are therefore compelled to offer some explanation of the language in Lk. i.27.

Two explanations are open to them. In the first place, it may be said that verse 27 has been tampered with by the same interpolator who inserted verses 34, 35, and that originally Mary was not here called a virgin. But against this explanation may be urged the fact that the word "virgin" occurs twice in the verse, and that if that word was not originally there the whole structure of the verse must have been different. The second possible explanation is that although the form of verse 27 which we now have is the original form—that is, although Mary was really designated there as a virgin—yet the mention of her marriage to Joseph has been omitted, by the interpolator of Lk. 1.34, 35, from the subsequent narrative. But it may be doubted whether this explanation quite accomplishes the purpose for which it is proposed. Even if the writer of Lk. i.27 were intending to introduce later on a mention of Mary's marriage to Joseph, his designation of her as a virgin would seem to be unnatural. In the Old Testament narratives of heavenly annunciations, the annunciations are represented as being made to married women; and if the narrator of Lk. i-ii intended the promised son to be regarded as having a human father as well as a human mother, as in those Old Testament narratives, why did he not, as is done there, represent the annunciation as being made to a married woman?

Why does he insist so particularly, by a repetition of the word, that it was made to Mary when she was a "virgin"? It must be remembered that according to all, or nearly all, of the advocates of the interpolation theory, the narrative is quite unhistorical; so that the narrator, according to their view, was not hampered by any historical consideration from placing the annunciation either before or after the marriage, exactly as he pleased. Why then does he insist so particularly that it took place before the marriage, or while Mary was still a "virgin," instead of representing it as taking place after the marriage? Surely this latter representation would have been far more natural, as well as more in accord with Old Testament analogy, if the narrator really intended the promised son to be regarded as being, in a physical sense, the son of Joseph.

A possible answer to this argument of ours might be based upon Lk. ii.7, where it is said that Jesus was the "firstborn son" of Mary, and upon Lk. ii.23, where there is recorded compliance in the case of Jesus with the Old Testament provisions about the firstborn. Perhaps, the advocates of the interpolation hypothesis might say, the emphasis in Lk. i.27 upon the virginity of Mary at the time when the annunciation was made to her, is due only to the desire of the narrator to show that she had not previously had children. But we do not think that this answer is satisfactory. Isaac was the firstborn son of his mother Sarah, in accordance with the Old Testament narrative; and yet the annunciation of his birth is represented as having come to his mother when she was already married. Similar is the case also with the birth of Samson and of Samuel. Why could not these models have been followed by the narrator of the birth of Jesus? Surely he could have represented Jesus as the firstborn son without placing the annunciation, in so unnatural and unprecedented a way, before instead of after His mother's marriage.

At any rate, whether we are correct or not in regarding this second explanation of Lk. i.27 as inadequate, it should be noticed that both explanations result in an overloading of the interpolation hypothesis. Whether it be held that Lk. i.27 has been tampered with, or that something has been removed by the interpolator at a later point in the narrative, in either case the activities of the interpolator must be regarded as having extended further than was at first maintained. What becomes, then, of the initial argument that a simple removal of Lk. i.34, 35 will suffice to make the narrative all perfectly smooth and easy as a narrative representing Jesus as being in a physical sense the son of Joseph?

Moreover, Lk. i.27 is not the only verse which requires explanation if Lk. i.34, 35 be removed. What shall be done with Lk. ii.5, which reads:

"to be enrolled with Mary who was betrothed to him, being great with child"? How could Mary be said to be only betrothed to Joseph, when she was already great with child? Certainly this form of expression, coming from a narrator who of course intended to record nothing derogatory to the honor of Mary, implies the virgin birth in the clearest possible way.

It is true, the matter is complicated in this case, as it was not in the case of Lk. i.27, by variants in the extant manuscript transmission. The reading, "who was betrothed to him," appears, indeed, in the best Greek uncials, including the typical representatives of the "Neutral" type of text, the Codex Vaticanus and the Codex Sinaiticus. It also appears in the Codex Bezæ, which is a representative of the "Western" type of text, and in a number of the versions. But certain manuscripts of the Old Latin Version and the "Sinaitic Syriac" manuscript of the Old Syriac Version read "his wife"; and a number of the later uncials with the mass of the cursive manuscripts, representing what Westcott and Hort called the "Syrian revision," read "his betrothed wife."

This last reading is generally rejected as being a "conflate reading"; evidently, it is held, some scribe combined the reading "betrothed" with the reading "wife" to make the reading "betrothed wife." But what decision shall be reached as between the other two readings?

The external evidence certainly seems to favor the reading "betrothed," which appears in the great early uncials, representative of the "Neutral" type of text, whereas the reading "wife" appears in no Greek manuscript at all, but is attested only in Latin and in Syriac. Despite all that has been said in criticism of Westcott and Hort's high estimate of the Neutral text, recent investigation has not really succeeded in invalidating that estimate.

Nevertheless, the combination of important Old Latin manuscripts with the Sinaitic Syriac in favor of the reading "wife" shows that that reading was in existence at a rather early time. It must, therefore, at least be given consideration.[12]

At first sight, transcriptional probability might seem to be in favor of it. If Mary at this point was in the original text spoken of as Joseph's "wife," it is possible to conceive of some scribe, who was eager to protect the virginity of Mary from any possible misunderstanding, as being offended by the word "wife" and so as substituting the word "betrothed" for it.

[12] The reading γυναικί, "wife," is favored by a number of recent scholars—for example, by Gressmann (*Das Weihnachts-Evangelium*, 1914, pp. 10 f.). It was favored by Hillmann, *op. cit.*, 1891, pp. 216 f. It is opposed, for example, by Holtzmann, *Die Synoptiker*, 3te Aufl., 1901, pp. 317 f., who thinks that ἐμνηστευμένῃ is probably to be read.

But it is possible also to look at the matter in a different light. If the word "betrothed" is read in this verse, then at least a verbal contradiction arises as over against the Gospel of Matthew; for without doubt Matthew lays great stress upon the fact that when Jesus was born Mary was in a legal sense not merely betrothed to Joseph, but actually his wife. The contradiction need not indeed be anything more than formal; for there is no reason why Luke may not be using a terminology different from that of Matthew, so that by the word "betrothed" he is designating the extraordinary relationship which according to Matthew prevailed after Joseph had obeyed the instructions of the angel—that is, the relationship in which Mary was legally the wife of Joseph but in which he "knew her not until she had borne a son." [13] But although the contradiction may not actually be more than formal, it might well have seemed serious to a devout scribe. The change from "betrothed" to "wife" may therefore fall into the category of "harmonistic corruptions."

This hypothesis, we think, is more probable than the alternative hypothesis, that "wife" was changed to "betrothed" for doctrinal reasons. Transcriptional considerations are thus not opposed to the reading of the Neutral text, and that reading should in all probability be regarded as correct.[14]

But if the reading "betrothed" at Lk. ii.5 is thus part of the earliest transmitted text, we have another overloading of the interpolation hypothesis with regard to Lk. i.34, 35: the advocates of that hypothesis must suppose that the interpolator tampered with Lk. ii.5 as well as with Lk. i.27 or with a supposed subsequent passage mentioning the marriage of Mary to Joseph. Obviously the removal of all mention of the virgin birth from Lk. i-ii is by no means so simple a matter as was at first supposed.

There is, of course, still another place in the Third Gospel where the virgin birth is clearly alluded to—namely, Lk. iii.23. The words, "as was supposed," in that verse—"being, as was supposed, the son of Joseph"—clearly imply that

[13] Mt. i.25. Compare Origen, *hom. in Luc.*, vi (ed. Lommatzsch, v, 1835, p. 104): "si enim non habuisset sponsum et, ut putabatur, virum. . . ."

[14] Loisy (*Les Évangiles synoptiques*, i, 1907, p. 348) supposes that "wife" in Lk. ii.5 was the original reading of the source, but that the Evangelist substituted "betrothed." The Evangelist, according to Loisy, would have no difficulty with the word "betrothed" because of the view that he had of the marriage: he supposed that both Joseph and Mary were determined to preserve Mary's virginity (*op. cit.*, i, pp. 270 f., 301), so that even the annunciation, according to him, may have taken place after Mary was already living in Joseph's house. This hypothesis regarding the marriage is faced with serious difficulties. See below, pp. 143 f. So far as the solution of the textual problem is concerned, it must be pronounced very unlikely that the reading of the source should have crept into manuscripts of the completed Gospel. Thus the change from "betrothed" to "wife" in certain manuscripts would still have to be explained as merely a harmonistic corruption, as indeed Loisy himself seems to explain it.

Jesus was only "supposed" to be the son (in the full sense) of Joseph, and that really his relationship to Joseph was of a different kind.

In this case there is no manuscript evidence for the omission of the words; the words appear in all the extant witnesses to the text, the variants (of order and the like) being unimportant for the matter now under discussion. The verse, therefore, constitutes an additional weight upon at least one form of the interpolation theory regarding Lk. i.34, 35; it constitutes a weight upon the hypothesis that those verses are an interpolation into the completed Gospel. For if Lk. i.34, 35 is an interpolation, the words, "as was supposed," in Lk. iii.23 must also be an interpolation; and the more numerous such interpolations are thought to be, the more difficult does it become to explain the disappearance from the many lines of documentary attestation of all traces of the original, uninterpolated text.

Of course, this verse, Lk. iii.23, has no bearing against the other principal form of the interpolation hypothesis, which supposes that the interpolation of Lk. i.34, 35 was made by the author of the Gospel himself into his source; for Lk. iii.23 does not stand within the infancy narrative. But even that form of the hypothesis is faced, as we have seen, by the difficulties presented by Lk. i.27 and ii.5. Thus it is not correct to say that if the one passage, Lk. i.34, 35, were deleted, the attestation of the virgin birth would be removed from the Lucan infancy narrative. If that passage is an interpolation, then at least one and probably two other passages must also be regarded as having been tampered with. But obviously every addition of such ancillary suppositions renders the original hypothesis less plausible.

Nevertheless, the advocates of the interpolation hypothesis may still insist that, although one or two verses in the infancy narrative outside of Lk. i.34, 35 do imply the virgin birth, yet the bulk of the narrative proceeds upon the opposite assumption that Jesus was the son of Joseph by ordinary generation. The arguments in favor of this contention may perhaps be classified under three heads. In the first place, it is said, the narrative traces the Davidic descent of Jesus through Joseph, not through Mary, so that it must regard Joseph as His father. In the second place, Joseph is actually spoken of in several places as the "father" of Jesus, and Joseph and Mary are spoken of as His "parents." In the third place, there is attributed to Mary in certain places a lack of comprehension, which, it is said, would be unnatural if she knew her son to have been conceived by the Holy Ghost.

The fact upon which the first of these arguments is based should probably be admitted; it is probably true that the Lucan infancy narrative traces the Davidic descent of Jesus through Joseph. Whether it does so depends to a considerable extent upon the interpretation of Lk. i.27.[15] Do the words, "of the house of David," in that verse refer to Joseph or to Mary?[16] It seems more natural to regard them as referring to Joseph. This is so for two reasons. In the first place, the words come immediately after the name of Joseph: and, in the second place, repetition of the noun, "the virgin," would not have been necessary at the end of the verse if Mary had just been referred to in the preceding clause; if "of the house of David" referred to Mary, the wording would be simply, "to a virgin betrothed to a man whose name was Joseph, of the house of David, and her name was Mary."

Some modern Roman Catholic scholars have indeed argued with considerable force against this conclusion.[17] The repetition of the word "virgin" instead of the use of the simple pronoun "her," they argue, is to be explained by the desire of the narrator not merely to mention, but to emphasize, the virginity of Mary; and since Mary is evidently the chief person in the narrative, it is natural, they say, to take the three phrases: (1) "betrothed to a man whose name was Joseph," (2) "of the house of David," and (3) "the name of the virgin was Mary," as being all of them descriptive of Mary. These arguments are certainly worthy of consideration—more consideration than they have actually received. And yet they are hardly sufficient to overthrow the *prima facie* evidence. It does seem more natural, after all, to refer the words, "of the house of David," to Joseph.

If so, the Davidic descent of Mary is not mentioned in the narrative. There is indeed nothing in the narrative to prevent us from holding, if we care to do so, that Mary was descended from David. Certainly her kinship with Elisabeth[18] does not preclude such an opinion; for intermarriage between the tribe of Levi, to which Elisabeth belonged, and the other tribes was perfectly permissible under the law. No positive objection, therefore, can be raised to the view, which is held even by some scholars who reject the reference of the words, "of the house of David," in Lk. i.27 to Mary, that the narrator means to imply in his account of the annunciation to the virgin that Mary as well as Joseph was descended from David. But certainly the Davidic descent of Mary, even

[15] Verses 26 f. read: *ἐν δὲ τῷ μηνὶ τῷ ἕκτῳ ἀπεστάλη ὁ ἄγγελος Γαβριὴλ ἀπὸ τοῦ θεοῦ εἰς πόλιν τῆς Γαλιλαίας ᾗ ὄνομα Ναζαρέθ, πρὸς παρθένον ἐμνηστευμένην ἀνδρὶ ᾧ ὄνομα Ἰωσήφ, ἐξ οἴκου Δαυείδ, καὶ τὸ ὄνομα τῆς παρθένου Μαριάμ.*

[16] The latter view was favored by Chrysostom, for example, in the early fifth century (*hom. in Matt.*, ii, ed. Montfaucon, vii, 1836, p. 29), and has been favored by many later writers, though the other view is held by the great majority of modern Protestant scholars (B. Weiss being an exception). Compare W. Bauer, *Das Leben Jesu im Zeitalter der neutestamentlichen Apokryphen*, 1909, p. 9.

[17] See especially Bardenhewer, "Mariä Verkündigung," in *Biblische Studien*, x. 5, 1905, pp. 75–77.

[18] Lk. i.36.

though it be held to be implied (which we for our part think very doubtful), is at any rate not definitely stated.[19]

If so, it looks as though the Davidic descent of Jesus were traced by the narrator through Joseph. But how could that be done if the narrator regarded the line as broken by the fact that Joseph was not really the father of Jesus?

In reply, it may be said that some persons in the early Church certainly did regard the two things—(1) the Davidic descent of Jesus through Joseph and (2) the virgin birth of Jesus—as being compatible. Such persons, for example, were the author of the first chapter of Matthew and the man who produced the present form of the first chapter of Luke, even though this latter person be thought to have been merely an interpolator. But if these persons thought that the two things were compatible, why may not the original author of the narrative in Lk. i-ii have done so? And if the original author did so, then the fact that he traces the Davidic descent through Joseph does not prove that he did not also believe in the virgin birth; so that the tracing of the Davidic descent through Joseph ceases to afford any support to the interpolation theory.

It is another question, of course, whether the virgin birth is *really* compatible with the Davidic descent through Joseph. All that we need to show for the present purpose is that it may well have been *thought* to be compatible by the author of the infancy narrative. However, it would be a mistake to leave the question, even at the present point in our argument, in so unsatisfactory a condition. As a matter of fact, there is, we think, a real, and not merely a primitively assumed, compatibility between the Davidic descent through Joseph and the virgin birth; the author of the first chapter of Matthew and also (if we are right in rejecting the interpolation theory) the author of the first two chapters of Luke had a perfect right to regard Jesus as the heir of the promises made to the house of David even though He was not descended from David by ordinary generation.

We reject, indeed, the view of Badham that, according to the New Testament birth narratives, although Mary was a virgin when Jesus was born, yet in some supernatural way, and not by the ordinary intercourse of husband and

[19] For the patristic opinions regarding the ancestry of Mary, see W. Bauer, *op. cit.*, 1909, pp. 8–16. Passages in the early patristic period declaring Jesus to belong to Levi as well as to Judah, Bauer says, do not mean that while Joseph was descended from Judah, Mary was descended from Levi; for the connection of Jesus with Levi was conceived of in a spiritual, not in a bodily, way. "In the time before Origen," says Bauer, "Mary is nowhere clearly designated as a daughter of Levi" (p. 11). On the other hand, the Davidic descent of Mary appears, Bauer points out, in the Protevangelium of James and other apocryphal Gospels, in Justin Martyr, Tertullian, etc., and in the Sinaitic Syriac manuscript of the Old Syriac Version of the Gospels.

wife, Joseph became even in a physical sense the father of Jesus.[20] This suggestion fails to do justice, no doubt, to the meaning of the narratives. In the first chapter of Matthew, and also really in the first chapter of Luke, the physical paternity of Joseph is clearly excluded.

Yet it ought to be observed, in the first place, that the Jews looked upon adoptive fatherhood in a much more realistic way than we look upon it. In this connection we can point, for example, to the institution of Levirate marriage. According to the Old Testament law, when a man died without issue, his brother could take the wife of the dead man and raise up an heir for his brother. Evidently the son was regarded as belonging to the dead man to a degree which is foreign to our ideas. Because of this Semitic way of thinking, very realistic terms could be used on Semitic ground to express a relationship other than that of physical paternity. Thus so eminent an expert as F. C. Burkitt, who certainly cannot be accused of apologetic motives, maintains that the word "begat" in the Matthæan genealogy does not indicate physical paternity, but only the transmission of legal heirship, so that even if the genealogy had ended with the words, "Joseph begat Jesus," that would not have afforded the slightest indication that the author did not believe in the virgin birth.[21] Certainly, according to Jewish usage, a child born to a man's wife, and acknowledged by him, was to all intents and purposes his son. The truth is that in the New Testament Jesus is presented in the narratives of the virgin birth as belonging to the house of David just as truly as if he were in a physical sense the son of Joseph. He was a gift of God to the Davidic house, not less truly, but on the contrary in a more wonderful way, than if he had been descended from David by ordinary generation.[22] Who can say that this New Testament representation is invalid? The promises to David were truly fulfilled if they were fulfilled in accordance with the views of those to whom they were originally given.

In the second place, the relation in which Jesus stood to Joseph, on the assumption that the story of the virgin birth is true, was much closer than is the case with ordinary adoption. By the virgin birth the whole situation was raised beyond ordinary analogies. In an ordinary instance of adoption there is

[20] F. P. Badham in a letter in *The Academy* for November 17, 1894 (vol. xlvi, pp. 401 f.). Compare also the curious suggestion of C. C. Torrey ("The Translations Made from the Original Aramaic Gospels," in *Studies in the History of Religions Presented to Crawford Howell Toy*, 1912, p. 303) that according to Matthew the Holy Spirit "anticipated Joseph," "yet the latter is quite as truly the father," so that "the child had thus three parents." Compare below, p. 187.

[21] Burkitt, *Evangelion da-Mepharreshe*, 1904, ii, pp. 260 f.

[22] See, for example, Strack-Billerbeck, *Das Evangelium nach Matthäus*, 1922, pp. 35 f. Compare Dalman, *Die Worte Jesu*, 1898, p. 263 (English translation, *The Words of Jesus*, 1902, p. 320); Box, *The Virgin Birth of Jesus*, 1916, p. 8.

another human being—the actual father—who disputes with the father by adoption the paternal relation to the child. Such was not the case with Joseph in his relationship to Jesus, according to the New Testament narratives. He alone and no other human being could assume the rights and the duties of a father with respect to this child. And the child Jesus could be regarded as Joseph's son and heir with a completeness of propriety which no ordinary adoptive relationship would involve.

Thus the fact that in the Lucan infancy narrative Jesus is presented as the descendant of David through Joseph does not at all show that the narrative in its original form contained no mention of the virgin birth.

Moreover, in refuting the first supposed proof of contradiction between the verses that attest the virgin birth and the rest of the narrative, we have really already refuted the second supposed proof. The second argument, as we observed, is based upon the application, in the second chapter of Luke, of the term "father" to Joseph and of the term "parents" to Joseph and Mary.[23] Of the instances where this phenomenon occurs, Lk. ii.48 clearly belongs in a special category; for there the term "father" is not used by the narrator in his own name, but is attributed by the narrator to Mary. Evidently, whatever may be the narrator's own view of the relationship of Joseph to Jesus, it is unnatural that even if the virgin birth was a fact, Mary should have mentioned the special nature of that relationship in the presence of her son. Thus in attributing the term "father" to Mary, in her conversation with Jesus, the narrator, if he did know of the virgin birth, is merely keeping within the limits of historical probability in a way which would not be the case if he had endeavored to make the virgin birth explicit at this point. But even the other occurrences of the term "father" or "parents" are thoroughly natural even if the narrator knew and accepted the story of the virgin birth. For, as we have just observed in connection with the matter of the Davidic descent, such terms could well be used on Semitic ground to describe even an ordinary adoptive relationship—to say nothing of the altogether unique relationship in which, according to the story of the virgin birth, Joseph stood to the child Jesus. Thus those manuscripts of the Old Latin Version which substitute in these passages the name "Joseph" for the term "father" and the phrase "Joseph and his mother" for the term "parents" are adopting an apologetic device which is altogether unnecessary. The absence of any such meticulous safeguarding of the virgin birth in the original text of Lk. ii shows not at all that the virgin birth was

[23] Lk. ii.33, "And His father and His mother were marvelling at the things which were being spoken about Him"; verse 41, "And His parents (γονεῖς) were in the habit of going year by year to Jerusalem at the feast of the Passover"; verse 43, "And His parents did not know it"; verse 48, "Behold, thy father and I seek thee sorrowing."

unknown to the author of that chapter, but only that the chapter was composed at an early time when naïvely direct narration had not yet given place to apologetic reflection.

The third supposed contradiction between Lk. i.34, 35 and the rest of the narrative, that has been detected by advocates of the interpolation theory, is found in those places where Mary is represented as being puzzled by evidences of the high position of her son. How could she have been surprised by such things, it is asked, if from the beginning she knew that the child had been conceived by the Holy Ghost?

With regard to this argument, it may be said, in the first place, that the argument proves too much. If the wonder, or lack of comprehension, which Mary is represented as displaying at various points of the narrative shows that she could not have been regarded by the narrator as having passed through the experience predicted in Lk. i.34, 35, it also shows that she could not have been the recipient even of the other angelic words. If Mary had had promised to her a son who was to be called a Son of the Most High[24] and of whose kingdom there was to be no end,[25] why should she have been surprised by the prophecies of the aged Simeon or have failed to understand the emergence in the boy Jesus of a unique filial consciousness toward God?[26] Surely the angel's words, even without mention of the virgin birth, might have provided the key to unlock all these subsequent mysteries. Logically, therefore, the argument with which we are now dealing would require excision, not merely of Lk. i.34, 35, but of the whole annunciation scene. But such excision is of course quite impossible, since the annunciation is plainly presupposed in the rest of the narrative and since the section Lk. i.26-38 is composed in exactly the same style as the rest. Evidently the argument with which we are now dealing proves too much.

But that argument faces an even greater objection. Indeed, it betokens, on the part of those who advance it, a woeful lack of appreciation of what is one of the most beautiful literary touches in the narrative and at the same time an important indication of essential historical trustworthiness. We refer to the delicate depiction of the character of Mary. These modern advocates of mechanical consistency seem to suppose that Mary must have been, or rather must have been regarded by the original narrator as being, a person of a coldly scientific frame of mind, who, when she had passed through the wonderful experience of the supernatural conception, proceeded to draw out the logical consequences

[24] Lk. i.32.

[25] Verse 33.

[26] Compare Hilgenfeld, "Die Geburts- und Kindheitsgeschichte Jesu Luc. I, 5–II, 52," in *Zeitschrift für wissenschaftliche Theologie*, xliv, 1901, pp. 177–235.

of that experience in all their minutest ramifications, so that thereafter nothing in heaven or on earth could affect her with the slightest perplexity or surprise. How different, and how much more in accord with historical probability, is the picture of the mother of Jesus in this wonderful narrative! According to this narrative, Mary was possessed of a simple and meditative—we do not say dull or rustic—soul. She meets the strange salutation of the angel with fear and with a perplexed question; but then, when mysteries beyond all human experience are promised her, says simply: "Behold the handmaiden of the Lord; be it unto me according to thy word." Then she journeys far to seek the sympathetic ear of a woman whom she can trust; and when she is saluted in lofty words, she responds with a hymn of praise which is full of exultation, but also full of reserve. Then when the child is born, and the shepherds come with their tale of the angelic host, others marvel, but Mary "kept all these words, pondering them in her heart." But when Simeon uttered his prophecy about the light which was to shine forth to the Gentiles, Mary, with Joseph, marvelled at the things which were spoken about her child. No doubt, if she had been a modern superman, she would have been far beyond so lowly an emotion as wonder; no doubt, since her son had been born without human father, she would never have been surprised by so comparatively trifling a phenomenon as an angelic host that appeared to simple shepherds and sang to them a hymn of praise. But then it must be remembered that according to this narrative Mary was not a modern superman, but a Jewish maiden of the first century, nurtured in the promises of God—the recipient, indeed, of a wonderful experience, but despite that experience still possessed of some capacity for wonder in her devout and meditative soul. And surely in the Palestine of the first century such a Jewish maiden is a more natural figure than the scientific monstrosity which some modern scholars seem to demand that she should be.

Finally, when she saw her twelve-year-old son in the Temple, in the company of the doctors of the law, she was astonished, and when her son said, "Wist ye not that I must be about my Father's business," she actually failed to understand. Truly that was unpardonable dullness—so we are told—on the part of one who knew that the child had been conceived by the Holy Ghost.

We can only say that if it really was dullness, that dullness has been shared from that day to this by the greatest minds in Christendom. Has the utterance of the youthful Jesus ever fully been understood—understood, we mean, even by those who have been just as fully convinced of the fact of the supernatural conception as Mary was convinced if the experience actually was hers? There are depths in this utterance which have never been fathomed even by the framers of the Nicene and Chalcedonian creeds. It will be a sad day, indeed, if the Church comes to suppose that *nothing* in this word of the boy Jesus can be understood; but it will also be a sad day if it supposes that *all* can be understood. Mary can surely be pardoned for her wonder, and for her failure to understand.

She had indeed passed through a unique experience; her son had been conceived in the womb without human father as none other had been conceived during all the history of the human race. But then when He had been born, with the mother's very human pangs, He was wrapped in swaddling clothes and laid in a manger; and then He grew up like other boys, in the Nazareth home. No doubt from the point of view with which we are now dealing His lowly birth and childhood ought to have caused no questioning or wonder in Mary's heart; no doubt she ought to have deduced from these things, when they were taken in connection with the miracle of His conception, the full Chalcedonian doctrine of the two natures in one person of the Lord; no doubt she ought to have been expecting the emergence, in the human consciousness of her child, of just such a sense of vocation and divine sonship as that which appeared when she found Him with the doctors in the Temple; no doubt she ought to have been far beyond all capacity for perplexity or surprise. But then we must reflect, from our modern vantage-ground, that Mary was just a Jewish woman of the first century. It is perhaps too much to expect that she should be a representative of the "modern mind." Perhaps she may even have retained the now obsolete habit of meditation and of quiet communion with her God; perhaps, despite her great experience, she may never have grasped the modern truth that God exists for the sake of man and not man for the sake of God; perhaps God's mercies had to her not yet come to seem a common thing. Perhaps, therefore, despite the miracle of the virgin birth, she may still have retained the sense of wonder; and when angels uttered songs of praise, and aged prophets told of the light that was to lighten the Gentiles, or when her child disclosed a consciousness of vocation that suddenly seemed to place a gulf between her and Him, she may, instead of proclaiming these things to unsympathetic ears, have preferred to keep them and ponder them in her heart.

So understood, the picture of Mary in these chapters is profoundly congruous with the verses that narrate the virgin birth. By the contrary argument modern scholars show merely that even for the prosecution of literary criticism something more is needed than acuteness in the analysis of word and phrase; one must also have some sympathy for the spirit of the narrative with which one deals. And if one approaches this narrative with sympathy, one sees that the supernatural conception is not only not contradictory to what is said about the thoughts of Mary's heart, but profoundly congruous with it. The words that recur like a refrain—"Mary kept all these words and pondered them in her heart," "Mary kept all these words in her heart"—place Mary before the readers in a way that is comprehensible only if she alone and not Joseph is the centre of interest in the narrative. And what made her the centre of interest save the stupendous wonder of the virgin birth? How delicate and how self-consistent is this picture of the mother of the Lord! Others might pass lightly over the strange events that occurred in connection with the childhood of her son; others might forget the angels' song; others might be satisfied with easy solutions of the problem presented by the consciousness of divine vocation which the youthful Jesus attested in the answer which He rendered in the Temple to His earthly parents. But not for Mary was such superficiality sufficient, not for the one who had been chosen of God to be the mother of the Lord. Others might be satisfied with easy answers to questions too deep for human utterance, but not so the one who had been overshadowed by the Holy Ghost. No, whatever others might do or say, Mary kept all these things and pondered them in her heart.

We are, indeed, as far as anyone from accepting the Roman Catholic picture of the Blessed Virgin. But we also think that Protestants, in their reaction against that picture, have sometimes failed to do justice to the mother of our Lord. Few and simple, indeed, are the touches with which the Evangelist draws the picture; fleeting only are the glimpses which he allows us into the virgin's heart. And yet how lifelike is the figure there depicted; how profound are the mysteries in that pure and meditative soul! In the narrative of the Third Gospel the virgin Mary is no lifeless automaton, but a person who lives and moves—a person who from that day to this has had power to touch all simple and childlike hearts.

Whence comes such a figure into the pages of the world's literature? Whence comes this lifelike beauty; whence comes this delicacy of reserve? Such questions will never be asked by those historians who reconstruct past ages by rule of thumb; they will never be asked by those who know the documents without knowing the human heart. But to historians fully worthy of that name the picture of Mary in the Third Gospel may seem to possess a self-evidencing power. Was such a picture the product of myth-making fancy, an example of the legendary elaboration which surrounds the childhood of great men? Very different, at least, were certain other products of such fancy in the early Church. Or is this picture drawn from the life; is the veil here gently pulled aside, that we may look for a moment into the depths of the virgin's soul; is the person here depicted truly the mother of our Lord?

Whatever answers may be given to these questions, whether the picture of Mary in these chapters is fiction or truth, one thing is clear—an integral part of that picture is found in the mention of the supernatural conception in the virgin's womb. Without that supreme wonder, everything that is here said of Mary is comparatively meaningless and jejune. The bewilderment in Mary's heart, her meditation upon the great things that happened to her son—all this, far from being contradictory to the virgin birth, really presupposes that supreme manifestation of God's power. That supreme miracle it was which rendered worth while the glimpses which the narrator grants us into Mary's soul.

Thus general considerations will certainly not prove Lk. i.34, 35 to be an interpolation; no contradiction, but rather the profoundest harmony, is to be found between these verses and the rest of the narrative. The Davidic descent could clearly be traced through Joseph, and was elsewhere traced through Joseph, even if Jesus was not regarded as being by ordinary generation Joseph's son; the term "father" as applied to Joseph does not necessarily imply physical paternity; the wonder in Mary's heart at various things that happened during the childhood of her son does not exclude the greater miracle of His conception in the womb, but on the contrary contributes to the picture of which that greater miracle is an integral part. It certainly cannot be said upon general principles, therefore, that the writer of the rest of the narrative could not have written Lk. i.34, 35.

But if such general considerations—such considerations based upon the central content of the verses—will not establish the interpolation theory, what shall be said of the two verses considered in detail and in the immediate context in which they appear? Is it possible to discern elements of style in these verses which designate them as foreign to the narrative in which they now appear; or else is it possible to exhibit between them and their present context imperfect joints which would disclose an interpolator's hand?

The former of these questions must certainly be answered in the negative. Harnack, it is true, discovers in the use of two conjunctions in the verses evidences of a hand other than that of Luke. One of these conjunctions,[27] he says, occurs, indeed, a number of times in Acts, but nowhere in the rest of the Third Gospel (unless it is genuine in Lk. vii.7);[28] and the other,[29] according

[27] διό.

[28] In Lk. vii.7 the words διὸ οὐδὲ ἐμαυτὸν ἠξίωσα πρὸς σὲ ἐλθεῖν are omitted by the "Western" text. They are no doubt genuine. The omission may be a harmonistic corruption to make the passage conform to Mt. viii.8.

[29] ἐπεί.

to the best text of Lk. vii.1 (where it is probably not genuine), occurs nowhere else in the Lucan writings.[30]

But surely the facts with regard to the former of these two words are rather in favor of Lucan authorship than against it; the word, on Harnack's own showing, does occur a number of times in Luke's double work. And with regard to the other word, it may simply be remembered that an author's choice of such words is seldom completely uniform. Bardenhewer[31] gives a list of other particles besides this one that occur only once in the Lucan writings. In general, it is significant that Zimmermann[32] and, more recently, Vincent Taylor[33] can point to the Lucan character of the diction in these verses positively in support of their view that Luke himself, and not some scribe, was the interpolator.

The truth is that the arguments of Zimmermann and Vincent Taylor, on the one hand, and of Harnack on the other, at this point simply cancel each other: the language of the two verses displays exactly the same combination of Jewish character with Lucan diction which appears everywhere else in the narrative. It is quite impossible to prove by stylistic considerations either that the verses are a Lucan interpolation into the source (or as Vincent Taylor would say into the original form of the Gospel) or a non-Lucan interpolation by a scribe. Nothing could be smoother, from a stylistic point of view, than the way in which these verses harmonize with the rest of the infancy narrative.

If, then, no support for the interpolation theory can be obtained from stylistic considerations, what shall be said of the way in which the thought of the two verses fits into the immediate context? May any loose joints be detected by which the verses have been inserted, or does the whole section appear to be of a piece?

In this connection, some of the arguments which have been advanced by advocates of the interpolation theory are certainly very weak. Thus when Harnack says[34] that the question and answer in Lk. i.34, 35 unduly separate the words, "Behold thou shalt conceive," in verse 31, from the corresponding words, "Behold, Elisabeth thy kinswoman has conceived, she also," in verse 36, surely he is demanding a perfect regularity or obviousness of structure which is not at all required in prose style. Even if verses 34, 35 are removed, still the two phrases that Harnack places in parallel are separated by the important

[30] Harnack, "Zu Lc. 1, 34, 35," in *Zeitschrift für die neutestamentliche Wissenschaft*, ii, 1901 p. 53.

[31] "Zu Mariä Verkündigung," in *Biblische Zeitschrift*, iii, 1905, p. 159.

[32] "Evangelium des Lukas Kap. 1 und 2," in *Theologische Studien und Kritiken*, lxxvi, 1903, p. 274.

[33] *The Historical Evidence for the Virgin Birth*, 1920, pp. 55–69.

[34] Harnack, *op. cit.*, pp. 53–55.

words of verses 32 f. As a matter of fact, it is by no means clear that the parallelism is conscious at all. But what is truly surprising is that Harnack can regard the *content* of this reference to Elisabeth as an argument in favor of the interpolation theory instead of regarding it as an argument against it. The words in verses 36 f., Harnack argues, obtain a good sense only if no mention of Mary's conception by the Holy Spirit has gone before; for if the most wonderful thing of all has already been promised, then it is weak and unconvincing, he thinks, to point, in support of this wonder, to the lesser wonder of Elisabeth's conception in her old age.[35]

Surely this argument should be exactly reversed. The fact that in verses 36 f. the angel points, not to the career of Elisabeth's son as the forerunner of Mary's greater son, but to something extraordinary in the manner of his birth, shows plainly that this example is adduced in illustration of the greater miracle involved in the conception of Jesus, entirely without human father, in the virgin's womb. If all that had been mentioned before was the greatness of a son whom Mary was to bear simply as the fruit of her coming marriage with Joseph, then nothing could be more pointless than a reference to the manner in which John was born. As a matter of fact, the plain intention is to illustrate the greater miracle (birth without human father) by a reference to the lesser miracle (birth from aged parents). It is perfectly true, of course, that there could be in the nature of the case no full parallel for the unique miracle of the virgin birth. But what the angel could do was to point to a happening that was at least sufficient to illustrate the general principle that "with God nothing shall be impossible."[36]

It is not surprising, therefore, that Hilgenfeld[37] apparently makes the reference to Elisabeth an argument, not against, but in favor of, the integrity of the passage and that Spitta[38] and others make it an argument for including verses 36 f. in the supposed interpolation.

[35] Compare Loisy, *op. cit.*, i, 1907, pp. 293 f.

[36] Lk. i.37. Clemen (*Religionsgeschichtliche Erklärung des Neuen Testaments*, 2te Aufl., 1924, p. 116) aptly quotes, as indicating the true connection in thought between verse 36 and what precedes, Evangelium de Nativitate Mariae, 3: "sicut ipsa (Maria) mirabiliter ex sterili nascetur, ita incomparabiliter virgo generabit altissimi filium."

[37] "Die Geburts- und Kindheitsgeschichte Jesu Luc. I, 5–II, 52," in *Zeitschrift für wissenschaftliche Theologie*, xliv, 1901, pp. 202 f.; "Die Geburt Jesu aus der Jungfrau in dem Lucas-Evangelium," *ibid.*, pp. 316 f.

[38] "Die chronologischen Notizen und die Hymnen in Lc. 1 u. 2," in *Zeitschrift für die neutestamentliche Wissenschaft*, vii, 1906, p. 289. Compare also Häcker, "Die Jungfrauen-Geburt und das Neue Testament," in *Zeitschrift für wissenschaftliche Theologie*, xlix, 1906, p. 52; Wilkinson, *op. cit.*, 1902, pp. 10 f.; Montefiore, *The Synoptic Gospels*, 1909, ii, p. 851 (but compare the second edition, 1927, pp. 368 f.). Häcker, Spitta, and the earlier edition of Montefiore are cited by Moffatt, *An Introduction to the Literature of the New Testament*, 3rd edition, 1918 (printing of 1925), p. 268 (footnote). Bultmann (*op. cit.*, 1931, pp. 321 f.) is an important recent advocate of the view that the interpolation (into the source by the author) embraces verses 34–37.

Against this latter hypothesis the argument from the stylistic congruity of the supposed interpolation with the remainder of the narrative tells with crushing force. That argument was strong even if only verses 34 f. were regarded as interpolated. But in that case it might conceivably (though even then not plausibly) be said that the interpolation is too brief to disclose the stylistic variations from the rest of the narrative which in a longer interpolation might be expected to reveal the interpolator's hand. But if the interpolator inserted so long a passage as verses 34-37, then it is truly a most extraordinary thing that he should have been able to catch the spirit of the infancy narrative so perfectly that nowhere in the whole course of his long insertion has he struck a single discordant note. Interpolators are not apt to be possessed of such wonderfully delicate skill. Moreover, it may turn out that there are still other special difficulties in the way of this modified form of the interpolation hypothesis.

But unlikely though this modification of the interpolation hypothesis is, it does at least show a salutary feeling for the weakness of the more usual view. Certainly verses 36 f. are connected with 34 f. in the most indissoluble way; it is inconceivable that the reference to Elisabeth's conception in her old age should be separated from the reference to Mary's conception by the Holy Ghost. What we have here is a rather clear instance of the fate that frequently besets interpolation theories. The critic starts hopefully to remove something from a literary production. At first he thinks it is an easy matter. But then he discovers, to his consternation, that great shreds of the rest of the book are coming up along with the thing that he is trying to remove; the book proves to be not an agglomeration but an organism. So it is with Lk. i.34, 35. At first it seems to be an easy matter just to remove these verses and so get rid of the disconcerting attestation of the virgin birth in a Palestinian narrative. But the thing proves to be not so easy as it seemed. For one thing, as we observed above, something has to be done with Lk. i.27 and probably with Lk. ii.5 and iii.23. And then here in the immediate context it is quite evident that if Lk. i.34 f. is to go, verses 36 f. must go, too. We may, before we have finished, discover connections with still other parts of the context. At any rate, it should certainly be disconcerting to the advocates of the interpolation theory that what Harnack regards as a loose joint, showing verses 34 f. to be no original part of their present context, is regarded by equally acute observers as being so very close a connection that if what appears on one side of the connection is interpolated, what appears on the other side must also go. If the interpolation theory were correct, we might naturally expect some sort of agreement among the advocates of it as to the place where the joints between the interpolation and the rest of the narrative are to be put.

Not much stronger, perhaps, though no doubt more widely advocated, than the arguments mentioned so far is the argument to the effect that verses 34 f. constitute a "doublet" with verses 31-33, and so could not originally have stood side by side with those former verses. In verses 31-33, it is said, Jesus is called Son of David and Son of the Most High; in verse 35 he is called Son of God because of the manner of his birth. If—so the argument runs—the writer had had in his mind the "Son of God" of verse 35, he would not have written the "Son of the Most High" and the "David His father" of verses 31-33.

With respect to this argument, it should be remarked in the first place that there is clearly no contradiction between the representation in verses 31-33 and that in verses 34 f. Offence has, indeed, been taken at the grounding of divine sonship in verse 35 upon the physical fact of divine paternity—"therefore also that holy thing which is begotten shall be called the Son of God." How different, it is said in effect, is the *Messianic* conception of divine sonship in verses 31-33!

But the question may well be asked whether the divine sonship of the child in verse 35 is grounded so clearly upon a physical fact of divine paternity as the objection seems to suppose. It is perfectly possible to take the word "holy" in that verse not as the subject but as part of the predicate. In that case, the words should be translated, "therefore also that which is begotten shall be called holy, Son of God." On this interpretation it is not particularly the divine *sonship* but the *holiness* of the child which is established by the physical fact of the supernatural conception, and the divine sonship becomes merely epexegetical of the holiness. The decision between the two ways of construing the word "holy" is difficult. But even if the word is regarded not as predicate but as subject, still we do not think that there is the slightest antinomy as over against verses 31-33. Even if the meaning is, "therefore also that holy thing that is begotten shall be called Son of God," we still do not see how such a grounding of the fact of divine sonship is contradictory to that which appears in the preceding verses. Certainly this verse does not intend to present the *only* way in which the divine sonship of the child is manifested. The verse says (in the construction that we are now discussing) that because of the supernatural conception the child shall be *called* Son of God; but it does not say that because of the supernatural conception the child shall *be* Son of God. We do not indeed lay particular stress upon this distinction. No doubt the distinction between "to be" and "to be called" is often not to be pressed; no doubt the passive of the verb "to call" in the New Testament sometimes implies not merely that a thing is designated as this or that, but that it is rightly so designated. So here, "shall be called Son of God" may be taken as meaning by implication, "shall be rightly called Son of God," and the emphasis may be upon the fact that justifies the calling rather than the calling itself. But whatever stress may be laid or may not be laid upon the distinction between "to be called" and "to be," it is certainly incorrect to take this sentence in an exclusive sense, as though it meant that the fact of the supernatural conception is the only reason why the child should "be called" or should "be" the Son of God. All that is meant is that the activity of the Holy Spirit at the conception of Jesus is intimately connected with that aspect of His being which causes Him to be called Son of God. One who was conceived in the womb by such a miracle must necessarily be the Son of God; a child who was conceived by the Holy Ghost could not be just an ordinary man. But clearly the verse does not mean that the supernatural conception was an isolated fact, and that it was the only thing that grounds the divine sonship of Jesus.

Certainly the modern, exclusive way of interpreting such an utterance is quite foreign to the Semitic mind, which could place side by side various aspects of the Messiah's person even before they were united in a systematic scheme. And at this point we are bound to think that the Semitic mind is preferable to the "modern mind." Nothing could be more consistent than the passage, verses 31-36, as it stands. First, the greatness of the promised child is celebrated in general terms; then, in response to Mary's question, the particular manner of His birth is mentioned, and mentioned in a way thoroughly congruous with the generally supernatural character which has been attributed to Him before. How the divine sonship which appears in verses 31-33 can be regarded as incongruous with the virgin birth, or as rendering superfluous the mention of it, is more than we can understand. Verses 34 f. are not a disturbing or unnecessary doublet as over against verses 31-33; but render more specific one point which is included in that more general assertion.

At any rate, it is quite incorrect to regard verse 35 as connecting the divine sonship of Jesus with the supernatural conception in any anthropomorphic way. It is the creative activity of the Holy Spirit, and not any assumption of human functions of fatherhood, which is in view. The chaste language of verse 35 is profoundly congruous with verses 31-33, and in general with the lofty monotheism of the Old Testament; and it is profoundly incongruous with the crassly anthropomorphic interpretation which has sometimes been forced upon it by modern scholars.

The arguments for the interpolation theory that have been mentioned so far are, we think, very easily refuted. Much more worthy of consideration is the argument with which we now come to deal. It is not, indeed, cogent as a support of the interpolation hypothesis; but at least it does call attention to a genuine exegetical difficulty which must be examined with some care.

We refer to the argument based upon Mary's question in verse 34, "How shall this be, seeing I know not a man?" This question has been regarded as being inconsistent with the context for two reasons. In the first place, why did not Mary simply assume that the child who has just been promised was to be the fruit of her coming marriage with Joseph? Since she was betrothed to Joseph, the fact that she was not yet living with him constituted no objection to the promise that she should have a child. In the second place, why is it that Mary should be commended, in the sequel, for her faith, if she had uttered this doubting question, which is very similar to the question for which Zacharias was so severely punished?

Of these two objections it is the former which most deserves attention. The latter objection, despite the great stress that has been laid upon it by many advocates of the interpolation hypothesis, can surely be dismissed rather easily. It is true, indeed, that in the narrative Zacharias is represented as punished for his question,[39] whereas Mary, despite her question, is praised.[40] But are the two questions the same?

In form, it must be admitted, there is a certain similarity. Both Zacharias and Mary, instead of accepting the lofty promises of the angel without remark, ask a question betokening at least bewilderment; and both of them ground their bewilderment in an explanatory clause. But there the similarity ceases. Zacharias' question reads, "According to what shall I know this?" That question cannot be interpreted as anything else than a definite request for a sign; the wonder that is promised must be able to exhibit an analogy with something else before Zacharias will consent to "know" it. Mary, on the other hand, says simply, "How shall this be?" She does not express any doubt but that it shall be, but merely inquires as to the manner in which it is to be brought to pass. Certainly she does not demand a sign before she will consent to "know" that what the angel has told her will be a fact.

To the modern reader, indeed, Mary's question may seem to indicate doubt. In our modern parlance, the words, "I do not see how that can be," or the like, may often mean that we do not think that it *will* be. Politeness, at the present time, is often a very irritating thing. But we have no right to attribute *such* politeness to Mary or to the writer who reports her words. And her question,

39 Lk. i.20.

40 Lk. i.45. "And blessed is she who has believed; because there shall be a fulfilment for the things that have been spoken to her from the Lord."

as it stands, attests not a refusal to believe without further proof, but only perplexity as to what is involved in the angel's words.

Even in its wording, then, Mary's question is different from that of Zacharias. But still greater is the difference in the situation which the two questions, respectively, have in view. Zacharias has been promised a son whom he had long desired, a son whose birth would bring him not misunderstanding and slander (as Mary's son might bring to her), but rather a removal of the reproach to which, by his childlessness, he had been subjected. Moreover, the birth of such a son, even in the old age of his parents, would be in accordance with the Old Testament analogies which Zacharias knew very well. What except sinful unbelief could lead, under such circumstances, to the request for a sign? Mary, on the other hand, when the angel, prior to her marriage, spoke of a son, was promised something which seemed at first sight to run counter to her maidenly consciousness. Old Testament analogies, moreover, could not give her, as they could give Zacharias, any help. Where in the Old Testament was it recorded that a son had been promised to a maid? Surely it is small cause for wonder that in such bewilderment she should have asked the angel for light.

Even, therefore, if the wording of the two questions were more similar than it actually is, the underlying mind of the two speakers may still have been quite different. Zacharias was promised that which was quite in accord with Old Testament analogies and would mean the fulfilment of hopes that he had cherished for many a year; Mary was promised a strange, unheard of, thing, which might subject her to all manner of reproach. And yet finally (and despite the strange explanation from the angel, which rendered the danger of that reproach only the more imminent) she said, in simple submission to the will of God, "Behold the handmaiden of the Lord, be it unto me according to thy word." It is surely no wonder that Zacharias was punished and Mary praised.

Much more worthy of consideration, we think, is the other one of the two objections to which Mary's question has given rise. Indeed, the former objection, as has just become evident in the last paragraph, receives what weight it may have only from this objection with which we shall now have to deal. We have argued that if the angel's promise to Mary seemed inconsistent with her maidenly consciousness, her question, unlike that of Zacharias, was devoid of blame. But, it will be objected, why should the promise have been interpreted by her in any such way; why should it have seemed inconsistent with her maidenly consciousness at all? The angel in the preceding verses has said nothing about anything peculiar in the birth of her son; why then did she not understand the promise as referring simply to her approaching marriage? If she was going to ask any question, surely it ought to have been—thus the objection runs—a question about the greatness of her son rather than about the manner of His birth; the thing which ought to have caused surprise in view of the preceding words is not the mere fact that she was to have a son (for in view of her approaching marriage that was to be expected), but that she was to have *such* a son—that the son of a humble maiden at Nazareth was to assume the throne of David, that He was to be called the Son of the Most High and that of His Kingdom there was to be no end. Her question, in other words, ought, in view of the context, to have been, "How shall this be, seeing I am a humble woman?," instead of, "How shall this be, seeing I know not a man?" As it is, verse 34, we are told, reveals clearly an interpolator's hand; it is entirely unnatural in view of the context, and merely constitutes a clumsy device for the introduction of an idea (the virgin birth) that was quite foreign to the original story.

To this argument Roman Catholic scholars have a ready answer.[41] The question of Mary in verse 34, they say, is to be explained by the fact that she had already either made a vow, or at least formed a fixed resolve, never to have intercourse with a man; the present tense, "I know," in the clause, "seeing I know not a man," is to be taken in a future sense, or rather as designating what was already a permanent principle of Mary's life. Thus the meaning of the verse is, "How shall this be, since as a matter of principle I have determined not to know a man?"[42]

This solution certainly removes in the fullest possible way the difficulty with which we now have to do. And no objection to it can be raised from a linguistic point of view; there seems to be no reason why the present indicative, "I know," could not be taken as designating a fixed principle of Mary's life that would apply to the future as well as to the present. But the question is whether in avoiding one difficulty this Roman Catholic solution does not become involved in other difficulties that are greater still. In the first place, this solution runs counter to the *prima facie* evidence regarding the brothers and sisters of Jesus, who are mentioned in a number of places in the New Testament. Despite the alternative views—that these "brethren of the Lord" were children of Joseph by a former marriage or that they were merely cousins

[41] See especially Bardenhewer, "Mariä Verkündigung," in *Biblische Studien*, x.5, 1905, pp. 120–131.

[42] Loisy (*op. cit.*, i, 1907, pp. 290 f.), who, unlike the Roman Catholic scholars, rejects the historicity of the narrative, is inclined to favor the Roman Catholic interpretation of the words as they stand; the author of the Gospel, he thinks, probably believed in the perpetual virginity of Mary, and that explains Mary's question.

of Jesus, the word "brother" being used in a loose sense—it still seems most probable that they were simply children of Joseph and Mary. This conclusion is in accord with Lk. ii.7, where Mary is said to have "brought forth her firstborn son"; for the word "firstborn" may naturally be held to imply that afterwards she had other children. The implication here is, indeed, by no means certain; for under the Jewish law the word "firstborn" was a technical term, which could be applied even to an only child, and in the sequel of this narrative stress is actually laid upon the fact that the legal provisions regarding the "firstborn" were fulfilled in the case of Jesus. Still, despite such considerations, the phrase does seem slightly more natural if Mary was regarded by the narrator as having other children. Such an interpretation would agree, moreover, with Mt. i.25, where it is said that "Joseph knew her not until she had borne a son." Here again the natural implication of the words can conceivably be avoided; it may be insisted that the author does not say that Joseph knew her *after* she had borne a son, but only that he did *not* know her before she had borne a son. And yet it does seem strange that if the narrator supposed that Joseph *never* lived with Mary as with a wife he should not have said that in simple words.

In rejecting the Roman Catholic solution of our difficulty, we are not merely influenced by the positive historical evidence for the existence of other sons of Mary. Equally cogent is the negative consideration that if the narrator in the first chapter of Luke had meant that Mary had formed a resolve of perpetual virginity, he would naturally have indicated the fact in a very much clearer way. Such a resolve in a Jewish maiden of the first century would have been an unheard-of thing. Asceticism, with the later prejudice against marriage and the begetting of children, was quite foreign to the Jewish circles that are depicted in Lk. i-ii in such a vivid manner. If, therefore, the narrator were intending to attribute so extraordinary a resolve to Mary, he would naturally have taken pains to make his meaning perfectly clear; he might, for example, have been expected to tell of the special divine guidance which alone could have led a Jewish maiden to depart in such an unheard-of way from all the customs and all the ingrained sentiments of her people. As a matter of fact, the narrator has done nothing of the kind. On the contrary, he has simply told us that Mary was betrothed to Joseph; and he has not hinted in any way whatsoever that the approaching marriage was to be a marriage in name only. Such a marriage is indeed set forth with great clearness in the apocryphal Protevangelium of James; but there is not the slightest hint of any such thing in our Third Gospel.

If, then, the Roman Catholic solution is to be rejected, what shall be put in its place? If when Mary said, "How shall this be, seeing I know not a man?", she was not giving expression to a resolve of perpetual virginity with which a child in her approaching marriage with Joseph would seem inconsistent, how shall her question be understood? Why did she not simply assume that the son whom the angel had promised would be the fruit of her approaching union with her betrothed?

Some modern scholars find an answer in the hypothesis of a mistranslation, in our Greek Gospel, of a Hebrew or Aramaic original of the angel's words. If the future, "thou shalt conceive", in verse 31, it is said, only were a present instead of a future, all would be plain; in that case the conception in Mary's womb would be represented by the angel as taking place at once, so that Mary could not understand it as referring to a marriage which still lay in the future, and so her bewildered question would easily be explained. Now, although in our Greek text, it is said, the word translated, "thou shalt conceive," is unequivocally future, the original of it in Hebrew or Aramaic would be a participle; and the participle might be meant to refer to the present as well as to the future—the decision in every individual case being determined only by the context. In the present passage, it is said, the participle was intended, in the Semitic source, to refer to the present; and the whole difficulty has come from the fact that the Greek translator, who gave us our present form of Lk. i-ii, wrongly took it as referring to the future. If, then, the Semitic original is here restored, Mary's question—since she could not explain a *present* conception in her womb by her *future* union with Joseph—becomes thoroughly suited to the context, so that there is no longer any indication of an interpolator's clumsy hand.

This solution, of course, assumes the existence of a Semitic original for the first chapter of Luke. That assumption is by no means improbable. But the question might arise how the Greek translator came to make the mistake. Would a translator be likely—for no particular reason, since the participle in the source *might* be translated by a present, even though it might also be translated by a future—would a translator be likely to introduce such serious confusion into the narrative in its Greek form? Obviously it would be more satisfactory, if possible, to find an interpretation which would suit the Greek narrative as it stands.

Such an interpretation, we believe, is actually forthcoming, though it appears in a number of slightly different forms, between which we may not be able to decide. This true interpretation of the Greek text is not without affinity with the hypothesis of mistranslation which has just been discussed;

indeed, what it actually proposes is to find in the Greek words a meaning rather similar to that which the advocates of the theory of mistranslation have found in the Hebrew or Aramaic original. The Greek word, "thou shalt conceive," is indeed future: but would it necessarily be referred by Mary to the time of her marriage with Joseph; might it not rather be referred by her to an *immediate* future?

The latter alternative, we think, is correct. Annunciations, as they were known to Mary from the Old Testament, were made to married women; and when such an annunciation came to her, an unmarried maiden, it is not unnatural that she should have been surprised. No doubt the influence upon her of the Old Testament narratives was not conscious; in the bewilderment caused by the angel's greeting it is not likely that she reviewed consciously in her mind the story of Hannah or of the wife of Manoah. But the unconscious effect of these stories may have been very great; they may well have served to create in her subconscious mind a close connection between angelic annunciations and the condition of a married woman as distinguished from that of a maid. Hence to her maidenly consciousness the promise of a son may well have occasioned her the utmost surprise.

If, indeed, she had looked at the matter from the point of view of cold logic, her surprise might possibly have been overcome. She could have reflected that, after all, she was betrothed, and that the annunciation could in her case, as was not so in the Old Testament examples, be taken as referring to a married state that was still to come. But would such reflection have been natural; is it not psychologically more probable that she should have given expression, in such words as those in Lk. i.34, to her first instinctive surprise?

We have, then, in the current objection to Mary's question another instance of that failure to understand the character of Mary, of that attempt to attribute to her, as she is depicted in this narrative, the coldly scientific quality of the "modern mind," which has already been noticed in another connection. Suppose it be granted that in her question to the angel Mary was not strictly logical; is that any objection either to the ultimate authenticity of the question as a question of Mary, or to its presence in the narrative in Lk. i-ii? We might almost be tempted to say that a certain lack of logic in Mary's words is a positive indication of their authenticity and of their original presence in this narrative. This absence of an easy, reasoned solution of all difficulties, this instinctive expression of a pure, maidenly consciousness, is profoundly in accord with the delicate delineation, all through this narrative, of the mother of the Lord.

But was maidenly instinct here really at fault; was Mary wrong in not simply referring the angel's promise to her approaching marriage? Was she wrong in thinking that an immediate conception in her womb was naturally implied in the angel's words? We are by no means certain that this is the case. On the contrary, the very appearance of the angel and his extraordinary greeting would seem clearly to indicate some far more immediate significance in that moment than could be found merely in a promise concerning the indefinite future. After all, it was really strange in itself, as well as an offence to the consciousness of the virgin, if a child to be born in the approaching union with Joseph should be promised before instead of after the marriage. The future tense, "thou shalt conceive," therefore, though not actually equivalent to a present, does refer most naturally to an *immediate* future. Thus the interpretation of the angel's previous words which is implied in verse 34 is a very natural interpretation, and cannot possibly stamp verses 34 f. as an interpolation.

This view avoids one difficulty that faces that theory of mistranslation which we have rejected. If the Hebrew or Aramaic participle of which the Greek, "thou shalt conceive", is a translation were intended in a strictly present sense, there would seem to be a contradiction with Lk. ii.21, where the name Jesus is said to have been given by the angel before the child had been conceived in the womb. If the conception were represented as taking place at the very moment when the word translated "thou shalt conceive" was uttered, then the name was given not before, but at the very moment of, the conception. On our view, on the other hand, it is possible to take Lk. ii.21 in the strictest way, and yet find no contradiction with Lk. i.31. The conception was represented by the angel as taking place in the immediate future, but not at the very moment when the word, "thou shalt conceive," was spoken. It is impossible to say just when the conception is to be put. Many have thought of the moment when Mary said, "Be it unto me in accordance with thy word;"[43] and this view has sometimes been connected with speculations about the necessity, for the accomplishment of the incarnation, of Mary's act of submission. The salvation of the world, it has sometimes been held, depended upon Mary's decision to submit herself to God's plan; here as elsewhere, it has been held, God had respect to human free will. Such a way of thinking is contrary to ours. Of course our rejection of it does not by any means involve rejection of the view that puts the moment of the conception at the time when Mary uttered her final words. Yet on the whole we think it better to treat the question as it is treated by the narrator—with a cautious reserve. All that

[43] Lk. i.38.

is involved in our view is that the "thou shalt conceive" in verse 31 refers to the near future, and would not naturally be taken by Mary as referring to her approaching marriage.

It is quite possible that at this point we have claimed too much; it is quite possible that Mary's question in verse 34 is not strictly logical; it is quite possible that she might well have taken the angel's promise as referring to her approaching marriage. But that admission would not at all seriously affect our argument. Even if Mary's question was not strictly logical, it was at least very natural; it was natural as expressing her bewilderment; like Peter at the transfiguration, she knew not what she said. She was terrified at the angel's greeting, and as a pure maiden she had not expected then the promise of a son. What wonder is it that her maidenly consciousness found expression in words that calm reflection might have changed? We are almost tempted to say that the less expressive of calm reasoning are Mary's words in verse 34, so much the less likely are they to be due to an interpolator's calculating mind, and so much the more likely are they to be due to Mary herself or to have been an original part of a narrative which everywhere depicts her character in such a delicate way.

So far, we have been considering the arguments that have been advanced in favor of the interpolation theory. It is now time to consider a little more specifically the positive arguments that may be advanced against it. What positive indications, as distinguished from the mere burden of proof against the interpolation theory, may be advanced in favor of the view that Lk. i.34 f. was an original part of the narrative in which it now stands?

The strongest indication of all, perhaps, is found in the total impression that the narrative makes. We have been accustomed to read Lk. i-ii with appreciation of its unity and of its beauty only because the virgin birth is in our mind. But if we could divest ourselves of that thought, if we could imagine ourselves as reading this narrative for the first time and reading it without Lk. i.34 f., it would seem disorganized and overwrought almost from beginning to end. The truth is that the child whose birth was prophesied by an angel and was greeted, when it came, by a choir of the heavenly host, is inconceivable as a mere child of earthly parents. No, what we really have here in this Christmas narrative is the miraculous appearance upon the earth of a heavenly Being—a human child, indeed, but a child like none other that ever was born. Not merely this detail or that, but the entire inner spirit of the narrative, involves the virgin birth.

Only partially can this total impression be analyzed. Yet such analysis is not without its value. It may serve to remove doubts, and so may allow free scope at the last for a new and more sympathetic reading of the narrative as a whole.

Some of the details in Lk. i-ii which presuppose the virgin birth are of a subsidiary kind. But their cumulative effect is very great. Thus it has been well observed that Mary's words of submission in Lk. i.38 are without point if there has been no prophecy of the virgin birth in what precedes. If all that the angel has said is a prophecy that in her coming marriage Mary is to be the mother of the Messiah, why should there be this parade of submission on her part? These words are natural only if what has been promised involves possible shame as well as honor; then only do they acquire the pathos which has been found in them by Christian feeling throughout all the centuries and which the narrator evidently intended them to have.

It is such considerations, perhaps, which have led a few advocates of the interpolation theory to suggest that verse 38, as well as verses 36 f., may be regarded as part of the interpolation. But this suggestion only heaps difficulty upon difficulty. Without Mary's final words of submission, the whole annunciation scene is left hanging in the air. Let the reader just imagine that verse 39 originally followed upon verse 33, and then let him see what effect is made by such an account of the scene. It will be evident enough that an artistic whole has been subjected to mutilation. What point is there, moreover, in the praise of Mary's faith in verse 45—"Blessed is she who has believed; for there shall be fulfilment of the things that have been spoken to her from the Lord"—if Mary has not in what precedes given any expression to her faith? Evidently verse 45 refers to verse 38 in the clearest possible way.

But verse 45 presupposes far more than verse 38; it also presupposes the stupendous miracle the promise of which Mary had believed. How comparatively insignificant would Mary's faith have been if all that had been promised her was that her son in her coming marriage was to be the Messiah! Is it not perfectly evident that the faith for which Mary is praised is something far more than that; is the reference not plainly to her acceptance of an experience that involved possible shame for her among men and that was quite unique in the history of the human race? We have here a phenomenon that appears in the narrative from beginning to end. The truth is that this account of the birth and infancy of Jesus is all pitched in too high a key to suit a child born by ordinary generation from earthly parents. The exuberant praise of Mary's faith, like many other features of the narrative, and indeed like the spirit of this narrative from beginning to end, seems empty and jejune unless the reader has in his mind the miracle which really forms the centre of the whole.

But this is not the only point at which the account of Mary's visit to

Elisabeth presupposes the virgin birth. Certainly the account of the visit constitutes a clear refutation at least of that form of the interpolation theory which includes in the interpolation verses 36 and 37. When the angel is represented in those verses as pointing to the example of Elisabeth, evidently the motive is being given for the journey that Mary immediately undertakes. "And Mary arose in those days and went with haste into the hill country into a city of Judah." Why did she go at all, and especially why did she go *in haste?* Is it not perfectly clear that it was because of the angel's words? Without verses 36 f. the whole account of the visit to Elisabeth is left hanging in the air.

Verses 36 f., therefore, were clearly in the original narrative. But, as we have already pointed out, verses 36 f. presuppose verses 34 f. in the clearest possible way. As it stands, the narrative hangs together; but when the supposed interpolation is removed all is thrown into confusion.

Hilgenfeld[44] has pointed out still another way in which the account of Mary's visit to Elisabeth presupposes Lk. i.34, 35. Evidently at the time of the visit the conception is regarded as already having taken place. When Elisabeth says to Mary: "Blessed art thou among women, and blessed is the fruit of thy womb. And whence is this to me, that the mother of my Lord should come to me?",[45] her words seem overwrought if the conception is still to come. But if the conception has already taken place at the time of Mary's journey, how is the journey to be explained? Surely it cannot be explained if Mary is regarded as already married to Joseph. In that case, as Hilgenfeld has well intimated, what would have been in place for Mary, if there was to be any journey at all, would have been a bridal tour with her husband, not a hasty journey far away from her husband to the home of a kinswoman.[46] Is it not perfectly clear that the whole account of Mary's visit to Elisabeth presupposes the supernatural conception? If Mary has passed through the wonderful experience promised in Lk. i.34, 35, then everything falls into its proper place; then it is the most natural thing in the world for the angel to suggest, and for Mary to carry out, a journey to visit her kinswoman, who

[44] "Die Geburts- und Kindheitsgeschichte Jesu Luc. I, 5– II, 52," in *Zeitschrift für wissenschaftliche Theologie,* xliv, 1901, p. 204.

[45] Lk. i.42 f.

[46] Loisy (*op. cit.*, i, 1907, p. 296) supposes that in the source (which he thinks did not contain verses 34, 35) an account of the marriage between Joseph and Mary came immediately after the account of the annunciation. But such suppositions overload the interpolation hypothesis, and the phrase ἐν ταῖς ἡμέραις ταύταις in verse 39 affords no sufficient reason for positing a wait between the departure of the angel and the visit to Elisabeth—a wait which was originally filled in by the marriage. Wilkinson (*op. cit.*, 1902, pp. 11 f.) agrees with Loisy in finding an antinomy between ἐν ταῖς ἡμέραις ταύταις and μετὰ σπουδῆς. The latter phrase, he thinks, has been added to the original account. But surely the difficulty in the narrative as it stands is not so serious as these scholars suppose.

also has passed through a wonderful, though of course far inferior, experience of God's grace. But if Lk. i.34 f. is omitted, everything is at loose ends.

Even at the very end of the infancy narrative, the virgin birth seems to be presupposed. When it is said in Lk. ii.51 that Jesus "went down with them, and came to Nazareth, and was subject unto them," the sentence seems perhaps to be without point if Jesus was born of Joseph and Mary by ordinary generation. Why should it be thought a thing so remarkable that a child of earthly parents, even if the child was the Messiah, should be subject to its parents? The very way in which the submission of the boy Jesus to His earthly parents is introduced in the narrative suggests that His relationship to them was such as to make the submission an extraordinary and noteworthy thing.

We should not, indeed, be inclined to lay particular stress upon this point if it were taken by itself. Perhaps one might say that if there was in the boy Jesus so extraordinary a consciousness of sonship toward God as is attested by His answer in the Temple, it was remarkable that He should subject Himself to earthly parents even if He were descended from them by ordinary generation. But that only pushes the difficulty in the way of an acceptance of the interpolation theory a step farther back. Is it likely that a son born of earthly parents by ordinary generation should have had such a stupendous consciousness of unique sonship toward God at all?[47] We are really led back again and again, wherever we start, to one central observation. That central observation is that only a superficial reading of Lk. i-ii can find in this narrative an account of a merely human child; when the reader puts himself really into touch with the inner spirit of the narrative, he sees that everywhere a supernatural child is in view. There is, therefore, a certain element of truth in the view advanced by the school of comparative religion to the effect that the child depicted in this narrative is a *Gotteskind*. That view is certainly wrong in detecting a polytheistic and mythological background for the stories of Lk. i-ii; but at least it is quite correct in observing that what the narrator has in view is no ordinary, merely human child. The whole atmosphere that here surrounds the child Jesus is an atmosphere proper only to one who has been conceived by the Holy Ghost.[48]

[47] Strauss (*Das Leben Jesu für das deutsche Volk bearbeitet*, 1864, 3te Aufl., unchanged, 1874, p. 387) found in the answer of Jesus in the Temple a reference to the story of the supernatural conception.

[48] The central place of the virgin birth in Lk. i–ii was recognized with special clearness nearly a century ago by Ch. Hermann Weisse (*Die evangelische Geschichte*, 1838, i, pp. 141–232). The myth of the virgin birth, he said in effect, is the central idea of the Lucan cycle: the rest of the cycle is built up around it; John the Baptist, for example, is brought in simply in order to make the importance of the birth of Christ clearer by the similarity and contrast over against the birth of John. Whatever may be thought of Weisse's mythical theory, there can be no doubt but that in making the virgin birth the central idea in the Lucan narrative he is displaying a true literary

But it is time to turn from such general considerations to an argument of a much more specific kind. The argument to which we refer is found in the remarkable parallelism that prevails between the account of the annunciation to Mary and that of the annunciation to Zacharias.[49] This parallelism shows in the clearest possible way that the verses Lk. i.34, 35 belong to the very innermost structure of the narrative. In both accounts we find (1) an appearance of the angel Gabriel, (2) fear on the part of the person to whom the annunciation is to be made, (3) reassurance by the angel and pronouncement of a promise, (4) a perplexed question by the recipient of the promise, (5) a grounding of the question in a causal clause, (6) reiteration of the promise with reference to something which in both cases is in the nature of a sign. The facts may best be indicated if we place the two sections in parallel columns:[50]

Lk. i.11-20	Lk. i.28-38
1	1
Verse 11	Verse 28
And there appeared unto him an angel of the Lord standing on the right side of the altar of incense.	And the angel came in unto her, and said, Hail, thou that art highly favoured, the Lord is with thee.
2	2
Verse 12	Verse 29
And when Zacharias saw him, he was troubled, and fear fell upon him.	And she was troubled at the saying, and cast in her mind what manner of salutation this might be.
3	3
Verses 13-17	Verses 30-33
But the angel said unto him, Fear not, Zacharias: for thy prayer is heard; and	And the angel said unto her, Fear not, Mary: for thou hast found favour with

insight as over against every form of the interpolation theory. Far from being an excrescence in the narrative, the virgin birth is really the thing for which all the rest exists. And that holds good no matter whether the narrative is mythical, as Weisse thought, or whether it is historical. If it is mythical, then the virgin birth explains the invention of the other elements; if it is historical, then the virgin birth explains the choice of the facts which are singled out for the narrative and also explains the way in which the narration is carried through. A return to Weisse would certainly, from the literary point of view, be desirable. And there is a sense in which that return, so far as the interpolation theory is concerned, is actually being effected in the most recent criticism of the infancy narratives.

[49] The parallelism was clearly recognized so early as 1841 by Gelpke (*Die Jugendgeschichte des Herrn*, pp. 41–51, 167–169) and was exhibited by him by at least a rudimentary use of parallel columns. Compare lso Sc hleiermacher, *Das Leben Jesu* (printed from reports of lectures delivered in 1832), 1864, pp. 53 f.

[50] The language of the following translation is for the most part that of the Authorized Version, corrected to conform to a better Greek text.

thy wife Elisabeth shall bear thee a son, and thou shalt call his name John. And thou shalt have joy and gladness; and many shall rejoice at his birth. For he shall be great in the sight of the Lord, and shall drink neither wine nor strong drink: and he shall be filled with the Holy Ghost, even from his mother's womb. And many of the children of Israel shall he turn to the Lord their God. And he shall go before him in the spirit and power of Elias, to turn the hearts of the fathers to the children, and the disobedient to the wisdom of the just; to make ready a people prepared for the Lord.

God. And behold thou shalt conceive in thy womb, and bring forth a son, and shalt call his name Jesus.

He shall be great and shall be called the Son of the Highest:

and the Lord God shall give unto him the throne of his father David: and he shall reign over the house of Jacob for ever; and of his kingdom there shall be no end.

4

Verse 18a

And Zacharias said unto the angel, Whereby shall I know this?

4

Verse 34a

Then said Mary unto the angel, How shall this be,

5

Verse 18b

for I am an old man, and my wife well stricken in years.

5

Verse 34b

seeing I know not a man?

6

Verses 19-20

And the angel answering said unto him, I am Gabriel that stand in the presence of God; and am sent to speak unto thee, and to shew thee these glad tidings.

And behold, thou shalt be dumb, and not able to speak, until the day that these things shall be performed, because thou believedst not my words, which shall be fulfilled in their season.

6

Verses 35-38

And the angel answered and said unto her, The Holy Ghost shall come upon thee, and the power of the Highest shall overshadow thee; therefore also that holy thing which is begotten shall be called the Son of God.

And behold, thy cousin Elisabeth, she also hath conceived a son in her old age: and this is the sixth month with her, who was called barren. For with God nothing shall be impossible.

And Mary said, Behold the handmaid of the Lord; be it unto me according to thy word. And the angel departed from her.

It may be remarked in passing that even this exhibition does not fully set forth the connection between the two accounts. It does not show, for example, that in both cases the name of the angel is Gabriel, that the description of Mary in verse 27 is very similar in form to that of the parents of John in verse 5, that the Holy Spirit is mentioned in connection with the beginning of the earthly life both of John and of Jesus, and that the two accounts are specifically linked together by the words, "in the sixth month", in Lk. i.26. But even in itself the parallelism, when the two accounts are set forth as above in parallel columns, is so striking as to render almost inconceivable the hypothesis that it came by chance. No one who really attends to the structure of both sections should doubt but that they came from the same hand. In both cases the narrative is cast in the same mould.

But if verses 34 and 35 were removed, this parallelism would be marred at the most important point. What, then, does the interpolation hypothesis involve? It involves something that is certainly unlikely in the extreme—namely, the supposition that an interpolator, desiring to insert an idea utterly foreign to the original narrative, has succeeded in inserting that idea in such a way as not only to refrain from marring the existent parallelism—even that would have been difficult enough—but actually to fill up in the most beautiful fashion a parallelism which otherwise would have been incomplete! We should have to suppose that the original narrator, though he did not include the virgin birth, left a gap exactly suited to its inclusion. And then we should have to suppose the appearance of an interpolator gifted with such marvellous literary skill as to be able, in the first place, to construct an interpolation that in spirit and style should conform perfectly to the body of the narrative, and then, in the second place, to insert that interpolation in just the place necessary to complete a parallelism which, when it is thus completed, makes upon the attentive reader the impression of being an essential element in the original framework of the narrative.

Surely this entire complex of suppositions is very improbable. How, then, can we possibly avoid the simple conclusion that the parallelism between the two accounts, including the part of it which appears in Lk. i.34 f., was due to the original narrator?

At this point, however, there may be an objection. May it not be said that the very perfection of the parallelism that appears if verses 34, 35 are included constitutes an argument not for, but against, the originality of those verses? Have we not, in other words, in the inclusion of verses 34 f., something in the nature of a "harmonistic corruption"? May not an interpolator, observing the large measure of parallelism between the accounts of the annunciations, have decided to make that parallelism a little more complete than it actually was?

A little reflection, we think, will show that these questions must be answered with an emphatic negative. The analogy with what is called a "harmonistic corruption" in textual criticism would not hold in this case at all. To show that it would not hold, we need only to glance at the harmonistic corruptions that actually appear in the text of the Synoptic Gospels. What is the nature of these corruptions? An example will make the matter plain. The verse Mt. xvii.21, "Howbeit this kind goeth not out but by prayer and fasting," in the account of the healing of the demoniac boy after the descent from the mount of the transfiguration, is omitted by the so-called "Neutral" type of text as attested by the Codex Vaticanus and the Codex Sinaiticus. It is universally recognized as a gloss. But if it were genuine it would not add anything to our knowledge of the incident; for in Mk. ix.29 very similar words are certainly genuine. It is perfectly evident that the text of Matthew has been made to conform to that of Mark. We have here, therefore, a typical example of a "harmonistic corruption." But how totally different is this case from the case of Lk. i.34 f., if these latter verses are really an addition to the original narrative! In the case of Mt. xvii.21, a sentence is taken over in a mechanical way from a parallel account; in the case of Lk. i.34 f., all that would be derived from the parallel account would be the sequence of question, grounding of the question, and answer: and the content of the interpolation would be of a highly original kind. Such originality would be quite unheard of among "harmonistic corruptions." What we should have here would be no mere obvious filling out of a narrative by the mechanical importation of details from a parallel account, but the addition of a highly original idea—by hypothesis foreign to the original narrative—and the expression of that idea in a way profoundly congruous, indeed, with the inner spirit of the narrative, but at the same time quite free from any merely literary dependence upon what has gone before or upon what follows. It is doubtful whether any parallel could be cited for such a phenomenon in the entire history of textual corruptions.

It appears, therefore—if we may use for the moment the language of textual criticism—that "intrinsic probability" and "transcriptional probability" are here in admirable agreement. On the one hand, the verses Lk. i.34 and 35 are really in the closest harmony with the rest of the narrative; but, on the other hand, that harmony is not of the obvious, superficial kind that would appeal to an interpolator. Indeed, the very difficulty that we found in the interpretation of Mary's question in verse 34 may be turned into an argument not for, but against, the interpolation theory. The difficulty is of a superficial kind that would probably have been avoided by an interpolator; the underlying harmony is of a kind worthy only of such a writer as the original composer of Lk. i-ii. Shall we attribute to an interpolator the delicate touch that is really to be found in Mary's question? Is not the question rather—we mean not the invention of the question but the preservation of it—to be attributed to the writer who has given us the rest of this matchless narrative?

In what has just been said, we have been using the language of textual criticism; we have been speaking of "intrinsic probability" and of "transcriptional probability" as though this were an ordinary question of the text. Such language would, of course, apply in fullest measure to that form of the interpolation hypothesis which finds in Lk. i.34 f. an interpolation into the completed Gospel; for in that case we should actually be dealing with scribal transmission in the strictest sense. But the language could really apply in some measure also to the other forms in which the interpolation hypothesis has been held. In any case, we have in Lk. i.34 f. an element that on one hand is in underlying harmony with the rest of the infancy narrative and yet, on the other hand, cannot be understood as being due to the effort of a later writer—whether the author of Luke-Acts or some one else—to produce that harmony by an insertion into this Palestinian narrative. *Real* harmony with the rest of the narrative, and *superficial* difficulty—these are the recognized marks of genuineness in any passage of an ancient work. And both these characteristics appear in Lk. i.34 and 35.

At any rate, whatever may be thought of our use of the terminology of textual criticism, the parallelism with the account of the annunciation to Zacharias stamps Lk. i.34 f. unmistakably as being an original part of the account of the annunciation to Mary. The argument comes as near to being actual demonstration as any argument that could possibly appear in the field of literary criticism. It is very clear that the two verses in question were part of the original structure of the narrative.

But before this phase of the subject is finally left, it will be necessary to consider the alternative view as to the extent of the interpolation, which was suggested by Kattenbusch and has been advocated by Weinel and others. According to these scholars, not the whole of Lk. i.34 f. constitutes the addition to the narrative, but only the four words translated "seeing I know not a man" [51] in verse 34.[52] If these four words are removed, it may be argued,

[51] ἐπεὶ ἄνδρα οὐ γινώσκω.

[52] Kattenbusch himself (*Das Apostolische Symbol*, ii, 1900, pp. 621 f.) did not insist upon the hypothesis of an actual interpolation of the words ἐπεὶ ἄνδρα οὐ γινώσκω into an underlying document, but contented himself with arguing that without those four words the narrative would

there is in Mary's question no reference to the manner in which her child is to be born; she is puzzled merely by the greatness of her promised son, and asks therefore, "How shall this be?"[53], without at all thinking of anything other than the son that she was to have in her approaching marriage with Joseph. In reply—so the hypothesis may be held to run—the angel in verse 35 points to an activity of the Holy Spirit securing the greatness and holiness of the son, without at all excluding the human agency in His conception in the womb: the child will be in a physical sense the son of Joseph and Mary; but just as the son of Zacharias was to be filled with the Holy Spirit at the very beginning of his life,[54] so the son of Joseph will be fitted by the same Spirit for a far higher function.

In comment upon this hypothesis, it may be said, in the first place, that the hypothesis hardly accomplishes what it undertakes to accomplish; it hardly succeeds in removing the supernatural conception from Lk. i.34, 35. Surely the minimizing interpretation which Weinel advocates for verse 35 is unnatural in the extreme. When Mary is told by the angel, "The Holy Ghost shall come upon thee, and the power of the Highest shall overshadow thee: therefore also that holy thing which is begotten shall be called the Son of God," it seems very improbable that no more is meant than a sanctifying action of the Spirit upon a child conceived by another agency in the womb. Why should it be said, "The Holy Ghost shall come upon thee," if the activity of the Spirit terminates upon the child in the womb rather than upon Mary? Why should not some expression like that in Lk. i.15—"He shall be filled with the

---

not necessarily involve the virgin birth, and that the emphasis in the narrative is not upon the virgin birth, but upon what he regarded as an independent idea—the activity of the Spirit in connection with the birth of the Messiah. Weinel ("Die Auslegung des Apostolischen Bekenntnisses von F. Kattenbusch und die neutestamentliche Forschung," in *Zeitschrift für die neutestamentliche Wissenschaft*, ii, 1901, pp. 37–39) made the suggestion of Kattenbusch definitely fruitful for the interpolation hypothesis. J. M. Thompson (*Miracles in the New Testament*, 1911, pp. 147–150) and Merx (*Die vier kanonischen Evangelien*, II. ii, 1905, pp. 179–181) advocate the same view. Compare the citation of the literature in Moffatt, *Introduction*, 1918 (1925), p. 269. This form of the interpolation hypothesis proceeds somewhat in the line of a remark which was made so early as 1817 by Schleiermacher. The reference to a supernatural conception, Schleiermacher said, becomes perfectly definite in the Lucan account of the annunciation to Mary only by means of Mary's question in Lk. i.34, which, moreover, interrupts the words of the angel in rather an unnatural manner—perhaps merely in order to prevent the angel from speaking too long. See Schleiermacher, *Ueber die Schriften des Lukas*, 1817, pp. 26 f. (English translation, *A Critical Essay on the Gospel of St. Luke*, 1825, p. 28). This remark of Schleiermacher's was opposed by Strauss (*Leben Jesu*, i, 1835, p. 167). Kattenbusch has recently (in *Theologische Studien und Kritiken*, cii, 1930, pp. 457 f., 462–474) defended essentially the same view of Lk. i.34b as that which he suggested in 1900. See above, pp. viii f.

[53] Merx (*op. cit.*, II. ii, p. 196, footnote 1) lays stress upon the insertion of *μοι* in Mary's question by certain manuscripts. Mary's modest question, "How shall this be to me?", becomes, Merx thinks, when the "to me" is omitted, a curious or astonished question concerning the physiological process. As a matter of fact, "to me" is plainly a gloss of the most harmless kind.

[54] Lk. i.15.

Holy Ghost"—be used if the work of the Spirit in both cases is essentially the same? Perhaps, indeed, the advocates of the hypothesis will maintain that in accordance with their view the work of the Spirit is not the same in both cases; perhaps they will say that in the case of John merely a sanctifying influence is meant, whereas in the case of Jesus, the Spirit, though working indeed with the human factor, becomes constitutive of the very being of the child. But when that is said we are getting back very close indeed to the view that the Spirit's action excludes the human father altogether. The truth is that in verse 35 the human father is quite out of sight; only two factors are in view—the mother, Mary, and the Spirit of God. "Conceived by the Holy Ghost and born of the virgin Mary" is really a correct summary of that verse. Even without the disputed words in verse 34, therefore, the following verse, verse 35, still presupposes the virgin birth. But if so, all ground for suspecting the words, "seeing I know not a man", disappears.

A second objection to Weinel's hypothesis is found in the parallelism with the annunciation to Zacharias to which attention has already been called. Weinel himself performed a very useful service by urging that parallelism as an objection to the ordinary form of the interpolation theory, which would remove all of verses 34 and 35. But he did not seem to observe that it tells also against his own view. If the words, "seeing I know not a man," are removed from verse 34, then there is nothing to correspond to the grounding of Zacharias' question in verse 18. Let it not be said that we are expecting too perfect a similarity between the two parallel accounts. On the contrary, we recognize to the full the freshness and originality of verses 28-38 as over against verses 11-20; there are many details in one account that are not also in the other; the parallelism is by no means mechanical. But the point is that if Mary's grounding of her question be removed from verse 34, it is not merely one detail that is subtracted, but an essential element in the structural symmetry of the passage. It is really essential to the author's manner of narrating the annunciation to Zacharias that Zacharias' question should not merely indicate bewilderment in general, but should point the way for the explanation that was to follow. It seems evident that a similar plan is being followed in the case of the annunciation to Mary. But that plan is broken up if the words, "seeing I know not a man," are not original in verse 34. Weinel's hypothesis would force us to suppose that the original narrator left a gap in the structure of one of his parallel accounts, and a gap so exceedingly convenient that when by the insertion of four words an interpolator introduced into the narrative a momentous new idea, the most beautiful symmetry of form was the result. Surely such a supposition is very unlikely. It is perfectly evident, on the contrary, that the symmetry that results when Mary's grounding of her question is retained is due not to mere chance or to what would be a truly extraordinary coincidence between a defect in the fundamental structure and an interpolator's desires, but to the original intention of the author.

In the third place, Mary's question in verse 34, in the shortened form to which Weinel's hypothesis reduces it, seems unnatural and abrupt even apart from any comparison with the parallel account. According to Weinel, Mary said merely, in reply to the angel's promise, "How shall this be?". In that form the question seems to have no point; it is a meaningless interruption of the angel's speech.[55] And it does not seem to prepare in any intelligible way for what follows in verse 35. No doubt there are narrators to whom such clumsiness could be attributed; but certainly the author of Lk. i-ii was not one of them. In this narrative such banality would be singularly out of place. It is perfectly evident that in verse 34 the author is preparing for verse 35 in some far more definite and intelligible way than by the meaningless words, "How shall this be?"; Mary's question is plainly intended to point the way to the special explanation that is given in the following verse. Thus on Weinel's hypothesis the original narrator would at this point have suddenly descended to banality; and the beautiful naturalness and symmetry which now appear in the passage would be due not to the author, but to an interpolator. Who can believe that such a supposition is correct?

Such objections would be decisive in themselves. But there is another objection that is perhaps even more serious still. It is found in the extraordinary restraint which Weinel's hypothesis is obliged to attribute to the supposed interpolator. An interpolator, we are asked to believe, desired to introduce into a Jewish Christian narrative of the birth of Jesus a momentous idea—the idea of the virgin birth—which by hypothesis was foreign to that narrative. How does he go to work? Does he insert any express narration of the event that he regarded as so important? Does he even mention it plainly? Not at all. What he does is simply to insert four words, which will cause the context into which they are inserted to appear in a new light, so that now that context will be taken as implying the virgin birth.

Where was there ever found such extraordinary restraint, either in an ordinary interpolator who tampered with the manuscripts of a completed book, or in an author like the author of Luke-Acts who desired to introduce a new idea into one of his sources? Is it not abundantly plain that if an interpolator

[55] If the question were in this short form, the remark which Schleiermacher (see above p. 157, footnote 52) wrongly made about it in its complete form might seem to apply; the question would actually seem to be a mere interruption, perhaps introduced merely in order to prevent the angel's speech from being too long.

desired to introduce the virgin birth into the narrative of Lk. i-ii he would have done so in far less restrained and far more obvious manner than Weinel's hypothesis requires us to suppose? On the ordinary form of the interpolation hypothesis, which includes in the supposed insertion all of verses 34 and 35, we were called upon to admire the extraordinary literary skill of the interpolator, which enabled him to construct a rather extensive addition that should be highly original in content and yet conform so perfectly to the innermost spirit of the rest of the narrative. On Weinel's hypothesis, on the other hand, it is the extraordinary restraint of the interpolator which affords ground for wonder. The surprising thing is that if the interpolator was going to insert anything—in the interests of the virgin birth—he did not insert far more.[56]

We have enumerated four special objections to the hypothesis of Weinel. With the exception of the one based on the parallelism with Lk. i.11-20, they apply only to this hypothesis and not also to the more usual view as to the extent of the interpolation. That more usual view is in turn faced by some special objections that the view of Weinel avoids. But it must be remembered that some of the weightiest objections apply to both hypotheses alike. All that we have said regarding the plain implication of the virgin birth in Lk. i.27 and ii.5, and regarding the subtler implication of it at other points in the narrative, tells against any effort to find in the original form of Lk. i-ii a narrative that presented Jesus as being by ordinary generation the son of Joseph and Mary.

What needs finally to be emphasized is that in holding the virgin birth of Christ to be an integral part of the representation in Lk. i-ii we are not dependent merely upon details. At least equally convincing is a consideration of the narrative as a whole. With regard to the results of such a general consideration, it may be well now to say a final word.

In what precedes, we have laid special stress upon the parallelism between the account of the annunciation to Mary and that of the annunciation to Zacharias. That parallelism, we observed, establishes Lk. i.34, 35 in the clearest possible way as belonging to the basic structure of the narrative; the (evidently intentional) symmetry of form between the two accounts is hopelessly marred if these verses, either as a whole or in part, are removed.

But what now needs to be observed is that the *difference* between the two accounts is at least as significant, in establishing the original place of the virgin

[56] Compare Vincent Taylor, *The Historical Evidence for the Virgin Birth*, 1920, p. 70: "To expand a narrative in the direction of the sense which it already bears is a conceivable suggestion. To transform it totally by merely adding four words is a theory which does not carry conviction. Was ever an interpolator so ingenious as this?"

birth in Lk. i-ii, as is the similarity. In fact, the very similarity finds its true meaning in the emphasis which it places upon the difference.

One obvious difference, of course, is that the annunciation of the birth of John comes to the father of the child, while the annunciation of the birth of Jesus comes to the mother. What is the reason for this difference? Is the difference due merely to chance? Is it due merely to the way in which the tradition in the two cases happened to be handed down—merely to the fact that, as Harnack thinks,[57] the stories regarding Jesus were preserved by a circle that held Mary in special veneration and had been affected in some way by the impression that she had made? If this latter suggestion is adopted, we have a significant concession to the traditional opinion, which has always been inclined to attribute the Lucan infancy narrative, mediately or immediately, to the mother of the Lord. Such an admission will probably not be made by many of those who reject, as Harnack does, the historicity of the narrative. And for those who will not make the admission, who will not admit any special connection of the narrative with Mary or with her circle, the central place of Mary instead of Joseph in the annunciation scene remains a serious problem. But even if we accept the Marianic origin of the narrative—and do so even in a way far more definite than that which Harnack favors—still the unique place of Mary in the narrative requires an explanation. The point is not merely that Mary receives special attention—that her inmost thoughts are mentioned and the like—but that she is given an actual prominence that would seem unnatural if the child belonged equally to Joseph and to her.[58]

The fact is that we find ourselves here impaled upon the horns of a dilemma. If, on the one hand, the narrative is quite unhistorical, and not based upon any tradition connected with the actual Mary, then we do not see how the narrative, or the legend lying back of it, ever came—since in this case it had full freedom of invention—to attribute such importance to the mother unless she was regarded as a parent of the child in some sense that did not apply to Joseph. Certainly the narrative displays no general predilection in favor of women as over against men; for in the case of John the Baptist the annunciation is represented as being made to Zacharias, not to Elisabeth. If, therefore, it regards the relation of Joseph to Jesus as being similar to that of Zacharias to John, why does it not make him, like Zacharias, the recipient of the angelic promise? So much may be said for one horn of the dilemma.

[57] Harnack, *Neue Untersuchungen zur Apostelgeschichte*, 1911, pp. 109 f. (English translation, *The Date of the Acts and of the Synoptic Gospels*, 1911, pp. 155 f.).

[58] The prominence of Mary as over against Joseph runs all through the narrative in Lk. i.5–ii.52, and it appears in the final scene. As Farrar (*Life of Christ*, i, 1874, p. 77) has observed, it is Mary, not Joseph, who addresses the boy Jesus in the Temple according to Lk. ii.48.

But if the other horn be chosen—if the narrator be regarded as being bound by historical tradition actually coming from Mary—still the prominence of Mary in the narrative remains significant. Are we to suppose that Mary attributed that prominence to herself without special reason? This supposition, in view of Mary's character, as it appears in the narrative itself, is unlikely in the extreme.

Thus, whatever view we take of the ultimate origin of the narrative, the prominence in it of Mary as compared with Joseph, which is so strikingly contrasted with the prominence of Zacharias as compared with Elisabeth, clearly points to something particularly significant in her relation to the promised child, something which Joseph did not share. In other words, it points to the supernatural conception, which is so plainly attested in Lk. i.34, 35. The removal of these verses by the advocates of the interpolation theory has really deprived us of the key that unlocks the meaning of the narrative from beginning to end.

There is, moreover, another way also in which the relation between the two accounts of annunciations presupposes the virgin birth. What sympathetic reader can fail to see that the relation between the two accounts is a relation of climax? It is clearly the intention of the narrator to exhibit the greatness of Jesus in comparison with His forerunner, John. But in the annunciation of the birth of John the manner of the birth is given special prominence. The child, it is said, is to be born of aged parents; and around this feature a large part of the narrative revolves. The unbelief of Zacharias and the punishment of that unbelief are occasioned not by the prediction of later events in the life of the promised child, but by the prediction of the wonderful manner of his birth. Are we to suppose that in the parallel account there was nothing to correspond to this central feature of the annunciation to Zacharias? Are we to suppose that after laying such special stress upon the unusual manner of the promised birth of John the narrator proceeded to narrate a promise of a perfectly ordinary birth of Jesus; are we to suppose that it is the intention of the narrator that while John was born of aged parents by a special dispensation of divine grace, Jesus was simply the child of Joseph and Mary? No supposition, we think, would more completely miss the point of the narrative. Verses 36 and 37 surely provide the true key to the relation between the two accounts; the angel there points to the coming birth of John the Baptist from an aged mother as an example of that omnipotence of God which is to be manifested in yet plainer fashion in the birth of Jesus. In the light of this utterance, the whole meaning of the parallelism between the two accounts of annunciations becomes plain. The very similarities between the two cases are intended to set off in all the greater plainness the stupendous difference; and the difference concerns not merely the relative greatness of the two children that are to be born, but also the manner of their conception in the womb. A wonderful, if not plainly supernatural, conception in the case of John followed by a merely natural conception in the case of Jesus, which the interpolation theory requires us to find, would have seemed to the composer of the narrative to involve a lamentable anticlimax. The entire structure of the narrative protests eloquently against any such thing.

At this point, however, an objection may possibly be raised. It is not an objection against our argument in itself, but an *argumentum ad hominem* against our use of it. We have insisted that there is a conscious parallelism between the account of the annunciation to Zacharias and that of the annunciation to Mary, and that the author evidently intends to exhibit the superiority, even in the manner of birth, that Jesus possesses over against John. But—so the objection might run—does not such a view of the author's intentions involve denial of the historicity of the narrative? If the author was ordering his material with such freedom as to exhibit the parallelism that we have discovered, and if he was deliberately setting about to show the superiority of Jesus over John, must he not, in order to pursue these ends, have been quite free from the restraint which would have been imposed upon him by information concerning what actually happened to Zacharias and to Mary? In other words, does not the artistic symmetry which we have discovered in the narrative militate against any acceptance of its historical trustworthiness? And since we are intending to defend its historical trustworthiness, have we, as distinguished from those who deny its trustworthiness, any right to that particular argument against the interpolation theory which we have just used?

In reply, it may be said simply that our argument has not depended upon any particular view as to the way in which the symmetry, upon which we have been insisting, came into being. It would hold just as well if the author merely reproduced a symmetry which he observed to be inherent in the divine ordering of the facts, as it would if he himself constructed the symmetry by free invention. In either case, the symmetry would be intentional in his narrative. Moreover, even in a thoroughly accurate narrative there is some possibility of such a selection and ordering of the material as shall bring certain features especially into view. A portrait, with its selection of details, is sometimes not less truthful but more truthful than a photograph. So in this case, the author, we think, was not doing violence to the facts when he presented the annunciation to Mary as in parallel with the annunciation to Zacharias. That parallelism, we think, was inherent in the facts; and the writer showed himself to be not merely an artist, but a true historian, when he refrained from marring it.

But the point is that, although the argument for the integrity of the passage which we have based upon the parallelism holds on the view that the narrative is historical, it holds equally well on the hypothesis that it is the product of free invention. In either case—however the parallelism came to be there—it certainly as a matter of fact *is* there; and an interpolation theory which holds that it was originally defective at the decisive point is faced by the strongest kind of objections that literary criticism can ever afford.

Our conclusion, then, is that the entire narrative in Lk. i-ii finds both its climax and its centre in the virgin birth of Christ. A superficial reading may lead to a contrary conclusion; but when one enters sympathetically into the inner spirit of the narrative one sees that the virgin birth is everywhere presupposed. The account of the lesser wonder in the case of the forerunner, the delicate and yet significant way in which Mary is put forward instead of Joseph, the lofty key in which the whole narrative is pitched—all this is incomprehensible without the supreme miracle of the supernatural conception in the virgin's womb. The interpolation hypothesis, therefore, not merely fails of proof, but (so fully as can reasonably be expected in literary criticism) is positively disproved.

Another attack upon the integrity of the Lucan narrative deserves separate consideration because it stands somewhat aside from the ordinary forms of the interpolation hypothesis. We refer to the theory of Daniel Völter, whose monograph appeared in 1911, but was based upon earlier studies.[59] Völter holds that there is embedded in Lk. i-ii, in addition to the Christian elements, a narrative that came from the sect of the disciples of John the Baptist. This narrative contained, of course, the account of the annunciation to Zacharias in Lk. i.5-25. But after that account it contained also—and here we come to the distinctive feature of the theory—an account of an annunciation by the angel Gabriel to Elisabeth, for which a Christian writer has substituted the episodes of the annunciation to Mary and of Mary's visit to Elisabeth. Why should "the sixth month" of Elisabeth's pregnancy be mentioned in Lk. i.26?, Völter asks. That way of fixing the time, he says, is natural only in an episode that concerns Elisabeth; yet in the narrative as it now stands the episode concerns not Elisabeth, but Mary. This incongruity, Völter argues, is evidently due to a redactor, and originally the annunciation in Lk. i.26-39 was an annunciation to Elisabeth. The real significance of the "sixth month" appears, Völter continues, in Lk. i.41; the sixth month marked the point of

[59] Völter, *Die evangelischen Erzählungen von der Geburt und Kindheit Jesu*, 1911.

time when the babe in Elisabeth's womb gave a sign of life. Originally, therefore, there came first an annunciation to Zacharias, the father, and then an annunciation by the same angel to Elisabeth, the mother. Then the babe leaped in the womb, and Elisabeth responded with the hymn of thanksgiving, the Magnificat, which now appears out of its original place and wrongly attributed (in nearly all manuscripts) to Mary. Thus, according to Völter, there stood in the original John-the-Baptist narrative, after the account of the annunciation of the birth of John to Zacharias, the following words:

> And in the sixth month the angel Gabriel was sent from God to the hill-country, to Bethlehem Judah. And he entered into the house of Zacharias and greeted Elisabeth and said: "Hail, thou favored one, the Lord is with thee." And behold thou shalt bear a son and shalt call his name John. And it came to pass, when Elisabeth heard the greeting of the angel, the child leaped in her womb, and Elisabeth was filled with the Holy Ghost and cried in exultation and said: . . .

Then followed the Magnificat, then the account of the birth and naming of John, and then a short form of the Benedictus without what Völter thinks are Christian interpolations that appear in the present form.

This account of the birth of John the Baptist which circulated originally among the (non-Christian) disciples of John was, Völter thinks, taken up by the Evangelist and incorporated, at first largely unchanged, in the Gospel; but the Evangelist put it at once in what he regarded as the proper light by placing an account of the birth of Jesus (Chapter ii of the Gospel) by its side. Then a later redactor gave the two chapters their present canonical form by substituting an annunciation to Mary and a visit of Mary to Elisabeth for the annunciation to Elisabeth, and by making other redactional changes. It was by this redactor that the idea of the virgin birth was first introduced into the narrative.

This theory[60] has recently been adopted in essentials by Eduard Norden in his important monograph which we shall discuss in Chapter XIV, and has won some additional support.[61]

In the criticism of the theory,[62] we may point, in the first place, to the

[60] In 1902 J. R. Wilkinson (*A Johannine Document in the First Chapter of St. Luke's Gospel*), working independently of Völter, some of whose studies had already appeared, propounded a theory which, although it is similar to Völter's in some respects, also presents differences. See especially pp. 34–40 of Wilkinson's booklet, and the discussion by the present writer in the article, "The First Two Chapters of Luke," in *Princeton Theological Review*, x, 1912, pp. 274 f.

[61] Norden, *Die Geburt des Kindes*, 1924, pp. 102–105; Klostermann, *op. cit.*, 2te Aufl., 1929, pp. 4 f. Compare also Bultmann, *op. cit.*, 1931, pp. 320–323. Apparently Norden, unlike Völter, attributes the redactional activity in the first chapter of Luke not to a later redactor, but to the Evangelist himself; but this difference does not affect the characteristic features of the theory.

[62] Compare the article just cited from *Princeton Theological Review*, x, 1912, pp. 272–275.

remarkable unity of style and spirit between the supposedly Johannine and the supposedly Christian parts of Lk. i-ii. Völter denies that unity, but despite his denial it is certainly present in striking measure. It is, indeed, true that Christian, as distinguished from pre-Christian, ideas are absent from the Johannine parts of the narrative, but so are they from the "Christian" parts—except of course what is involved in the fact that the child Jesus is represented as the virgin-born Messiah. In the second place, we may point to the weakness of Völter's detailed arguments—particularly the argument derived from the mention of the "sixth month" in Lk. i.26. As Bultmann[63] has pointed out, it is not true that that note of time is important only for Elisabeth and not for Mary; for it marks the time when the sign to which the angel pointed in the annunciation to Mary[64] could be observed by the leaping of the child in the womb.[65] The narrative as it stands really hangs together, and there is not the slightest reason to reverse the impression of unity which is undoubtedly made upon the unprejudiced reader by the style and spirit of the whole section. In general, it may be said that Völter's theory serves only to demonstrate anew the uncertainty of the ordinary forms of the interpolation hypothesis. "The verses, Lk. i.34 f.," Völter correctly says,[66] "cannot be separated from their context. They are presupposed not only in verses 36 f., but in the whole of verses 26-33; without them the whole annunciation to Mary loses its point." Indeed, the whole of the passage, Lk. i.26-41 (or 42a), Völter says, is due to one hand. Thus this latest denial of the integrity of Lk. i-ii holds that what previous critics regarded as loose joints in the narrative are really organic connections. It is not possible to remove verses 34-35 alone, nor verses 34-37. Völter has correctly observed that much. But it cannot be said that his own very venturesome theory is unworthy of the rejection which it has so generally received.

One solid observation underlies the theory of Völter regarding the first chapter of Luke—the observation that specifically Christian ideas are absent from Lk. i.5-25 and from other parts of the narrative that relate to John the Baptist. Harnack[67] has used this same observation, not indeed to propound an elaborate documentary analysis like that of Völter, but to commend the view that these Johannine parts of the narrative do come from a tradition preserved among John's disciples. The narrative in Lk. i, he thinks, is derived

[63] In a review of Norden's book, in *Theologische Literaturzeitung*, xlix, 1924, col. 323.

[64] "And behold, Elisabeth, thy kinswoman, she also has conceived a son in her old age" (Lk. i.36).

[65] Lk. i.44.

[66] *Op. cit.*, pp. 20–22.

[67] For what follows, see the article cited from *Princeton Theological Review*, x, 1912, pp. 275–277.

not merely from two chief sources, but even ultimately from two religious camps; for the narrative of the birth of John the Baptist,[68] which still shows that it was not originally composed as an introduction to the story of Jesus, but had independent value, must have arisen in the circle of John's disciples, where also Lk. iii.1 ff. (in so far as it goes beyond Mark and Q), including the great chronological note, evidently originated. The passage, Lk. i.39-45, 56 (so Harnack's hypothesis continues), unites the two birth narratives, which were originally quite distinct. The former of these narratives originally celebrated the Baptist not as forerunner of Jesus the Messiah, but as preparing the way for the coming of Jehovah in redemption.[69] The birth narrative of John is accordingly very old, and presents the tradition of John's disciples in Lucan spirit and style.[70]

This hypothesis of Harnack is not altogether devoid of plausibility. But it can be established, if at all, only if Lk. i is unhistorical. For if Mary was really related to Elisabeth, as is asserted in Lk. i.36, and if the two mothers really came into contact in the way described in Lk. i.39 ff., then a family history of the birth of Jesus could hardly have been composed without including also the events connected with the birth of the forerunner. In Lk. i.5-25 John appears, indeed, as the forerunner not specifically of the Messiah, but of Jehovah. That fact might be explicable if the narrative were composed by a non-Christian disciple of John. But it is equally explicable if the description of the work of John in Lk. i.15-17 is not a *vaticinium ex eventu,* but a genuine prophecy. For in prophecy definiteness is not to be demanded. The Old Testament, according to one element of its teaching, connected the future redemption with a coming of Jehovah. In just what way Jehovah was to come had not yet been revealed with perfect definiteness, either in Old Testament times or at the time just preceding the birth of Jesus. The non-Christian character of Lk. i.5-25, therefore, may establish not its origin in a non-

[68] Lk. i.5–25, 46–55, 57–80.

[69] Lk. i.16 f.

[70] See Harnack, *Neue Untersuchungen zur Apostelgeschichte*, 1911, pp. 108 f. (compare the English translation, *The Date of the Acts and of the Synoptic Gospels*, 1911, pp. 153 f.). In a footnote (*ibid.*) Harnack says: "It is not improbable that Luke, before he united himself with the Christian community, belonged to the disciples of John the Baptist [Anhänger der Täuferbewegung gewesen ist] and had already pursued historical investigations which he afterwards used for his Gospel. The attitude which he assumes in the Gospel (and also in Acts) toward the Johannine movement [Täuferbewegung] and toward the 'Spirit' tends to support this hypothesis. Furthermore, in Lk. iii.15, 'And as the people were in expectation, and all men mused in their hearts of John, whether he were the Christ, or not' [we have given the English translation here instead of the Greek original which Harnack quotes], Luke has probably given expression to experiences of his own, which, after the narrative in Lk. i, seem altogether natural. This narrative can only have originated in the circle of the Baptist's disciples and could have been placed at the beginning of the history of Jesus only by one who was connected with that circle."

Christian sect, but merely its historicity. It could not have been composed by a Christian writer, but must have been composed by a Johannine writer—unless the Christian writer was telling the truth.

At any rate, this hypothesis of Harnack, as to Johannine tradition in Lk. i, must be sharply distinguished from a documentary theory like that of Völter and Norden. Harnack's theory might be held in a form compatible with the historicity of the narrative; for there is no reason why a circle of John's disciples (if indeed such a circle existed) might not have preserved genuine historical information about the birth of the one to whom the sect appealed, and why a Christian writer might not have connected that historical information about John with equally historical information about Jesus, so as to produce the narrative that we now have in Lk. i-ii. Very different in its implications is the theory of Völter, which represents those parts of Lk. i that concern Jesus (including the mention of the virgin birth) as secondary elements in a process of literary manipulation. It is this theory which we are really concerned to refute. And it can be refuted, as we have observed, in no uncertain way. There is no reason, then, for us to reverse the conclusion at which we arrived after considering the ordinary forms of the interpolation hypothesis. All the attacks upon the integrity of Lk. i-ii which would represent the mention of the virgin birth as a secondary element in the narrative have signally failed.

Chapter VII

THE NARRATIVE IN MATTHEW

IN THE five preceding chapters we have been dealing with the Gospel according to Luke. It is now time to turn to the other of the two Gospels that attest the virgin birth of Christ—namely, the Gospel according to Matthew.

This Gospel, unlike the one with which we have just dealt, keeps the personality of the author entirely in the background. In Luke-Acts, the author, although he does not mention his name, does introduce himself personally in his two prologues and does (at least according to the only natural interpretation of his words) indicate by the use of the first person plural the places where he was an eye-witness of the events that he narrates. In the First Gospel, on the other hand, no such phenomena are to be observed. On the contrary, it would be hard to find a book where the personality of the author is kept more completely out of view. It may be possible to detect significance in the way in which the call of Matthew (or Levi) is narrated in this Gospel as compared with the others, if one has already accepted the traditional view of the authorship; but certainly these peculiarities would never in themselves establish that view unless it had already been suggested by other considerations. The decision about the authorship of this Gospel, therefore, depends not upon any specific indications of authorship in the book itself—for there are none—but upon our estimate of early Christian tradition on the subject, when taken in connection with the character of the material which the book contains.

Nevertheless, although the First Gospel keeps the personality of its author in the background, it does indicate, by the character of its contents, something of the destination which the author had in mind when he wrote. It is widely held that this Gospel is addressed particularly to the Jews. Its Jewish destination appears, for example, in the peculiar prominence which it assigns to the fulfilment of Old Testament prophecy in the events of the life of Jesus, and also, perhaps, in certain answers which it seems to give to specific Jewish attacks.

Exaggerations, indeed, should be avoided at this point. On the one hand, all of the Gospels—not merely this Gospel—are interested in the fulfilment of Old Testament prophecy; and on the other hand, this Gospel is certainly not

Jewish in the sense that it stands in any disagreement with the principles of the Gentile mission in the early Church or in the sense that it obtrudes into the history in any disturbing way its answers to Jewish attacks. But despite such qualifications, the essentially Jewish character of the Gospel does seem to stand firm. The differences from the other Gospels in this respect are, indeed, not at all sharp; they are subtle differences of emphasis, rather than clear-cut differences of treatment. Possibly the Gospel from the beginning was intended for Gentiles as well as for Jews; and certainly it was admirably suited to the needs of both. But a certain special Jewish reference cannot be denied.

In this Gospel, as in the Gospel according to Luke, the account of the birth and infancy of Jesus is found in the first two chapters. There can be no doubt but that these chapters formed an original part of the book. Abortive efforts have, indeed, been made in the course of modern criticism to establish a contrary conclusion; but the evidence against them is overwhelming.

Hilgenfeld,[1] for example, argues that Mt. iii.1 would not be natural if the third chapter was originally joined to what now goes before; the public appearance of John the Baptist, he says in effect, took place many years after the settlement of Joseph and Mary at Nazareth, which is narrated at the close of the second chapter; so that the phrase, "in those days," as fixing the time of John's appearance, could hardly have been intended to refer back to that event. Accordingly, Hilgenfeld supposes, the phrase referred originally to the close of the genealogy, Mt. i.18-ii.23 being a later addition. In comparison with the long period of time covered by the genealogy, he thinks, it would be perfectly natural to mean by the phrase, "in those days", merely "in the time of Jesus" as distinguished from the many previous generations.

But, surely, it may be said in reply, this reference of Mt. iii.1 to the genealogy seems rather unlikely; for the genealogy is the expression of one idea, and attention is not fixed, at the end of it, upon one period of time as distinguished from preceding periods. Rather does the phrase, "in those days", require that something in the nature of a narrative should have gone before, and this requirement is not satisfied by the genealogy. Surely it is much more natural to suppose that the period to which "in those days" refers is the period of residence at Nazareth following upon the settlement of Joseph and Mary there,

[1] "Friedrich Loofs gegen Ernst Haeckel," in *Zeitschrift für wissenschaftliche Theologie*, xliii, 1900, p. 269. So also Merx, *Die vier kanonischen Evangelien nach ihrem ältesten bekannten Texte*, II.i, 1902, pp. 14 f. The following discussion of critical attempts to separate Mt. i-ii, in whole or in part, from the rest of the Gospel is similar to the treatment by the present writer in "The New Testament Account of the Birth of Jesus", second article, in *Princeton Theological Review*, iv, 1906, pp. 61-63.

which is narrated in Mt. ii.23. According to Hillmann,[2] indeed, who supposes that the whole of the first two chapters and not merely Mt. i.18-ii.23 constitutes the later addition, some chronological note similar to that in Lk. iii.1 was left off at Mt. iii.1 by the redactor who added chapters i and ii: the redactor was so far from the time described that he would take no offence at applying the phrase, "in those days", to what really happened after an interval of thirty years. But in reply it may be said that possibly the author of the Gospel would himself, when he wrote his book, have been looking back over a long enough interval not to have objected to the phrase, especially in view of the loose way (so far as chronology is concerned) in which the incidents are coupled together all through this Gospel. In reality, Mt. ii.23, though it directly relates only an event that took place long before the event narrated in Mt. iii.1, really implies a long period of residence at Nazareth following upon that event. It is that period which is in view in the phrase, "in those days." Meyer,[3] moreover calls attention to the fact that Mt. iv.13 (where, in distinction from the other Gospels, Nazareth is mentioned) clearly presupposes the settlement of the holy family at Nazareth in Mt. ii.23.

Thus the way in which the third chapter begins does not at all stamp the first two chapters as an addition to the Gospel. Equally unconvincing are the arguments which have been based upon the contents of the section itself. Hilgenfeld[4] enumerates, as indications that Mt. i.18-ii.23 is the work of some one other than the author of the Gospel, (1) the Old Testament pragmatism, (2) the friendly attitude toward the heathen, (3) the view of Christ as being born Son of God. But the "Old Testament pragmatism" rather reveals the hand of the author of the whole Gospel, who is interested throughout in showing the fulfilment of Old Testament prophecy. The friendly attitude toward the Gentiles proves nothing if the story of the magi is essentially true; for in the mere form of the story, as distinguished from its content, there is no evidence of a desire to magnify the Gentile visitors at the expense of the Jews. Moreover, why may not the author of the whole book himself have felt the contrast between the rejection of the gospel by the Jews and its acceptance by the Gentiles? Finally, with regard to Hilgenfeld's third point, it may simply be said that the author of the Gospel, as well as a redactor, may have held the view that Christ was born Son of God. Some one—that is, the redactor at least—held to both the Davidic sonship and the virgin birth. Why, then, may not the author have done so?

[2] "Die Kindheitsgeschichte Jesu nach Lucas," in *Jahrbücher für protestantische Theologie*, xvii, 1891, pp. 259 f.

[3] *Kritisch-exegetischer Kommentar über das Neue Testament*, 6te Aufl., i, 1876, p. 70.

[4] *Loc. cit.*

Against all such hypotheses of later insertion regarding Mt. i-ii may be urged in the first place the unanimity of documentary attestation, and in the second place the striking similarity of language and style that prevails between this section and the main body of the Gospel.

The unanimity of documentary attestation has been questioned by Conybeare[5] and Hilgenfeld,[6] who find in a certain Syriac tract, extant in a sixth-century manuscript,[7] evidence to the effect that A.D. 119 or 120 was the earliest date when Mt. ii.1-13 could have been inserted into the text of the Gospel. The tract is attributed to Eusebius and purports to be an account of the Star and the Magi, the history being said to have been written down at a time which can be identified as A.D. 119. According to Conybeare, "the Syriac author of this tract . . . had in his hands a precanonical Greek source of 119 or 120," to which belonged the colophon that gives the date. No doubt the document is interesting, but the conclusions drawn from it are, to say the least, problematical and seem to have won no noteworthy acceptance among modern scholars.[8] We may therefore fairly insist that the documentary attestation of Mt. i-ii as a part of the First Gospel is for all practical purposes unanimous. If there was ever a form of the Gospel without these chapters, it has left no trace in any of the widely divergent lines of transmission in which the text has come down to us.

This weight of external evidence is amply confirmed by the stylistic characteristics of the section, which display a marked affinity with the rest of the First Gospel. This affinity was pointed out one hundred years ago by Gersdorf, in the book to which reference has already been made;[9] and subsequent investigation has not served at all to overthrow his conclusion. One peculiarly Matthæan characteristic which will be noticed even by the casual reader is the formula of Old Testament citation, "that it might be fulfilled which was spoken by the Lord through the prophet," which occurs several times in Mt. i-ii. Hilgenfeld is able to avoid the cogency of this link between the infancy section and the rest of the Gospel only by supposing that the occur-

[5] "Mr. Headlam and the Protevangel," in *Guardian,* lviii, 1903, p. 469; "The Protevangel,' *ibid.*, p. 608.

[6] "Die Einführung des kanonischen Matthäus-Evangeliums in Rom," in *Zeitschrift für wissenschaftliche Theologie,* xxxviii, 1895, pp. 447–451; "Friedrich Loofs gegen Ernst Haeckel," *ibid.*, xliii, 1900, p. 269.

[7] The manuscript was published by William Wright in *Journal of Sacred Literature,* ix (new series), 1866, pp. 117–136; and a translation was published by the same writer in the same journal. x, 1867, pp. 150–164.

[8] Against Conybeare's argument, see Moffatt, *Introduction to the Literature of the New Testament,* third edition, 1918, printing of 1925, pp. 251 f. Moffatt regards Mt. i-ii as an original part of the Gospel (*op. cit.*, pp. 250 f.).

[9] Gersdorf, *Beiträge zur Sprach-characteristik der Schriftsteller des Neuen Testaments,* 1816.

rences of the formula in the body of the Gospel are due to a redactor. In this supposition he has not, so far as we know, been followed by any later investigators.

In view of the conjunction of external and internal evidence it is not surprising that few, if any, contemporary scholars of note are inclined to follow Hillmann,[10] Hilgenfeld, and Merx[11] in regarding Mt. i.18-ii.23 or the whole of the first two chapters as a later addition. There is today no doubt general agreement with the view which J. Weiss expressed[12] in 1903 to the effect that there never were forms of the Gospels of Matthew and Luke without the infancy sections.

As for the attempt of Charles[13] to prove that the genealogy, as distinguished from the narrative of the birth and infancy, is an addition to the Gospel made at about A.D. 170, that is interesting only as a curious example of the way in which more usual critical theories are sometimes reversed. Conybeare[14] has shown in reply how impossible it would have been for the genealogy to have been added at that late date, when interests other than the interest in the Davidic descent were predominant; and Badham[15] has argued with some weight against separating Mt. i.1-17 from Mt. i.18-ii.23 at all. Certainly there can be no doubt whatever but that the genealogy was part of the original Gospel, and (when this conclusion is taken in connection with what has been said above) that the whole of Mt. i-ii is genuine.

The Matthæan account of the birth and infancy is not possessed of quite so marked literary characteristics as those which appear in the corresponding narrative in Luke. In particular we miss here any such striking contrast as that which exists between the Lucan prologue and the narrative that immediately follows. That contrast served to set off the Semitic character of Lk. i.5-ii.52 with special clearness. Even apart from the absence of such contrast, moreover, the style of Mt. i-ii is perhaps less markedly Semitic than that of the Lucan section. Here, as elsewhere, the First Gospel preserves, linguistically, a sort of middle course; in the infancy section, as elsewhere, it lacks the roughness of Mark, the Greek literary touches that appear at various places in Luke-Acts, and the Old Testament poetic beauty of the Lucan infancy narrative.

[10] "Die Kindheitsgeschichte Jesu nach Lucas," in *Jahrbücher für protestantische Theologie*, xvii, 1891, pp. 259 f.

[11] *Die vier kanonischen Evangelien nach ihrem ältesten bekannten Texte*, II. i, 1902, pp. 14 f.

[12] J. Weiss, in *Theologische Rundschau*, vi, 1903, p. 208.

[13] "The New Syriac MS. of the Gospels," in *Academy*, xlvi, 1894, pp. 447 f.; "The New Syriac Codex of the Gospels," *ibid.*, pp. 556 f.

[14] "The New Syriac Codex of the Gospels," *ibid.*, pp. 474 f.

[15] *Ibid.*, p. 513.

Nevertheless, the essentially Jewish and Palestinian character of Mt. i-ii is scarcely less plain than that of Lk. i-ii. Here, as in the Lucan narrative, we find as great simplicity of sentence-structure as might be expected even in a direct translation from a Semitic source. The parataxis is, indeed, less strongly marked than in Lk. i-ii; there are fewer definite Hebraisms or Aramaisms, perhaps none in the strict sense at all: but on the other hand there is nothing in the style of this section that would seem unnatural for a Jew who knew both Aramaic and Greek. The content of the narrative, moreover, is even more clearly Jewish than the form. There is here, as in Lk. i-ii, a complete understanding of Jewish feeling, and a complete absence of anything that would seem natural only in a Gentile environment or only in a late period in the history of the apostolic Church. Familiarity with Jewish custom is seen especially in the way in which betrothal is treated as being in so far equivalent to marriage as that it could be broken off only by a formal divorce. In that respect the Jewish law was not only totally unlike our modern institutions, but also totally unlike the prevailing institutions in the Græco-Roman world. What is at this point presented as a matter of course in Mt. i.18-25 would have seemed very strange to a Gentile writer of the first century.[16] Old Testament prophecy is cited in Mt. i.18-ii.23 no less than five times, despite the brevity of the section; and the genealogy is presented in a way thoroughly consonant with Jewish ideas. But such observations in detail are only supplementary to the more subtle, but even more convincing, evidence of a Jewish origin that is to be found in the entire spirit and outlook of the narrative.

One recent writer, Box, has endeavored to characterize a little more precisely the Jewish form of this section; he sees in the first two chapters of Matthew, as in the corresponding section in Luke, a typical Jewish Midrashic narrative, in which certain fundamental historical information (notably that concerning the virgin birth) is elaborated in a legendary way.[17] One may perhaps employ the observations of Box as to the Jewish character of the narrative without relinquishing, as he does, the historicity of the secondary features. Why may not the form of Jewish narration have been preserved even if in this case there was genuine historical information to cover not merely the central events but also those things which formed their setting? Box has certainly performed a useful service in showing by independent observation that the Matthæan narrative of the birth and infancy is of a genuinely Jewish character.

[16] See Merx, *Die vier kanonischen Evangelien nach ihrem ältesten bekannten Texte*, II. i, 1902, pp. 9–13; Strack-Billerbeck, *Kommentar zum Neuen Testament aus Talmud und Midrasch*, i, 1922, pp. 51–53; ii, 1924, pp. 393–398.

[17] Box, *The Virgin Birth of Jesus*, 1916, especially pp. 7–33.

In the case of Matthew, we are not called upon, as we were in connection with Luke, to face any serious denial of the integrity of the section. Efforts have indeed been made to show that the second chapter possesses a certain independence as over against the first. Bethlehem, it has been said, for example, is first mentioned at Mt. ii.1, instead of at the beginning of the narrative in Mt. i.18, as might be expected if the section were all of one piece.[18] But this objection depends upon the view—which we think erroneous—that the birth narrative in Matthew represents Bethlehem rather than Nazareth as the original home of Joseph and Mary. If the narrator was not engaging in free invention, but was bound by the facts, and if the facts at this point were what they are represented as being in the parallel narrative in Luke, then Bethlehem could not have been mentioned at Mt. i.18, for the simple reason that it was not as a matter of fact the place at which most of the events recorded in Mt. i.18-25 took place. There is nothing surprising, therefore, in finding the first mention of Bethlehem in Mt. ii.1. Indeed, even if the narrator supposed Bethlehem and not Nazareth to have been the original home of Joseph and Mary, and even if he were not bound, in Mt. i.18-25, by a source of information that took account of the opposite view, still we do not think that the failure to mention Bethlehem before Mt. ii.1 would be at all surprising. After all, it was as the place of the birth and not as the place of preceding events that Bethlehem was important to the narrator; for it was to the birth that the Old Testament prophecy, as used by the narrator, referred. Moreover, Bethlehem needed to be mentioned at the beginning of the story of the magi because the geographical facts were important for the understanding of the story that follows. From every point of view, therefore, and even aside from the question whether Nazareth was or was not recognized in the narrative as the place of the preceding events, Mt. ii.1 and not Mt. i.18 is the place where the first mention of Bethlehem was naturally to be expected.

A positive connection between Mt. ii and Mt. i.18-25 is perhaps to be found in the way in which throughout the story of the magi Joseph and Mary and Jesus are designated. Joseph is never designated as the father of Jesus, though Mary is designated as His mother; Jesus is never designated as Joseph's son; and Mary is never designated as Joseph's wife. Instead, Joseph is told by the angel to take "the young child and His mother," and the same phraseology is used in connection with the carrying out of the commands. Why are the terms "son" and "wife" so carefully avoided? The latter term occurs, indeed, a number of times in the preceding chapter;[19] and, no doubt, if it had occurred

[18] Schmiedel, art. "Mary," in *Encyclopædia Biblica*, 1902, iii, cols. 2959 f.

[19] Mt. i.20, 24. Compare also the use of "husband" in Mt. i.16, 19.

in Mt. ii, it would not at all have involved a denial of the supernatural conception. Yet we cannot help feeling that its non-occurrence is significant. The manner in which the relationship of Joseph to Mary and the child is treated throughout the story of the magi is natural only if there was something unique in that relationship; Joseph is represented as the guardian of the mother and the child, but by various subtle touches is set over against them in a way which would perhaps be strange if he were regarded as being in a physical sense the father of Jesus. The most natural conclusion is that Mt. ii presupposes the virgin birth as it is narrated in Mt. i.18-25. Finally, the two passages are bound together by the most striking similarity of style and spirit. The unprejudiced reader receives an overpowering impression that the whole infancy section is of a piece. We have here a strikingly Jewish and clearly unitary narrative of the birth and infancy of Jesus.

That narrative certainly contains an account of the virgin birth. There can be no thought of removing the supernatural conception from this narrative by an interpolation hypothesis, as was attempted in the case of Luke. The entire section, Mt. i.18-25, is intended to set the virgin birth clearly over against a birth by ordinary generation from Joseph and Mary.

Nevertheless, although the virgin birth obviously cannot be removed from this narrative by any mere deletion of a few verses, an attempt has been made to discover in Mt. i.16 a witness to the contrary view that would make Jesus in a physical sense a son of Joseph. This attempt has been based upon a peculiar reading of the so-called "Sinaitic Syriac," an individual manuscript of the Old Syriac version of the Gospels, which was discovered in the monastery of St. Catherine on Mt. Sinai in 1892. The reading has been translated by F. C. Burkitt [20] as follows:

> Jacob begat Joseph; Joseph, to whom was betrothed Mary the Virgin, begat Jesus called the Messiah.

There, it has been said, is an important testimony against the supernatural conception of Jesus; the Sinaitic Syriac contains the momentous words, "Joseph . . . begat Jesus."

Subsequent discussion has altogther failed to confirm the importance which was formerly, and no doubt to some extent is still, attributed to this reading by popular opponents of the doctrine of the virgin birth. But undoubtedly the reading is interesting, and deserves to be examined with some care.[21]

[20] *Evangelion da-Mepharreshe*, ii, 1904, p. 263.

[21] Use has been made, in the following treatment of the text of Mt. i.16, of the article (by the present writer), "Matthew 1:16 and the Virgin Birth," in *The Presbyterian*, for March 18, 1915.

The Sinaitic Syriac manuscript,[22] in which the reading is found, is a "palimpsest"; the vellum was used a second time after the original writing had been partly obliterated. The upper writing, which treats of the lives of certain Syrian saints, was produced in the eighth century; the under writing, with which alone we are concerned, constitutes an ancient copy of the Gospels in the Syriac language. The under writing was probably produced about the beginning of the fifth century or possibly a little earlier. It is not true, therefore, as has sometimes been popularly supposed, that the Sinaitic Syriac is our earliest copy of the Gospels; for two of the Greek manuscripts, the Codex Vaticanus and the Codex Sinaiticus, are to be dated earlier still. Nevertheless, it is very ancient and deserves the most careful attention.

The Sinaitic Syriac displays a marked similarity to another Syriac manuscript of the Gospels, the so-called "Curetonian Syriac," which was probably produced a little later. The widespread agreement of these two manuscripts is due, no doubt, to the fact that they are copies of the same translation of the Greek Gospels into Syriac, the Curetonian being a much less faithful copy than the Sinaitic. This translation, which is called the "Old Syriac," to distinguish it from the "Peshitta," the well-known Syriac translation of the early part of the fifth century, was probably made as early as A.D. 200. Another early form of the Gospels in Syriac was the Syriac form of the "Diatessaron" of Tatian. The Diatessaron, however, was not a translation of the four Gospels complete, but was a kind of Gospel harmony, the material of the four Gospels being pieced together in such a way as to form one continuous life of Christ. Unfortunately, the original text of the Diatessaron can be reconstructed only in a very imperfect manner. It seems clear that there is some direct relation between the Diatessaron and the Old Syriac, but it is not clear whether the Diatessaron used the Old Syriac, or the Old Syriac the Diatessaron. If the Diatessaron used the Old Syriac—that is, if the Old Syriac was produced first—then the production of the Old Syriac translation must be placed near the middle rather than at the close of the second century. The reverse relation, however, seems to be somewhat more probable.

In the light of what has just been said, it will be observed that in order for a peculiar reading of the Sinaitic Syriac to be regarded as preserving the original text of a passage in the Gospels, the following assumptions, normally at least, must be made:

(1) In the first place, the Sinaitic Syriac must be supposed to reproduce accurately, at the point in question, the original Old Syriac translation. Of

[22] The following presentation of the facts concerning the Syriac versions is not based upon independent research, but is simply a summary of the opinions of the experts in this field.

course this assumption is sometimes not in accord with the facts; we do not know how many copyings of the Old Syriac intervened before the production of our Sinaitic manuscript; probably there were many opportunities for mistakes to be made.

(2) In the second place, supposing that the Sinaitic Syriac does represent accurately the original Old Syriac translation, it must further be assumed that the Old Syriac translation is a literal and accurate translation, at the point in question, of the Greek manuscript from which it was made. Unless it is a literal and accurate translation, a re-translation of it into Greek will not allow us to draw any inference as to the underlying Greek text, and it is just that underlying Greek text with which we are concerned.

(3) In the third place, supposing that the Sinaitic Syriac does represent accurately the original Old Syriac translation, and supposing that that Old Syriac translation does represent accurately the underlying Greek text, it must further be assumed that the underlying Greek text, at the point in question, has reproduced accurately the autograph of the New Testament book. The underlying Greek text from which the Old Syriac translation was made was a text of about A.D. 150 to 200; we do not know how many copyings had intervened between the New Testament autographs and the manuscripts of that time; undoubtedly within the interval there was abundant opportunity for error to creep in.

Such, in general terms, is the character of the witness which the Sinaitic Syriac bears to the original Greek text of the Gospels. It remains to consider the particular problem of Mt. i.16. This verse appears in the witnesses to the text of the New Testament in the following three forms, of which the second and third are, formally at least, very much alike:

I. And Jacob begat Joseph, the husband of Mary, of whom was born Jesus who is called Christ.

This reading is attested by almost all of the many hundreds of Greek manuscripts (including the Codex Vaticanus and the Codex Sinaiticus, and other representatives of the so-called "Neutral" type of text), and by all the translations except the Old Latin and the Old Syriac.[23] Such a consensus of testimony would show clearly that the reading is at least as early as the second century, and a quotation by Tertullian confirms that conclusion.

II. And Jacob begat Joseph, to whom having been betrothed the Virgin Mary bare Jesus who is called Christ.

[23] Merx (*op. cit.*, II. i, pp. 13 f.) supposes that the earliest form of the Armenian translation constitutes another exception. It is not important for us to consider whether this supposition is or is not correct.

This reading is attested by the so-called "Ferrar Group," consisting of a number of Greek cursive manuscripts, and, in essentials, by the manuscripts of the Old Latin translation, which was made probably in the latter part of the second century in North Africa. The reading of the Curetonian Syriac is also very similar; Burkitt translates that reading as follows: "Jacob begat Joseph, him to whom was betrothed Mary the Virgin, she who bare Jesus the Messiah."

III. Jacob begat Joseph; Joseph, to whom was betrothed Mary the Virgin, begat Jesus called the Messiah.[24]

This reading is attested by the Sinaitic Syriac, and by it alone. Other evidence for a text containing the words, "Joseph . . . begat Jesus," has proved to be illusory.[25] It should be observed that even the reading of the Sinaitic Syriac clearly implies the virgin birth of Christ (because it speaks of Mary *the virgin*), though it also contains an apparent contradiction of it.

If we had to choose between I and II, the choice would certainly fall upon I.

In the first place, although both readings are ancient, the attestation of I is far stronger. The high estimate which Westcott and Hort placed upon the so-called "Neutral" type of text, relatively to the other types, has at the very most been somewhat modified by subsequent investigation; it has certainly not been overthrown.

In the second place, the first reading looks in itself far more as though it were correct than does the second. If the author of the Gospel had written II, it is hard to see how any scribe would have been led to substitute I for it; whereas if I was genuine, it is easy to explain the substitution of II. It will be observed that I does not definitely refer to the virgin birth. Of course, when it is contrasted with the rest of the genealogy, and especially when it is taken in connection with Mt. i.18-25, it implies the virgin birth in the clearest possible way; but the words themselves do not actually exclude the view that Jesus was in a physical sense the son of Joseph; indeed Joseph is called without explanation the "husband" of Mary. Now some later readers of the Gospels were inclined to look askance upon any such even merely apparent ambiguity; they were inclined to avoid the word "husband" in referring to Joseph; they were inclined to emphasize the virginity of Mary at every point, leaving nothing to the intelligence of the reader. To copyists of this way of thinking,

[24] The translations from the Syriac in the present part of our discussion are those of Burkitt, *Evangelion da-Mepharreshe*, ii, 1904, pp. 262–264.

[25] See William P. Armstrong, "Von Soden's Text and Matthew i.16," in *Princeton Theological Review*, xiii, 1915, pp. 465–468.

Mt. i.16, in the form to which we are accustomed, would have given difficulty. Most copyists, indeed, fortunately did not allow their own reflections to interfere with their duties as scribes; they simply copied the text faithfully, without asking questions. But evidently some one scribe in the second century proceeded in a different way; he apparently jumped to the conclusion that Matthew could not have written what stands in reading I, and therefore thought that he was correcting some previous copyist's error when he substituted reading II. To us, this seems to be a very remarkable procedure, but it did not seem so to a certain class of ancient scribes; it is analogous to what may be observed elsewhere in the history of the New Testament text. From the faulty copy thus produced by a second-century scribe the extant witnesses to reading II have descended; from the correct copies have come the great mass of our manuscripts.

Thus the first of the three readings will explain the origin of the second, but the second will not explain the origin of the first; the second, but not the first, can be explained as due to the mistake of a scribe. But if the first reading cannot be explained as due to the mistake of a scribe, it can be explained only as due to the author—in other words, as part of the original text. There is no difficulty whatever about such an explanation; for the first reading is admirably in accord with the context. Some unintelligent copyist took offence because this reading represented Joseph, without explanation, as the "husband" of Mary. But in reality, such a representation is exactly in accord with the author's purpose. In the whole of the first chapter, the author is interested, not only in showing that Jesus was not in a physical sense the son of Joseph, but also (and just as earnestly) in showing that Jesus was the legal heir of David and Abraham through Joseph. In order that this second point might be proved, it was necessary to show clearly that Joseph was Mary's husband at the time when Jesus was born. The second reading, therefore, is not only, in its extreme clumsiness of sentence-construction, out of harmony with Matthew's style; it also obscures the main point of the genealogy.

Thus from every point of view the first of our three readings is vastly more likely to be correct than the second. The first looks unmistakably like the work of the original author, and the second looks unmistakably like the error of a scribe.

But how is it with the third reading, the reading of the Sinaitic Syriac? The answer is really very plain. The third reading is nothing in the world but a variety of the second reading, and therefore shares in the condemnation which that second reading has just received. If the third reading were part of the original text of the Gospel, the origin of the second reading might be explained; but the origin of the first reading, for the reasons that have just been set forth, would at least be very puzzling. A scribe who, out of zeal for the virgin birth, set about changing the reading, "Joseph . . . begat Jesus," would not have been likely to remove the word "virgin," which already stood in that reading, and insert instead, without explanation, the word "husband." On the other hand, if the first reading was part of the original text, both the other readings may be explained as due to the mistakes of scribes. The second reading was derived from the first in the way which has been explained above; and as for the derivation of the third from the second, that may have happened in any one of a number of ways.

Possibly, for example, the third reading may have been derived from the second by a mere careless blunder, of the kind called "dittography." There is a striking monotony in the wording of the genealogy—"Abraham begat Isaac, and Isaac begat Jacob, and Jacob begat . . ." The mistake of the scribe of the Sinaitic Syriac (or of some ancestor of it) may have consisted simply in letting this monotony run away with him—simply in carrying it one step too far. It will be observed that every name in the genealogy up to Joseph is written twice in succession.[26] What, then, was more natural than for a careless scribe to write this name twice also, and thus to be led to produce the reading of the Sinaitic Syriac? If the mistake had appeared in a Greek manuscript, or if it could be regarded with any plausibility as having been originally produced in the course of the Greek transmission, we should be rather positive in advocating this first explanation; in Greek, the word used for "bare" (referring to the mother) in the reading of the Ferrar Group (II) is exactly the same as the word for "begat"; thus the reading of the Sinaitic Syriac in Greek would be derived from the reading of the Ferrar Group by little more than the mere insertion of the words "And Joseph."[27] In Syriac, the difference seems to be somewhat greater; but if a scribe had once made the initial mistake of repeating the word "Joseph", he might naturally, and half unconsciously, proceed to any slight further changes that might be involved.

Another explanation—that of Burkitt—is that the reading of the Sinaitic Syriac was produced by a mistranslation in the original Old Syriac translation of about A.D. 200; and still other explanations have been proposed. Clearly, at

[26] In Greek the word "and" is not inserted, as in English, between the two successive occurrences of each name. The genealogy runs, Ἀβραὰμ ἐγέννησε τὸν Ἰσαάκ, Ἰσαὰκ δὲ κ. τ. λ.

[27] It would also, perhaps, have been necessary to change μνηστευθεῖσα to ἐμνηστεύθη. But in the first place that change would be easy; and in the second place μνηστευθεῖσα might conceivably be allowed to remain as a predicate nominative with a verb "to be" understood. No doubt this latter usage would be an unwarrantable use of an aorist participle; but it might well escape notice by a careless scribe.

any rate, the reading of the Sinaitic Syriac, in one way or another, may be understood as a mere mistake in the transmission of the text. And if it *may* be so understood, surely it *must* be. It must always be remembered that the reading of the Sinaitic Syriac does not compete for our favor on anything like equal terms with the other readings. Both the other readings are widely attested; both of them must have originated at least as early as the second century. The reading of the Sinaitic Syriac, on the other hand, is not found at all in the original language of the New Testament; and it is entirely isolated, being found only in one manuscript. Such isolated readings must always be viewed with great suspicion; they may be due to the mere careless, uncorrected blunder of the scribe of the individual manuscript in question. If the reading of the Sinaitic Syriac had strong and early attestation, it might be a debatable question whether it was not part of the original text, and the other two readings pious emendations made by orthodox scribes; but since, as a matter of fact, its attestation is not strong and early, and since it can be accounted for plausibly as arising merely by an ordinary blunder in the course of the transmission, this latter explanation of its origin is certainly to be accepted.

The view, therefore, that the Sinaitic Syriac at Mt. i.16 represents the original text of the Gospel can be maintained only by textual criticism of the most adventurous and unscientific mind. The reading of the Sinaitic Syriac cannot with certainty be traced back of A.D. 400, while the common reading is clearly attested at the beginning of the third century, and certainly was present considerably before that time; the reading of the Sinaitic Syriac looks as though it may well be the mere mistake of a scribe or translator, while the common reading looks unmistakably like the work of the author of the Gospel, and defies any other explanation of its origin.[28]

Thus if we have to choose between the attested readings at Mt. i.16, it is clear that the familiar reading of the "Neutral" type of text deserves acceptance. But at this point an objection may be raised. Why, it may be asked, do we have to choose merely between the attested readings? Why may we not posit as original a reading which, even though it does not appear in any of our witnesses to the text, will account for the origin of all of the readings that do so appear? Such a reading, it may be said, could be found in the words, "Joseph begat Jesus." If in the original text of the Gospel those words appeared

28 It is therefore extremely misleading when James Moffatt, in his popular translation of the New Testament, following von Soden's Greek text, reproduces the reading of the Sinaitic Syriac at Mt. i.16 without any explanation. In criticism of von Soden's text at other points, see the article by William P. Armstrong to which reference has already been made, "Von Soden's Text and Matthew i.16," in *Princeton Theological Review*, xiii, 1915, pp. 461–468.

without explanation, they would naturally give offence to orthodox scribes; there was, therefore, a strong motive for the introduction of some sort of explanatory gloss. As a matter of fact—so the hypothesis runs—two lines of emendation appeared in the course of transmission. One is found in the words, "to whom was betrothed the virgin Mary," which seemed to safeguard the virgin birth. At first these words were allowed to stand as a modifier of the word "Joseph" in the sentence, "Joseph begat Jesus"; thus we have the reading of the Sinaitic Syriac, "Joseph, to whom was betrothed Mary the Virgin, begat Jesus called the Messiah." But then it came to be observed that this text involves a contradiction: how could it have been said that "Joseph begat Jesus," if Joseph was only "betrothed" to Mary and if Mary was a "virgin"? As a result of such reflections, the word "Joseph," as subject of the verb translated "begat," was omitted; and "Mary," not "Joseph," was made the subject of that verb. The verb would then have, of course, to be translated, in English, "bare" instead of "begat." Thus we have the reading of the Ferrar group, of certain manuscripts of the Old Latin version, and of the Curetonian Syriac. But parallel with this whole line of emendation—so the hypothesis continues—another line was chosen by the ancestor of our earliest Greek manuscripts—another method of bringing the original text, "Joseph begat Jesus," into conformity with the doctrine of the virgin birth. This method was the omission of the words, "Joseph begat Jesus," and the substitution for them of the words, "the husband of Mary, of whom was born Jesus."

Thus, it is said, a reading, "Joseph begat Jesus," will account admirably for the origin of all the extant variants, and so must be regarded as original. Such, in essentials, is the hypothesis of Merx, in his work on the "earliest known text" of the Gospels.[29]

In reply, it may be said, in the first place, that the method of conjectural emendation, which is here followed, can be applied only with the greatest caution to a work which has so extraordinarily rich a documentary attestation as has the Gospel according to Matthew. In the case of many classical authors, where we have only one or two late and obviously very imperfect manuscripts, an editor is often justified in rejecting the transmitted text of a passage and in substituting for it a reading which shall best account for the obviously incorrect wording of those manuscripts that happen to be extant. But in the case of the Gospels, the extant documentary attestation is so very abundant, and the various lines of transmission began to diverge at such an

[29] Merx, *Die vier kanonischen Evangelien nach ihrem ältesten bekannten Texte*, II. i, 1902, pp. 5–19.

early time, that one has difficulty in understanding how the original text could have been so completely obliterated as to leave no trace. There may indeed be such instances, where all of our extant witnesses to the text have been corrupted; but surely they are very few. Thus although conjectural emendation cannot be excluded in principle from the textual criticism of the New Testament, it should certainly be employed there in the most sparing possible way. The employment of it in any passage should be regarded as a counsel of desperation, to be resorted to only when all ordinary methods fail. If it is possible to regard any one of the extant variants as original, that alternative should be chosen; and the critic should not undertake to reproduce by conjecture a text which has actually left no trace.

In the case of Mt. i.16, if there is any truth in what has been said above, we are by no means reduced to such desperate expedients. It is perfectly possible to understand the reading attested by our earliest Greek manuscripts as belonging to the original text of the Gospel, and both the variants as having been produced from that reading in the course of the transmission by well-known causes of textual corruption. But if such a solution of the problem is possible, it is surely—in view of the wealth of documentary attestation—decidedly preferable. What need is there of going so far afield to solve a problem for which a satisfactory solution lies near at hand?

There is, however, another objection to Merx's theory as to Mt. i.16. It is found in the contents of the section, Mt. i.18-25, which immediately follows. That section is not in harmony with the proposed reading, "Joseph begat Jesus," at Mt. i.16. We do not mean that the disharmony is an altogether irreconcilable one. The words, "Joseph begat Jesus," could, as we shall see, be understood in a sense congruous with the account of the virgin birth that follows. But, after all, the reader may naturally suppose that an author who had the contents of the following section in mind would have prepared for that section at the point where the birth of Jesus is first mentioned—namely, at the close of the genealogy in Mt. i.16. Thus it is the reading of our earliest Greek manuscripts, and not the conjectural reading proposed by Merx, which really suits the context.

Merx is able to overcome this objection only by supposing that Mt. i.18-25—indeed, the whole of Mt. i.18-ii.23—formed no original part of the Gospel. Thus the change in Mt. i.16 would in accordance with his view be only one manifestation of a serious interpolating activity which reversed the entire representation of the birth of Jesus with which the Gospel begins. We have already noticed the insuperable objections to any such hypothesis; Mt. i.18-ii.23, we observed, is united to the rest of the Gospel in the most unmistakable way.

Thus Merx's view with regard to Mt. i.16 depends upon a quite untenable view with regard to the entire infancy section; and for that reason, in addition to other reasons, must certainly be rejected. There is really not the slightest ground for departing from the best-attested text at Mt. i.16.

We have not yet, however, quite finished our discussion of this verse. We have shown that the reading of the Sinaitic Syriac was not part of the original text of the Gospel; but even if so much should be granted—even if it should be granted that the reading of the Sinaitic Syriac is due, not to the author, but to a copyist—it might still be maintained that that reading is historically valuable. How did a copyist come to introduce the startling sentence, "Joseph . . . begat Jesus"? Only, it has sometimes been said, because there was lying back of the genealogy in the first chapter of Matthew a written source, or at any rate an oral tradition, which represented Jesus as being in a physical sense the son of Joseph; the scribe who produced the reading, "Joseph . . . begat Jesus," has caused the original representation of the birth of Jesus to shine through even in a Gospel which has itself striven to obliterate that representation. But surely the evidence for such a view is exceedingly slender. The reading of the Sinaitic Syriac can be explained as due to the ordinary processes of textual corruption; what need is there, therefore, of resorting to so far-reaching an hypothesis? Indeed, the action of the hypothetical scribe who allowed himself to be influenced by the supposed tradition of the physical paternity of Joseph is quite inconceivable. That scribe himself was surely convinced of the opposite view of the birth of Jesus; otherwise he would not have retained Mt. i.18-25 in its present form:[80] why, then, did he gratuitously introduce contradiction? It is unscientific to resort to a difficult and complicated explanation of a textual error when a perfectly simple explanation lies ready to hand.

Evidently, therefore, the common reading at Mt. i.16 represents correctly the original text of the Gospel, and the variants are to be explained as due to the ordinary processes of corruption. It should now be observed, finally, that this textual question is not by any means so important as has sometimes been maintained. Suppose we were quite wrong with regard to it, suppose that Mt. i.16 originally contained the words attested by the Sinaitic Syriac, suppose even that the original text had simply "Joseph begat Jesus" without qualification (a reading which as a matter of fact is found in no manuscript), even then no conclusion derogatory to the attestation of the virgin birth would necessarily follow. The word "begat" in the genealogy in Matthew clearly is

[80] It should always be remembered that the Sinaitic Syriac narrates the virgin birth in this section just as clearly as does any other manuscript.

not to be taken in the physical sense. As Burkitt pertinently remarks, "the contemporaries of the Evangelist knew their Bible at least as well as we do"; "they knew that there were more than fourteen generations between David and the Captivity, that Joram did not beget Uzziah, and that Josiah did not beget Jeconiah." The word "begat" in the genealogy means simply "had as a legal heir." At any rate, it certainly had that meaning to the Evangelist, if he did write "Joseph begat Jesus"; for certainly Mt. i.18-25, the passage that immediately follows, excludes the physical paternity of Joseph in the clearest possible terms. Of course, the case would be different if Mt. i.18-25 were no original part of the Gospel of Matthew; but for such a view there is not a jot of manuscript evidence, and the passage in question exhibits in a very striking way the characteristics of the Gospel. Evidently, therefore, if the author of the Gospel wrote "Joseph begat Jesus," he meant nothing derogatory to the virgin birth, but used the word "begat" in a broad sense. Such a use of the word would have been far more natural among the Jews of the first century than it would be in the Western world of today; an adoptive relationship, as we have seen, meant more to them than it does to us; to the Jewish mind a son born of Joseph's wife, and acknowledged by him as his heir, was to all intents and purposes his son.

The reading of the Sinaitic Syriac at Mt. i.16 is accordingly without bearing upon the question of the historicity of the virgin birth; even if the author wrote "Joseph begat Jesus," he did not mean to assert the physical paternity of Jesus.[31] But this whole latter part of our discussion has been merely for the sake of the argument. As a matter of fact, the author did not write "Joseph begat Jesus," or any such thing, but he wrote exactly what we find in our Bibles. He was, indeed, very much interested in showing that Jesus was heir of David through Joseph. But he was just as much interested in showing that Jesus was not son of Joseph by ordinary generation. Jesus belonged, indeed, to the house of David; in Him the promises were fulfilled. But He belonged to that house in a more wonderful way than could easily have been foreseen; He was a gift granted to the house of David by a mysterious act of God.[32]

[31] In coming to this conclusion we can appeal to the authority of Burkitt, who certainly is not influenced by any apologetic motive. See Burkitt, *op. cit.*, ii, p. 261. The curious interpretation proposed by C. C. Torrey ("The Translations Made from the Original Aramaic Gospels," in *Studies in the History of Religions Presented to Crawford Howell Toy*, 1912, p. 303) to the effect that according to Matthew the Holy Spirit "anticipated Joseph," so that the child "had thus three parents," is surely quite impossible. Compare above, pp. 128 f.

[32] On the textual question regarding Mt. i.16, see especially Zahn, *Einleitung in das Neue Testament*, 3te Aufl., ii, 1907, pp. 298–300 (English translation, ii, 1909, pp. 565–567); and Burkitt, *op. cit.*, ii, pp. 258–266.

A number of peculiar readings occur in the Sinaitic Syriac in Mt. i.18-25. Thus in verse 21 this manuscript reads, "she shall bear *to thee* a son"; and in verse 25 it omits the words, "knew her not until," and reads simply, "And she bore *to him* a son." In these readings, when they are taken in conjunction with the reading, "Joseph . . . begat Jesus," in verse 16, some scholars have detected an "Ebionite" tendency, which, they think, exalts Joseph's place with reference to the child Jesus and perhaps preserves traces of an original representation that made Joseph actually the father. But closer examination renders the matter to say the least very doubtful. The addition of the words "to thee" and "to him" is quite consonant with the supernatural conception; Joseph was the heir of David, and the child, though born without his agency, was born in a real sense "to him." A scribe may well have allowed the familiar words "to thee" and "to him"[33] to creep in, without observing that their omission in Matthew was significant.

As for the omission by the Sinaitic Syriac of the words, "knew her not until," in Mt. i.25, that has, if anything, exactly the opposite significance to the significance which has been attributed to it. It rather looks as though an orthodox scribe had been offended by the implication which might seem to lie in the words, "knew her not until," to the effect that after Mary had brought forth her son Joseph did live with her as with his wife, so that she had other children.[34] This implication would be removed by the omission of the words, as in the Sinaitic Syriac. Thus the reading of the Sinaitic Syriac may conceivably be explained as a doctrinal correction, intended to safeguard the perpetual virginity of Mary. At any rate, it certainly cannot be explained with any plausibility as an Ebionite correction or as preserving any original tradition of a physical paternity of Joseph.

[33] Compare Gen. xvii.19 and Lk. i.13.

[34] Compare above, p. 144.

Chapter VIII

THE RELATION BETWEEN THE NARRATIVES

IN THE preceding chapters we have adduced evidence in support of the following three propositions: (1) the infancy narratives both in Matthew and in Luke are no later additions, but original parts of the First and Third Gospels; (2) they are both (and particularly the one in Luke) strikingly Jewish Christian and Palestinian in form and in content; (3) they really contain in their original form an account of the virgin birth.

The question now arises whether any literary relationship can be established between them. And that question must clearly be answered in the negative.

It is evident, in the first place, that neither narrative is dependent upon the other; for if there had been such dependence, the difficulties which now face an attempt to fit the two narratives together would never have been permitted to arise. Those difficulties are not indeed, as we shall see, sufficient to establish actual contradiction; but they do suffice to show independence. In fact, one of the chief arguments which have been relied upon to exhibit the mutual independence of the Gospels of Matthew and Luke has been found in the obvious independence of the sections with which these Gospels begin. There can be no reasonable doubt but that the author of the infancy narrative in Matthew was writing in complete independence of the infancy narrative in Luke, and vice versa. It is significant that Pfleiderer, who at one time maintained a contrary view, was led later to abandon his theory.[1]

Equally unlikely is the view that the two infancy narratives were derived from a common written source. The efforts which have been made by Resch,

[1] Compare Pfleiderer, *Das Urchristenthum*, 1te Aufl., 1887, pp. 480 f., with the second edition of the same book, i, 1902, pp. 550 f. (English translation, *Primitive Christianity*, ii, 1909, pp. 303 f.). See "The New Testament Account of the Birth of Jesus," first article, in *Princeton Theological Review*, iii, 1905, pp. 647 f. Bruno Bauer in his earlier work, *Kritik der evangelischen Geschichte der Synoptiker*, i, 1841 (pp. 84–89, 121), held that Matthew's birth narrative is dependent on Luke's, but in a later book, *Kritik der Evangelien*, i, 1850 (pp. 333 f.), he held, apparently, a more complicated hypothesis as to the relation between the two narratives. The rise of such complicated hypotheses only serves to show anew that the narratives are really independent. The independence of the narratives is no doubt admitted by the majority of scholars, though there have been notable exceptions, such as, for example, Holtzmann (*Die Synoptiker*, 3te Aufl., 1901 p. 41) who held that the author of the Third Gospel knew Mt. i–ii, thus reversing Pfleiderer's original hypothesis.

Conrady, and Reitzenstein[2] to establish such a common source have received little or no support from other scholars. Resch[3] attempted to reconstruct a Hebrew "Book of the Generations of Jesus Christ," from which both infancy narratives were derived and upon which the prologue of the Fourth Gospel constitutes a theological reflection; but although the wealth of material which he collected in support of his thesis possesses real and permanent value in helping to establish the Semitic character of the two narratives, his thesis itself no doubt deserves the universal rejection that it has received. Even more obviously wrong was the thesis of Conrady,[4] who actually found in the apocryphal Protevangelium of James the source of both canonical narratives. There can be not the slightest doubt but that the universal judgment of other scholars is correct when they insist against Conrady that far from our canonical narratives being derived from the Protevangelium, the Protevangelium is derived from them.

The theory of Reitzenstein[5] differs from that of Conrady in that it represents the supposed common source of the two infancy narratives as being for the most part lost; and it differs from that of Resch in that it makes no effort to reconstruct the lost source in detail. Reitzenstein's hypothesis is based largely upon a poorly preserved Egyptian fragment of about the sixth century, which contains in its first part the dialogue between the angel and Mary in a different form from the one given by Luke. The Egyptian fragment, Reitzenstein argues, cannot be derived from the narrative of Luke; for on that theory the differences cannot well be explained, and Luke's narrative is in itself incomprehensible and clearly secondary. Rather, he continues, the fragment was derived from a Gospel older than any that we now possess. A notable difference from Luke is the omission of the words, "thou shalt conceive in the womb," in the promise of the angel. These words being omitted, Reitzenstein says, Mary would naturally, in accordance with ancient usage, understand the angel's greeting, "Hail, highly favored one; thou hast found favor with God," and the words, "thou shalt bear a son," to mean that she was already pregnant. Her question, therefore, which appears in the form, "Whence shall this happen to me, seeing I know not a man?"[6], becomes perfectly natural, whereas (Reitzenstein insists) in the narrative of Luke, where the conception

[2] On these theories, see "The New Testament Account of the Birth of Jesus," first article, in *Princeton Theological Review*, iii, 1905, pp. 648–650; second article, *ibid.*, iv, 1906, pp. 39–42.

[3] "Das Kindheitsevangelium," in *Texte und Untersuchungen*, x. 5, 1897.

[4] *Die Quelle der kanonischen Kindheitsgeschichte Jesus'*, 1900.

[5] *Zwei religionsgeschichtliche Fragen*, 1901, pp. 112–131.

[6] *πόθεν μοι τοῦτο γε[νήσεται, ἐπεὶ ἄνδρα οὐ γινώσκω]*. The letters enclosed in brackets do not appear in the manuscript, but are supplied by conjecture.

is put in the indefinite future, the question is meaningless.[7] This representation that the narrative of the annunciation is itself a narrative of the conception —a representation which, according to Reitzenstein, appears in Origen, in those early Christian documents which speak of a conception from the Logos, and notably in a certain prayer discovered at Gizeh [8]—is brought by Reitzenstein into connection with a contemporary religious idea according to which one god produces another through his speech.[9] Starting with this religious idea—so the hypothesis runs—the writer of the Gospel from which this fragment is derived constructed the first account of the conception; his account, however, was often misunderstood, and two examples of such misunderstanding appear in our canonical narratives. In Matthew the miracle is announced only after it has happened, whereas in the original account it was in indissoluble connection with the annunciation itself. In Luke the miracle is announced beforehand, in order that it may be brought into parallel with the case of John the Baptist. In both cases the original significance of the annunciation is lost.

To this theory one obvious objection is the late date of Reitzenstein's fragment as compared with our canonical Gospels. Even Reitzenstein himself seems to be unable to trace back the Gospel upon which the fragment is based to a date earlier than the last part of the second century; [10] and our canonical Gospels certainly cannot be put so late as that. Moreover, the fragment, as interpreted by Reitzenstein, certainly does not contain such internal evidence of its primary character as Reitzenstein seems to attribute to it. For example, Mary, according to Reitzenstein's interpretation, understands the words of the angel to mean that she is already pregnant; yet the angel takes care to inform her that the wonder is dependent upon her consent—in which rather intricate progress of the narrative the steps are by no means clearly marked.[11] In general, we must say that entirely too much is built upon an extremely meagre foundation for the theory to become in the slightest degree plausible. The fragment in question is itself very badly preserved, so that even from the outset much has to be left to conjecture. For example, the most fundamental thing of all for Reitzenstein's theory is that the fragment should not contain the words, "thou shalt conceive in the womb"; yet there is a gap at the proper place. The gap is thought not to be large enough; very possibly it is not large enough. But the fact remains that even with regard to such a fundamental point we are not dealing with definite certainty. Or suppose (as indeed seems

[7] See, however, above, pp. 145-148.
[8] Jacoby, *Ein neues Evangelienfragment*, 1900.
[9] Reitzenstein, *op. cit.*, p. 124; compare p. 83.
[10] Reitzenstein, *op. cit.*, p. 126.
[11] See Anrich, in *Theologische Literaturzeitung*, xxvii, 1902, cols. 304 f.

probable) that Reitzenstein is right in thinking that the words, "thou shalt conceive in the womb," were absent. Even then it is by no means certain that the author had any different view of the annunciation from that of Luke; for the omission may have arisen merely from loose quoting of our Third Gospel. Indeed, "thou shalt conceive," in connection with "thou shalt bring forth," may have seemed almost like unnecessary fullness of expression, so that one of the phrases may easily have been omitted.

Moreover, if we thus find reasons for doubt in connection with the very basis of the hypothesis, how much more is that the case with the remoter conclusions—for example, the conclusion that Matthew as well as Luke represents a weakening of the original account. In general, it is abundantly clear that Reitzenstein's fragment has contributed nothing whatever toward solving the vexed problem of the sources of our canonical infancy narratives. And that means, we may remark in passing, that the fragment has also contributed nothing toward explaining the origin of the ideas that our narratives contain. In themselves the narratives contain no hint whatever of the religious idea of creation by the Word; if, therefore, their connection with the source that is supposed to contain that idea breaks down, we have no reason whatever to regard them as based on an attempt to embody that idea in narrative form.

The fact is that every attempt to exhibit a common written source for Mt. i-ii and Lk. i-ii must result in failure. The two narratives, though they agree with regard to certain central facts such as the virgin birth and the birth in Bethlehem, are quite different for the most part both in style and in content. Thus their witness to those facts about which they do agree is a double witness; the two narratives cannot be reduced to one.

But if that be so, the question naturally arises whether the independence of the narratives amounts to contradiction. At this point we begin to leave the sphere of literary criticism, and enter at last into that sphere of historical criticism to which everything that we have said so far has been leading up. If the narratives are contradictory, then their witness—even their witness to those things about which they are agreed—will be greatly weakened. The question of harmony between the two narratives must, therefore, be considered with some care.

In the minds of many modern scholars this question seems almost to be settled in advance. What right have we, they say, to insist that two ancient narratives must be so interpreted as that they shall agree; why should we not interpret each of them by itself, according to the interpretation that is inherently most probable, and entirely without reference to the other; is not this whole business of harmonization a mere unscientific apologetic expedient?

But surely such a method of approach begs the question in a very unscientific way. In countless cases, where we hear two independent and perfectly trustworthy witnesses, A and B, testify to the facts regarding the same event, there are questions that arise in our mind. We say to A: "How is that? I do not understand; you say one thing, and B says another, and I do not see how your testimony agrees with that of B." And then in countless cases a few words of explanation will clear the whole matter up, and our difficulty results only in a clearer and more complete account of the course of events. In such cases the harmonizing method is not unscientific at all. What is true, moreover, with regard to contemporary testimony is also true with regard to ancient documents. If we have two historical documents, for whose trustworthiness there is any evidence at all, it is not unscientific, but on the contrary in accordance with sound common sense, to favor, other things being equal, that interpretation of each of them which will permit us to regard both of them as true. We may well ask, with Andrews,[12] "Is there any consistent history which is not the result of harmonistic expedients?" Surely, then, we should approach without unfavorable prejudice the question of the harmony between the infancy narratives in Matthew and in Luke.

Some of the contradictions that have been discovered between the two narratives disappear at once upon a little examination. Thus we may safely pass over without much discussion such objections as those of Usener, to the effect that "the divinity of Christ is attested in Lk. by the angel's words to the shepherds and the song of the heavenly host, in Mt. by the appearance of the star in the East; the new-born Messiah receives his first adoration in Lk. from the shepherds, in Mt. from the magi."[13] The obvious answer in the former case is that there might be more than one attestation of the divinity of Christ. In the latter case, after the word "first" (for which there is no warrant) has been removed, a similar answer might be made; the new-born Messiah might have received adoration *both* from the shepherds and from the magi, and the narrative in Matthew does not say or imply that the particular act of adoration which it relates was the first.

It is objected with more insistence, and with more show of reason, that "Joseph's home in Mt. is Bethlehem, in Lk. Nazareth."[14] But, after all, the contradiction which is here detected is not a contradiction between an assertion of one narrative and an assertion of the other, but a contradiction between an assertion of one narrative and the silence of the other. Such contradictions in

[12] *The Life of Our Lord*, 2nd edition, 1891, p. ix.
[13] Usener, article "Nativity," in *Encyclopædia Biblica*, iii, 1902, col. 3343.
[14] Usener, *loc. cit.*

countless cases are apparent rather than real. Matthew does not say that Joseph's home was Bethlehem before the birth of Jesus. Indeed, the mention of Bethlehem at Mt. ii.1 rather than at i.18 might possibly suggest the contrary; for if the events of Mt. i.18-25 took place at Bethlehem (that is, at the ancestral home of the Davidic house) why was that significant fact not mentioned in connection with those events? We are indeed far from desiring to lay stress upon this particular consideration. Quite possibly the reason why the place of the events was not mentioned before Mt. ii.1 is that only at that point is the place directly important for the details of the narrative. In order to understand the journeyings of the magi, the inquiry at Jerusalem, the reference to Old Testament prophecy by the Sanhedrin, it is necessary to know that Jesus was born at Bethlehem; hence it is in connection with Mt. ii that the place of the birth is mentioned. Moreover, it was the localizing of the *birth* at Bethlehem, and not that of previous events, which was important as a fulfilment of prophecy. At any rate, the absence of geographical information in Mt. i.18-25 is no proof that all the events there narrated are regarded as having happened at the place which is mentioned at the beginning of the following section. It is not until ii.1 that Matthew displays any geographical interest at all.

No doubt the objector will point in triumph to Mt. ii.22 f., where it is intimated that after the return from Egypt Joseph and Mary were intending to dwell in Judæa, were prevented from doing so only by the fear of Archelaus, and thus were forced to enter into Galilee and dwell "in a city called Nazareth." If Nazareth had been their original home, would they not have returned there without seeking to enter into Judæa at all? And would Nazareth have been referred to simply as "a city called Nazareth," if it had been regarded as the scene of the events already narrated in Mt. i.18-25?

The objection is by no means so formidable as might at first sight appear. The intention of Joseph and Mary to live in Judæa after the return from Egypt is quite comprehensible even if Nazareth had been their original home. Mary's child, Jesus, was, according to the narrative, the promised king of David's line; and that fact was known to Mary and to Joseph. What could be more natural than that they should desire to bring the child up in His ancestral home until the time when His kingship should publicly appear? Residence at Bethlehem or at Jerusalem would seem altogether fitting to those who were the earthly parents of the Messiah. So much lies upon the surface of the narrative. There is also of course ample room for surmise. It has often been held, for example, that Joseph may have possessed property in Bethlehem. The suggestion is perfectly possible; and it helps to explain the intention to dwell in Judæa. But it is not necessary. One may well understand the situation without it. At any rate, Matthew certainly does not say that the original home of Joseph and Mary was not Nazareth but Bethlehem. Whether the Evangelist (or the one who gave the narrative in Mt. i-ii essentially its present form) was aware of the original residence at Nazareth it is perhaps impossible to say. But even if the narrator was not aware of it, his narrative is free of any contradiction with Luke on this point. Silence is a very different thing from contradiction.

Another evidence of contradiction has often been detected in the fact that according to Luke the annunciation is made to Mary, whereas according to Matthew it is made to Joseph. Of course, the obvious answer is that it might have been made to both.[15] But, it will be said, if Mary had already been informed of the miracle of the supernatural conception, would she not have repeated to Joseph what the angel had said to her? In that case, could Joseph ever have formed the intention of putting her away? Would not the annunciation to Joseph, in other words, have been unnecessary if the annunciation to Mary had already taken place?

Here again the supposed contradiction disappears as soon as it is at all carefully examined. Suppose Mary had told Joseph what the angel had said to her. Would he have believed so wonderful a tale? And even if he had believed it, would he have proceeded to take Mary as his wife? She was to become the mother of the Messiah by a stupendous miracle. Was it then right that she should live with a husband as other women do?

We must not, indeed, lay too much stress upon these last considerations. Mary had been told that the child was to be the promised king of David's line. If the descent was traced through Joseph, it was essential that Joseph should be her husband when the child was born. Hence Joseph might have thought, even though he was not to be in a physical sense the father of the child, that it was God's will for him to take Mary as his wife. It is only fair, however, to notice that this reasoning is not quite conclusive. Must Mary have traced the Davidic descent through Joseph when she listened to the angel's words in Lk. i.32 f.? May she not—if, as is not impossible, she also was descended from David—have traced the Davidic descent through herself, so that her marriage with Joseph would no longer be necessary? And if her marriage was no longer necessary, may not Joseph have formed exactly the plan that is

[15] This answer was the one given by Chrysostom in the late fourth century (*hom. in Matt.*, iv, ed. Montfaucon, vii, 1836, p. 63). Many too artless men, Chrysostom says, have detected a contradiction between the two accounts, "in that Luke says that the good news came to Mary, while Matthew says it came to Joseph. But in doing so they have not observed that as a matter of fact both things were done. This it is necessary for us to keep in mind throughout the whole story; for in doing so we shall resolve many seeming contradictions."

attributed to him in Mt. i.19? The child was not his child; yet the mother was without blame. May he not have decided to break off the betrothal—which, under the Jewish law, could be done only by a formal divorce—yet in doing so to avoid putting the innocent virgin to shame?

As we have already said, this suggestion is conjectural. We mention it as a possibility and nothing more. Also possible is the view that Joseph did not believe Mary when she told him of the angel's words. But most likely of all, perhaps, is it to suppose that Mary never told him at all.[16] What would the virgin be likely to do after she had passed through the wonderful experience that is narrated in Lk. i.26-38? Would she tell Joseph of that experience? Perhaps she might have done so if she had been a woman of coarser mould. But if she was really the kind of person who is depicted with such wonderful verisimilitude in Lk. i-ii, any such action would be open to objections of a very serious kind. To tell Joseph of her experience would be to expose herself to disbelief. Her experience, after all, was entirely unique; nothing like it had been heard of in the whole history of the world. Even she herself, in the very presence of the angel, had failed to understand; even she, in her maidenly consciousness, had shrunk from what her own ears had heard. How then could she ever hope that Joseph would believe? What would she do under such circumstances? Surely it is obvious what she would do. She would wait for a vindication from God. The messenger who had spoken to her could speak also to her betrothed. It all depended upon God's will. Meanwhile she could bear patiently the burden which she had accepted when she said: "Behold the handmaid of the Lord; be it unto me according to thy word." She was content to wait for God's good time.

Far from being in contradiction, therefore, the two narratives supplement each other in the most remarkable way. Neither is thoroughly comprehensible without the other. Mary's attitude is not explained in Matthew, and Joseph's attitude is not explained in Luke; but when the two narratives are put together the course of events in all essentials is fairly clear. When the wonderful promise came to her, Mary went not to Joseph, but to a sympathizing woman friend. But she did not go of her own motion; she went only because of the angel's express words. Elisabeth, too, the angel had said, had passed through a marvellous experience. In that quarter, therefore, and in that quarter only, could Mary hope to find credence; what she could tell Elisabeth would be confirmed by what Elisabeth herself had passed through. How wonderfully natural the

[16] This is the solution favored by Chrysostom (*op. cit.*, iv, ed. Montfaucon, vii, 1836, p.6) Mary, he supposes, did refrain from telling Joseph, in order that he might not fall into the sin of Zacharias; Mary foresaw that Joseph would not believe.

narrative is, how exactly in accordance with the meditative and sensitive nature attributed by the Lucan narrative to the mother of the Lord!

Then came the return to Nazareth and the hour of Mary's trial. But she was content to await God's time; she was content to bear the burden which God had asked her to bear. Her faith was not in vain. Joseph, too, was made the recipient of a divine message and took unto him his wife. God had provided a human protector for the maiden and her child. Here as elsewhere the seeming contradictions in these wonderful narratives lie only on the surface; the underlying harmony and the underlying verisimilitude are profound.[17]

Finally, it has been objected that the narrative in Luke leaves no place for the visit of the magi and the sojourn in Egypt. Forty days after the birth in Bethlehem, according to Luke, there was the presentation in the Temple. The visit of the magi could hardly have taken place during this forty-day interval; for it would have been impossible to take the child into the Temple when the wrath of the king was so aroused—that would have been to face the very jaws of death. Evidently, therefore, the flight into Egypt took place immediately after the magi had come; no visit to the Temple could have intervened. If, therefore, the two narratives are to be harmonized, we must suppose that when the presentation in the Temple had been completed, Joseph and Mary returned with the child to Bethlehem, received there the visit of the magi, and then fled into Egypt.

There is nothing at all unnatural in this suggestion. The only difficulty arises in connection with Lk. ii.39, where it is said: "And when they had performed all things according to the law of the Lord, they returned into Galilee, to their own city Nazareth." These words seem at first sight to require an immediate return to Nazareth after the presentation in the Temple, and therefore seem to exclude a prior return to Bethlehem and a sojourn in Egypt.

But does not such a view involve an undue pressing of the Evangelist's words? The author of Lk. ii.39 is interested in pointing out the fact that the requirements of the law were satisfied in the case of the infant Jesus. He knew that the childhood of Jesus was passed for the most part at Nazareth.

[17] Some noteworthy scholars have, indeed, taken a somewhat different view of the course of events from that which has just been set forth. It has been held, for example, by Ebrard (*Wissenschaftliche Kritik der evangelischen Geschichte*, 3te Aufl., 1868, p. 271) and by Riggenbach (*Vorlesungen über das Leben des Herrn Jesu*, 1858, pp. 169, 172) that the marriage took place before and not after the visit of Mary to Elisabeth. That view is no doubt less natural, as it is far less commonly held, than the one which we have adopted (see the discussion in Chapter IX, pp. 233 f.). But we are not concerned here to argue the point. It is enough for our present purpose if it can be shown that there are various ways in which, if our knowledge were more complete, the harmony between the two narratives could be exhibited.

But what he is interested here in observing is that that well-known residence in Nazareth did not begin until after the requirements of the law had been satisfied in Bethlehem and in Jerusalem. In fact, he is not interested just at this point in anything else at all; he would not care, for the moment, how many events took place between the presentation in the Temple and the return to Nazareth, provided only the return to Nazareth did not take place before the accomplishment of the requirements of the law. The representation in Matthew, therefore, does not contradict the real point of Lk. ii.39. No doubt that verse gives eloquent testimony to the independence of Luke as over against Matthew; if the Third Evangelist had had the account of the flight to Egypt before him when he wrote, he would hardly have put the verse in its present form. But here again the silence of one narrative regarding events recorded in another is quite a different thing from actual contradiction.

Thus the supposed contradictions have succeeded only in demonstrating the complete independence of the two narratives. No doubt if one writer had had the work of the other before him, the task of fitting the narratives together would have been made much easier than it is. But such ease of harmonizing would have diminished rather than increased the value of the testimony which these infancy narratives render to the central things that they both record. As it is, we have not only two witnesses to the virgin birth and the birth in Bethlehem, but two *independent* witnesses.

It is perfectly possible, moreover, despite superficial difficulties, to put the narratives together in such a way as to produce a natural account of the course of events. When that is done, we have the following order of events: (1) annunciation to Zacharias, (2) annunciation to Mary, (3) visit of Mary to Elisabeth, (4) return of Mary to Nazareth, (5) discovery of her condition, (6) annunciation to Joseph, (7) marriage of Joseph and Mary, (8) journey to Bethlehem on account of the census, (9) birth of Jesus, (10) visit of the shepherds, (11) circumcision at Bethlehem eight days after birth, (12) presentation in the Temple at Jerusalem forty days after birth, (13) return to Bethlehem, (14) visit of the magi, (15) flight to Egypt, (16) return to Nazareth. No doubt this order of events is in a few particulars not altogether certain; but it is at least perfectly possible; and if other arrangements also are possible, that is not at all derogatory to the harmony between the two accounts.

But even though this much should be granted, even though it should be admitted that the two narratives are not actually contradictory, they are at least *different;* and their mere difference, as distinguished from contradiction, might conceivably be regarded as an argument against their historicity. The source of information about events concerning the birth of Jesus, it might be argued, was, in the very nature of the case, unitary; it could be found only in the testimony of Mary. How, then, could two such different accounts as those which are found in Matthew and in Luke ever have been produced? If the information all came from Mary, how could any narrative which was derived from her have been so incomplete, as each one of our two narratives, when it is taken by itself, certainly is?

Of course it may be answered that there was another possible source of information—namely, the testimony of Joseph. But in the first place, Joseph does not appear in the Gospels in connection with the public ministry of Jesus; and therefore it has been conjectured that he died at an early time. And in the second place, the testimony of Joseph, even if he lived long enough to give it to the disciples, could hardly have been so independent of the testimony of Mary as to produce an entirely distinct cycle of tradition. Mary and Joseph lived together; there must have been, after the birth of Jesus, the fullest possible exchange of testimony between them. Even, therefore, if the narrative in Matthew goes back to the testimony of Joseph, as distinguished from the testimony of Mary which appears in the narrative in Luke, it still seems surprising that the Joseph-narrative does not contain more of Mary's experiences, and the Mary-narrative more of Joseph's. How did two such distinct cycles of tradition ever originate if the ultimate source of information was essentially one?

This objection was put in a particularly striking way by E. F. Gelpke in 1841.[18] Writing not long after the appearance of Strauss's "Life of Jesus," Gelpke sought to add to the merely negative criticism of Strauss some positive understanding of the infancy narratives as works of art. But this understanding, according to his view, was not favorable to the historicity of the accounts. On the contrary, he said, the very difference between the two narratives, the distinct artistic unity of each when it is taken by itself, would be impossible if the narrators were giving an account of facts. How could facts that were so closely connected in themselves be so completely separated in the tradition? The two narratives, Gelpke insisted, are written from two distinct points of view, and set forth two distinct pictures. "The narrative of Luke," says Gelpke, "presupposes, as it were, the notion that earth as well as heaven recognized the pure virgin, and found in her condition no reason for offence, but on the contrary, as was the case with Elisabeth, only an occasion for joy." Very different, on the other hand, is the narrative of Matthew. There we have, instead of the simple joy that prevails in Luke, the bitter hostility of the world-rulers; and instead of an intimate idyl of family life, a mighty drama in which enemies

[18] Gelpke, *Die Jugendgeschichte des Herrn*, 1841, pp. 127, 162 f., 167 ff., 172 ff.

seek the life of the new-born king. No one, Gelpke insists, would want to take the incidents of one narrative and put them into the gaps left in the other. To do so would be to destroy the artistic beauty of each of the two stories. It would be like jumbling together a drama of world-history with an intimate picture of family life.[19]

In commenting upon this argument, we may freely admit that Gelpke does display a certain amount of true appreciation of the artistic beauty of the narratives. It may be freely admitted, within certain limits, that each narrative constitutes an artistic unity which might be spoiled by the addition of incidents taken from the other account. But what of it? What Gelpke has not observed—if we may use a figure of speech which Gelpke in his day could not have employed—is that although a portrait is different from a photograph it may be just as faithful a representation of the person that it depicts. In many cases a portrait would be spoiled by the addition to it of the wealth of details that a photograph contains. Those details belong truly to the person whose portrait is being made; yet they would detract not merely from the artistic beauty of the picture, but also from the faithfulness of its representation. A portrait, in other words, as distinguished from a photograph, is selective; by omitting some details it enables the eye to grasp those details that remain; and thus it brings us into far closer and far truer spiritual contact with the person whom it sets forth.

So it may well be with the infancy narratives of Matthew and of Luke. Even if we admit that either of the narratives would be spoiled by the addition of the incidents narrated in the other, that does not mean that both of the narratives are the product of free invention; but it only means that they are portraits rather than photographs; they present two distinct aspects of the birth and infancy of Jesus, but each of the two aspects may well be in accordance with the facts. Thus we deny that the artistic distinctiveness of the narratives is at all incompatible with their historical truth.

With regard to the specific reasons for the divergence in the tradition, various views may be held. A process of artistic selection may, as has just been intimated, well be given a certain place. It is, indeed, improbable, as we pointed out at an earlier stage of our discussion, that the two infancy narratives are dependent upon a common written source. But even if there was no dependence upon a common written source, there may well have been depend-

[19] Compare the anonymous work, *The Jesus of History*, 1869 (of which the author was Sir Richard Davis Hanson), p. 130: "In the one picture, all is peace and hope—in the other, all is violence and terror." Here also this difference in the two narratives is regarded as furnishing an argument against their historicity. A. Réville (*Jésus de Nazareth*, 2ième édition, 1906, p. 340) calls the narrative in Matthew a tragedy; that in Luke, an idyl.

ence upon a common oral tradition; the author of each narrative may well have selected from a common fund of oral information those incidents that belonged to the particular aspect of the birth and infancy of Jesus which he was interested in setting forth. Such selection, we think, is not really inimical to historical trustworthiness; and in this case we have the advantage of being able to let one narrative supplement the other. We can be thankful, therefore, for the twofold account of these events. Each picture is partial; even the combined picture formed when both are taken together is partial; but when we have first sunk ourselves in the sympathetic contemplation of each, and then have put our impressions together, we discover that the two accounts are not contradictory but supplementary, and that when we use both of them we learn just those things that we most need to know.

But the selective process that led to the distinctiveness of the two narratives was hardly of a merely literary kind. On the contrary, it probably began at a time prior to literary fixation. It is probably a true instinct that has led many readers to suppose that Joseph is the source of the narrative in Matthew and Mary the source of that in Luke. In the latter case, the indications seem to be particularly clear. In the Lucan infancy narrative, Mary's inmost thoughts are revealed—not, it is true, in an indelicate or verbose manner, but in a way quite consonant with the character that is here attributed to the mother of the Lord. And the whole narrative is presented from her point of view. Of course these facts might conceivably be explained by the inherent importance of Mary for the events that are here narrated, an importance which would appeal to some other narrator as well as to Mary herself. And yet such an explanation does not seem to go quite the whole way. There is such delicacy in the touches by which Mary's part in the events is set forth, and such intimacy in the glimpses which are granted into her inmost soul, that the sympathetic reader will hardly be able to rid himself of the conviction that this narrative is derived mediately or immediately from her. Even Harnack has not kept altogether free of this impression. His naturalistic principles will not, indeed, permit him to accept as historical the deeper elements in the narrative; and of course, therefore, he cannot believe that the story of the birth of Jesus, as we have it, comes really from the mother of Jesus. But at least he admits that Luke *regarded* it as coming from Mary, and that it presupposes an impression which Mary had made upon the circle from which it came.[20] Evidently what we have here in Harnack's thinking is a struggle between his naturalistic principles,

[20] Harnack, *Neue Untersuchungen zur Apostelgeschichte*, 1911, pp. 109 f. (English translation, *The Date of the Acts and of the Synoptic Gospels*, 1911, pp. 154–156). When Harnack says that since Jesus' family did not believe on Him during His lifetime, this story could not in its present form have been produced before Mary's death, his argument is unconvincing. See below, pp. 245–248.

and his perfectly correct instinct in the sphere of literary criticism. If we do not share his naturalistic principles—if, unlike him, we are ready to admit the entrance of the supernatural in the life of Jesus—then we shall have no difficulty in following the leading of the literary indications which at this point he so convincingly sets forth; and so we shall hold that this narrative is really derived from Mary, the mother of our Lord.

Of course, even then the exact course of the transmission will still be in doubt. Did the author of the Gospel himself come into contact with the mother of Jesus? Even that view is perhaps not altogether impossible. Or was it an earlier writer of a Jewish Christian source who received the essentials of the story from Mary's lips? That view again is perfectly possible. Or was there a brief course of oral transmission between Mary and the one who first put the story into literary form? Some modern scholars have thought in this connection of Philip and his prophesying daughters, with whom the author of Luke-Acts (if he be indeed the same as the author of the we-sections) came into direct contact according to Acts xxi.8 f. To Philip's daughters would then be due, in part at least, the womanly touch which has been detected in the narrative. This view, again, is not impossible, but like the other views it is not certain. The womanly touch in the narrative is perhaps adequately explained by the supposition that the information came ultimately from Mary, whether or not it passed through other lips before it was finally put into literary form. What really stands firm is that the narrative is written from Mary's point of view, and therefore in some sort claims to come from her. We see no reason whatever to reject that claim.

In Matthew, on the other hand, everything is presented from the point of view of Joseph. His scruples it is that are silenced by the appearance of the angel; he is the one who receives heavenly guidance as to the movements of the mother and the child. Was he, then, the ultimate source of this narrative as Mary was the source of the narrative in Luke? The objection to this view, as has been intimated above, is that Joseph does not appear in connection with the public ministry of Jesus and therefore may be supposed to have died at an early time. Could he then have delivered his testimony before he died? There are perhaps difficulties in the way of an affirmative answer. During the earthly life of Jesus, the virgin birth—even supposing it was a fact—would, as we shall see, naturally remain secret. To have spoken of it would have given rise only to slander and misunderstanding. If, then, Joseph died long before the resurrection of Jesus and the founding of the Church in Jerusalem, to whom could he have handed on his marvellous tale? Must he not have died before his secret had passed his lips? How then can we have in Mt. i-ii a narrative of

Joseph independent of that testimony of Mary which is preserved in the first two chapters of Luke?

The objection is perhaps not quite conclusive. In the first place, may not Joseph have committed the story to writing before he died? That is perhaps not quite beyond the bounds of possibility. In the second place, may he not have confided his testimony to some one who could be trusted not to make it known until the proper time? That the persons chosen for such confidence should have been the younger brethren of Jesus is indeed unlikely in itself, as well as out of accord with their attitude as it is recorded in the Gospels. But there may well have been others whom he might trust to the full, and in whom it might be fitting (as it was not in the case of Jesus' brothers) for him to confide.

Of course it remains possible that Mary is the source of both our infancy narratives. Even then the difference between the two accounts may conceivably be explained. Joseph no doubt confided in Mary; he told her of his experiences as they are recorded for us in Mt. i-ii: Mary would then include these experiences of Joseph in what she told to sympathetic ears when finally she broke the silence that she had previously preserved. But some of her hearers might be interested in some features of what she told, and some in others. Relatives of Joseph, for example, would be interested in those features that concerned Joseph and that were based ultimately upon his testimony; and thus it is those features, especially, which they would transmit. In this way an early divergence in the tradition might well come to pass.

The difference of our two narratives from each other is therefore probably to be explained, not exclusively by separateness in the ultimate sources of information, and not exclusively by a selective process either in the course of the transmission or at the time of the final literary fixation, but by both causes combined. The exact proportions in which the two causes were operative can never be determined; there is room for various perfectly possible conjectures. But if so, it cannot be said that the difference in the two narratives disproves the historicity of both. Not merely one explanation, but various perfectly reasonable explanations, can be given of the way in which the tradition came to diverge.

One of the most serious questions of harmony between the representations of the birth of Jesus in Matthew and in Luke has not been discussed so far, because it belongs in a somewhat different category from those questions with which we have just dealt. The difference is that this question, unlike those others, concerns not the relation between the two infancy sections, but the relation between one infancy section and a detail contained in a later chapter of the Gospel that contains the other. We refer to the matter of the two genealogies in Mt. i.1-17, and Lk. iii.23-38.

At first sight, the genealogies may seem to be in hopeless contradiction. From Abraham to David they run alike; but the son of David through whom the line is traced is, according to Matthew, Solomon, and according to Luke, Nathan, and from that point on two divergent lists of names are given down to the father of Joseph, the husband of Mary. How can the divergence of the two lines be explained? How, in particular, could the father of Joseph be Jacob (as Matthew says) and also Heli (as he is said to be by Luke)? The two genealogies seem to be directly contradictory even with regard to a point so near at hand as that.

According to one solution of the difficulty, the genealogy in Luke is not really a genealogy of Joseph at all, but a genealogy of Mary. In that case, the difficulty regarding the divergence at the end of the genealogies disappears: Jacob was simply the father of Joseph and Heli the father of Mary.

But is this solution exegetically possible? The verses at the beginning of the Lucan genealogy read, according to the usual interpretation, when literally translated, as follows:

> And Jesus Himself was, when He began, about thirty years old, being the son, as was supposed, of Joseph, who was the son of Heli, who was the son of Matthat, etc.[21]

According to this rendering, Heli was the father of Joseph. But some scholars, who find in this genealogy a genealogy of Mary, remove the comma between "as was supposed" and "of Joseph," and translate somewhat as follows: "being the son (of Joseph as was supposed) of Heli, of Matthat, etc." That is, Jesus was *supposed* to be the son of Joseph, but was *really* the son of Heli, etc. Heli would then be the father of Mary, and the word "son" would be taken in the wider sense of "descendant," the name of the mother of Jesus being omitted because it was not customary for women to be included in a genealogy.[22]

Undoubtedly this interpretation would remove a difficulty in the comparison between the two genealogies; and it has won the support of noteworthy scholars, including, for example, Bernhard Weiss.[23] But on the whole it seems rather unnatural. The strictly parenthetical interpretation of "as was supposed

[21] *καὶ αὐτὸς ἦν Ἰησοῦς ἀρχόμενος ὡσεὶ ἐτῶν τριάκοντα, ὢν υἱός, ὡς ἐνομίζετο, Ἰωσὴφ τοῦ Ἡλεὶ τοῦ Ματθάτ, κ.τ.λ.* Lk. iii.23 f.

[22] According to this view the article *τοῦ* which recurs at every link in the genealogy would agree with the *following* name. On the usual view, on the other hand—the view that makes the genealogy the genealogy of Joseph—the article in every case would agree with the *preceding* name; that is, it would mean "the (son of)."

[23] "Die Evangelien des Markus und Lukas," in Meyer's *Kommentar*, 9te Aufl., 1901, pp. 331 f.

of Joseph" would hardly occur to a reader who had not the advantage of modern marks of punctuation. And instead of taking every name in the genealogy as depending directly upon the initial word "son" (in the sense of "descendant"), it surely seems more natural to take every name as depending upon the immediately preceding name.

A more natural way of interpreting the genealogy as a genealogy of Mary is to say that Joseph is here represented as having become "son" or heir of Heli by his marriage to Mary. If Mary was Heli's daughter, and if she had no brothers, then she would become an heiress in accordance with the provisions of Num. xxvii.1-11; xxxvi.1-12. In the former passage, it seems to be provided that the "name" of a man who had daughters but no sons should be preserved. This could be accomplished if the husband of one of the daughters should become identified with the family of his wife.[24] Conceivably, therefore, Joseph may be designated in the Lucan genealogy as the son of Mary's father, Heli. This interpretation would at least have the advantage of avoiding the linguistically unnatural treatment of the words, "as was supposed of Joseph," which is involved in the view just mentioned; every link in the genealogy would now be joined naturally to that which precedes; Jesus would be represented as the "son" of Joseph, Joseph as the "son" of Heli, Heli as the "son" of Matthat.

On the whole, however, it seems better to follow the usual view, in accordance with which the genealogy is the genealogy of Joseph. This view is in accordance with what we saw to be the more natural interpretation of Lk. i.27. If in that verse the author of the Third Gospel calls attention to the Davidic descent of Joseph, and does not call attention to the Davidic descent of Mary, it is natural to find that the genealogy which he inserts at a later point in his book is a genealogy of Joseph and not of Mary.

But if the Lucan genealogy is a genealogy of Joseph, how shall we explain the apparent discrepancy with the genealogy in Matthew? How shall we explain the fact that according to Luke Joseph's father is Heli, and according to Matthew, Jacob?

The most probable answer is that Matthew gives the *legal* descendants of David—the men who would have been legally the heir to the Davidic throne if that throne had been continued—while Luke gives the descendants of David in that particular line to which, finally, Joseph, the husband of Mary, belonged. There is nothing at all inherently improbable in such a solution. When a kingly line becomes extinct, the living member of a collateral line inherits the throne. So it may well have been in the present case.

[24] An interesting account of such a custom in modern Japan is given by Thomas C. Winn, "Oriental Customs Substantiate Truth," in *The Bible Champion*, xxxiii, 1927, pp. 423–425.

The first objection to this view which might occur to a modern reader is found in the use of the word "begat" by Matthew. How could that word be used if merely legal heirship and not physical descent were intended? But an examination of Semitic usage soon shows that this objection is entirely without force. Indeed, it is clear in the course of the genealogy itself that the word "begat" is used in a very broad sense. Thus any reader of the Old Testament would know that in the strict sense Joram did not "beget" Uzziah, but that three generations are here omitted between these two kings. As Burkitt has pointed out, it is probable that the author of the genealogy knew his Old Testament as well as we do. Evidently, therefore, he is using the word "begat" in a broader sense than that in which we employ the English word.[25]

Lord Hervey,[26] who adopts this general solution of the problem of the harmony between the genealogies, cites a number of instances of double genealogies in the Old Testament—that is, a number of cases where a man was reckoned with the family of one who was not in a physical sense his father. This incorporation into another family was practised, he thinks, when a man came into possession of property which belonged to some one other than his own father.

It is not necessarily an objection to this view of the relation between the genealogies that they coincide, in the middle of the divergent sections, in two names, Shealtiel (Salathiel) and Zerubbabel; for we should only have to suppose either that Jeconiah, who is said to have "begotten" Shealtiel, had no son, or else that his son, because of the curse recorded in Jeremiah xxii.30,[27] could not be the heir to the Davidic throne, so that Shealtiel (the living representative of the collateral line recorded in Luke) had to be inserted next by Matthew in the kingly line. Then, at the death of Zerubbabel, or of Abiud (if he is the same person as the Joda of Luke), the line of descent of Joseph's ancestors began to diverge again from the line of legal heirs to the throne, because the (potentially) reigning line came to an end with Jacob, who is said to have "begotten" Joseph, so that Joseph, who was the son, not of Jacob but of Heli, became legally Jacob's heir.

Of course, we cannot say, on this view, how many times in the genealogy of Matthew, between Zerubbabel and Joseph, the line of descent was broken;

[25] F. C. Burkitt, *Evangelion da-Mepharreshe*, 1904, ii, pp. 260 f. The whole of Burkitt's treatment of the word "begat" in Matthew's genealogy, and of the underlying Semitic notion of fatherhood, is illuminating in the present connection.

[26] *The Genealogies of our Lord and Saviour Jesus Christ*, 1853.

[27] "Thus saith the Lord, Write ye this man childless, a man that shall not prosper in his days: for no man of his seed shall prosper, sitting upon the throne of David, and ruling any more in Judah."

for all that we can tell, there may be several places in Mt. i.13-16 where a family came to an end and thus had to take a descendant of a collateral line into itself as its heir. But it would only be at the end that a representative of that particular line to which Joseph, the foster-father of Jesus, belonged became heir to the Davidic throne.

A difficulty, indeed, does arise at this point, when we examine the Old Testament records. In I Chron. iii.19, according to the Hebrew text, Zerubbabel is represented as the son of Pedaiah and as the nephew, not the son, of Shealtiel, so that when he is elsewhere in the Old Testament called Shealtiel's "son," the word "son" designates an adoptive, not a physical, relationship. How then, if Luke in his genealogy is giving the line of physical, rather than merely legal, descent of Joseph, could he have designated Zerubbabel as the son of Salathiel, as he does in Lk. iii.27?

Three answers are possible. In the first place, one may hold that the "Zorobabel" and the "Salathiel" of Lk. iii.27 are different persons from the "Zorobabel" and the "Salathiel" of Mt. i.12 and from the "Zerubbabel" and the "Shealtiel" of the Old Testament. That opinion has actually been held, but in view of the juxtaposition of the two names it seems perhaps to be unlikely. In the second place, one may follow certain manuscripts of the Septuagint at I Chron. iii.18 f., instead of following the Hebrew text. In that case, Pedaiah drops out as the father of Zerubbabel, and Zerubbabel may be regarded as the actual son of Shealtiel. But it is certainly far more likely that the Hebrew text is correct. Probably, therefore, the third of our three alternatives is to be chosen. By that third alternative, we shall simply have to modify our view of the Lucan genealogy. We shall have to say that there is at least one link in that genealogy in which something other than actual physical paternity is designated. This admission would not involve the total abandonment of our hypothesis; it would not involve the relinquishment of our distinction between the Lucan and the Matthæan genealogy. We should still be able to say that, while the Matthæan genealogy traces the successive heirs to the throne of David from David to Joseph, the Lucan genealogy traces the ancestors of Joseph back to David. Suppose, as is quite possible, that Pedaiah "raised up seed" to his brother, Salathiel, in accordance with the legal provisions about Levirate marriage, which we shall speak of in a moment. The Lucan genealogy could then designate Pedaiah's son, Zerubbabel, as being the son of Salathiel, without at all becoming confused with the Matthæan genealogy, supposing that that genealogy involved breaks where the scion of a more or less widely separated collateral line had to be taken into the succession of the heirs to the throne. Luke's genealogy would not, indeed, in its successive links, always indicate actual physical paternity, but it would mean that every successive link did involve at least a very close adoptive relationship between the two persons named.

Thus the difficulty about Shealtiel and Zerubbabel requires a modification, rather than an abandonment, of our hypothesis. We shall still be able to say that the difference between the two genealogies, taken broadly, is due to the fact that for the most part—perhaps even in every link except one—the Lucan genealogy traces the actual physical ancestors of Joseph back to David, while the Matthæan genealogy enumerates the successive heirs to the Davidic throne. The Lucan genealogy, in other words, starts with the question, "Who was Joseph's 'father'?" The answer to that question is, "Heli." Then, in the course of the genealogy, we come to the question, "Who was Zerubbabel's 'father'?" The answer is, "Salathiel," even though the relationship of Salathiel to Zerubbabel was not that of physical paternity. And so on up to David. In the Matthæan genealogy, on the other hand, we start with the question, "Who was the heir to David's throne?" The answer is, "Solomon," and so on down to Joseph. When we consider the matter in this way, it becomes evident that our distinction between the two genealogies does not depend upon the assumption that actual physical descent is designated in the Lucan genealogy in every link, though no doubt it is designated in the vast majority of the links. There may well have been two perfectly valid ways of exhibiting Joseph's Davidic descent, even though the general principle of one at least of these two ways—supposing that general principle was the exhibition of actual physical paternity—was not followed with complete uniformity throughout.

The correctness of this view of the purpose and meaning of each genealogy is confirmed by the fact that the genealogy in Luke begins at the end and works backward, whereas the genealogy in Matthew begins at the beginning. Where the point was to trace the actual descent of Joseph back to David, that could be done by recording the tradition of the family as to his actual father, Heli, and then the actual father of Heli, and so on up to Nathan the son of David. But where the point was to mention the successive heirs of the Davidic throne, it was natural to begin with David and work down.

The view which we have set forth above as to the latest links in the two genealogies is based upon the assumption that the Matthan of Mt. i.15 is *not* the same person as the Matthat of Lk. iii.24. If these two names do refer to the same person, then a difficulty seems to arise. For if Jacob[28] and Heli[29] were both sons of the same person, why should not the elder of them have been

[28] Mt. i.15.
[29] Lk. iii.23.

the heir? And if Jacob was the elder, how could Joseph, the son of the younger, Heli, have been in the line of legal heirship?

This difficulty, however, is quite readily removed. We should need only to suppose that Jacob died without issue, so that his nephew, the son of his brother Heli, would become his heir. One could also think, at this point, of the institution of Levirate marriage, in accordance with which when a man died without issue his brother married the widow and "raised up seed" to the deceased. The question which the Sadducees addressed to Jesus about this matter shows that the custom was not forgotten, whether or not it was frequently practised, in the time of Christ. Possibly, therefore, Heli married Jacob's widow, so that the children, while physically his own, belonged legally to his dead brother.[30]

If Matthan and Matthat are *not* the same person, then it is less natural to appeal to Levirate marriage; for if Heli was the brother of Jacob, how could he have had a different father (Matthat instead of Matthan)? The only answer, apparently, would be the ancient one that Jacob and Heli were half-brothers—that is, that they had the same mother but not the same father. But then the question might be raised whether Levirate marriage was practised in the case of half-brothers, and in general the hypothesis would seem to be overloaded.

If Matthat and Matthan *are* the same person, then the question how different persons could each be the father of the same man, which on the other view arises in connection with the father of Joseph, arises in the case of the father of Matthat (Matthan). And here again it would be unnatural to appeal to Levirate marriage; because that would assume that Levi, the father of Matthat (Matthan) according to Luke, and Eleazar, the father of the same man according to Matthew, were brothers—in which case their father ought to be the same. If, therefore, Matthat and Matthan are the same person, it seems best to explain the divergence regarding their father, not by Levirate marriage, but by the fact that the kingly line became extinct with Eleazar, who is said by Matthew to have "begotten" Matthan (Matthat), so that a scion of a widely divergent collateral line became his heir. Matthat (Matthan) would thus be the legal heir of Eleazar, but the actual son of Levi, who appears in the genealogy in Luke.

Thus on the view that Matthat and Matthan are the same person, the custom of Levirate marriage may plausibly be cited to explain the divergence

[30] This appeal to Levirate marriage would help to explain the use of the word "begat," as referring to an heir who was not an actual son. But the help is not necessary. It would probably not be out of accord with Semitic usage in such a genealogy to use the word "begat" with reference to the mere relation between uncle and nephew if that relationship involved legal heirship.

as to the father of Joseph (Heli in one genealogy, Jacob in the other), but not to explain the divergence as to the father of Matthat (Matthan). On the view that Matthat and Matthan are *not* the same person, Levirate marriage is probably not to be appealed to at all.[81]

We are not endeavoring to discuss the intricate question of the genealogies with even the slightest approach to completeness. But enough, we think, has been said to show that the differences between the two genealogies are not irreconcilable. Reconciliation might conceivably be effected in a number of different ways. But on the whole we are inclined to think that the true key to a solution of the problem (however the solution may run in detail) is to be found in the fact that Matthew, in an intentionally incomplete way, gives a list of incumbents (actual or potential) of the kingly Davidic throne, while Luke traces the descent of Joseph, back through Nathan to David. Thus the genealogies cannot properly be used to exhibit contradiction between the Matthæan and the Lucan accounts of the birth and infancy of our Lord. Here, as in the other features of the two accounts, there is complete independence, but no contradiction.

[81] Even if Matthat and Matthan are the same person, there is no necessity of citing the custom of Levirate marriage; and if the Lucan genealogy itself involves a case of Levirate marriage, when it designates Zerubbabel as Shealtiel's son, then it seems better perhaps not to call in Levirate marriage to help explain the peculiarity of Matthew's genealogy over against Luke's. On the whole question of the genealogies, compare K. Bornhäuser, "Die Geburts- und Kindheitsgeschichte Jesu," in *Beiträge zur Förderung christlicher Theologie*, 2. Reihe, 23. Band, 1930, pp. 6–36.

Chapter IX

THE INHERENT CREDIBILITY OF THE NARRATIVES

TWO important conclusions have been reached in the preceding chapter. The two New Testament accounts of the birth of Jesus, it has been shown, are on the one hand completely independent, but on the other hand not at all contradictory. So far as the relation between them could lead us to judge, they might be regarded as two independent and trustworthy accounts of the same event.

But now the question arises whether this favorable judgment is borne out by a separate examination of each of the two narratives. The relation between them does not prevent us from regarding both as trustworthy; but how is it when they are considered (1) in themselves and (2) in relation to secular history and to the rest of the New Testament? These questions must now be considered in order. We shall in the present chapter consider the narratives in themselves. Is the content of them such that they can plausibly be regarded as trustworthy? Then we shall consider them in comparison with secular history and with the rest of the New Testament.

When we examine the narratives in themselves, one fact, of course, stares us in the face. It is that the content of the narratives is strikingly supernatural; the New Testament accounts of the birth and infancy of Jesus are suffused with the miraculous.

This fact has often been held to settle the question at the start. If miracles have never happened and never can happen, or if, granting the abstract possibility of their happening, the presumption against their having happened in any particular case is so great that the evidence could never be sufficient to establish them, then of course a narrative that contains miracles can hardly be historical.

Conceivably, indeed, such a narrative might be historical in part; it might be held to reproduce the facts except where the miraculous intrudes. In that case, all that would be necessary in order to arrive at the historical content would be to subtract the miracles and nothing else. This method of treatment was applied to the infancy narratives by the rationalizing treatment of one hundred years ago. The infancy narratives, it was held, contain accounts of real events; only these events were not really supernatural: the narrators, or even the witnesses upon whose testimony the narratives are ultimately based, have put a false, supernaturalistic construction upon purely natural happenings. Thus, according to the rationalizing treatment of Paulus,[1] Zacharias really went into the Temple at the hour of incense, as he is said to have done in the first chapter of Luke; while he was there, the glow of the fire or something of that sort seemed to him to take the form of an angel; when he came out, he did not use his voice, because, thinking that dumbness was the punishment that had been imposed upon him for his unbelief, he did not even try to speak.

The most formidable criticism of this whole way of treating the narratives came not, perhaps, from conservative or orthodox scholars, but from David Friedrich Strauss in his famous "Life of Jesus."[2] The polemic of Strauss was turned not merely against the supernaturalistic view, that the narratives are historical as they stand, but also (and with equal sharpness) against the rationalizing method of Paulus and others. If, Strauss said in effect, the miracles are rejected, it is useless to seek a factual basis for the details of the narratives; for in the narratives as they stand the miracles are really central, and the other details are brought in merely for their sake. Rather, said Strauss, the narratives must be regarded as the embodiment in narrative form of certain fundamental ideas. In other words, these stories of the birth and infancy of Jesus are not misunderstood accounts of real happenings, but they are "myths."

This "mythical" theory of Strauss has been dominant throughout the whole course of subsequent criticism, except so far, of course, as it has been rejected by the advocates of the supernaturalistic view. It was not, indeed, always applied, even with respect to the infancy narratives, so thoroughly as was done by Strauss himself; and here and there attempts were made[3] to rescue many details in the narratives as historical even though the central miracle was given up. Nevertheless, it did seem as though the rationalizing method of Paulus had succumbed permanently to Strauss's vigorous attack. Instead of seeking any factual basis for the miracles narrated in the infancy narratives of Matthew and Luke, subsequent scholars applied themselves to the task of understanding historically the origin of the myths. Strauss, it was thought, had performed a necessary negative task: he had disposed of the view that the miracles really happened as they are said in the Gospels to have happened; and he had also

[1] *Philologisch-kritischer und historischer Commentar über das neue Testament*, 2te Ausg., i, 1804, pp. 26–32; compare *Das Leben Jesu*, I. i, 1828, pp. 71–80.

[2] Strauss, *Leben Jesu*, 1835.

[3] For example, by Beyschlag, *Leben Jesu*, 4te Aufl., i, 1902, pp. 159–174. See "The New Testament Account of the Birth of Jesus," second article, in *Princeton Theological Review*, iv, 1906, pp. 37–39.

shown how useless it is to look for a factual basis in the details of a narrative whose main point, for which the details exist, had already been rejected. He had, therefore, it was thought, been quite correct in regarding the infancy narratives of Matthew and Luke as "myths"—that is, as the embodiment in historical form of certain religious ideas. But he had failed to show in sufficient detail just what these ideas were; he had failed to exhibit positively the full meaning of the myths. This positive task, therefore, it was held, needed to be undertaken by others.

The most impressive effort at such a positive understanding of the New Testament "myths"—the motives that led to their formation and their place in the history of thought—was the construction of F. C. Baur and his associates of the "Tübingen school." But the leaders of the Tübingen school for the most part devoted comparatively little attention to the infancy narratives of Matthew and Luke. In that field, the positive evaluation of the supposed myth was undertaken particularly by Ch. Hermann Weisse, in a book which in some respects deserves much more attention than it is receiving at the present time.[4] Weisse observed that the virgin birth, far from being an excrescence in the infancy narrative of Luke, is at the very centre of the whole, as of course it is also in the first chapter of Matthew; in the story of the virgin birth, he supposed, we have a poetic expression of a great idea—the idea of the incarnation of the Divine. But this central idea had to build around it its own mythical cycle. The details of the infancy narratives are, therefore, not to be explained by any dependence upon facts, but by their relationship to the central idea.

Exception may well be taken to the way in which this relationship is set forth in detail: Weisse saw in the details of the infancy narratives a wealth of symbolism which certainly goes far beyond what later scholars have for the most part been willing to detect. A profound symbolism, for example, underlies, according to Weisse, the genealogy in Matthew, especially Mt. i.16: Judaism, as symbolized by Joseph, stands merely in the relation of stepfather to Christianity; it was not able actually to beget the divine Son, but was only able to foster the Son who had been immediately begotten by the Spirit.[5] John the Baptist, Weisse says further, represents Jewish prophecy and the Jewish nation in general, which stand in connection, but also in contrast, with Christ and with Christianity;[6] Zacharias and Elisabeth are represented in the narrative as aged, because new ideas come up only when the ideas from which they

[4] Weisse, *Die evangelische Geschichte*, 1838, i, pp. 141–232. Compare also Bruno Bauer, *Kritik der evangelischen Geschichte der Synoptiker*, i, 1841, pp. 1–127; *Kritik der Evangelien*, i, 1850, pp. 253–336.

[5] Weisse, *op. cit.*, pp. 172 f.

[6] Weisse, *op. cit.*, pp. 187–190.

immediately sprang are old and powerless; Zacharias was dumb, because the priestly wisdom of the Israelites was made dumb in the time just before the coming of Christ on account of their failure to believe in the promises of the Lord; their tongue was loosed when the ancient prophecies began to be fulfilled.[7] In the story of the magi, Weisse found the crown of all these mythical representations: the spirit of old-world priests and poets, he said, is here represented as bringing gifts of symbolic poetry and art to the new religion; the magi failed to return to Herod, because the worldly power was deserted by the religious substance, by the priestly wisdom, of ancient heathenism.[8]

In many of these details, Weisse has not been followed by more recent adherents of the mythical theory. But the mythical theory itself, as over against the rationalizing method of a Paulus or a Venturini,[9] has been dominant throughout the whole course of subsequent naturalistic criticism. It has seemed quite clear to most of those who deny the entrance of the supernatural in connection with the birth and infancy of our Lord that the supernatural elements are quite central in the narratives as we now have them, and that it is useless to seek for non-miraculous events as forming the basis upon which a false supernaturalistic construction was built up.

One objection to such a view would be found in an early date of the narratives; for the production of myths ordinarily requires a certain lapse of time. This objection was expressly urged by Paulus in 1828.[10] We might, he said, be inclined to think that the Lucan infancy narrative is a mythical story; but such a view is excluded by the early date of the Third Gospel. The Book of Acts was written at the end of the two-year period in Rome with which the narrative of the book closes; and the "we" shows that Luke, the author, spent a considerable time in Palestine, where he would have had opportunity to gather material. Hence, Paulus concludes, the mythical interpretation must be given up; and the events narrated in the infancy section must be understood

[7] Weisse, *op. cit.*, pp. 190–196. In the discovery of such symbolism in the narrative, Weisse was anticipated to some extent by the great exponent of allegorical exegesis in the third century—namely, by Origen. So, for example, Origen (*hom. in Luc.*, v, ed. Lommatzsch, v, 1835, pp. 100–102) says that the silence of Zacharias is the silence of the prophets in the people of Israel (the word of prophecy having passed over to the Christians), and that the making of signs at the time of the circumcision of John the Baptist represents the ceremonies of the Jews for which they can give no reason. It is scarcely necessary to remark, however, that the view of Origen as to the way in which the symbolism is supposed to have entered into the narrative has no affinity with the mythical theory of Weisse.

[8] Weisse, *op. cit.*, pp. 219–230.

[9] See below, pp. 273 f.

[10] Paulus, *Das Leben Jesu*, I. i, 1828, pp. 77 f. Compare also the very early dating advocated for the Gospel of Luke by Bahrdt, in his book, *Briefe über die Bibel im Volkston* (p. 49), which appeared anonymously in 1782. Bahrdt, like the later adherents of the rationalizing method, admitted as much of the narrative to be historical as was consistent with his rejection of the supernatural.

as actual, though non-miraculous, happenings upon which the observers in good faith put a supernaturalistic interpretation.

This objection to the mythical view was in the subsequent period overcome by the general denial of the Lucan authorship and early date of the Third Gospel. The Tübingen school, in particular, adopted a very late dating for the Gospel of Luke, as also for others of the New Testament books. But it is very interesting to observe how the modern development of literary criticism has gradually led to a recession from this position, and even to a return, here and there at least, to a position regarding the date of the Third Gospel not unlike that of Paulus. A. von Harnack and C. C. Torrey, for example, have come to believe, as Paulus did one hundred years ago, that Luke-Acts was actually written by Luke, a companion of Paul, and that the second part, the Book of Acts, was written immediately after the point of time reached in the narrative itself. This conclusion about Luke-Acts, moreover, is important also for Matthew; for Harnack holds that the First Gospel was written in the same general period as the Gospel of Luke.

The question then arises what these scholars do with the objection which caused Paulus in his day to reject the mythical theory regarding the narratives and to have recourse to the rationalizing method which has made his name almost an object of opprobrium and ridicule ever since. Now certainly we are as far as possible from accusing such a scholar as Harnack of anything like the prosaic baldness which makes the works of Paulus seem such curious reading to men of the present day. Nevertheless, when we find Harnack suggesting—after some eighty years' dominance of the mythical theory—that possibly the birth in Bethlehem and the journey to Egypt may be historical, that even the visit of the magi from the East is perfectly conceivable, and that possibly there may be a kernel of truth in the story of the massacre at Bethlehem,[11] we cannot help having a feeling that naturalistic criticism is in danger of finding itself, like a man lost in a forest, back in the place where it started out. This feeling is deepened when we examine what Harnack says about the central feature of the Matthæan narrative, the virgin birth. He does not, indeed, abandon the mythical explanation of the story of the virgin birth, but holds to it in a form which will concern us at a later stage of our discussion. Nevertheless, his treatment does show, in some respects, a most interesting tendency to return to the method of Paulus and of the other rationalizers of one hundred years ago. The author of Mt. 1.18-25, Harnack says, admits, as over against the Jewish slander regarding an illegitimate birth of Jesus, that Jesus was born only

[11] Harnack, *Neue Untersuchungen zur Apostelgeschichte*, 1911, pp. 105 f. (English translation, *The Date of the Acts and of the Synoptic Gospels*, 1911, pp. 149 f.).

a few months after Mary had gone to live in the house of Joseph. How did that admission come to be made? Conceivably it might have been made merely in the interests of the virgin birth; that is, the notion that Mt. i.18-25 is polemic against Jewish attacks may be incorrect; and thus the "admission" would be no admission at all, but merely a thing that the writer insists upon to safeguard the truly miraculous character of the conception of Jesus in Mary's womb. But Harnack is inclined to be dissatisfied with this explanation. How could the brothers and younger relatives of Jesus have been expected to accept such a narrative if, as a matter of fact, they knew that Jesus had not been born until Mary had lived for a long time in Joseph's house? Thus Harnack seems clearly to lean to the view that the conception took place by agency of Joseph before Mary had come to live in her husband's house. There would be nothing immoral, he insists, in such intercourse of Joseph and Mary; for betrothal was then equivalent to marriage, and gave, in principle, to the man who had entered into the relationship a husband's rights.

It may be doubted whether Harnack has quite succeeded in removing the opprobrium which would seem to rest upon Joseph and Mary through an acceptance of such a view. Indeed, he himself admits that a premature entrance into the marriage relationship—after betrothal, but before the reception of the bride into the husband's house—though it was perfectly moral, did nevertheless expose the wife more readily to slander; for in such a case it might be said that she had had an adulterous union with another man. Why should Mary have been willing to expose herself to such slander? For her to have done so does seem, despite all the difference between the Hebrew notion and ours (and quite irrespective of the question how far Harnack's view of the Hebrew notion is correct), to cast a certain stain upon her character.

Of course, the mere fact that Harnack's suggestion is repugnant to Christian feeling will not be held by modern historians to prove that it is not true. And yet, on second thought, it does seem to be a sound historical instinct which leads the vast majority of modern scholars to shrink from any such thing. The way in which Jesus came forward in later life, and his entire character, are better explained, just on naturalistic principles, if his parents were far above any such unseemly conduct as that which Harnack is inclined to attribute to them.

At any rate, whatever may be thought of the probability of Harnack's suggestion, the making of it involves a return to a rationalizing treatment of the narratives that was generally thought to be abandoned long ago. It may fairly be held that if David Friedrich Strauss could read Harnack's latest book on the Lucan writings, he would think that he had lived in vain. The gradual "return to tradition" in the sphere of literary criticism has led to a method of treating the miracles which Strauss thought that he had demolished nearly one hundred years ago. And as over against Harnack we cannot help feeling that Strauss would be right. It does seem clear that the narratives of the birth and infancy must be accepted as they stand, including the miraculous element, or else must be relegated as a whole to the realm of myth. If the miracles are rejected—that is, if we reject the thing for which the narratives exist—it is useless to look for any basis of the miracle-stories in misunderstood natural events. The rationalizing treatment of the narratives, as Strauss and his successors have observed, is radically wrong.

Very different from such a rationalizing treatment is the treatment which has been applied to the narratives by such a scholar as G. H. Box.[12] Like the rationalizers, Box believes that the narratives are partly historical and partly not. But the difference is that the rationalizers reject the central thing, the miracle of the virgin birth, and retain only things which to the narrator himself would have seemed quite subordinate, whereas Box retains the central thing and rejects only subordinate features. Our narratives of the birth and infancy of Jesus, Box believes, are midrashic in character—that is, they are built up by fanciful elaboration of a few central facts. But without those central facts, he thinks, they cannot be explained. The central facts in question, the facts which Box regards as the historical basis upon which the midrashic narratives have been built up, include the miracle of the virgin birth. Without that fact the narratives would be left hanging in the air; a midrashic elaboration presupposes something around which the elaboration shall grow.

This separation between fact and fancy is, we think, unnecessary, since we see no valid reason to reject the historicity of the narratives as they stand. But the theory of Box is at any rate not to be confused at all with the rationalizing treatment with which we have just been dealing. In order to understand the difference, it is only necessary to compare Box with Beyschlag, who (at a time long after the golden age of rationalism) carried out the rationalizing method in some detail. Beyschlag accepted the details of the narratives and rejected the main point; Box accepted the main point and rejected many details. That is the difference between the rationalizing treatment, on the one hand, and supernaturalism on the other—even an unduly concessive supernaturalism. As between the two, we certainly prefer the view of Box.

The alternative presented by Strauss in 1835, therefore, still, we think, holds good. Either accept the narratives as they stand, including their supernatural content; or else, without seeking a historical basis in detail, regard them

[12] *The Virgin Birth of Jesus*, 1916.

as myths—that is, as the embodiment, in historical form, of certain fundamental religious ideas. We are not concerned here with the positive elaboration of the second of these two alternatives; we are not concerned with the question how the supposed myths came to be produced, or what are the particular ideas of which they are the embodiment. Those questions will be dealt with, to some extent at least, in the latter part of our discussion. Here we have been interested merely in showing that the supernatural element is quite at the centre of these narratives, and that if the supernatural element is rejected the direct historical value of the narratives is gone. If Jesus was the son of Joseph and Mary by ordinary generation, then the New Testament account of His birth and infancy must be regarded, as Strauss regarded it, as a myth.

But are we, as a matter of fact, shut up to such a conclusion? This question, we think, should be answered in the negative; but certainly it should not be lightly answered. It is perfectly evident that an enormous weight of presumption rests against our holding that at any designated point in history there has been an intrusion, into the order of nature, of the creative power of God. And we are quite unable to comfort ourselves by any lower definition of "miracle" or any lower understanding of the virgin birth of Christ. Efforts have sometimes been made to exhibit the supernatural conception in Mary's womb as standing in some sort of analogy with what occurs in the realm of nature; apologists for the virgin birth have sometimes pointed to the "parthenogenesis" which is said to occur among some of the lower forms of life. But such apologetic efforts really defeat their own purpose. If the virgin birth is reduced to the level of a biological triviality, it becomes quite unbelievable; the weight of presumption against it is too powerful to be overcome. Parthenogenesis certainly does not occur in the higher forms of life, and there is no conceivable reason why such a curious natural phenomenon should have appeared in the case of Jesus. But if the virgin birth represents the beginning of a new era in the course of the universe, a true entrance of the creative power of God, in sharp distinction from the order of nature,[13] then, we think, when it is taken in connection with the entire phenomenon of Jesus' life and particularly in connection with the evidence of His resurrection, it is no longer a meaningless freak, but becomes an organic part of a mighty redeeming work of God, the reality of which is supported by a weight of evidence adequate even to overcome the initial presumption against it. As a natural phenomenon the

[13] This correct definition of miracle was given, with specific reference to the virgin birth, by the ancient commentator, Chrysostom (*hom. in Matt.*, iv, ed. Montfaucon, vii, 1836, p. 66), who says of that which was announced by the angel to Joseph that it was "above the laws of nature" (*ἀνώτερον τῶν τῆς φύσεως νόμων*). Our sharp distinction between the natural and the supernatural is certainly no mere modern invention.

virgin birth is unbelievable; only as a miracle, only when its profound meaning is recognized, can it be accepted as a fact.[14]

We are well aware that such a definition of miracle, and such a belief in the actuality of miracle in this particular case, depend upon a certain definite type of philosophy. There is no greater mistake, we think, than to suppose that the Christian religion can get along with the most widely diverse types of philosophical theory. On the contrary, the Christian gospel has as its necessary presupposition that particular view of the world which is called, in the fullest sense, "theistic"; it presupposes not merely the existence of a personal Being, creator of all things that are, but also the existence of a real order of nature, an order of nature created, indeed, by God and forever dependent upon Him, yet at the same time possessed of a true regularity and unity of its own. Without the existence of a true order of nature, there can be no distinction between natural and supernatural; and if there be no distinction between natural and supernatural, then an event like the virgin birth loses all significance, and losing all significance ceases to be believable as a fact. We do not mean, indeed, that although supernatural events are caused by God, natural events are not caused by Him; but we do mean that He has seen fit to create a true order of nature and to make use of it in the accomplishment of certain of His purposes. Back of that order of nature there lies a creative act of God; and even after that act of creation, God has never abandoned His freedom in the presence of the things that He has made. So, at His own good time, there did enter, we think, into the course of this world a creative work for the redemption of sinful man, a creative work which was begun by the stupendous miracle of the virgin birth. It is only as such a stupendous miracle, only as a part of such a work of redemption, that the virgin birth of Christ can ever be accepted as a fact by reasonable men.

But when it is so accepted, it is accepted, we must insist, as a fact of history. We are often told, indeed, that if the virgin birth is accepted, it can only be accepted as a matter of "faith," and that decision about it is beyond the range of historical science. But such a distinction between faith and history is, we think, very unfortunate. Underlying it, no doubt, there is a certain element of truth. It is certainly true that in order to believe in the virgin birth of Christ one needs to do more than merely examine the immediate documentary evidence; for one needs to take the documentary evidence in connection with a sound view of the world and with certain convictions as to

[14] We agree thoroughly with J. J. van Oosterzee (*Disputatio theologica de Jesu, e virgine Maria nato*, 1840, p. 13), when, in comment on Lactantius' appeal in support of the virgin birth to the animals said by Virgil (*Georgics*, iii. 272–275) to conceive by wind and air, he says: "Quibus nisi meliora scripsisset, Lactantius non fuisset Lactantius."

the facts of the human soul. But the sharp separation between the documentary evidence on the one hand and these presuppositions about God and the soul on the other is far from being truly scientific. A science of history that shall exist by itself, independent of presuppositions, is an abstraction to which no reality corresponds. As a matter of fact, scientific history as well as other branches of science rests upon presuppositions; only, the important thing is that the presuppositions shall be true instead of false.

So it is an unwarranted narrowing of the sphere of history when history is made to deal only with those events which stand within the order of nature, as distinguished from events that proceed from an exercise of the immediate, or creative, power of God. The true sphere of history is the establishment of all facts, whatever they are, that concern human life—the establishment of these facts and the exhibition of the relations between them. So if the virgin birth is a fact at all, by whatever means it may be established, it is a fact of history. No doubt we may sometimes find it convenient to isolate certain particular methods of research and follow those methods for the moment without using others. But ultimately, if we are to be truly scientific, there must be a real synthesis of truth; there can scarcely be a greater error than that of keeping different kinds of truth in separate water-tight compartments in the mind; there can scarcely be a greater error than that of regarding "religious truth," for example, as in some way distinct in kind from "scientific truth." On the contrary, all such distinctions are at best merely provisional and temporary; all truth, ultimately, is one. And we must continue to insist, even in the face of widespread opposition, that if the virgin birth is a fact at all, it belongs truly to the realm of history.

We are not afraid, therefore, of admitting the miraculous or supernatural character of the event narrated in the first two chapters of Matthew and Luke. There is a presumption, indeed, against the supernatural; but that presumption, in the case of Jesus, has, we think, been gloriously overcome.[15]

But although the supernatural appears in these birth narratives, it does not appear in any excessive or unworthy form. In order to exhibit that fact it is necessary only to compare these narratives with those that appear in the apocryphal Gospels. When the child Jesus is represented, as in the Arabic Gospel of the Infancy, as striking His companions dead for slight offences, when He is represented as using His power in trivial or cruel fashion, we certainly find ourselves, as we read, in an entirely different atmosphere from that which prevails in the narratives of Matthew and Luke. Even in the Protevangelium of James, which is the earliest and by far the most interesting

[15] See below, pp. 266–268, 380–382.

of these apocryphal Gospels of the infancy, we miss the wonderful sobriety and beauty of the canonical narratives. A certain impressiveness does indeed appear in this Gospel here and there; as when, for example, all nature and all of human life are represented as standing still at the moment of the birth of the holy child. But that representation, despite its grandeur, does involve a certain excessiveness of the supernatural which is very different from the restraint of the New Testament accounts. And in other particulars—for example, in the evidence of the midwife concerning the birth of our Lord—the Protevangelium enters on a path which the New Testament entirely avoids. According to the New Testament, the *birth* of Jesus, as distinguished from the conception in the womb, may be regarded as a purely natural event; in the Protevangelium we have a heaping up of the miraculous in a way that endangers the true humanity of our Lord.

Thus a comparison with the apocryphal Gospels serves to place in all the clearer light the sober and worthy form in which the supernatural appears in the narratives of Matthew and Luke. Here a wonderful simplicity prevails throughout. A stupendous event is represented as taking place; the Saviour has entered into the world by a creative act of God. But that event takes place not with flare of trumpets or crash of forces, but in the quietness of God. Such was the divine condescension of Him who was to save His people from their sins.[16]

In two particulars, indeed, this sobriety has sometimes been thought to be deserted; modern readers have objected especially first to the angels and second to the star of the magi.

"When angels," says Gressmann at the beginning of his book on the "Christmas Gospel," "descend from heaven and appear to men, we have no historical narrative but a legend, whose historical background is painted over with the golden colors of fabulous imagination." [17] This attitude unquestionably is shared by very many modern men. And yet we question very much whether it can stand the test of sober reflection. Why should it be thought a thing incredible that there should exist in the universe personal beings other than man? Why should it be thought incredible that these beings should hold intercourse

[16] There is wisdom in the words of the ancient preacher Chrysostom (*hom. in Matt.*, viii, ed. Montfaucon, vii, 1836, pp. 143 f.): "If He had exhibited marvels in His earliest years, He would not have been thought to be a man. For this cause, neither was a temple [*i.e.*, of His body?] simply formed (οὐδὲ ἁπλῶς ναὸς πλάττεται); but there was conception and the nine-months time, there were birth-pangs and child-bearing and suckling and quiet throughout all that time. So He awaited the age [or stature] suited to men, in order that by all means the mystery of the divine dispensation might be capable of being well received." The signs that *were* done at the beginning, Chrysostom goes on to say, were for the sake of Joseph, etc., and of the Jews.

[17] Gressmann, *Das Weihnachts-Evangelium*, 1914, p. 1.

with men? Especially in an age when spiritualism is so much in vogue as it is at present, this skepticism about the angels may seem to be out of place. We do not, indeed, desire to underestimate the objection; and our reference to spiritualism is at best an *argumentum ad hominem* which may conceivably be turned back against us. We ourselves do not accept as actual the phenomena with which spiritualism deals; why then, it may be asked, should we believe that in the first century of our era angels descended from heaven and held converse with men?

The answer is that it is simply a question of the adequacy or inadequacy of the evidence in either case. The strong point of spiritualism is that it appeals to what is certainly an abstract possibility—namely, the communion of men with spirits who are in some state of existence different from ours. But we do not think—from all that we can learn—that this abstract possibility has been converted into actuality in the phenomena to which spiritualists appeal. For one thing, a certain triviality seems to affect the entire complex of supposed facts, a triviality which seems somehow to be inconsistent with what might reasonably be expected in a spirit world. But it is not our purpose here to discuss spiritualism; indeed, that discussion would be one in which we are singularly ill qualified to engage. What we are interested in observing is that in the case of the New Testament accounts concerning angels, the evidence is not limited, as it is in the case of modern spiritualistic claims, to the sheer, unrelated testimony about these particular facts, but embraces confirmatory evidence of a very convincing kind. The confirmatory evidence is found in the connection between the appearances of angels and the whole redemptive work of God culminating in the resurrection of the Lord Jesus Christ. The angels appear in the New Testament, not in disconnected or trivial fashion, but as accompanying a mighty, supernatural, redemptive work. When once that work is accepted as a fact, then the appearance of heavenly messengers will no longer give offence. If Jesus was no mere man but the eternal Son of God, incarnate for our redemption, then it is altogether fitting that His birth should have been heralded by a song of the heavenly host.

When the angelic appearances are once considered in this light—as accompaniments of the redeeming work of God—certain detailed objections will seem scarcely worthy of notice. Thus the earlier opponents of miracles used to pour out the vials of their ridicule upon the name "Gabriel," which is applied in the Gospel of Luke to the angel of the annunciation. Is Hebrew, it was asked, the language of heaven; are the angels that stand around God's throne called by Hebrew names? This particular objection, we think, will hardly appeal very strongly to the men of the present day. It will hardly be thought necessary for us to repeat the obvious remark that the name Gabriel ("man of God" or "hero of God") is no mere appellation, but designates in human language the nature of the heavenly being.[18]

All such objections, surely, are trivial. The real objection is that angels do not appear to us today; why, then, should we suppose that they appeared to the people of Palestine nineteen hundred years ago? But to that objection the answer has already been given. The angels do not appear today—that is true. But neither does the incarnate Son of God. Once accept the incarnation, in any true, unique sense, and the angels will altogether cease to be a hindrance to faith. The real question is whether Jesus Christ was just a man like the rest of men, or a heavenly Being, the eternal Son of God, come voluntarily to earth for our redemption. Once admit the absolute uniqueness of Jesus, admit not merely that He was One who has not as a matter of fact been surpassed, but that He was One who can never by any possibility be surpassed, and you have taken the really decisive step. But if you take that step, you should have no difficulty in accepting the exultant supernaturalism of the New Testament narratives as they stand.

Mediating views with regard to this matter are really in a condition of unstable equilibrium. The Ritschlians, for example, tried to maintain the absolute, eternally normative uniqueness of Jesus in the moral sphere without accepting the miracles in the external world. But by an inexorable logic they are pushed in one direction or the other. If they hold to Jesus' moral uniqueness, they will finally have no difficulty with the accompaniments of that moral uniqueness in the external world. Or else, if they insist on giving up the accompaniments of the moral uniqueness, they will soon find that the moral uniqueness itself will have to go. This latter step is being taken by the radicals of the present day. And unquestionably the radicals have the logic of the situation on their side. It is impossible to bring the supernatural in by a back door as the Ritschlians did. If it is to be brought in at all, it demands the central place.

We are not, indeed, without sympathy for those who, unlike the Ritschlians, accept the central miracle of the virgin birth, and yet have difficulty with the angelic accompaniments. Their view may be a useful stepping-stone to higher things; it is not theoretically impossible. Conceivably the New Testament narratives about angels may record inner experiences, objectified, after the manner of those days, by those who passed through them. But for our part we

[18] So, for example, C. J. Riggenbach (*Vorlesungen über das Leben des Herrn Jesu*, 1858, p. 163) speaks of the angel as "a messenger from heaven whose nature is indicated in human language by the name 'Gabriel,' 'hero of God.'"

must discard such mediating views. If once we accept the stupendous miracle of the incarnation, the angelic appearances seem to us to be wonderfully and beautifully in place.

The other point at which the particular form of the miraculous in the birth narratives has given rise to objection is found in the star of the magi. How could a star in the heavens possibly go before men as they walked upon the earth; how could it possibly serve as their guide to point out a particular house? At this point, it is said, we have not merely what is miraculous, but what cannot even be conceived.

With regard to this objection, the first question that arises is an exegetical one. Has the objector interpreted correctly the Matthæan narrative about the star? Does the narrative really mean that the star literally went before men as they walked upon the earth; does it really mean that it pointed out to them the house in which Mary and the child were found? The answer is by no means so certain as is sometimes assumed.

It is perfectly clear, at any rate, that if the star ever served directly as a guide from one point to another, it did not do so continuously. When the magi arrived at Jerusalem, they were obliged to inquire their way; evidently they had no direct supernatural guidance to lead them to Bethlehem. As they started out on the last stage of their journey, Old Testament prophecy and not the star served as their guide.

But, it may be said, why should they ever have come to Jerusalem in the first place, unless they had been directly guided by the star? What except a moving star could ever have led them away from their own country, and particularly just to the country of the Jews? This objection is by no means so formidable as it seems. As has often been pointed out, the heavens were divided by ancient astrology into regions corresponding to regions on the earth's surface. A celestial phenomenon in one particular part of the heavens, therefore, might well have been connected by the magi with an earthly happening in the West. But even if that were so, how could they have come to think particularly of Judæa? The answer can plausibly be found in the wide spread of the Messianic expectation. Whatever may be thought of the positive testimony with regard to that, whatever view may be held of the famous assertion of Suetonius and Tacitus that there was throughout the East an expectation of world-rulers to come from Judæa,[19] it may be regarded as inher-

[19] Suetonius, *vit. Vesp.*, iv; Tacitus, *hist.*, v. 13. Zahn (*Das Evangelium des Matthaus*, 1903, p. 91, footnote 80), for example, thinks that the value of this testimony is diminished by its evident dependence upon Josephus, *de bell. Jud.*, VI. v. 4; III. viii. 9: but he also thinks that the expectation among Eastern astrologers of a world ruler to appear in the West is otherwise well attested.

ently very probable that Hebrew prophecy should have been widely known throughout many regions of the Eastern world. Ever since the time of the exile, there had been Jews in Babylonia; and it may well have been from Babylonia that the magi came. But in the possession of a Jewish population Babylonia was by no means unique; almost everywhere a Jewish dispersion was to be found. It should never be forgotten, moreover, that in the first century of our era and in the preceding century Judaism was an active missionary religion; through the agency of its synagogues it was making converts in many parts of the world. But its influence was by no means limited to the winning of proselytes in the full sense. Also very important was the effect which it had upon those who were by no means ready to take the decisive step of becoming Jews. The Book of Acts repeatedly mentions such persons—the "God-worshippers" or "God-fearers," who attended the Jewish synagogues and accepted some features of the Jews' religion without becoming circumcised or giving up their own national affiliations. But there is not the slightest reason to think that this Jewish influence was exerted always to the same degree or in the same way. An almost infinite variety, no doubt, characterized the effect which Judaism had upon the Gentile populations with which it came into contact in the Hellenistic age. So there is abundant room, in the life of that period, for Gentile astrologers who either directly, by a perusal of the Old Testament, or more probably indirectly, had heard of the Messianic hope, had on the basis of it come to expect the appearance of a world-ruler in Judæa, and thus were able to interpret a celestial phenomenon, astrologically connected with the West, as announcing the birth of the promised "king of the Jews."

So far, therefore, it is quite possible, in perfect loyalty to the meaning of the narrative, to regard the star of the magi as being merely a natural phenomenon, a conjunction or a comet or a new star, which the magi interpreted by the principles of their art as referring to the Messianic king. This interpretation is admirably in accord with the account of what happened in Jerusalem. The narrator seems at that point to have no thought that the star might have been a guide to the magi to direct them to the exact spot where the child was born. On the contrary, they had to inquire their way; and it was only on the basis of Messianic prophecy, interpreted by experts, that they started out for Bethlehem.

When they started out, they saw the star again; and, seeing it, they rejoiced. Then it "went before them until it came and stood over the place where the young child was."[20] It is these words alone which really give any

[20] Mt. ii.9, *καὶ ἰδοὺ ὁ ἀστὴρ, ὂν εἶδον ἐν τῇ ἀνατολῇ, προῆγεν αὐτοὺς ἕως ἐλθὼν ἐστάθη ἐπάνω οὗ ἦν τὸ παιδίον.*

serious difficulty to the natural, as distinguished from the supernatural, way of interpreting what is said about the star. How could the star "go before" them, how could it stand over a particular place, if it was a natural phenomenon in the heavens? Do not these words clearly indicate that the narrator conceives of the star as a phenomenon near to the earth, and thus (to use our modern terminology) as clearly supernatural? [21]

Plausible though such considerations are, we do not think that they are at all decisive. They fail to take account of the poetical, oriental way of describing events that we should describe in very different terms. Do Matthew's words mean anything more than that when the magi started out by night upon their journey to Bethlehem they were cheered on their way by the star which shone down upon them from the heavens? Does the narrator intend to do more than picture for us that last stage of the long journey and describe for us the joy that filled the magi's hearts? Or even if a fresh appearance of the star is meant, as distinguished from an appearance that had been taking place every night, might that not be explained by the reappearance of a phenomenon which had been invisible for some months? They had been in doubt whether they were really on the right way; the star had appeared in the East, but then had disappeared; and in Jerusalem they had been obliged in their perplexity to go about seeking advice. But now when they started out for Bethlehem, perhaps uncertain whether the information that had been given them was correct, the star which they had seen in the East was up there again in the heavens, lighting them on the way. It seemed to go before them while they journeyed, as celestial bodies do when one moves upon the earth; and at last, when they came to Bethlehem and had found by inquiry the house where there was a new-born babe, there stood the star in the heavens still, shining down upon them as they entered into the house.

No doubt, when we propose such an interpretation, we may be faced by a charge of inconsistency. We have been very severe, it may be said, upon the rationalizers, who regarded the narratives as historical but explained the

[21] Modern objections to the explanation of the star as a natural phenomenon were anticipated by Chrysostom (*hom. in Matt.*, vi, ed. Montfaucon, vii, 1836, pp. 101–103). It was not an ordinary star, says Chrysostom, for the following reasons: (1) it moved from north to south, (2) it appeared in the daytime, overcoming the rays of the sun, (3) it appeared and disappeared (disappearing when the magi were in Jerusalem, appearing again when they needed it, and thus showing intelligence), (4) it must have come down low in order to indicate the place where the young child lay. Of these arguments, only the last is really worthy of consideration. With respect to it, we may remark that Chrysostom has a very extreme view of the nearness of the star to the ground; he supposes (*op. cit.*, vii, ed. Montfaucon, vii, 1836, p. 127) that the star stood over the very head of the child. The second argument is based upon the assumption that the star appeared in the daytime, for which there is no evidence in the text.

miracles away; and now here we are ourselves proposing a natural interpretation which shall make the story of the magi more palatable to modern men!

In reply, we may say that we never denied the possibility of a wide range of figurative interpretation, especially in oriental books. What we objected to in Paulus and the rationalizers was something quite different. It was not by figurative interpretation that they endeavored to remove the supernatural from the New Testament books; on the contrary, so far as exegesis was concerned, they held a thoroughly supernaturalistic view. They held that the narrators for their part were quite convinced that the happenings were supernatural, but that this view which the narrators held was false. We, on the other hand, if we really decide to adopt the interpretation set forth above, are maintaining that the narrator himself intended to designate a star in the heavens rather than one that actually moved along with travellers upon the earth, and that if we interpret his expressions in a literal sense we are simply failing to get his meaning. It is rather strange that we defenders of the Bible should often be designated as "literalists," and still more strange that we should be said to favor "literalistic interpretation." As a matter of fact, in many cases it is those who deny the truthfulness of the Bible who are the real literalists; in many cases they insist upon a baldly literal interpretation which is really quite absurd. To indicate what we mean, it is only necessary to point to those popular opponents of Christianity who ridicule the representation of "the Lamb's wife" in order to discredit the Book of Revelation. But we might also point, perhaps, to more academically respectable examples of what we mean. Thus when Old Testament scholars interpret such an utterance as "I will have mercy and not sacrifice" as indicating opposition on the writer's part to the sacrificial system, we are bound to say that that seems to us to be an extreme literalism which is quite unjustified in the interpretation of an oriental book—and indeed for that matter in the interpretation of any book. The truth is that there can be no hard and fast rule for the decision between literal and figurative interpretation. What we must try to do in any individual case is to read the passage in question sympathetically, so as to enter into the mind of the writer. When we do so, we may perhaps be able to decide with perfect impartiality whether the passage was literally or figuratively meant.

So it is in the present case. We have suggested a figurative interpretation which would permit us to regard the star of the magi as a natural phenomenon. But we are not conscious, in doing so, of any apologetic bias. The reason why we are not conscious of any apologetic bias is that if the figurative interpretation should prove to be wrong and the literal interpretation right—that is, if the writer of the second chapter of Matthew regarded the "star," not as a conjunction or the like, but as something so near to the earth that it could actually go along with an observer as he walked from Jerusalem to Bethlehem and could actually stand still over a particular house—we should still have no objection of principle against regarding the narrative as true. When once we have accepted the entrance of the supernatural in connection with the appearance of Jesus in this world, we are no longer interested in setting exact limits to the extent to which the supernatural is to be found. Of course it would be different if in any particular the supernatural element in the narrative appeared in a form that could be regarded as unworthy of God. But that would not be the case with the star, even if it was supernatural in the fullest sense. If a sound exegesis of the Gospel of Matthew should show that the Evangelist regarded the star as having literally gone before the magi as the pillar of fire went before the Israelites in the desert, we should have no objection of principle against accepting that as a fact. But, as it is, we think that the matter is in doubt. The figurative interpretation is, on the one hand, by no means certain; but on the other hand it cannot be called impossible. If, unlike ourselves, any modern readers hold that the historicity of the narrative can be maintained only if the figurative interpretation is right, and if (as we think they ought to do) they find independent reasons for maintaining the historicity of the narrative, then we think they are perfectly justified in adopting the figurative interpretation. For ourselves, we cannot find, on the basis of either interpretation, anything in the narrative that is unworthy of God.

A moral objection is, indeed, sometimes raised against the story of the magi. If, it is said, the magi were guided aright by astrological calculations, if their conception of the relation between the movements of the heavenly bodies and events upon the earth actually led them in this case to the feet of the new-born king, then the stamp of God's approval would be put upon a harmful pseudo-science; the magi and those who came into contact with them would be confirmed in their superstition. Such confirmation of what is false, it is said, would be unworthy of the God of truth.

This objection has had a great vogue all through the course of modern naturalistic criticism. But we are unable to regard it as very serious. Who can say how far God could or could not stoop to human weakness in his treatment of the wise men from the East? In countless cases, as we know, error has become the stepping-stone to truth; even astrology, as has often been observed, was the ancestor of true astronomical science. No, we are unable to regard it as unworthy of God when these strangers were led by their searching of the heavens to bring their gifts to the infant Saviour. It was not astrology, moreover, which played the decisive part; what really led the magi to the feet of

Jesus was not astrological calculation, but the prophecies of God's Word—the prophecies which spread abroad throughout the East the expectation of a Messianic king.[22]

We shall not pause here to examine the various hypotheses which have been proposed regarding the star. Many attempts have been made to identify it with some known phenomenon of the heavens, and thus to fix the year of Jesus' birth. The most famous of such attempts was that of Kepler, who thought that a conjunction of the planets Jupiter and Saturn in the constellation of the Fish, which took place in the year 7 B.C., was the occasion of the magi's journey.[23] This hypothesis has recently been defended as altogether possible, with abundant references to astrological speculation, by the Roman Catholic scholar, Steinmetzer.[24] Certainly something is to be said for it; and the date which it fixes for Jesus' birth is not at all impossible.

We do not at all unite in the scorn which some modern scholars have expressed for such attempts to identify the star of the magi. But certainty has at any rate not been attained by any one of them. And the present writer is quite without the expert knowledge which would be necessary in order that he might enter fruitfully into the discussion. Many views are possible with regard to this matter; but enough perhaps has been said to show that, whether the star be regarded as natural or as supernatural, there is no decisive reason why the appearance of it should not be regarded as historical.

Neither the miraculous character of the narratives in general, therefore, nor the account of the angels or the star in particular, is sufficient to cast discredit upon the New Testament accounts of the birth and infancy of our Lord. There is, indeed, a presumption against the supernatural; but that presumption has, in this case, we think, been overcome. The supernatural happenings recorded in the first two chapters of Matthew and Luke would no doubt be unbelievable if they stood alone; but it is different when they are taken in con-

[22] With regard to the moral objection against the story of the magi, Chrysostom (*hom. in Matt.*, vi, ed. Montfaucon, vii, 1836, pp. 103–107) is still worth reading. The purpose of the star, Chrysostom says, was that the Jews might be deprived of all excuse if they did not believe in Christ. They rejected great prophecies; the magi believed a lesser witness. God used the star, because He desired to use what the magi would heed. It was an act of extreme condescension (σφόδρα συγκαταβαίνων). Compare, Chrysostom continues, Paul's speech on Mars Hill. And compare the whole Jewish dispensation. The sacrifices, etc., originated in the dullness of the nations; but God used them, with changes, to lead up gradually to a higher religion. So God led the magi up from the star to an angel. [It must be admitted that here Chrysostom departs a little from what is surely given in the text.] Compare, also, Chrysostom says further, the way in which God answered the Philistine soothsayers about the Ark of the Covenant; and compare also other analogous acts of God. The knowledge was brought to the magi not only by the star, but also by God who moved their soul.

[23] See Box, art. "Star," in Hastings, *Dictionary of Christ and the Gospels*, ii, 1908, p. 675.

[24] *Die Geschichte der Geburt und Kindheit Christi und ihr Verhältnis zur babylonischen Mythe*, 1910, pp. 84–109.

nection with the entire New Testament representation of the person of the Lord.

But even if we have thus overcome the initial presumption against the supernatural, are there not independent objections against the historicity of these infancy narratives? Or do the narratives, irrespective of the supernatural, look as though they might be correct? Are they in accord with what might reasonably be expected? Is the information that they contain, even about what is not supernatural, of a kind that might have been founded in fact? Are the actions attributed to the characters in accordance with psychological probability?

These questions were partly answered when we considered, for example, the integrity of Lk. i-ii and the relation between that narrative and the narrative in the Gospel according to Matthew. But a few points still call for brief comment.

In the first place, what shall be thought of the genealogies? We have considered the relation between them, and have endeavored to show that they are not contradictory. But aside from the relation between them, are they inherently likely to be correct? Is it probable that genuine information should have been preserved about the lineage of Joseph, and that such information has actually been recorded in the genealogies of Matthew and Luke?

There is really no reason whatever for answering these questions in the negative. At first sight, indeed, it may perhaps seem strange that a person in such humble circumstances as was Joseph should have had preserved to him the record of his ancestors for many generations back. But such an objection ignores the remarkable tenacity of genealogical traditions in the East. Whatever may be thought of the assertion by Julius Africanus to the effect that Herod the Great had commanded the public genealogical records of the Jews to be destroyed, such a command would not affect private records.[25] That there were genealogical records after the time of Herod is shown by the matter-of-course way in which Josephus speaks of his own ancestry.[26] Certainly it is not at all antecedently improbable that a tradition of Davidic descent could have been preserved in the family of Joseph, and that such a tradition would be correct.[27]

There is nothing improbable, moreover, in the actual genealogies as they

[25] Julius Africanus, in Eusebius, *hist. eccl.*, I. vii.13.

[26] Josephus, *vita*, i (ed. Niese, iv, 1890, pp. 321 f.). Josephus, it may be remarked in passing, appeals to public records in support of his genealogy, despite what Julius Africanus says about the destruction of such records by Herod. See also *contr. Ap.*, i.7. Compare E. L. Curtis, art. "Genealogy," in Hastings, *Dictionary of the Bible*, ii, 1906, p. 121.

[27] See especially Zahn, *Das Evangelium des Matthäus*, 3te Aufl., 1910, pp. 45 f. (footnote 6).

stand in the Gospels. If, indeed, the genealogy in Matthew were intended as a complete record of actual physical descent, it would present serious difficulties; for the number of generations between the Exile and the time of Christ is much smaller than would be expected in view of the length of the time. But as a matter of fact that genealogy is not intended to be taken in any such way. In the genealogy in Luke, on the other hand, the number of generations is just about what might naturally be expected.

It has often been asked whether the genealogies existed separately before they were incorporated in the Gospels. And if they did exist separately, did they in their separate form contain any reference to the virgin birth or did they simply make Jesus the son of Joseph without hint of anything peculiar in that relationship? Did the Matthæan genealogy, for example, simply end with the words, "Joseph begat Jesus"?

Even if this question should be answered in the affirmative, we should not have any denial of the virgin birth; for, as has already been observed, the words, "Joseph begat Jesus," could be understood in the same putative or legal sense as that in which similar words are to be understood elsewhere in the genealogy. Moreover, even if the person who compiled this genealogy thought, when he included the words, "Joseph begat Jesus," that Jesus was in a physical sense the son of Joseph, that fact would not militate against the fact of the virgin birth; for there certainly was a time—during the earthly ministry of Jesus—when the virgin birth, even if it was a fact, was unknown among Jesus' disciples.

But we think that the question whether the genealogies existed in separate form prior to their incorporation in the Gospels is wrongly put when the separate genealogies are regarded as being necessarily genealogies of Jesus. Rather should it be said that the genealogies were genealogies of Joseph before they became genealogies of Jesus; they represented a family tradition which was added to from generation to generation.

A special question is raised by the mention of four women in the Matthæan genealogy; Thamar, Rahab, Ruth, and the wife of Uriah. The view has often been held that these women are mentioned by way of answer to a Jewish slander regarding Mary the mother of Jesus; [28] the Jews, it is said, had maintained, in caricature of the Christian story of the virgin birth, that Jesus was born out of wedlock; and now Matthew answers this slander by

[28] This hypothesis was held so early as the middle of the eighteenth century, by Wettstein (*Novum Testamentum Graecum*, i, 1751, pp. 226 f.). See Ebrard (*Wissenschaftliche Kritik der evangelischen Geschichte*, 3te Aufl., 1868, p. 250), who rejects the suggestion. A prominent recent advocate of the hypothesis in question is Th. von Zahn (*Das Evangelium des Matthäus*, 3te Aufl., 1910, pp. 64–67.

pointing to the irregularities which had already prevailed in the case of certain women in the kingly line; Thamar and Rahab and the wife of Uriah were connected with shameful stories, and Ruth was a foreigner; hence there was no reason for the Jews to reject the Messiahship of Jesus even if they were right in supposing that there was something shameful about his birth.

This hypothesis, if correct, would only increase, if anything, the weight of the Matthæan testimony to the virgin birth of Jesus; for it would show that belief in the virgin birth had had a considerable history before this infancy narrative was written; it would show that the Jewish opponents of Christianity had already recognized the doctrine of the supernatural conception as one of the essential beliefs of the early Church against which they needed to direct their attack. Such a development—thesis, attack, answer to the attack—could not already have been completed if the belief of the disciples in the virgin birth was any new thing. As a matter of fact, however, we doubt very much whether the hypothesis, so far as it is based upon the names of the women in the genealogy, is correct. Would the compiler of the genealogy, or the author who inserted it at the present place, ever have consented, even for the moment and for the sake of the argument, to compare the mother of Jesus with women in whose lives any shameful thing could be found? Perhaps it might be said in reply that the reference would be one of contrast rather than of analogy: if even shameful relationships with women could be used by God in the transmission of the kingly line, the author might be intending to say, how much more the creative action of the Holy Spirit! But this reply would not be altogether satisfactory. After all, the writer would still be bringing Mary the mother of Jesus into a sort of connection with shameful things; and that he would probably have shrunk from doing. On the whole, therefore, it is at least very doubtful whether the mention of the women in the genealogy has any polemic reference against Jewish slander. It remains perfectly possible that the women were mentioned even before the last link of the genealogy was added, and that they were mentioned not because they were shameful, but merely because for one reason or another they were noteworthy. The problem presented by the mention of these women is as yet unsolved.[29]

[29] Origen (*hom. in Luc.*, xxviii, ed. Lommatzsch, v, 1835, p. 191) finds in the mention of the women ("Thamar, quae cum socero fraude concubuit: et Ruth, Moabitis, nec de genere Israel: et Raab, quae unde sumta sit scire nequeo: et conjux Uriae, quae violavit mariti torum") the thought that since Jesus was to bear our sins, He was born of a sinful race (as is shown also by the mention of Solomon, Rehoboam, etc.). Similarly, Jerome (*com. in Matt.*, i, on Mt. i.3, ed. Vallarsius et Maffæius, vii, 1845, col. 21): "Notandum in genealogia Salvatoris nullam sanctarum assumi mulierum; sed eas quas Scriptura reprehendit, ut qui propter peccatores venerat, de peccatoribus nascens, omnium peccata deleret." Compare also Chrysostom (*hom. in Matt.*, iii,

Another minor problem is presented by the division of the Matthæan genealogy into three groups of fourteen generations each. We are not concerned here with the purpose of this division, but only with the fact that the last of the three groups seems at first sight to contain only thirteen generations instead of the specified fourteen. One solution of the problem is to say that Mary is counted as a "generation"—that is, as a link in the genealogy—between Joseph and Jesus. There is really nothing preposterous about this suggestion, in view of the author's broad use of the term "generation" and of the related term translated "begat." On the whole, however, it seems better to adopt the solution which was favored by Edward Robinson, in his Harmony of the Gospels.[30] According to that solution, David is counted both at the end of the first division and at the beginning of the second. The second division then ends with Josias, and the third division begins with Jechonias and, including Jesus, embraces the fourteen "generations," or members of the genealogy, that are sought. There is justification for this hypothesis in the language that is employed when the enumeration is made. The first division is said to include the generations from "Abraham to David"; the expression names both Abraham and David and thus indicates that both are to be counted. Similarly, David is named in the expression designating the second group, and so is to be counted there also. But what designates the end of the second group and the beginning of the third is not a person but an epoch—"the exile to Babylon"—and therefore "the persons who are reckoned as coeval with this epoch . . . are not reckoned before it. After the epoch the enumeration begins again with Jechoniah, and ends with Jesus."[31]

Certainly, therefore, when the true character and purpose of this genealogy are understood, there is no objection against supposing that the information that it contains is correct, as there is no objection to a similarly favorable estimate of the genealogy in Luke.

---

ed. Montfaucon, vii, 1836, pp. 40–42), who says that the shameful women are mentioned to show the humiliation undergone by Christ for our salvation, and who also develops the edifying thought that what is really important is not that a man should come from good ancestors, but that he should be good himself. In passing, it may be remarked that even if the hypothesis of Zahn and others regarding the women be rejected, one may still hold to the polemic reference of the first chapter of Matthew as a whole. It is quite possible that this author, in recounting Joseph's doubts about Mary and the way in which they were overcome, is intending to refute the Jewish slander which attributed the birth of Jesus to an adulterous union. But although that is possible, it is certainly not proved. The writer's own interest in establishing the legal Davidic descent of Jesus and the inherent importance of the facts would no doubt explain the choice of material without any anti-Jewish polemic reference.

[30] Robinson, *A Harmony of the Four Gospels in Greek*, revised edition, with additional notes by M. B. Riddle, [1885], p. 206.

[31] Robinson, *loc. cit.*

But if the genealogies appended to the narratives contain nothing that may not well be true, what shall be said of the narratives themselves? Do they contain psychological or historical absurdities, or do they bear the marks of truth?

The latter estimate, we think, should be adopted. There are, of course, points in these narratives where some things are left unexplained; there are places where the motives of the characters are not perfectly clear. But such difficulties often constitute an argument not against, but in favor of, the historicity of a narrative. A manufactured narrative tends to be perfectly plain: since it is the product of invention, one point in it naturally grows out of another. But a true narrative, on the other hand, often gives rise to many questions; the characters in it do not move in accordance with the logic of the narrator's mind, but in accordance with the infinite complexity of actual life, of which only a fraction can ever be recorded. Thus if in these infancy narratives there are some things that are not perfectly clear, that fact in itself does not show at all that the narratives are not true.

What are the points that have been thought to be unnatural? Some of them have already been considered in connection with our discussion of the integrity of the Lucan narrative. We showed in that connection that the attitude of Mary the mother of Jesus, though unnatural if Jesus was the son of Joseph, is perfectly natural on the basis of the virgin birth. Objection has, indeed, sometimes been raised to her going to Elisabeth as recorded in Lk. i.39. How could a merely betrothed Jewish maiden make a long journey like that alone? Would such a journey have been in accord with the custom of those days? Because of such objections, some scholars have supposed that the events recorded in Mt. i.18-25, including the marriage of Joseph and Mary, are to be put before instead of after Mary's visit to Elisabeth.[32] But in that case are we to suppose that Joseph accompanied Mary to Elisabeth's home? He might have been expected to do so if the marriage had already taken place; but then it becomes strange that he is not mentioned in Lk. i.39-56. This latter consideration is perhaps not altogether decisive; it is barely possible that in view of the subordinate place of Joseph in the whole narrative his presence on this occasion might be passed over without mention—just as even Zacharias is here out of view. On the whole, however, the hypothesis of a marriage prior to the visit of Mary to Elisabeth will be felt to raise more difficulty than it removes; the natural impression which the reader of Lk. i.39 receives is that Mary visited Elisabeth at once after the annunciation and without waiting for any determination regarding her relations with Joseph. The events of Mt.

[32] See above, p. 196, footnote 17.

i.18-25 are in all probability to be put not before, but after, Mary's three months in Judæa.

But even if that be so, the journey of Mary does not become incredible. To say that a betrothed Jewish maiden of the first century could not under any circumstances make a journey unaccompanied by the man to whom she was betrothed is to claim a degree of familiarity with the customs of that day that far transcends our actual knowledge. And it must always be remembered that the circumstances of this case were very peculiar; Mary had just passed through a stupendous experience, and the heavenly messenger who had appeared to her had himself suggested by implication her visit to her relative in Judæa.

Even less important are the objections that have been raised against the story of the birth and circumcision of John.

If it is asked, for example, how Zacharias could have continued his ministrations at the Temple, in accordance with Lk. i.23, if he was dumb and so could no longer satisfy the Mosaic requirements of physical perfection for the priests, we may simply say two things. In the first place, Lk. i.23 does not necessarily mean that Zacharias continued active in the Temple ministry, but may mean only that he continued in Jerusalem during the week's period of service of his course; and, in the second place, it may well be doubted whether a lack of the power of speech which was unaccompanied by any obvious physical imperfections and which might be regarded as purely temporary, would unfit a priest even for active service.

In connection with Lk. i.60, it is quite trivial to ask how Elisabeth could know that the child's name was John, since Zacharias was dumb and so could not tell her of the directions given him by the angel. The context provides a sufficient answer. The answer simply is that the art of writing was not unknown in those days! Then it is asked why the bystanders should have had to make signs to Zacharias,[33] since we have been told only that he was dumb and not that he was deaf. But surely that difficulty also is trivial. As has often been observed, it is natural to use signs in communicating with one who can reply only with signs. Moreover, the signs in this case would be of the very simplest sort; it would only be necessary to turn to Zacharias with a gesture of interrogation. Such little touches as that tell in favor of the historicity of the narrative rather than against it: they are really very natural as describing an actual scene, but might have been avoided in a fictitious account.

In the second chapter of the Lucan narrative, objection has sometimes been

[33] Lk. i.62.

raised against Mary's journey with Joseph to Bethlehem at the time of the enrolment. If the notion of the writer is that an enrolment of women was necessary, as well as of men, that, we are told, is contrary to all historical probability. And otherwise how could Mary have decided to make such a journey just before the birth of her child; would not her condition have made it natural for her to stay at home? An obvious answer to this question is that it was just her condition that made it natural for her not to stay at home, but to go with Joseph to Bethlehem. In the first place, she would desire not to be deprived of the protection of Joseph at such a time; in the second place, she expected her son to be the Messiah, and so might naturally desire that He should be born at Bethlehem. Her journey, moreover—whether this last point was in her mind or not—may actually have served the purpose of averting the slander which might have come upon her at Nazareth because of the apparently premature birth of her child. We are not saying that these are just the considerations that determined Mary's journey.[84] But they are sufficient, at least, to show that various motives for the journey may be suggested; the representation in the narrative at this point, therefore, presents no psychological or historical improbabilities.

Such improbabilities, however, are often found especially in the story of the magi. We have already discussed those difficulties—real or supposed—in that story which concern the supernatural element; but now we must consider the difficulties that are found in the realm of psychology. Quite aside from the question of the supernatural, it is said, the actions of the characters in the story, especially of Herod, are quite out of accord with all psychological probability.

In the first place, when the magi came to Jerusalem with their inquiry for a king of the Jews, would Herod have fanned the flames of Messianic hopes by calling a meeting of the "chief priests and scribes"[85] to ask where the Messiah was to be born? And, indeed, before that, would the magi have been naïve enough to ask so politically dangerous a question in such a public way under the very eyes of a suspicious king? Then, after the scribes had pointed to Bethlehem, why did Herod use secrecy in calling the magi to him? The whole city, according to Mt. ii.3, had already been set in an uproar; what possible purpose, therefore, could secrecy now serve? And did Herod actually think the magi childlike enough to suppose that he would really want to wor-

[84] B. Weiss (*Leben Jesu*, 4te Aufl., i, 1902, pp. 231 f.; English translation, *The Life of Christ*, i, 1883, p. 252) suggests that Joseph took Mary with him to Bethlehem because he wanted the child to be listed at once as his in the public registers.

[85] We cannot be certain that the author regards it as a formal meeting of the Sanhedrin. See Andrews, *The Life of our Lord*, second edition, 1891, p. 97.

ship a king of the Jews who would be a claimant to his own throne? Why did he not simply send spies after them, so that when they reached their destination he could put the child out of the way?

These difficulties are not so formidable as at first sight they may seem to be. They are all based upon the erroneous assumptions that the magi were animated by motives of worldly wisdom and that Herod in his declining years was as cool and calculating as a modern psychological expert. No doubt the magi were very incautious in making their inquiry in Jerusalem. If they had employed the intelligence service of whatever country it was from which they came, they might have learned enough about Herod to know that he would not look with favor upon inquiries about a king of the Jews. But then it must be remembered that the thoughts of those magi were centred upon the heavens and not upon political conditions on this earth. There were many impractical men in the strange, complex religious life of those days; in such an age, we may well find room for these children of the East with their disconcerting questions. Incautious, moreover, as their questions no doubt were, we have no right to assume that Herod would have thought it safe just to kill them out of hand. The Messianic hope, after all, was very widely held in those days; and Herod knew that it could not possibly be put down by force. Harsh and cruel though he was, he never altogether relinquished the pose of being a Jewish, rather than a foreign, king. Who can say what trouble he may have had if he had stopped the mouths of the magi by a public act of violence? On the whole, there was something to be said for the cunning method that he actually adopted—a method, moreover, which is quite in accordance with his character as it appears in the pages of Josephus. He pretended to be devout in his attitude toward Old Testament prophecy, but meanwhile planned to make Old Testament prophecy harmless by secret measures of his own.

As for the reason why he used secrecy in calling the magi to him, that is fairly obvious. He did not want to let the people know of his hypocritical words about worship of the new-born child; such words might deceive these strangers, but it would hardly deceive those who knew Herod well. And in general he did not want to give the matter any greater publicity than it already had. The meeting of the chief priests and scribes may have been necessary in order that he might show his devoutness as a Jew; and then it may also have been necessary because of his own superstitious fears. He really feared, perhaps, the rise of a Messianic king; and perhaps he really thought that the expert judgment of the scribes would help him to find that king in order that he might kill him when he was still a child. Hence the meeting may have seemed to him to be necessary for the accomplishment of his plan. But that meeting over, the less publicity that should be given to the magi the better it would be.

But why did not Herod have the magi "shadowed" instead of trusting them so naïvely to bring back word to him after they had found the child? No doubt that other plan might have appealed to the modern police. But there may have been difficulties connected with it. If the magi had observed that they were being followed, might they not have been discouraged in their search, and so might not the chance of finding the dangerous child have been lost? Why, then, did not Herod send some one along with the magi under pretence of friendly assistance? [36] That ruse also might have been detected. Something may perhaps be said, here again, for Herod's plan. Perhaps indeed he was unwise; but then was Herod always wise in his mad closing years? [37] Who can say, moreover, whether an attempt may not actually have been made to spy upon the magi as they went to the house where they found the child, and whether such an attempt may not have failed? If it failed, then Herod's purpose could be accomplished only by wholesale murder; and from such murder no one who knew Herod in that last period of his life could suppose that he would shrink.

There is no reason, therefore, for saying that this narrative contains psychological absurdities. The actions, no doubt, are not in all cases what modern men would have done, and in some cases, no doubt, they are very foolish or incautious; but as attributed to men of that time, and to those particular persons, they cannot be shown to be impossible.

[36] "Officii praetextu"—Calvin, on Mt. ii.7.

[37] There is perhaps some truth in the remark which Chrysostom (*hom. in Matt.*, vii, ed. Montfaucon, vii, 1836, p. 126) makes to explain Herod's failure to see that the magi would detect his deceit: "A soul made captive by wickedness becomes more foolish than all things else." Compare also Calvin (*loc. cit.*), who appeals, in explanation of Herod's folly, to the stupor which God inflicted on him for the protection of the infant Christ. Bruno Bauer (*Kritik der evangelischen Geschichte der Synoptiker*, i, 1841, pp. 108–110) praises Calvin for his recognition of the difficulty but does not think highly of his solution.

Chapter X

THE BIRTH NARRATIVES AND SECULAR HISTORY

IT HAS been shown in the preceding chapter that there is nothing in the first two chapters of Matthew and Luke which does not in itself look as though it could be historical. That conclusion will of course be denied by those who are opposed on principle to an acceptance of the supernatural, or else do not believe that the presumption which everywhere prevails against the acceptance of the supernatural has as a matter of fact been overcome in the case of the life of Jesus and the beginnings of Christianity. But if a man is once impressed with the evidence in favor of a supernatural origin of Christianity, he should find no special objection to those particular miracles that are narrated in the infancy narratives of the First and Third Gospels; and the non-miraculous elements of the stories also are by no means devoid of psychological and historical probability.

But if these narratives are thus not condemned by their own inherent qualities, how is it when they are compared with secular history and with the rest of the New Testament?

Under the former head—comparison with secular history—two points have been thought to offer difficulty. They are, first, the massacre of the infants at Bethlehem and, second, the census of Quirinius.

The former point can be dismissed very quickly. It is true that Josephus, our informant about Jewish history, says nothing about the massacre of the innocents; and it is also true that the passages in the works of historians that actually mention this event are so late and so likely to have been derived from the Gospel of Matthew as to possess little value. But the argument from silence is in this case altogether devoid of weight. No doubt, from our point of view, the massacre of young children would be a particularly atrocious form of murder, which would have to be mentioned in any detailed account of current events—even, perhaps, in Chicago! But in ancient times, when the exposure of infants was a common practice, which is alluded to, for example, in one of the non-literary papyri, in the most casual possible manner as an ordinary feature of the life of that day,[1] the murder of children would

[1] See Milligan, *Selections from the Greek Papyri*, 1910, p. 33.

probably not be regarded with any special horror. Moreover, we ought not to exaggerate the number of the infants who would be killed. If Bethlehem was a small village, as it probably was, then the number of male children in it under two years of age would not exceed perhaps twenty or thirty. In the orgies of blood and cruelty that marked the closing years of Herod's reign, the removal of a score of children in an obscure village might well escape the notice of our one historian. But even if Josephus knew of the incident, and even if he thought it in itself worthy of remark, there was in this case a special reason for his silence. The incident involved Jewish Messianic hopes; and without doubt Josephus purposely avoided the mention of such things in the history that he wrote for Roman readers. There is no reason, therefore, for supposing that if the massacre of the innocents had really happened Josephus would necessarily have included it in his historical work.

But something more positive needs also to be said. Although the massacre of the innocents is not directly attested by secular history, it is exactly in accord with what we know of the character of Herod in his declining years. Herod the Great was an able monarch, but in the last years of his reign he entered upon a career of cruelty that reached the verge of madness. His actions in putting to death his own children and his beloved wife, and his plan (interrupted only by his death) of butchering all the leading citizens of Jerusalem in the theatre, possess just exactly that quality of wild and useless bloodthirstiness which appears in the massacre of the innocents at Bethlehem. Never was a story more completely in character than this. In general we may say that the difficulty which has been found in the silence of secular history about the bloody deed at Bethlehem amounts to nothing at all.

Far more important is the other of the two objections which have been drawn from secular history against the truthfulness of our narrative—namely, the difficulty regarding the census of Quirinius.[2] At that point we have a problem which, despite a certain amount of light that has been shed upon it in recent years, has not yet quite been cleared up.

The account of the census to which exception has been taken is found in Lk. ii. 1-5. In this account, verse 1 presents no real difficulty. When it is said that "in those days a decree went forth from Cæsar Augustus that all the world should be enrolled," that does not at all mean that a census was to be taken, in the modern fashion, in all parts of the Empire in the same manner and on the same day. On the contrary, the language of the verse is fully satisfied if we think only of the announcement by Augustus of a general

[2] On this subject see especially W. P. Armstrong, art. "Chronology of the New Testament," in *International Standard Bible Encyclopædia*, i, 1915, pp. 645 f.

policy of enrolment for the Empire. It is not at all necessary to suppose that this policy was carried out in any uniform manner, or even that it was carried out in every one of the provinces and vassal kingdoms at all. In accordance with the wise Roman policy of adaptation to local circumstances, a large amount of liberty would naturally be allowed to the several administrators and vassal monarchs. In Egypt, where, because of the discovery of the non-literary papyri, our information is particularly abundant, we find a census being taken under a regular fourteen-year cycle; a census was also taken, we know, in Italy and in Gaul and other provinces; and the census in Judæa in A.D. 6 is mentioned not only by the New Testament but also by Josephus.[3] In some provinces, indeed, modern historians have asserted that no census was taken. But it is quite unnecessary for our present purpose to discuss the question whether this assertion is correct: for Luke says only that the decree of Augustus was issued; he does not say that it was completely carried out. Certainly the issuance of such a decree is altogether in accord with Augustan policy; there is a great abundance of evidence to show that this emperor was greatly concerned with an inventory both of the material resources of the Empire and of its man power. The "decree" mentioned in Lk. ii.1, though not directly attested elsewhere, is quite in line with all that we know with regard to Augustus' reign. There is not the slightest reason to think that it is not historical.

The real difficulty in the passage is found in connection with verse 2. This verse is to be translated as follows: "This happened as a first enrolment when Quirinius was governing Syria," or "This became a first enrolment when Quirinius was governing Syria."[4] The expression is certainly peculiar; and the linguistic difficulty in it has been reflected in changes introduced by copyists. It is no wonder that conjectural emendations of so difficult an expression have been attempted in ancient and modern times; and the possibility that some primitive corruption has crept in cannot altogether be excluded. But since the best-attested text is not absolutely impossible, that text must be made the basis of our discussion.

The verse as it stands seems to distinguish the enrolment here referred to from one or more subsequent enrolments; it seems to mean that this enrolment was either the first that was made in the Empire as a whole or else the first among two or more that were made during the rule of Quirinius over Syria. Since in Acts v.37 the well-known enrolment under Quirinius in A.D. 6 is mentioned by this same writer, it is natural to think

[3] For these facts, see the evidence cited by Armstrong, *op. cit.*, p. 645.

[4] *αὕτη ἀπογραφὴ πρώτη ἐγένετο ἡγεμονεύοντος τῆς Συρίας Κυρηνίου.*

that he is in our passage distinguishing an earlier event from that. Thus he seems to mean that there was an earlier enrolment under Quirinius as distinguished from the enrolment in A.D. 6. That earlier enrolment must apparently have taken place during the reign of Herod the Great. Herod is mentioned in Lk. i.5, and there is no evidence to show that he is regarded as having died in the interval between the time referred to in that passage and the time of the birth of Jesus. No doubt, therefore, Luke as well as Matthew regards the birth of Jesus as having taken place before the death of Herod in 4 B.C.; and since the birth of Jesus was connected with the census, the latter too must apparently have taken place at the same time.

The problem, therefore, if the narrative is to be regarded as accurate at this point, is to find room for a census during the rule of Quirinius over Syria and yet prior to the death of Herod the Great.

Some progress toward the solution of this problem has been made by the patient researches of recent years. It has been rendered altogether probable, on the basis of information quite independent of the Third Gospel, that Quirinius was actually legate of Syria at a time prior to his well-known legateship that began in A.D. 6. This former legateship of Quirinius is accepted by some scholars who are as far as possible removed from any desire of rescuing the trustworthiness of the Gospel according to Luke.

But the difficulty is that the former legateship of Quirinius apparently cannot be put quite early enough. Saturninus, we know, was legate of Syria from 9 to 6 B.C.; and Varus was legate from 6 B.C. until after the death of Herod in 4 B.C. The former legateship of Quirinius, therefore, cannot be put earlier than about 3-2 B.C. How, then, can a census under Quirinius have taken place, as the Lucan narrative seems to represent it as having taken place, in the days of Herod the Great?

With respect to this difficulty, two things may be said. In the first place, one may suppose that although the enrolment began during the reign of Herod, it was not brought to completion until after his death. In favor of this suggestion may perhaps be urged the very peculiar expression that is used by Luke. "This became a first enrolment," Luke says, according to one possible interpretation of his words, "when Quirinius was governing Syria"; or "This took place [that is, was brought to completion, was actually carried out] when Quirinius was governing Syria." Possibly the intention is to distinguish the earlier stages of the process of enrolment—during which earlier stages the journey of Joseph and Mary to Bethlehem took place—from the consummation or final carrying out of the decree, so far as Judæa was concerned, under the (earlier) legateship of Quirinius. This solution of the problem is perhaps not quite impossible.

More probable, however, is the other suggestion that has been made in this connection—the suggestion, namely, that the rule of Quirinius in Syria which is here referred to is not his legateship, but a special commission of a military kind which he held during the legateship of Saturninus or Varus. There are some slight indications that Quirinius did hold such a special commission; and there is at any rate nothing that absolutely forbids us to suppose that he did so. The special commission of Quirinius might include expressly the duty of taking a census. Hence it might be possible for the author of the Third Gospel to speak of a census taken in Palestine in the closing years of Herod the Great as being the former of two enrolments under Quirinius.[5]

Our conclusion, then, is that although the problem of the enrolment has not as yet been fully solved, there is no reason to think that it might not be solved if our knowledge should become more complete than it is at present. Certainly the example of other places in which the Lucan writings were formerly thought to be inaccurate about matters of civil administration, but have now been vindicated in the most thoroughgoing way, should make the historian very cautious about asserting the presence of an error at this point.

Objection has indeed sometimes been raised not merely to the mention of Quirinius, but also to the manner in which the census is represented as being taken. A method of enrolment by which every man, wherever he should be living at the time, should have to go to his ancient ancestral home would, it is said, be quite impractical; it would involve the necessity of "a regular migration."[6]

In reply to some such objections, Ramsay[7] has appealed to an Egyptian papyrus document[8] which directs that for the purposes of enrolment every person shall go from the place where he is residing at the moment to the place where his home is found. But of course the analogy is not quite complete. It is one thing for a man to go to the place where he owns a home and another thing for him to go, as is apparently meant in Lk. ii.4 f., to the home of his remote ancestry. It has often been suggested, indeed, that Joseph owned property in Bethlehem; and if so, that fact would provide a more obvious

[5] It is probable that πρώτη could be used, instead of προτέρα, even where there were only two members in the series referred to. But the argument is not essentially changed if this enrolment is designated as the first among a whole series of enrolments in Palestine and not merely as the former of two enrolments under Quirinius.

[6] "Eine wahre Völkerwanderung." See Keim, *Geschichte Jesu von Nazara*, i, 1867, pp. 390 f.

[7] "The Morning Star and the Chronology of the Life of Christ," in *Expositor*, seventh series, v, 1908, pp. 19 f.

[8] *Greek Papyri in the British Museum*, iii, 1907, pp. 124–126.

official reason for this journey. We are by no means certain that the assumption of such an official reason is contrary to the language used by Luke. If the reason for the journey was Joseph's possession of property in Bethlehem, and the reason for his possession of property in Bethlehem was, in turn, his belonging to the family of David, then perhaps it was not inaccurate for the historian, omitting the immediate cause, to say simply that he went up to Bethlehem because he was of the house and lineage of David.

On the whole, however, it seems better, rejecting the analogy of the Egyptian census, to regard this enrolment as taking place in accordance with a Jewish method by which family relationships determined the classification. There is no real absurdity in such a supposition; for it need not be assumed that all members of the Jewish people could trace their lineage so far back as could Joseph. In Joseph's family the tradition of Davidic descent was preserved from generation to generation; Bethlehem, therefore, retained its position for that family as the ancestral home and as the place to which recourse needed to be had in any tribal census. But in the case of other families, where only the nearer ancestry could be given, no such journeyings would be required. A census conducted by the tribal method would therefore not require a "regular migration" as Keim supposed.[9]

That a census should have been required in the dominions of Herod by Roman decree is altogether in accord with what we know of the thoroughly subservient position of this vassal king; but that Herod should have been allowed to carry out the decree by a method which would respect the customs of his people is also in accord with the Roman policy of adaptation to local circumstances. When in A.D. 6 a census was carried out in Judæa by the distinctly Roman method, discontentment and disorder were the result; but the earlier census, since it was not so obviously a foreign measure, did not arouse the hostility of the people.

Our treatment of the intricate question of the census has been of the most cursory kind. But enough, perhaps, has been said to show that if on the basis of a general examination we have come to have a high view of the trustworthiness of Luke-Acts, and particularly a high view of the trustworthiness of the infancy section, the difficulty about the census does not furnish any adequate reason why we should reverse that favorable estimate.

[9] The narrative does not say that everyone went to the place where his family originated, but only that everyone went "to his own city" (Lk. ii.3). The reason why Bethlehem was Joseph's "own city" was that it was the home of his ancestors (verse 4); but that in all other cases the place of enrolment, the city to which a man belonged, was determined in the same way is not said.

Chapter XI

THE BIRTH NARRATIVES AND THE REST OF THE NEW TESTAMENT

IN THE preceding chapter it has been argued that there is no contradiction between the two infancy narratives and secular history. But what shall be said about their relation to the rest of the New Testament? That question must now be examined with some care.

It will be convenient to begin with what the Gospels permit us to learn regarding the attitude of Jesus' contemporaries—the attitude, that is, of those who came into contact with Him during His life upon earth. Was that attitude such as to exclude the historicity of the first two chapters of Matthew and Luke?

In this connection it may freely be admitted that according to the Gospels there was no general knowledge of the virgin birth of Christ among the people of Palestine during the period of the public ministry; the people of Nazareth, for example, are represented in Mt. xiii.55 as saying with respect to Jesus, "Is not this the carpenter's son?", and are similarly represented in Lk. iv.22. Evidently Jesus was generally regarded simply as the son of Joseph. But what of it? Surely Joseph and Mary would not have spoken publicly about a thing which in the nature of the case could not be proved, and which, therefore, could, until Jesus' claims should be vindicated in some palpable way, only give rise to suspicion and slander. There is not the slightest evidence in Lk. i-ii and Mt. i-ii to show that the story of the supernatural conception was narrated by Joseph or Mary to the shepherds, to the magi, or to Simeon. We have, indeed, found it not improbable that Mary confided in her kinswoman Elisabeth; indeed, she must certainly be supposed to have done so if the greeting in Lk. i.42-45 indicates knowledge on Elisabeth's part that the child was already conceived in Mary's womb, and if, as is probable, Elisabeth knew that the marriage, as distinguished from the betrothal, of Joseph and Mary had not yet taken place. But such confidence of Mary in Elisabeth, to whom she had by implication been directed by the angel, is very different from any general publication of her strange experience; and there is not the slightest reason to suppose that Elisabeth betrayed Mary's confidence by telling others of what Mary had told her. Moreover, Elisabeth and Zacharias were both of them aged at the time when John the Baptist was born; they probably did not long continue to live. For many reasons, therefore, it is unlikely that the story of the virgin birth should by their agency have become known. As for Mary herself, the implication, of the Lucan narrative at least, is that she, in her quiet, meditative way, kept the wonderful secret locked in her heart. There was, therefore, no reason why, even if the virgin birth was a fact, the contemporaries of Jesus during the public ministry should have had any knowledge of it. Hence their ignorance, as attested by the Gospels, provides no argument at all against the historicity of the infancy narratives.

A similar consideration is valid also in the case of the brothers of Jesus. In the Gospel of John we are told expressly that at a certain period, at least, in the public ministry, Jesus' brothers did not believe on Him; and this general representation of their attitude is on the whole confirmed by the scanty references to them in the Synoptic Gospels. Such an attitude on their part would perhaps hardly have been likely if they had known of the virgin birth, though conceivably it might be said that even if they had been told of it, they might have disbelieved the story. But is it likely that Joseph or Mary would have told them of the wonderful event? This question must certainly be answered in the negative. If there were any persons who would not be told, it was just the younger brothers of Jesus. Surely what Mary would do with her knowledge of the wonderful, unbelievable event would be to keep it as a secret until the time when the lofty destiny of her son should be made known by God in some unmistakable way.

The case would of course be different if Mary herself[1] displayed ignorance of the virgin birth; for of course she at least could not be ignorant of it if it was a fact. Such ignorance on the part of Mary has been found by many scholars in Mk. iii.21, 31. In Mk. iii.21 it is said that Jesus' friends[2] "went out to lay hold on him; for they said, He is beside himself." The expression rendered in the English Bible, "his friends," is really incapable of translation; it means "those who came from his home," "his people," "those who were connected with him." Now ten verses further on, in Mk. iii.31, it is said: "Then came his mother and his brethren and standing without sent to him, calling him." If the former passage is interpreted by the latter, then the persons who, according to verse 21, thought that He was beside himself[3] turn out to be His mother and His brothers. But how could His mother have thought that

[1] Joseph passes out of view, and presumably had died before the beginning of the public ministry.

[2] οἱ παρ' αὐτοῦ.

[3] ὅτι ἐξέστη.

He was beside Himself if she knew that He had come into the world by a stupendous miracle? Thus this passage, it is said, shows clearly that Mary was unaware of the virgin birth; and that fact shows, of course, that the virgin birth had never taken place.[4]

Few arguments against the virgin birth of Christ have been more persistently used than this. And yet upon any careful examination the argument is seen to be extraordinarily weak. Almost every step in it is doubtful. In the first place, it is doubtful who are meant by "his people" or "his friends" in Mk. iii.21. The expression is of a rather general character; that it designates only those who lived under the same roof with Jesus is by no means clear. In the second place, it is very doubtful whether verse 21 is to be interpreted by verse 31—that is, whether "His mother and His brethren," who sought Him according to verse 31, are represented as being the same as the persons who, according to verse 21, supposed that He was beside Himself. A passage of considerable length has intervened between the two verses, a passage in which is discussed the attitude of a class of persons quite distinct both from those who are mentioned in verse 21 and from those who are mentioned in verse 31. What indication is there that after turning aside to discuss the attitude of the scribes who had come down from Jerusalem,[5] the author intends to return in verse 31 to exactly the point at which he had left off in verse 21? There is really no clear indication to this effect at all.

Indeed, we might almost argue that there is an indication to the contrary; we might almost argue that if the author had been intending to return to the point at which he had left off he would have had to express himself differently, that he would have had to indicate in some way that Jesus' mother and brethren, introduced into the narrative as though for the first time in verse 31, are the same persons as "His people" or "His friends" mentioned in verse 21. If the same persons are meant, why is such different terminology used? Of course the terminology in verse 31 is fixed by the utterance of Jesus that follows; but why could that same terminology not have been used in verse 21? Perhaps it may be said that the terminology in each case was fixed in the tradition at a time when the incidents were narrated separately, and that when the incidents were combined in the Gospel the original terminology was allowed to remain. That suggestion is possible enough. But what right have we, then, to interpret one incident by the other? Is there any evidence whatever that the Evangelist meant to identify the persons mentioned in one

[4] See especially Clemen, *Religionsgeschichtliche Erklärung des Neuen Testaments*, 2te Aufl., 1924, p. 114, with the account of recent discussion given in footnote 7

[5] Mk. iii.22–30.

incident with the persons mentioned (with very different terminology) in the other? We do not think that any such evidence can be found.

Even, therefore, if the persons referred to in verse 21 are members of the household in which Jesus had lived, and not merely persons who were connected with Him in some broader sense, it is still not clear that verse 31 mentions just those and only those particular members of the household who were designated in that former verse. The persons who, according to verse 21, thought that Jesus was beside Himself may therefore have been His brothers without any inclusion of His mother.

It should be observed that in verses 31-35 there is not the slightest indication of any unsympathetic attitude on the part of Jesus' mother toward Him or of any unsympathetic attitude on His part toward her. His mother and His brethren are represented as seeking Him, but that this was done in a hostile way is certainly not said. And Jesus' utterance, "Behold my mother and my brethren," is seriously misinterpreted if it is regarded as derogatory to His relationship with the family circle in which He had lived. By placing the tie that united Him with the disciples on the same plane as that which united Him with His brethren and sisters and mother, our Lord was not debasing the latter relationship, but was gloriously exalting the former.

Finally, suppose it should even be admitted for the sake of the argument (as in point of fact we do not admit at all) that Mary was present with those who said that He was beside Himself, would that fact exclude knowledge on her part of the miracle of the virgin birth? We are very doubtful whether it would. It must be remembered that Mary's faith had suffered severe trials; Jesus had not lived at all the life that might have been expected of one who had been conceived by the Holy Ghost and was destined to occupy the throne of David for ever. Long quiet years had passed without the expected burst of glory; and now was begun a kind of public ministry that seemed to involve naught but opposition and suffering. Who can wonder if Mary was troubled by what she saw? Her perplexity would be the greater just because of her knowledge of the miracle of Jesus' birth. How great was the contrast between what she had expected in those first glorious days and what the years had actually brought forth! It is indeed unlikely that she would actually lose faith; it is unlikely that she would actually agree with those who said of her son that He was beside Himself. But that she might have stood quietly with them when they sought to halt Jesus in what they considered to be a mad career is not altogether beyond the bounds of possibility. No doubt her thoughts, because of her knowledge of what they did not know, were widely different from theirs; but she, too, because of her perplexity, might hope that Jesus would be led into a different career. We must remember that despite the stupendous destiny of her son and the miracle of His birth, Mary had actually been in a position of authority over Him during the long years when, according to Lk. ii.51, He had been subject to His earthly parents. Was it God's will that all guidance on her part was now to cease? Perhaps the thing may not have been quite so clear to her as some modern scholars think that it should have been.

What we have just been saying, however, has been said merely for the sake of the argument. Even if Mary was in some sort associated, no doubt silently, with those who said that Jesus was beside Himself, that would not exclude knowledge, on her part, of the miracle of His birth. But as a matter of fact there is no evidence that she was associated with them at all. It is only by the most adventurous kind of reasoning, therefore, that the third chapter of Mark has been made to furnish an argument against the virgin birth of Christ. Rightly interpreted, the passage is quite consistent with the historicity of the birth narratives in Matthew and Luke.

A similar remark might be made about all the other indications which the Gospels afford regarding the attitude of Jesus' contemporaries. John i.31, it is true, where John the Baptist is represented as saying with respect to Jesus: "And I knew him not: but that he should be made manifest to Israel, therefore am I come baptizing with water," has often been thought inconsistent with the first chapter of Luke. How could John the Baptist have failed to know Jesus if he was actually a relative of His, as he is said to have been in Lk. i, and if the two children were so closely linked together by a series of wonderful events? But the objection is by no means insuperable. Zacharias and Elisabeth are expressly declared in Lk. i.7 to have been old at the time when John was born; it is not impossible that they died before their child came to years of discretion. Some thirty years had passed before Jesus came to the baptism; it is not necessary to suppose that John and Jesus had ever come into contact during that period. Moreover, it is not clear whether the verb "knew" in the sentence, "I knew him not," in John i.31 is used of ordinary acquaintanceship. It may possibly be used of a profound understanding which might have been lacking even though John was acquainted personally with Jesus, and perhaps even though he knew Him to be the promised Messiah. The passage may possibly intend only to contrast John's lack of understanding of the full meaning of his own baptizing work with the true purpose of that work as it existed in the mind of God. At any rate, the verse will certainly not bear the weight that has been hung upon it. It is perfectly capable of being understood in a way that involves no contradiction with the relation between John and Jesus as it is set forth in the first chapter of Luke.

Still more clearly must a similar conclusion be reached with regard to John's question, "Art thou he that should come, or look we for another?", in Mt. xi.3; Lk. vii.19. It may seem surprising that John should have doubted the Messianic mission of Jesus if there had occurred in his own family the event narrated in Lk. i.39-56. But the difficulty is diminished by considerations similar to those that we have just adduced. How much of those wonderful events would have become known to John even if they had happened in the manner that is set forth in the first chapter of Luke? We cannot definitely say. At any rate, the argument from John's perplexed question militates against the account of the baptism of Jesus in Mt. iii.17 and John i.32-34, as much as it does against the infancy narrative. If John the Baptist really saw the heavens opened at the baptism of Jesus, and heard the voice from heaven, his doubting question in Mt. xi.3; Lk. vii.19 might at first sight seem to be impossible. But a little reflection serves to diminish this objection. Just because John's expectations about Jesus were set so high (not only by what he may have learned regarding what is recorded in the first chapter of Luke, but also by the event at the baptism), he was perplexed at the strange and apparently indecisive character of Jesus' ministry. Who can say that in his perplexity he may not have sought light by the question recorded in Matthew and Luke?

One other point, however, deserves to be mentioned before we leave the present phase of our subject. It has perhaps not received from opponents of the virgin birth quite the amount of attention that it deserves relatively to their other arguments. The point to which we refer concerns the attitude of the people of Nazareth, and, reflecting their attitude, the attitude of Jesus' opponents generally, toward the legitimacy of His birth. That attitude, so far as we can judge, was one of complete acquiescence in the view that Jesus was the son of Joseph and Mary. We have already considered this acquiescence so far as any possible knowledge of the story of the virgin birth is concerned; it would have been quite unnatural for the contemporaries of Jesus to have been told the story of the virgin birth even if that story was true; hence their ignorance of the story does not show at all that it was false. But here we are considering the matter from a slightly different angle. Suppose the events concerning the birth of Jesus were as they are recorded in the infancy narratives of Matthew and Luke. Our present point is not that those events might have given rise to a general belief in the virgin birth, but on the contrary that they might have given rise to slander. If the conception in Mary's womb really took place three months before her marriage with Joseph, then the birth, from the point of view of ordinary observers, was premature; and if the birth was premature, would not slander have resulted; and if slander had resulted, would it not have been revived during the public ministry by the bitter enemies of Jesus; and if it had been revived by the enemies of Jesus, would it not have been recorded in the Gospels as were other attacks? But since as a matter of fact there is no hint in the Gospels that any slander was raised against the birth of Jesus, and since, on the contrary, the objection of unbelievers was merely to the obscurity of His birth as a child of the carpenter, Joseph, must we not suppose that all even apparent basis of such slander was absent, and therefore that the virgin birth of Jesus as narrated in Lk. i-ii and Mt. i-ii, which must have given rise to slander, is unhistorical? In other words, does not the same consideration, absence of slander, which excludes a *really* illegitimate birth of Jesus also exclude an *apparently* illegitimate birth such as the birth of Jesus would have been if the story in the birth narratives in Matthew and Luke were true?

These considerations are not without their importance. But they are important not because they really cast discredit upon the story of the virgin birth, but rather because they give us a salutary sense of the limitations of our knowledge. Are we to suppose, on the basis of the first chapter of Luke, that the conception in Mary's womb took place before her journey to Elisabeth? The answer even to that question is perhaps not entirely certain. There are indeed several considerations which make an affirmative answer very probable. It seems more natural in itself, in view of the whole character of the annunciation, to suppose that the conception took place immediately after the annunciation was given; the greeting of Elisabeth to Mary in Lk. i.42-45 looks rather as though the child were already in Mary's womb as her own child was in her womb; above all, the difficulties of Joseph are perhaps best explained if Mary's pregnancy had lasted for some time before the marriage took place. The first two of these considerations would be satisfied if we should suppose the marriage to have occurred before and not after Mary's visit to Elisabeth. In that case, the conception might have taken place immediately after the annunciation and prior to Elisabeth's greeting, and yet not have caused an apparently premature birth. But the last of the three considerations does seem to make an apparently premature birth highly probable. The perplexity which Joseph experienced because of Mary's condition does seem to indicate that her pregnancy had continued some time before the marriage took place.

Even so, however, it is not clear that a birth only six months after the marriage must necessarily have given rise to slander. It must be remembered that according to the narrative in Luke the birth occurred at a place remote from Nazareth, where the mother would not be under the gaze of prying eyes. How long a time was occupied by the journey from Nazareth to Bethlehem we do not know. It may, furthermore, have been some years after the birth before the family returned to Nazareth. Would the (apparently) premature time of the birth then be known? But what we need to remember above all is that Joseph acknowledged Jesus as his son. There is to be found the real barrier against slander. If Joseph was really a "just" man, as he is said to have been in Mt. i.19, his character would be known and his acknowledgment of the child would prevent all likelihood of slander. In the early period, there would be no particular reason for occasion of slander to be sought; for Joseph and Mary had then, for all we know, the good will of the inhabitants of Nazareth. And in the later period, after thirty years' acceptance of the birth of Jesus as a child of Joseph and Mary, it would be too late for the basis of slander to be found.

We have indeed insisted, in another connection, that Joseph would not gratuitously have exposed Mary to even the possibility of slander by a premature union with his wife. But it is one thing to say that such a possibility of slander would naturally be avoided, so far as it could be avoided by seemly conduct on the part of Joseph and Mary, and quite another thing to say that when possibility of slander arose by a mysterious act of God, the possibility must necessarily have been converted into actuality. Thus the most that can be admitted is that the virgin birth of Christ, if it was really a fact, involved the *risk* of slander. To say that it involved the *certainty* of slander is going far beyond the truth. But if it did not involve the certainty of slander, and still more clearly if it did not involve even the probability of slander, then the absence of slander does not at all prove that the virgin birth was not a fact.

We may hold, then, without fear of successful contradiction, that the attitude of Jesus' contemporaries during the period of the public ministry, as that attitude is recorded in the Gospels, is congruous with the truth of the birth narratives. But how is it with the attitude of the authors themselves? Do the authors of the Gospels confirm or do they contradict the wonderful incidents that are recorded in the first two chapters of Matthew and Luke? In particular, do they confirm or contradict those assertions which place the birth at Bethlehem and attribute the conception in Mary's womb to the Holy Ghost?

In the case of the First and Third Gospels this question was already answered when we proved that the first two chapters of each of those Gospels really belonged to the original form of the book. If the authors really included Mt. i-ii, Lk. i-ii in their books, then of course they held the contents of these chapters to be true. The most that might still be alleged is that in the body of their works they have carelessly retained elements found in their sources, which with regard to the birth in Bethlehem and the supernatural conception were hostile to the view that the final authors themselves held. But this allegation cannot be substantiated. It is true that Matthew and Luke do not refer to the virgin birth from the third chapter to the end of their books (except in the words, "as was supposed", in connection with the genealogy in Lk. iii.23). But this fact is altogether without significance. Why should they mention again and again a thing that had already been narrated plainly enough at the proper place? And when they leave without correction the utterance of the inhabitants of Nazareth, "Is not this the son of Joseph?", or, "Is not this the carpenter's son?", their doing so merely shows the faithfulness with which they have reported the conditions that prevailed during the public ministry of Jesus; it does not at all show any ignorance, on their own part or on the part of their sources, of the fact of the virgin birth.

So much may be said with regard to Matthew and Luke. But how is it with regard to Mark and John?

Unlike the other two Synoptic Gospels, the Gospel according to Mark contains no account of the virgin birth of our Lord. Great capital has been made out of that fact by many modern scholars. But seldom has the argument from silence been more incautiously used. Certainly the Gospel according to Mark contains no account of the virgin birth; but then the fact is that it contains no account of the birth of Jesus at all, and for it to have contained such an account would have been to run counter to the purpose and plan of the book. This Gospel was not intended to provide intimate details about Jesus, but it was intended rather to produce an overpowering impression by the rehearsal of incidents which for the most part were matters of public observation. Typical of the contents of the book is the scene in the synagogue at Capernaum which is depicted with such vividness in the first chapter. The readers of the Second Gospel are not asked to sit quietly at the feet of Jesus and listen to extended discourses from Him, as in the Gospel according to Matthew, nor are they asked, for the most part, to hear things which in the nature of the case could be attested only by one or two persons; but they are asked to share the astonishment of those who first listened to the strange new teaching in the synagogue and beheld the works of power. We do not mean that this choice of material is carried out in any pedantically exclusive way. But still, when the Gospel is taken as a whole, Jesus does appear here primarily as the mighty One whose authoritative words and mighty deeds could make their impression upon all who were willing to hear and see. In such a Gospel the intimate story of the birth and childhood of our Lord certainly had no necessary place.

That does not mean that the author of the Second Gospel regarded the virgin birth as less important than the events of the public ministry. The most important thing that needs to be told is not always the first thing; and Mark seems to be concerned especially with the first things: he desires in this book to implant in the minds of his readers a first impression of the majesty of Jesus' person, in order that then they may proceed to more intimate and no doubt equally important teaching.

Another reason also, in addition to the one that has just been set forth, has apparently determined the choice of material in the Second Gospel, and particularly the omission of the virgin birth. We refer to the desire of this author to set forth only or chiefly those things to which his informant could testify as an eyewitness. According to the information which Papias, in the former part of the second century, received from "the Presbyter" [6], the Gospel according to Mark contains the teaching of Peter. It is not unnatural, therefore, that this Gospel should contain almost exclusively those things to which Peter could testify on the basis of personal observation. To those things, of course, the events connected with the birth and infancy of Jesus did not belong.

At one point the Gospel according to Mark has often been thought actually to show knowledge of the virgin birth. At Mk. vi.3, namely, in a connection where Matthew has, "Is not this the carpenter's son?", and Luke has, "Is not this the son of Joseph?", Mark reads merely, "Is not this the carpenter?". Does the Second Gospel here purposely avoid calling Jesus the son of Joseph? It has often been supposed that he does. Matthew and Luke, it is said, could report the words of the people of Nazareth in a form that made Jesus the son of Joseph, because in their case all fear of misunderstanding was removed by the express narration of the virgin birth which they had placed at the beginning of their Gospels: but Mark had no such safeguard, since it had not been part of his plan to narrate the birth of Jesus; and therefore, in order to avoid the possibility that his readers might suppose Jesus to be really the son of Joseph, and in order also to avoid the awkwardness of correcting in his own name the utterance of the people of Nazareth (a procedure which would be quite contrary to the style of all the Synoptic Gospels), he simply substitutes the words, "Is not this the carpenter?", for the offending words, "Is not this the son of the carpenter?".

This view would not necessarily imply any untruthfulness on the part of the author of the Second Gospel. No doubt the words of the people of Nazareth may have been put by the people themselves in a number of different forms; it is altogether natural that they would say, "Is not this the carpenter?",

[6] Eusebius, *hist. eccl.*, III. xxxix.15.

as well as, "Is not this the son of the carpenter?"; and quite possibly Peter, Mark's informant, may have heard them put the question in both forms. It would be quite allowable, therefore, for the author of the Gospel to choose for reporting in his account that one of the two forms which would not cause misunderstanding in the minds of his readers. But although we have no decisive objection to the view of Mk. vi.3 which has just been discussed—the view that regards as intentional the author's omission of any reference to Joseph—yet we are not inclined to lay any particular stress upon it. What is really clear, at any rate, is that the whole plan and purpose of the Second Gospel prevented any narration of the birth and infancy of Jesus; the silence of this Gospel about the virgin birth, therefore, does not afford the slightest argument against the truthfulness of the birth narratives in Matthew and Luke.

The Gospel according to John, like the Gospel according to Mark, has usually been held to contain no reference to the virgin birth of Christ. But here again the omission—supposing for the moment that it really exists—is altogether without significance. The real key to the choice of material in the Fourth Gospel is found in the words, "we beheld his glory," in John i.14. It is an altogether unwarranted sublimation of these words to take them in any merely "spiritual" or figurative sense; it is altogether out of accord with the thought of the writer to take them as referring merely to a spiritual apprehension of the Logos on the part of believers generally. On the contrary, the root idea of this Gospel is that "the Word became flesh" and that because He became flesh He could actually be seen and heard and touched by the men who lived with Him upon earth, the original disciples of Jesus to whom the writer himself belonged. There is, indeed, a sense in which Clement of Alexandria was correct when he called this book "the spiritual Gospel"; [7] but the word "spiritual" must not be understood in any exclusive sense. The idea of the book is not the independence of the spiritual life as over against things that have happened in the world of sense, but, quite the contrary, it is the profound dependence of the spiritual life upon things that happened in the world of sense. There is no book in the New Testament which lays greater stress than this book does upon the plain testimony of the senses. The author claims to be an eyewitness of the incarnate Word, and upon that claim the whole book is based. "The Word became flesh and *we beheld his glory*"—that utterance is at the very heart of this wonderful Gospel, and the whole meaning of the Gospel is missed when the utterance is explained away.

But if that be so—if the purpose of the book was to record the direct personal testimony of the author regarding what was said and done by the in-

[7] Eusebius, *hist. eccl.*, VI. xiv.7.

carnate Word—then it would have been quite out of place for the author to have included an account of the birth and infancy of the Lord. Of these events the author was not an eyewitness, and therefore a narration of these events did not belong in the book.

We are not forgetting the fact that the Fourth Gospel does include an account of some happenings at which the author himself was not present. One can think in this connection, for example, of the conversations of Jesus with Nicodemus and with the woman at the well. But it was one thing for the author to include such events—events that fell within at least the general purview of his own observations and that had repercussions which he himself immediately observed—and quite a different thing for him to include a whole complex of facts which was quite outside that period of Jesus' life with which his testimony could deal. Despite all cautions and exceptions, therefore, we are brought back ever anew to our initial observation. The Fourth Gospel contains not everything that could be said about Jesus, but rather the testimony of an eyewitness to the things that he had seen and heard. He had had the inestimable privilege of seeing with his eyes and hearing with his ears the glory of the Word made flesh. That privilege he desires, by his testimony, to make available for others, in order that they too, like him, may believe. In such a book there was no place whatever for a narration of events that took place long before the author came into contact with Him whose visible glory he desires to set forth. Quite naturally the narrative of the book begins not with an account of the birth and infancy of Jesus, but with an account of the way in which the author ceased to follow John the Baptist and became, instead, an eyewitness of the incarnate Word.

The book does begin, it is true, with a prologue—a prologue which deals, not, indeed, in detail, but in summary fashion, with things that formed the necessary presupposition of that incarnate life of the eternal Son which the body of the book was to set forth. Is there any reference in this prologue to the peculiar manner in which the only begotten Son of God came into the world; is there any reference in the prologue, in other words, to the virgin birth of our Lord?

Such a reference is found by some modern scholars of widely differing types of opinion [8] in John i.13. In that verse the great mass of our witnesses to the text (including all the Greek manuscripts) read, "who [that is, those who have received the Logos] were begotten not of bloods, nor of the will

[8] Notably Th. von Zahn (*Das Evangelium des Johannes*, 1908, pp. 72–77, 700–703) and A. von Harnack (*Neue Untersuchungen zur Apostelgeschichte*, 1911, p. 103; English translation, *The Date of the Acts and of the Synoptic Gospels*, 1911, p. 148).

of the flesh, nor of the will of man, but of God."[9] But in accordance with the express testimony of Tertullian there was at least as early as the second century another reading which had the singular instead of the plural—that is, not "who were begotten" or "they were begotten," but "who was begotten" or "he was begotten." This reading, which is favored by Tertullian himself and may be traced also in other early patristic references, would involve nothing less than an express assertion of the virgin birth of Christ. When applied to believers (as is done in the ordinary reading) the expressions of course refer to the spiritual new birth; but when applied to Christ they could not refer to any such thing, since of course this author did not suppose Christ to have experienced a new birth, which was necessary for other men only because of sin. Conceivably, indeed, the expressions might refer to an eternal, pre-incarnation begetting of the Son of God; but such an interpretation would be very unnatural. Why should an eternal begetting of the Son be set forth with such express and insistent exclusion of any human factor—"not of bloods, nor of the will of the flesh, nor of the will of man, but of God"? It remains far more likely, indeed practically certain, that if this reading is correct the author is intending to deny any physical human paternity in the case of Jesus and to assert the virgin birth in the clearest possible way.

A plausible argument may perhaps be constructed in favor of this reading on the basis of intrinsic probability. The plural reading, "who were begotten . . . ," it is said, is unnatural because it involves a disturbing digression; it diverts attention from the presentation of the person of Christ, which forms the real subject of the prologue, to an elaborate distinction between the ordinary, physical birth of men and the new birth by which they become in a high sense children of God. What possible motive could the author have had for thus insisting just in this strange place upon such a distinction, which, moreover, is in itself so obvious as not to need any such elaborate exposition? If, however—so the argument runs—the singular is read instead of the plural, if the expressions are applied not to believers but to Christ, then all is plain. The subject in this verse would be the same as the subject of the whole prologue—namely, the Logos who appears in verse 1.

It cannot be said that this argument is altogether convincing. In the first place, the thought of verse 13, if the ordinary reading is correct, finds a rather close parallel in the answer of Jesus to Nicodemus' question in John iii.4. When Nicodemus asks: "How can a man be born when he is old? Can he enter the second time into his mother's womb and be born?", and when Jesus in the course of His answer says: "That which is born of the

[9] *οἳ οὐκ ἐξ αἱμάτων οὐδὲ ἐκ θελήματος σαρκὸς οὐδὲ ἐκ θελήματος ἀνδρὸς ἀλλ' ἐκ θεοῦ ἐγεννήθησαν.*

flesh is flesh; and that which is born of the Spirit is spirit," we have something of the same explicit contrast between the natural, physical birth of all men and the spiritual new birth of believers which appears in our passage if the ordinary reading is adopted. That ordinary reading, therefore, is not altogether out of analogy with what appears elsewhere in the same book. It is also perhaps not altogether unnatural in its present context. In John i.13 the two spheres—the heavenly and the earthly—are contrasted; and this leads the author to speak in verse 14a of the descent of the Logos from the heavenly to the earthly. Verse 14 describes, then, the connection formed between the two spheres, by means of which the new birth described in verse 13 is made possible.[10] The other reading, moreover, would be by no means devoid of difficulty. It would involve a certain anticipation of the utterance in the next verse, "The Word became flesh," which does not seem to be altogether natural. It is true, the event of verse 14 has already, according to the most probable interpretation, been referred to in verse 11 and possibly even in the preceding verses. But verse 13, if the singular reading is right, would describe the event in detail, in a way which seems rather out of place before the summary statement in verse 14 has been made. Intrinsic probability, therefore, does not tell in any clear way against the ordinary text or in favor of the other reading.

As for transcriptional probability, one may of course hold that Tertullian was right when he accused the Gnostics of inventing the plural reading in the interests of their doctrine of a special class of "spiritual" persons.[11] But, as has been pointed out with some force, the plural reading does not suit the Gnostic teaching very perfectly; for that reading would seem to imply that all believers are "spiritual" persons, whereas the Gnostics reserved that term for a special class as distinguished from ordinary Christians. It remains perfectly possible, moreover, that the reading of the singular was introduced by some scribe either in order to remove all possible support from the Gnostic doctrine of a class of spiritual persons or else simply in order to provide a testimony to the virgin birth of Christ. There would be a certain tendency on the part of scribes to apply such language as is used in John i.13 to Christ rather than merely to believers: the language would seem to a scribe to suit Him who was begotten without human agency by the power of the Holy Spirit; and so, perhaps in perfect good faith and without any consciousness of falsification, the singular instead of the plural may have been allowed to slip in.

[10] See "The New Testament Account of the Birth of Jesus," first article, in *Princeton Theological Review*, iii, 1905, pp. 660 f.

[11] Tertullian, *de carne Christi*, xix. See the discussion of this passage in Zahn, *op. cit.*, pp. 700 f.

If the plural is to be read, we should probably not see in the verse any reference to the virgin birth of Christ. Such a reference was indeed found in it by Zahn (before he came to his present view that the singular is to be read) and also by Grützmacher.[12] John meant to say in John i.13 f., Zahn argued, that what is true of the new birth of the children of God is true of the physical birth of Christ. But such an interpretation perhaps attributes to the Evangelist a confusion between the spiritual and the physical spheres, or rather an elaborate parallel between them, which, if intended, would probably have had to be more clearly marked.

We are not inclined, therefore, to lay any great stress upon John i.13 as a testimony to the virgin birth of Christ.[13] But what we do affirm with some insistence is that the view of the Fourth Gospel with regard to the person of Christ and with regard to His entrance into the world is profoundly congruous with the story of the virgin birth and profoundly incongruous with the view that Jesus was in a physical sense the son of Joseph. Certainly there is not the slightest reason to suppose that this author rejected the representation which had already appeared in the Gospels of Matthew and Luke. His silence is altogether without significance as a testimony against the virgin birth; for the narration in detail of the manner in which the Son of God entered into the world was quite outside the scope of his book.

One passage in the Fourth Gospel has, it is true, often been used as a testimony, not indeed against the virgin birth, but against the birth in Bethlehem. The passage to which we refer is found in John vii.41 f., where a certain group in the Jerusalem crowd is represented as saying: "Does the Messiah come out of Galilee? Has not the Scripture said that the Messiah comes of the seed of David and from the village where David was?" What we are concerned with here is not the attitude which this passage attributes to Jesus' contemporaries. It is not surprising that even if Jesus had been born at Bethlehem, the Jerusalem crowd, or a certain group in it, should have designated Him as having come from Galilee. After all, He had lived for many years at Nazareth; His birth in Bethlehem, if it was a fact, was not generally known, and could not easily be proved. If it had been proved, one might still have

[12] Zahn, *Das apostolische Symbolum*, 1893, pp. 62–64; Grützmacher, *Die Jungfrauengeburt*, 1906, pp. 13 f. For early anticipations of this view, that John i.13 (with the ordinary reading) alludes to the virgin birth of Christ, see J. J. van Oosterzee, *Disputatio theologica de Jesu, e virgine Maria nato*, 1840, pp. 177–179, 191 f., 225 f.

[13] On the whole question of John i.13 in its relation to the virgin birth, see especially Geerhardus Vos (*The Self-Disclosure of Jesus*, 1926, pp. 210–213), who thinks that the virgin birth is here referred to whether the plural or the singular reading is correct. We are not intending to reject that view in any confident way, but are merely pointing out certain objections that may be urged against it.

supposed it strange that the Messiah should have deserted His ancestral home and lived for long years in an obscure Galilean village. But what we are concerned with here is the attitude of the Evangelist. If he had accepted the story of the birth of Christ in Bethlehem, would he have been obliged to correct the false opinion of the Jerusalem group and attest the true fact at this point in his narrative?

This question has often been answered in the affirmative. But to answer it so really involves a serious misunderstanding of the whole method and purpose of this Evangelist. It is not in accordance with the method of this writer to correct in his own name false views expressed in the narrative by the opponents of Christ. There was no need, moreover, for him to mention the birth in Bethlehem; for he was writing in supplement to the Synoptic Gospels and was presupposing their narrative as known. At the time when the Fourth Gospel was written, the birth of Christ in Bethlehem was a matter of course; and there was no reason for the author of this Gospel to inform his readers of what they already knew.

In the Book of Acts, the few apologetic or missionary speeches of Peter and Paul that are inserted in the narrative contain no reference to the virgin birth. But that omission is of course quite without significance. Even if the virgin birth was a fact, it would be the most unnatural thing in the world for it to be referred to before hostile or uninstructed audiences; and the author of the book did not at all need to supplement these speeches by remarks of his own, especially since he had already narrated the virgin birth plainly at the beginning of his double work.

But how is it with Paul? Two passages in the Epistles have sometimes been supposed to have some special bearing upon his attitude to the virgin birth of Christ. These passages are Gal. iv.4 f. and Rom. i.3 f.

In Gal. iv.4 f. Paul says: "But when the fullness of time came, God sent forth his Son, born of a woman, born under the law, in order that he might redeem those who were under the law, in order that we might receive the adoption of sons." This passage has sometimes been held to show that Paul did not believe in the virgin birth, and sometimes also has been held to show that he did do so. As a matter of fact, both opinions are probably wrong; the passage does not enable us to draw any conclusion with regard to Paul's belief in the matter one way or the other.

If Paul had accepted the virgin birth, would he have been obliged in this passage to say, "born of a virgin," or the like, instead of "born of a woman"? We do not think so at all. On the contrary, for him to use such an expression would have been to obscure the point of the passage. What the Apostle is speaking of here is the humiliation of Christ—the likeness to us men which He assumed for our redemption. Part of that likeness to us was His human birth. But the words, "born of a virgin," would have emphasized not the similarity of Christ's birth to ours, but, on the contrary, the difference between His birth and ours. Such a phrase, therefore, would have run directly counter to the whole thought that the Apostle here has in mind. Certainly the expression which is actually used does not at all contradict the story of the birth of Jesus in the Gospels of Matthew and Luke. It should never be forgotten that according to the New Testament representation, although the conception was supernatural, the birth itself was natural. Paul had a full right, therefore, even though he accepted the virgin birth as it is narrated for us in the early chapters of Matthew and Luke, to say that Christ was "born of a woman."

On the other hand, although we can find no evidence in this verse against a belief on Paul's part in the virgin birth of Christ, we can also find no direct evidence in favor of it. If Paul had not believed in the virgin birth, would he have been obliged in this passage to mention the human father as well as, or instead of, the human mother? We are not inclined to think so. All that can be said is that as a matter of fact neither in this passage nor anywhere else in the Pauline Epistles does Paul mention the human father of Jesus. This silence about the human father may or may not be significant. But we are prepared to assert that it is just as likely to be significant as is the silence about the virgin birth. We are certainly not endeavoring on our part to use the argument from silence; but what we are prepared to say is that if it is to be used at all, it should not be used merely on one side.

The other Pauline passage which is often mentioned in the same connection is Rom. i.3 f., which reads as follows: ". . . concerning his Son, who was born of the seed of David according to the flesh, who was declared to be the Son of God in power according to the Spirit of holiness by the resurrection of the dead. . . ." In this passage, it is argued, Paul connects the higher nature of Jesus with the resurrection, not with the birth, as he would have been obliged to do if he had believed in the supernatural conception. But such reasoning is very vulnerable indeed. Let us suppose for a moment, just for the sake of the argument, that Paul accepted exactly the same view of the birth of Jesus as that which appears in the infancy narratives of Matthew and Luke. What is there in Rom. i.3 f. that is inconsistent with such a view? We really cannot see that there is anything at all. It still remains true on the basis of Mt. i-ii, Lk. i-ii that Jesus was "born of the seed of David according to the flesh"; the Davidic descent appears in those infancy narratives as well as in Paul, and we have already pointed out that it is not contradictory to the virgin birth which also appears in the same narratives. Moreover, it is particularly clear just in Paul, in accordance with his use of the word "flesh," that when he says "according to the flesh" he may well be referring to something other than unbroken physical continuity. The question, therefore, whether Mary as well as Joseph was a descendant of David does not need to be answered one way or the other by one who desires to defend both the Davidic descent (in the Pauline, and generally New Testament, sense) and the virgin birth. Moreover, if it remains true on the basis of Lk. i-ii, Mt. i-ii that Jesus was born of the seed of David according to the flesh, it also remains true that He was "declared to be the Son of God in power by the resurrection of the dead." Jesus was indeed Son of God, according to Lk. i.35, prior to the resurrection and indeed from the very beginning of His earthly life, to say nothing of a life prior to His entrance into the world. But did Paul hold any other view? Does he mean to set forth any other view in this passage? Most emphatically he does not. Unquestionably Paul believed that Jesus was Son of God during His earthly life. What He became at the resurrection was Son of God *in power*. It does not make much difference whether we put the emphasis thus upon the words "in power" or upon the word which may be translated "declared to be" or "established as being."[14] Whether the meaning of the passage is "established as being Son of God *in power*" (as distinguished from the sonship that He had had in His state of humiliation before the resurrection), or "*declared* to be Son of God," "*vindicated* as being Son of God" (as distinguished from a sonship that was concealed from men by the conditions of His earthly life), in either case there is not the slightest disharmony between this passage and the story of the virgin birth. The contrary view is based upon the same incorrect, exclusive way of regarding the activity of the Holy Spirit that we noticed in the case of a certain modern way of treating the baptism of Jesus.[15] Why should it have seemed incredible to Paul, and why should it seem incredible to us, that the Holy Spirit should have been operative in connection with our Lord not in one way, but in many ways? Why should Paul not have believed that the Spirit was active both in the conception in Mary's womb and also in the mighty act of the resurrection? These questions are really unanswerable. There is not the slightest contradiction between the significance of the resurrection as it is set forth in this passage and the account of the virgin birth that is given in the birth narratives of Matthew and Luke.

These individual passages in the Pauline Epistles cannot rightly be ap-

[14] ὁρισθέντος.

[15] See above, pp. 50-56.

pealed to either for or against the view that Paul believed in the virgin birth. But how is it with the general fact of Paul's silence? If Paul had accepted the virgin birth, would he have been obliged to mention it in his Epistles?

We do not think that this is the case. It must always be remembered that in the Epistles Paul mentions very few events in the life of Jesus on earth. And yet the incidental way in which he does mention some things shows clearly that he knew many other things of which he finds no occasion to speak. The institution of the Lord's Supper, for example, would never have been narrated except for the appearance of certain abuses at Corinth; and if it had not been narrated, one may well shudder at the inferences which would have been drawn from Paul's silence. A similar remark may be made about the account which Paul gives in I Cor. xv.3 ff. of the appearances of the risen Christ. If it had not been for that one passage, which was written only because of the emergence of certain errors in the church that is addressed, modern scholars would certainly have drawn from Paul's consciousness of independence as it is set forth in the first chapter of the Epistle to the Galatians the inference that the resurrection of Christ was established in Paul's teaching on the basis of the Apostle's own testimony alone; and yet, as it is, the appeal to the testimony of Peter and others is seen to have been part of the "first things" that Paul gave to his churches. These examples should certainly make us extremely cautious about applying the argument from silence to our treatment of Paul's attitude toward the virgin birth. If things so very important to the Apostle as the institution of the Lord's Supper and the appearances of the risen Christ appear in the whole extent of the Epistles only once each—because of what from the human point of view was the mere chance of the emergence of certain errors—how can we draw from the non-appearance of other things the inference that Paul knew nothing about them? It does not follow at all, therefore, that because Paul says nothing about the virgin birth in his Epistles he knew nothing about it.

What is clear, at any rate, is that, although the virgin birth is not directly mentioned in the Epistles, it is profoundly congruous with Paul's teaching about Christ. Paul clearly regarded Jesus Christ as no mere product of what had gone before Him, but as an entirely new beginning in humanity, the second Adam, the Founder of a new race. Could such a Person have been derived by ordinary generation from the men who had existed before Him upon the earth; could He, in the ordinary sense, have had a human father? One should of course be cautious about saying what might or might not have been. And yet to think of the Christ of the Pauline Epistles as the son of Joseph and Mary involves an incongruity from which the mind naturally shrinks. The virgin birth is not explicitly mentioned in the Epistles, but it does seem to be implied in the profoundest way in the entire view which Paul holds of the Lord Jesus Christ.

Conceivably, indeed, we might derive from this consideration an argument not for but against Paul's knowledge of the virgin birth. If, it might be said Paul's doctrine is so perfectly in accord with the virgin birth, why does he not mention a thing which fits in so well with his teaching; why does he not make use of so welcome a support for his views?

This reasoning ignores one of the outstanding facts about the Paulin-Epistles—the fact, namely, that Paul does not argue in the Epistles about his conception of the person of Christ. About other things there was debate, but, at least during the period of the earlier Epistles, there was no debate whatever about this; apparently Paul assumes that his own stupendous view of Jesus as a supernatural Person, come voluntarily into the world for our redemption, now risen from the grave and living in glory, was the view of everyone in the Church. Apparently even the Judaizers, the bitter opponents of Paul, raised no objection to the Apostle's teaching on this point. This extraordinary unanimity with regard to the person of Christ, this extraordinary absence of any struggle between the lofty Pauline view of Christ and any lower, merely human conception, may be puzzling to modern naturalistic historians—indeed it constitutes the great central problem that faces any naturalistic reconstruction of primitive Christianity—but however puzzling it may be, it must certainly be recognized as a fact. It is certainly true that Paul does not feel called upon to defend in his Epistles that view of Christ which is the basis of all his thinking and all his life. But if so, why should he have been obliged to mention the virgin birth? He might have mentioned it if he had been living in the time of Irenæus, when it was subject to attack. He may actually have mentioned it when he was dealing with opponents of Christianity. But the extant Epistles, it should never be forgotten, were addressed not to opponents of Christianity, but to professing Christians; and in them are contained those things about which professing Christians needed to be set right. Thus the absence of the virgin birth from the Epistles, though it might conceivably mean that Paul did not believe in the virgin birth, may also mean that the fact was so universally accepted as to require no defence.

From the foregoing review of the evidence, it appears that the virgin birth was not known during the earthly life of Jesus and even after the resurrection probably did not form a part of the missionary preaching of the earliest apostolic Church. But these observations are not inconsistent with acceptance of the virgin birth as a fact. Let us suppose for a moment, for the sake of the argument, that Jesus was really born without a human father as He is said to have been born in the infancy narratives of Matthew and Luke. On that supposition, what would the course of development naturally be? According to the infancy narratives there were only two persons who at first certainly knew of the virgin birth, namely, Joseph and Mary, nor is there any definite record that they confided in anyone else. That Mary confided in Elisabeth is indeed probable; but the very reason why she would naturally confide in Elisabeth was that she could not confide in others. The report of the shepherds and of Anna need not have reached a very wide circle, and, like the visit of the magi (in which case there were also special reasons for silence), took place in Judæa, far from Nazareth, the subsequent home of the family, and perhaps several years before their return. It has been further suggested by Ramsay that fear of Herod Antipas may have been a special reason for silence after their return.[16] In any case, there is no evidence whatever that the shepherds or the magi or Simeon or Anna knew of the virgin birth. Probably Joseph died before Jesus reached maturity, since he does not appear in the record of the public ministry; and Elisabeth is expressly said to have been old at the time of Mary's momentous visit in the Judæan home.[17] Not improbably, therefore, Mary was left as the sole keeper of the secret of Jesus' birth.

This "secret," it is true, is often regarded as an apologetic expedient; why should Mary not have told of the virgin birth if it had been a fact? But a little exercise of the historical imagination will show how inconclusive this reasoning is. One great fault of the modern treatment of the subject is that not enough sympathetic attention has been given to the personal equation. Would it have been in accord with the character of Mary, as it is depicted in such lifelike colors in the infancy narrative of Luke (the truth of which we are assuming just now for the sake of the argument), that after she had undergone experiences of the most mysterious kind and had submitted to a command which ran counter to every instinct of her soul, she should proceed to engage in idle gossip about the matter, thereby subjecting herself and her holy child to the basest slander? Some women might have acted so, but hardly the one who "kept all these sayings, pondering them in her heart." There is every reason to suppose, on the contrary, that she would keep the secret even from her younger sons—or rather, perhaps, most carefully of all from them. So the years went by; and He who was to rule over the house of Jacob forever continued to labor at a carpenter's bench until the time of His majority had come

[16] Ramsay, *Was Christ born at Bethlehem?*, 1898, p. 76.
[17] Lk. i.7.

and gone. Must not the miraculous events of thirty years ago have come to be to Mary like a wonderful dream? We will not say, indeed, that her faith ever failed; but certainly it suffered trial. And then when her son did come before the nation, how different was His coming from that which she had pictured! How strange and perplexing were the ways of God! From every point of view, there was reason that her silence should not be broken. Perplexity leads some persons to ask questions of every passer-by, but others keep their bewilderment locked in their own souls. To this latter type belonged Mary the mother of the Lord. As in the early days, she kept all these things and pondered them in her heart. But finally she learned, like the disciples, the true nature of Jesus' work. When Pentecost had come and gone, and the company of the disciples were praying together, comforted by the Spirit whom Jesus had sent, she must have continued to ponder over all these things, but now in a very different way. Now at last had come the time for her to speak; now the claims of Jesus had been vindicated; now she would be believed. So, within the little circle of believing and sympathetic women or near friends, she may have been led to breathe things too sacred and mysterious to be spoken of to mortal ears before. These things, of course, were not repeated at once to the official governors of the Church, like the progress of daily collections. Still less were they included in missionary sermons, where the great effort was to adduce facts which could be attested directly by all, and where the humble woman's mystery would have brought nothing but slander and scorn. But when the story was finally told, there is no evidence that it aroused any opposition at all from those who were already disciples of Christ. And so, possibly supplemented by a record that Joseph had left, the marvellous tale of the mother of the Lord found its way into the Gospel tradition and creeds of the Church, and into the inmost hearts of Christians of all the centuries.[18]

[18] This hypothesis appears here in essentially the same form as that in which it appeared in the article by the present writer, "The New Testament Account of the Birth of Jesus," first article, in *Princeton Theological Review*, iii, 1905, pp. 663 f. See Ramsay, *Was Christ Born at Bethlehem?*, 1898, pp. 73–91; Sanday, article "Jesus Christ," in Hastings, *Dictionary of the Bible*, ii, 1906, pp. 643 f.; Gore, *Dissertations on Subjects Connected with the Incarnation*, 1895, p. 13. Somewhat similar considerations are set forth, in a very interesting passage, by Chrysostom (*hom. in Matt.*, iii, ed. Montfaucon, vii, 1836, pp. 37–39). The virgin birth, Chrysostom points out, was quite unparalleled, and hence the story of it would be naught but an offence to all who had not already come to believe in Jesus. "For a man who had once been persuaded that He [Jesus] is the Son of God had no reason to doubt about this thing either; but anyone who thought that He was a deceiver and in opposition to God—how would he not be offended by this thing all the more . . .? For this reason even the apostles do not tell of this right at the beginning, but discourse much and often concerning the resurrection, since of this there were examples (ὑποδείγματα) in previous times, although not such examples as this; but that He was born of a virgin they do not continually (οὐ συνεχῶς) say." So even the mother, Chrysostom continues, did not venture to speak of the virgin birth; and it was not told to the shepherds by the angels.

What we maintain, therefore, is not that the extant attestation of the virgin Birth of Christ is as early and as abundant as the attestation of certain other events, such as the resurrection, but only that it is as early and as abundant as the attestation of this particular event might with any certainty have been expected to be. In the very nature of the case this event could not be attested by many persons; and in the nature of the case the one person who could certainly attest it would have the strongest reason, in the early period, for silence. The limited extent of the attestation, therefore, is not inconsistent with the hypothesis that the virgin birth was a fact.

But at that point an objection may arise. In our effort to explain the silence of Jesus' contemporaries and of great sections of the New Testament, have we not involved ourselves in an apologetic peril that is far greater than the one which we have endeavored to avoid? We have pointed out that, even if the virgin birth was a fact, the attestation of it would not necessarily be any greater than that which our New Testament contains. But in order to do so have we not been obliged to admit that the attestation of such an event must in the nature of the case be very small? And does not that mean that, in view of the miraculous character of the event, the attestation of it could never possibly be sufficient to convince a cautious mind?

This objection might possibly be conclusive if the attestation of the virgin birth stood alone. Unquestionably there is an enormous initial presumption against the view that any human being was born without human father; and the direct testimony, being limited, in the very nature of the case, to one person, would hardly be sufficient in order that this initial presumption should be overcome. If the question were simply whether a man about whom otherwise we knew nothing was born without human father, no doubt that question would have to be answered in the negative. But as a matter of fact that is not the question at all. The question is not whether an ordinary man was born without human father, but whether Jesus was so born. And this question is quite different from the other. It is indeed highly improbable that any ordinary man came into this world in the supernatural manner which is set forth in the infancy narratives of Matthew and Luke; but then Jesus was like no other man that ever has lived. So unique a person, it might well be argued, may well have had an unique entrance into this world. Moreover, it is not merely the moral uniqueness of Jesus to which our argument appeals. There are in the life of Jesus as narrated in the Gospels plainly miraculous elements whose attestation is not at all subject to the limitations which we have found in the case of the virgin birth. Particularly is that true with regard to the supreme miracle of the resurrection. A mass of convergent testimony leads, we think, to the conviction that on the third day after the death of Jesus on the cross His tomb became empty by a supernatural act of God. But if the supernatural has been accepted at any one point in connection with Jesus, the presumption has been overcome against accepting it at other points. And in particular the presumption has been overcome against accepting it in connection with the birth. Having once come to the conclusion that Jesus was a supernatural person, that the miraculous element which is so abundant in the Gospel account of Him cannot be explained as due to the myth-making fancy of the early Church, but truly represents a creative activity of God quite distinct from God's works through nature, we shall have no difficulty about supposing that He was supernaturally conceived in the virgin's womb. On the contrary, the story of the virgin birth is profoundly congruous with the whole New Testament account of Jesus. If Jesus was at all the sort of person that He is represented as being in the whole New Testament, then it is an altogether believable thing that He came into the world in the manner described in the early chapters of the Gospels of Matthew and Luke; and it is an exceedingly improbable thing that He was the son, by ordinary generation, of Joseph and Mary.

We do not mean that the story of the virgin birth ever could have been constructed merely by inference from the facts in the later life of Jesus; indeed, in the following section of our discussion, we shall adduce reasons to show that such could not have been the case. The birth narratives retain a wonderful originality as over against all the fancies of that day; and they are of a character that in itself commands respect. What we do mean is not that the direct attestation of the virgin birth is unnecessary in order that we may accept the fact, but only that it is in itself perhaps insufficient. It becomes convincing only when it is taken in connection with the entire account which the New Testament gives of the person of Jesus Christ.

But when it is actually taken in that connection, it becomes convincing indeed. These birth narratives bear many unmistakable indications of truth. Their wonderful restraint, their lofty moral tone, their delicacy of language, their primitive and Palestinian character, their lifelike depiction of the personalities involved, their mutual independence, and their agreement—these and many other characteristics create in the sympathetic reader an overpoweringly favorable impression. Such an impression might have to be resisted if these narratives stood alone. But when they are taken in connection with the whole majestic and self-evidencing portrait of Jesus Christ as it is contained in the

New Testament, the necessity for resistance is gone. The reader can now abandon himself without sacrifice of his scientific conscience to the spell of these matchless chapters, and can believe that the marvellous things that they narrate are sober truth. If Christ really rose from the dead, if He really was at all the kind of person that He is represented in the New Testament as being, then there is every reason to think that He was conceived by the Holy Ghost and born of the virgin Mary.

Chapter XII

ALTERNATIVE THEORIES: PRELIMINARY CONSIDERATIONS

IN THE preceding chapters we have dealt with one of the two ways in which the Christian belief in the virgin birth has been explained; we have examined the hypothesis that the belief was founded on fact. The attestation, it has been argued, is as early and as strong as it could naturally be expected to have been if the virgin birth actually took place; and although there is an enormous initial presumption against the occurrence of such a miracle, that presumption can be overcome if the investigator bears in mind the uniqueness of Jesus' person and the total phenomenon of the origin of the Christian religion. Thus there is good ground, we think, to hold that the reason why the Christian Church came to believe in the birth of Jesus without human father was simply that He was as a matter of fact so born.

This conclusion is very widely rejected at the present day even within the confines of the Church. But when it is rejected, the question arises what is to be put into its place. The historian has by no means completed his task when he has decided to reject the New Testament attestation of the virgin birth of Christ; for the initial problem still demands solution. How was it that the Christian Church ever came to believe in the virgin birth? Whatever may be thought of the content of the belief, the belief itself is a fact of history which no one can possibly deny. It is a fact that for some nineteen hundred years a large part of the human race has believed that Jesus of Nazareth, a person living in the full light of history, was born without human father, being conceived in the womb of the virgin by the immediate exercise of the power of God. How did that strange belief ever arise? This question is of course answered at once if the belief was founded upon fact; if Jesus really was born of a virgin, it is not difficult to understand how the Church came to believe that He was so born. But if this obvious answer be rejected, the question to which it is an attempted answer still remains. If Jesus of Nazareth was not really born of a virgin, how did the Church come to believe that He was born in that way? The question does seem to be a fair question for all who reject the testimony to the fact of the virgin birth. An important part of all discussions of our subject is to be found, therefore, in the discussion of alternative theories as to the way in which the *idea* of the virgin birth is to be explained if the *fact* of the virgin birth is denied.

At this point, Vincent Taylor, the author of the latest important monograph on the subject, dissents from the usual view. The importance of the question about "alternative theories," he thinks, has been greatly exaggerated; apologists have made a great mistake in attempting to argue the historic character of the virgin birth tradition "by dwelling upon the incongruities and contradictions of alternative theories"; men may agree in rejecting a tradition or belief and yet be at variance about the origin of it, and that they "agree upon the one point is more significant than that they differ upon the other."[1]

But surely this objection runs counter to sound common sense. In appraising any kind of testimony, one instinctively asks the question how the witness came to testify thus. If (supposing the testimony to be false) the motive of the false witness is clear, or if the way can be detected in which even an honest witness could have fallen into error in the particular case in question, then the testimony is discredited to a degree that would not otherwise be the case. Instinctively, therefore, in a court of law or in the ordinary affairs of life, one does ask the question regarding a witness: "How did he come to say this or that if it is not true?"

Until that question is answered, the testimony is often felt not to be finally disposed of; but when it is answered, the mind of the hearer is set at rest with regard to that particular testimony, and the question will be decided altogether on the basis of other evidence.

So it is also in historical investigations. It is not enough to deny the truthfulness of a tradition; one must also try to exhibit the manner in which the tradition arose. Until that is done, one cannot altogether put out of the way the possibility that the tradition, supposing it to possess any claims to credibility at all, may be true.

This principle is indeed not of universal application; for we do constantly reject stories without at all explaining how they arose. The world is full of tales that no one believes, yet the origin of which no one can explain; if we endeavored to account for all of them, we should have no time for the serious business of life. So much may readily be granted to Vincent Taylor

But the Christian tradition about the virgin birth belongs in a very different category. In the case of many stories the reason why the origin of the stories has not been discovered is simply that the investigation is not worth while. The evidence in support of the stories is so very slight, or the stories deal with matters of such little importance, that no one takes the trouble to

[1] Vincent Taylor, *The Historical Evidence for the Virgin Birth*, 1920, pp. 124–127.

ask how the stories came into being. Very different is the situation with regard to the story of the virgin birth. That story has formed the subject of scholarly investigation for many years; the best efforts of modern scholarship have been devoted to the question how the story arose. Under such circumstances, surely it is not altogether without significance that so far these efforts have resulted in failure, and that no unanimity has been attained on the question how, if the virgin birth is not a fact, the Christian Church came to believe in it.[2]

It must be admitted, indeed, that this argument from the failure of alternative theories cannot possibly stand alone. Certainly we cannot arrive at the truth of the New Testament testimony merely by a process of elimination; we cannot simply say that since no other satisfactory explanation has yet been discovered for the origin of the idea of the virgin birth, therefore, whatever the strength or weakness of the positive testimony may be, the idea must be founded on fact and the New Testament at this point must be true. Such a method of reasoning would be precarious in the extreme. It is perfectly conceivable that the origin of a myth may be obscure; and so it is perfectly conceivable that a belief like that in the virgin birth of Christ may have originated in some manner beyond the reach of modern research.

But this consideration does not do away with the value of the argument with which we now have to deal. That argument is inconclusive when it stands alone; but when taken in connection with the positive attestation of the virgin birth it may be very powerful indeed. What the historian has to do is not to consider the theories of mythical origin of the virgin birth tradition by themselves, but to balance these theories over against the theory that the tradition is true. The less satisfactory the alternative theories are in detail, and the greater is their disagreement with one another, the more favorably disposed the historian will be toward the simple hypothesis that the idea of the virgin birth arose because the virgin birth was a fact.

The cogency of this method of reasoning is tacitly recognized by opponents of the New Testament testimony. No argument against the virgin birth, perhaps, is used with more confidence or more effectiveness by popular preachers than the argument drawn from the supposed ease with which the virgin birth tradition could have been produced in the first century of our era. "In those

[2] Compare H. R. Mackintosh, *The Doctrine of the Person of Jesus Christ*, New York, 1916, p. 529: "For history the really strong argument in favour of the virgin-birth is the difficulty of accounting for the story otherwise than on the assumption of its truth." This sentence, it must be admitted, does seem to involve an exaggeration of the value of the argument from the failure of alternative theories, as compared with other evidence. The argument from the failure of alternative theories, we hold, though exceedingly important, is yet only subsidiary to the direct evidence for the truth of the New Testament story. Compare the review of our book by the same writer, in *British Weekly*, for July 17, 1930.

days," it is said in effect, "many great men were thought to be virgin-born; so when the early Christians came to think Jesus supremely great it was only natural that they should regard Him too as having been born in that way." This argument is, as we shall see, extremely crude; scholarly investigators, even those who oppose the virgin birth, are usually not inclined to think the matter quite so simple as that. Nevertheless, the preachers who use the argument display a sound methodological instinct; they at least tacitly recognize the fact that the idea of the virgin birth is a fact of history which requires explanation, and that those who deny the factual basis of the idea must endeavor to account for the idea in some other way.

In opposition to Vincent Taylor's protest, therefore, we must insist upon the relevance of the discussion upon which we shall now try to enter. The historical question about the virgin birth will finally be determined by a comparison of the hypothesis that the idea of the virgin birth was founded upon fact with the most plausible form of the hypothesis that it was founded upon some kind of error. The former member of this comparison has been considered in the preceding chapters: the positive attestation of the virgin birth, we have endeavored to show, is by no means contemptible, and when it is taken in connection with the total phenomenon of the life of Christ and the beginnings of Christianity, there is no insuperable objection against regarding it as true. But how is it with the other alternative? If, despite the arguments that we have adduced in defence of the tradition, the virgin birth is not a fact, how shall we explain the origin of the idea? This question must now be considered with some care.

One method of explanation may be dismissed rather quickly—namely, the rationalizing method which was popular one hundred years ago. It is now for the most part admitted that unless the virgin birth actually occurred it is vain to seek any considerable factual basis for the story as it appears in Matthew and Luke. At first sight, indeed, the search for such a factual basis might have seemed to offer some likelihood of success. It is perfectly true that a false supernaturalistic interpretation has sometimes been put, even by the observers themselves, to say nothing of later narrators, upon events that were in point of fact purely natural. So the effort of Paulus and the other rationalizers of the early part of the nineteenth century to reconstruct a natural course of events in connection with the birth and childhood of Jesus as the basis for the supernaturalistic account given in Matthew and Luke was only to be expected when once the actuality of miracles was given up. But it is now generally admitted that the effort was a failure. The New Testament birth narratives do not lend themselves at all to such treatment; for in them the miracles are not mere excrescences, but represent the element for which all the rest exists, and the natural happenings which are supposed to have been the basis for the stories are quite trivial and incapable of giving rise to the narratives as they stand. Thus the rationalizing method of treating the narratives, which was considerably in vogue a century ago, has now for the most part been abandoned, at least among scholars. But since there are just now interesting signs that it may be revived, even in scholarly discussion, and since it has always flourished in an underground realm of popular attack upon Christianity, we may do well to consider briefly the application of it to the specific question of the virgin birth.

The essence of the rationalizing method is to discover a natural happening, preferably unusual, which, when interpreted supernaturalistically, could give rise to the narratives as they stand. But what natural happening could have been distorted into the view that Jesus was born without human father by the power of the Holy Ghost? What was there so unusual in the birth of Jesus that this strange story could have seemed necessary to explain it? Only one plausible answer can be given; it can only be said that Jesus was not the son of Mary's husband, Joseph, and that, therefore, to avoid the shameful implications of such a fact, the early Christians came to believe in the supernatural conception in the virgin's womb.

Some of the early rationalizers did not shrink from the full implication of such a view; Jesus, they said, was born out of wedlock, His mother having been deceived, perhaps, by a man who passed himself off as a messenger of God.[3] In essentially the same category with these rationalizing reconstructions is to be put the ancient Jewish "Panthera" story, which, as we have seen,[4] is attested by Origen and the Talmud and culminates in the mediæval Tōl'dōth Jēshū; the ancient Jewish slander, like the more modern romances, was intended as a naturalistic explanation of the Christian story of the virgin birth. But such solutions of the problem, despite sporadic revivals in modern times,[5] have been rejected by practically all serious scholars.[6] The entire attitude of

[3] So, for example, Venturini, *Natürliche Geschichte des grossen Propheten von Nazareth*, 2te Ausg., 1806, i, pp. 126–130; and Paul de Régla (P. A. Desjardin), *Jésus de Nazareth*, nouvelle édition, no date, 1896 or after, pp. 44, 51–54.

[4] Above, p. 10.

[5] As, for example, by the biologist Haeckel. See "The New Testament Account of the Birth of Jesus," second article, in *Princeton Theological Review*, iv, 1906, p. 37, with the literature there cited. See also above, p. 11.

[6] No doubt there is an underground literature in which the ancient slander, in one form or another, is still exploited. Schweitzer (*Geschichte der Leben-Jesu-Forschung*, 2te Aufl. des Werkes "Von Reimarus zu Wrede", 1913, p. 48) said that Venturini's romance was still appearing almost yearly in new editions, and that the type which it created was followed directly or indirectly by all romance-like lives of Christ. The book, he said, is copied as is no other life of Christ, though it is never cited.

Jesus' contemporaries, particularly the character of the polemic against Him, is inexplicable if there was such a stain upon His birth. It is perfectly clear that, however the idea of the virgin birth is to be explained, it cannot be explained by a prior knowledge, on the part of the early Christians, of something abnormal in the way in which Jesus was born.

Yet it is very interesting to observe that certain scholars who repudiate the thought of anything shameful in the manner of Jesus' birth have been unwilling to relinquish altogether the rationalizing method. Thus Paulus held that Joseph did not beget Jesus,[7] and that what gave Mary confidence that she was to be the mother of the Messiah was "something external."[8] What that something was is left quite vague, and Paulus assures us that in any case Mary was innocent;[9] but such assurances give very little comfort when the whole tendency of Paulus' view leads straight to some such revolting (and quite improbable) story as that which is to be found in Venturini and in the underground literature that has not altogether been eliminated since his day. Even vaguer than Paulus is Schleiermacher; and yet even Schleiermacher, if the implications of his vagueness be examined, may be found to have taken the first step in the downward path. A veil is left over the birth of Jesus, says Schleiermacher in effect;[10] nothing sinful could have entered into the origin of the life of Christ; and the Panthera story is false[11]: yet the basis in tradition for the poetical New Testament narrative is that before the birth of Jesus Mary did become aware, in an extraordinary manner, that she was to bear the Son of God.[12] What does Schleiermacher mean by his curiously vague language? Does he mean nothing more than that Joseph and Mary became convinced that the child which was to be the fruit of their marriage was to be the Messiah? If so, it is difficult to see how such an expectation on the part of Joseph and Mary could possibly have had any part whatever in producing the story of the virgin birth. On the whole, the criticism which Neander[13] directed against Schleiermacher must be pronounced just. If, when the miracle is rejected, a factual basis is sought for the story of the virgin

[7] Paulus, *Leben Jesu*, I. i, 1828, p. 92.

[8] *Op. cit.*, p. 80.

[9] *Op. cit.*, p. 81.

[10] Schleiermacher, *Ueber die Schriften des Lukas*, i, 1817, p. 47 (English translation, *A Critical Essay on the Gospel of St. Luke*, 1825, p. 50).

[11] Schleiermacher, *Leben Jesu* (lectures of 1832, published from notes in 1864, in *Sämmtliche Werke*, I.vi), pp. 62 f.

[12] Schleiermacher, *Ueber die Schriften des Lukas*, i, 1817, p. 46 (English translation, *A Critical Essay on the Gospel of St. Luke*, 1825, p. 49). Compare *Leben Jesu*, p. 77.

[13] *Leben Jesu Christi*, 7te Ausg., 1874, p. 15 (English translation, *The Life of Jesus Christ*, from the fourth German edition, New York, 1848, p. 14).

birth, that factual basis must in the nature of the case be something of a repulsive (and thoroughly improbable) kind.

Yet one of the most distinguished scholars of the present day, A. von Harnack, of Berlin, a scholar who may perhaps be regarded as the ablest living representative of the "Liberal" or Ritschlian view of the New Testament and the beginnings of the Christian Church, has recently ventured to take a first step on this same dangerous, rationalizing path. Possibly, Harnack says in effect, there may have been a slight factual basis for the New Testament account of the virgin birth after all; possibly there may have been this much that was extraordinary in the way in which Jesus came into the world, that He was begotten by Joseph after the "betrothal" but before the marriage. "Betrothal" among the Jews, Harnack points out, was not at all what we mean by this word, but was equivalent to marriage. Even before Joseph took Mary into his house, she was his wife; so that there is nothing at all derogatory to Mary, Harnack insists, in the possibility which he suggests. The form of the narrative in Matthew may be partly explained, Harnack thinks, if the author is admitting, over against Jewish slanders, that Jesus was conceived in the womb of Mary before she was actually brought into Joseph's house.[14]

Harnack does not, indeed, exploit this suggestion as a means of explaining how the belief in the virgin birth arose. He holds, no doubt, still to his theory of a mythical origin of that belief. Nevertheless, the suggestion does indicate a certain tendency to return to the old rationalizing treatment of the narratives which was prevalent one hundred years ago. It is possible that under the influence of the "return to tradition," which is found here and there in recent literary criticism of the Gospels, the revival of the rationalizing method of treatment may soon go to much greater lengths.

If such a revival does take place, it will certainly be strangely perverse. And the present suggestion of Harnack, as has already been pointed out,[15] is faced by objections of the most serious kind. It does not really preserve the mother of Jesus from blame; for even if during "betrothal" she was really Joseph's wife, still the kind of conduct which Harnack is inclined to attribute to her would have subjected her at least to suspicion. And the existence of such suspicion is inconsistent with all that we know of the later life of Jesus and of the attitude of His contemporaries toward Him.

An objection may, indeed, be raised against our reasoning at this point. Are we not, it may be said, proving too much? If a premature birth of Jesus would necessarily have given rise to suspicion, and if that would have been

[14] With von Harnack compare von Baer, *Der Heilige Geist in den Lukasschriften*, 1926, pp. 122 f.

[15] See above, p. 215.

inconsistent with what we know of the attitude of Jesus' contemporaries toward Him, is not the story of the virgin birth, as we have it in Matthew and Luke, itself stamped as unhistorical? According to that story, just as much as according to the hypothesis of Harnack, the birth of Jesus was, to any ordinary observer, premature; and if either a really or an apparently premature birth is inconsistent with the attitude of Jesus' contemporaries, have we not, in condemning the hypothesis of Harnack, really condemned also our own view that the narratives in Matthew and Luke are true?

This objection is by no means insuperable. The point of our present argument against the hypothesis of premature birth as a basis for the virgin birth story is not that premature birth *might* have given rise to suspicion among the inhabitants of Nazareth, but that it must actually have done so if it is to be made the basis of the story of the virgin birth in Matthew and Luke. If the fact that the birth was premature was concealed from neighbors and friends and enemies, then how could it ever have given rise to suspicion; and if it gave no rise to suspicion, if, in other words, it never became something which to the early Christians required explanation, then how could the story of the virgin birth ever have arisen as an explanation of it? Or are we to suppose that after concealing the premature birth all through the time of Jesus' youth and of His public ministry Mary revealed the fact at some time after the beginning of the apostolic preaching, and that *then* suspicion arose and the story of the virgin birth was evolved as a means of allaying it? Surely such conduct on Mary's part is unnatural in the extreme.

If, on the other hand, the virgin birth was a fact, the situation becomes very different. In this case, the apparently premature time of the birth may never have become known to the inhabitants of Nazareth, for the reasons that have already been set forth in another connection;[16] there is no reason to suppose that suspicion would have arisen during the public ministry. But after the resurrection, there was in this case abundant reason why the secret of Jesus' birth should be revealed. It was not in this case a trivial (if not shameful) thing, but was a glorious manifestation of God's power; about it Mary could no longer keep silent. On the hypothesis of a virgin birth, therefore, the initial absence of suspicion and the final disclosure of the secret are both explained; whereas on the hypothesis of an ordinary premature birth an initial presence of suspicion is needed to explain the final emergence of the virgin birth story, and that initial presence of suspicion is clearly excluded by all that we know of the attitude of Jesus' contemporaries during His public ministry.

[16] See above, p. 250 f.

The attitude of Jesus' contemporaries, therefore, does provide an argument against Harnack's hypothesis of a premature birth, and yet does not provide an argument against the story of the supernatural conception as it appears in Matthew and Luke. But perhaps an even stronger argument against the hypothesis of a premature birth is to be found in somewhat more intangible and yet very powerful considerations regarding the character of Joseph and Mary. Are we to suppose that they would lightly have exposed Mary to the suspicion to which, even on Harnack's view of Jewish betrothal, a premature entrance upon the marriage relationship might well have subjected her? The suggestion is, after all, derogatory to their character; and such a defect in them does seem to be contrary to all that we should naturally expect to be the case. It does seem that the whole phenomenon of Jesus' life is better explained (especially on naturalistic principles, but also when He is regarded as truly the Son of God) if He grew up in what from the human point of view was a blameless home. And the attitude of His contemporaries both toward Him and toward the household in which He had lived does seem to be more natural if the conduct of Joseph and Mary was of a really, and not merely apparently, worthy kind.

At any rate, we have at this point the support of the vast majority of modern investigators of all shades of opinion. Most modern scholars who reject the virgin birth are agreed, for whatever reason, in rejecting the thought of anything unusual or suspicious in connection with the birth of Jesus. Indeed, the chief interest of Harnack's suggestion is to be found not in any inherent merit in it, but in the fact that Harnack has been led to make it. If, after nearly one hundred years' dominance of the purely mythical theory of the birth narratives, so distinguished a leader of the modern Church and so accomplished a scholar feels compelled to return, to some extent at least, to the old rationalizing method of treatment, we may find there an indication that when the fact of the virgin birth is given up it may not be quite so easy as was formerly supposed to account for the New Testament narratives as they stand. Harnack's suggestion may be important, in other words, as indicating the defects of the dominant mythical view.

It is of course quite without warrant when popular defenders of the virgin birth alarm their hearers by presenting the hypothesis of illegitimate birth as being the only alternative to acceptance of the miracle; for probably ninety-nine out of a hundred among those who deny the virgin birth (at least among the educated classes of society) do so without thought of any such thing, and on the contrary believe that Jesus was simply the son of Joseph and Mary. Yet on that view that Jesus was the son of Joseph and Mary the origin of the belief in the virgin birth does become more difficult to explain than would be the case if there were actually something unusual in the manner of His birth. We are indeed precluded from this latter solution of the problem by historical considerations of the most compelling kind, and thus are forced back, if we still reject the historicity of the miracle, to the purely mythical view; but the difficulties of that view, as we shall see, are so serious that now and then there will always probably be some men who, like Harnack, will be led to have some recourse again to the rejected rationalizing method and will try to find some sort of factual basis which would help account for the extraordinary narratives in Matthew and Luke.

Nevertheless, such help is altogether rejected by the overwhelming majority of those who reject the fact of the virgin birth. It is almost universally admitted that if Jesus was not born of a virgin, He was the son of Joseph and Mary, born in wedlock and without anything which could give rise to question or suspicion with regard to the manner of His birth. The conditions of the problem, then, are in the minds of most scholars quite definitely fixed. How is it to be explained that one of the sons in a Jewish family, about whose birth there was really nothing extraordinary, came to be regarded as having been conceived in the womb of a virgin by a supernatural act of God? The story of the virgin birth, it is admitted, is not a distortion of actual happenings. What then is it; how did it arise?

The answer to this question that has been dominant since the days of Strauss is that the New Testament story of the virgin birth is a myth—that is, it is the expression, in supposedly historical form, of a religious idea. About the question what particular religious idea it is that the story expresses there have been some differences of opinion, but those differences are not so important as they might possibly have been expected to be. Bruno Bauer, it is true, supposed that the story expresses the idea of the divine initiative in the establishment of the unity between the Christian community and God. The Christian community, he supposed, was conscious of the unity of the divine and the human; this unity could not come from sinful man, but from God; the community, therefore, regarded itself as something produced by God without human help; and finally this thought was transferred from the community to the person of the Founder.[17] But such highly specialized accounts of the idea that is supposed to be expressed by the myth are at best isolated; and in general the advocates of the mythical theory content themselves with pointing simply to the Christian conviction regarding the greatness of Jesus' person (especially His divine sonship) or regarding the overpowering debt which believers owe

[17] Bruno Bauer. *Kritik der evangelischen Geschichte der Synoptiker*, 1841, pp. 37f.

to Him, as being the thought which the myth expressed. One so great as Jesus, it is said, could not, in the circles in which this myth arose, be regarded as born in the ordinary human way, but had to be thought of as owing even His conception in His mother's womb to an act of God.

But of course this general exhibition of the thought that was expressed by the myth does not suffice to explain the myth itself. Why was the greatness of Jesus celebrated in just this particular way? At this point opinions begin to diverge.

Chapter XIII

THE THEORY OF JEWISH DERIVATION

IT HAS been observed in the preceding chapter that in the opinion of the great majority of those who reject the historicity of the virgin birth story, the story is to be regarded as a myth. It is, in other words, to be regarded as the expression in narrative form of a religious conviction—the Christian conviction regarding the greatness of Jesus Christ. But whence did this particular myth come; how, specifically, did the idea of the virgin birth of Christ arise?

The most obvious suggestion unquestionably is that the idea arose on Jewish Christian ground. The narratives that contain the idea are, as we have seen, strikingly Jewish and Palestinian in character; what is more natural, therefore, than to suppose that the idea was formed on the basis of Jewish elements of thought? It is not surprising to discover that the Jewish Christian origin of the doctrine of the virgin birth has been defended by noteworthy scholars such as Keim, Réville, Lobstein and Harnack.

But what are the Jewish elements out of which the idea of the virgin birth of Christ is thought to have been formed?

In the first place, there are the Old Testament stories regarding heroes like Isaac and Samson and Samuel who were born of aged parents or at least of mothers who had previously been barren. In the case of such births, the course of nature was broken through; Sarah, for example, had given up all expectation of having children of her own; yet in a wonderful way God's power was manifested, and she conceived a son in her old age. Thus in the case of Isaac God's power, and not the ordinary course of nature, was the determinative thing. Was it not, then, an easy step to exclude the human father altogether and to hold that one greater than Isaac was conceived in the womb of a virgin by an immediate exercise of the power of God?

Such considerations might seem to be confirmed by the juxtaposition of the birth of Jesus with the birth of John in the infancy narrative in Luke. John the Baptist, like Isaac, was born of aged parents, and it is the intention of the narrative to present Jesus as greater than John. But if the superior greatness of Jesus is to be reflected in the manner of His birth, and if John was born of aged parents by an extraordinary manifestation of divine grace, what is there more natural than that in the case of Jesus the human father should be excluded altogether and that the child should be represented as conceived in the womb by the power of God? If John was to be filled with the Holy Spirit even from his mother's womb,[1] what is there more natural than that in the case of the one greater than John, the Holy Spirit in the womb of the mother should bring about the very existence of the child?

This parallelism between the wonder in connection with the birth of John the Baptist and the greater wonder in connection with the birth of Jesus would seem to be plainly indicated by the angel's words in Lk. i.36 f., where, in confirmation of the promise of the supernatural conception, Mary has pointed out to her the experience that her kinswoman Elisabeth has passed through: "And behold, thy kinswoman Elisabeth, she also hath conceived a son in her old age; and this is the sixth month with her who was called barren. For no word from God shall fail of power." Was it not, then, for persons who were impressed by the supreme greatness of Jesus, an easy step from a conception brought about in the womb of an aged woman by a special dispensation of God to a conception brought about in the womb of a virgin by an immediate exercise of God's creative power?

Despite the plausibility of such considerations, we answer that it was not an easy step at all—certainly not to a Jew. An essential point in the story of Isaac's birth was the paternity of Abraham; and the paternity of Zacharias is emphasized to the full in the case of John the Baptist. It is to Zacharias, the father of John, that the announcement of the approaching birth is made; and although the divine favor shown to Elisabeth does appear also in the narrative, in Lk. i.13, 24 f., 43 f., yet in general it may be said that Zacharias is the prominent figure. Evidently the narrators both in the Old Testament books and in the first chapter of Luke regard it as quite an essential part of the divine favor that the husband should actually beget a son who should be his very own.

This attitude of these particular narrators is quite in accord with the general Jewish attitude toward the begetting of children. All through the Old Testament, the possession of a large family is regarded as a signal mark of divine favor, and there is no trace of an ascetic attitude toward the marriage relationship. Moreover, there can be little question but that the attitude of the Old Testament at this point was also the prevailing attitude of later Judaism. Josephus does mention, indeed, as one of the three Jewish sects the ascetic order of the Essenes, and there have been efforts here and there to bring the life of Jesus and particularly the story of the birth into some sort of connection

[1] Lk. i.15.

with them; but in general such efforts have sprung only from dilettantism and have been rejected by the main trend of modern scholarship. The whole picture of the Judaism in which Jesus lived during his public ministry is just as remote as possible from the Essenism that Josephus describes. When we read the Gospels, with their lifelike descriptions of Pharisees and Sadducees, we feel that those strange Essenic companies with their asceticism, their curious observances, and their monastic life, belong altogether to a different world. Not only are the Essenes not mentioned in the Gospels, but evidently they are not at all in view. In the infancy narratives of Matthew and Luke the possibility of Essenic influence becomes particularly remote; the whole spirit of the narratives is contrary to any such thing. Certainly it is improbable in the extreme that Essenic asceticism should have exerted the slightest influence upon the circles from which these narratives came; those circles plainly belonged to a type of Jewish life that drew its inspiration from the Old Testament Scriptures. And part of the Old Testament tradition was the attitude toward the marriage relationship and the begetting of children which we have characterized above. Indeed, that attitude was no doubt shared, among the Jews, by friends of early Christianity and foes alike.

At that point, then, is to be found one barrier against the exclusion of the human fatherhood in the case of Jesus. Another barrier is to be found in the Jewish attitude toward God. To a Jew nothing could be more abhorrent than anything which would seem to bring God into degrading contact with the world. Indeed, it has often been remarked that the transcendence of God, which is fundamental even in the Old Testament, was exaggerated in later Judaism until it even seemed to forbid the mention of God's name. Particularly abhorrent would have been the notion that God could take the place of a human father and beget children after the manner of the divinities of the pagan world. No such notion as that appears, indeed, in Lk. i-ii, Mt. i-ii. But even the story of the virgin birth which does appear there might well have seemed to a Jew to move in somewhat the same direction—the direction of a breaking down of the full transcendence of God. Pre-Christian Judaism did, indeed, have some idea of a fatherhood of God; for such an idea is found in the Old Testament. "Thou art my son; this day have I begotten thee," says Jehovah to the Messianic king, according to the Second Psalm.[2] But this verse plainly refers not to the birth of the Messianic king, but to His induction into office; and it is as far as possible removed from excluding the human paternity. The fatherhood of God according to the Old Testament Scriptures (at least as they were understood by later Judaism), whether it refers to God's

[2] Ps. ii.7.

relationship to the nation or to God's relation to the king, is a relationship into which God enters by a gracious act; to set it over against the paternity of a human father is to have recourse to an entirely different circle of ideas. And to a Jew it might well seem to be derogatory to the transcendence of God as over against the world.

A word of caution must, indeed, be interjected at this point. We are insisting upon the incongruity between the Jewish doctrine of the transcendence of God and the story of the virgin birth. Does not that incongruity militate against the New Testament birth narratives themselves as much as against the view of their origin which we are now criticizing? Do we mean to say that the doctrine of the supernatural conception in Matthew and Luke is really contrary to the doctrine of the transcendence of God, which is certainly taught in the Old Testament as well as in later Judaism? And if it is not contrary to that doctrine, then why may not the Jewish Christians, in perfect loyalty to the Old Testament idea of God, have come to believe in the virgin birth of Christ?

In reply, we point out simply that there is a vast difference between acceptance of an idea when it is presented in some imperative way and evolution of that idea without such compulsion. There is no doubt a certain antinomy between the transcendence of God and the virgin birth of Christ; it is no doubt a supreme wonder that not some lesser one, but the eternal Son of God, He through whom the world was made, should not despise the virgin's womb, but should consent to be born as a man and dwell among us; it is no doubt a wonder, too, that the manner in which He should come should be found in a creative act of God's Spirit in Mary's womb. These stupendous antinomies do not, indeed, amount to contradiction; and in the wonderful narratives of Matthew and Luke they are so presented that neither member of the antinomy is sacrificed at all. It is not by some lower conception of God that God is thought of as excluding the human father when our Saviour entered into the world; it is not a god of Greek mythology, begetting children after the manner of men, but the Holy Spirit Himself, in His creative activity, who brought about the beginning of the human life of Jesus in the virgin's womb. There is an antinomy here; but is it not at bottom merely the antinomy which is involved of necessity in the incarnation of the Son of God? "So the All-Great were the All-Loving too"—what wonder could be greater than that? Yet it is a wonder in which the Christian can rest.

Thus the antinomy in the Gospel narratives is not only created, but transcended, by the stupendous fact. The lofty Old Testament conception of God is preserved to the full; and yet that God, by His creative power, has formed in the virgin's womb the body of Him who was to be both God and man. The antimony has truly been overcome here—overcome by a mighty act of God.

Could it have been overcome in any other way? We think not; and because we think not we have rejected the Jewish Christian derivation of the supposed myth of the virgin birth. It is one thing to say that when Jesus was actually conceived by the Holy Ghost in the womb of the virgin Mary, that fact could be harmonized by divine revelation with the awful transcendence of God; and it is quite a different thing to say that a Jew, beginning with the transcendence of God, would ever have been able, without compulsion of fact, without the enlightenment of revelation, to arrive at the wonderful representation that appears in Matthew and Luke. All that we know of Judaism is contrary to such a possibility as that. A Jew could accept the virgin birth when it actually occurred, but that is very different from evolving the notion of it from existing ideas. Very hostile to such an evolution of the notion was the whole tendency of the Jews' thought about God.

A subsidiary obstacle to the Jewish Christian derivation of the virgin birth story is to be found in the fact that the word for "spirit" in Hebrew is feminine. Would it have been natural, in view of this fact, for a Jew with an Old Testament background to evolve the notion that a supernatural conception was accomplished by the Holy Spirit? Would a feminine noun naturally be used to designate the divine power that took the place of the male factor in the birth of Jesus? Against such a supposition has often been urged especially the fact that in the Jewish Christian Gospel according to the Hebrews, the Holy Spirit is actually represented not as the father but as the mother of Jesus.

This argument should undoubtedly be used only with caution. In the birth narratives in Matthew and Luke, the Spirit is not represented as taking the place of the male factor in any anthropomorphic way, but as entering upon a creative activity. And we found reason to believe that the Gospel according to the Hebrews, despite its strange designation of the Holy Spirit as the mother of Jesus, did contain an account of the virgin birth—presumably, though of course not certainly, in much the same form as that which appears in the canonical Gospels. If, then, in the Gospel according to the Hebrews the feminine gender of the word for "spirit," and even the exploitation of that gender by the designation of the Spirit as Jesus' mother, did not prevent the inclusion of the story of the supernatural conception by that same Spirit, would the feminine gender of the noun have prevented the formation of the story in the first place?

Such considerations do not altogether destroy the argument against which they are directed. It is perfectly true that the feminine gender of the word for "spirit" in Hebrew would not necessarily prevent the acceptance by men of Semitic background of the story of the supernatural conception if that story came to them already formed. We have already pointed out that the lofty representation in Matthew and Luke does not at all imply the discharge of human functions by the Holy Spirit, but has reference to the Spirit's creative work. If that representation was rightly understood, therefore, it could easily be accepted by men of Jewish race despite the feminine gender of the Hebrew word. But if the story was to be evolved without basis in fact, on the basis of the kind of reflection regarding the presence or absence of the human father which is attributed to the Jewish Christian originators of the story by advocates of the theory with which we are now concerned, then we think that the feminine gender of the word might be a great obstacle indeed. Rightly understood, the story (when it is taken as true) is fully harmonious with the feminine gender of the word for "spirit"; but the theory of Jewish Christian mythical derivation supposes that the story at the beginning was understood in a very different way. Thus the gender of the Hebrew word does provide a valid, though undoubtedly subsidiary, argument against the theory of a Jewish Christian derivation of the supposed myth.

A far more important argument is to be found in the Jewish expectation of the Davidic descent of the Messiah. Surely that expectation would constitute a powerful barrier against any evolution of the idea of the virgin birth on Jewish Christian ground. If the story of the virgin birth stands in antinomy with the transcendence of God as it appears in the Old Testament and as it appears in one-sided and exaggerated form, perhaps, in later Judaism, even more obviously does it stand in antimony with the promise of the king that was to come from David's line. In the narratives of Matthew and Luke, as we have seen, the Davidic descent is traced through Joseph, and not, in accordance with the most probable interpretation, through Mary. How then, except under the compulsion of fact, could Jewish Christians like the authors of these narratives, Jewish Christians who laid such stress upon the Davidic descent of Jesus, ever have evolved the notion that Jesus was not the son of Joseph, after all, but was born without human father, being conceived by the Holy Ghost?

Here again the antinomy is not incapable of being resolved in a higher unity. We have argued in another connection that when Jesus was born in Joseph's house—not in a physical sense his son but conceived in the womb of the virgin Mary by a stupendous act of God, and yet born when Mary was already Joseph's wife—He was, in accordance with the promises, truly the heir of David. Even mere adoption, we argued, meant more to the Jews than it does to us; and the relation of Jesus to Joseph, if the story of the virgin birth be true, is more than mere adoption as it exists ordinarily among men. Thus Jesus, though virgin-born and not in the ordinary sense Joseph's son, was yet Joseph's heir, and heir to the promises of God concerning the Messianic king. According to the New Testament narratives, then, Jesus belonged truly to the house of David; only, He was a gift of God to the house of David in a far more wonderful way than if He had been in a physical sense Joseph's son.

But if the antinomy may be resolved so readily in this way, if the promises were really fulfilled by the birth of Jesus as it is narrated in Matthew and Luke, and fulfilled in accordance with the ideas of those to whom they were made, have we then, after all, any basis for an argument against the Jewish Christian derivation of the myth of the virgin birth? However it may seem to *us,* would the story of the virgin birth have seemed to *a Jew* to stand in any antinomy at all with the Davidic descent of Jesus through Joseph?

Here again, as in the case of the Jewish doctrine of God, we answer that it is one thing to be able to resolve an antinomy when once it is created by the compulsion of facts and quite a different thing to create the antinomy in the first place without impelling cause. No doubt the Davidic descent of Jesus through Joseph can be harmonized with the story of the virgin birth; no doubt when that latter story was once heard, any student of the Old Testament, and especially a Jew, could see that the virgin-born Messiah, born in Joseph's house, not only belonged truly to the house of David, but belonged to the house of David in an even more wonderful way than if He had been descended from David by ordinary generation. No doubt God's promises could be seen to have been fulfilled even more fully and even more gloriously than if they had been fulfilled merely as they were originally understood. All that is perfectly true, when once the story of the virgin birth was received. But until that story was received, would the story ever have been evolved by those whose thought concerning the Messiah centred in the promise that He should be descended from David's line? Surely this supposition is unlikely. Unless all indications fail, the expectations of the Jews regarding the Messiah, especially such Jews as the original authors of the narratives in Mt. i-ii, Lk. i-ii may be conceived to have been, were running in a direction quite remote from the thought of any even apparent break in the Davidic descent of the Messiah, like that which is involved in the story of the virgin birth. We insist, therefore, that the representation of the birth of Jesus in Matthew and Luke does stand in an antinomy with the Jewish doctrine of the Davidic descent as well as with the Jewish doctrine of the transcendence of God—an antinomy which militates strongly against a Jewish Christian origin of the supposed myth of the virgin birth. By what impulsion could such obstacles in the Jewish mind to the story of the virgin birth be overcome?

They could be overcome, of course, by the impulsion of fact. If the virgin birth really occurred, then it is not difficult to see how it might have been accepted even by men of Jewish race. But if that explanation be rejected, as it is of course rejected by the advocates of the theory now under consideration, what may be put in its place? Was there any other impulsion—other than the impulsion of fact—which could have led the Jewish Christians, despite their inherited view of the awful transcendence of God and despite the stress that they laid upon the Davidic descent of the Messiah, to accept, or rather themselves to evolve, the story of the virgin birth?

Only one answer to this question can possibly be suggested. Might not the impulsion to the notion of the virgin birth of Jesus have been found in the prophecy in Is. vii.14? [3] When the Jewish Christians read in the Scriptures the words, "Behold the virgin shall conceive, and bear a son, and shall call his name Immanuel," what was there more natural, it may be said, than that they should interpret these words, with their mention of a virgin mother, as being a prophecy of the virgin birth of the Messiah; and since prophecy, according to their view, must be fulfilled, what more natural than that they should suppose that *this* prophecy had actually been fulfilled in the case of the true Messiah, Jesus, who therefore must have been born of a virgin as is narrated in the story that has been preserved for us in Matthew and Luke? Thus, according to this hypothesis, the doctrine of the virgin birth of Jesus was evolved in order to show fulfilment of a prophecy contained, or supposed to be contained, in one verse in the seventh chapter of Isaiah. The hypothesis is thought to be strongly supported by the actual quotation of Is. vii.14 in Mt. i.22 f. There we have, it is supposed, an indication by the author of the First Gospel himself of the way in which the doctrine of the virgin birth was evolved; in the search for Messianic proof-texts the Jewish Christians hit upon the Immanuel prophecy in Isaiah, and the Immanuel prophecy produced the story of its supposed fulfilment.

In our consideration of this suggestion, it is necessary to distinguish sharply between the question how the passage in Isaiah ought really to be interpreted

[3] Certainly the impulsion could not have been found in any other passage. The use of Ps. ii.7 ("Thou art my son; this day have I begotten thee") by Strauss in this connection (Strauss, *Leben Jesu*, 1835, i, p. 177) has remained quite sporadic, and was apparently abandoned by Strauss himself in his later work, *Das Leben Jesu für das deutsche Volk bearbeitet* (3te Aufl., 1874).

and the question how it actually was interpreted by men of Jewish race in the first century after Christ.

With regard to the former question, we hold very strongly that the author of the First Gospel is entirely correct in taking the Immanuel passage as a true and very precious prophecy of the virgin birth of our Lord. Against this view has been urged, indeed, the fact that the word translated "virgin"[4] in the Septuagint means in Hebrew not "virgin" but simply "young woman of marriageable age"; it is not ***bethulah*** but *'almah*. This objection is at least as old as the middle of the second century; for Justin Martyr, writing at that time, represents his Jewish opponent, Trypho, as insisting, against the Christian doctrine of the virgin birth of the Messiah, that the Septuagint translation at Is. vii.14 is wrong, and that *'almah* should have been translated by the Greek word for "young woman" and not by the Greek word for "virgin."[5] Then the second-century Jewish versions of the Old Testament by Theodotion, Aquila, and Symmachus actually have the former translation, apparently in conscious opposition to the Christian use of the Septuagint at this point; and in the opinion of many modern scholars these versions are right. Thus if the second-century Jews and their modern supporters are correct about the interpretation of Is. vii.14, the doctrine of the virgin birth, on the hypothesis of Jewish Christian origin, would seem to have been evolved from a mistranslation of a Hebrew word, which the Septuagint happened to have made at Is. vii.14. In the Hebrew original, it is said, there is nothing whatever in this passage about a virgin birth of the Messiah.

But is this ancient Jewish, and modern critical, interpretation of the Isaiah passage really correct, or is the First Gospel correct in taking that passage as a prophecy of the virgin birth? The question, we think, cannot be settled merely by a consideration of the meaning of the Hebrew word *'almah*.

It has been urged, indeed, on the one hand that the Hebrew language has a perfectly unmistakable word for "virgin," ***bethulah***, and that if "virgin" had been meant that word would have been used. But as a matter of fact there is no place among the seven occurrences of *'almah* in the Old Testament where the word is clearly used of a woman who was not a virgin.[6] It may readily be admitted that *'almah* does not actually indicate virginity, as does *bethulah;* it means rather "a young woman of marriageable age." But on the other hand one may well doubt, in view of the usage, whether it was a natural word to use of anyone who was not in point of fact a virgin.

[4] παρθένος.

[5] That is, by νεᾶνις, not παρθένος. See Justin Martyr, *dial.*, 67.

[6] Prov. xxx.19 and Cant. vi.8, which have been appealed to for an opposite view, seem not really to constitute exceptions.

C. F. Burney aptly compares our English use of "'maiden' and 'damsel,' terms which do not in themselves connote virginity, yet would scarcely be used of any but an unmarried woman."[7] If a married woman were referred to in Is. vii.14, it does seem as though some other word than *'almah* would naturally be used.[8]

But even if that conclusion were incorrect, even if the word were in itself quite neutral as to whether a young married woman or a virgin in the strict sense were in view, still we think that the context would point strongly in the latter direction. According to the immediately preceding verses, Ahaz, the king of Judah, has been told by the prophet (by direct command of Jehovah) to ask for a "sign," to ask it "either in the depth, or in the height above." Ahaz declines to do so, and then comes the passage with which we are concerned:

> Therefore the Lord himself shall give you a sign: behold, a virgin[9] shall conceive, and bear a son, and shall call his name Immanuel. Butter and honey shall he eat, when he knoweth to refuse the evil, and choose the good. For before the child shall know to refuse the evil, and choose the good, the land whose two kings thou abhorrest shall be forsaken. Jehovah will bring upon thee, and upon thy people, and upon thy father's house, days that have not come, from the day that Ephraim departed from Judah—even the king of Assyria.[10]

What does the first verse in this passage mean? Who is the *'almah* whose child-bearing constitutes the "sign" that Jehovah gives?

Various answers to this question have been given in the long history of the exegesis of this famous passage. A very ancient answer is that the *'almah,* or "young woman," who is meant is the prophet's wife. A few verses below, at the beginning of the eighth chapter, it is said that the prophet's wife bore a son, whose name, Maher-shalal-hash-baz, is significant of impending polit-

[7] C. F. Burney, "The 'Sign' of Immanuel," in *Journal of Theological Studies*, x, 1909, p. 583.

[8] See especially for the use of *'almah, bethulah*, etc., and the translations of these words in the versions, R. D. Wilson, "The Meaning of 'Alma (A. V. 'Virgin') in Isaiah vii. 14," in *Princeton Theological Review*, xxiv, 1926, pp. 308–316. For a different view see John H. Raven ("The Sign Immanuel," in *Biblical Review*, ii, 1917, pp. 213–240), who holds that Is. vii.14 is not really, and was not taken by Matthew as being, a prophecy specifically of the virgin birth, the point of the (true) prophecy being found not in the manner of the birth, but in the child Himself and in His significant name.

[9] It should be observed that in the original Hebrew, as well as in the Greek translation (both in the quotation in Mt. i.23 and in the Septuagint), the important word in the passage has the article; it is *the 'almah*, not *an 'almah*. According to some scholars, it is true, the article is not to be pressed, and the translation should be "a virgin" (or "young woman"). But the translation by the English definite article is, from the linguistic point of view, equally allowable, to say the least, and the context clearly favors it. The margin of the American Revised Version, which substitutes "the" for "a," is therefore clearly to be preferred to the translation in the text.

[10] Is. vii.14–17, according to the American Revised Version (with omission of the alternative renderings and marginal notes).

ical events. May not another son have been given the still more significant name, Immanuel, to signalize the discomfiture of the two kings, Rezin, king of Syria, and Pekah, king of Israel, who had come up against Ahaz to battle? But why should the prophet's wife, who is designated in the later passage, very naturally, as "the prophetess," be designated here as "the young woman of marriageable age," even supposing that the word *'almah* means no more than that? Surely the designation is rather strange.

Another interpretation finds in the *'almah* the wife of Ahaz the king, so that the promised child is Ahaz's son, Hezekiah. This interpretation, which is attested in Justin Martyr's Dialogue with Trypho as being the one favored by the non-Christian Jews in the second century, was refuted by Jerome some centuries later,[11] who pointed out that since Hezekiah must have been born before Ahaz came to the throne his birth could not have been referred to within the reign of Ahaz as lying still in the future. Moreover, the reference to Hezekiah is not favored by anything in the context, to say nothing of the fact that, as on the first interpretation, the choice of the word seems very strange.

A third interpretation abandons all such identifications of the *'almah* and holds that *any* young woman is meant. "Let us suppose," the prophet, according to this third interpretation, would say, "that a young woman, at this moment when I speak, is conceiving; then before the child whom she shall bear shall come to years of discretion the land whose two kings have threatened the land of Judah shall be forsaken, and because of that deliverance that is to take place before the child shall grow up, the child might appropriately be called, 'God with us.'" Thus the prophecy would merely indicate, in a pictorial sort of way, the shortness of the time within which deliverance was to come to Judah. A little reflection, we think, will reveal the inadequacy of this view. After all, the attention of the readers, as of the original hearers of the prophet, is directed to the young woman and her child-bearing in a way that seems very strange if she is introduced merely as a sort of measure of the time that must elapse before the danger to the kingdom will be averted; and the reference to Immanuel in Is. viii.8, when taken in connection with our passage, clearly shows that a definite person is meant.

The truth is that all these interpretations which find in the child-bearing of the *'almah* only an ordinary birth are opposed by the way in which the promise is introduced. Why should an ordinary birth be regarded as a "sign"? That word naturally leads us to think of some event like the turning back

[11] Justin M., *dial.*, 43; Jerome, *com. in Isaiam,* on Is. vii.14, ed. Vall et Maff., iv, 1845, col. 109.

of the sun on Hezekiah's dial, or the phenomena in connection with Gideon's fleece. But it is not merely the use of this one word which would lead us to expect something miraculous in that which the prophet proceeds to announce. Equally suggestive is the elaborate way in which the "sign" is introduced. The whole passage is couched in such terms as to induce in the reader or hearer a sense of profound mystery as he contemplates the young woman and her child.[12]

At this point, as at other points in connection with the Old Testament, we receive, in the field of exegesis, an unexpected ally in the ultra-modern school of comparative religion. That school, as represented, for example, by Gressmann, is inclined to return to the traditional exegesis of our passage by finding in the Immanuel prophecy at least no mere trivial reference to events in the immediate vicinity of the prophet, but a presentation of a stupendous divine personage, whose birth transcends the ordinary human sphere.[13] We cannot agree with Gressmann as to the source from which this presentation comes; for he finds the source in a widespread oriental myth of a divine redeemer, while we find it in genuine revelation from the one living and true God. But at least there is a certain agreement in the exegetical sphere. The modern school of comparative religion at least agrees with devout readers of the Old Testament in rejecting the minimizing interpretation of the Old Testament prophecies which has been in vogue in the dominant critical school. No doubt a sound exegetical instinct is here at work. It is certainly clear that something more than the Israelitish people is meant by the figure of the "Servant of Jehovah" in the latter part of Isaiah; and it is certainly clear that something more is meant by "Immanuel" in our passage than the child of the prophet or of Ahaz or of any ordinary young woman of that time. A really sympathetic and intelligent reader can hardly, we think, doubt but that in

[12] This argument is as old as Justin Martyr, who in the Dialogue with Trypho, at the middle of the second century, writes as follows (*dial.*, 84): "For if this one was to be born of the union between the sexes, as all the other first-born sons are born, why did God say that He would produce a sign, which is not common to all first-born? But anticipating through the Holy Spirit that which is truly a sign and was destined, to be sure, for the race of men—that is, that the first-born of all created things should by incarnation through a virgin's womb truly become a child—He proclaimed it aforehand in one and another fashion (as I have set forth to you), in order that when it happened it might appear to have happened by the power and purpose of the maker of all things." No doubt this argument may have to be supplemented in the light of subsequent investigation, but whether it has really been invalidated may be seriously doubted. Conceivably, indeed, the term "sign" may be used in different ways; conceivably it may, for example, denote an event in itself natural which becomes a sign only because of its harmony with what has been supernaturally predicted. But when one takes the Isaiah passage as a whole, such an interpretation is here seen to be clearly inadequate.

[13] See Gressmann, *Der Ursprung der israelitisch-jüdischen Eschatologie*, 1905, pp. 272–278, 289. Similarly Hans Schmidt, "Die grossen Propheten" (in *Die Schriften des Alten Testaments*), 1915, pp. 74 f.

the "Immanuel" of the seventh and eighth chapters of Isaiah, in the "child" of the ninth chapter, whose name shall be called "Wonderful, Counsellor, Mighty God, Everlasting Father, Prince of Peace," in the "branch" of the eleventh chapter, one mighty divine personage is meant. The common minimizing interpretations may seem plausible in detail; but they disappear before the majestic sweep of the passages when they are taken as a whole.

At this point, however, an objection lies ready to hand. If the passage in the seventh chapter of Isaiah constitutes a real prophecy of Christ, what shall be done with the plain reference in the sixteenth verse to events belonging to the prophet's own time?[14] How can the coming of Christ to years of discretion some seven centuries later be made to fix the time for the forsaking of the land of Israel and Syria? Surely some more immediate birth of a child must be in view.

In reply, either one of two things may be said.[15] In the first place, it may be held that the prophet has before him in vision the birth of the child Immanuel, and that irrespective of the ultimate fulfilment the vision itself is present. "I see a wonderful child," the prophet on this interpretation would say, "a wonderful child whose birth shall bring salvation to his people; and before such a period of time shall elapse as would lie between the conception of the child in his mother's womb and his coming to years of discretion, the land of Israel and of Syria shall be forsaken." This interpretation, we think, is by no means impossible. It is difficult, indeed, to set it forth adequately in our bald modern speech; but the objections to it largely fall away when one reads the exalted language of the prophet as the language of prophetic vision ought really to be read.

In the second place, one may hold that in the passage some immediate birth of a child is in view, but that that event is to be taken as the foreshadowing of the greater event that was to come. Does an immediate reference to a child of the prophet's own day really exclude the remoter and grander reference that determines the quotation in the first chapter of Matthew? Certainly it does so in accordance with the prevailing view of the Old Testament prophets, the view which rejects altogether the typology in which the Church of all the ages has found so much of beauty and so much of the grace of God. But has that prevailing view really penetrated to the full meaning of these Old Testament books? We think not; and because we think not (or else because we adopt the other of the two possible interpreta-

[14] "For before the child shall know to refuse the evil, and choose the good, the land whose two kings thou abhorrest shall be forsaken."

[15] They are well distinguished and expounded by J. A. Alexander, in *The Prophecies of Isaiah*, 1865, i, pp. 169–172.

tions that have just been set forth) we are able to accept still the use which the First Evangelist makes of the prophecy in the seventh chapter of Isaiah. That does not mean that we desire to return at all to the allegorical interpretation which in Philo and in Origen had such a baleful influence upon the readers of the Old Testament Scriptures. On the contrary, we adhere with full conviction to the method of grammatico-historical exegesis. But grammatico-historical exegesis does not demand the exclusion of all allegory from ancient books; it only demands that allegory shall not be discovered where no allegory was meant. So also grammatico-historical exegesis does not demand the exclusion of all typology from the exalted language of the Old Testament prophets; the question whether all typology is to be excluded is a question which should be settled, not by the mechanical application of modern exegetical methodology, but only by patient and sympathetic research. And when such patient and sympathetic research is applied to the Old Testament, the result, we think, will be that in the dealings of God with His covenant people will be found a profound and supernatural promise of greater things to come. So, in our passage, the prophet, when he placed before the rebellious Ahaz that strange picture of the mother and the child, was not merely promising deliverance to Judah in the period before a child then born should know how to refuse the evil and choose the good, but also, moved by the Spirit of God, was looking forward, as in a dim and mysterious vision, to the day when the true Immanuel, the mighty God and Prince of Peace, should lie as a little babe in a virgin's arms.

But such a reading of prophecy will not be induced, in those who have abandoned it, by any considerations that we can now bring forth; indeed, it will come only when there is a mighty revulsion from the shallowness of our present religious life, and when men are again ready to listen to the voice of the living God. Certainly for us now to attempt any defence of it would lead us far away from our present subject. For what is now relevant to our argument is not at all that Is. vii.14 really is a prophecy of the virgin birth of the Messiah. Upon that point we have touched merely in passing, lest there should be any misunderstanding of the position that we hold with regard to the Evangelist's use of a prophecy that we think was given truly by inspiration of God. What is really relevant to our present argument is quite a different thing; it is the fact that, whatever the true interpretation of Is. vii.14 may have been, the *actual* interpretation of that prophecy which was prevalent among the Jews in the first century after Christ was, unless all indications fail, as far as possible from finding in the prophecy any prediction of the virgin birth of the Messiah.

It may perhaps at first sight seem strange that if Is. vii.14 is really a prophecy of the virgin birth of the Messiah, the later Jews should have so completely failed to interpret it in that way. But a parallel case is found in Is. liii. If there is any one passage in the Old Testament which seems to the Christian heart to be a prophecy of the redeeming work of Christ, it is that matchless fifty-third chapter of Isaiah. We read it today, often even in preference to New Testament passages, as setting forth the atonement which our Lord made for the sins of others upon the cross. Never, says the simple Christian, was there a prophecy more gloriously plain. Yet the historian must admit that as a matter of fact the later Jews did not interpret the prophecy in any such way. Nothing seems to have been more foreign to later Judaism than the thought of the vicarious sufferings and death of the Messiah. The profound meaning of the Old Testament had at this point been missed; Jewish thought about the Messiah was moving along entirely different lines. So also it may have been, and with vastly better excuse, in the case of the mysterious prophecy in Is. vii.14. That was really a prophecy of the virgin birth; but it was couched in such terms as to be fully intelligible only after the event. At any rate, whatever may have been the reason, it seems perfectly clear that the later Jews did not interpret Is. vii.14 as referring to the virgin birth of the Messiah.

One indication of that fact is to be found in the attitude of the Jew Trypho, who in Justin Martyr's Dialogue with Trypho is the exponent of Jewish polemic against the Christian faith. What Trypho urges against the Christian doctrine of the virgin birth is not at all that, although prophecy requires the Messiah to be born of a virgin, Jesus of Nazareth was as a matter of fact not so born and so could not be the one to whom prophecy looked. On the contrary, Trypho's argument is that the Old Testament never predicted the virgin birth of the Messiah at all, and particularly did not do so at Is. vii.14. Neither Justin Martyr nor his Jewish opponent displays the slightest acquaintance with any non-Christian Jews who expected the Messiah to be born of a virgin or who interpreted Is. vii.14 in accordance with any expectation of that sort. This fact is worthy of careful consideration; for there can be little doubt but that the Dialogue with Trypho does represent faithfully the state of Jewish opinion in the second century after Christ. It makes very little difference whether Trypho is a real or an imaginary figure; for even if he is an imaginary figure the arguments which Justin puts into his mouth are plainly arguments which the Christians actually had to meet in the conflicts of that day. Evidently Justin is not engaged in knocking down a man of straw; the Jewish attack upon Christianity which he attributes to Trypho is not an attack which *might* be made, but an attack which actually *was* made. Thus the Dialogue does provide extremely valuable information about the Judaism of that day. The fact is not unimportant, therefore, that the Dialogue displays no knowledge whatever of any Jewish doctrine of the virgin birth of the Messiah, or any corresponding Jewish interpretation of Is. vii.14. But if the doctrine of the virgin birth and the Matthæan interpretation of Is. vii.14 were thus so contrary to Jewish opinion, what starting-point would Jewish Christians have for the evolution of the virgin birth story that is recorded for us in Matthew and Luke?

An objection to this argument is, indeed, ready to hand. Justin Martyr, it will be said, may be admitted to give us information about the Judaism of the second century; but what right have we to suppose that the Judaism of the second century was the same as the Judaism of the preceding period, in which the Christian story of the virgin birth arose? In opposition to Christianity, it will be said, and especially after the calamities to the Jewish state, Judaism would eliminate those elements of thought which would tend to support Christian contentions, and in particular would oppose to the Christian view of the supernatural Christ a purely humanitarian view of the Messiah as a king of David's line. Might not this process of elimination have been applied to the special question of the Messiah's entrance into the world? What right have we, therefore, to conclude that because second-century Judaism held to a purely natural birth of the Messiah, first-century Judaism may not have had on the contrary a doctrine of the virgin birth?

Unquestionably this objection possesses considerable force. It is no doubt true that a process of impoverishment did go on in Jewish thought about the Messiah after the founding of the Christian Church. Trypho, for example, is represented by Justin as denying the preëxistence of the Messiah. But we know from certain "apocalypses," such as the Ethiopic book of Enoch, that in the pre-Christian period there were some Jewish circles in which the Messiah was believed to have existed in heaven before his appearance upon the earth. At that point, then, the Dialogue with Trypho does fail to represent the full richness and variety of earlier Jewish thought. Why may not the case be similar with reference to the virgin birth? May there not have been, despite the contrary opinion of Trypho, some Jewish circles in the earlier period that expected the Messiah to be virgin-born?

But although this objection does correct an undue reliance upon Justin's testimony for our purpose, it does not destroy the value of that testimony altogether. Even with regard to the preëxistence of the Messiah and His superhuman character, the Dialogue with Trypho does unite with other indications to show that these elements in Jewish Messianic expectation probably did not belong, even in the pre-Christian period, to the main current of Jewish thought, and that the prevailing view probably was that the Messiah was to be an earthly king of David's line.[16] So the polemic of Trypho against the virgin birth, though it cannot of itself prove the complete absence of a virgin birth doctrine in the Jewish Messianic expectation of the preceding period, yet does tend strongly in that direction, and may be valuable in confirming other evidence to the same effect.

Such other evidence is in this case easily to be adduced. It is to be found in the complete silence, in all our sources of information, about any Jewish belief in the virgin birth of the Messiah, coupled with the marked antinomy in which, as we have already shown, that belief would stand over against the whole current of Jewish thought. Let it not be said that we have here a mere instance of the argument from silence to which we ourselves have objected strongly in other connections. The point is that the burden of proof in this case rests upon our opponents in the debate. They have asserted that the myth of the virgin birth of Jesus arose on the basis of Jewish ideas. Surely it is fair to ask them positively to point out what those ideas were and to adduce the evidence of their existence. Their contention would be greatly strengthened if they could show that the belief in the virgin birth of the Messiah did not need to be evolved *de novo* by Jewish Christianity, but had already existed in pre-Christian Judaism. So far the proof has not been forthcoming. We have considerable information about pre-Christian Jewish thought regarding the Messiah; yet in that information a virgin birth of the Messiah has no place; the silence of our sources of information is complete.[17]

At one point, indeed, that silence has been thought by several recent scholars to have been broken; the virgin birth of the Messiah, they maintain, is implied by the Septuagint translation of Is. vii.14. The Septuagint introduction of the word "virgin" in that passage is, according to these scholars, quite unwarranted; but just because it is unwarranted some reason must be sought for such an extraordinary mistake. What reason could there be except that when the Septuagint translation was made there had already arisen a doctrine of the virgin birth of the Messiah and that this doctrine had already been read into Is. vii.14 or was now read into that passage by the Septuagint translators themselves?

But surely the making of this suggestion only reveals the dearth of real evidence for that which is to be proved. The Septuagint translates the word

[16] See *The Origin of Paul's Religion*, 1921, pp. 184–186.

[17] It is generally admitted that the Rabbinical passages which have been adduced in this connection are altogether without value. See Strack-Billerbeck, *Kommentar zum Neuen Testament aus Talmud und Midrasch*, i, 1922, pp. 49 f.

'almah in one other place in the Old Testament[18] by the Greek word for "virgin." Since in that place no profound calculation underlies the translation, why should such mysteries be read into the same translation at Is. vii.14? It is true that in that other passage the word *'almah* designates an unmarried woman, so that it may be argued that the translation "virgin" was natural enough in that passage, whereas in Is. vii.14, where conception and child-bearing are mentioned, some special cause was needed to determine the choice of the word. But a little consideration will reveal the weakness of this argument. The use of the Greek word for "virgin" to translate the Hebrew word *'almah* in a clearly non-Messianic passage does seem to show that in the minds of translators like the translators of the different parts of the Septuagint there was an affinity between these two words. It shows at least that when *'almah* was translated by "virgin" at Is. vii.14, that was no such crass offence against linguistic usage as would necessarily need to be explained in some special way. The same Greek word for "virgin," moreover, is used in several other places in the Septuagint to translate a Hebrew word (other than *'almah*) which means simply "young woman" or "maiden."[19] On the whole, it seems evident that the Septuagint is inclined to use the Greek word for "virgin" in rather a loose way, or in places where no special emphasis upon virginity appears. The word, therefore, might well have crept into the translation at Is. vii.14 without any special cause, or certainly without influence from any Jewish doctrine of a virgin birth of the Messiah. It must be remembered that such a doctrine is entirely without attestation elsewhere. To find it merely in the Septuagint translation of *'almah* by "virgin," a translation that appears in another passage where there is no suspicion of any doctrinal significance, and that is paralleled by the occasional use of the same Greek word to translate a simple Hebrew word for young woman, is surely venturesome in the extreme. There is not the slightest direct evidence, therefore, in support of the view that there was in the pre-Christian Judaism of the time subsequent to the Old Testament any expectation of a virgin birth of the Messiah.

At this point, however, it becomes necessary to refer to the indirect support which has sometimes been found for such a view in the writings of Philo, the Jewish Alexandrian philosopher, who was a contemporary of our Lord.

[18] Gen. xxiv.43, where Abraham's servant is represented as praying that the maiden (*'almah*) who should come to the fountain and give to drink to him and to his camels, should be the wife destined for Isaac. See Thayer, *Greek-English Lexicon of the New Testament*, s. v. παρθένος. Wade (*New Testament History*, first published in 1922, p. 362, footnote 1) points out that παρθένος is in one place used by the Septuagint of a young woman who was not a virgin (Gen. xxxiv.3). The Hebrew original there has *na'arah*.

[19] *na'arah*.

Philo does not, indeed, attest anything like a virgin birth of the Messiah; such a thing stands entirely aside from the whole scope and method of his thought. So much, of course, must be admitted. But although he does not attest a virgin birth of the Messiah, he does speak of a virgin birth, or at least of a divine begetting, of certain Old Testament characters; and if these Old Testament characters could thus be spoken of by a Jew, Philo, as born without human father, might there not have been Jews who could also think of the greater One to come as being so born?

The Philonic passages which may be appealed to in this connection are fairly numerous.[20] The most important and most extensive one of them is that which is found in the "De Cherubim." Since serious misunderstanding may arise, and actually has arisen, from a consideration of Philo's references to divine begetting apart from their context, it becomes advisable to quote the passage, or at least the most important part of it, in full. This passage, then, is as follows:[21]

"And Adam knew his wife; and she conceived and brought forth Cain, and said, 'I have gotten a man by the instrumentality of God.' And again she bore his brother Abel." Those men whose virtue the lawgiver has attested he does not introduce as knowing women—namely Abraham, Isaac, Jacob, Moses, and any others of like zeal. For inasmuch as we regard "woman" in our symbolic interpretation as representing "sense-perception,"[22] and inasmuch as knowledge exists by estrangement from sense-perception and from the body,[23] he will represent the lovers of wisdom as rejecting sense-perception rather than choosing it. And is that not natural? For those who dwell with these lovers of wisdom are in name[24] "women" but actually[25] virtues—Sarah ruling and sovereign virtue, Rebekah patience in things that are good, Leah rejected and laboring in the continuity of discipline[26] (which every foolish person denies and shuns and turns away from), and Zipporah, the wife of Moses, hastening up from earth unto heaven and considering the divine and blessed creatures[27] that are there (she is called "little bird"). But that we may tell of the conceiving and travailing of the virtues, let superstitious persons shut their ears or else depart; for

[20] See the passages cited by Leisegang, *Pneuma Hagion*, 1922, pp. 43 (Anm. 2), 45 (Anm. 1), 49 (Anm. 1), 52. See also the extensive collection of passages (many of which, it is true, are hardly relevant in the present connection) by Carman, "Philo's Doctrine of the Divine Father and the Virgin Mother," in *American Journal of Theology*, ix, 1905, pp. 491–518.

[21] Philo, *de cherub.*, 12–15, ed. Cohn et Wendland, i, 1896, pp. 179–183. For the translation compare Cohn, *Die Werke Philos von Alexandria*, iii. Teil, 1919, pp. 182–185; Yonge, *The Works of Philo Judæus*, i. 1854, pp. 185–188; F. H. Colson, in Colson and Whitaker, "Philo," ii, 1929, pp. 32–41, in the *Loeb Classical Library*.

[22] αἴσθησις. Yonge translates "outward sense."

[23] ἀλλοτριώσει δ' αἰσθήσεως καὶ σώματος ἐπιστήμη συνίσταται.

[24] λόγῳ. [25] ἔργῳ.

[26] Or "fainting and weary at the long continuance of exertion." So Yonge. Cohn translates, "Lea die verschmähte und bei beständiger Tugendübung sich abmühende." Colson translates, "'rejected and faint' through the unbroken discipline." Text and interpretation are difficult.

[27] φύσεις. Colson translates, "the nature of things divine and blessed."

we teach divine mystic rites[28] to the initiates who are worthy of the most sacred mysteries, and these are the men who practise without arrogance the true and really existing unadorned godliness; but to those other men we will not be hierophants—namely, to those who are bound by an incurable evil, by arrogance in words and greediness for names and claptraps in manners, and who measure by nothing else that which is pure and holy.

Here then must the initiation be begun. A man in accordance with nature comes together with a woman, a male of the human race with a female, to enter upon those embraces that lead to the generation of children; but in the case of virtues, which bring forth numerous and perfect offspring, it is not lawful for a mortal man to possess them. Yet they will never of themselves alone, without receiving seed from any other, bring forth offspring. Who then is the one who sows in them the things that are good unless it be the Father of existing things, the uncreated God who Himself begets all things? This God, then, sows, indeed, the seed, but on the other hand bestows as a gift His own offspring which He has sown; for God begets nothing for Himself, because He has need of nothing, but He begets all things for him who needs to receive them. I will adduce as sufficient surety of the things that I am saying the most holy Moses; for he introduces Sarah as being then with child when God visited her after she had been left solitary, but as being with child not to Him who made the visitation, but to him who desired to attain wisdom—and this latter is called Abraham. And in the case of Leah he teaches that more plainly, saying that God indeed opened her womb—and to open the womb is the function of a husband—but that she, when she conceived, brought forth not to God—for God is competent in Himself and self-sufficient—but to Jacob, who endures toil for the sake of the good, so that virtue received from the First Cause [29] the divine seeds, but brought forth the child unto whichever one of her lovers should be preferred to all the other suitors. Again, when the all-wise Isaac entreated God, Rebekah, who is perseverance, became pregnant from Him who was entreated. And without entreaty and prayer Moses, taking winged and lofty virtue, Zipporah, finds her with child from no one [30] mortal at all.[31] These things, O initiates with purified ears, receive ye as indeed holy mysteries in your own souls, and divulge them to no uninitiated person, but storing them up in your own keeping guard them as a treasure—not a treasure in which gold and silver, perishable substances, are kept, but one in which is kept the most beautiful of true possessions, the knowledge of the First Cause and of virtue and of that third thing which is the offspring of both. And if ye chance upon any one of the initiated persons, embrace him with gentle insistence, that he hide not from you any new mystery which he may know, until ye be taught it clearly. For I also, though I had been initiated into the great mysteries under the guidance of Moses beloved of God, nevertheless when I saw Jeremiah the prophet and perceived that he was not only an initiate but also a competent hierophant, did not delay having recourse to him; but he, as one who often was possessed

[28] *τελετὰς γὰρ ἀναδιδάσκομεν θείας.*

[29] *τοῦ αἰτίου.* Compare Cohn: "von dem (göttlichen) Urheber"; Colson: "the Creator." A few lines below, Colson translates the same expression by "the Cause."

[30] Or "nothing."

[31] *εὑρίσκει κύουσαν ἐξ οὐδενὸς θνητοῦ τὸ παράπαν.*

by the divine frenzy, uttered a certain oracle in the name of God, saying this to most peaceful virtue: "Hast thou not called me as a house and father and husband of thy virginity?"—clearly showing that God is both a house, an immaterial dwelling-place of immaterial ideas, and the father of all things, as having begotten them, and the husband of wisdom sowing the seed of blessedness for the mortal race into good and virgin soil. For it is fitting for God to hold converse with a nature undefiled and untouched and pure, the nature truly virgin, in a manner different from our manner; for in the case of men the union for the begetting of children makes virgins to become women, but whenever God begins to converse with a soul, even if the soul was a woman before, he makes it again a virgin, since, destroying and putting out of the way the low-born and unmanly lusts, by which the soul had been made effeminate, He introduces instead of them genuine and undefiled virtues. With Sarah, therefore, He will not hold converse until she has ceased from all the ways of women and has returned to the rank of a pure virgin. But it is possible, perhaps, for even a virgin soul to be polluted by undisciplined passions and put to shame; wherefore the oracle is careful to say, not that God was the husband of *a virgin*—for a virgin is changeable and mortal—but that He is the husband of *virginity*—that is, of the idea which always remains the same.[32] For while things that are of this sort or that are subject by nature to beginning and to decay, the powers that have given the imprint to the individual things have received an immortal inheritance. Wherefore it is fitting that the uncreated and unchangeable God should sow the ideas of immortal and virgin virtues into virginity, which never changes into the form of a woman. Why then, O soul, it being required of thee to live as a virgin in the house of God and to cling to knowledge, dost thou leave these things and give thy greetings to sense-perception, which makes thee effeminate and corrupt? For this cause thou shalt bring forth as thy utterly hybrid and utterly ruined offspring that Cain who murdered his brother and was accursed—a possession that is not worthy to be possessed (for "Cain" means "possession").

At first sight, this passage, and other similar passages in Philo, might seem to provide a rather close parallel to the New Testament account of the birth of Jesus. In both cases there is begetting by divine agency; in both cases the human paternity seems to be excluded; and in both cases emphasis is laid upon the virginity of the mother.

This similarity should not, indeed, be overestimated. The form which the divine agency takes is different in Philo from that which appears in Matthew and Luke; for Philo says nothing about an activity of the *Holy Spirit* in the birth of Isaac and of the others about whom he speaks. It is God, not specifically the Spirit of God, who causes the conception of the child in the womb of Sarah and of the other three women.

F. C. Conybeare, indeed, has tried to bridge this gap between the two

[32] *τῆς ἀεὶ κατὰ τὰ αὐτὰ καὶ ὡσαύτως ἐχούσης ἰδέας*. Cohn translates: "der sich stets gleich bleibenden Idee." Compare Colson: "of virginity, the idea which is unchangeable and eternal."

representations.[33] In another passage [34] in Philo, he points out, the Alexandrian philosopher speaks of the individual man as being "compounded of earthly substance and of divine Spirit" [35] and of his soul as arising "out of nothing created whatsoever, but from the Father and Controller of all things." [36] Here there is a verbal similarity to our passage in the "De Cherubim"; the phrase, "from nothing [or "no one"] created at all," [37] corresponds with the phrase "from nothing [or "no one"] mortal at all." [38] But if there is such similarity in the way in which the human element is excluded in the two passages, must there not also be a connection in Philo's mind—so the argument might run—between what the two passages designate as the divine element? Thus the activity of God in the begetting of Isaac according to the "De Cherubim" passage would be identified with the activity of "the divine Spirit" mentioned in the passage in the "De Opificio Mundi." Accordingly, we should have in Philo, after all, the idea of a begetting by the Spirit of God; and the parallel with Matthew and Luke would become even closer than at first sight it seems to be.

This reasoning is, however, very precarious. The passage in the "De Opificio Mundi" does not say that the soul of man came not from anything mortal, but from the divine Spirit; it says rather that the soul of man came not from anything mortal, but from the Father and Ruler of all things. What it does say about "spirit" is that the individual man is compounded of earthly substance and divine spirit. Here the divine spirit appears not as the power which begat the soul, but as the substance of which the soul is compounded. In exposition of Gen. ii.7, where the Scripture says that God breathed into man's nostrils (Greek, "face") the breath of life, Philo identifies the soul, as distinguished from the body, with the breath or spirit [39] of God:

> For that which he breathed in was nothing else than the divine spirit sent as a colonist from that blessed and happy nature for the aid of our race, in order that even if the race is mortal in its visible part yet at least in its invisible part it may be made immortal.[40]

[33] Conybeare, "The Newly Found Sinaitic Codex of the Gospels," in *Academy*, xlvi, 1894, pp. 400 f.

[34] *De opificio mundi*, 46, ed. Cohn et Wendland, i, 1896, pp. 46 f.

[35] *σύνθετον . . . . ἔκ τε γεώδους οὐσίας καὶ πνεύματος θείου.*

[36] *τὴν δὲ ψυχὴν ἀπ' οὐδενὸς γενητοῦ τὸ παράπαν, ἀλλ' ἐκ τοῦ πατρὸς καὶ ἡγεμόνος τῶν ἁπάντων.*

[37] *ἀπ' οὐδενὸς γενητοῦ τὸ παράπαν.*

[38] *ἐξ οὐδενὸς θνητοῦ τὸ παράπαν.*

[39] The Septuagint uses *πνοή*; Philo in his exposition *πνεῦμα*. The two words are closely related. It is noteworthy that G. H. Whitaker (in Colson and Whitaker, *op. cit.*, i, 1929, p. 107) translates *πνεῦμα θεῖον* in the passage in the *De opificio mundi* not by "Divine Spirit," but by "Divine breath."

[40] *De opif. mundi, loc. cit.* Compare the translation in Colson and Whitaker, *loc. cit.*

Very different is the representation in Mt. i.18-25; Lk. i.35. In the New Testament passages the Holy Spirit certainly does not appear as a substance which is breathed by God into the virgin Mary for the formation of the soul, as distinguished from the body, of the child. On the contrary, the Spirit is here the source or agent of the act of begetting by which the body of the child was formed in the womb.

Moreover, that passage in the "De Opificio Mundi" is not really relevant to the present discussion. There what is in view is something that belongs to empirical "man" as such. But what we are seeking if we are to obtain a parallel for the New Testament narrative of the virgin birth of Christ is something that is attributed only to specially exalted men—something, therefore, that might conceivably be designated as belonging especially to the Messiah. It is noteworthy that in the passages where Philo lays stress upon the absence of the human paternity in the case of certain special Old Testament personages he does not speak at all of the "divine spirit," but says only that those personages were begotten by "God." We are not denying that the thought of the "De Opificio Mundi" passage is connected with the thought that appears in the "De Cherubim." In both cases Philo is thinking of facts regarding the human soul. The individual characters mentioned in the "De Cherubim" do not appear, as we shall see, at all for their own sakes, but solely for what they represent in Philo's allegorical exegesis. But our point is that it is not the underlying meaning of the "De Cherubim" passage which might conceivably be regarded as affording a basis for the New Testament virgin birth doctrine, but only the external form of expression with its reference to Isaac and the rest. The "De Opificio Mundi" passage in itself affords not the slightest parallel to the New Testament narrative. Only such passages as the one in the "De Cherubim" can by any chance be cited in that connection. It is, therefore, quite unjustifiable to import the phrase "the divine spirit" from that former passage into the latter, in order by this means to make more complete the parallel with Matthew and Luke. It does remain true, therefore, that the divine agency is not designated in the same way in the *really* relevant Philonic passages as in the New Testament account of the virgin birth of Christ.

But even with this limitation there seems at first sight to be similarity enough. Both Philo and the New Testament seem to exclude the human agency in the act of begetting, and they both emphasize the virginity of the mother. Moreover, one of the Old Testament characters to whom Philo refers is Isaac, who according to the Old Testament was born of aged parents, as was John the Baptist, whose birth is in the Lucan infancy narrative brought into such close parallel with that of Jesus. Have we not here a clear indication of the path by which the idea of the virgin birth of the Messiah could enter into Jewish or Jewish Christian belief? First the Old Testament spoke of the birth of Isaac as being in some sort supernatural, since his parents were past age; then this supernatural element in the birth of Isaac was in some Jewish circles actually held to involve exclusion of the human father in the case of Isaac himself (Philo), while in other Jewish (or else in Jewish Christian) circles it could lead to the notion that if not Isaac himself at least one greater than Isaac, the Messiah, was born without human father.

The argument is plausible at first sight; but upon closer examination it breaks down. Here as elsewhere verbal parallels beween Philo and the New Testament are found to mask a wide divergence of thought.

Did Philo really believe that Isaac and the other Old Testament characters in question were actually born without human father by the direct agency of God? So far as we are aware, no one today holds that to be the case; no present-day scholar, so far as we know, maintains that the Alexandrian philosopher actually believed that historical personages such as Isaac were virgin-born. To maintain such a view would be to misunderstand the whole nature of Philo's allegorical exegesis. As soon as one attains the slightest insight into the allegorical method of using the Old Testament, one sees clearly that when Philo speaks of a virgin birth or a divine begetting in the passages which are now in view, he is thinking of a divine begetting of the soul of man, or a divine begetting of certain virtues in the soul of man, and not at all of a divine begetting of human beings of flesh and blood who actually lived upon this earth.

Suppose we came to Philo, after our perusal of the passage in the "De Cherubim," with the question what he actually thought the manner of birth of the historic personage, Isaac, to have been—in particular with the question whether he did or did not think that Abraham was in a physical sense the father of this son. In the first place, it is perfectly evident that by the very asking of such a question we should, in the judgment of our philosopher, have completely forfeited our right to be taken seriously; we should have forfeited our right to become candidates for initiation into the "great mysteries." In the presence of the Alexandrian teacher we moderns with our boasted grammatico-historical exegesis, with our interest in the question what actually happened long ago, would have seemed to be very profane persons indeed; it is very doubtful whether Philo would have wasted much time with questioners like us. But if he had answered our question, no doubt it would have been to the effect that his teaching at this point was not intended for children, and that if we wanted to hear about historical personages as historical personages, we should turn either to other teachers or to his own simpler works, but as for reading the "De Cherubim," or the "De Opificio Mundi," that could only confuse our minds to no profit at all. No, there is not the slightest probability that Philo ever believed in, or even for one moment thought of, an actual virgin birth of a man of flesh and blood.

At first sight, indeed, it might seem to an uninitiated reader as though he did hold such a belief. Certain sentences in his writings seem to be perfectly explicit; and apparently he uses certain utterances of the Old Testament to construct a veritable argument against the view that Isaac and the others were begotten by the human beings who were the husbands of their mothers. Moses, Philo says, speaks of God as opening the womb of Leah; but to open the womb is the function of the husband; therefore—so Philo's argument seems to run—God it was, and not Jacob, who begat Leah's child. Or else it is an argument from the silence of Scripture which leads Philo to the same conclusion; Scripture does not speak of Abraham and certain others as knowing their wives; therefore they cannot be regarded as having begotten the children whom their wives brought forth.

At this point F. P. Badham departs in a curious way from the ordinary interpretation.[41] Philo's real meaning, he says, is that although Isaac was actually born of the seed of Abraham, yet by the divine agency that seed was conveyed to the mother in a way other than by the ordinary intercourse of the sexes. Thus, according to this interpretation, the mother could be a virgin, although the child was Abraham's child. This same interpretation is applied by Badham to the New Testament narratives: the real meaning of Matthew and Luke, he holds, is that although Mary was a virgin, yet Joseph was actually in a physical sense the father of Jesus; God caused the act of begetting to be accomplished without any intercourse between husband and wife.[42]

It is scarcely necessary to point out that this view does justice neither to Philo nor to the New Testament. In the case of Philo, Badham lays stress upon the fact that the "De Cherubim" passage says that the children, though begotten by an act of God, were born to Abraham and the other human beings regarded as their fathers. But does this really mean that God caused Abraham to be in a physical sense the father of Isaac, and Jacob the father of Leah's child, though in some more wonderful way than by the intercourse between husband and wife? Surely such an interpretation is impossible. The real

[41] Badham, "The New Syriac Gospels: The Account of the Nativity," in *Academy*, xlvi, 1894, p. 513; "The New Syriac Gospels," *ibid.*, xlvii, 1895, pp. 14 f., 151.

[42] "God took from Joseph's loins: ὁ παρθένος ἐγέννησε" (*Academy*, xlvi, 1894, p. 513). Compare the view of C. C. Torrey mentioned above, pp. 129, 186.

meaning plainly is that although God and God alone performed the act of begetting, yet the children were born in the house of Abraham and of Jacob and belonged to them as would be the case with other children. Equally impossible is Badham's interpretation of Matthew and Luke. It is true that the New Testament narratives lay stress upon the Davidic descent of Jesus through Joseph; but, as we observed in an earlier chapter,[43] the Davidic descent of Jesus through Joseph does not at all require us to suppose that Jesus was in a physical sense Joseph's son. And the actual wording of Mt. i.18-25 and Lk. i.34,35 makes Badham's interpretation very improbable. The meaning seems clearly to be not that the agency of Joseph was mediated in some unusual and miraculous fashion, but that that agency was altogether excluded.

To return, then, to Philo, we must plainly insist against Badham that what Philo is speaking of is an actual exclusion of the human paternity in the case of Isaac and of the other children of whom he speaks. But it is also perfectly clear that the exclusion of the human paternity belongs altogether to the allegorical sphere and is not intended at all to refer to the actual historical personages whose names are used. When Philo uses details of the Old Testament narrative to support his interpretation, that is quite in accord with the allegorical method. An isolated phrase, such as the phrase referring to the opening of Leah's womb, is seized upon quite apart from its context, and quite apart from the literal or historical sense of the passage, in order to afford a starting-point for the treatment of spiritual mysteries concerning the soul of man and the things of the unseen world. A sympathetic perusal of the passage in the "De Cherubim" and of other similar passages will show that when Philo speaks of virginity and of the divine begetting he is not really thinking at all of Sarah or Isaac or Leah or Zipporah, but of the facts concerning the soul of man and its relations to God. The whole representation goes back to certain spiritual, or, as modern men might put it, psychological, facts. The soul clogged with representations coming from the senses is sterile; it must be freed from these things and thus become truly virgin before it can receive the true seed; and it can receive the true seed not from man, but from God. But when the virgin soul has thus received by inspiration the seed that comes from God it can bring forth virtue. Such are the things with which Philo is really dealing in these passages. There is indeed a bewildering variety in detail.[44] At times it is the soul that is represented as the mother; at times it seems rather to be virtue—virtue that brings forth true

[43] See above, pp. 128-130.

[44] Part of this variety is exhibited by Leisegang (*op. cit.*, 1922, p. 52) by means of a table listing in three columns the designations (1) of the male principle, (2) of the female principle, and (3) of the offspring.

blessedness. It is useless to seek in Philo any one scheme in which all of his representations will fit; the exuberance of his language defies any attempt at complete systematization of his teaching. But at any rate it is perfectly clear that when he speaks about children begotten of God he is not for one moment thinking of beings of flesh and blood.

So much is admitted; it is generally admitted that Philo did not mean to say that Isaac or any of these other Old Testament personages was born of a virgin mother by a divine act of begetting. We do not find in Philo's own thinking, therefore, any notion that would form a parallel for the story of the virgin birth of Jesus in Matthew and Luke.

How then, if at all, may the Philonic passages be used in the search for such a parallel? A very definite answer to this question was given by F. C. Conybeare in the course of the correspondence to which reference has already repeatedly been made.[45] Although Philo may not himself be referring to a physical as distinguished from a spiritual pregnancy,[46] yet these passages "certainly imply among Philo's contemporaries a belief in actual parthenogenesis—*i.e.*, in the possibility of virgins bearing children *to* earthly fathers, yet not *by* them conceived, but by the Divine Spirit."[47] "Granted the existence among the Jews of the first century of such a belief," Conybeare goes on to say, "the rise and development in regard to Jesus of the entire story which we have in the first chapter of Matthew is seen to be a natural and almost a necessary outcome of his age." Thus, according to Conybeare, there were in the time of Philo Jews who actually believed in the virgin birth of certain patriarchs; however sublimated Philo's own view may have been, he is making use, in the passages to which we have referred, of a Jewish tradition as to actual virgin births. This Jewish tradition, Badham surmises,[48] may well have been found in Palestine as well as elsewhere. If so, we find attested in the Philonic passages a pre-Christian Palestinian belief in the virgin birth of Isaac and other Old Testament characters, which may well have been the basis for the belief in the virgin birth of the Messiah that appears in Matthew and Luke.

This hypothesis as to a Jewish tradition of parthenogenesis underlying the Philonic passages received the support of Carl Clemen in the first edition of his work on "Primitive Christianity and Its Non-Jewish Sources."[49] But it

[45] Conybeare, "The New Syriac Gospels," in *Academy*, xlvii, 1895, pp. 58, 150.

[46] Conybeare leaves the question open whether Badham's interpretation of Philo, which we have mentioned above, is to be accepted or not.

[47] Conybeare, *op. cit.*, p. 150. We have already seen how unwarranted is Conybeare's introduction of "the Divine Spirit" in this connection.

[48] F. P. Badham, "'Virgo concipiet,'" in *Academy*, xlvii, 1895, pp. 486 f.

[49] Clemen, *Religionsgeschichtliche Erklärung des Neuen Testaments*, 1909, p. 231 (English translation, *Primitive Christianity and Its Non-Jewish Sources*, 1912, pp. 297 f.).

seems to be dropped by Clemen in the second edition of his work.[50] At any rate, it must surely be pronounced very improbable. It is perfectly clear that when Philo speaks of virgin births and divine begettings he is thinking of facts concerning the soul, not of events in Old Testament history. His Scriptural attestation of his doctrine is found by an ingenious allegorical method of using certain Old Testament passages, for which it is quite idle to seek any support in Jewish tradition. Indeed, to seek such support is to show misunderstanding of Philo's whole attitude of mind.

There is, then, no evidence in the Philonic passages to show that there ever were Jews in the pre-Christian period who believed in the virgin birth of any being of flesh and blood. But may not those passages at least afford a hint as to the way in which such a belief might conceivably have originated? We have seen that Philo's references to the birth of Abel and Isaac and the others, when isolated from their context and taken literally, look very much as though they meant that those men were actually virgin-born. May there not then have been some persons, either in pre-Christian Judaism or in the Jewish Christian Church, who, misunderstanding such allegorical exegesis in that literal way, derived from these passages or from passages like them in other allegorical writers the notion that there had been, or at least might be, men born without human father by a creative act of God? May not, in other words, allegorical exegesis like the exegesis which is preserved for us in Philo have given to literally-minded men of Jewish race the idea of a virgin birth, which could then easily be applied to the Messiah?

This suggestion is opposed by the very great difference of atmosphere which separates Philo, on the one hand, from the New Testament infancy narratives, on the other. It would be difficult to imagine a greater contrast. That contrast is no doubt rooted in the difference which prevailed in general between Alexandria and Palestine—a difference which was well insisted upon by R. H. Charles in his controversy with Conybeare.[51] But it appears in a particularly acute form when we compare with Philo's writings and indeed with the other products of Alexandrian Judaism the Palestinian narratives that are contained in the first two chapters of Matthew and Luke. Are we to suppose that those narratives, with their simplicity and directness, have derived their most distinctive feature from a misunderstanding of an allegorical exegesis like that of Philo? The hypothesis certainly seems to be very unlikely.

[50] Clemen, *op. cit.*, 2te Aufl., 1924, p. 121. Against it, see I. Heinemann, "Die Lehre vom Heiligen Geist im Judentum und in den Evangelien", in *Monatsschrift für Geschichte und Wissenschaft des Judentums*, lxvi, 1922, pp. 272–279, especially p. 278.

[51] R. H. Charles, "The New Syriac Codex of the Gospels," in *Academy*, xlvi, 1894, pp. 556 f. Charles well speaks of "the gulf that divides Palestinian and Egyptian Judaism."

To avoid this difficulty we might try to find the basis for the New Testament story, not in a misunderstood allegorical exegesis of the passages concerning Abel and Isaac, but in the general notion, attested by Philo, that a man's soul is derived from God, while his body comes by the ordinary intercourse of the sexes. Such apparently was Conybeare's first suggestion about the matter.[52] The original purport of the story underlying the New Testament documents was, Conybeare supposed, "to represent Mary as owing the soul of the Messiah to the Holy Spirit, and His flesh to the natural human intercourse." Then there was foisted upon this original version of the story—so the hypothesis runs—the notion attested by Mt. i.19 f., that the activity of the Holy Spirit excludes the human fatherhood altogether.[53]

But surely this hypothesis hardly represents any improvement over that which we have just discussed. In the first place, it does not do justice to the New Testament narratives; for not merely the single passage, Mt. i.19 f., but the whole account of the annunciation and conception in Matthew and Luke really involves the exclusion of the human fatherhood. A reflection like that in Philo's "De Opificio Mundi," that the soul of *every* man comes from God really leads away from, and not toward, the New Testament narratives; for the point of the New Testament narratives is that there was something different in the birth of Jesus from that which is found in the birth of other men. In the second place, the hypothesis does not do away with the argument drawn from the difference of atmosphere that prevails between Philo and the New Testament. Even the underlying notion about the source of the soul of man as distinguished from the body is not—at least in the form in which it could become fruitful for the hypothesis, as distinguished from the form in which it had a true Old Testament basis—such that we should naturally attribute it to Palestinian Jews. Conybeare himself says that according to his hypothesis Mt. i.18-25 "must be explained by help of the Jewish theosophy current at the time." [54] Is it natural to find the basis of such a Palestinian narrative in "Jewish theosophy"? The question must certainly be answered in the negative. If, on the other hand, we reduce the supposed underlying notion about the source of the soul of man to such general terms that it could be found in the Old Testament and so on Palestinian soil, then the specific idea of the virgin birth is left altogether hanging in the air. We are therefore

[52] Conybeare, "The Newly Found Sinaitic Codex of the Gospels," in *Academy*, xlvi, 1894, pp. 400 f.

[53] Thus, according to Conybeare, "the Christian dogma is a materialisation of a philosophical myth found in Philo" ("The New Syriac Gospels," in *Academy*, xlvii, 1895, p. 58).

[54] Conybeare, "The Newly Found Sinaitic Codex of the Gospels," in *Academy*, xlvi, 1894, p. 401.

impaled upon the horns of a dilemma: either make the supposed underlying notion such that it could be derived from the Old Testament, in which case the origin of the idea of the virgin birth is left without explanation; or else put into the supposed underlying notion elements found in Philo's peculiar philosophic doctrines, in which case the presence of that underlying notion in Palestine and the influence of it in Matthew and Luke become improbable in the extreme.

Thus it cannot be said that Philo's treatment of the divine begetting of the human soul affords any plausible explanation of the New Testament doctrine of the virgin birth of Christ. Before we turn away from Philo, however, it is necessary to consider for a moment another suggestion which Conybeare made. This suggestion concerned not the divine begetting of human souls, but the divine begetting of the Logos. According to Philo, says Conybeare, the Logos was begotten by God and born of Sophia, "Wisdom," who was an "ever-virgin, gifted with an incontaminate and unstainable nature."[55] This birth of the Logos is spoken of, for example, in one passage as follows:[56]

> Accordingly we shall immediately say with justice that the One who has wrought this universe is both Fashioner and Father of that which has come into being; and we shall say that the mother is the Knowledge[57] of Him who has created it, with whom God having intercourse not after the manner of man sowed His creation. But she having received the seed of God brought forth with final birth-pangs the only and beloved visible son, this world.

In the light of such ideas, what could be more natural, says Conybeare, than that when Jesus was thought to be the Logos incarnate He, like the Logos, should be thought of as being born of a virgin mother?

One obvious objection to this hypothesis is that there is no trace of a Logos doctrine in the birth narratives of Matthew and Luke. Whether the Alexandrian Logos doctrine influenced any part of the New Testament is another question, with which we shall not now attempt to deal; but surely at any rate it did not influence the Palestinian narratives which mention the virgin birth of our Lord. Thus to derive the story of the virgin birth of Christ from speculations about the Logos is to relinquish all the advantages which belong to theories of Jewish origin as over against theories of pagan origin. We should at once have on our hands the question how such an obviously non-Palestinian notion came to be attested just in the most strikingly Pales-

55 Conybeare, "The New Syriac Codex of the Gospels," in *Academy*, xlvi, 1894, p. 535.

56 Philo, *de ebrietate*, 8, ed. Cohn et Wendland, ii, 1897, p. 176. Compare the translation by Conybeare, *op. cit.*, p. 534.

57 ἐπιστήμη, to be identified according to the context with Sophia, Wisdom.

tinian narratives in the whole New Testament. Conybeare says in commendation of his hypothesis:

> In the year of Rome 743 was born Jesus of Nazareth, a man in whom, because of his moral and thaumaturgic pre-eminence, his followers, so far as they were Aramaic-speaking Jews, quickly recognised their promised Messiah; while such of them as were Greek Jews and proselytes acclaimed in him the Divine Word, which, many times before in their history, had come down from heaven and assumed human form.[58]

The trouble is that the story of the virgin birth appears in the New Testament, despite the final Greek form of the story as we have it, in an underlying Aramaic-speaking, not Greek-speaking, environment.[59] But it is by no means merely a question of language. The whole spirit of Mt. i-ii, Lk. i-ii is as far as possible removed from the spirit of Philo. To find any influence of an Alexandrian Logos doctrine in these narratives is to do violence to any sound canons of literary and historical criticism.

This conclusion is amply confirmed when we examine the Philonic teaching in detail. Charles points out, in answer to Conybeare, that there are two representations of the Logos in Philo. According to one representation, which Charles calls Logos I, the Logos is the immanent reason of God; according to the other (Logos II), it is the material world. But it is only the Logos in the former sense that by any chance could be identified with the person, Jesus Christ; while it is only the Logos in the latter sense that is spoken of as having been begotten by God and born of the divine Wisdom.[60] Conybeare's answer apparently is that it is by a comparison of Logos I with Logos II on the part of the Christian teachers that the Christian Logos doctrine could come into being.[61] But surely that answer does not altogether remove the objection. The fact remains that when Philo speaks of the Logos or the "beloved son" of God as having been born of the virgin Wisdom, he is thinking not of a person, but of the material universe. It would be difficult to imagine any complex of ideas more utterly remote from what we find in the birth narratives in Matthew and Luke.

In much of what has just been said about Philo and the virgin birth we have really been anticipating the discussion in our next chapter, where we shall deal with the hypothesis of pagan, as distinguished from Jewish, origin of the virgin birth idea. Conybeare, for example, does not for a moment believe that

[58] Conybeare, *op. cit.*, p. 534.

[59] This point is well made by Charles ("The New Syriac Gospels," in *Academy*, xlvii, 1895, pp. 13 f.) in criticism of Conybeare. Conybeare's reply (*ibid.*, p. 58) is hardly satisfactory.

[60] Charles, "The New Syriac Gospels," in *Academy*, xlvii, 1895, p. 14.

[61] Conybeare, *ibid.*, p. 58.

the idea was originally Jewish: although he finds it attested in Jewish sources, he holds that ultimately it is a bit of "pagan folk-lore." [62] Certainly if any use is to be made, in this connection, of what is characteristic in Philo's teaching, the extra-Jewish origin of the idea will stand firm; for Philo's teaching is essentially derived from pagan sources—from Greek philosophy, and, as recent scholars are inclined to believe, from the popular mystical religion of the Hellenistic world. We shall have to return to Philo, therefore, when we come to deal with the theory of pagan derivation of the virgin birth idea. We shall then have to discuss the question whether Philo does or does not help us to reconstruct a type of pagan religion from which the Christian idea of the virgin birth of Christ may ultimately have come.

Here our interest in the great Alexandrian teacher has been of a more limited kind. Philo, after all, was a Jew; and when he speaks of the virgin birth of certain patriarchs or of the Logos, the question arises whether he attests the presence in pre-Christian Judaism of an idea which might have afforded the basis for our narratives in Matthew and Luke. The ultimate source of the idea is another question, with which we shall afterwards have to deal. Here we have considered merely the question whether, whatever its ultimate origin, the virgin birth idea is shown by the Philonic passages to have actually been found in Judaism, especially in Palestinian Judaism, at a time prior to that in which the New Testament story appeared.

That question we have answered with an emphatic negative. In the first place, Philo does not speak at all of a virgin birth of the Messiah, but only of a virgin birth of certain Old Testament characters. In the second place, when he speaks of a virgin birth of those Old Testament characters, he is not dealing with them at all as historical personages, as men of flesh and blood, but only with what they represent in his allegorical exegesis. There is not the slightest likelihood that either Philo himself or any Jews of his day believed that Isaac or any of the others of whom he speaks in this connection were born without human father. In the third place, there is no evidence whatever, and it is most improbable, that any Jews ever obtained from Philo's philosophical teaching about the human soul or about the origin of the universe the notion that the Messiah or any other man had been born or would be born of a virgin.

Thus Philo gives to those who derive the Christian story of the virgin birth of Christ from pre-Christian Jewish notions regarding the Messiah not the slightest real support. We are brought back to the main thread of our argument at exactly the point at which we left off. There is no indication in Philo, as there is no indication elsewhere, that in pre-Christian Judaism of the

[62] Conybeare, "'Virgo concipiet,'" in *Academy*, xlvii, 1895, p. 508.

period subsequent to the Old Testament there was any thought of a virgin birth of the Messiah.

To do justice to those who hold that the idea of the virgin birth was derived from really Jewish elements of thought, it should be remarked that they do not, so far as we have observed, often have recourse to the supposition that we have just been discussing: they do not usually seem to hold that the idea of the virgin birth had already existed in pre-Christian Judaism with reference to the Messiah; but they maintain rather that it was evolved with specific reference to Jesus by the Jewish Christian Church.[63] The existence of a pre-Christian Jewish doctrine of the virgin birth of the Messiah has been argued for the most part not by those who believe that the doctrine of the virgin birth was derived from Jewish elements of thought, but by a certain group among those who hold the doctrine to be of pagan origin—the group, namely, that regards the idea of the virgin birth as a pagan idea which entered into the Christian Church by means of a previous assimilation in Judaism. This latter theory will more conveniently be considered at a later point in our discussion. But of course if it could be shown that the idea of the virgin birth, whether its ultimate origin was Jewish or pagan, was actually found in pre-Christian Judaism, that fact would militate in favor of any theory of Jewish Christian derivation of the belief in the virgin birth of Jesus, including the theory of Keim and Lobstein and Harnack with which this chapter has to do. It is very important, therefore, to observe even at the present point in the discussion that there is not the slightest reason to suppose that there was ever in pre-Christian Judaism any expectation of the virgin birth of the Messiah. If the idea of the virgin birth emerged in the Jewish Christian Church, it did not emerge as an inheritance from Judaism, but must have been evolved by the Jewish Christian Church itself with specific reference to Jesus.

In particular, if Is. vii.14 was interpreted by the Jewish Christian Church as referring to the virgin birth, that interpretation, too, was an innovation over against pre-Christian Jewish exegesis. Is it likely that such an exegetical innovation should arise? Of course it could readily arise if Jesus was actually born of a virgin. But could it arise if that was not the case; and if it had arisen, could it have then produced the story of the virgin birth of Christ?

Such an hypothesis is certainly faced by objections of the most serious kind. Certain general objections have already been indicated in the former

[63] Harnack (*Neue Untersuchungen zur Apostelgeschichte*, 1911, p. 103; English translation, *The Date of the Acts and of the Synoptic Gospels*, 1911, pp. 147 f.) constitutes an exception. He regards it as "probable that brooding over the original text of Is. vii even in the pre-Christian period had brought many full-Jews to the opinion that the text was speaking of a virgin as mother of the Messiah."

part of the present chapter; the discovery of a virgin birth prophecy in Is. vii.14 would be faced, in Judaism, by the same obstacles as those which opposed the idea of a virgin birth in general. But there would also be special obstacles in the way of the supposed new interpretation of this verse.

One obvious objection, for example, is found in the language presumably used by those who originated the new interpretation. That language, on the theory of a Jewish Christian derivation of the idea of the virgin birth, was no doubt Aramaic, not Greek; and on the part of Aramaic-speaking Christians a knowledge of the Hebrew Old Testament may probably be assumed. But in the Hebrew original the interpretation of Is. vii.14 as referring to the virgin birth of the Messiah is by no means so obvious as it is in the Greek translation, where the word "virgin" is used. Few would be so bold as to maintain that the verse in the original ever could have given rise among Jewish Christians to the story of the virgin birth of Jesus. Certainly most advocates of the view with which we are now dealing cannot do so, since no doubt they share the common view that the Hebrew word *'almah* does not mean "virgin" at all. The theory, therefore, cannot possess even plausibility except on the basis of the Septuagint; it is the Greek translation alone which can be supposed to have led to the evolution of the virgin birth story as a fulfilment of the prophecy in Is. vii.14. But if that be true, what becomes of the Palestinian origin of the story, which seems to be demanded by the Palestinian character of the narratives in Lk. i-ii, Mt. i-ii? The chief advantage possessed by the theory of Jewish Christian origin of the idea of the virgin birth, as compared with other theories with which we shall presently deal, is that it does justice to the Palestinian style and content of the narratives in which in the New Testament the virgin birth is attested. But now that advantage seems to be lost by the necessity of supposing that the idea could have originated only on the basis of the Greek translation, as distinguished from the Hebrew original, of Is. vii.14.

Let it not be said that the origination of the idea of the virgin birth of Jesus might have been accomplished in Palestine and yet by Greek-speaking persons.[64] No doubt there were many such persons in Palestine; but the trouble is that the linguistic character of Lk. i-ii, Mt. i-ii seems to be strongly against the supposition that it was in those Greek-speaking circles that the idea of the virgin birth arose. Indeed, in Mt. i.21, immediately before the introduction of the virgin-prophecy from Isaiah, we have an interpretation of the name

[64] This suggestion is made by Harnack (*loc. cit.*), in addition to his suggestion, noted above, that even the original text of Is. vii.14 may have been interpreted by pre-Christian Jews to involve a virgin birth of the Messiah.

"Jesus" which is intelligible only on the basis of Hebrew.[65] But that detail only confirms the evidence of a Semitic background which is found in the whole character of the narratives. On the theory, then, that the virgin birth tradition arose out of a translation in the Septuagint at Is. vii.14, supposed to be contrary to the Hebrew original, we have upon our hands the immense difficulty of understanding how an idea which would have arisen only among those who spoke Greek should be attested just by the most markedly Semitic parts of the New Testament.

But even aside from this linguistic consideration, the whole notion that the doctrine of the virgin birth came from the desire to show a fulfilment of one Old Testament prophecy is very improbable. At this point we have the overwhelming support of recent investigators. If there is any one critical method that has fallen into disfavor in recent years, it is this method of deriving the supposed myths of the New Testament from Old Testament prophecy. That method was in full vogue in Strauss's first "Life of Jesus," which appeared in 1835. Even then, it is true, Strauss did not ignore the supposed pagan analogies for the virgin birth; but in addition to them he pointed with great insistence not only to Is. vii.14, but even to Ps. ii.7, and apparently found in those Old Testament passages the real propulsion toward the forming of the idea.[66] In his later work there is a striking change. The inadequacy of the prophetic passages in explaining the origin of the myth is now clearly recognized.[67] Thus even the most famous advocate of the theory by which New Testament stories are supposed to have been produced through a desire to show fulfilment of Old Testament prophecies felt compelled to modify very seriously his original attitude. Even more striking has been the change in the general trend of scholarship. It is now very generally held that the Old Testament prophecies quoted in the New Testament did not for the most part produce the New Testament stories, but on the contrary were brought in as supposed Scriptural confirmation for stories that had arisen in an entirely different way. First came the myths, it is held, and then the searching of Scriptures for all sorts of fanciful support of them. So it is thought to be in the case of the virgin birth. Is. vii.14 never in the world, it is said, would have been taken as a prophecy of the virgin birth of the Messiah unless the story of the virgin birth had been established already in the mind of the writer. The very fancifulness of Matthew's interpretation of the verse in

[65] "Thou shalt call his name Jesus: for he shall save his people from their sins."

[66] Strauss, *Leben Jesu*, 1835, pp. 173–180, especially pp. 176 f.

[67] Strauss, *Das Leben Jesu für das deutsche Volk bearbeitet*, 3te Aufl., 1874, pp. 349–351 (English translation, *The Life of Jesus for the People*, second edition, 1879, ii, pp. 41–44).

Isaiah shows, it is said, that the Old Testament passage never could have been the source of the story of which it is supposed to be a prophecy.[68]

Now for our part we do not think that Matthew's interpretation of Is. vii.14 is fanciful. On the contrary, for reasons partly set forth above, we hold that it is profoundly true. But although it is true, it is certainly not obvious. Here, as in many other cases, prophecy was not intended to permit the hearers to map out the course of future events, but on the contrary became fully intelligible only after the fulfilment had come. We can agree, therefore, *mutatis mutandis* with the argument that has just been set forth, the argument that has led to the practically universal rejection of the view that Is. vii.14 is the principal germ out of which the myth of the virgin birth arose.

With the rejection of that view about Is. vii.14 has gone the very general rejection of the whole Jewish Christian derivation of the idea of the virgin birth. It is admitted by the overwhelming majority of modern scholars that the myth of the virgin birth never arose in the Jewish Christian Church on the basis of purely Jewish ideas. The general opinion is voiced by Merx, when he says that the idea of the virgin birth is "as un-Jewish as possible."[69]

That general opinion, we are convinced, is correct so far as later Judaism is concerned. No doubt the Old Testament teaching is profoundly congruous with the virgin birth of Christ, but later Jewish thought was moving along entirely different lines. It is significant, as B. Weiss has remarked,[70] that the denials of the virgin birth which are attested in the early Church came just from men of Jewish race. There are, of course, those who will tell us that those denials by the "Ebionites" were based upon genuine historical tradition, but another hypothesis is vastly more probable. When one compares the negative attitude of the non-Christian Jews toward the preëxistence and virgin birth of the Messiah, as that attitude is attested by Justin Martyr's Dialogue, with the similar attitude of the Ebionites, one receives the irresistible impression that both the Ebionites and the non-Christian Jews are simply reflecting a profound antipathy of later Judaism to anything like the story that is found in Mt. i-ii, Lk. i-ii. No doubt, as in our first chapter we found reason to believe, many

[68] The prevailing attitude toward Is. vii.14 was expressed in typical form by Usener in 1889 (*Das Weihnachtsfest*, p. 75). "It would be," Usener said, "to turn the natural course of affairs around if we should regard this prophetic utterance as the occasion and point of departure for the formation of the legend: rather was it the seal which was impressed upon the finished material."

[69] "So unjüdisch als möglich"—Merx, *Die vier kanonischen Evangelien*, II. i, 1902, p. ix.

[70] B. Weiss, *Leben Jesu*, 4te Aufl., 1902, i, p. 210 (English translation, *The Life of Christ*, 1883, i, p. 229).

men of Jewish race overcame that antipathy, and became not Ebionites, but in the full sense Christians. But that some should have stuck in the halfway position of the Ebionites does provide one more indication, in addition to many others, that the Judaism of the early Christian era was a soil in which a myth of a virgin birth would be as unlikely as possible to spring up.

Chapter XIV

THE THEORY OF PAGAN DERIVATION

IT HAS been shown in the last chapter that the theory of Jewish derivation of the idea of the virgin birth has been rejected by the great majority of contemporary scholars and that such rejection is well grounded. If, therefore, the factual basis of the idea is still to be thought inadmissible, some other theory of origin is to be sought.

Before we examine the theory that is dominant at the present time, it will be advisable to consider briefly one possibility that has perhaps not received quite the amount of attention that it deserves. That possibility was suggested especially by Kattenbusch in 1900,[1] after some anticipation by Pfleiderer in 1887.[2] The idea of the virgin birth, Kattenbusch suggested, may have been developed within the early Church on the basis of Pauline teaching. Thus the idea would not be strictly Jewish Christian, and yet to account for it we should not have to have recourse to the pagan world. In the development of the account of Jesus' birth which we have in the first two chapters of Matthew and Luke, two stages, according to Kattenbusch, are to be distinguished. In the former stage came the idea of conception by the Holy Spirit; in the second stage the idea of the virgin birth. The former idea, which is the dominant one in the Lucan narrative,[3] might well have been suggested, Kattenbusch thinks, by the Pauline intimation that the Spirit was active in the entrance of Jesus into the flesh; the latter idea, the idea of the virgin birth, was fostered by Paul's doctrine of Christ as the second Adam, had its final form imparted to it by the prophecy in Is. vii.14, and then was important in making acceptable the Pauline doctrine of the preëxistence of Christ.

This theory is interesting in various ways. In the attention which it gives to the positive side of the New Testament representation of the birth of Jesus, as over against the negative side—that is, the activity of the Holy Spirit in the

[1] Kattenbusch, *Das Apostolische Symbol*, ii, 1900, pp. 620–624. Compare his later article in *Theologische Studien und Kritiken*, cii, 1930, pp. 462–474. See above, pp. viii f.

[2] Pfleiderer, *Das Urchristenthum*, 1te Aufl., 1887, pp. 419 f. Afterwards Pfleiderer modified his view. See "The New Testament Account of the Birth of Jesus," first article, in *Princeton Theological Review*, iii, 1905, p. 648 (with footnote 1); second article, *ibid.*, iv, 1906, pp. 69 f.

[3] Indeed, Kattenbusch's treatment suggested, though it did not quite expressly propose, the theory that the other idea, the idea of the virgin birth, came into the Lucan narrative only by the interpolation of the four words, ἐπεὶ ἄνδρα οὐ γινώσκω, in Lk. i.34. See above, pp. viii f., 156 f.

supernatural conception as over against the exclusion of the human father—it is anticipatory of the most recent elaborate theory as to the origin of the virgin birth tradition.[4] In its insistence upon the connection that exists between Pauline teaching and the doctrine of the virgin birth it displays a genuine insight that contrasts very favorably with some modern treatments of the subject. Particularly refreshing is its rediscovery of the close connection between the doctrine of the virgin birth and the doctrine of the preëxistence of Christ. That connection unquestionably exists;[5] and we have never been able to understand how the two doctrines ever could have come to be regarded, as they certainly are in much modern discussion, as standing in any relation of antinomy or contradiction. It is certainly true that if a man is convinced that Jesus of Nazareth existed before He came to this earth, he is facing a serious difficulty if he holds Jesus to have been by ordinary generation the child of Joseph and Mary. It is difficult to believe that a voluntary entrance of a heavenly being into this world could have been accomplished without a break in the ordinary process of the propagation of the human race. There is a profound connection also, as Kattenbusch observes, between the Pauline doctrine of the second Adam and the story of the virgin birth. The doctrine of the second Adam represents Jesus as a new beginning in humanity, just as He is represented when He is said in the Gospels of Matthew and Luke to have been conceived by the Holy Ghost.

But here again it is one thing to recognize the connection between two ideas when both are given, and quite a different thing to evolve one of them from the other. Could the story of the virgin birth ever have been evolved from the elements of Pauline teaching to which reference has just been made? That story is a very concrete thing; its details hardly look as though they were arrived at merely by reflection upon the activity of the Spirit in connection with the human life of Jesus or upon Christ as the second Adam. Indeed, it would be more plausible, if the choice had to be made, to suppose that the designation of Christ as the second Adam grew out of the fact of the virgin birth than that the story of the virgin birth grew out of that designation. Even to one who held the Pauline view of Christ, the evolution of so concrete a representation as that which appears in Matthew and Luke would be anything but a matter of course.

To support the theory at this point, therefore, Kattenbusch is obliged to call in the assistance of Is. vii.14. That verse, he supposes, provided for the

[4] Leisegang, *Pneuma Hagion*, 1922, pp. 14-72. See below, pp. 363-379.

[5] It appears clearly at such an early time as the middle of the second century, when, in Justin Martyr's Dialogue with Trypho, the virgin birth and the preëxistence of Christ are linked together as the things that are attacked by Trypho and defended by Justin.

early Church the solution of the problem which was presented by the Pauline teaching about Christ. Thus although Kattenbusch begins by saying that Is. vii.14 was not the source of the virgin birth story, he is obliged in the end to have recourse to that verse. Such recourse is forbidden by the considerations which we have already adduced.

The suggestion of Kattenbusch, interesting and suggestive though it is, has not, so far as we have observed, obtained any considerable support. It is time, therefore, to consider what has become the dominant theory as to the origin of the idea of the virgin birth. That theory is the theory of pagan derivation. The doctrine of the virgin birth of Christ, according to the overwhelming majority of those who today deny the factual basis of it, did not come from Jewish or purely Christian elements of thought, but it came from pagan ideas.

This theory of pagan derivation has appeared in many forms. But before the individual forms are considered in detail, it should be observed that two objections would seem to face all of them alike.

The first objection is found in the separation between the early Christian Church and the paganism that surrounded it in the Græco-Roman world. That separation was maintained by Gentile Christianity as well as by Jewish Christianity. The converts from paganism, as Paul says in the First Epistle to the Thessalonians, "turned to God from idols, to serve the living and true God."[6] Would those converts so readily have turned back again just to the most degrading features of that polytheism which their conversion caused them to detest? We say "the most degrading features" advisedly, since exactly so are to be characterized those elements in pagan mythology which modern scholars have brought into parallel with the virgin birth. Would the pagan converts have returned so readily to the pit from which they had been digged?

We are well aware of the fact that in the apostolic age a great battle had to be fought against the paganism which in subtle ways sought to merge the life of the first Gentile Christian churches with the life of the world. The First Epistle to the Corinthians, in particular, attests the seriousness of that battle. The Corinthian converts were tempted to fall back not merely into pagan habits of life, but also into pagan ways of thinking; they were tempted, for example, to sublimate the Christian doctrine of the resurrection of the body into the pagan doctrine of the immortality of the soul. At many points, the apostle Paul had a battle on his hands against the paganism which was seeking to obtain a foothold within the Church.

[6] 1 Thess. i.9.

Yet there are evidences that that battle was fought through to victory and that paganism was actually prevented from obtaining any firm foothold in the Church. Moreover, even when the battle was sorest, even when paganism threatened to engulf the little groups of converts that had recently turned to Christ, it does not seem to have been the polytheistic forms of paganism that exerted the really dangerous appeal. In Corinth, for example, the dangerous thing was the Greek pride of intellect and the subtle attraction of a philosophy falsely so called. So far as we can see, there was no tendency at all for the converts to return to the worship of many gods; polytheism did not at all constitute the serious menace against which the apostle Paul had to contend. There may have been differences of opinion as to what was demanded, in the complex life of that day, by the new allegiance to the one Lord and the one God: could the converts conscientiously buy in the markets meat that had been technically offered to idols; could they accept meat when they were guests at the house of a friend; could they accept invitations to dinner when those invitations were technically in the house of some heathen god? No doubt serious dangers lurked beneath such questions; compromise of principle, or even of what is falsely regarded as principle, is always dangerous to the Christian life. But the dangers did not spring from any theoretical friendliness to polytheism. There might be differences of opinion as to the practical consequences of the opposition to polytheism; even Paul himself, it must be remembered, advised that when a Christian was a guest in an unbeliever's house he should eat the meat that was offered to him without asking whether it had been offered to idols or not. Certainly such problems were very perplexing indeed. But whatever differences of opinion there may have been about the practical consequences of opposition to polytheism, about the necessity of that opposition itself there was no doubt. Indeed, what was most obviously distinctive, perhaps, in the Gentile Christian Churches was the monotheism of the converts, which contrasted in the most striking way with the boundless syncretism and tolerance of the surrounding world.[7]

Could such churches have fallen so readily a prey to influences from just the most degrading features in polytheistic mythology, as we are required to believe by the theory of pagan origin of the idea of the virgin birth of Christ? And could this influence not merely have made itself felt here and there among the rank and file, but even have celebrated its triumph

[7] On the interesting but mistaken attempt of McGiffert (*The God of the Early Christians*, 1924) to represent the early Gentile converts as being devoted to Jesus as Saviour without being expressly devoted to monotheism or concerned to deny the existence of other gods, see the dis cussion by the present writer in *What Is Faith*, 1925, pp. 54–66, and the more extended discussion in *Princeton Theological Review*, xxii, 1924, pp. 544–588.

by inclusion in the Gospels of Matthew and Luke and in the fourfold Gospel canon? Could it, at the time and in the manner which we know must have been the case, have attained universal acceptance in the early Catholic Church and inclusion in the Apostles' Creed? These questions are deserving of much more careful attention than they have usually received from advocates of the theory of pagan origin of the idea of the virgin birth of Christ. In a later period, when the Church had obtained possession of the throne of the Cæsars, no doubt pagan influences came in like a flood; no doubt the saints became in many places the successors of the heathen gods. But against such influences in the early period, the opinion which Harnack, for example, enunciated in 1889 [8] is still worthy of the most careful consideration.

Such considerations are, indeed, quite contrary to what has come to be the dominant trend in the treatment of the early history of the Christian Church by those who deny the historicity of miracles. That dominant trend is represented by the school of comparative religion, which regards Christianity as being from the beginning a syncretistic religion and finds pagan influences even at the very centre of the teaching of Paul. But because a contention is fashionable, it does not follow that it is true; and the contention of the school of comparative religion is faced by objections of the most serious kind. These objections cannot, of course, be set forth here.[9] All that we can do now is to remark that the theory of pagan origin of the virgin birth story involves the entrance of just that particular kind of pagan influence which would be least likely to make itself felt; it involves the influence of pagan mythology in its most degrading features. Are we to suppose that despite the horror of polytheism, which was undoubtedly felt by the Church in the first century, the Church yet opened its doors, not merely to other pagan beliefs, but also to just the most crassly polytheistic elements in the myths of the heathen gods? We do not think that this question can be waved lightly aside.

Thus one barrier which would be interposed against reception of pagan influences in the story of the birth of Jesus is found in the separation of the early Christian Church in general from the pagan world. Another barrier is found in the clearly Palestinian character of the New Testament narratives in which the story of the virgin birth is told. Whatever may be thought of the hospitality of the Gentile Church to pagan ideas, are we really to suppose that pagan ideas found a place just in the most clearly Jewish and

[8] Harnack, review of Usener, *Das Weihnachtsfest*, in *Theologische Literaturzeitung*, xiv, 1889, col. 205.

[9] Some of the objections have been set forth by the present writer in *The Origin of Paul's Religion*, 1921, pp. 211–317.

Palestinian narratives in the whole New Testament? Are we to suppose that the authors of the narratives in Mt. i-ii, Lk. i-ii, with their high monotheism and their Old Testament piety, actually gave a place to an idea derived from the most degrading parts of pagan mythology? Surely there is an immense incongruity between the whole atmosphere of these narratives and the pagan ideas which are supposed by the theory now under discussion to have formed the basis for the doctrine of the virgin birth. How can this incongruity be explained?

One effort to explain it is found, as we observed, in the interpolation theory with regard to Lk. i.34, 35. The Lucan infancy narrative, it is said, is indeed Palestinian; but the pagan idea of the virgin birth got into it by interpolation. It is no wonder, according to this theory, that there is an incongruity between the pagan influence with regard to the virgin birth and the Jewish character of the rest of the narrative; for the verses in which the virgin birth is recorded were no part of the narrative as it was originally composed.

But this interpolation theory, as was set forth in Chapter VI, can be refuted in the most overwhelmingly decisive way; it can be shown clearly that the verses attesting the virgin birth in Lk. i-ii are no later addition, but belong to the fundamental structure of the narrative. The initial problem, then, remains, not only with regard to Matthew but also with regard to Luke. How did a crassly pagan and polytheistic idea ever find a place, not merely in Gentile Christian documents but in the most strikingly Jewish and Palestinian narratives in the whole New Testament?

A new solution of this problem has been coming increasingly into vogue within recent years. The interpolation theory, it is usually admitted by the advocates of this new solution, must be abandoned;[10] the verses attesting the virgin birth are an integral part of the Lucan narrative, to say nothing of the narrative in Matthew. How, then, could the pagan idea of the virgin birth have found a place in these distinctly Jewish narratives? The answer which these recent scholars propose is that the idea was already naturalized in pre-Christian Judaism and so could appear in Mt. i-ii and Lk. i-ii as a Jewish idea, although ultimately it was of pagan origin; back of the Jewish Christian belief in the virgin birth of Jesus lies a pre-Christian Jewish expectation of a virgin birth of the Messiah.[11]

[10] Cheyne (*Bible Problems*, 1904, pp. 91, 244 f.) is an exception. He regards Lk. i.34 f. as a later insertion.

[11] This hypothesis was brought into prominence especially by Gunkel (*Zum religionsgeschichtlichen Verständnis des Neuen Testaments*, 1903, pp. 65–70) and Cheyne (*op. cit.*, 1904, pp. 65–100) who, however, were anticipated by F. C. Conybeare (see especially *Academy*, xlvii, 1895, p. 508). The hypothesis has subsequently been favored by Gressmann, Petersen, and others.

But what evidence is there of the existence of such a Jewish expectation? What evidence is there that pre-Christian Jews ever supposed that the Messiah would be born without human father? The Rabbinical passages sometimes supposed to attest such an expectation are, it is generally admitted, without value. If any pre-Christian attestation is to be found at all, it can only be found in the Septuagint translation of Is. vii.14. In translating *'almah* by "virgin," does not the Septuagint attest a Jewish belief that the "Immanuel" of the Isaiah passage was to be identified with the Messiah and that the mother of the Messiah was to be a virgin? We have already observed in the last chapter how extremely precarious such a view is, and how precarious also is the view that certain passages in Philo attest a Palestinian belief in the virgin birth of Old Testament characters such as Isaac. Certainly all that we know of pre-Christian Judaism is distinctly unfavorable to the view that it cherished an expectation of the virgin birth of the Messiah.

If, therefore, the existence of such an expectation is still to be established, that must be done not on the basis of positive evidence, but simply in the interests of a theory as to the pagan derivation of the Christian doctrine of the virgin birth. It is impossible to see how a pagan idea could have crept into Jewish Christian narratives unless it had already had a place in pre-Christian Judaism; therefore we must assume, despite the absence of direct evidence, that it had such a place—such is the reasoning. No doubt it may seem convincing to those who are already convinced that the idea of the virgin birth is a pagan idea; but by those who do not share that conviction the reasoning will be regarded as dubious in the extreme. Certainly the necessity of supposing without any positive evidence, and even in sharp contradiction to all the indications that we possess, that a belief in the virgin birth of the Messiah was present in pre-Christian Judaism hangs as a dead weight upon the most recent theories of pagan origin of the virgin birth doctrine as it appears in the New Testament books.

Yet that weight can be shaken off only by a return to the interpolation theory; and such a return is precluded by considerations of the most decisive kind. Thus the advocates of a pagan origin of the virgin birth idea are shut up to two equally unsatisfactory alternatives. In order to explain the presence, in the most strikingly Jewish Christian narrative in the New Testament, of what on their hypothesis is a pagan idea, they must suppose either (1) that the words attesting the pagan idea have crept into the Jewish Christian narrative by interpolation, or else (2) that the pagan idea was already so completely naturalized in pre-Christian Judaism that in the first century it could form an integral part even of a Palestinian narrative. The former of these two alternatives has been adopted particularly by those who look to Greek mythology for the source of the virgin birth doctrine; the latter, by those who look rather to the East. But both alternatives are faced by objections of the most serious kind. It would perhaps be fruitless to debate the question which of them is the least unlikely.

When, therefore, we consider the supposed pagan parallels, we do so only for the sake of the argument. Those parallels might be vastly closer than they actually are without at all justifying the view that in them the origin of the Christian doctrine of the virgin birth is to be found. There would still remain the powerful objection that, whatever may be said of the early Church in general, Jewish Christian narratives like Lk. i-ii could hardly have given a place to a crassly pagan idea. Unless this objection is overcome, an immense burden of proof rests upon the theory of pagan derivation. Are the pagan parallels really so close that this burden of proof can be overcome? That is the question with which we must now undertake to deal.

The simplest form in which the theory of pagan derivation has been held is that the doctrine of the virgin birth of Christ was evolved on Gentile Christian ground under the influence of Greek stories of heroes who were begotten by the gods.[12] In the earliest years of the Christian Church—so the theory runs—Jesus was called "Son of God." This title in the Jewish Christian Church was of course as far as possible from excluding a human father or involving a special physical derivation from God; the Jewish Christians used the term, no doubt, in a sense analogous to its Old Testament usage by which it could be a title of the Messiah, or they used it to designate that warm filial relationship of a moral kind in which Jesus felt Himself to stand toward God. But when the Gentile Christians, as distinguished from the Jewish Christians, heard this title applied to Jesus in the instruction that they received in their new faith, they would naurally interpret it in accordance with their previous habits of thought. Those previous habits of thought of the Gentile Christians attributed a very different sense to the title, "Son of God," from that which was attributed to it in Judaism; the Gentile Christians found implied in the title an actual physical sonship analogous to the relation of a man to his human father. Zeus, according to the previous beliefs of these Gentile converts, was father of gods and men; and both he and other gods are represented as begetting children by human mothers. Similar stories were current with regard to the birth of great men of historic times; Alexander, Plato, Augustus, and

[12] This theory was presented in classic form by Usener (whose *Weihnachtsfest* appeared, in its first edition, in 1889), though of course the theory is far from having been originated by him. It has subsequently been supported, in varying forms, by a large number of recent scholars, particularly by Eduard Meyer (*Ursprung und Anfänge des Christentums*, i, 1921, pp. 54-57).

others were regarded as having been begotten by gods. These great men were "sons of gods." Could Jesus, in the mind of the Gentile converts, be less than they? And if they were sons of pagan gods, must not Jesus, in somewhat similar fashion, be the Son of the one true God in whom these converts had at their conversion come to believe?

In considering this hypothesis, it will hardly be necessary to examine the individual stories in any great detail; for they have often been collected and are well known. Some of the collections must indeed be sifted before they can be of use for the present purpose. Thus when Petersen [13] includes in his list of sons of gods in Greek mythology heroes who were born of divine mothers as well as begotten by divine fathers, he is obviously going far afield. Obviously the only stories which by any chance can be brought into comparison with the virgin birth of Christ are the stories that tell of the union of a divine father with a human mother. But even such stories are not wanting. We may think, for example, of Perseus, whose mother Danaë was beloved of Zeus and conceived by means of a rain of gold which descended upon her in her seclusion; or of Hercules, who also was the child of Zeus and of a mortal woman.

Much more stress is usually laid, however, upon the stories that relate not to demigods of mythical antiquity, but to historical personages. Most interesting of these, perhaps, is the one regarding Plato. This story is reported by Diogenes Laertius, who flourished probably in the third century after Christ, as follows:

> Speusippus, Plato's nephew, in his work called *Plato's Funeral Feast,* and Clearchus in the *Encomium on Plato,* and Anaxilaïdes in the second book of his work *On Philosophy,* say that there was a report at Athens to the effect that Ariston [Plato's father] sought to have union with Perictione [Plato's mother], who was then of marriageable age, and did not attain his end; and that when he ceased from his violence he saw the appearance of Apollo; wherefore he kept her pure from marriage until she brought forth her child.[14]

The same story is mentioned by Origen [15] and by certain other writers.[16] A somewhat similar story is reported by Plutarch regarding Alexander the Great: [17]

> It seemed to the bride [Olympias, Alexander's mother], before the night when her marriage with Philip was consummated, that there was a clap of thunder, that a

[13] *Die wunderbare Geburt des Heilandes*, 1909, pp. 34–36.

[14] Diogenes Laertius, iii.2. Compare the translation by R. D. Hicks in "Diogenes Laertius," i, 1925, p. 277, in the *Loeb Classical Library*. The Greek text also is found in that edition.

[15] *Contra Celsum*, i. 37.

[16] See Usener, *Das Weihnachtsfest*, 2te Aufl., 1911, pp. 72 f.

[17] *Vit. Alex.*, ii.2–4.

bolt fell upon her womb, and that from the stroke a great fire was kindled, and then, breaking out in all directions into sparks, was quenched; then later, after the marriage, Philip saw himself in a dream placing a seal over his wife's womb; and the carving of the seal, as he thought, had the figure of a lion; and when the other seers viewed the vision with suspicion, as meaning that Philip should keep careful watch over things concerning his marriage, Aristander of Telmessus said that the woman was with child (since nothing that was empty required a seal) and that she would bring forth a son who would be high-spirited and like a lion in his nature. And on one occasion there appeared also a serpent stretched out beside Olympias' body as she slept, and they say this especially dulled the love of Philip and his ardor so that he did not thereafter often approach her—either because he feared certain sorceries that might be practised upon him, or because he avoided her on the ground that she belonged to one greater than he.[18]

There was also a report, Plutarch says, which attributed Philip's loss of one of his eyes to his having applied it to the crack of the door when the god was with his wife. Olympias, according to Eratosthenes (reported by Plutarch) told Alexander the secret of his birth when he was going forth to his campaign, and bade him show a spirit worthy of such an origin. But according to another report, Olympias rejected the story and said, "Will not Alexander cease slandering me to Hera?"[19]

The prevalence of such stories of the love of gods for mortal women is attested sometimes in indirect ways. Thus, after the adultery of Alcibiades with the wife of Agis king of Sparta, the king is said to have given credence to the report, because, having been frightened by an earthquake, he had rushed out of his wife's chamber and had avoided her for ten months, after which he declared that the child Leotychides was not his son.[20] After citation of this story Usener[21] calls attention to the poetic phrases in which a lover speaks of his beloved as worthy of the love of Jupiter, and also to the report of Seneca that in the days of Nero women sat in the Capitol at Rome, hoping to be loved by Jupiter, and were not even deterred by the fear of Juno's wrath.[22] More specific is the scandalous story[23] of Paulina, reported by Josephus.[24] In the time of Tiberius, says Josephus, a noble Roman lady, Paulina, wife of Saturninus, was beloved by Decius Mundus. Being unable to secure his end by

[18] Some use has been made, here and in the following quotations, of the translation by Bernadotte Perrin, "Plutarch's Lives," vii, 1919, in the *Loeb Classical Library*. The Greek text also is found in that edition.

[19] Plutarch, *vit. Alex.*, iii. 2.

[20] Plutarch, *vit. Alc.*, xxiii. 8.

[21] *Op. cit.*, pp. 26 f.

[22] Seneca, quoted by Augustine, *de civ. dei*, vi.10, ed. Hoffmann, 1899, i, p. 296. See Usener, *op. cit.*, p. 77.

[23] Also referred to by Usener, *loc. cit.*

[24] *Antiq. Jud.*, XVIII. iii.4 (ed. Niese, 1890, iv, pp. 152–155).

the ordinary processes of corruption, Mundus had recourse to the priests of Isis. They, induced by bribery, told Paulina that she was beloved by the god Anubis, who invited her to come to him. The credulous Paulina reported the story to her husband, who consented that she should share the god's "bed and board." [25] The husband, in other words, knowing his wife's reputation for chastity, readily consented that she should spend a night in the temple. This she did; and there she was deceived by the lover, Mundus, who pretended to be the god. After the event, Paulina boasted openly of the favor which the god had shown her, until she was undeceived by Mundus, who divulged to her the true fact.

Such a story, it is said, when taken with other indications, shows the wide credence which was given, even in the upper classes of society, to the stories of the union of mortal women with gods. May we not, then, have in such stories the origin of the Christian story of the virgin birth of Christ?

A favorable presumption in behalf of this hypothesis may at first sight seem to be created by the fact that the pagan stories are brought into connection with the New Testament stories by certain early Christian writers. Thus Justin Martyr, in the middle of the second century, commends the Christian story of the virgin birth of Christ to his pagan readers by pointing out the analogy in which it stands to the story of the birth of Perseus. "And if also we hold," Justin says, "that He was born through a virgin, let this also be something that He has in common with Perseus." [26] In Justin's Dialogue with Trypho, the pagan stories are introduced in a somewhat different way. Trypho, the Jew, is represented as making their similarity to the Christian story of the virgin birth of Christ a ground of objection to the latter:

> And in the myths of those who are called Greeks it is said that Perseus was born of Danaë, who was a virgin, the one who is called among them Zeus having come upon her in a golden flood; [27] and you, when you say the same things as they, ought to be ashamed, and ought rather to say that this Jesus was born as a man from men; and if you show from the Scriptures that he is the Christ, you ought to say that he was counted worthy of being chosen to be Christ because of his lawful and perfect life, instead of daring to tell stories of portents, in order that you may not be convicted of folly like that of the Greeks.[28]

To this attack Justin Martyr replies by developing the theory that the similarities which the heathen myths exhibit as over against the Old Testament prophecies about Christ are due to imitation of the prophecies induced in the

[25] *δεῖπνον . . . καὶ εὐνήν.*
[26] Justin Martyr, *apol.*, i. 22 (ed. Goodspeed, *Die ältesten Apologeten*, 1914, p. 41).
[27] *ἐν χρυσοῦ μορφῇ ῥεύσαντος ἐπ' αὐτήν.*
[28] Justin Martyr, *dial.*, 67 (ed. Goodspeed, 1914, p. 174).

authors of the myths by Satan and the evil spirits. In a list of such imitations,[29] Justin includes the birth of Dionysus from Zeus and Semele, and the birth of Hercules from Zeus and Alcmene; and finally, at the end of the passage, he refers to the birth of Perseus:

> And whenever I hear, O Trypho, I said, that Perseus was born of a virgin, this also I understand to have been due to imitation on the part of the deceiving Serpent.

A similar treatment of the heathen myths appears in Origen's treatise against Celsus. There is no reason, Origen says, why the Greeks should regard the virgin birth of Christ as unbelievable; for something analogous appears even among the lower animals; and by the Greeks themselves not all men were regarded as having been born of both man and woman. The basic passage may well be quoted in full:

> Furthermore, it should be said to the Greeks who disbelieve in the birth of Jesus from a virgin that the Creator, in the origin of the various kinds of animals, showed that it was possible for Him, if He desired, to do what He did in the case of one animal also in the case of the others and even in the case of men. For there are found certain female animals that do not have union with males, as writers on natural history say is the case with vultures; this animal preserves the continuity of its kind without the union of the sexes. What, then, is there strange, if when God wished to send a divine teacher to the race of men He caused Him to come into the world in another manner than that in which other men come, who are born by the union of men with women? [30] And according to the Greeks themselves not all men are born of man and woman. For if the world had a beginning, as many of the Greeks have supposed, it follows of necessity that the first men were produced not by the union of the sexes but from the earth, their spermatic elements being found there [31]—which I think is harder to believe [32] than the birth of Jesus which was half like that of other men. And there is nothing unreasonable about using Greek stories in arguing with Greeks, in order that we may not be thought to be the only ones who narrate this strange story. For some have chosen, not in connection with stories of remote antiquity about the heroes, but in connection with things that have happened in our own times, to write (for example) that even Plato was born of Amphictione, Ariston being prevented from approaching her until she should bring forth the one who was begotten by Apollo. But these things are really myths; the authors of them were moved to invent some such thing concerning a man whom they supposed to have greater wisdom and power than the generality of mankind and so supposed to have received from greater

[29] Justin Martyr, *op. cit.*, 69–70 (ed. Goodspeed, 1914, pp. 178–181).

[30] For the translation at this point, compare Koetschau, *Des Origenes ausgewählte Schriften*, ii, 1926, p. 51; and Crombie, "The Writings of Origen" (in *Ante-Nicene Christian Library*, x), i, 1869, p. 437.

[31] Compare Crombie, *loc. cit.*

[32] *παραδοξότερον*.

and more divine seed the beginning of the formation of his body—this being thought fitting for those who surpassed human standards. But since Celsus has introduced his Jew arguing with Jesus, and bringing forth in the course of his attack upon what he regards as Jesus' merely pretended virgin birth the Greek myths concerning Danaë and Melanippe and Auge and Antiope, it should be said that these words are worthy of a buffoon and not of one who is writing in a serious tone.[33]

The last part of this passage is regarded by Usener as particularly instructive. The authors of the stories about Plato and others reasoned, according to Origen, that a man who stood above the generality of men must have had something more than a purely human birth. Quite so, says Usener in effect; and so it was also in the case of Jesus. Of course, Origen says that the Greek stories are merely myths whereas the story about Jesus is true. But those who believed the Greek stories and disbelieved the story about Jesus would, it is argued, reverse this judgment; and in reality the origin of the stories is in both cases, we are told, the same. Superhuman achievement or character demands as its explanation superhuman birth—there we have, according to the advocates of the theory now under discussion, the hidden impulse for the formation of the virgin birth story as it appears in Matthew and Luke. A flood of light is thought to be cast upon that hidden impulse by the naïve words of Origen in his effort to defend the Christian doctrine against pagan attack.

But are not all the passages that we have cited from Justin Martyr as well as from Origen similarly instructive in the present connection? Is it not highly significant that these early Christian writers, instead of pointing out dissimilarity between the virgin birth story and these pagan myths, insist upon the similarity and make use of it in their argument against pagan opponents? Is it not significant that when the argument is turned against them by Jewish, as distinguished from pagan, opponents—when the similarity to pagan myths is made the basis of Jewish attack—the Christian writers meet the attack by the desperate expedient of attributing the pagan myths to demoniac imitation of the Old Testament prophecies concerning the virgin birth of the Messiah? Can modern writers be blamed for detecting an analogy which was also detected by early Christian writers who stood in close contact with both sides of the comparison, Christian writers who on the one hand lived at a time not so very remote from the time when the story of the virgin birth of Christ first appeared and on the other hand were familiar with circles where the stories about Plato and other heroes were still narrated and where the current of thought that produced the stories was still alive?

[33] Origen, *contr. Cels.*, i. 37 (ed. Koetschau, i, 1899, pp. 88 f.). The happy translation of the last phrase is that of Crombie (*op. cit.*, i, 1869, p. 438), who has also been consulted elsewhere.

This argument may seem plausible at first sight. But it will not stand the test of a closer examination. We should never forget that the appeal of Justin Martyr and Origen to the pagan stories of divine begetting is an *argumentum ad hominem*. "*You* hold," Justin and Origen say in effect to their pagan opponents, "that the virgin birth of Christ is unbelievable; well, is it any more unbelievable than the stories that you yourselves believe?"

Now we are perfectly ready to admit that the *argumentum ad hominem* is at times a very dangerous thing; we are perfectly ready in the present case, with regard to Origen's appeal to Plato—and to the vultures—to quote, as van Oosterzee [34] does in a similar connection, the line:

nec tali auxilio, nec defensoribus istis.

But however dangerous it may be, the *argumentum ad hominem* of Justin and Origen was very natural under the circumstances, and is far from justifying the consequences that have been deduced from it by modern writers.

In the first place, the closeness of Justin and Origen to the time when, at the latest, the story of the virgin birth of Christ must have arisen, should not be exaggerated. We have seen that that story was certainly, to say the least, in existence before the end of the first century, and by any sound process of literary criticism must be dated many decades before that time. Justin Martyr, on the other hand, lived in the middle of the second century, and Origen in the early half of the third.

But what is far more important than this merely temporal remoteness is the spiritual remoteness of these writers from the authors of the New Testament birth narrative. Between that narrative, indeed between the New Testament in general, on the one hand, and Justin Martyr on the other, a very important change has taken place. The period of origination has passed, and the period of conscious and systematic defence has set in.

At this point, indeed, we desire not to be misunderstood. There is certainly defence of Christianity in the New Testament; the New Testament gives no color of support to the feeble modern notion that preaching should be positive but never negative, or that the Christian preacher can dispense with an answer to the intellectual objections that arise against the Christian faith. The Epistles of Paul are certainly full of argument; and argument is also found in the teaching, and even the admittedly authentic teaching, of our Lord. "If God so clothe the grass of the field, which to day is, and to morrow is cast into the oven, shall he not much more clothe you, O ye of little faith?" "If ye then, being evil, know how to give good gifts unto your children, how

[34] *Disputatio theologica de Jesu, e virgine Maria nato*, 1840, p. 16.

much more shall your Father which is in heaven give good things to them that ask him?" These familiar passages, and others like them in the teaching of Jesus, consist of argument. Nor is there lacking argument of a distinctly polemic kind. "If Satan cast out Satan, he is divided against himself; how shall then his kingdom stand?" Here we have a truly argumentative way of meeting attack. Let not that fact seem to the simple Christian to be derogatory to the dignity of our Lord. It involves, no doubt, a marvellous condescension; He who was endued with all authority in heaven and on earth consents actually to *reason* with the children of men. But such condescension is no mark of weakness, but rather a supreme manifestation of glory. There can be without argument no clear, and no reasonable, presentation of a message. And the presentation of the Christian message in the whole New Testament is profoundly reasonable. We do not mean that the content of the message can be deduced by human reasoning from the observed facts in nature; at the centre the message is sheer revelation from God. But though the content of the revelation cannot be deduced by human reasoning, the credentials of the revelation become clear to a human reason that has been freed from the blinding effect of sin. And even the content of the revelation, though it cannot be deduced by reason, can be shown, and should be shown, not to be contrary to reason. So it is in the New Testament. From the very beginning, acceptance of the gospel was commended as a truly reasonable thing.

Thus the difference between the New Testament and Justin Martyr cannot be expressed by any such simple formula as that whereas Justin Martyr engages in argumentative defence of Christianity the New Testament does not. The New Testament as well as Justin defends the gospel against argumentative attack. But we must go further still. Not only does the New Testament engage in argument, but in the argument it seeks, here and there at least, a meeting-ground in the previous beliefs of those with whom the argument is being carried on. Thus in Paul's speech on Mars Hill, as reported in the seventeenth chapter of Acts, the Apostle appeals to the element of truth that was to be found in Stoic pantheism, and at the beginning of the speech he even uses, in a *captatio benevolentiae,* the unsatisfied longing attested by a polytheistic altar "to an unknown god." In the Epistles, as is to be expected in writings addressed not to the unconverted, but to Christians, such arguments do not, to any great extent at least, appear. But even in the Epistles there are not altogether wanting references of an argumentative kind to the pagan world.

Thus, in contrasting Justin and Origen, on the one hand, with the New Testament, on the other, certain cautions need to be borne in mind. But even when such cautions receive their full due, the contrast is still striking enough.

The New Testament does contain argument; it does set the true religion over against the false beliefs of the surrounding world. But in the New Testament this element is merely subordinate; it is completely overshadowed by a triumphant, positive presentation of the redeeming work of God through the Lord Jesus Christ. The New Testament writers present the truth over against the dark background of pagan error, but they do not pause to analyze that pagan darkness into its component parts. No New Testament writer, and no one of the apostles whose teaching is reported in the New Testament, would have thought of engaging in detailed and conscious study of pagan beliefs as a preparation for missionary work. But it is just such detailed and conscious study that underlies the works of Justin Martyr and of Origen. Here we have Christian scholars, who studied not merely the Old Testament, and not merely the words of our Lord and of the apostles, but also the religion and the philosophy of the pagan world. That is true to some extent of Justin Martyr; and it is true to a much greater extent of Origen. The great Alexandrian teacher was the foremost scholar of his time; he was as much, or almost as much, at home in Greek philosophy and in the history of pagan religion as he was in the teachings of the Old and New Testaments. And he seeks to commend Christianity by a detailed comparison with, and refutation of, the beliefs of the pagan world.

In other words, in coming from the New Testament to Justin Martyr and Origen, we leave the joyous outdoor air and enter into the study-chamber. In formulating the transition in that way we must not be understood as passing any unfavorable judgment upon the study-chamber. Manifold is the work of the Christian Church, and without the patient labors of the Christian scholar, whether in the third century or in the twentieth century, the Christian cause is sure to suffer. There is a diversity of gifts, but the same Spirit. Sad would it be for the Church if she had only scholars and no evangelists; but sad would it also be if she had only evangelists and no scholars. For the work of the Christian scholar, moreover, there is ample justification even in the New Testament. Very foolish is the modern notion that Paul, for example, was a "practical Christian worker" in the shallow modern sense—a man who preached without previous meditation, or who presented a religion that was not based upon theology. Still, after all has been said, there remains a profound difference of emphasis and of atmosphere between all the New Testament writings, on the one hand, and those of an apologist like Justin Martyr or an Alexandrian scholar like Origen on the other. It does not follow, therefore, that because Justin or Origen, in their diligent and conscious search for analogies that would commend the new faith to the pagan world, can detect an analogy between the birth of Jesus and that of Perseus or of Plato, such an analogy must have produced the New Testament story of the birth of Jesus in the first place.

If anyone is tempted to draw such an inference, let him simply read the passages in Justin and in Origen in their wider context. He will then see that these writers were determined to find analogies whether they did or did not really exist. The theory of demoniac imitation of Old Testament prophecies had a baleful attraction for these Christian writers. It served to exhibit the venerable antiquity of the Old Testament books as over against the great names of pagan philosophy; it served to make all that was good in pagan thinking conducive to an acceptance of the Christian faith. So that theory is certainly overworked by these writers. Very fanciful, it will be admitted by anyone who will really look into the matter, are some of the analogies that are discovered in the interests of the theory. So it may well be in the case of the virgin birth. It is one thing to say that when the story of the virgin birth of Christ had once come to be believed, and when Christian apologists were once engaged in a learned search for elements in pagan religion that could show analogies to elements in the Christian faith, such an analogy could be found between the New Testament story and the story of the birth of Perseus or Alexander or Plato; and it is quite a different thing to say that those analogies could have given rise in the first place to the naïve and beautiful narrative in Matthew and Luke. Have we not here, in other words, in this theory of the pagan origin of the virgin birth story, merely another example of the same error as that which appeared in the theory of Jewish derivation? The meaning of the Old Testament prophecy about the birth of the Messiah, we observed when we considered the latter theory, could well be detected after the story of the virgin birth was already known and believed; but it never could have produced that story; and indeed the pre-Christian interpretation of prophecy was moving in an entirely different direction. So it is also in the case of the pagan analogies to the virgin birth—with the difference that those pagan analogies were *supposed* analogies only, whereas the Old Testament prophecy was, according to our view, a real prophecy. Those pagan analogies might well be detected by men like Justin and Origen, who were on the search for analogies of all sorts; but could they, in the minds of first-century Christians who, as the hypothesis demands, knew only the tradition that Jesus was the son of Joseph and Mary, ever have produced in the first place the strange belief that Jesus was not in a physical sense the son of Joseph, but was born without human father? Could simple Christians of the first century—not apologists, not Alexandrian scholars, not students of pagan antiquity, but men who had a wholesome horror of the degraded mythology of the pagan world—ever have derived from the story that Perseus owed his birth to the lust of Zeus for Danaë, or Plato owed his birth to the lust of Apollo for Perictione, the belief that Jesus was conceived in the womb of the virgin Mary by the power of the Holy Ghost? That it is which seems to us unlikely. The passages in Justin and Origen do not really justify any inference at all regarding the origination of the story of the virgin birth.

Finally, it should be observed that these early Christian writers are not really unaware of the profound difference between the pagan stories of the births of gods and demigods and the Christian story of the birth of Jesus. They regard the pagan stories with horror not merely because they are demoniac imitations of prophecy, but also because of their content. Thus in a passage just before the one which we first cited above, Justin Martyr displays a true moral indignation against the view that the gods, who supposedly are worthy of imitation, should have become slaves of pleasure and should have entered into adulterous unions.[35] Here Justin seizes upon the really important point: the analogies between the pagan stories on the one hand and the Christian story on the other, however useful they may be in an *argumentum ad hominem,* are superficial merely; and at bottom the two representations are different in kind. Still more significant is the following passage:

> But lest certain men, not understanding the aforementioned prophecy,[36] should bring the same objection against us that we brought against the poets when we said that Zeus approached women for the sake of carnal pleasure, we shall try to make the words clear. The words, "Behold the virgin shall conceive," signify that the virgin conceived without intercourse; for if she had had intercourse with anyone whatever, she would no longer be a virgin. But the power of God coming upon the virgin overshadowed her and caused her to conceive though she was a virgin. . . . Accordingly the Spirit and the power which was from God must be understood as nothing else than the Logos, who also is the firstborn of God, as Moses the aforementioned prophet declared; and this, coming upon the virgin and overshadowing her, caused her to be with child not by intercourse but by power.[37]

Here we find stated with all requisite clearness the real difference between the pagan myths of the births of demigods on the one hand and the New Testament story of the virgin birth of Christ on the other. Justin sees clearly

[35] Justin Martyr, *apol.*, i.21 (ed. Goodspeed, 1914, pp. 40 f.).

[36] Is. vii.14.

[37] Justin Martyr, *apol.*, 33 (ed. Goodspeed, p. 49). For the translation some use has been made of M. Dods, in the *Ante-Nicene Christian Library*. T. Allan Hoben ("The Virgin Birth," in *American Journal of Theology*, vi, 1902, pp. 489 f.) cites the passage and makes some very judicious remarks regarding it.

that the pagan stories are not stories of virgin births at all, but have at the very heart of them the notion of the carnal lust of the gods for mortal women, and that the New Testament narrative is different in kind. It is perfectly evident, therefore, that the argument from analogy with the pagan stories, which he uses elsewhere, is an *argumentum ad hominem* merely and does not touch the real centre of his conviction.[38] Surely men like the one who wrote the passage just quoted would have been the last in the world to derive the Christian story of the virgin birth from the pagan stories which they regarded with such horror. When we examine this theory of derivation, therefore, we do so without any favorable presumption from the passages in Justin Martyr, but on the contrary with the feeling that the second-century apologist may prove to have refuted the theory in advance. With that understanding, we turn now to an examination of the pagan stories themselves.

At the very beginning of the examination, it can be noted, as we have just seen that Justin Martyr noted, that the pagan narratives do not contain any account of a *virgin* birth at all.[39] That appears even in the form of the narratives; for in the pagan sources the word "virgin" does not seem to occur. It could not well occur in the story of Alexander; for according to that story the mother was already married when the conception occurred, and no stress, to say the least, seems to be laid upon the absence of previous intercourse between the mother and the human father before the divine begetting took place. In the case of Plato, the divine begetting does seem to be represented by Plutarch as taking place before any union of the human husband with his wife; and in the case of the mythical Danaë, it is an integral part of the story that Danaë was carefully guarded from male society until Zeus found access to her chamber by means of the rain of gold. But even in those stories the word "virgin" does not appear.

That word does appear, indeed, in references of the *Christian* writer, Justin, to the pagan sources. It appears in the passages cited above, where Justin says that the extraordinary birth of Jesus is something that He has in common with Perseus,[40] and where he alludes to the report that "Perseus was born of a virgin."[41] It appears also in the passage where Justin represents the Jew Trypho as alluding to the myth that "Perseus was born of Danaë who was a virgin."[42] But the reason why it appears in a Christian writer like Justin

[38] Compare T. Allan Hoben, *loc. cit.*

[39] See especially Sweet, *op. cit.*, p. 188; Orr, *The Virgin Birth of Christ*, 1907, pp. 167–171.

[40] Justin Martyr, *apol.*, i. 22 (ed. Goodspeed, 1914, p. 41).

[41] Justin Martyr, *dial.*, 70 (ed. Goodspeed, 1914, p. 181).

[42] *Ibid.*, 67 (ed. Goodspeed, 1914, p. 174).

Martyr is not far to seek.[43] The reason simply is that Justin is insisting upon the analogy of the pagan stories to the Christian story of the virgin birth, and in order the better to exhibit the analogy expresses the pagan representation in Christian terms. Let us not be too severe upon the second-century Apologist for such a procedure; he was doing only what is frequently being done by scientific students of comparative religion today. Even in the enlightened twentieth century, advocates of the theory of syncretistic origin of the Christian religion sometimes commend their theory by describing in Christian terms the pagan beliefs or practices that they are bringing into comparison. We are far from impugning the good faith of scholars either ancient or modern who err in that way. It is so very hard to distinguish sharply one's own interpretation of the sources from what the sources themselves actually say. But however the error may arise, an error it certainly is. There is every reason to believe that Justin Martyr has fallen into such an error; there is every reason to suppose that when Justin, or the Jew whom he is making the spokesman of Jewish polemic against Christianity, refers to the birth of Perseus as a birth from (or through) a virgin, he is going beyond what the pagan sources contained. There seems to be no clear evidence that pagan sources used the word "virgin" as referring to the mothers of heroes, mythical or historical, who were represented as being begotten by the gods.

It is not, however, upon this observation that we are inclined to lay the chief stress. Far more important than the terminology of the pagan stories is their content; and far more important than the question whether the mothers of the pagan heroes were represented as virgins before their union with the gods is the question whether, even if they were virgins before, they ceased to be virgins because of that event.

This latter question must be answered by an emphatic affirmative. The clear representation of the pagan stories is that the union of the gods with the women who bore children to them was closely analogous to the union between the sexes in human life. The stories of the amours of Zeus and other gods were certainly of a crassly anthropomorphic kind. It was because the Olympic gods were regarded as exercising human functions and possessing human passions that they could be regarded as begetting children like Perseus or like Hercules. Nothing could be farther from the whole spirit of the stories than to represent the births of such children of the gods as being "virgin births." Exactly the same observation is to be made, moreover, regarding the stories

[43] It does not appear in the basic passage in Origen (*contr. Cels.*, i. 37, ed. Koetschau, i, 1899, pp. 88 f.), cited in full above. Is that fact due to the greater accuracy of the learned Alexandrian scholar?

that relate, not to demigods of mythical antiquity, but to historical personages such as Plato and Alexander. These latter stories are clearly formed on the basis of the mythological and anthropomorphic representations in the works of poets and dramatists. When the admirers of Alexander desired to represent him as a demigod like Hercules, they conceived of his mother as being beloved, as Hercules' mother was, by Zeus. Thus the entire background of these stories is anthropomorphic polytheism of the crassest possible kind.

It is true that the manner of the divine begetting may sometimes be represented as being different from that which prevails among men. Ordinarily, indeed, that difference does not appear. It certainly does not appear when the embraces of Ares and Aphrodite are represented as provoking the laughter of the Homeric gods. It certainly does not appear when Paulina, in the passage cited above from Josephus,[44] after receiving the very human embraces of her lover Mundus, could suppose that those were the embraces of a god. But Zeus, it will be said, entered into Danaë's chamber not in human form, but in the form of a shower of gold; and a serpent, not a lover, was seen by Olympias' side. There is, moreover, an interesting passage in Plutarch where the part of the gods in such cases of divine begetting seems to be sublimated into the production of "certain beginnings of generation" in the mortal women from whom the hero-children were to be born.[45] And with regard to the story of Paulina it may perhaps be said that although Paulina herself held a crassly anthropomorphic view of her divine lover, yet her husband must have held a different view, else he would not have been so willing that his wife should share the god's "bed and board."

In some such cases, it may perhaps be doubted how much is merely symbol or prophecy of the god's presence and how much is the god's presence itself. Thus when a serpent appeared by Olympias' side, does that mean that the act of begetting was actually accomplished by the serpent in her bosom, or does it mean that the vision of the serpent merely showed that the god had already been there, as the vision of the sealed womb which Philip saw indicated that the divine-human child had already been conceived in the womb? The answer to such questions is not always quite clear.

Nevertheless, it does seem probable that in some cases of divine begetting in the Greek stories the act of begetting is regarded as having taken place in some way other than that which ordinarily prevails among men. These cases would then be brought into connection with the mass of instances which Hartland has gathered from the most diverse ages and the most diverse peo-

[44] See above, pp. 326 f.

[45] Plutarch, *vita Numae*, iv. 4.

ples, where the act of conception is represented as taking place in strange and unusual ways.[46] There is conception by eating or drinking, conception by the touch, conception by a ray of light, conception by the breath, conception by bathing in water where the fructifying seed has long ago been placed, and so on in bewildering variety. But for our present purpose it will not be necessary to examine or to sift that mass of material; for certainly in the Greek stories with which we now have to deal the essential anthropomorphism of the stories is not affected by anything unusual or abnormal that there may be in the manner by which the act of begetting takes place. Zeus may have union with Danaë not in human form, but in a shower of gold, but all the same the union is a satisfaction of his lust for the human maid. Everywhere it is the love of the god for the mortal woman, and not merely the exclusion of a human father of the child, which stands in the forefront of interest.

But what a gulf that places between these pagan stories and the New Testament story of the virgin birth of our Lord! Could anything be more utterly remote from the representation in Matthew and Luke than these stories of the amours of Zeus? The true spirit of those stories is found, even when they deal with historical personages, in the words attributed to Olympias in one of the accounts reported by Plutarch. "Will not Alexander cease slandering me to Hera?," the mother of Alexander is represented as saying when her son boasted of being a child of Zeus. There we have the true atmosphere in which those stories arose and from which they never really became free—the polytheistic and anthropomorphic atmosphere of an Olympus where the gods are naught but more powerful men, with human lusts, human jealousies, and human hates. Was it from such an atmosphere that the early disciples derived the story of the virgin birth of our Lord? Christian feeling answers, No. And Christian feeling is confirmed and not invalidated by patient research.

In the pagan stories of divine begetting, polytheism is not merely incidental; it is the centre and core of the whole complex of ideas. But in the New Testament story of the virgin birth of Christ, the lofty Old Testament monotheism is abated not a whit; the awful transcendence of God, the awful separateness of God from the world, is never lost from view. Where in the New Testament story is there found any hint of a love of God for the maid of Nazareth, which could be analogous to the love of a husband for his wife? The question can scarcely even be asked, by any man of literary taste—to say nothing of any devout Christian—without a shudder. Yet it would have not only to be asked, but also to be answered in the affirmative, if the theory with which we are now dealing were correct. The love of the gods for mortal women is the very point

[46] Hartland, *The Legend of Perseus*, 1894–1896, and *Primitive Paternity*, 1909–1910.

of the pagan stories—the thing without which they could not possibly exist. To mention any such thing in connection with the narratives in Matthew and Luke is to do violence to the whole spirit of those narratives. The truth is that when we read these narratives we are in a totally different world from that which produced the pagan stories of the loves and hates of the gods.

Thus the most obvious form that has been taken by the theory of pagan derivation breaks down when the evidence is examined with a little care. The New Testament story of the virgin birth of Christ certainly cannot be explained as a simple reflex, in Gentile Christian circles, of the Greek and Græco-Roman stories of the birth of heroes from human mothers and from gods. If we are to find the origin of the virgin birth story on the hypothesis that the story is untrue, we must at least go somewhat farther afield.

In recent years, a number of scholars have turned, in this connection as in other connections, to the religions of the East. In some of the Eastern religions parallels have been discovered which, it has been thought, may explain the origin of the Christian doctrine of the virgin birth.

Some of these parallels may be dismissed very quickly. That is the case, for example, with the parallel which was detected by Seydel[47] and others in the Buddhist story of the birth of Gautama, the founder of the Buddhist religion. Gautama[48] lived about five hundred years before Christ. Our earliest source of information about his life and teaching is found in the writings of the Pāli canon, which, it is thought, was formed at the time of Asoka in the third century before Christ, though it did not attain its present written form until a later time. In the Pāli canon, nothing is said about the birth of Gautama which could by any possibility be brought into comparison with our story of the virgin birth. But in the introduction to the Jātaka book, which dates from the fifth century after Christ, we have the well-known story of the white elephant that entered into the body of Māyā, Buddha's mother, at the time when her child was conceived; and the white-elephant story seems to be shown by inscriptional evidence to have been current as early as the reign of Asoka in the third century before Christ. In its earliest form, the story appears as the narration of a dream; Māyā *dreamed* that a marvellous white elephant entered into her side. In this form of the story, obviously, there is no parallel to the virgin birth of Christ; for the white elephant represented merely the

[47] *Das Evangelium von Jesu in seinen Verhältnissen zu Buddha-Sage und Buddha-Lehre*, 1882, pp. 110–135; *Die Buddha-Legende und das Leben Jesu*, 2te Aufl., 1897, pp. 11 f.

[48] In our brief presentation of the facts about the Buddhist tradition and literature we are of course entirely dependent upon the experts in this field. See especially Winternitz, *Geschichte der Indischen Litteratur*, II. i, 1913, and E. Windisch, "Buddha's Geburt und die Lehre von der Seelenwanderung," in *Abhandlungen der phil.-hist. Klasse der königl. sächsischen Gesellschaft der Wissenschaften*, xxvi, 1908.

"gandhabba" whose presence was necessary for the birth of the child. According to Buddhist belief, three factors are regularly involved in the birth of a child—the father, the mother, and the gandhabba—the last-named being that which came from the previous existences, whether animal or human, through which the child had passed.[49] Edmunds, indeed, did attempt to bring this Buddhist doctrine of the gandhabba into connection with the "Holy Spirit" appearing in the narrative of Luke; but his attempt was half-hearted at best, and apparently has won not the slightest acceptance among subsequent scholars.[50] As Oldenberg pertinently asks, what has the gandhabba, which is concerned in the birth of *every* child, to do with the Holy Spirit,[51] whose activity in the case of Jesus marked Him as quite unique? It is of course needless to say that the Buddhist doctrine of the gandhabba, even in the form in which it appears in Māyā's dream, does not at all exclude the part of the human father, Suddhodana, in the birth of Gautama.

In later Buddhist sources, what had originally been regarded as a dream of Māyā came to be regarded as an actual happening.[52] A white elephant, it came to be narrated, actually entered the body of the mother of Gautama. But even this form of the story does not of itself involve any exclusion of the human father; the coming of the gandhabba in the form of a white elephant could simply be regarded as waiting for the moment of a union between husband and wife. The way in which the exclusion of the human father seems to have grown up in Buddhist legend is rather through the development of the idea of Māyā's purity and sanctity. At first the vow of chastity which she took is represented as taking place after the conception of her child, Gautama; but in the later story apparently it is represented as taking place *before* the conception. But, in the first place, this development appears only in late sources; so that if there were any relationship of dependence between the New Testament story and this Buddhist story, the dependence might well be dependence of the Buddhist story upon the New Testament rather than vice versa.[53] And, in the second place, the Buddhist story is so totally unlike the New Testament story that it is quite unnecessary to posit any relationship between the two. As Louis de la Vallée Poussin remarks, Māyā in Buddhist legend comes to be a

[49] See Windisch, *op. cit.*, p. 12.

[50] Albert J. Edmunds, *Buddhist and Christian Gospels*, fourth edition, i, 1908, pp. 167 f.

[51] Oldenberg, in *Theologische Literaturzeitung*, xxxiv, 1909, col. 627.

[52] Windisch, *op. cit.*, pp. 5 f., 157.

[53] See A. S. Geden, "Buddha, Life of the," in Hastings, *Encyclopædia of Religion and Ethics*, ii, 1910, p. 881, footnote: "The story of the virginity of Maya, the mother of the Buddha, is late, and owes its inspiration, it can hardly be doubted, to Christian sources."

virgin only when she ceases really to be the mother of the Buddha.[54] In the riot of the miraculous which is found in the late Sanskrit tradition, it was thought to be derogatory to Gautama for him to have had anything like a human birth at all. The heavenly being is represented as entering into Māyā's womb in the form of the white elephant, then as seated there visibly as in a sort of transparent receptacle, then as emerging with the utmost pomp and circumstance. Anything like a human birth has really been lost from view; what we have is merely the appearance of a divine being upon earth with the profusion of marvels so characteristic of later Buddhist legend. It would be difficult to imagine anything more unlike the New Testament story of the virgin birth of Christ.

No weight, therefore, is to be attached to the words of Jerome at the end of the fourth century, when he says that "among the Gymnosophists of India, as it were on the basis of this view [namely, the superiority of virginity to the marriage relationship],[55] the authority of this tradition is handed down, that a virgin brought forth from her side Buddha, the originator of their teaching."[56] We have seen how little place the "virginity" of Māyā really occupies in Buddhist tradition. Evidently the fourth-century advocate of Christian monasticism, in his search for justification of the monastic ideal, has let his zeal run away with him and has, in referring to Buddha, used a terminology which the Buddhist sources themselves did not justify.

In view of the facts as they have just been outlined, it is not surprising that few recent scholars have been inclined to press the supposed Buddhist parallel as an explanation of the way in which the Christian story of the virgin birth arose. Even van den Bergh van Eysinga, despite his radical denial of the historicity of the Gospel picture of Jesus, was not inclined to lay stress upon the comparison with Buddhism at this particular point;[57] and Edmunds also adopted a somewhat similar attitude. A comprehensive refutation of the theory of Buddhist influence was accomplished by E. Windisch in his monograph on Buddha's birth. Windisch's conclusion is that if we are going to speak of Buddhist parallels to the Gospel narrative, we must use the word "parallel" in its original sense, according to which "parallels are lines which do not touch or intersect each other."

[54] Louis de la Vallée Poussin, "Le Bouddhisme et les évangiles canoniques," in *Revue biblique*' nouvelle série, iii, 1906, p. 376.

[55] "quasi per manus hujus opinionis." E. Windisch (*op. cit.*, p. 220, footnote) translates "gleichsam an der Hand dieser Anschauung (von dem Vorzug der Jungfräulichkeit vor dem ehelichen Leben)."

[56] Jerome, *adv. Jovinianum*, i. 42 (ed. Vall. et Maff., ii, 1845, col. 273).

[57] Van den Bergh van Eysinga, *Indische Einflüsse auf evangelische Erzählungen*, 2te Aufl., 1909, p. 26.

At this point, however, a word of caution needs to be uttered. Is Windisch correct when he goes on to explain the "parallels" (in the above sense) between the Buddhist and the Christian traditions by the observation that the thoughts of mankind are everywhere the same? [58] Is it true that a similarity of development can be discovered in the Buddhist and in the Christian stories regarding the births, respectively, of Gautama and of Jesus? We think that in this connection a striking difference can be discovered, which is far more instructive than all the similarities which, rightly or wrongly, have been found.

The difference does not concern merely the content of the stories that finally appeared, though even in that respect the difference, as we have seen, is great enough. Just as striking is the difference in the time at which the stories appeared. The earliest information that we have about the life of Gautama is found in the Pāli canon, which is thought to have been compiled in the time of Asoka, over two centuries after Buddha's death. A corresponding period in Christian history would be, roughly speaking, the time of Origen in the third century after Christ. But in the Pāli canon no story of any strictly supernatural birth of Gautama seems to have appeared. The story of the supernatural birth—at least in anything like the form in which it could be appealed to in the connection in which we are now interested—cannot be traced back to a point earlier than (let us say) five to ten centuries after the time when Gautama lived. Many centuries seem to have been necessary in Buddhism for the story of supernatural birth to be formed.

In the Christian tradition, on the other hand, we are confronted by a totally different state of affairs. Even if we should accept the most unfavorable conclusions at which recent scholars have arrived with regard to the New Testament documents attesting the virgin birth of Christ, still those documents would have to be assigned to a time only seventy years or so after the death of Jesus. And as a matter of fact such a late dating of the documents is improbable in the extreme. The tradition of the virgin birth can easily be shown to have been in existence only a few decades from the time when Jesus lived upon earth. In the case of Jesus, therefore, we find a story of supernatural birth appearing at a time when information concerning Jesus' life may be supposed still to have been abundant. Very striking is the difference as over against the late emergence of the Buddhist stories.

But this difference is only one particular illustration of a difference which concerns the entire representation in Buddhism and in Christianity of Gautama and of Christ. In the Buddhist tradition, the deification of the founder of the religion appears many centuries after the time when he lived upon earth; in

[58] Windisch, *op. cit.*, p. 221.

the Christian tradition, the deification of the Founder (if deification indeed it be, and not recognition as divine of One who really was divine) appears with the utmost clearness in the very first generation in the Epistles of Paul, which, furthermore, presuppose the prevalence of essentially the same view among the intimate friends of Jesus Himself. That is a stupendous difference indeed. The deification of Gautama—quite aside from the fact, which for the moment we are leaving out of account, that it was quite different in kind from the Christian doctrine of the deity of Jesus—appears as a development which it took centuries to produce; the Christian view of Jesus as a divine Redeemer, who had come into the world for the salvation of men, pervades the primitive records from beginning to end, and all efforts to represent it as a development from an original account of a purely human Jesus have signally failed. Can we speak of a "parallel" between Buddhism and Christianity when the difference is so striking as that?

Apologists for Christianity have, indeed, never denied all significance to the deification of Gautama and perhaps of certain other founders of religions. On the contrary, that deification shows no doubt a deep-seated longing in the human heart for contact, in human form, with a person who was more than man. But a comparison of the tardy and fantastic way in which the ascription of deity appears in the case of Gautama with the primitive and assured way in which it appears in the case of Jesus raises the question whether what men had vainly longed for in many countries and in many religions has not in Jesus become sober fact. We do not think that that time-honored argument for the truth of Christianity has suffered at all from the modern study of religion. No doubt the form of the argument may have to be modified in detail; but at the basis of the argument there lies a profound truth. And that truth is illustrated in particular by a comparison of the Buddhist story of the birth of the Buddha with the Christian story of the birth of Christ.

Thus it is quite clear that wherever the origin of the virgin birth may be found, it cannot be found in Buddhist tradition. Equally negative is the result when the examination turns to the religion of Persia. Böklen, indeed, has pointed in this connection to the wonderful birth of the coming deliverer, Saoshyant;[59] but the parallel, if parallel it can be called, is exceedingly remote. Saoshyant is to be born by means of the seed of Zoroaster. The seed is preserved in a wonderful manner; but the fatherhood of Zoroaster is plainly taught, and of a virgin birth there is not the slightest trace. So it is also with what is said about the birth of Zoroaster himself; there is no real thought in either case of

[59] Böklen, *Die Verwandtschaft der jüdisch-christlichen mit der parsischen Eschatologie*, 1902, pp. 91 f.

anything like a virgin birth.[60] As for the birth of Mithras from the rock, it is difficult to see how any parallel with the Christian story could possibly be found there.[61]

Babylonia does not really afford any better support than does Persia or India to the hypothesis with which we are now concerned. It is not surprising, indeed, that the enthusiastic pan-Babylonianism of a certain group of modern scholars should have been extended into the New Testament field and particularly into the discussion of the virgin birth; but the plain fact is that no real evidence of any belief in virgin births has been discovered in Babylonian sources. The ground has been well covered by Franckh[62] and by Steinmetzer,[63] and upon these writers we are mainly dependent in the brief sketch that follows.

Little stress, surely, can be laid upon the fact that the constellation of the "virgin" is said to rise on December 25th at midnight. A host of questions arise before any conclusions for our subject can be drawn from this fact. Was the constellation of the "virgin" ever connected by anyone in ancient times with the notion of a true virgin who brought forth a son? Was the birth of Jesus connected with the twenty-fifth of December at an early time or only (as is usually supposed) centuries after the New Testament story of the virgin birth arose? Evidently we are moving here in a sphere of the most uncertain combinations and inferences. And, as Franckh insists, Marduk, the Babylonian redeemer-king, is most emphatically *not* represented as virgin-born. The astrological theory is that events in the starry heavens correspond with events upon the earth. Hence it might be supposed that the constellation of the virgin would correspond with an earthly virgin who should bear a son. But Marduk, the god whose astral character ought to be clear, turns out not to be born of a virgin at all. The sources desert the seeker for parallels with the New Testament narrative just at the decisive point.

It is true that great personages in Babylon are represented as standing in a filial relation to various female deities, who are more or less identified with, or go back to, Ishtar, the female deity *par excellence*. But is Ishtar represented as a virgin? That is emphatically not the case. She has no continuing male consort; but if the term "virgin" is applied to her, it is only in a vague sense

[60] Clemen, *Religionsgeschichtliche Erklärung des Neuen Testaments*, 2te Aufl., 1924, p. 117.

[61] Clemen, *op. cit.*, pp. 117 f.; Steinmetzer, *Jesus, der Jungfrauensohn, und die altorientalische Mythe*, 1917, pp. 31–34; Steinmann, *Die Jungfrauengeburt und die vergleichende Religionsgeschichte*, 1919, pp. 20–25.

[62] "Die Geburtsgeschichte Jesu Christi im Lichte der altorientalischen Weltanschauung," in *Philotesia Paul Kleinert zum LXX. Geburtstag dargebracht*, 1907, pp. 201–221.

[63] *Die Geschichte der Geburt und Kindheit Christi und ihr Verhältnis zur babylonischen Mythe*, 1910; *Jesus der Jungfrauensohn und die altorientalische Mythe*, 1917, pp. 24–31.

which is as far as possible from what the New Testament means by the word.[64] There is, indeed, in Babylonian sources the notion that certain great personages were children of unknown fathers; but that notion is compatible with illegitimate birth just as much as with virgin birth, and there is at any rate not the slightest evidence that it was ever connected with the latter.

Stress, indeed, is laid upon a passage in which Sargon, the founder of Babylon, is represented as saying: "My mother was *enitu,* my father unknown."[65] But what is meant by *enitu?* It has sometimes been thought to mean "vestal-virgin," and so "virgin"; but opinions of the experts differ widely, and there is really no certainty about the matter. It would be a very unwarranted procedure to base far-reaching conclusions on a word the meaning of which is so obscure. And even if the word did turn out to mean vestal-virgin, it might be used in such a broad sense as not at all to connote real virginity.

Equally without importance for our subject is the passage in which Gudea is represented as saying to the goddess Gatumdug: "I have no mother, thou art my mother; I have no father, thou art my father . . . in a holy [or "secret"] place thou hast brought me forth."[66] The father of Gudea is mentioned immediately after these words;[67] and no idea of a fatherless birth is really to be found in the passage. We have here merely a drastic expression of the peculiarly intimate relation in which these Babylonian personages stand to the mother-goddess.

The real result of the examination is that no idea of a virgin birth is to be found in Babylonian sources and that the origin of the New Testament doctrine certainly cannot be found there. Thus the great religions of India, Persia, and Babylonia, with regard to which we have abundant sources of information, have signally failed to provide the desired parallels to the Christian story of the virgin birth of Christ.

It is not surprising, therefore, that at least one noteworthy modern scholar should have had recourse in this connection to a much more obscure cult. We refer to the use which has been made by Bousset of the cult of the Arabian god, Dusares.[68] Bousset intimates, indeed, that the parallels to the Christian virgin birth tradition are really too numerous to mention;[69] but we have already seen how little weight is to be attributed to such general intimations, and thus we are interested rather in the parallel with which Bousset specifically

[64] See Franckh, *op. cit.*, pp. 213 f.

[65] See A. Jeremias, *Babylonisches im Neuen Testament*, 1905, pp. 28 f.

[66] Jeremias, *op. cit.*, p. 29.

[67] Steinmetzer, *Die Geschichte der Geburt und Kindheit Christi*, 1910, pp. 53 f.

[68] Bousset, *Kyrios Christos*, 2te Aufl., 1921, pp. 271–274. Compare also Cheyne, *Bible Problems*, 1904, pp. 73–76.

[69] Bousset, *op. cit.*, p. 270.

deals. Despite the wealth of parallels from which we might choose, says Bousset in effect, it is not impossible that we ought to find the immediate occasion for the development of the Christian virgin birth dogma in the legend of the virgin birth of Dionysus-Dusares.

That legend is attested by the fourth-century Christian writer, Epiphanius. In the course of his refutation of heresies, Epiphanius writes as follows:

> For also, being compelled to confess a part of the truth, those who are ringleaders in idol-worship and deceivers, in order that they may lead astray the idolaters who obey them, practise in many places a great feast in the very night of Epiphany, to the end that they may put their hope in error and thus may not seek the truth. This is done, in the first place, in Alexandria in the so-called Coreium, which is a very great temple—that is, the sacred precinct of Core. For having passed all the night singing to the idol with certain songs accompanied by the flute, and having thus finished night-vigil, they come together after cockcrowing with torches into a certain underground shrine and carry up a certain wooden image lying naked on a litter, which image has a certain gilded seal or a cross upon its forehead and other two similar seals upon its two hands and other two on its two knees—in all five seals stamped with gold—and they carry the image about seven times, making the circuit of the innermost temple with flutes and drums and hymns, and after the festival they carry it down again into the underground place. And when asked what this mystery is, they answer and say that at this hour Core (that is the virgin) brought forth Aeon. And this takes place also in the city of Petra (the metropolis of Arabia, which is called Edom in the Scriptures) in the idol-temple which is there; and in the Arabian tongue they sing hymns to the virgin, calling her in the Arabian language *Chaamou* [70] (that is, "maiden" [71] or "virgin" [72]) and to "Dusares" (that is, "only-begotten of the master") who was born of her. And this takes place also in the city of Elusa on that night, as it does there in Petra and in Alexandria.[73]

The same cult is also referred to in somewhat similar terms by the eighth-century writer, Cosmas of Jerusalem, who says that the worshippers, when they came forth, cried: "The virgin has brought forth; the light increases." [74]

These passages are no doubt interesting, and the discussion of them might be instructive in many ways. But here we are concerned only with the question whether they really attest anything like a pre-Christian belief in the virgin birth of Dusares, the Arabian god, or his Hellenized adaptations. And surely that question should be answered by an emphatic negative.

[70] Χααμοῦ.

[71] Κόρην.

[72] παρθένον.

[73] Epiphanius, *haer.*, li. 8–11 (ed. Holl, ii, 1922, pp. 285–287).

[74] Ἡ παρθένος ἔτεκεν, αὔξει φῶς, Cosmas Hierosolymitanus, *in carm. Greg. Naz.*, in Migne, *Patrologiae cursus completus*, series Græca prior, xxxviii, col. 464.

The plain fact is that the only sources[75] calling the mother of Dusares a "virgin" are two Christian sources, of which the earlier dates from the fourth century after Christ, and the later from the eighth century. What possible right have we to suppose that the title attested only in these late sources was applied to this goddess in pre-Christian times? We have already seen that the application of the term "virgin" to pagan mothers by Christian writers is in general to be viewed with suspicion, since there was a tendency on the part of these writers to seek parallels for Christian beliefs in pagan religion.[76] This suspicion attaches in fullest measure to the use of the term by Epiphanius in the passage with which we are now concerned. Wellhausen may well be right in thinking that Epiphanius has been influenced in his choice of language by his desire to show a connection with Mary and Jesus.[77]

Indeed it has been suggested, with some show of reason, that the word "virgin" was introduced simply by a misunderstanding of an Arabic word which appears in Epiphanius as *Chaamou,* or as some scholars prefer to read *Chaabou.* So Wellhausen[78] says that the assertion (of Epiphanius) that *Chaabou* means "maiden" is of no more value than the assertion (by the same writer) that "Dusares" means "the only-begotten of the Lord"; and suggests that the parthenogenesis from the *Chaabou* may simply go back to the fact that the inhabitants of Petra, perhaps under the influence of Mithraism, thought of Dusares as a god who was born of the sacred stone. Similarly, Dalman suggests that what we have is a word-play between Arabic *ḳaʿb,* "dice-shaped stone," and *ḳāʿibe,* "mature virgin," though it is not clear whether he means to derive the whole tradition of the virgin birth of Dusares from this word-play.[79] At any rate, this latter step was apparently taken by Clemen in the first edition of his "Primitive Christianity and Its Non-Jewish Sources";[80] and although Clemen has now abandoned it[81] in deference to Bousset's objection,[82] there is still perhaps something to be said in its favor.

What is really important to observe, however, is that even if this particular way of dealing with the Epiphanius testimony be rejected, it is still quite

[75] See the collection of passages referring to Dusares which was made by Mordtmann ("Dusares bei Epiphanius," in *Zeitschrift der Deutschen Morgenländischen Gesellschaft,* xxix, 1876, pp 103–106).

[76] See above, pp. 103–106.

[77] Wellhausen, *Skizzen und Vorarbeiten,* iii, 1887, p. 46.

[78] *Loc. cit.*

[79] Dalman, *Petra und seine Felsheiligtümer,* 1908, p. 51.

[80] Clemen, *Religionsgeschichtliche Erklärung des Neuen Testaments,* 1909, pp. 228, 277 (English translation, *Primitive Christianity and Its Non-Jewish Sources,* 1912, pp. 293, 356).

[81] Clemen, *op. cit.* 2te Aufl., 1924, p. 119.

[82] Compare W. Robertson Smith, *Lectures on the Religion of the Semites,* new edition, 1894, pp. 56 f., footnote 3.

unjustifiable to use that testimony as establishing any pre-Christian belief in a real virgin birth of the Arabian god. The use of the term "virgin" by Christian writers, and particularly by Christian writers of such a late date, still remains open to the gravest suspicion; it is all too likely to be due simply to the well-established desire of such writers to find perverse imitations of Christian beliefs in pagan religion. We really have no valid evidence whatever to show that the term was actually used in the pagan worship of Dusares three centuries before the time when Epiphanius lived. Furthermore, even if the term was used in the pre-Christian worship of Dusares, that would not show at all that it was used in the sense in which we use it and in which it was used by Matthew and Luke. On the contrary, it would merely designate a mother-goddess like Ishtar, "unmarried, or rather choosing her temporary partners at will,"[83] or like Tanith-Artemis, "the heavenly virgin, *i.e.,* the unmarried goddess,"[84] whose obscene rites Augustine mentions with such disgust,[85] or like "the great mythic mother-goddess" who "was independent of the marriage-tie."[86] In other words, the term "virgin,".if it really was applied in pre-Christian times to the mother of Dusares, meant, no doubt, almost the exact opposite of what that term means in the New Testament account of the birth of our Lord.[87]

We may therefore venture to maintain that Bousset's appeal to Dusares-Dionysus is valuable chiefly as indicating the weakness of the more usual hypotheses. If so learned and able a scholar, in seeking pagan parallels to the virgin birth of Christ as narrated in the New Testament, is obliged to have recourse to a virgin birth story attested only in Christian writers many centuries later than the time when the New Testament story was produced, surely we have here an eloquent testimony to the absence of real parallels. If modern research had really discovered any circle of ideas from which the virgin birth tradition, supposing it not to be true, could conceivably have come, we doubt whether it would have been necessary for Bousset to appeal to Dusares-Dionysus and to the exceedingly dubious testimony of a fourth-century Christian writer.

At least two notable attempts have been made in recent years to find the source of the New Testament virgin birth story in Egypt; and it will perhaps be instructive to examine these two attempts in some detail. They have been

[83] W. Robertson Smith, *op. cit.*, p. 56.

[84] *Loc. cit.*

[85] Augustine, *de civ. dei*, ii. 4. See W. Robertson Smith, *loc. cit.*, on the probability of the identifications involved.

[86] Cheyne, *Bible Problems*, 1904, p. 75.

[87] Compare Clemen, *op. cit.*, 2te Aufl., 1924, p. 119.

made by Hugo Gressmann, the well-known student of the Old Testament, and by Eduard Norden, who is one of the most distinguished philologians of the present day.

The book of Gressmann,[88] in which the theory concerning the virgin birth appears, is devoted primarily, not to the annunciation (as it is narrated in the first chapters of Matthew and Luke), but to the birth narrative in Lk. ii.1-20. That narrative, says Gressmann, must be treated by itself, in complete isolation from all the other stories about Jesus. The earliest units of legendary tradition, he insists, are detached legends, not legendary cycles; and for that reason, as well as in view of certain special evidences of original independence between Lk. ii.1-20 and its present context, we must treat this narrative as though it were the only story that we possessed concerning Jesus.

At this point, the reader may perhaps be permitted a slight pause to get his breath. Is it not making a considerable demand upon our docility to ask us to interpret this narrative as though it contained all that we knew about Jesus? Does not the word "Jesus" appear in the narrative as the name of a person who is assumed to be known to the hearers or readers, certainly as the name of a person known to the narrator? Is it right, therefore, to treat that name as though it were simply an *x* or a *y*? But if that name is the name of a person otherwise known both to the narrator and to his hearers, then surely we should interpret the narrative in the light of the further information about that person which we may suppose the first narrator and the first hearers to have possessed. We find it difficult, therefore, to fulfil at the start the requirement of complete detachment of this narrative from other narratives dealing with the same person. The reason why that demand is important in Gressmann's book becomes, indeed, plain in the sequel; it is because he is going to show, or attempt to show, that originally the narrative had nothing to do with Jesus and that the references to Jesus have been imported into it at some later time. But surely it seems unwarranted to ask us to assume at the beginning what can be established, if at all, only by the whole course of the following argument. Surely it is quite conceivable that the first man to tell this story should have been a person who already had a fund of information about Jesus and presupposed such a fund of information in his readers or hearers. That possibility may turn out in the course of the investigation not to be actuality; but until it turns out not to be actuality, it should surely not be ignored. We do not think, therefore, that it is at all a matter of course that this narrative should be interpreted as though it were the only narrative that we possessed about Jesus, and certainly we do not think that the positive

[88] *Das Weihnachts-Evangelium*, 1914.

indications which Gressmann adduces for an original independence between this narrative and the narrative in the first chapter of Luke are at all decisive.

Our dissent at this point is closely connected with another dissent. When we get back to the original form of the narrative, says Gressmann, we must assume that the narrative is a perfect work of art. "Every interpretation proceeds as a matter of course upon the assumption that the narrative with which it happens to be concerned is a perfect work of art, on which it is justified in making the highest demands." But why should any such assumption be made? Is every legend, in its original, pre-literary form, a perfect work of art, whose elements hang together with complete artistic and logical necessity? If that is so, surely it is a most extraordinary fact, that runs directly counter to all considerations of antecedent probability. Yet apparently our author, far from proving his remarkable assertion, gives not the slightest hint as to the way in which proof of it could be found. Until such proof is forthcoming, we may surely be doubtful about assuming the artistic perfection of every narrative with which we have to do. Such an assumption, of course, almost excludes the possibility that the narrative possesses historical trustworthiness; for history seldom proceeds in perfect accord with considerations of artistic propriety. But even if the narrative be assumed to be purely legendary, so that the narrator would not have been hampered by any dependence upon the facts, still we do not see how it follows that the canons of artistic construction must have been followed with perfect consistency. Why must every popular story have been a perfect story? We suspect that real life may not always be found to follow the strict canons that modern literary critics seek to impose upon it. It is only with caution, therefore, that we proceed to examine Gressmann's analysis of the narrative in detail.

That analysis eliminates at the start any large share of the final author of the Gospel in giving the narrative its present form. Where this author's sources are known, says Gressmann, it is found that he merely retouches them here and there; and the Jewish Christian character of this particular narrative as it appears in the Gospel of Luke is so clear as to make it evident that the Gentile author has left the underlying Jewish Christian narrative for the most part unchanged. The author, therefore, Gressmann concludes, is here following closely a written or oral source; and in that source there stood not merely the narrative in Lk. ii.1-20, but the whole cycle in which that narrative now stands, the final author of the Gospel not even having taken the trouble to smooth out the contradictions among the (originally independent) legends composing the cycle.

With regard to the Jewish Christian character of these narratives in Lk. i-ii, and the part which the final author of the Gospel had in giving them their present form, the measure of our agreement has already been indicated in Chapters II-VI. More dubious is the further analysis by which Gressmann seeks to penetrate to the original form of the narrative in Lk. ii.1-20.

Evidently, he says, the census of Quirinius is a later addition; for the prose tone of this part of the story contrasts sharply with the poetic tone of the rest; and with the census the whole incident of a journey of the child's parents becomes open to suspicion. Even in the rest of the narrative, he continues, there are rough edges. When the shepherds go to see the child, why do they not bring him gifts, as, for example, the magi do in the second chapter of Matthew? As it is, their visit seems to be without purpose or meaning. Indeed, one does not see exactly why the shepherds should be brought in at all: they do not seem to perform any particular function with reference to the child. Yet in the narrative as it stands they, and not the parents of the child, are really the chief personages. Moreover, why should the mere fact that the child was lying in a manger be regarded as a "sign"? A "sign" obviously is a strange, if not necessarily a miraculous, occurrence; but for a child to lie in a manger hardly seems to be so very strange. What, moreover, became of the parents after they laid the child in the manger? Did they themselves remain in the inn, or did they change altogether the place of their abode? The narrative, Gressmann thinks, is curiously vague at this point. Why, moreover, is the manger so much emphasized in the narrative? We think of a manger as being in a stall for cattle; but the narrative says nothing about a stall. Finally we should naturally expect the manger to have something to do with the shepherds to whom announcement of the birth of the child is made; yet in the narrative as it stands the shepherds and the manger are far apart.

All of these defects in clearness, all of these loose ends, in the present narrative, lead, Gressmann supposes, to one conclusion—namely, that in the original form of the legend no parents of the child appeared. Without the parents, everything becomes perfectly clear. The child was a foundling child; hence the shepherds had the very necessary function of bringing it up: the manger was the particular manger that belonged to these particular shepherds. The whole trouble in the narrative as it stands is that the parents are dragged in so as to usurp the place belonging originally to the shepherds. But why were the parents dragged in? The answer, Gressmann thinks, is obvious. They were dragged in only because the historical personage, Jesus, with whom the child of the original legend was now to be identified, had well-known parents who could not be ignored. But originally this was a foundling child, whose legend was connected with Bethlehem; and the contradictions in the present narrative are due to the fact that a pre-Christian Jewish legend, which originally had nothing to do with Jesus, was seized upon by Jewish Christians to do honor to Him who had become the object of their reverence.

In seeking, therefore, the ultimate origin of the story, we must seek, according to Gressmann, not the origin of a story specifically about Jesus, but the origin of a pre-Christian Jewish story about a foundling child. An interesting detail in this pre-Christian story, Gressmann thinks, is contributed by the extra-canonical mention of a cave as the place of Jesus' birth.[89] It is impossible to suppose that the cave was derived either from the New Testament canonical narratives or from Old Testament prophecy: evidently, therefore, we have in the mention of the cave a remnant of the pre-Christian story; that story was connected not merely with Bethlehem, but with one particular cave near Bethlehem.

The child in the pre-Christian birth story was, according to Gressmann, clearly a *royal* child: in the first place, because foundling legends are for the most part stories about kings, a favorite point being the contrast between the destiny of the child and his lowly upbringing by humble folk; in the second place, because the story was connected with Bethlehem, the ancestral seat of the Davidic line from which the Messiah was to come; and, in the third place, because the terms "saviour," "gospel," and "peace," which occur in the narrative as it stands, are well-known elements in the "court style" used to do honor to the Roman Emperor, while the term "Christ" ("anointed"), which also occurs in the narrative, is the regular designation of the Messianic king. Plainly, therefore, Gressmann concludes, we have in the pre-Christian story a Jewish story regarding the king who was to come of David's line and be the deliverer of His people.

Ultimately, however, according to Gressmann, this story was not of Jewish origin. It did not appear on Jewish ground before the Hellenistic age, Gressmann argues, since it is not found in the Old Testament; and in the Hellenistic age a Jewish origin of such a story is unnatural, while importation from outside of Judaism, with adaptation to Jewish conditions, becomes in that period easy to understand. What is decisive, however, for an extra-Jewish origin is, according to Gressmann, not merely such general considerations, but the presence at the very heart of the narrative of the technical terms, "saviour" and "gospel," which never could have originated on Jewish ground.[90]

[89] See Justin Martyr, *dial.*, 78; *Protevangelium Jacobi*, 18.

[90] Gressmann admits (pp. 20 f., footnote 2) that these terms appear in the Old Testament but insists that their technical use does not appear there. The distinction, we think, can hardly be maintained; and the terms as used in Lk. ii.1–20 are, we think, quite comprehensible on the basis of Old Testament ideas.

From what source, then, was this originally non-Jewish narrative ultimately derived? Gressmann has a very definite answer to this question; the story was derived ultimately, he holds, from the Egyptian story of the exposure and lowly upbringing of Osiris, the well-known Egyptian god. That story appears in Plutarch's treatise "Concerning Isis and Osiris" in two variants as follows:[91]

> On the first day [that is, the first of the intercalary days at the close of the year] Osiris is said to have been born, and a voice is said to have fallen from on high[92] to the effect that the Lord of all was coming forth into the light. Some, however, say that a certain Pamyles in Thebes, while he was drawing water, heard a voice from the temple of Zeus,[93] commanding him to proclaim with a shout that a great king, the benefactor, Osiris, is born; and that for this cause Pamyles brought up Osiris, who had been entrusted to him by Cronus,[94] and therefore the festival of the Pamylia was celebrated in his honor—a festival similar to phallic festivals.

There are, of course, differences between this narrative and the one in Lk. ii.1-20; but these differences, Gressmann insists, are merely due to changes in the setting which became necessary when the legend was transplanted from one country to another. In the Theban landscape, which was dominated by the Nile, it had of course to be a drawer of water who fished the foundling child from the river, while in pastoral Judæa shepherds were of course the natural persons to perform a corresponding function; the swaddling-clothes, in which the child was wrapped according to the Lucan narrative, also are due in all probability to the peculiarity of Palestinian custom.

But, says Gressmann, how great, as over against these differences, are the similarities! In both cases the birth of the child is immediately announced by a divine voice; the divinity is watching over the child and summons the necessary rescuer; in both cases the child is designated as "Lord" (*Kyrios*), and the title "benefactor" in the Egyptian story is closely related to the title "Saviour" in Luke; in both cases the divine announcement is passed on, in the Egyptian story by express command, in the Lucan story without it; in both cases the recipients of the divine announcement are laymen, belonging to the lower classes of the people. But more important than such similarities in detail is, according to Gressmann, the similarity in the entire structure of the two stories. That similarity does not appear, indeed, in the present form of the Lucan story; but in the original form of the story it is clear: the Christ-child

[91] Plutarch, *De Iside et Osiride*, xii.

[92] The Greek has *συνεκπεσεῖν*. Gressmann, following Norden, supplies "from on high" or "from heaven."

[93] "Zeus," says Gressmann, is the Egyptian Amon, the chief divinity of Thebes.

[94] Cronus, according to Gressmann, is the Egyptian Geb, the father of Osiris.

is born in wonderful fashion; it is without human parents (being a divine child that sprang from divine parents); suddenly it lies far from men, helpless and wrapped in swaddling-clothes, in a manger; but meanwhile the shepherds, who happen to be in the field, are made aware of the event and are sent to the manger; and since they know that the foundling is of divine origin and is destined for great things, they spread abroad the angelic announcement and take the foundling under their protection, giving him milk to drink, and bringing him up.

Accordingly, we find here, Gressmann concludes, essentially the same story attested by Plutarch and by Luke; there is clearly a relation of definite dependence between the Egyptian and the Jewish form in which the story appears. But there can be no doubt, Gressmann thinks, but that the dependence is on the side of the Jewish form. In the first place, the loose joints and breaks in the Lucan story show that that story has passed through a long history, whereas such breaks are lacking in the Osiris legend;[95] in the second place, the fact that the foundling is a king is in the Christ legend merely implied, while in the Osiris legend it is plainly stated; in the third place (what is most important), the fact that the *royal* child has at the same time divine rank, as is indicated in the Lucan narrative by the angelic announcement, is as completely out of accord with native Jewish ideas as it is completely in accord with the Egyptian deification of the monarch, which was prevalent in Egypt from the earliest times.

The localization of the birth legend in a cave near Bethlehem requires, according to Gressmann, a word of special explanation. That the legend should be connected with Bethlehem is of course natural so soon as it was applied to the Messiah; but why should it be connected particularly with this particular cave? It would be tempting, Gressmann says, simply to regard the Adonis-Tammuz worship in the cave of the nativity, which is attested for post-Christian times by Jerome,[96] with a pre-Christian worship of Osiris (who was merged with Adonis on Egyptian ground) in that same cave; but this connection is not proved, he says, and on the whole is improbable. All that we can say, therefore, is, according to Gressmann, that a peculiar sanctity attached for some obscure reason to the Bethlehem cave, so that it became natural to localize in that cave the birth legend which was imported by pre-Christian Judaism from Egypt and was attached to the Messiah.

Finally, Gressmann confirms his Egyptian derivation of the narrative by

[95] At this point Gressmann might seem to have forgotten that he has previously attributed the breaks in the Lucan narrative not to the original Jewish legend, which he is comparing with the Osiris story, but to the trouble caused by the introduction of the Christian elements.

[96] Jerome, *epist.*, lviii.3 (ed. Hilberg, I. i, 1910, p. 532).

comparison with the legends of other countries. The foundling *motif*, of course, is common, and so are stories of the births of gods; but nowhere except in Egypt, says Gressmann, have we the peculiar combination of the foundling *motif* with the notion of the king as a god, which appears in the legend underlying Lk. ii.1-20. Egypt, moreover, is *par excellence* the land where the notion of the divine child (for example, "Horus, the Child") engrosses the thoughts and sentiments of the people. To Egypt, therefore, and to Egypt alone, must we look for the origin of the "Christmas gospel" in the second chapter of Luke.

It will not be necessary for us to criticize this theory in detail; for it lies somewhat aside from the specific subject with which our discussion is concerned. The virgin birth, Gressmann holds, does not appear in Lk. ii.1-20 or in the Egyptian-Jewish legend underlying that section; so that perhaps we might have spared our readers the rather detailed exposition of Gressmann's analysis which we have just brought to a close. Nevertheless, we believe that that exposition has by no means been without value for the understanding of the modern method of dealing with the subject of the virgin birth. Gressmann's comparison of Lk. ii.1-20 with the Plutarch passage from the "De Iside et Osiride" is so perfect an example of the method followed by modern students of comparative religion that it becomes highly instructive when we come to evaluate the treatment, by Gressmann himself and by others, of the closely related subject with which specifically the present volume is concerned.

That modern method proceeds first by inference from the extant form of a narrative to an original form existing prior to literary fixation. Then the narrative so reconstructed is brought into comparison with some other narrative which, like the former narrative, is not actually given in the extant sources, but is derived from those sources by a process of elaboration or subtraction. In the application of this method, Gressmann begins with the Lucan narrative. That narrative says nothing whatever about a foundling child; but the foundling child is put into it by an hypothesis which may or may not be correct. Then it is the turn of the narrative in Plutarch. That narrative also says nothing very plainly about a foundling child; at least it says nothing about the fishing up of that child from the Nile. Again these elements are introduced into it by inferences which may or may not be correct. Then the two narratives thus reconstructed are treated as though they were actually attested and are compared with each other with a gratifyingly positive result. Grave questions certainly arise with regard to the whole procedure; it may well be questioned whether a cautious historian will not have to adhere more closely to the sources as they actually are.

But it is time now to turn to the treatment by the same author of the subject of the virgin birth. It will soon be observed that our author's conclusions about this latter subject are very similar, even in detail, to his conclusions with regard to the story in the second chapter of Luke.

In treating the New Testament *motif* of the supernatural conception, it is important, Gressmann says, to find the particular passage where that *motif* has its original seat. But this passage is not the first chapter of Matthew, which is plainly secondary, but rather verses 26-38 in the first chapter of Luke. It is true that even in this passage the virgin birth is not narrated, but merely presupposed; yet at least it does form the subject of the annunciation which was made by the angel Gabriel to Mary the mother of Jesus. Here, then, we have to start, Gressmann says, in our effort to discover the origin of the myth.

As in the story of the birth, in Lk. ii.1-20, so here in the story of the annunciation, Gressmann detects loose ends and contradictions in the narrative as it stands. One of these loose ends, he says, of course stares us in the face in Mary's question in Lk. i.34. Mary was betrothed to Joseph, the descendant of David; why, then, did she not interpret the angel's promise as referring to her coming marriage with Joseph; why did she ask, instead: "How shall this be, seeing I know not a man?" The truth is, says Gressmann, that the entire representation of the Davidic descent of Jesus as son of Joseph is quite contrary to the virginity of Mary which appears plainly in Lk. i.27 and is implied in the following verses. Yet Gressmann rejects emphatically the interpolation hypothesis regarding Lk. i.34 f. The Semitic form of these verses, he says, shows clearly that they were an original part of the narrative, as does also their agreement with the emphasis on the virginity of Mary in verse 27 and with the surprise which Mary felt at the angel's greeting. How, then, is the contradiction in the narrative really to be explained?

Gressmann has a very definite answer to this question. The contradiction arose, he thinks, from the introduction of Joseph and Mary, as parents of the child, into a legend in which originally they had no place. Originally the legend had to do merely with a virgin mother, a divine father, and a divine-human child destined to be a king. That legend was in pre-Christian Judaism applied to the Messiah. Then it was seized upon by Jewish Christians to do honor to the one whom they regarded as the Messiah, namely Jesus. But the parents of Jesus, Joseph and Mary, were well known; they had to be brought somehow into the story; and the confusion which we find in the Lucan narrative was the inevitable result.

Thus Gressmann rejects the view that the idea of the virgin birth of Christ originated in Gentile Christian circles. The Semitic character of the narratives containing that idea protests strongly, he observes, against any such view. But, on the other hand, Jewish Christians who already believed in Jesus were not the originators of the idea; for then the contradictions in Lk. i.26-38 could not be explained. The only possible conclusion, Gressmann thinks, is that the legend was already applied to the Messiah in the Judaism of pre-Christian times.

Ultimately, however, Gressmann continues, the legend could not have been of Jewish origin; for with its crass mythology it is contrary to the very heart and core of Jewish monotheism. In Luke, the mythological notion is perfectly clear; the "Holy Ghost" is parallel to "the power of the Most High," so that God Himself is regarded as having performed the act of physical begetting. In Matthew, on the other hand, Gressmann thinks, there is a greater degree of concession to Jewish feeling, since the "Holy Ghost" of the Matthæan narrative is regarded as a male being subordinate to God. But it is a mistake, Gressmann continues, to regard the introduction of the Holy Spirit as a Jewish Christian modification of some grosser pagan representation; for the pagans had not only the notion of begetting by a god, but also the notion of begetting by the divine Spirit.[97] Thus even the form in which the divine activity in begetting appears in the New Testament narratives has, according to Gressmann, its counterpart in pagan belief.

From what particular pagan source, then, did this pre-Christian Jewish notion of divine begetting ultimately come? In answering this question, as in answering the question regarding the ultimate source of Lk. ii.1-20, Gressmann turns with some confidence to Egypt. What we are seeking, he says, is not a story of birth from a divine mother, but a story of birth from a human mother after begetting by a divine father. That consideration narrows somewhat the range of our search. The range is, indeed, according to Gressmann, still fairly broad; for there are many stories in which a human mother is represented as having brought forth a divinely begotten child. But one further feature of the New Testament story enables us to fix a particular one of the parallels and to eliminate the others—the feature, namely, that according to the New Testament narrative the divine-human child is to be a great *king*. If we give due weight to this feature and at the same time confine our attention to those countries that came into contact with Palestine, we are led inevitably, Gressmann says, to Egypt. In Egypt, both in ancient times and during the period of the Ptolemaic dynasty, it was the current belief that every new king sprang from a human mother and from the highest god, Amon-Rā, who appeared to

[97] Plutarch, *vita Numae*, iv. 4: *καίτοι δοκοῦσιν οὐκ ἀπιθάνως Αἰγύπτιοι διαιρεῖν ὡς γυναικὶ μὲν οὐκ ἀδύνατον πνεῦμα πλησιάσαι θεοῦ καί τινας ἐντεκεῖν ἀρχὰς γενέσεως, κ.τ.λ.*, "And yet it seems to be not unbelievable when the Egyptians assert it to be possible for the spirit [or breath] of God to approach a woman and engender certain beginnings of generation."

the young queen in his divine form, had intercourse with her, and then promised her that she should bring forth a son who should be king over Egypt. The similarity of this legend to that which is found in the New Testament is, Gressmann thinks, striking; it appears both in the structure of the whole and in details. The "power of the Most High" in Luke answers to the "highest god," Amon-Rā, in the Egyptian legend; the Egyptians, as we know from Plutarch, believed that the "divine spirit" could have intercourse with a woman and thus beget a child, so that the "divine spirit" is in Egypt a substitute for Amon-Rā, as it is among the Jews for Jehovah; in the Egyptian legend as in the Gospels there is closely connected with the conception of the child in the womb the promise that the child should possess the kingdom. These similarities, Gressmann thinks, can only be explained by the dependence of the Jewish story upon the Egyptian story of the birth of the king.

Gressmann admits, indeed, that the Egyptian legend contains no mention of the virginity of the mother. His explanation is that no one in Egypt doubted the intercourse of the god with the queen; whereas when the legend was transferred to other persons, whose intercourse with divinity was not a matter of course, there needed to be emphasis upon the mother's virginity and purity.[98] Such emphasis appears, for example, says Gressmann, in the case of the birth legend of Plato, which may well be connected in some way with the Egyptian legend; and it appears also in the story in Matthew and Luke.

Surely this explanation, it may be remarked in passing, is quite inadequate; and the absence of any notion of the virginity of the mother in the Egyptian story does constitute a very important difference, in addition to other still more important differences closely connected with it, between the Egyptian belief as to the divine origin of the king and the New Testament narrative of the supernatural conception of Jesus in the womb of the virgin Mary.

Before we proceed to criticize this hypothesis of Egyptian origin of the virgin birth story, it will be necessary to notice the form in which the hypothesis has appeared in the learned monograph by Eduard Norden, on "The Birth of the Child."[99] Norden's book is devoted primarily to a study of the Fourth Eclogue, the so-called "Messianic eclogue" of Virgil. In that eclogue, Norden insists, we have no mere celebration of some noble Roman child contemporary with the poet, but a poetic treatment of an ancient myth. The original home of that myth, certainly the place from which Virgil's form of it came, was Egypt; a man of genius has here given poetic expression to an ancient theologoumenon which with various changes had been scattered abroad from its

[98] For the alternative explanation proposed by Norden, see below, pp. 359 f.
[99] Norden, *Die Geburt des Kindes*, 1924.

Egyptian home into various lands and among various peoples. The myth or theologoumenon in question was the myth of the Divine Child.

In ancient Egyptian sources, that myth appears in the story of the begetting of the heir to the kingdom by the god Amon-Rā. The god is represented as taking the form of the reigning monarch and as thus having intercourse with the queen. The result of this union is the conception and then the birth of the new monarch. In this story the various scenes are depicted with much detail on the monuments: various gods and goddesses are represented as taking part in the different functions connected with the birth and the suckling of the child.[100]

According to Moret,[101] this notion of divine begetting was connected with *every* king (not merely with kings whose right to the throne was for some reason in doubt), and it persisted down into very late times. A late product of it is found in the story in Pseudo-Callisthenes in the third century after Christ. According to that story, Alexander the Great was begotten by Nectanebes, the last of the Pharaohs, who gained access to Olympias, wife of Philip of Macedon, under the pretence that he was the god Amon. From the Alexander story there have come many expressions of the same *motif*. In a few of them, as in the incident of Paulina and Mundus,[102] an actual event underlies the story; unscrupulous men used the ancient story about the deceit of Nectanebes as a suggestion of the way in which they could gratify their own lust. But most of the stories in which the Nectanebes *motif* appears are pure fiction, as in Boccaccio and in most of the other examples which Weinreich has adduced.[103]

The ancient Egyptian belief in divine begetting is attested, according to Norden, by Plutarch and by Philo. But there are two important differences, Norden says, between these two attestations. In the first place, Philo says nothing about the "spirit" in this connection, while Plutarch says that according to the Egyptians "it is not impossible for the spirit of God to approach a woman and engender certain beginnings of generation."[104] In the second place, Plutarch says nothing about virginity, which is strongly emphasized by Philo.[105] These differences, Norden says, are to be explained by the difference between the Egyptian and the Hellenistic forms of the theologoumenon: the notion of the "spirit," or life-giving breath, of the god is Egyptian; while

[100] See A. Moret, "Du caractère religieux de la royauté pharaonique," (in *Annales du Musée Guimet*, xv), 1902, pp. 39–73.

[101] *Op. cit.*, pp. 59–68.

[102] See above, pp. 326 f.

[103] Weinreich, *Der Trug des Nektanebos*, 1911.

[104] See above, p. 357, footnote 97.

[105] In the passage quoted at length above, pp. 298–300.

the notion of virginity is Greek. A union of these two factors, Norden concludes, took place in the Græco-Egyptian religion of the Ptolemaic period; and so was produced the form of the myth which underlies the passages in the first chapters of Matthew and Luke—"God begets a son in pneumatic union with a virgin."

Of course, when that myth was transplanted to Jewish soil, it must be admitted that certain changes became necessary in order to adapt it to the Jewish idea of God. Thus instead of the appearance of the god himself to perform the act of begetting we have in the Gospels the appearance of a messenger merely to announce it; and instead of the exultation of the mother in the joy of her union with the god we have merely the words addressed to the messenger: "Behold the handmaiden of the Lord; be it unto me according to thy word." Nevertheless, Norden insists, the original myth still shines through from beneath its Jewish Christian dress. It appears even in the detail that the mother in the Jewish Christian story is a married woman at the time when the conception takes place. That detail introduces an element of unexplained contradiction, Norden says, into the Jewish Christian story, whereas in the original Egyptian story of the divine begetting of the king it had a logical and necessary place. And in general, Norden thinks, the story in the Gospels gives clear evidence of its secondary character, clear evidence of being an adaptation to monotheistic requirements of the ancient Egyptian myth of the theogamy of Amon-Rā with the reigning queen.

Our criticism of this hypothesis may well find its starting-point in the word "theogamy" which Norden himself uses. The Egyptian story is indeed the story of a theogamy; and being the story of a theogamy it has nothing to do with the New Testament story of the virgin birth of Christ. In Egypt the carnal union of the god with the queen is no mere detail which could be removed without destroying the essential character of the myth; on the contrary, the sources linger upon it with great insistence, and it appears as quite central in all the many later stories to which the ancient myth has given rise.

Norden himself gives us a hint as to the weakness of his own hypothesis when he writes as follows:

> The *motif* of a supernatural birth is found—though without the Græco-Egyptian and Judæo-Christian peculiarities, which form a closed circle of their own—in many peoples of quite diverse forms of culture. Wherever trustworthy tradition is extant, the mystery is without exception clothed in the form that the god himself appears to the mortal woman with whom he desires to enter into the marital relationship. "I will descend into thy bosom"—thus or in some similar way he speaks

to her, and she gives herself willingly to him. The Gospel narrative exhibits by its peculiarity a conscious departure from a type.[106]

This passage is not altogether clear; we do not quite understand what Norden means by saying that the Græco-Egyptian and Judæo-Christian peculiarities "form a closed circle of their own." Does he mean that the Græco-Egyptian peculiarities form one closed circle and the Judæo-Christian peculiarities another, or that they both form one closed circle when they are taken together? If, as seems probable, he means the latter, then we fail to see the exact relevance of the words that follow. For surely the actual appearance of the god to the woman with which he will have union is a characteristic of the Egyptian story just as much as it is of the many other stories to which Norden alludes. Indeed, it is found in the Egyptian story in an especially crass and detailed form. Yet in the Judæo-Christian story it appears not at all. Surely, then, it is misleading to say that the closed circle embraces the Græco-Egyptian and the Judæo-Christian peculiarities in distinction from other myths of divine begetting. In reality there are two circles: one embraces the many pagan stories of the carnal union of a mortal woman with a god; the other contains only the New Testament story of the supernatural conception of our Lord. And the two circles are entirely distinct.

This distinctness is made clear by Norden, as though against his will, in the following revealing passage, which appears almost immediately before the passage that we have just quoted above:

> How touching, through their expression of submission, are those words of the woman to whom an incomprehensible experience has been announced: "Behold the handmaid of the Lord; be it unto me according to thy word." [107] We would not do without them, although we now, I think, recognize that they are a substitute for the proud and exultant words which a woman rejoicing in her love-union with the god addresses to the god himself. Perhaps, indeed, many religious souls will even think that the majesty of the divine in the Gospel narrative, which leaves the divine in mysterious unapproachableness, is loftier than in the basic story in which the god approaches the marriage bed in the form of the king and lays his heart upon that of the woman, who now in his arms, pervaded in all her members by his magic life-giving power, becomes a goddess. The Egyptian theologoumenon breathes still the sturdy, grand style of a myth; while the Gospel narrative is surrounded by the entrancing fragrance of a delicate legend, which is only quite from afar still touched by a shadow from an ancient time.

Does not this passage show more clearly than could be done by any argument of ours the abysmal difference between the Egyptian story and the one that is

[106] Norden, *op. cit.*, p. 91.
[107] We have here translated the quotation from Lk. i.38, which Norden quotes in Greek.

found in Matthew and Luke? Between the words of Mary to the messenger of the Most High God and the exultant words of the queen in her carnal union with an anthropomorphic god, what a gulf is fixed! Norden himself admits that the New Testament narrative is unique. In all the other stories of supernatural birth, the god himself appears to the woman with whom he will have union; here only nothing of the sort appears. Is the difference to be explained merely by the adaptation of the pagan story to monotheistic conditions? Such an explanation is quite inadequate. The trouble is that the supposed "adaptation" would really mean the removal of the very heart and core of the pagan myth; for the heart and core of the pagan myth is found in the carnal union of the god with the woman of his choice. Can that be adaptation which really produces the very opposite of the thing from which the adaptation is supposed to have taken place? Is it not perfectly clear, on the contrary, that in the Egyptian myth, on the one hand, and the New Testament narrative of the virgin birth of our Lord, on the other, we have phenomena which spring from two separate and distinct roots?

If anyone desires to confirm this conclusion, if anyone desires to detect with a new clearness the difference between the New Testament account of the virgin birth of Christ and the pagan myth, let him read the learned book by Weinreich to which allusion has already been made;[108] let him trace the history of these stories that really do have a common root. Let him observe how, though in many varying forms, there always appear both the content and the spirit of the same lascivious tale. And then let him turn to the lofty monotheism of the infancy narratives in Matthew and Luke. Let him compare these narratives with the ancient Egyptian myth. If he then still thinks there is dependence, it can only be because, despite Weinreich's services, he has not yet learned what real dependence is.

This distinctness of the New Testament doctrine, it is true, is not perceived with equal clearness by all men. But perhaps that is because all men have not equal organs of perception. We may perhaps appeal in this connection to Norden himself. The prologue of the Fourth Gospel, says Norden, is a test of a man's power of forming judgments in the sphere of comparative religion; he who does not find in that prologue an echo of Heraclitus shows merely that his ear is not sufficiently sharp to hear these ancient tones. We confess that our ear is not sufficiently sharp for that. But we may perhaps venture upon a retort. We may perhaps say that he who does not see that there is something radically wrong when Norden gravely debates the question whether Mary's pure words of submission are or are not higher from the

[108] Weinreich, *Der Trug des Nektanebos*, 1911.

religious point of view than the exultant words of the Egyptian queen in her amorous embraces with the god; he who does not see that the lofty monotheism of the New Testament narrative is removed by an infinity of difference from the Egyptian tale; he who does not see that the conception of the holy child Jesus by the creative power of God is the very opposite of the theogamy of Amon-Rā with a mortal woman—he who does not see these things shows thereby that his eye has never been sharpened by any really sympathetic contemplation of the religion of Israel or of the wonderful narratives in the first two chapters of Matthew and Luke. For a true comparison between the New Testament, on the one hand, and pagan religions on the other, something more than a knowledge of pagan religions is required. One must also try to enter into the inner spirit of the New Testament books. And when one does that, one sees clearly that the hypothesis of Gressmann and Norden altogether breaks down.[109]

Perhaps the most elaborate effort that has ever been made to explain the genesis of the New Testament idea of the virgin birth, supposing the idea not to be based on fact, is the effort of Hans Leisegang in his monograph on the passages in the Synoptic Gospels which deal with the Holy Spirit.[110] This monograph appeared two years before the work of Eduard Norden, which has just been discussed; but we have reserved consideration of it to the last because its elaborate character makes it in some sort the culmination of the entire treatment by modern naturalism of the New Testament story of the birth of Christ.

Previous treatments of the subject, Leisegang says, have erred in ignoring, or giving insufficient attention to, the positive side of the New Testament representation; the investigators have attended to the fact that in that representation the human father is excluded, but they have not considered sufficiently that which is substituted for the human father—namely, the activity of the Holy Spirit. It is this positive side of the New Testament representation, just as much as the negative side, which the student of comparative religion is called upon to explain.

[109] This conclusion is not invalidated by the Plutarch passage (see above, p. 357) where the "spirit of God" is given a part in the begetting of a child. At first sight it might seem as though this were a close parallel with the New Testament account of conception by the Holy Ghost. But the plausibility of such a suggestion disappears when we observe that what Plutarch means by the "spirit" or "breath" of God is no doubt something of a material kind, in accordance with the usual meaning of the term in Greek pagan thought. See Burton, *Spirit, Soul, and Flesh*, 1918, especially pp. 134 f. Norden himself seems to give us a hint that "spirit" in Plutarch is to be taken in a material sense; for he says that Philo avoids the term just because of its usage to designate something material (Norden, *op. cit.*, p. 80).

[110] Leisegang, *Pneuma Hagion, Der Ursprung des Geistbegriffs der synoptischen Evangelien aus der griechischen Mystik*, 1922, pp. 14–72.

Now the New Testament representation appears, according to Leisegang, in two distinct forms: one in Matthew, the other in Luke. If we began with the one in Matthew, he says further, the explanation might at first sight seem to be very simple; at first sight it might seem to be discoverable on purely Jewish ground. The words, "from the Holy Spirit," in the sentence, "she was found with child from the Holy Spirit,"[111] clearly designate the "Holy Spirit" as performing the act of begetting. But in the original Greek the expression "Holy Spirit" has no article with it; the meaning, therefore, may be not *"the* Holy Spirit," but *"a* holy spirit"; and what would be designated would be not the Spirit of God, but a subordinate being, a "holy spirit," different, indeed, in moral quality from the unclean spirits frequently mentioned in the Gospels, but not essentially different from them in his place in the scale of being. But if this be the meaning, if the Gospel of Matthew attributes the act of begetting to a personal being, a "spirit," subordinate to God, then, says Leisegang, we can find striking parallels on Semitic ground. The parallels do not, indeed, appear in literary sources from ancient times; but popular beliefs in certain remote districts in Bible lands are known to be conservative, so that even modern sources in those countries may give correct information about ancient beliefs. The particular beliefs to which Leisegang refers are the beliefs in carnal union between a woman and certain spirits or "welis"; barren women are said to have recourse to certain places which such spirits haunt. So the conception of Jesus by "a holy spirit" in Mary's womb might conceivably be nothing more than one particular instance of this sort. "One cannot get rid of the thought," says Leisegang, "that the angel of the Lord, who announces the conception, and the holy spirit, that carries it out, are originally in the popular belief one and the same person, an arch-weli who undertakes the act of begetting in place of God."[112] In this way the Semitic opposition to making God Himself the physical father of a child would come to its rights, while yet the notion of supernatural birth would be preserved.

Despite what he regards as the attractiveness of this theory, Leisegang is not inclined to find in it the ultimate explanation of the New Testament representation of the virgin birth of Christ. It was only in the lower circles of Judaism, he says, that notions about the fatherhood of subordinate spirits could subsist; and although these lower circles, with their crude superstition, were much more influential in the formation of New Testament legends than is popularly supposed, still we can hardly hold that so crude a belief, vigorously opposed by official Judaism, attained the high place in early Christian

[111] Mt. i.18.
[112] Leisegang, *op. cit.*, p. 21.

thought that was actually attained by the virgin birth idea. For the ultimate origin of that idea, therefore, we must look farther afield. And inevitably we are led away from Judaism out into the Hellenistic world.

This wider search into which we are thus led can only be begun, Leisegang says, through the assistance of the narrative in Luke. In the Third Gospel, as is not the case in the First, the activity of the Spirit in the begetting of Jesus is connected with a whole circle of other activities in which also the Spirit has the central place. These other activities are concerned with prophecy; the Spirit in the Lucan narrative appears specifically as the source of prophetic inspiration. Thus the angel announces to Zacharias that the prophet John will be "filled with the Spirit from his mother's womb," and that he will go before the Lord "in the Spirit and power of Elias." It is in close parallel with this annunciation to Zacharias that the same angel says to Mary: "The Holy Spirit will come upon thee and the power of the Most High will overshadow thee; therefore also that holy thing which is begotten shall be called Son of God." Whoever comes into contact with Mary while she is bearing the child in her womb, or comes into contact afterwards with the child Himself, experiences the activity of the Holy Spirit. When Mary greets Elisabeth, the child leaps in Elisabeth's womb, and Elisabeth herself is filled with the Holy Spirit and breaks forth into prophetic words.[113] To Simeon, upon whom the Holy Spirit is said to have rested, it is announced by the same Spirit that he should not see death before he had seen the Messiah. "In the Spirit" he comes into the Temple, takes the child Jesus into his arms, and breaks forth into prophetic words of praise. Finally we hear of the boy Jesus in the Temple and of his extraordinary spiritual gifts. Also in the parallel history of John the Baptist the *motif* of the Holy Spirit is not forgotten: Zacharias became full of the Holy Spirit and prophesied; and the child himself "grew and waxed strong in the Spirit."

The conclusion from these observations, which, themselves also, we have just reproduced almost in exact translation of Leisegang's own words, is as follows:

> We observe: the two passages which here speak of an activity of a "Holy Spirit" (1) during the pregnancy of Elisabeth [114] and (2) in connection with the conception in Mary's womb [115] are by Luke intertwined and interwoven with a wealth of expressions in which the "Holy Spirit" is quite clearly to be understood as the

[113] Originally, says Leisegang, the Magnificat was attributed to Elisabeth. This representation (on p. 24 of Leisegang's book) seems at first sight to be in rather strange contradiction with a passage on the very next page where stress is laid on the fact that Mary, not Elisabeth, speaks the prophetic verses of this psalm. But see below, pp. 376 f.

[114] *πνεύματος ἁγίου πλησθήσεται ἔτι ἐκ κοιλίας μητρὸς αὐτοῦ*, Lk. i.15.

[115] *πνεῦμα ἅγιον ἐπελεύσεται ἐπὶ σέ*, Lk. i.35.

gift of the prophetic Spirit, the vehicle of inspiration. At the same time there is lacking here any occasion for regarding the Spirit as a person. The drastic representation of a conception by a holy spirit,[116] in which the "spirit" takes the place of a male being who carries out the act of begetting, is here, in contrast with the representation in Matthew, carefully avoided. Instead of that, we have here in the description of the act of begetting (in addition to the thrice appearing expression, "to be filled with the Holy Spirit") the words, "The Holy Spirit shall come upon thee, and the power of the Most High shall overshadow thee." But the expressions, "to be filled with the Holy Spirit" and "the Holy Spirit to come upon someone," suggest inevitably the expressions (known also in the Greek literary language), "full of God," and "to breathe upon,"[117] "a breathing upon,"[118] which in turn lead us into the sphere of Dionysiac orgiasm—to be specific, into the sphere of enthusiastic manticism, a well-known form of Greek prophetism. And as a matter of fact the same "Holy Spirit," which accomplishes the conception of the child by Mary, makes Mary at the same time, according to the Lucan composition, a prophetess, who breaks forth into the enthusiastic verses of a psalm. It is at the same time the "prophetic Spirit" that broods over the persons active in the two birth narratives and is powerful in them.[119]

We are led in the same direction, Leisegang continues, by a consideration of the expression, "The power of the Most High shall overshadow thee." Whence comes the figure of speech involved in the word "overshadow"? It comes, according to Leisegang, from Hellenistic mysticism as attested by Philo. In certain passages[120] Philo connects the coming of the divine Logos for the inspiration of man with a darkening of the human understanding; only when the sun of human reason has set can the divine light shine upon the soul. The word "overshadow" is not indeed used in these passages; but it occurs in a passage where the inspiration that takes place when the human reason is darkened is an inspiration not by God, but by evil angels.[121] These passages, coupled with certain other indications, show, according to Leisegang, that the figure underlying the word "overshadow" in Lk. i.35 is the figure of a spiritual winged being that overshadows with his wings the human recipient of inspiration. "From this conception," says Leisegang, "there was developed first the general use of the word 'overshadow' to designate the approach of any spiritual being and then (in mystical circles) the special use to designate the darkening of the human understanding in the interests of the divine

[116] Leisegang here uses the Greek words, ἐκ πνεύματος ἁγίου, as he also uses the Greek word in other similar cases in this passage.

[117] ἐπιπνεῖν.

[118] ἐπίπνοια.

[119] Leisegang, *op. cit.*, pp. 24 f.

[120] *Quis rer. div. heres*, liii (ed. Cohn et Wendland, iii, 1898, p. 60); *de somniis*, I. xix (ed. Cohn et Wendland, iii, p. 230).

[121] *Quod deus sit immut.*, i (ed. Cohn et Wendland, ii, 1897, p. 56).

influence. Just by the choice of this word, therefore, the description of the pneumatic conception by Mary is very closely connected with the Greek notions of the communion of human beings, especially of women, with the world of spirits."[122]

But how, then, was it possible that the "Holy Spirit," regarded as a gift of inspiration, as "prophetic Spirit," became at the same time the cause of Mary's pregnancy? To answer this question we must search, according to Leisegang, in the sphere toward which the expressions used by Luke or by his source have already pointed us—namely, in the sphere of Greek prophetism.

In that sphere, it is no obscure phenomenon which first arrests our attention, but the well-known figure of the prophetess at Delphi, the Pythia. When that prophetess, a virgin, is represented as sitting on a tripod over the cavern from which the prophetic "spirit" came, it is perfectly plain, Leisegang thinks, from the attitude of the prophetess, from the expressions that are used by Greek writers, from the scornful words of Christian writers, that the prophetic spirit is represented in drastic fashion as being received into the *womb*. But it is not only from this secret of Greek manticism that the Christian apologists remove the veil; they also disclose, Leisegang says, the notion of pagan antiquity that a bearer of the divine spirit, a prophet, can by a carnal union transfer this gift to a woman, whereby the woman in turn becomes a prophetess. So Irenæus relates concerning the Gnostic prophet Marcus.[123] What Marcus is here represented as practising is nothing else than the transference into practice of the Greek speculation about the mystic union of the human soul with its heavenly bridegroom—in other words, the Greek speculation about the "sacred marriage." But it is well-known, says Leisegang, that this speculation had its origin in the religion of Dionysus and particularly in the mysteries.

Thus it is established to Leisegang's satisfaction "that between the prophetic spirit and the impregnation of a woman there is a fixed connection in thought; the divine 'spirit' is regarded as being capable of transmission, by means of a carnal union (either directly by the divinity himself or by a prophet who possesses the spirit), to a woman who thereby becomes herself a prophetess."[124]

But there still remains, Leisegang admits, a considerable gulf between the New Testament story of the supernatural conception by the Holy Spirit and these pagan notions as they have so far been set forth. The difference is that what Mary brings forth by her reception of the Spirit is an actual child, while what the pagan prophets or prophetesses bring forth are only prophetic words.

[122] Leisegang, *op. cit.*, pp. 28 f.

[123] Irenæus, *haer.*, I. xiii.3 (ed. Stieren, i, 1853, pp. 148–151), quoted in Epiphanius, *haer.*, xxxiv.2 (ed. Dindorf, ii, 1860, pp. 219 f.).

[124] Leisegang, *op. cit.*, p. 34.

Thus ventriloquists in antiquity were regarded as those who spoke "from out of the belly";[125] the words were forced out of them by a cramp-like impulse coming from the under part of the body; and that impulse was regarded as due to prophetic inspiration. The effect of divine or demoniac entrance into the belly or the womb was therefore the utterance of prophetic words, not the birth of a divine or demoniac child. Apparently, therefore, we have here something quite different from the New Testament representation.

It is in the effort to bridge this gulf that Leisegang develops the most distinctive part of his theory.

He points in a preliminary way, first, to the myth of the prophet-god Dionysus. Semele has union with Zeus; thereby she enters into an enthusiastic condition; all who touch her body are full of the god. And then she brings her divine child to the birth—her divine child who is himself a prophet and a dispenser of the divine spirit. In this myth Leisegang finds a special similarity to the Lucan narrative in that in both cases the mother during her pregnancy is represented as being herself in an enthusiastic condition and as transferring this condition to others who come into contact with her.[126]

The same *motif* appears also, Leisegang says, though in slightly different form, in the myth of Branchus, the founder of the Branchidic oracle. But it is not in the references to either of these myths that we find the real heart of Leisegang's theory. That is found, rather, in the use which Leisegang makes of certain passages in Philo, including the passage in the "De Cherubim" which we have quoted at length above.[127] In these passages, we have the notion of divine begetting coupled with the notion of virginity; only with a virgin soul, or rather with the archetypal idea of virginity, can God, according to Philo, have union for the bringing forth of that which is good. It is a great mistake, Leisegang says, to seek the origin of these ideas in any precedent Jewish belief regarding a virgin birth of the patriarchs;[128] rather is Philo led to his exegesis of the Old Testament passages by his desire to find Scriptural warrant for the Hellenistic notion of what a prophet should be. "Not because in a precedent tradition (indeed, that lacks all attestation) the Jewish patriarchs are virgin-born, do they become to Philo men of God and

[125] They were ἐγγαστρίμυθοι, "Bauchredner."

[126] Very unconvincing is Leisegang's reference in this connection to a passage in Eusebius (*demonstr. ev.*, VII. i. 96; ed. Heikel, in "Eusebius Werke", vi, 1913, p. 316, in *Die griechischen christlichen Schriftsteller*), in which, according to Leisegang, Eusebius in his treatment of the famous passage in Is. vii.14 "thinks it necessary" to call attention to the fact that the "virgin" in Isaiah is a "prophetess." Surely the use of the term "prophetess" is due simply to the fact that Eusebius is making capital of Is. viii.3, where that word is used of the prophet Isaiah's wife.

[127] Pp. 298–300.

[128] Compare above, pp. 298–300.

prophets. Rather because Moses and the patriarchs, especially Isaac, are to be made to correspond with the Hellenistic prophets and hierophants, there is interwoven with the story of their lives, by means of allegorical exegesis, the *motif* of divine begetting and virgin birth."[129] So clearly were the ideas of divine begetting and virgin birth connected with each other in the Hellenistic belief upon which Philo was dependent that he felt obliged to preserve their connection in his allegorical interpretation, no matter what violence was thereby done to the Old Testament narrative.

But still we have not yet penetrated, according to Leisegang, to the real root of this whole aspect of Philo's teaching. The real root of the whole complex of ideas was not found, Leisegang thinks, in anything that Philo had received from books, or that he had gleaned from a learned examination of pagan religion or philosophy. But it was found in a mystic experience through which Philo himself had passed—a mystic experience which was determinative of the whole character of his most important writing. Philo was no mere student of mysticism, but was himself a mystic—that conviction Leisegang shares with what seems to be the main trend of modern Philonic studies. In great sections of his works, indeed, the Alexandrian teacher writes in a vein very different from mysticism; he engages in a pedantic kind of argumentation that suggests the study-chamber rather than the place of religious exaltation. But from such sections of his works, Leisegang thinks, there are clearly to be distinguished the passages where mystical illumination is allowed free course. Philo was conscious of moments when suddenly there descended upon him a divine power which took him out of himself, placed his ordinary reasoning faculties in abeyance, and made of him a prophet and a seer. And to describe such experiences—to describe what, properly speaking, was indescribable—he had recourse to the well-known language about theogamy, divine begetting and virgin birth. In certain moments of his life he felt his soul to be suddenly fructified, quite without his own volition, by a stream of divine influence that caused him to bring forth ideas of which he would otherwise have been quite incapable.

Leisegang quotes in this connection the following passage where Philo describes such mystic experiences:[130]

For the things with which the soul is in travail of its own motion are for the most part abortions and untimely born; but as many things as God waters with snows from above are born perfect and whole and best of all things. I am not ashamed to tell of my own experience which I am conscious of having had many,

[129] Leisegang, *op. cit.*, p. 46.

[130] Philo, *de migr. Abr.*, 7 (ed. Cohn et Wendland, ii, 1897, p. 275). The translation is ours, with some use of Leisegang's renderings.

many times.[131] There have been times when, wishing to proceed according to the way of writing customary for philosophical doctrines, and knowing well what needed to be set down, I have yet found my mind impotent and barren[132] and so have desisted without accomplishing my purpose. Then I have blamed my mind for its false pretensions, but have wondered at the might of God,[133] in whose power lies the opening and shutting of the womb of the soul. But also there have been times when, coming empty to my task, I have suddenly become full by means of the thoughts that have mysteriously come down upon me like snow or like seed from above, so that in a divine possession[134] I have been filled with Corybantic frenzy and have lost awareness of everything—of the place, of my companions, of myself, of the things that were being said, of the things that were being written.

There we have, says Leisegang, the warm description, by a true mystic, of a personal experience of inspiration. The example of his own experience presses itself upon this writer's attention when he comes to speak of a fructification of the soul by God.

But how was the transition effected from the figure of divine begetting, which Philo uses to describe such mystical experiences, to the actual fact of a begetting of a human child by divine seed? The answer is found, Leisegang thinks, in a consideration of the pagan mysteries. In the mysteries—in the Dionysus religion with its Mænads, in the Delphic prophetess who brought forth mysterious words from her body without knowing what she was saying, in the liturgic pictures of the theogamy of the soul, in the cultic actions that suggested or even drastically set forth the union of God with a human being—in these things Philo discovered what he needed for the description of his own mystic experiences. Thus we have "everywhere the same thing: a sexual union between God and man—but in the greatest possible variety between the extreme of concrete sensuous action and spiritualized symbolism almost sublimated away into a mere rhetorical figure of speech."[135]

So, according to Leisegang, the importance of Philo lies in the insight that he gives us into the structure of Hellenistic mystical religion. At bottom, Leisegang says, what Philo has in mind is the personal experience of a stream of new power, supposedly supernatural, suddenly descending into the human soul. To describe this experience he makes use of the figures of divine begetting that appeared in the mysteries; and sometimes, says Leisegang, we can almost hear in his rhythmic words the chant of the initiates who in ecstasy,

[131] *μυριάκις.*
[132] *ἄγονον καὶ στεῖραν.*
[133] Literally, "of the One that is," *τοῦ ὄντος.*
[134] *ὑπὸ κατοχῆς ἐνθέου.*
[135] Leisegang, *op. cit.*, p. 47.

with lifted hands, pray for pneumatic conception and virgin birth.[136] This same figure he applies to the Old Testament narrative by means of allegorical exegesis; and thus are to be explained the passages where he speaks of the divine begetting of Isaac and of other Old Testament characters.

But Philo applies the same idea of divine begetting in another sphere also—namely, in the sphere of abstract speculation. Not only does he speak of a divine begetting of Isaac and other Old Testament characters, representing states of the human soul, but also he speaks of a divine begetting of the Logos, which represents the sensible world: from the impregnation of the mother, Wisdom, by the Father, God, the Logos comes forth as the first-born son. Here we have, according to Leisegang, nothing else than the projection of the mystic experience of a union of the human soul with God out into the region of the hypostases that exist outside of the sensible world—in other words (if we may use Platonic language for what is not really in accord with Plato's teaching), into the region of "ideas."

Thus we have in Philo the idea of divine begetting and virgin birth in two parallel spheres—in the sphere of the human soul and in the sphere of super-sensible hypostases. In both spheres the variety in which the idea appears is bewildering, as can be observed in the tabulation which Leisegang provides.[137] Everywhere there is (1) a male principle, (2) a female principle, and (3) the thing that is begotten; but the terms in which these three factors are set forth are so diverse that at first sight the whole complex of ideas might seem to be simply a mass of arbitrarily chosen fragments from various systems. But such an estimate would, according to Leisegang, be altogether unjust. We ought never to forget, he says, that Philo was a mystic, and that some of his writing was done in an ecstatic condition of the writer's soul. The bewildering variety of his utterances about divine begetting is to be explained, therefore, as the effort of a true mystic to express what is really inexpressible. Back of all such utterances is the mystic experience by which the soul, with its own faculties in abeyance, is suddenly fructified by an irresistible stream of divine power.

[136] Leisegang (*op. cit.*, p. 50) quotes one such rhythmic passage where very drastic language is used (*de somniis*, i.34; ed. Cohn et Wendland, iii, 1898, p. 248):

ἐπιβαίνετε οὖν οἱ σοφίας ὀρθοὶ λόγοι πάντες,
ὀχεύετε, σπείρετε,
καὶ ἣν ἂν ἴδητε ψυχὴν βαθεῖαν,
εὔγειον, παρθένον,
μὴ παρέλθητε,
καλέσαντες δ' εἰς τὴν ὁμιλίαν καὶ συνουσίαν ἑαυτῶν
τελειώσατε
καὶ ἐγκύμονα ἀπεργάσασθε.

[137] Leisegang, *op. cit.*, p. 52.

We are now in a position, says Leisegang, to trace the whole progress of the development of which the birth narratives of Matthew and Luke form a part.[138] Back of the whole development, Leisegang says, there lies "the mystic experience of an immediate and sudden union of the human soul with the Divine, the disappearance of the human consciousness in the presence of a power conceived of as supernatural—a power entering into the human soul from the outside and bringing forth religious enthusiasm, joy in the Spirit, and the gift of ecstatic speech."[139] In ancient Greece, in the early period, this mystic experience was prevalent especially among women, whose addiction to the wild, orgiastic religion of Dionysus is well known. Not unnaturally, therefore, the entrance of the divine power could be conceived of in such circles as the entrance of a demon who penetrated into a woman's body and performed with her the sacred act of begetting; and ancient popular belief would be favorable to such a view.

From the Dionysus cult, Leisegang continues, the *motif* of divine begetting entered into the sphere of enthusiastic manticism and of the mysteries. The priestess of the Pythian oracle is a typical example of a prophetess who as a result of pneumatic conception comes into an ecstatic condition and predicts the future. In the mysteries, the same experience was at least suggested, even if not always drastically set forth. In the myths also, as well as in the cults, we find the same belief; the birth of a prophet is preceded by an act of begetting on the part of a prophet-god, and thus is united the notion of prophetic speech as the result of a conception by a "spirit" with the notion of the birth of a divine child who possesses the prophetic gift. Thus the woman who bears the child becomes both herself a prophetess and also a prophet's mother.

Against this primitive popular belief, indeed, the poets and philosophers uttered emphatic protests:

> They condemned the mysteries; they sought other explanations for enthusiastic manticism; they interpreted the myths by allegorical methods. But wherever even in philosophical circles mysticism came to life and sought for means of describing the mystic-religious experience, recourse was had to the ancient representations, and use was made of them as of welcome figures of speech. When that was done, the distinction between man and woman fell away: the soul is now the female principle, the Divine the male principle, the spirit is the seed that proceeds as mystic power from God.[140]

[138] Before proceeding to this summary of the development, Leisegang enters upon a treatment of the Prologue of the Fourth Gospel and of the Protevangelium of James, the consideration of which would here lead us too far afield.

[139] Leisegang, *op. cit.*, p. 67.

[140] Leisegang, *op. cit.*, p. 69.

Through the growing spiritualizing of the idea of God under the influence of Platonic teaching, the act of begetting is more and more removed from the ordinary world and placed in the super-sensible world of hypostases or ideas.

> God in the region of the Beyond begets with the idea of virginity (which appears as wisdom, as virtue, as science, as everything beautiful and good) the world-creating power, the Logos. At this point there offer themselves rich possibilities of combination, which are the more exploited the richer and more varied are the myths and the figures of the sacred stories that are to be allegorically interpreted and thereby lifted into the region of mystic speculation. So there is a begetting and fructifying without end: God begets in Wisdom; He Himself, the Logos and all other heavenly powers beget in the human soul. Where the philosophic speculation is not understood and there is on the other hand a close relation to the popular belief still living in the lower classes of society—the popular belief from which the abstract figurative language of the philosophers originally came—a hopeless confusion runs riot. A man like Philo who is acquainted with the doctrine of hypostases would never put in the place of Wisdom or of the divine-human soul a bodily virgin living on this earth, and would never put in place of the Logos a human child of flesh and blood. . . . But to the layman who ventured into this field, who was equipped only with his subjective conviction of the truth-content of his own [mystic] experience that he found reflected both in the belief of the people and in the teachings of the philosophers—to him [or in his hands] all this must have come to be a hopeless tangle.[141]

As such laymen, says Leisegang, we must regard both Luke and the authors of the First and Fourth Gospels. The only difference is that the degree of their naïveté[142] in the things of Greek religion was not the same. Upon the lowest plane there stands the compiler of the birth-narrative in Matthew; for he simply seizes material that came to him from the Hellenistic world, understands it in accordance with popular Semitic belief, and inserts it as best he can into his narrative. Luke, on the other hand, displays a detailed acquaintance with the Greek beliefs of the lower classes and also with the prophetism that was developed from that belief. The few words with which he sets forth the pneumatic conception by Mary are the vehicle of his treatment of the mystic process which, often by only slight improvements and additions, he has imported into the infancy narrative. Over and in all the persons that appear in the narrative he causes the breath of the Spirit and its activities to blow. The Spirit for him, as in Greek manticism, is especially the prophetic Spirit. Its double activity—in ecstatic speech and in the birth of a divine child who Himself is distinguished by the gift of prophecy—is inserted into the

[141] Leisegang, *op. cit.*, pp. 69 f.
[142] "Harmlosigkeit."

narrative by subtle touches. Just as is the case with personages in the Greek myths, Mary is in Luke both a prophetess and the mother of a prophet. But of an acquaintance with philosophic speculation there is no trace.

Such is the theory of Leisegang. It constitutes certainly an imposing effort at solution of a problem which naturalistic historians have hitherto found unsoluble. But is it really any more successful than the theories that preceded it? That question must be answered in the negative.

There are, in the first place, various weaknesses in detail, which can hardly fail to appear to the careful reader. Particularly glaring is the weakness in the treatment of the Matthæan narrative. When Leisegang interprets *pneuma hagion* in Matthew as meaning "*a* holy spirit" and as referring to a personal being subordinate to God, surely he is departing from all sound principles of interpretation.[143] Where can he find a parallel for such a usage of the phrase either in the Biblical books or in related writings? The parallel passage in Luke gives him no help; for he admits that in that passage *pneuma hagion* has a very different meaning from the meaning that he attributes to it in Matthew. Surely a sound method would interpret the less definite passage by the help of the more definite,[144] since after all the two passages are closely parallel, and since not the slightest parallel can be found in related sources for the other interpretation of the Matthæan phrase. The Gospels do, indeed, speak of certain subordinate beings as "spirits"; but of the application of the word "holy" to any of these subordinate beings no trace can be found.

Leisegang thinks, indeed, that he can find parallels on Semitic ground for the notion of the birth of a child as the fruit of a union between a woman and a subordinate "spirit." But the Biblical passages which he cites in this connection—the passage in Gen. vi.1,2 where the "sons of God" and the "daughters of men" are spoken of, and the passage in I Cor. xi.10 regarding the angels—are obscure; and the illustrations upon which apparently he places chief reliance are found not in ancient, but in modern times. This latter circumstance might at first sight seem to be disconcerting; it might at first sight seem to be an objection to Leisegang's argument that the facts upon which it relies—the facts about fructification of women by "arch-welis" and the like—are attested not in ancient records, but in a description by S. I. Curtiss of modern conditions.[145] The truly advanced student of comparative religion, it is true, makes short shrift of such objections; he seldom allows the flow of his thought to be troubled by questions of date. But questions of date will persist in

[143] In criticism of Leisegang at this point, compare von Baer, *op. cit.*, pp. 114–120; F. Büchsel, *Der Geist Gottes im Neuen Testament*, 1926, p. 194.

[144] Supposing, for the sake of the argument, that Matthew really is less definite than Luke.

[145] S. I. Curtiss, *Primitive Semitic Religion To-day*, 1902.

arising in the minds of those who do not belong to the innermost circle of the comparative-religion school; and when they are allowed to arise at all they will place serious obstacles in the way of Leisegang's argument at this point.

Another objection to Leisegang's theory is found in the transition, in his treatment of Greek prophetism, from the notion of the bringing forth of inspired words to the notion of the bearing of an actual child. Leisegang himself is apparently aware of the difficulty that besets his theory at this point. "The Pythias," he says,[146] "the Sibyls, the Gnostic prophetesses, the participants in the mysteries receive the Spirit likewise in their body, come thereby into an enthusiastic condition, and bring forth—well, certainly not a child." After this correct observation, Leisegang proceeds to a five-page treatment of that which the Greek prophetesses and ventriloquists do bring forth—namely, prophetic words. Then he returns to the point at which he has left off, and seeks to bridge the gap between these prophetic or enthusiastic words and the actual bearing of a child. But it cannot be said that the evidence that he adduces is very abundant or very convincing.[147] He points, indeed, to the birth of the prophet-god Dionysus: Semele has union with Zeus, comes thereby into an enthusiastic condition, and brings forth a child who is both a prophet and the bestower of the divine spirit upon others. But is it really clear in this myth that the enthusiastic condition of Semele was due to her union with Zeus as such; may it not have been due rather to the fact that the particular child whom she was to bear was a prophet-god? After all, it is natural that the mother of a prophet-god should herself, during her pregnancy, have been possessed of the prophetic gift. We still do not see any very close connection here between the bringing forth of a child and that bringing forth of prophetic words which Leisegang has treated at such length. Even less convincing is the reference to Eusebius' comment on Is. vii.14, which has been dealt with above.[148] And with regard to the birth of Branchus, which Leisegang cites next, an observation may be made somewhat similar to that which has just been made with regard to the birth of Dionysus: Branchus was a prophet, and it was natural that he should be begotten by the prophet-god Apollo. The gift of prophecy, to put the thing in prosaic language, could be inherited like any other gift; but what does not seem to be clear is that there was any necessary connection between the bringing forth of prophetic words through divine inspiration and the bringing forth of an actual child.

Another detail in which Leisegang's exposition is open to criticism is his

[146] *Op. cit.*, p. 35.
[147] Compare Heinemann, *op. cit.*, lxvi, 1922, pp. 273 f.; Büchsel, *op. cit.*, pp. 199 f.
[148] See above, p. 368, footnote 126.

treatment of the word "overshadow" in Lk. i.35. The interpretation of this word by reference to a special mystical usage, in which it designates the darkening of the human understanding in the presence of divine inspiration, and ultimately by reference to the notion of a winged spiritual being who overshadows a man or woman with his wings, is certainly, to say the least, not clearly established. In the Philonic passages to which appeal is made, the actual word "overshadow" is not used of divine inspiration; but appears only in one passage, where the light of reason is said to be "overshadowed" so that the inhabitants of darkness can come into the soul and beget a baleful offspring by union with the passions. Surely we need not look to such a passage as this for an explanation of the Lucan word.[149]

But it is not such faults in detail that constitute the really central objection to Leisegang's theory. That central objection is found, rather, in the treatment of the Lucan narrative itself. Leisegang's whole construction depends on the connection which he detects in the first two chapters of Luke between prophetic inspiration and the conception of the child in Mary's womb. This connection does not exist; and hence the whole theory falls to the ground.[150]

According to Leisegang's theory, the child who is the product of the Spirit's activity in Mary's womb ought to be designated above all things as a prophet, and Mary herself ought to be represented as being filled with the Spirit whenever she speaks. But as a matter of fact these are just the things which do *not* appear. Nowhere in this narrative is Jesus designated as being "filled with the Spirit" or as being destined to speak by the Spirit when He should grow up. A similar observation may be made regarding Mary; in her case, as in the case of Jesus, the narrative says nothing about inspiration by the Holy Spirit. She is represented, indeed, as speaking the Magnificat, which may no doubt plausibly be regarded as an inspired song; but even at this point the narrator does not call attention to her being filled with the Spirit.

The attitude of Leisegang toward the Magnificat is not altogether clear. At first he says that Elisabeth, not Mary, was originally represented as the speaker of it; and yet on the following page he lays stress on the fact that

149 Compare Bultmann, review of Norden, *Die Geburt des Kindes*, 1924, in *Theologische Literaturzeitung*, xlix, 1924, col. 322: "The derivation of ἐπισκιάζειν (Lk. i.35) from mystical religion [Norden and Leisegang hold similar views about this] appears to me to fall down not only because the word in the only place where so far as I know it appears in Philo in a mystical sense is differently construed from the way in which it is construed in Lk. i.35, but especially because if this derivation were correct the expression would have to be supposed to have forced its way out of the realm of mystical religion, in which it is comprehensible, into the realm of mythology, in which it would not be comprehensible." Compare also Heinemann, *op. cit.*, lxvii, 1923, p. 33, footnote 2; von Baer, *op. cit.*, pp. 127–129; W. K. Lowther Clarke, *New Testament Problems*, 1929, pp. 71–75; Kattenbusch, in *Theologische Studien und Kritiken*, cii, 1930, pp. 463 f.

150 Compare Bultmann, as quoted below, p. 378; also Büchsel, *loc. cit.*

Mary breaks forth, in the Magnificat, into an enthusiastic psalm and that thus she, as well as Elisabeth, is represented as being possessed of the prophetic gift.[151] At first sight, it looks like a mere contradiction, due to careless use of the Magnificat in a double way; but apparently Leisegang's meaning is that while the Magnificat was attributed to Elisabeth in the underlying narrative it was transferred to Mary by the Evangelist-redactor who also apparently gave it its present form.[152] This transfer of the Magnificat to Mary seems to be represented as part of the redactional activity by which the Evangelist inserted reference to the mystical process into the infancy narrative.[153] We confess, however, that the matter is still not quite clear. It still looks a little as though Leisegang were using the Magnificat in one place to prove that Elisabeth, and in another place to prove that Mary, is represented in the narrative as a prophetess. Surely such a double use of the psalm is quite without warrant.

At any rate, what is plain is that even in the completed narrative, with the introduction of the "mystical process" all finished, still Mary is not represented as the possessor of prophetic inspiration when she spoke her word of praise. It is not sufficient to say that such a psalm must no doubt be regarded by the narrator as being spoken under the influence of the Spirit; our point is that according to Leisegang the purpose of the Evangelist was to connect the conception of the child in the womb with the prophetic Spirit which the mother possessed, and if that is so we should certainly expect the connection to be explicit and not merely implicit. If the final author was dominated by the idea that the Spirit in Mary was both the source of prophetic inspiration and also the source of her conception of her child in the womb, it does seem strange that he has so carefully avoided saying that that was the case. Why should what Leisegang regards as the central thought of the narrator be so carefully concealed in the narrative as it stands?

It may of course freely be admitted that in the Lucan infancy narrative as a whole the presence of the prophetic Spirit is noted in the case of a number of the personages—John the Baptist,[154] Elisabeth, Zacharias, Simeon. But, in the first place, as Bultmann has remarked, these passages do not go beyond the Old Testament-Jewish doctrine of the Spirit,[155] and therefore do not re-

151 Leisegang, *op. cit.*, pp. 24 f. Compare also p. 41.

152 Elisabeth, according to Leisegang (*op. cit.*, pp. 23 f.), "speaks prophetic words, which have been moulded by Luke into the form of a psalm."

153 Leisegang, *op. cit.*, p. 70.

154 Quite unwarranted, it is true, is Leisegang's use, in this connection, of Lk. i.80: for when it is said that John "waxed strong in spirit," surely "spirit" is simply in contrast with "body," or the like, and does not refer to the Spirit of God.

155 Bultmann, in his review of Leisegang's book in *Theologische Literaturzeitung*, xlvii, 1922, col. 426.

quire us to have recourse, for their elucidation, to the Hellenistic mystical notions which Leisegang sets forth in such an extensive and such an interesting way; and, in the second place, there is no real trace in the Lucan narrative of any *connection* between these manifestations of the Holy Spirit in prophecy and the special act of the same Holy Spirit in bringing about the conception of the child in Mary's womb. It is this latter fact which is most obviously decisive against Leisegang's theory. We may, indeed, read Leisegang's book with interest; we may learn much from him about the history of Greek mystical religion; but, after all, the bearing of the whole complex of facts upon our subject depends upon the exegetical question whether in the Lucan narrative there is any special connection between prophetic inspiration and the supernatural conception in the virgin's womb. That question must be answered in the negative, and therefore the foundation of Leisegang's whole theory as to the origin of the virgin birth idea is destroyed.

That this estimate of Leisegang's theory need not be attributed merely to apologetic zeal on our part may perhaps be shown by a quotation from one of the most distinguished contemporary New Testament scholars—namely, from Rudolf Bultmann, who certainly cannot be accused of any apologetic bias. In a review of Leisegang's book Bultmann says:[156]

> The crucial point in the argumentation [of Leisegang] is, however, the question whether in Lk. i there is really to be found a connection between the Spirit as "prophetic Spirit"[157] and as power of fructification. This is in my judgment not the case. That which in Lk. i (aside from verses 34-37) is said concerning the Spirit does not seem to go beyond Old Testament-Jewish ideas; moreover, neither is Mary represented as a pneumatic prophetess (even if verses 46 ff. belong in her mouth), nor is Jesus, the miraculously conceived child, represented as a prophet, as ought to be the case according to the analogies. Above all, however, the verses 34-37 (or 34-35), which contain the *motif* of the miraculous conception, are probably an insertion into the source, so that the connection which Leisegang maintains does not exist at all. In my opinion the *motif* of the supernatural conception in Luke as well as in Matthew comes from a very much more primitive sphere than that of Hellenistic mysticism; and it seems to me to be a very artificial proceeding to explain Mt. i.18-21 from crassly misunderstood Greek pneuma-speculation adapted to Semitic popular beliefs.

In general Bultmann holds Leisegang's book, despite its instructiveness in detail, to be mistaken.[158]

[156] Bultmann, in *Theologische Literaturzeitung*, *loc. cit.* Compare also R. Asting, *Die Heiligkeit im Urchristentum*, 1930, pp. 119 f.
[157] We have here translated the words which Bultmann quotes in Greek.
[158] "Verfehlt"—Bultmann, *op. cit.*, col. 427.

Certain questions arise in our mind as we read these words of Bultmann's—notably the question whether Leisegang's theory as to the composition of the narrative is as different as the reviewer seems to think it is from the interpolation theory which the reviewer himself holds. We have already observed that Leisegang seems to find back of Lk. i an underlying narrative which was subtly transformed by the Evangelist through the addition of various touches, until it became the vehicle of the notion about the Spirit which Leisegang supposes the present form of the narrative to teach. But it is far from clear in Leisegang's exposition how much is to be attributed to the source and how much to the Evangelist; and in particular it is far from clear whether, according to Leisegang, the source, as distinguished from the completed Gospel, presented or did not present a doctrine of prophetic inspiration similar to that which Leisegang sets forth. We have mentioned above one particular instance of this lack of clearness—namely, the treatment of the Magnificat. But the fault may be found to be more far-reaching than that. As Bultmann seems correctly to observe, Leisegang's explanation of the virgin birth idea by reference to other elements in the first chapter of Luke apparently requires acceptance of the integrity of the narrative; yet it is a grave question how far Leisegang himself accepts that integrity. We may well ask, in other words, whether Leisegang, in view of his distinction between the parts due to the source and the parts due to the Evangelist, really has any right to use the whole of the narrative as casting light upon Lk. i.34,35.

At any rate, the rejection of Leisegang's theory by Bultmann is not without interest. It shows us anew that those who deny the historicity of the virgin birth have never been able to agree upon any one theory as to the origin of the virgin birth idea. Very imposing is Leisegang's construction; but there is not the slightest reason to think that it is destined to win any more general acceptance, among those who share its author's naturalistic presuppositions, than has been won by the constructions that preceded it. The problem of the virgin birth idea has not been solved by this most elaborate of all attempts, any more than it was solved by the many previous theories that have succeeded one another in the long history of modern naturalistic criticism. The conclusion to which we are obliged to come after examination of the whole subject of "alternative theories" is that if the doctrine of the virgin birth of Christ did not originate in fact, modern critical investigation has at any rate not yet succeeded in showing how it did originate.

Chapter XV

CONCLUSION AND CONSEQUENCES

IN THE preceding discussion we have considered, first, the virgin birth tradition itself, and, second, the attempts which have been made to account for it, supposing it not to be true.

We have shown, under the former head, that in the early patristic period no gradual formation of the tradition can be traced, but that the tradition appears just as firmly established at the beginning of the second century as at the close. We have shown that in the New Testament it does not appear as a late addition, but had an original place in the First and Third Gospels and was plainly attested in Palestinian sources, oral or written, underlying those Gospels. We have shown that the two infancy narratives containing it are independent but not contradictory. We have shown that it is not contradicted by the rest of the New Testament and that it is as strongly attested as we should expect it to be on the assumption that it is true.

Under the second head, we have shown that if the virgin birth tradition is not true the efforts at explaining the origin of it have so far resulted in failure. It did not originate on the basis of Jewish ideas or in order to show fulfilment of a misunderstood prophecy. It was no mere reflex among Gentile Christians of the pagan notions about children begotten by the gods. It was no ancient pagan idea already naturalized in the pre-Christian Jewish doctrine of the Messiah. The advocates of one of these theories are often the severest critics of the advocates of another; and none of the theories has obtained anything like general assent.

What, then, shall be said about the central historical question: was Jesus of Nazareth born without human father or was He born as all other men are born? That question obviously cannot be answered when it is considered in isolation from everything else; it cannot be answered unless it is taken in connection with what we know in general concerning Jesus Christ.

Even in isolation, indeed, the story of the virgin birth should give the thoughtful historian pause. There is a startling beauty and vividness and originality about the first chapters of Matthew and Luke. Only superficiality can detect a similarity here to the coarse and degrading stories which are found in the surrounding world. Whence came this supremely beautiful tale, so unlike the products of human fancy, so unlike the myths of all the peoples that have lived upon the earth? Whence came such a story not in later generations, but in close proximity to the time of the narrated events? Whence came the self-evidencing quality of this narrative, so simple yet so profound?

These questions, we think, are unanswerable. Even if the story of the virgin birth stood alone, it would at least present an insoluble problem to the man who would regard it as untrue. But it would be hard for this bewilderment to issue in belief. The story of the virgin birth is the story of a stupendous miracle, and against any such thing there is an enormous presumption drawn from the long experience of the race.

As it is, however, that presumption can be overcome; it can be overcome when the tradition of the virgin birth is removed from its isolation and taken in connection with the whole glorious picture of the One who in this tradition is said to be virgin-born. What shall we think of Jesus Christ? That is the question of all questions, and it can be answered aright only when the evidence is taken as a whole. It is a fact of history, which no serious historian can deny, that in the first century of our era there walked upon this earth One who was like none other among the children of men. Reduce the sources of information all you will, and still that mysterious figure remains, that figure who is attested in the Epistles of Paul, that figure who walks before us in lifelike, self-evidencing fashion in the Gospels, that figure upon whom the Christian Church was built. Many have been the efforts to explain Him in terms of what is common to mankind, to explain Him as a product of forces elsewhere operative in the world. Those explanations may satisfy the man who treats the evidence, in pedantic fashion, bit by bit; but they will never satisfy the man who can view the whole. View Jesus in the light of God and against the dark background of sin, view Him as the satisfaction of man's deepest need, as the One who alone can lead into all glory and all truth, and you will come, despite all, to the stupendous conviction that the New Testament is true, that God walked here upon the earth, that the eternal Son, because He loved us, came into this world to die for our sins upon the cross.

When you have arrived at that conviction you will turn with very different eyes to the story of the virgin and her child. Wonders will no longer repel you. Rather will you say: "So and so only did it behoove this One, as distinguished from all others, to be born."

At this point, indeed, a misunderstanding lies ready at hand. Are we not arguing that a man will accept the story of the supernatural conception in the virgin's womb only when he is already convinced, on other grounds, of the supernatural dignity of Him about whom that story is told? Do we then mean that the tradition of the virgin birth hangs as a dead weight upon the man who accepts in general the New Testament account of Jesus Christ; do we mean that a man can believe in the supernatural person of Christ merely despite, and not at all because of, the story of the virgin birth?

As a matter of fact, that is not our meaning at all. To our mind, the story of the virgin birth, far from being an obstacle to faith, is an aid to faith; it is an organic part of that majestic picture of Jesus which can be accepted most easily when it is taken as a whole. The story of the virgin birth will hardly, indeed, be accepted when it is taken apart from the rest; but when taken in connection with the rest it adds to, as well as receives from, the convincing quality of the other things about Jesus which the New Testament tells.[1]

At this point we are brought to the last question with which it is necessary for us to deal—the question, namely, as to the importance of belief in the virgin birth to the Christian man. That question is being argued eagerly at the present day; there are many who tell us that, though they believe in the virgin birth themselves, they do not think that that belief is important for all men or essential even to the corporate witness of the Church.

This attitude, we are convinced, is radically wrong, and with a brief grounding of this conviction regarding it our discussion may properly be brought to a close. What is the importance of the question of the virgin birth?

In the first place, the question is obviously important for the general question of the authority of the Bible. It is perfectly clear that the New Testament teaches the virgin birth of Christ; about that there can be no manner of doubt. There is no serious question as to the *interpretation* of the Bible at this point. Everyone admits that the Bible represents Jesus as having been conceived by the Holy Ghost and born of the virgin Mary.[2] The only question is whether in making that representation the Bible is true or false.

[1] Compare B. B. Warfield, "The Supernatural Birth of Jesus: Is It Essential to Christianity?", in *American Journal of Theology*, x, 1906, p. 21: "I certainly make no question that additional evidence of tremendous weight is brought to this fact by its place in the system of Christianity, commended as this system as a whole is by the entire body of proof which we call the 'Christian evidences.' But I do not believe that it needs this additional evidence for its establishment. And I prefer my readers to understand that I proceed to the consideration of its place in the Christian system with it in my hands, not as a hypothesis of more or less probability (or improbability), but as a duly authenticated actual occurrence, recognized as such on its own direct evidence, and bringing as such its own quota of support to the Christian system of which it forms a part." See also, with regard to the connection of the virgin birth with the whole New Testament account of Jesus Christ, J. A. Faulkner, "The Miraculous Birth of our Lord," in *The Aftermath Series*, Number 10, 1924, p. 473.

[2] The curious views of Badham and C. C. Torrey (see above, pp. 128 f., 304 f.) may surely be left out of account. Even they do not eliminate the supernatural from what they regard as the thought of the authors of the First and Third Gospels.

If the latter alternative is chosen, if the Bible is regarded as being wrong in what it says about the birth of Christ, then obviously the authority of the Bible, in any high sense, is gone. It is true, men use that word "authority" in very loose senses today. Why may not the Bible be authoritative, they say, even though what it says about the birth of Jesus without human father is not true? Why may not the Bible be authoritative in the sphere of religion even though it is not authoritative in the sphere of history or of science? May not Jesus still be the Master of human hearts even though the Gospels of Matthew and Luke are wrong about the way in which He came into the world? May not even these stories of His birth, which we are obliged to reject as history, possess a profounder authority as expressions of the homage due to Him who led men into communion with the Father God?

Such is the attitude of many modern men. Give the Bible its proper place, they say, as a book of religion and not of science, as a book of inspiration and not of external history, and its authority will be quite independent of all that historical science can say. Thus the modern denial of the virgin birth, as of other elements in the Gospel account of Jesus, so disturbing at first to devout Christian feeling, may, it is thought, turn out to be a blessing in the end. By removing false notions of Bible authority it may establish a true authority which will stand forever firm.

What shall we say of such an attitude as that? Briefly we can say this of it—that if it is correct the Christian religion, as it has existed for some nineteen hundred years, must now at length be given up. It is not this or that element of the Christian religion that is here at stake, but all elements of it, or rather the Christian religion as an organic whole. What is this modern religion that is founded upon a Bible whose authority is altogether in the sphere of inspiration and not at all in the sphere of external fact? Is it not a religion whose fundamental tenet is the ability of man to save himself? Give us the moral and spiritual values of the Christian religion, it is said in effect, give us the inspiration of the teaching and example of Jesus, and we have all that is needed for our souls; not for us is there any need of dependence upon the question what happened or did not happen in the external world nineteen hundred years ago. Dependence upon those things belonged to the childhood stage of religion, but we, as distinguished from the men of past ages, find our God here and now in the depths of our own souls. What care we how Jesus entered into the world? However that may be, His teaching stirs our souls and leads us out into a larger life.

Such is the modern religion that is independent of events like the virgin birth. The adherents of it are, indeed, seldom quite consistent; for if they were consistent they could not depend upon the example of Jesus, as many of them do. The authority of the Bible, they say, lies altogether in the sphere of religion and ethics and not at all in the sphere of external history. But what is the logical result of a principle like that? Is it not to make the authority of the Bible and to make the Christian religion independent of the question whether such a person as Jesus ever lived upon this earth? That Jesus lived in Palestine nineteen hundred years ago is surely an assertion in the sphere of external history; and if so the authority of the Bible and the truth of the Christian religion cannot, according to the principle with which we are now dealing, be staked upon it. Thus upon this principle we have logically what B. B. Warfield aptly called a "Christless Christianity"; [3] even the very existence of Jesus is unnecessary to this sublimated religion that is independent of events in the external world.

There are some modern men, like D. C. Macintosh in America,[4] who do not shrink from this logical result of their position; Christianity, they say, could conceivably exist in its inmost essence even if no such person as Jesus ever lived. But many men shrink from a logic that is so thoroughgoing as that. They say, on the one hand, that Christianity and the authority of the Bible are quite independent of events in the external world; and yet on the other hand they do make both of these depend upon certain external events, after all. We shall not endeavor to explain how otherwise intelligent persons can stick in a halfway position that is so utterly inconsistent and absurd; but stick in it they certainly do, and they must be reckoned with in any complete account of the modern religious world. They are indeed losing ground rapidly at the present time; a Christianity dependent upon the so-called "historical Jesus" is gradually giving place to a Christianity that is dependent upon no Jesus at all—a Christianity that is content to use the ethical and religious ideas contained in the Gospels without settling the question whether the person who is said to have enunciated these ideas ever really walked upon the earth. But such consistency, even though it is being attained among scholars, has not yet won any general acceptance among popular exponents of "Liberalism" in the Church; and such popular exponents of Liberalism, with disregard of all logic, go cheerfully on asserting that the authority of the Bible lies altogether in the sphere of ideals (or what they call "religion"), while all the time they do regard as essential to the Bible its attestation of the existence of Jesus and so its attestation of an external fact.

At any rate, even such an attitude, though it shrinks from the full conse-

[3] Warfield, "Christless Christianity," in *Harvard Theological Review*, v, 1912, pp. 423–473.
[4] *The Reasonableness of Christianity*, 1926, pp. 135–138.

quences of the radical principle with which it begins, is, itself also, quite contrary to the Christian religion. What is this religion that is founded upon a historical Jesus, and yet is independent of events like the virgin birth? Is it not still a religion whose fundamental tenet is the ability of man to save himself? Jesus attained to sonship with God, say the adherents of this religion in effect, and we, if we will only follow Him, can attain to that sonship, too. Certainly men who think thus will not be much interested in the fact of the virgin birth. Indeed, if they are interested in it at all, they can be interested only in rejecting it. The fundamental notion of their religion is that Jesus showed us what man can do; but if so it is important for our encouragement that He should be thought to have begun where we too must begin. If He was born of a virgin He had an advantage which we do not possess; how, then, can we in that case be sure that we, who were not virgin-born, can do what He did? Carpocrates and the Ebionites of Epiphanius have here come to life again in the modern world. We can all be Christs if we will only follow Christ's example—that is the essence of this religion of the imitation of Jesus. Such a religion, both in ancient and modern times, will, if it be logical, have nothing to do with the story of the miracle in the virgin's womb.

It seems never to have occurred to the adherents of this religion that there is such a thing as sin, and that sin places an awful gulf between man and God. But those convictions, though they are unpopular at the present time, are certainly quite central in the Christian religion. From the beginning Christianity was the religion of the broken heart; it is based upon the conviction that there is an awful gulf between man and God which none but God can bridge. The Bible tells how that gulf was bridged; and that means that the Bible is a record of facts. Of what avail, without the redeeming acts of God, are all the lofty ideals of Psalmists and Prophets, all the teaching and example of Jesus? In themselves they can bring us nothing but despair. We Christians are interested not merely in what God commands, but also in what God did; the Christian religion is couched not merely in the imperative mood, but also in a triumphant indicative; our salvation depends squarely upon history; the Bible contains that history, and unless that history is true the authority of the Bible is gone and we who have put our trust in the Bible are without hope.

Certainly, whatever we may think of it, that is the view of Bible authority which the Bible itself takes. The authors of books like the Gospels are not intending merely to give their readers inspiring poetry or an instructive philosophy of religion; they are intending to narrate facts. The prologue of the Third Gospel is really typical of the Bible; faith, according to the Bible, is founded upon an account of things that have happened in the external world, and it is the purpose of the Biblical writers to set forth those things in an orderly and trustworthy way. The Bible, in other words, does not merely tell us what God is, but it also tells us what God did; it contains not merely permanent truths of religion and ethics, but also a gospel or a piece of good news.

An integral part of that piece of news, to the authors of the First and Third Gospels, was the fact that Jesus Christ was conceived by the Holy Ghost and born of the virgin Mary. If that fact is rejected, then the witness of these writers—and hence the witness of the Bible—is in so far not true.

If, therefore, the virgin birth be rejected, let us cease talking about the "authority of the Bible" or the "infallibility of Scripture" or the like. Let us rather say plainly that that authority and that infallibility are gone. We may indeed hold that many things which the Bible says are true, even though this thing that it says is untrue. Many earnest souls—if we may for the moment speak in general terms and without reference to the virgin birth—adopt such a mediating position. They hold that, although the Bible is wrong in many particulars, although it displays no supernatural freedom from the errors that beset other books, yet it contains some things that are true, and upon those things we can ground our hope for time and for eternity. Far better is it to say that these men are right, to say that the Bible is not infallible but only partly true, than to say that the Bible is infallible in the sphere of religion and ethics, and that the external happenings that it relates are matters of indifference to our souls. Many earnest Christians hold the former position; but a man who really holds the latter position cannot logically be a Christian at all. Christianity is founded upon the redeeming work of Christ which was accomplished in Palestine nineteen hundred years ago; to be indifferent to the record that sets forth that work is to reject the gospel in which Christ is offered as our Saviour from sin and wrath.

But even if the former position is taken, even if we do continue to rest for salvation upon part of the record of facts which the Bible contains, still, if we reject other parts, our belief in the authority of the Bible is gone. We may hold that many things which the Bible tells us are true, but we can no longer depend upon the Bible *as such*. We can no longer say, as many simple Christians say, "I believe this or that because God has told it to me in His book."

We are not now arguing the question whether this attitude of simple "Bible Christians" is right or wrong; we are not arguing the question whether the infallibility of Scripture can really be maintained in the modern world. But what we are saying is that if the infallibility of Scripture is to be abandoned, there should be no concealment from simple Christians of the full seriousness of the step. Let us stop speaking of the "infallibility" of a book that we hold to be in considerable measure untrue. Really the issues are too momentous, and human souls are too deeply concerned, to permit of any such trifling as that. A man may hold what opinion he will about the doctrine of Biblical infallibility, he may denounce it all he pleases, as involving us in a slavish religion of a book; but the importance of the doctrine he cannot possibly deny. It is a thing to which countless souls cling today, for weal or for woe. If it is a bad thing, let it by all means be abandoned, but let it be abandoned at least in a perfectly straightforward and open way.

Certainly that doctrine of Biblical infallibility is involved in the question of the virgin birth. It seems strange that we should ever have been obliged to argue the matter at all, but there are scarcely any limits to the confusion of religious discussion at the present day. The Bible teaches the virgin birth of Christ; a man who accepts the virgin birth may continue to hold to the full truthfulness of the Bible; a man who rejects it cannot possibly do so. That much at least should be perfectly plain.

In the second place, the question of the virgin birth is important as a test for a man to apply to himself or to others to determine whether one holds a naturalistic or a supernaturalistic view regarding Jesus Christ. There are two generically different views about Jesus, and they are rooted in two generically different views about God and the world. According to one view, God is immanent in the universe in the sense that the universe is the necessary unfolding of His life; and Jesus of Nazareth is a part of that unfolding, a supreme product of the same divine forces that are elsewhere operative in the world. According to the other view, God is the Creator of the universe, immanent in it but also eternally separate from it and free; and Jesus of Nazareth came into the universe from outside the universe, to do what nature could never do. The former view is the view of modern naturalism in many different forms; the latter view is the view of the Bible and of the Christian Church.

How can it be determined which of these two views is held by any particular modern man? Obviously that question is best answered when it is made concrete, and it is best made concrete when it deals with the supernatural as it appears in the New Testament books. But at what point may the issue best be raised; what question may be asked to determine whether a man holds a naturalistic or a supernaturalistic view of Jesus Christ?

The matter is by no means so simple as at first sight it might appear. Perhaps the first question which might occur to the layman, as being the question to ask, is the question, "Do you believe in the deity of Christ?" But that question obviously will not do at all. It is difficult to imagine any assertion more utterly meaningless in the religious parlance of the present day than the assertion, "I believe in the deity of Christ," or the assertion, "I believe that Jesus is God." These assertions have meaning only when the terms that they contain are defined; the assertion, "Jesus is God," depends for its significance altogether upon what is meant by "God."

But unfortunately that term, like the term "deity," is often defined today to mean something entirely different from what the simple Christian holds it to mean. The simple Christian, like Jesus of Nazareth, is a convinced theist; indeed, he is such a convinced theist that no other view of God save the theistic view ever comes into his mind. But many leaders of the modern Church and hosts of modern ministers, unlike the simple Christian and unlike Jesus of Nazareth, are not theists at all. They are either pantheists or positivists, and their pantheistic or positivistic opinions determine what they mean by "God."

If they are pantheists, "God" means to them the mighty process of the world itself or else (if their pantheism is not quite consistent and complete) the spiritual purpose that pulsates through the world. On that view Jesus is God in a sense not essentially different from that in which all men are God. Efforts may be made to preserve for Him some sort of uniqueness; He may be regarded as the supreme manifestation of the divine life or the like; but, after all, according to such a view the presence of the divine life in Him is not essentially different from its presence in other men.

If positivism rather than pantheism is the way of thinking that is chosen, then the assertion, "Jesus is God," merely means that Jesus is the highest thing that we moderns know. We have given up the old notion, it is said in effect, that there is a personal Creator and Ruler of the world; such things belong, at any rate, merely to metaphysics, and not at all to religion, and upon such speculations little reliance can be placed. But the word "God" is a useful word; it releases certain worthy emotions of reverence and love which humanity cannot afford to do without; we shall therefore retain it to designate the highest thing that we know. But the highest thing that we moderns know is not a mysterious Creator and Ruler, or indeed anything else that is beyond the confines of the universe; for in such a Creator and Ruler we have ceased to believe, and beyond the confines of the universe we are no longer bold enough to look. So the highest thing that we moderns know must be something that we can see and hear, something within the course of this world. But within such limits the highest thing that we know, the thing most worthy to evoke our reverence, is the moral life of Jesus of Nazareth. To that moral life of the man Jesus, therefore, we do honor by applying to Jesus the word "God."

It should be perfectly clear that the adherents of both of these ways of thinking are far more remote from the Christian faith than were the older Unitarians; for the older Unitarians, in something like a Christian sense, no doubt still believed in God. The man who says, "There is a God who is Creator and Ruler of the world, and Jesus is not that God," is far nearer to the Christian faith than the man who says, "There is no God who is Creator and Ruler of the world, but Jesus is 'God' in our modern sense." In countless cases the assertion, "Jesus is God," is not the most Christian, but almost the least Christian, thing that modern religious teachers say. Yet the plain man often goes away from his hearing of such utterances much impressed. When he goes away much impressed, we have the distinct feeling that he has been trifled with. About such serious matters there should be, above all, great plainness and openness of speech. At any rate it is perfectly clear that the question, "Do you believe in the deity of Christ?," or the question, "Do you believe that Jesus is God?," is in itself quite valueless today to determine whether a man holds a Christian or a non-Christian, a supernaturalistic or a naturalistic, view of Jesus Christ.

Evidently, therefore, if we want to discover anyone's position in the great religious issue of the present day, we must be more specific; we must single out some particular manifestation of the supernatural as the point at which the issue shall be raised. But where shall such a point be found; what particular miracle shall be singled out to find whether a man believes in the supernatural or not?

Our first impulse might be to single out the supreme miracle in the New Testament—namely, the resurrection of Christ. Surely, it might be held, if a man is willing to say, "I believe in the resurrection of Christ," he has parted company with modern naturalism and has taken his stand squarely with the despised believers in the supernatural Person whom the New Testament presents.

But here again first appearances are deceptive, and an assertion that to the plain man seems to be very definite is in modern parlance not definite at all. The assertion, "I believe in the resurrection of Christ," has in itself today almost as little meaning as the assertion, "I believe that Jesus is God," so abysmal is the intellectual morass into which we have been flung by the modern business of "interpreting" perfectly plain language in a sense utterly different from the sense in which it has always hitherto been used. The truth is that the expression, "resurrection of Christ," is used in widely different senses today. Some men mean by it merely the continued influence of Jesus; others use it in a mystical sense to indicate the presence of "the living Christ" in human souls; others mean by it the continued personal existence of Jesus, or what might formerly have been called the immortality of His soul.

We do not for one moment mean to say that these new interpretations of the expression are justifiable in the least. Surely we are bound, in our use of the word "resurrection" as applied to Jesus, by the meaning which the earliest sources attribute to the term. And about what that meaning is there can really be little doubt. Evidently the New Testament books do not mean by the resurrection of Jesus merely His continued personal existence. In that sense the disciples believed in His resurrection even during the sad three days when they were in such despair. They were certainly not Sadducees; they did not believe that Jesus' personal identity was lost, and no doubt they believed that He would rise from the dead as all other men would rise at the end of the age. But it never occurred to them to call that continued existence of Jesus "resurrection," and only when they became convinced of the real resurrection, the actual emergence of the Lord's body from the tomb, did they become the instruments in founding the Christian Church. To use the word "resurrection" in any other way than this way in which it is used by the New Testament books is merely to confuse our discussion of this theme.

Nevertheless, it cannot be denied that such other uses of the word, however unjustifiable they may be, are very common at the present time; so that for a man to say that he believes in the "resurrection" of Christ means in itself, prior to careful definition, practically nothing at all.

But it is somewhat different when we come to deal with the virgin birth. If a man affirms that Jesus was born without human father, being conceived by the Holy Ghost in the virgin's womb, it is difficult to see how he can escape the plain meaning of such terms; and thus when he makes that affirmation, he has taken the momentous step of affirming the entrance of the supernatural into the course of this world. Misguided apologetics, we know, may sometimes have obscured the issue; defenders of the virgin birth have sometimes talked about "parthenogenesis" and thus have sought to bring the conception by the Holy Spirit in Mary's womb into some sort of analogy with what nature can produce. But such apologetic expedients, fortunately, are rare; and certainly they are contrary to sound sense. It still remains true in general that the question of the virgin birth brings us sharply before the question of the supernatural, and that a man who accepts the virgin birth has taken his stand squarely upon supernaturalistic ground. There is possibility of evasion even here, but it is much less serious than in the case of many other points at which the issue might be raised.

We do not mean that a modern man who accepts the virgin birth has necessarily accepted all of Christianity. Certainly that is far from being the case; for sometimes acceptance of the virgin birth is an isolated Christian survival in a man's thinking, which goes along with a rather general rejection of the Christian view of Christ. At any rate, the importance of the virgin birth should never blind our eyes to the importance of other things; and we are in little agreement with those who make the Apostles' Creed, in which the virgin birth is contained, the be-all and the end-all of their Christian profession. Just as important is the Christian doctrine of redemption—the Christian doctrine of sin and grace—about which the Apostles' Creed says scarcely a word.

But the two elements of Christian truth belong logically together; the supernatural Person of our Lord belongs logically with His redemptive work; the virgin birth belongs logically with the Cross. Where one aspect is given up, the other will not logically remain; and where one is accepted, the other will naturally be accepted, too. There may be halfway positions for a time, but they are in unstable equilibrium and will not long be maintained.

Certain it is that men who reject the virgin birth scarcely ever hold to a really Christian view of Christ. Conceivably, indeed, a man might reject this miracle and yet accept other miracles that the New Testament contains; conceivably a man might hold Jesus to be a supernatural Person and yet reject the Gospel story about the manner of His entrance into this world. But it would perhaps be difficult to find a single New Testament student of any prominence who holds to such a view today.[5] In the overwhelming majority of cases those who reject the virgin birth reject the whole supernatural view of Christ. They often profess belief in the "incarnation"; but the word is apt to mean to them almost the exact opposite of what the New Testament means when it says that "the Word became flesh." To these modern men the incarnation means that God and man are one; to the New Testament it means rather that they are *not* one, but that the eternal Son of God became man, assumed our nature, by a stupendous miracle, to redeem us from sin. Seldom does any real belief in the incarnation go along with a rejection of the miracle of the virgin birth.

Thus we have held that the virgin birth is important, in the first place, because if it is rejected the authority of the Bible is denied, and, in the second place, because it brings before a man in particularly unambiguous fashion

[5] Compare James Orr, *The Virgin Birth of Christ*, 1907, pp. 18 f., 183 f.

the great question of the supernatural in connection with the person of our Lord. But that is by no means all that needs to be said. It is not true that the virgin birth is important only as a test of Bible authority or as a test case of the supernatural. On the contrary, it has an importance of its own, which the Christian man can ill afford to miss. Without the story of the virgin birth there would be something seriously lacking in the Christian view of Christ.[6]

It is important at this point to make clear exactly what we mean, since in recent discussion there has often been considerable confusion of thought. We do not mean, in the first place, merely that the virgin birth was important for God's plan; for that goes without saying if the virgin birth was a fact. If Jesus Christ was really born without human father, if that was really God's way for our Saviour to enter into the world, then it may certainly be assumed that it was the best way and that any other way would have been wrong. We are not concerned now to assert anything so self-evident as that. But what we do assert now is not only that the virgin birth was important as an event, but that it is important for us to know—that we could not have remained ignorant of it without loss.

In the second place, we do not mean merely that it is important for us to accept the story of the virgin birth now that it is presented to us in the Gospels of Matthew and Luke. To assert that would be merely to repeat what has already been said. We have already argued that a man cannot reject the testimony of the New Testament at this point without serious peril to his soul. But what we are now proposing is to imagine the case of a man who had never heard of the virgin birth at all, and yet had accepted everything else that the New Testament contains. Would such a man be worse off or not worse off than the devout Christian who possesses and accepts our existing New Testament, including the first two chapters of Matthew and of Luke?

It can hardly be emphasized too strongly that such an hypothetical case is quite different from any case which can actually arise at the present day. Never to have heard of the virgin birth is an entirely different thing from rejecting it after one has heard it attested by the New Testament books. Yet these two entirely different cases are frequently confused by those who today represent acceptance of the virgin birth as a matter of indifference to the Church. These persons frequently maintain that there was a time in the primitive days of Christianity when true disciples did not know of the virgin

[6] On the whole subject of the doctrinal importance of the virgin birth, see especially, in addition to the article by B. B. Warfield, which has been cited in the preceding footnote, the full and illuminating discussion by Orr (*op. cit.*, pp., 16–29, 182–227).

birth, and that if those primitive disciples got along without accepting the virgin birth we can do so today.

Of course, if the primitive time referred to in this argument is the time prior to the crucifixion and resurrection of our Lord, then the argument at once falls to the ground for anyone who believes in our Lord's redeeming work. No one who believes that our Lord came into the world to redeem men by His death upon the cross and to complete His redeeming work by His glorious resurrection from the dead can possibly desire to return now to the preliminary, pre-Pentecostal days when the disciples walked with Jesus on Galilean hills. The full meaning of redemption could be made clear only after the redeeming work was done. Thus the whole custom of appealing to the faith of those who met Jesus in Galilee as though it could be an example for faith today does despite to the thing that Jesus came into the world to do.

But even if the supposed primitive Christians who got along without knowledge of the virgin birth are to be put after the death and resurrection and not before, still their case was entirely different from the case of men who do not believe in the virgin birth today. They (supposing they ever really existed) had never heard of the virgin birth; but these modern men reject that of which they have heard full well. The real question at this point is not whether there were primitive Christians who had never heard the story of the virgin birth, but whether there were primitive Christians who rejected the story when once it was heard. It is this latter point which has not been proved. The Ebionite deniers of the virgin birth have never been traced back to primitive times, and it has never been shown that they were at heart Christians at all.

Thus in considering the case of the man who has never heard of the virgin birth, as distinguished from the man who has heard of it and rejected it, we are considering a purely hypothetical case which can hardly be actual in the modern world. Yet the consideration of that purely hypothetical case is not without value; for it will show whether our knowledge of the virgin birth possesses independent value or whether it is important merely because of its connection with the question of the authority of the Bible or with the question whether the supernatural has or has not entered into the course of the world in the person of Jesus Christ. Would our knowledge of our Saviour be essentially complete if the New Testament did not contain the passages which narrate the virgin birth?

That question, we think, should be answered with an emphatic negative; without the story of the virgin birth our knowledge of our Saviour would be impoverished in a very serious way.

Exaggerations, indeed, should be avoided at this point. Even without the infancy narratives we should have much upon which to rest our faith. Christ would still be presented in the New Testament as both God and man in two distinct natures and one person forever; the significance of His Cross would still stand out in all its glorious clearness; He would still be offered to us in the gospel as our Saviour.

Yet there would be a serious gap in our knowledge of Him, and questions would arise which would be full of menace for the souls of men. How did this eternal Son of God enter into the world? Did the Son of God unite with the man Jesus at the baptism as the Gnostics supposed; was the man Jesus received up gradually into union with the eternal Son? Erroneous answers to such questions would, without the story of the virgin birth, be all too ready to hand. No doubt those erroneous answers would still be capable of refutation to a mind ideally logical and really filled with the convictions which all the Gospels and Epistles would provide. Yet they would be only too natural to the minds of men as they actually are. Without the story of the virgin birth we should be living constantly in a region of surmises like the errors of the heresiarchs in the ancient Church.

Such surmises would deprive us of the full doctrine of the incarnation upon which our souls can rest. To that doctrine it is essential that the Son of God should live a complete human life upon this earth. But the human life would not be complete unless it began in the mother's womb. At no later time, therefore, should the incarnation be put, but at that moment when the babe was conceived. There, then, should be found the stupendous event when the eternal Son of God assumed our nature, so that from then on He was both God and man.

Our knowledge of the virgin birth, therefore, is important because it fixes for us the time of the incarnation. And what comfort that gives to our souls! Marcion, the second-century dualist, was very severe upon those who thought that the Son of God was born as a man; he poured out the vials of his scorn upon those who brought Christ into connection with the birth-pangs and the nine months' time. But we, unlike Marcion and his modern disciples, glory just in the story of those things. The eternal Son of God, He through whom the universe was made, did not despise the virgin's womb! What a wonder is there! It is not strange that it has always given offence to the natural man. But in that wonder we find God's redeeming love, and in that babe who lay in Mary's womb we find our Saviour who thus became man to die for our sins and bring us into peace with God.

Moreover, the knowledge of the virgin birth is important because of its bearing upon our view of the solidarity of the race in the guilt and power of sin. If we hold a Pelagian view of sin, we shall be little interested in the virgin birth of our Lord; we shall have little difficulty in understanding how a sinless One could be born as other men are born. But if we believe, as the Bible teaches, that all mankind are under an awful curse, then we shall rejoice in knowing that there entered into the sinful race from the outside One upon whom the curse did not rest save as He bore it for those whom He redeemed by His blood.

How, except by the virgin birth, could our Saviour have lived a complete human life from the mother's womb, and yet have been from the very beginning no product of what had gone before, but a supernatural Person come into the world from the outside to redeem the sinful race? We may not, indeed, set limits to the power of God; we cannot say what God might or might not have done. Yet we can say at least that no other way can be conceived by us. Deny or give up the story of the virgin birth, and inevitably you are led to evade either the high Biblical doctrine of sin or else the full Biblical presentation of the supernatural Person of our Lord. A noble man in whom the divine life merely pulsated in greater power than in other men would have been born by ordinary generation from a human pair; the eternal Son of God, come by a voluntary act to redeem us from the guilt and power of sin, was conceived in the virgin's womb by the Holy Ghost.

What, then, is our conclusion? Is belief in the virgin birth necessary to every man if he is to be a believer in the Lord Jesus Christ? The question is wrongly put when it is put in that way. Who can tell exactly how much knowledge of the facts about Christ is necessary if a man is to have saving faith? None but God can tell. Some knowledge is certainly required, but exactly how much is required we cannot say. "Lord, I believe; help thou mine unbelief," said a man in the Gospels who was saved. So today there are many men of little faith, many who are troubled by the voices that are heard on all sides. It is very hard to be a Christian in these times; and there is One who knows that it is hard. What right have we to say that full knowledge and full conviction are necessary before a man can put his trust in the crucified and risen Lord? What right have we to say that no man can be saved before he has come to full conviction regarding the stupendous miracle narrated in the first chapters of Matthew and Luke?

We desire, however, at this point not to be misunderstood. We do not mean by what we have just said that denial of the virgin birth is to be treated as a matter of indifference by the wise pastor of souls. The soul of man in its depths, indeed, is beyond our ken; our judgments regarding those depths are not the judgments of Him who "needed not that any should testify of man," because "He knew what was in man." Yet if we are to help our fellow-men we must give counsel on the basis of the best knowledge that we in our weakness can obtain. And certainly even with that weakness we can say that perhaps not one man out of a hundred of those who deny the virgin birth today gives any really clear evidence of possessing saving faith. A man is not saved by good works, but by faith; and saving faith is acceptance of Jesus Christ "as He is offered to us in the gospel." Part of that gospel in which Jesus is offered to our souls is the blessed story of the miracle in the virgin's womb.

One thing at least is clear: even if the belief in the virgin birth is not necessary to every Christian, it is certainly necessary to Christianity. And it is necessary to the corporate witness of the Church. Sad is it when men who will not affirm this doctrine are sent out into the ministry to lead Christ's little ones astray. Such men are learners, it is said; they will grow in knowledge and in grace; let us deal patiently with them and all will be well. Now we have all sympathy with those who are immature in the faith, and we hope that by the blessing of God they may be led into clearer and stronger convictions as to the truth of His Word. But the place for such learning, so far as the basic things are concerned, is not the sacred office of the Christian ministry. Let these men learn first by themselves, let them struggle, let them meditate, with such help as we and others can give them; and then, if God leads them aright, let them aspire to the holy ministry of the Word. But to send them out before they have attained such convictions, as official representatives of a Church whose faith they do not share—that is simply to trifle with human souls.

Let it never be forgotten that the virgin birth is an integral part of the New Testament witness about Christ, and that that witness is strongest when it is taken as it stands. We are not averse, indeed, to a certain logical order of apologetics; and in that order the virgin birth certainly does not come first. Before the virgin birth come the things for which testimony in the very nature of the case can be more abundant than for this. To those things no doubt the inquirer should be directed first, before he comes to consider this mystery which was first attested perhaps only by the mother of the Lord. But though that is true, though theoretically a man can believe in the resurrection, for example, without believing in the virgin birth, yet such a halfway conviction is not likely to endure. The New Testament presentation of Jesus is not an agglomeration, but an organism, and of that organism the virgin birth is an integral part. Remove the part, and the whole becomes harder and not easier to accept; the New Testament account of Jesus is most convincing when it is taken as a whole. Only one Jesus is presented in the Word of God; and that Jesus did not come into the world by ordinary generation, but was conceived in the womb of the virgin by the Holy Ghost.

INDEX

NAMES AND SUBJECTS

II BIBLICAL PASSAGES

OLD TESTAMENT